C# 10.0

ALL-IN-ONE

C# 10.0

ALL-IN-ONE

by John Paul Mueller

C# 10.0 All-in-One For Dummies®

Published by: **John Wiley & Sons, Inc.,** 111 River Street, Hoboken, NJ 07030-5774, www.wiley.com

For general information on our other products and services, please contact our Customer Care Department within the U.S. at 877-762-2974, outside the U.S. at 317-572-3993, or fax 317-572-4002. For technical support, please visit https://hub.wiley.com/community/support/dummies.

Wiley publishes in a variety of print and electronic formats and by print-on-demand. Some material included with standard print versions of this book may not be included in e-books or in print-on-demand. If this book refers to media such as a CD or DVD that is not included in the version you purchased, you may download this material at http://booksupport.wiley.com. For more information about Wiley products, visit www.wiley.com.

Library of Congress Control Number: 2021951074

ISBN: 978-1-11-983907-1 (pbk)

ISBN 978-1-11-984012-1 (ebk); ISBN 978-1-11-983908-8 (ebk)

SKY10032337_010622

Contents at a Glance

Table of Contents

Introduction

C# is an amazing language that is currently ranked the fifth most popular language in the world, according to the Tiobe Index (`https://www.tiobe.com/tiobe-index/`)! You can use this single language to do everything from desktop development to creating web applications and even web-based application programming interfaces (APIs). In addition, C# now makes it possible to target a multitude of platforms, including macOS and Linux. While other developers have to overcome deficiencies in their languages to create even a subset of the application types that C# supports with aplomb, you can be coding your application, testing, and then sitting on the beach enjoying the fruits of your efforts. Of course, any language that does this much requires a bit of explanation, and *C# 10.0 All-in-One For Dummies* is your doorway to this new adventure in development.

So, why do you need *C# 10.0 All-in-One For Dummies* specifically? This book stresses learning the basics of the C# language before you do anything else. With this in mind, the book begins with all the C# basics in Books 1 through 3, helps you get Visual Studio 2022 installed in Book 4, and then takes you through more advanced development tasks, including basic web development, in Books 5 through 6. Using this book helps you get the most you can from C# 10.0 in the least possible time.

About This Book

Even if you have past experience with C#, the new features in C# 10.0 will have you producing feature-rich applications in an even shorter time than you may have before. *C# 10.0 All-in-One For Dummies* introduces you to all these new features. For example, you discover how to work with both Universal Windows Platform (UWP) and Windows 10 and above applications (besides using all the old standbys). You also find all the new features provided for object-oriented development, and new IDE features designed to make your development experience easier. Make sure you don't miss out on the new `Record` type discussed in Book 2, Chapter 11. This book is designed to make using C# 10.0 fast and easy; it removes the complexity that you may have experienced when trying to learn about these topics online.

To help you absorb the concepts, this book uses the following conventions:

- Text that you're meant to type just as it appears in the book is in **bold**. The exception is when you're working through a step list: Because each step is bold, the text to type is not bold.
- Words for you to type that are also in *italics* are meant as placeholders; you need to replace them with something that works for you. For example, if you see "Type ***Your Name*** and press Enter," you need to replace *Your Name* with your actual name.
- I also use *italics* for terms I define. This means that you don't have to rely on other sources to provide the definitions you need.
- Web addresses and programming code appear in `monofont`. If you're reading a digital version of this book on a device connected to the Internet, you can click the live link to visit a website, like this: `www.dummies.com`.
- When you need to click command sequences, you see them separated by a special arrow, like this: File ➪ New File, which tells you to click File and then click New File.

Foolish Assumptions

You might have a hard time believing that I've assumed anything about you — after all, I haven't even met you yet! Although most assumptions are indeed foolish, I made certain assumptions to provide a starting point for the book.

The most important assumption is that you know how to use Windows, have a copy of Windows properly installed, and are familiar with using Windows applications. Even though this book covers developing applications that run on multiple platforms, the development environment always assumes that you're working with Windows. If installing an application is still a mystery to you, you might find this book a bit hard to use. While reading this book, you need to install applications, discover how to use them, and create simple applications of your own.

You also need to know how to work with the Internet. Many of the materials, including the downloadable source, appear online, and you need to download them in order to get the maximum value from the book. In addition, Book 6 assumes that you have a certain knowledge of the Internet when working through web-based applications and web-based services.

Icons Used in This Book

As you read this book, you encounter icons in the margins that indicate material of special interest (or not, as the case may be!). Here's what the icons mean:

Tips are nice because they help you save time or perform some task without a lot of extra work. The tips in this book are time-saving techniques or pointers to resources that you should try so that you can get the maximum benefit when performing C#-related tasks.

I don't want to sound like an angry parent or some kind of maniac, but you should avoid doing anything that's marked with a Warning icon. Otherwise, you might find that your configuration fails to work as expected, you get incorrect results from seemingly bulletproof processes, or (in the worst-case scenario) you lose data.

Whenever you see this icon, think advanced tip or technique. You might find these tidbits of useful information just too boring for words, or they could contain the solution you need to get a C# application running. Skip these bits of information whenever you like.

If you don't get anything else out of a particular chapter or section, remember the material marked by this icon. This text usually contains an essential process or a bit of information that you must know to work with C#.

Beyond the Book

This book isn't the end of your C# learning experience — it's really just the beginning. I provide online content to make this book more flexible and better able to meet your needs. Also, you can send me e-mail at `John@JohnMuellerBooks.com`. I'll address your book-specific questions and tell you how updates to C# or its associated add-ons affect book content through blog posts. Here are some cool online additions to this book:

- **Cheat sheet:** You remember using crib notes in school to make a better mark on a test, don't you? You do? Well, a cheat sheet is sort of like that. It provides you with some special notes about tasks that you can do with C# that not every other person knows. To find the cheat sheet for this book, go to `www.dummies.com` and search for *C# 10.0 All-in-One For Dummies Cheat Sheet.* It contains really neat information such as how to figure out which template you want to use.

- **Updates:** Sometimes changes happen. For example, I might not have seen an upcoming change when I looked into my crystal ball during the writing of this book. In the past, this possibility simply meant that the book became outdated and less useful, but you can now find updates to the book at `www.dummies.com`.

  In addition to these updates, check out the blog posts with answers to reader questions and demonstrations of useful book-related techniques at `http://blog.johnmuellerbooks.com/`.

- **Companion files:** Hey! Who really wants to type all the code in the book manually? Most readers prefer to spend their time actually working with C#, creating amazing new applications that change the world, and seeing the interesting things they can do, rather than typing. Fortunately for you, the examples used in the book are available for download, so all you need to do is read the book to learn C# development techniques. You can find these files at `www.dummies.com` and at `http://www.johnmuellerbooks.com/source-code/`.

Where to Go from Here

Anyone who is unfamiliar with C# should start with Book 1, Chapter 1 and move from there to the end of the book. This book is designed to make it easy for you to discover the benefits of using C# from the outset. Later, after you've seen enough C# code, you can install Visual Studio and then try the programming examples found in the first three minibooks. (Note that Book 1, Chapter 1 provides a brief overview of using Jupyter Notebook instead of Visual Studio 2022, but many of the new examples won't work with this setup.)

This book assumes that you want to see C# code from the outset. However, if you want to interact with that code, you really need to have a copy of Visual Studio 2022 installed. (Some examples will not work at all with older Visual Studio versions.) With this in mind, you may want to skip right to Book 4 to discover how to get your own copy of Visual Studio 2022. To help ensure that everyone can participate, this book focuses on the features offered by Visual Studio 2022 Community Edition, which is a free download. That's right, you can discover the wonders of C# 10.0 without paying a dime!

The more you know about C#, the later you can start in the book. If all you're really interested in is an update of your existing skills, check out Book 1, Chapter 1 to discover the changes in C#. Then, scan the first three minibooks looking for points of interest. Install C# by using the instructions in Book 4, Chapter 1, and then move on toward the advanced techniques found in later chapters. You definitely don't want to miss out on the Windows 10 and above development topics in Book 5, Chapter 5. In addition, Book 6 is entirely new for this edition, so even if you saw the previous edition of the book, you don't want to miss out on this new content.

1
The Basics of C# Programming

Contents at a Glance

IN THIS CHAPTER

» Getting a quick introduction to programming

» Creating and examining a simple console application

» Saving code for later

» Working online and in other environments

Chapter 1
Creating Your First C# Console Application

A console application is one that you run at the command prompt; it doesn't rely on any sort of fancy GUI to provide a pretty interface. Console applications are useful for all sorts of utilitarian tasks, and many people with low-level computer knowledge prefer them because they're extremely efficient to use. However, many people use console applications without even knowing it because console applications often play a role in configuration tasks. Because console applications are also easier to write than any other application type, you see them used quite often to demonstrate general C# (pronounced *see-sharp*) coding principles that really matter, like saying, "Hello World!"

Part of working with code is knowing how to perform basic tasks using the Integrated Development Environment (IDE). For example, you need to know how to create a new application and then save it to disk when you're done. This book assumes that you're using Visual Studio 2022 Community Edition. However, you might want to be different and use something else. That's why you see the IDEs for different people at the end of the chapter. Oddly enough, you can use some of these IDEs with your mobile device. Why write application code in your stuffy office when you can bask in the Maui sun?

REMEMBER

You don't have to type the source code for this chapter manually. In fact, using the downloadable source is a lot easier. You can find the source for this chapter in the `\CSAIO4D2E\BK01\CH01` folder of the downloadable source. See the Introduction for details on how to find these source files.

Getting a Handle on Computer Languages, C#, and .NET

Computers will do anything you ask them to (within reason). They do it extremely fast, and they're getting faster all the time. Unfortunately, computers don't understand anything that resembles a human language. Oh, you may come back and say something like, "Hey, my telephone lets me dial my friend by just speaking a name." Yes, a tiny computer runs your telephone, but that's a computer *program* that parses English into tokens that the computer matches to patterns of things to do. Never does the computer understand English or whatever other language you speak.

The language that computers truly understand is *machine language.* It's possible for humans to write machine code directly, but doing so is extremely difficult and error prone. So, programmers developed languages that are easier for people to use but are easily translated into machine code. The languages occupying this middle ground — C#, for example — are *high-level* computer languages. (*High* is a relative term here.)

What's a program?

What is a program? In a practical sense, a Windows program is an executable file that you can run by double-clicking its icon. For example, Microsoft Word, the editor used to write this book, is a program. You call that an *executable program,* or *executable* for short. The names of executable program files generally end with the extension `.exe`. Word, for example, is `Winword.exe`.

But a program is something else as well. An executable program consists of one or more *source files.* A C# source file, for instance, is a text file that contains a sequence of C# commands that fit together according to the laws of C# grammar. This file is known as a source file probably because it's a source of frustration and anxiety.

Uh, grammar? There's going to be grammar? Just the C# kind, which is much easier than the kind most people struggled with in junior high school.

What's C#?

Programmers use the C# programming language to create executable programs. C# combines the range of the powerful but complicated C++ (pronounced *see plus plus*) with the ease of use of the friendly but more verbose Visual Basic. A C# program file carries the extension `.cs`. Some people have pointed out that C sharp and D flat are the same note, but you shouldn't refer to this new language as *D flat* within earshot of Redmond, Washington. C# is

- **Flexible:** C# programs can execute on the current machine, or they can be transmitted over the web and executed on some distant computer.
- **Powerful:** C# has essentially the same command set as C++ but with the rough edges filed smooth.
- **Easier to use:** C# error-proofs the commands responsible for most C++ errors, so you spend far less time chasing down those errors.
- **Visually oriented:** The .NET code library that C# uses for many of its capabilities provides the help needed to create complicated display frames with the controls commonly seen in specific environments such as the desktop, using technologies like Windows Forms, Windows Presentation Foundation (WPF), and Universal Application Platform (UAP).
- **Internet-friendly:** C# plays a pivotal role in the .NET Framework, Microsoft's current approach to programming for Windows, the Internet, and beyond.
- **Secure:** Any language intended for use on the Internet must include serious security to protect against malevolent hackers.

Finally, C# is an integral part of .NET (which includes the .NET Framework, .NET Core, and other elements of the .NET ecosystem).

REMEMBER

This book is primarily about the C# language. If your primary goal is to use Visual Studio, program Windows 8 or 10 apps, or ASP.NET, the *For Dummies* books on those topics go well with this book; go to `www.dummies.com` to find them. You can find a good amount of information later in this book on how to use C# to write traditional Windows, WPF, UAP, web, and service applications.

What's .NET?

Think of .NET as the foundation of the application you want to build. It contains all the low-level features you need to create an application, but C# builds on to that foundation to make development easier. .NET began as Microsoft's strategy to open the web to mere mortals like you and me. Today, it encompasses everything Microsoft does. In particular, it's the way to program for Windows and other platforms. It also gives C# the visual tools that made Visual Basic so popular. For the purposes of this book, .NET includes these subelements:

- **.NET Framework:** This is the Windows-only, feature-complete version of .NET that you use for the majority of the book's examples.
- **.NET Core:** This is the multiplatform, less functional version of .NET that you use to implement some C# 9,0 and C# 10.0 features. It allows you to use the same application on Windows, Linux, macOS, and mobile devices (via Xamarin). The article at `https://stackify.com/net-core-vs-net-framework/` provides a great overview of the differences between the .NET Framework and .NET Core, but this book tells you about them from a real-world perspective.

What is Visual Studio 2022?

(You sure ask lots of questions.) The first "Visual" language from Microsoft was Visual Basic. The first popular C-based language from Microsoft was Visual C++. Like Visual Basic, it had Visual in its name because it had a built-in graphical user interface (GUI — pronounced "GOO-ee"). This GUI included everything you needed to develop C++ programs.

Eventually, Microsoft rolled all its languages into a single environment — Visual Studio. As Visual Studio 6.0 started getting a little long in the tooth, developers anxiously awaited version 7. Shortly before its release, however, Microsoft decided to rename it Visual Studio .NET to highlight this new environment's relationship to the .NET Framework (.NET Core wasn't available then).

That sounded like a marketing ploy to a lot of people — until they started delving into it. Visual Studio .NET differed quite a bit from its predecessors — enough to warrant a new name. Visual Studio 2022 is the eleventh-generation successor to the original Visual Studio .NET. (Book 4 is full of Visual Studio goodness, including instructions for customizing it. You may want to use the instructions in Book 4, Chapter 1 to install a copy of Visual Studio before you get to the example later in this chapter. If you're completely unfamiliar with Visual Studio, reviewing all of Book 4 is helpful.)

Creating Your First Console Application

Visual Studio 2022 includes an Application Wizard that builds template programs and saves you a lot of the dirty work you'd have to do if you did everything from scratch. (The from-scratch approach is error prone, to say the least.)

Typically, starter programs don't really do anything — at least, not anything useful. However, they do get you beyond that initial hurdle of getting started. Some starter programs are reasonably sophisticated. In fact, you'll be amazed at how much capability the App Wizard can build on its own, especially for graphical programs.

REMEMBER

The following instructions are for Visual Studio 2019 configured for C# development. (There are other configurations you can use, including a general configuration if you use a number of languages.) If you use anything other than Visual Studio, you have to refer to the documentation that came with your environment, such as Jupyter Notebook (described in the "Working with Jupyter Notebook: The Short Version" section, near the end of the chapter). Alternatively, you can just type the source code directly into your C# online environment (described in the "Interacting with C# Online" section, later in this chapter).

Creating the source program

To start Visual Studio, press the Windows button on your keyboard and type **Visual Studio**. Visual Studio 2022 appears as one of the available options. Complete these steps to create your C# console app:

1. **Open Visual Studio 2022.**

   You see a list of options, as shown in Figure 1-1. (If this is the first time you've used Visual Studio 2022, you won't see any recent files and you may also see an additional Get Started option or two.) Notice that you can connect to various source code locations, open a recently opened project or solution, or create something new.

2. **Click the Create a New Project link.**

   You see a rather long and confusing list of project types. However, you can easily prune away the projects you don't want.

3. **Select C# in the Language drop-down list box, Windows in the Platform drop-down list box, and Console in the Project Type drop-down list box.**

   Visual Studio presents you with entries representing the different types of applications you can create, as shown in Figure 1-2. Notice that each entry shows a language and the platforms that it supports.

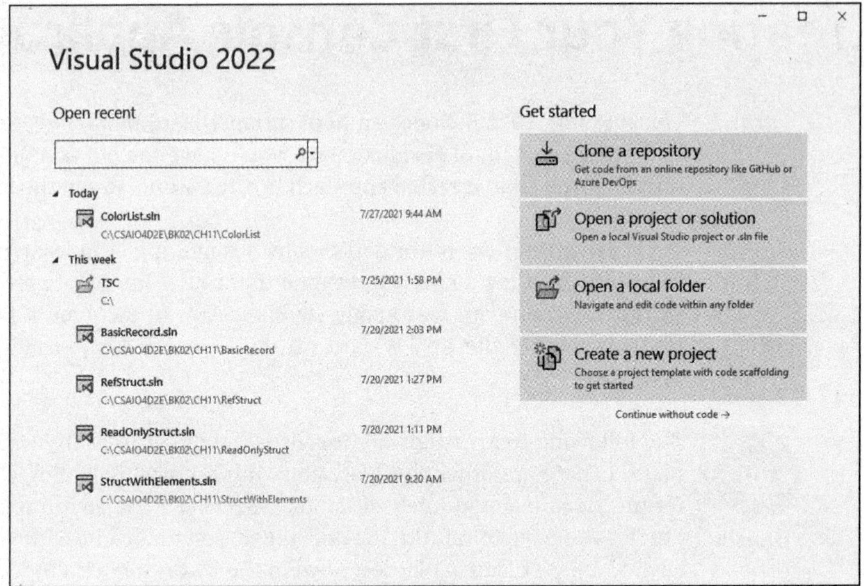

FIGURE 1-1: Creating a new project starts you down the road to a better Windows application.

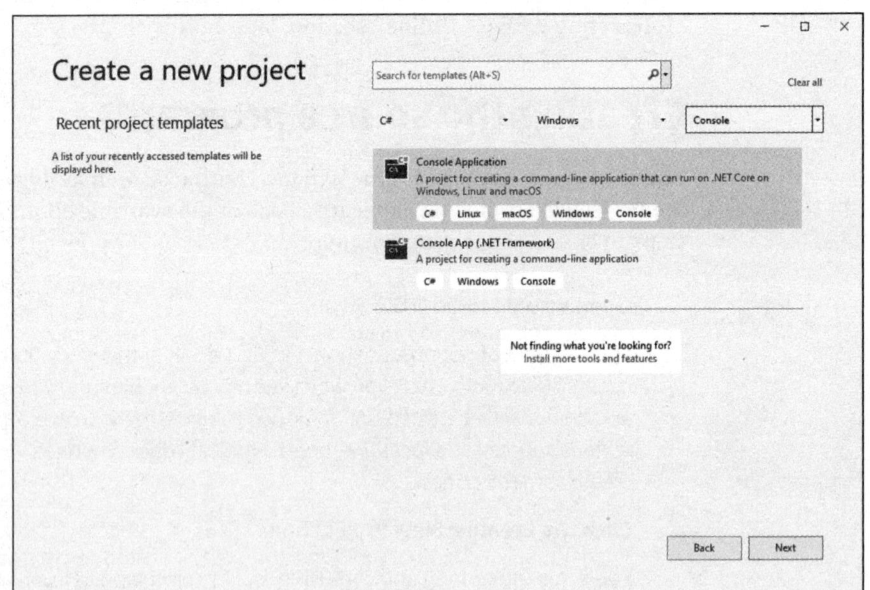

FIGURE 1-2: The Visual Studio App Wizard is eager to create a new program for you.

4. **In the Create a New Project window, select the Console App (.NET Framework) entry.**

REMEMBER

Visual Studio requires you to create a project before you can start entering your C# program. A *project* is a folder into which you throw all the files that go into making your program. It has a set of configuration files that help the compiler do its work. When you tell your compiler to build (*compile*) the program, it sorts through the project to find the files it needs in order to re-create the executable program.

TECHNICAL STUFF

Visual Studio 2022 provides support for both .NET Framework and .NET Core applications. A .NET Framework application is the same as the C# applications supported in previous versions of Windows; it runs only in Windows and isn't open source. A .NET Core application can run in Windows, Linux, and Mac environments and relies on an open source setup. Although using .NET Core may seem ideal, the .NET Core applications also support only a subset of the .NET Framework features, and you can't add a GUI to them. Microsoft created the .NET Core for these uses:

- Cross-platform development
- Microservices
- Docker containers
- High performance and scalable applications
- Side-by-side .NET application support

5. **Click Next.**

You see a Configure Your New Project dialog box, as shown in Figure 1-3. This is where you tell the wizard how to create the basics of your application.

6. **The default name for your first application is** `ConsoleApp1`**, but change it this time to** Program1 **by typing in the Name field.**

TIP

The default place to store this file is somewhere deep in your `Documents` directory. For most developers, it's a lot better to place the files where you can actually find them and interact with them as needed, not necessarily where Visual Studio wants them.

7. **Type** C:\CSAIO4D2E\BK01\CH01 **in the Location field to change the location of this project.**

TIP

If you don't have permission to create folders in the root directory of your drive where they're easy to access, create the same folder on your desktop by typing **C:\Users\<*Your Username*>\Desktop\CSAIO4D2E\BK01\CH01**. The point is to make your source code easy to access, and the default setting doesn't do that very well — it hides things.

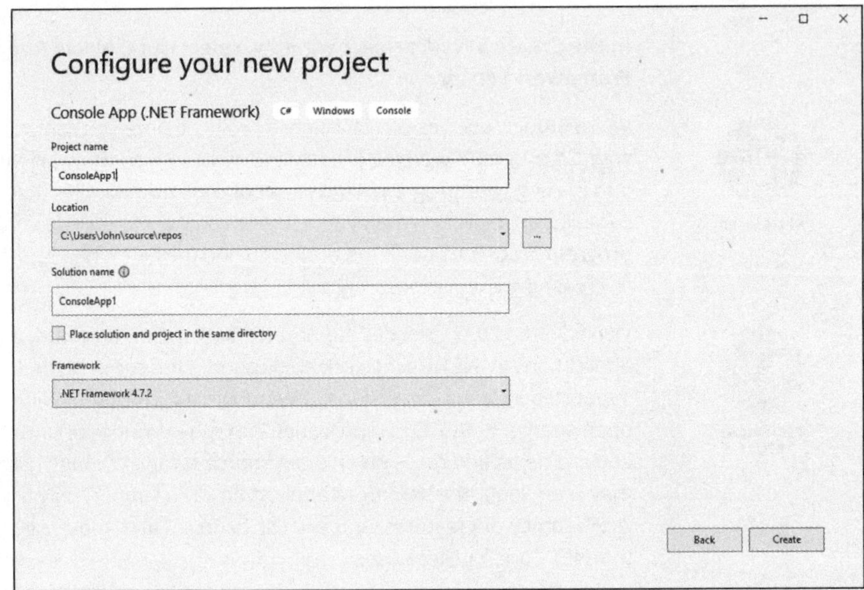

FIGURE 1-3: The Visual Studio App Wizard is eager to create a new program for you.

8. **Select Place Solution and Project in the Same Directory.**

   You use this option to make solutions that contain just one project simpler. A *solution* is a container for multiple projects when you want to create a complex application. For example, you might want to create a console application that also includes a special library contained in a `.dll` file.

9. **Click the Create button.**

   After a bit of disk whirring and chattering, Visual Studio generates a file named `Program.cs`. (If you look in the window labeled Solution Explorer, shown in Figure 1-4, you see some other files; ignore them for now. If Solution Explorer isn't visible, choose View ➪ Solution Explorer.)

   C# source files carry the extension `.cs`. The name `Program` is the default name assigned for the program file.

The contents of your first console app appear this way (as shown in Figure 1-4):

```
using System;
using System.Collections.Generic;
using System.Linq;
using System.Text;
using System.Threading.Tasks;

namespace Program1
{
    class Program
```

```
    {
        static void Main(string[] args)
        {
        }
    }
}
```

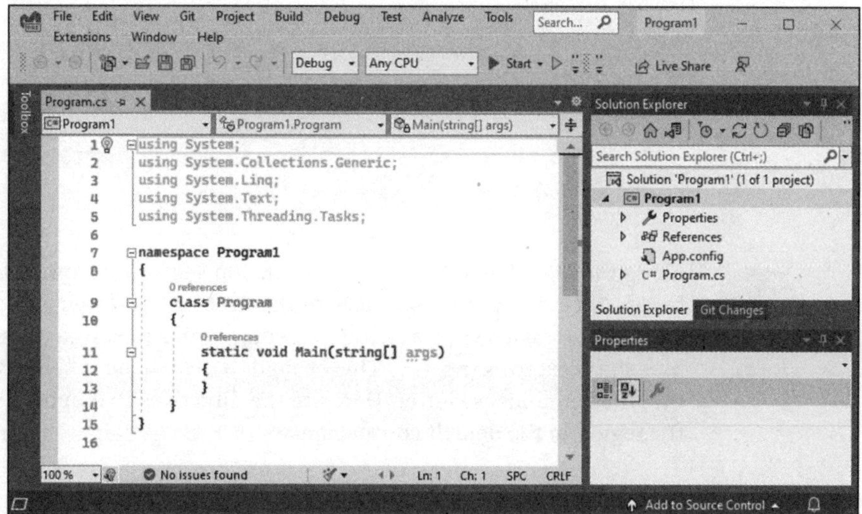

FIGURE 1-4: Visual Studio displays the project you just created.

TIP

You can manually change the location of the project with every project. However, you have a simpler way to go. When working with this book, you can change the default program location. To make that happen, follow these steps after you finish creating the project:

1. **Choose Tools ⇨ Options.**

   The Options dialog box opens.

2. **Choose Projects and Solutions ⇨ Locations.**

3. **Select the new location in the Project Location field and click OK.**

   (The examples assume that you have used `C:\CSAIO4D2E` for this book.)

You can see the Options dialog box in Figure 1-5. Leave the other fields in the project settings alone for now. Read more about customizing Visual Studio in Book 4.

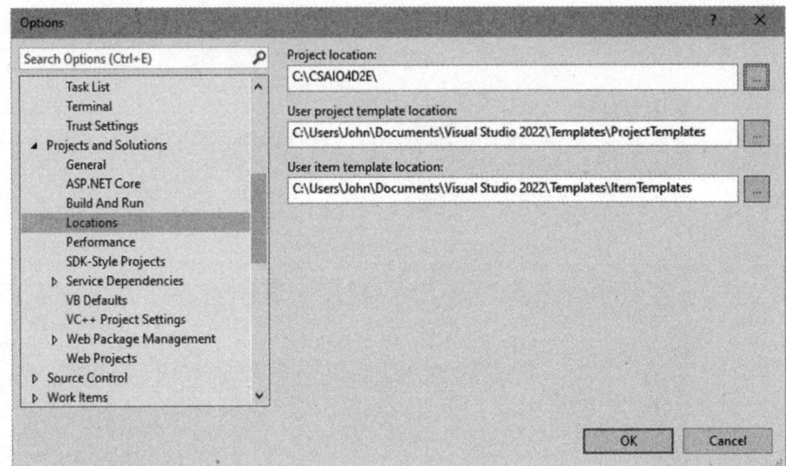

FIGURE 1-5: Changing the default project location.

REMEMBER

Along the left edge of the code window, you see several small minus signs (–) in boxes. Click the minus sign next to the first `using` statement, and all the `using` statements collapse into a `using ...` entry with a plus sign (+) next to it. Click the plus sign next to `using ...`. This expands a *code region*, a handy Visual Studio feature that minimizes clutter. Here are the directives that appear when you expand the region in the default console app:

```
using System;
using System.Collections.Generic;
using System.Linq;
using System.Text;
using System.Threading.Tasks;
```

Regions help you focus on the code you're working on by hiding code that you aren't. Certain blocks of code — such as the namespace block, `class` block, methods, and other code items — get a +/– automatically without a `#region` directive. You can add your own collapsible regions, if you like, by typing `#region` above a code section and `#endregion` after it. It helps to supply a name for the region, such as `Public methods`. This code section looks like this:

```
#region Public methods
... your code
#endregion Public methods
```

REMEMBER

This name can include spaces. Also, you can nest one region inside another, but regions can't overlap.

For now, `using System;` is the only `using` directive you really need. You can delete the others; the compiler lets you know whether you're missing one.

Taking it out for a test drive

Before you try to create your application, open the Output window (if it isn't already open) by choosing View ➪ Output. To convert your C# program into an executable program, choose Build ➪ Build Program1. Visual Studio responds with the following message:

```
1>----- Build started: Project: Program1, Configuration: Debug Any CPU -----
1>  Program1 -> C:\CSAIO4D2E\BK01\CH01\Program1\bin\Debug\Program1.exe
========== Build: 1 succeeded, 0 failed, 0 up-to-date, 0 skipped ==========
```

The key point here is the `1 succeeded` part on the last line.

TIP

As a general rule of programming, `succeeded` is good; `failed` is bad. The bad — the exceptions — is covered in Chapter 9 of this minibook.

To execute the program, choose Debug ➪ Start Debugging. The program brings up a black console window and terminates immediately. (If you have a fast computer, the appearance of this window is just a flash on the screen.) The program has seemingly done nothing. In fact, this is the case. The template is nothing but an empty shell.

TIP

An alternative command, Debug ➪ Start Without Debugging, behaves a bit better at this point. Try it out. You press Enter to dismiss the window.

Making Your Console App Do Something

Edit the `Program.cs` template file until it appears this way:

```
using System;

namespace Program1
{
  public class Program
  {
    // This is where your program starts.
    static void Main(string[] args)
    {
      // Prompt user to enter a name.
      Console.WriteLine("Enter your name, please:");

      // Now read the name entered.
      string name = Console.ReadLine();
```

```
            // Greet the user with the name that was entered.
            Console.WriteLine("Hello, " + name);

            // Wait for user to acknowledge the results.
            Console.WriteLine("Press Enter to terminate...");
            Console.Read();
        }
    }
}
```

TIP

Don't sweat the stuff following the double slashes (//) and don't worry about whether to enter one or two spaces or one or two new lines. However, do pay attention to capitalization.

Choose Build ⇨ Build Program1 to convert this new version of `Program.cs` into the `Program1.exe` program. Choose Debug ⇨ Start Without Debugging. The black console window appears and prompts you for your name. (You may need to activate the console window by clicking it.) Then the window shows `Hello`, followed by the name entered, and displays `Press Enter to terminate ....` Pressing Enter twice closes the window.

TECHNICAL STUFF

You can also execute the program from the DOS command line. To do so, open a Command Prompt window by opening the Windows Run dialog box, typing **cmd.exe**, and pressing Enter; then enter the following:

```
cd \CSAIO4D2E\bk01\ch01\Program1\bin\debug
```

Now enter **Program1** to execute the program. The output should be identical to what you saw earlier. You can also navigate to the `\CSAIO4D2E\bk01\ch01\Program1\bin\debug` folder in Windows Explorer and then double-click the `Program1.exe` file.

TIP

To open a Command Prompt window in Visual Studio, try choosing Tools ⇨ Command Line ⇨ Developer Command Prompt.

Reviewing Your Console Application

In the following sections, you take this first C# console app apart one section at a time to understand how it works.

The program framework

The basic framework for all console applications starts, as shown in Figure 1-4. The program starts executing right after the statement containing `Main()` and ends at the closed curly brace (}) following `Main()`. (You find the explanation for these statements in due course. Just know that they work as they should for now.)

REMEMBER

The list of `using` directives can come immediately before or immediately after the phrase `namespace Program1 {`. The order doesn't matter. You can apply `using` to lots of things in .NET. You find an explanation for namespaces and `using` in the object-oriented programming chapters in Book 2.

Comments

The template already has lots of lines, and the example code adds several other lines, such as the following (in boldface):

```
// This is where your program starts.
public static void Main(string[] args)
```

C# ignores the first line in this example. This line is known as a *comment.*

TIP

Any line that begins with // is free text, and C# ignores it.

Why include lines if the computer ignores them? Because comments explain your C# statements. A program, even in C#, isn't easy to understand. A programming language is a compromise between what computers understand and what humans understand. These comments are useful while you write the code, and they're especially helpful to the poor sap — possibly you — who tries to re-create your logic a year later. Comments make the job much easier. Comment early and often.

The meat of the program

The real core of this program is embedded within the block of code marked with `Main()`, like this (the additional two lines at the end deal with the window automatically closing when you choose Debug ➪ Start Debugging):

```
// Prompt user to enter a name.
Console.WriteLine("Enter your name, please:");

// Now read the name entered.
string name = Console.ReadLine();

// Greet the user with the name that was entered.
Console.WriteLine("Hello, " + name);
```

TIP

Save a ton of routine typing with the C# Code Snippets feature. Snippets are great for common statements like `Console.WriteLine()`. Press Ctrl+K,X to see a pop-up menu of snippets. (You may need to press Tab once or twice to open the Visual C# folder or other folders on that menu.) Scroll down the menu to `cw` and press Enter. Visual Studio inserts the body of a `Console.WriteLine()` statement with the insertion point between the parentheses, ready to go. When you have a few of the shortcuts, such as `cw`, `for`, and `if`, memorized, use the even quicker technique: Type **cw** and press Tab twice. (Also try selecting some lines of code, pressing Ctrl+K, and then pressing Ctrl+S. Choose something like `if`. An `if` statement *surrounds* the selected code lines.)

The program begins executing with the first C# statement: `Console.WriteLine("Enter your name, please:");`. This command writes the character string `Enter your name, please:` to the console.

The next statement reads in the user's answer and stores it in a *variable* (a kind of workbox) named `name`. (See Chapter 2 of this minibook for more on these storage locations.) The last line combines the string `Hello,` with the user's name and outputs the result to the console.

The final three lines cause the computer to wait for the user to press Enter before proceeding. These lines ensure that the user has time to read the output before the program continues:

```
// Wait for user to acknowledge the results.
Console.WriteLine("Press Enter to terminate...");
Console.Read();
```

This step can be important, depending on how you execute the program and depending on the environment. In particular, running your console app inside Visual Studio, or from Windows Explorer, makes the preceding lines necessary — otherwise, the console window closes so fast you can't read the output. If you open a console window and run the program from there, the window stays open regardless.

Replacing All that Ceremonial Code: Top-Level Statements

TECHNICAL STUFF

C# uses a lot of what is termed as *boilerplate code*, which is code that appears everywhere and really is quite necessary, but it's boring because you write it every time. C# 9.0 and above lets you get rid of some of that code. If you're using Visual Studio 2022 with C# 9.0 and above support, you could create the previous application using just this code (which is also available in the Program2 project in the downloadable source):

```
using System;

// Prompt user to enter a name.
Console.WriteLine("Enter your name, please:");

// Now read the name entered.
string name = Console.ReadLine();

// Greet the user with the name that was entered.
Console.WriteLine("Hello, " + name);

// Wait for user to acknowledge the results.
Console.WriteLine("Press Enter to terminate...");
Console.Read();
```

There is only one problem with this whole scenario. Visual Studio 2022 doesn't allow you to choose a language version when you create a project, so you have to jump through a terrifying hoop as a novice programmer. After you create your project shell and save it, choose File ⇨ Close Solution. Doing so saves your project to disk and ensures that nothing is in use. Next, you need to open the `.csproj` file associated with your project, such as `Program2.csproj` for this example, which is in `C:\CSAIO4D2E\BK01\CH01\Program2`. Go to the end of the file and insert the following lines shown in bold to change the language version from the default of 7.3 to 9.0.

```
  <PropertyGroup>
    <LangVersion>9.0</LangVersion>
  </PropertyGroup>
</Project>
```

Introducing the Toolbox Trick

The key part of the program you create in the preceding sections consists of the final two lines of code:

```
// Wait for user to acknowledge the results.
Console.WriteLine("Press Enter to terminate...");
Console.Read();
```

The easiest way to re-create those key lines in each future console application you write is described in the following sections.

Saving code in the Toolbox

The first step is to save those lines in a handy location for future use: the Toolbox window. With your `Program1` console application open in Visual Studio, follow these steps:

1. **In the `Main()` method of class `Program`, select the lines you want to save — in this case, the three lines mentioned previously.**
2. **Make sure that the Toolbox window is open on the left.**

   If it isn't, open the Toolbox by choosing View ⇨ Toolbox. You must also pin it by clicking the thumbtack icon so that it remains open.
3. **Drag the selected lines into the General tab of the Toolbox window and drop them. (Or copy the lines and paste them into the Toolbox.)**

   The Toolbox stores the lines there for you in perpetuity.

Reusing code from the Toolbox

Now that you have your template text stored in the Toolbox, you can reuse it in all console applications you write henceforth. Here's how to use it:

1. **In Visual Studio, create a new console application as described in the section "Creating the source program," earlier in this chapter.**
2. **Click in the editor at the spot where you'd like to insert some Toolbox text.**
3. **With the `Program.cs` file open for editing, make sure that the Toolbox window is open.**

   If it isn't, see the procedure in the preceding "Saving code in the Toolbox" section.
4. **In the General tab of the Toolbox window (other tabs may be showing), find the saved text you want to use and double-click it.**

   The selected item is inserted at the insertion point in the editor window. (Note that you can also click and drag the text from the Toolbox to any point in the code.)

With that boilerplate text in place, you can write the rest of your application above those lines. That's it. You now have a finished console app. Try it for about 30 seconds.

Interacting with C# Online

You might find yourself trying to understand some C# concept or needing to review some code. Perhaps you just want to play for a while. Fortunately, there are online resources that will make discovering everything you can about C# considerably easier:

- **Microsoft's interactive tutorials (**`https://docs.microsoft.com/en-us/dotnet/csharp/tour-of-csharp/tutorials/`**):** You can find a lot of quick ways to put applications together that let you actually type the code in and interact with it. The tutorials begin with easy tasks like writing Hello World and move on to complex topics like working with Language Integrated Query (LInQ).
- **W3Schools tutorials (**`https://www.w3schools.com/cs/default.asp`**):** This site provides a more comprehensive listing of C# features than the Microsoft site, but it's also less interactive. Most of the sections end with a quick exam to test your skills.
- **OneCompiler (**`https://onecompiler.com/csharp`**):** If you want to try working with some code but all you have is a tablet, you can use this site instead. This site is pretty amazing because you select a language (and there are many) and then write your code and run it. There are limitations, though — don't expect a full-blown Visual Studio environment.

Working with Jupyter Notebook: The Short Version

A lot of people love Jupyter Notebook because it uses an entirely different programming paradigm than Visual Studio called the literate programming technique. Donald Knuth (`https://www-cs-faculty.stanford.edu/~knuth/lp.html`) introduced this technique as a means to make programming simpler. Usually you use it with languages like Python, but now it's also available (with limitations) for C# developers. In addition to Jupyter Notebook's ease of development, its output can look more like a report than a programming file, so it's an excellent means of developing code for something like a presentation.

You can get a better idea of how this all works by reading the post at `https://devblogs.microsoft.com/dotnet/net-interactive-is-here-net-notebooks-preview-2/`. The screenshots in the post give you an idea of just how different Jupyter Notebook is when compared to working with Visual Studio directly. The post also tells you how to make the setup work. Microsoft calls this new way of programming .NET Interactive, and you can get the source files for it at `https://github.com/dotnet/interactive`.

Even though this book doesn't use the Jupyter Notebook form of coding with C#, you owe it to yourself to try it at some point. It won't solve every problem and may not be what you want in an IDE, but it really can be amazing.

IN THIS CHAPTER

» Using C# variables, such as integers, as storage lockers

» Declaring other types of variables — dates, characters, strings

» Handling numeric constants

» Changing types and letting the compiler figure out the type

Chapter 2

Living with Variability — Declaring Value-Type Variables

The most fundamental of all concepts in programming is that of the variable. A C# variable is like a small box in which you can store things, particularly numbers, for later use. (The term *variable* is borrowed from the world of mathematics.)

Unfortunately for programmers, C# places several limitations on variables — limitations that mathematicians don't have to consider. However, these limits are in place for a reason. They make it easier for C# to understand what you mean by a particular kind of variable and for you to find mistakes in your code. This chapter takes you through the steps for declaring, initializing, and using variables. It also introduces several of the most basic data types in C#.

Declaring a Variable

Mathematicians work with numbers in a precise manner, but in a way that C# could never understand. The mathematician is free to introduce the variables as needed to present an idea in a particular way. Mathematicians use algorithms, a set of procedural steps used to solve a problem, in a way that makes sense to other mathematicians to model real-world needs. Algorithms can appear quite complex, even to other humans, much less C# (it doesn't understand algorithms except what you tell it in code). For example, the mathematician may say this:

$$x = y^2 + 2y + 1$$
$$\text{if } k = y + 1 \text{ then}$$
$$x = k^2$$

Programmers must define variables in a particular way that's more demanding than the mathematician's looser style. A programmer must tell C# the kind of value that a variable contains and then tell C# specifically what to place in that variable in a manner that C# understands. For example, a C# programmer may write the following bit of code:

```
int n;
n = 1;
```

The first line means, "Carve off a small amount of storage in the computer's memory and assign it the name *n*." This step is analogous to reserving one of those storage lockers at the train station and slapping the label *n* on the side. The second line says, "Store the value 1 in the variable `n`, thereby replacing whatever that storage location already contains." The train-locker equivalent is, "Open the train locker, rip out whatever happens to be in there, and shove a 1 in its place."

REMEMBER

The equals symbol (=) is called the *assignment operator.*

TECHNICAL STUFF

The mathematician says, "*n* equals 1." The C# programmer says in a more precise way, "Store the value 1 in the variable `n`." (Think about the train locker, and you see why that's easier for C# to understand.) C# operators, such as the assignment operator, tell the computer what you want to do. In other words, operators are verbs and not descriptors. The assignment operator takes the value on its right and stores it in the variable on the left. You discover more about operators in Chapter 4 of this minibook.

What's an int?

In C#, each variable has a fixed type. When you allocate one of those train lockers, you have to pick the size you need. If you pick an integer locker, for instance, you can't turn around and hope to stuff the entire state of Texas in it — maybe Rhode Island, but not Texas.

For the example in the preceding section of this chapter, you select a locker that's designed to handle an integer — C# calls it an `int`. Integers are the counting numbers 1, 2, 3, and so on, plus 0 and the negative whole numbers –1, –2, –3, and so on.

REMEMBER

Before you can use a variable, you must *declare* it, which means creating a variable with a specific name (label) using code and optionally assigning a value to that variable. After you declare a variable as `int`, it can hold integer values, as this example demonstrates:

```
// Declare a variable named n - an empty train locker.
int n;
// Declare an int variable m and initialize it with the value 2.
int m = 2;
// Assign the value stored in m to the variable n.
n = m;
```

The first line after the comment is a *declaration* that creates a little storage area, `n`, designed to hold an integer value. The initial value of `n` is not specified until it is *assigned* a value, so this locker is essentially empty. The second declaration not only declares an `int` variable `m` but also *initializes* it with a value of 2, all in one shot.

REMEMBER

The term *initialize* means to assign an initial value. To initialize a variable is to assign it a value for the first time. You don't know for sure what the value of a variable is until it has been initialized. Nobody knows. It's always an error to use a variable before you initialize it.

The final statement in the program assigns the value stored in `m`, which is 2, to the variable `n`. The variable `n` continues to contain the value 2 until it is assigned a new value. (The variable `m` doesn't lose its value when you assign its value to `n`. It's like cloning `m`.)

Rules for declaring variables

You can initialize a variable as part of the declaration, like this:

```
// Declare another int variable and give it the initial value of 1.
int p = 1;
```

This is equivalent to sticking a 1 into that `int` storage locker when you first rent it, rather than opening the locker and stuffing in the value later.

TIP

Initialize a variable when you declare it. In most (but not all) cases, C# initializes the variable for you — but don't rely on it to do that. For example, C# does place a 0 into an uninitialized `int` variable, but the compiler will still display an error if you try to use the variable before you initialize it. You may declare variables anywhere (well, almost anywhere) within a program.

WARNING

However, you may not use a variable until you declare it and set it to some value. Thus the last two assignments shown here are *not* legal:

```
// The following is illegal because m is not assigned
// a value before it is used.
int n = 1;
int m;
n = m;
// The following is illegal because p has not been
// declared before it is used.
p = 2;
int p;
```

Finally, you cannot declare the same variable twice in the same scope (a function, for example).

Variations on a theme: Different types of int

Most simple numeric variables are of type `int`. However, C# provides a number of twists to the `int` variable type for special occasions.

All integer variable types are limited to whole numbers. The `int` type suffers from other limitations as well. For example, an `int` variable can store values only in the range from roughly –2 billion to 2 billion.

A distance of 2 billion inches is greater than the circumference of the Earth. In case 2 billion isn't quite large enough for you, C# provides an integer type called long (short for long int) that can represent numbers almost as large as you can imagine. The only problem with a long is that it takes a larger train locker: A long consumes 8 bytes (64 bits) — twice as much as a garden-variety 4-byte (32-bit) int. C# provides several other integer variable types, as shown in Table 2-1.

TABLE 2-1 **Size and Range of C# Integer Types**

Type	Bytes	Range of Values	In Use
sbyte	1	-128 to 127	sbyte sb = 12;
byte	1	0 to 255	byte b = 12;
short	2	-32,768 to 32,767	short sh = 12345;
ushort	2	0 to 65,535	ushort ush = 62345;
int	4	-2,147,483,648 to 2,147,483,647	int n = 1234567890;
uint	4	0 to 4,294,967,295	uint un = 3234567890U;
long	8	-9,223,372,036,854,775,808 to 9,223,372,036,854,775,807	long l = 123456789012L;
ulong	8	0 to 18,446,744,073,709,551,615	ulong ul = 123456789012UL;

As explained in the section entitled "Declaring Numeric Constants," later in this chapter, fixed values such as 1 also have a type. By default, a simple constant such as 1 is assumed to be an int, unless the value won't fit in an int, in which case the compiler automatically selects the next largest type. Constants other than an int must be marked with their variable type. For example, 123U is an unsigned integer, uint.

Most integer variables are called *signed*, which means they can represent negative values. Unsigned integers can represent only positive values, but you get twice the range in return. As you can see from Table 2-1, the names of most unsigned integer types start with a u, while the signed types generally don't have a prefix.

TECHNICAL STUFF

C# 9.0 and above also support a new native integer type, nint, that you use as nint MyInt = 9. The unsigned version appears as nuint. Native integer values are useful for low-level programming, such as when you want to interact with the Windows operating system directly. You won't use them in this book. Should you want to know more about native integers, the article "Native-sized integers - C# 9.0 specification proposals | Microsoft Docs (https://docs.microsoft.com/en-us/dotnet/csharp/language-reference/proposals/csharp-9.0/native-integers) tells you more about them.

TECHNICAL STUFF

MAKING NUMBERS EASIER TO WORK WITH

Starting with C# 7.0, you can use the underscore (_) between numbers in place of the usual commas. For example, `long MyLong = 123_456_789L` is perfectly acceptable.

In addition, sometimes you need to represent numbers in other bases, such as binary or hexadecimal. To do this in C#, you need to prefix the value with `0` and either a `b` for binary or an `x` for hexadecimal, which is called an *integer literal*. Consequently, `MyHex = 0x0019_F0A1` places the decimal value 1700001 in `MyHex`. Notice that you can also use the underscore in hexadecimal numbers. For a binary number, when you use something like `MyBin = 0b1000_1000_1100`, C# places the decimal value 2,188 in `MyBin`. Note that the `0b` syntax requires C# 7.0 or above.

It's also important to note that integer literals are always positive. For example, the value 0xFFFF_FFFF equates to a decimal value of 4,294,967,295. However, it could also represent the value -1 depending on how C# interprets it. To produce the negative form of the number, you need to convert the positive form (a `uint,` for example) to a form that allows negative numbers (an `int`) using `unchecked((int)0xFFFF_FFFF)`.

Representing Fractions

Integers are useful for most calculations. However, many calculations involve fractions, which simple integers can't accurately represent. The common equation for converting from Fahrenheit to Celsius temperatures demonstrates the problem, like this:

```
// Convert the temperature 41 degrees Fahrenheit.
int fahr = 41;
int celsius = (fahr - 32) * (5 / 9);
```

This equation works just fine for some values. For example, 41 degrees Fahrenheit is 5 degrees Celsius.

Okay, try a different value: 100 degrees Fahrenheit. Working through the equation, 100−32 is 68; 68 times 5 is 340; 340 / 9 is 37 when using integers. However, a closer answer is 37.78. Even that's wrong because it's really 37.777 . . . with the 7s repeating forever.

REMEMBER

An `int` can represent only integer numbers. The integer equivalent of 37.78 is 37. This lopping off of the fractional part of a number to get it to fit into an integer variable is called *integer truncation*.

TECHNICAL STUFF

Truncation is not the same thing as *rounding.* Truncation lops off the fractional part. Goodbye, Charlie. Rounding picks the closest integer value. Thus, truncating 1.9 results in 1. Rounding 1.9 results in 2.

For temperatures, 37 may be good enough. It's not like you wear short-sleeved shirts at 37.7 degrees but pull on a sweater at 37 degrees. But integer truncation is unacceptable for many, if not most, applications.

Actually, the problem is much worse than that. An `int` can't handle the ratio 5/9 either; it always yields the value 0. Consequently, the equation as written in this example calculates `celsius` as 0 for all values of `fahr`.

Handling Floating-Point Variables

The limitations of an `int` variable are unacceptable for some applications. The range generally isn't a problem — the double-zillion range of a 64-bit-long integer should be enough for almost anyone. However, the fact that an `int` is limited to whole numbers is a bit harder to swallow.

In some cases, you need numbers that can have a nonzero fractional part. Mathematicians call these *real numbers.* (Somehow that always seemed like a ridiculous name for a number. Are integer numbers somehow unreal?)

REMEMBER

Note that a real number *can* have a nonzero fractional part — that is, 1.5 is a real number, but so is 1.0. For example, 1.0 + 0.1 is 1.1. Just keep that point in mind as you read the rest of this chapter.

Fortunately, C# understands real numbers. Real numbers come in two flavors: floating-point and decimal. Floating-point is the most common type. You can find a description of the decimal type in the section "Using the Decimal Type: Is It an Integer or a Float?" later in this chapter.

Declaring a floating-point variable

A floating-point variable carries the designation `float`, and you declare one as shown in this example:

```
float f = 1.0;
```

After you declare it as `float`, the variable `f` is a `float` for the rest of its natural lifetime.

Table 2-2 describes the two kinds of floating-point types. All floating-point variables are signed. (There's no such thing as a floating-point variable that can't represent a negative value.)

TABLE 2-2 Size and Range of Floating-Point Variable Types

Type	Bytes	Range of Values	Accuracy to Number of Digits	In Use
float	8	$1.5 * 10^{-45}$ to $3.4 * 10^{38}$	6 to 7	float f = 1.2F;
double	16	$5.0 * 10^{-324}$ to $1.7 * 10^{308}$	15 to 16	double d = 1.2;

REMEMBER

You might think that `float` is the default floating-point variable type, but actually the `double` is the default in C#. If you don't specify the type for, say, 12.3, C# calls it a `double`.

The Accuracy column in Table 2-2 refers to the number of significant digits that such a variable type can represent. For example, 5/9 is actually 0.555 . . . with an unending sequence of 5s. However, a `float` variable is said to have six significant digits of accuracy — which means that numbers after the sixth digit are ignored. Thus 5/9 may appear this way when expressed as a `float`:

```
0.5555551457382
```

Here you know that all the digits after the sixth 5 are untrustworthy.

The same number — 5/9 — may appear this way when expressed as a `double`:

```
0.55555555555555557823
```

The `double` packs a whopping 15 to 16 significant digits.

TIP

Use `double` variable types unless you have a specific reason to do otherwise. For example, here's the equation for converting from Fahrenheit to Celsius temperatures using floating-point variables:

```
double celsius = (fahr - 32.0) * (5.0 / 9.0);
```

Examining some limitations of floating-point variables

You may be tempted to use floating-point variables all the time because they solve the truncation problem so nicely. Sure, they use up a bit more memory. But memory is cheap these days, so why not? But floating-point variables also have limitations, which you discover in the following sections.

Counting

You can't use floating-point variables as counting numbers. Some C# structures need to count (as in 1, 2, 3, and so on). You know that 1.0, 2.0, and 3.0 are counting numbers just as well as 1, 2, and 3, but C# doesn't know that. For example, given the accuracy limitations of floating-points, how does C# know that you aren't *actually* saying 1.000001?

REMEMBER

Regardless of whether you find that argument convincing, you can't use a floating-point variable when counting things.

Comparing numbers

You have to be careful when comparing floating-point numbers. For example, 12.5 may be represented as 12.500001. Most people don't care about that little extra bit on the end. However, the computer takes things extremely literally. To C#, 12.500000 and 12.500001 are not the same numbers.

So, if you add 1.1 to 1.1, you can't tell whether the result is 2.2 or 2.200001. And if you ask, "Is `doubleVariable` equal to 2.2?" you may not get the results you expect. Generally, you have to resort to some bogus comparison like this: "Is the absolute value of the difference between `doubleVariable` and 2.2 less than .000001?" In other words, "within an acceptable margin of error."

TECHNICAL STUFF

Modern processors play a trick to make this problem less troublesome than it otherwise may be: They perform floating-point arithmetic in an especially long `double` format — that is, rather than use 64 bits, they use a whopping 80 bits (or 128-bits in newer processors). When rounding off an 80-bit `float` into a 64-bit `float`, you (almost) always get the expected result, even if the 80-bit number was off a bit or two.

Calculation speed

Integers are always faster than floats to use because integers are less complex. Just as you can calculate the value of something using whole numbers a lot faster than using those pesky decimals, so can processors work faster with integers.

TECHNICAL STUFF

Intel processors perform integer math using an internal structure called a general-purpose register that can work only with integers. These same registers are used for counting. Using general-purpose registers is extremely fast. Floating-point numbers require use of a special area that can handle real numbers called the Arithmetic Logic Unit (ALU) and special floating-point registers that don't work for counting. Each calculation takes longer because of the additional handling that floating-point numbers require.

Unfortunately, modern processors are so complex that you can't know precisely how much time you save by using integers. Just know that using integers is generally faster, but that you won't actually see a difference unless you're performing a long list of calculations.

Not-so-limited range

In the past, a floating-point variable could represent a considerably larger range of numbers than an integer type. It still can, but the range of the `long` is large enough to render the point moot much of the time.

WARNING

Even though a simple `float` can represent a very large number, the number of significant digits is limited to about six. For example, `123,456,789F` is the same as `123,456,000F`. (For an explanation of the `F` notation at the end of these numbers, see "Declaring Numeric Constants," later in this chapter.)

Using the Decimal Type: Is It an Integer or a Float?

As explained in previous sections of this chapter, both the integer and floating-point types have their problems. Floating-point variables have rounding problems associated with limits to their accuracy, while `int` variables just lop off the fractional part of a variable. In some cases, you need a variable type that offers the best of both worlds:

- » Like a floating-point variable, it can store fractions.
- » Like an integer, numbers of this type offer exact values for use in computations — for example, 12.5 is really 12.5 and not 12.500001.

Fortunately, C# provides such a variable type, called `decimal`. A `decimal` variable can represent a number between 10^{-28} and 10^{28} — which represents a lot of zeros! And it does so without rounding problems unless you're dealing with extremely large numbers.

Declaring a decimal

Decimal variables are declared and used like any variable type, like this:

```
decimal m1 = 100; // Good
decimal m2 = 100M; // Better
```

The first declaration shown here creates a variable m1 and initializes it to a value of 100. What isn't obvious is that 100 is actually of type int. Thus, C# must convert the int into a decimal type before performing the initialization. Fortunately, C# understands what you mean — and performs the conversion for you.

The declaration of m2 is the best. This clever declaration initializes m2 with the decimal constant 100M. The letter *M* at the end of the number specifies that the constant is of type decimal. No conversion is required. (See the section "Declaring Numeric Constants," later in this chapter.)

Comparing decimals, integers, and floating-point types

The decimal variable type seems to have all the advantages and none of the disadvantages of int or double types. Variables of this type have a very large range, they don't suffer from rounding problems, and 25.0 is 25.0 and not 25.00001.

The decimal variable type has two significant limitations, however. First, a decimal is not considered a counting number because it may contain a fractional value. Consequently, you can't use them in flow-control loops, as explained in Chapter 5 of this minibook.

The second problem with decimal variables is equally serious or even more so. Computations involving decimal values are significantly slower than those involving either simple integer or floating-point values. On a crude benchmark test of 300,000,000 adds and subtracts, the operations involving decimal variables were approximately 50 times slower than those involving simple int variables. The relative computational speed gets even worse for more complex operations. Besides that, most computational functions, such as calculating sines or exponents, are not available for the decimal number type.

Clearly, the decimal variable type is most appropriate for applications such as banking, in which accuracy is extremely important but the number of calculations is relatively small.

Examining the bool Type: Is It Logical?

Finally, here's a logical variable type, one that can help you get to the truth of the matter. The Boolean type `bool` can have two values: `true` or `false`.

WARNING

Former C and C++ programmers are accustomed to using the `int` value 0 (zero) to mean `false` and nonzero to mean `true`. That doesn't work in C#.

You declare a `bool` variable this way:

```
bool thisIsABool = true;
```

No direct conversion path exists between `bool` variables and any other types. In other words, you can't convert a `bool` directly into something else. (Even if you could, you shouldn't because it doesn't make any sense.) In particular, you can't convert a `bool` into an `int` (such as `false` becoming 0) or a `string` (such as `false` becoming the word "false").

Checking Out Character Types

A program that can do nothing more than spit out numbers may be fine for mathematicians, accountants, insurance agents with their mortality figures, and folks calculating cannon-shell trajectories. (Don't laugh. The original computers were built to generate tables of cannon-shell trajectories to help artillery gunners.) However, for most applications, programs must deal with letters as well as numbers.

C# treats letters in two distinctly different ways: individual characters of type `char` (usually pronounced *char*, as in singe or burn) and strings of characters — a type called, cleverly enough, `string`.

The char variable type

The `char` variable is a box capable of holding a single character. A character constant appears as a character surrounded by a pair of single quotation marks, as in this example:

```
char c = 'a';
```

You can store any single character from the Roman, Hebrew, Arabic, Cyrillic, and most other alphabets. You can also store Japanese katakana and hiragana characters, as well as many Japanese and Chinese kanjis.

In addition, `char` is considered a counting type. That means you can use a `char` type to control the looping structures described in Chapter 5 of this minibook. Character variables do not suffer from rounding problems.

WARNING

The character variable includes no font information. So you may store in a `char` variable what you think is a perfectly good kanji (and it may well be) — but when you view the character, it can look like garbage if you're not looking at it through the eyes of the proper font.

Special chars

Some characters within a given font are not printable, in the sense that you don't see anything when you look at them on the computer screen or printer. The most obvious example of this is the space, which is represented by the character `' '` (single quotation mark, space, single quotation mark). Other characters have no letter equivalent — for example, the tab character. C# uses the backslash to flag these characters, as shown in Table 2-3.

TABLE 2-3 Special Characters

Character Constant	Value
'\n'	Newline
'\t'	Tab
'\0'	Null character
'\r'	Carriage return
'\\'	Backslash

The string type

Another extremely common variable type is the `string`. The following examples show how you declare and initialize `string` variables:

```
// Declare now, initialize later.
string someString1;
someString1 = "this is a string";
```

```
// Or initialize when declared - preferable.
string someString2 = "this is a string";
```

A `string` constant, often called a *string literal*, is a set of characters surrounded by double quotation marks. The characters in a `string` can include the special characters shown in Table 2-3. A string cannot be written across a line in the C# source file, but it can contain the newline character, as the following examples show (see boldface):

```
// The following is not legal.
string someString = "This is a line
and so is this";
// However, the following is legal.
string someString = "This is a line\nand so is this";
```

When written out with `Console.WriteLine()`, the last line in this example places the two phrases on separate lines, like this:

```
This is a line
and so is this
```

A `string` is not a counting type. A `string` is also not a value type — no "string" exists that's intrinsic (built in) to the processor. A computer processor understands only numbers, not letters. The letter *A* is actually the number 65 to the processor. Only one of the common operators works on `string` objects: The + operator concatenates two strings into one. For example:

```
string s = "this is a phrase"
        + " and so is this";
```

These lines of code set the `string` variable `s` equal to this character string:

```
"this is a phrase and so is this"
```

WARNING

The `string` with no characters, written `""` (two double quotation marks in a row), is a valid `string`, called an empty `string` (or sometimes a null `string` by those who like to be confusing). However, an empty `string` (`""`) is different from a null `char ('\0')`, a real null string (where string `s1 = null`), and from a `string` containing any amount of space, even one (`" "`).

TIP

A best practice is to initialize strings using the `String.Empty` value, which means the same thing as `""` and is less prone to misinterpretation:

```
string mySecretName = String.Empty; // A property of the String type
```

USING THE VERBATIM STRING LITERAL

There are exceptions to many rules, and the verbatim string literal provides one of those exceptions for C# developers. While this string is illegal:

```
string someString = "This is a line
and so is this";
```

this string is legal because of the addition of the @ sign:

```
string someString = @"This is a line
and so is this";
```

The @ sign, or verbatim string operator, tells the compile to interpret a sting literally so that you don't have to deal with things like escape sequences. For example, normally you must use \\ to indicate a single \. However, with a verbatim string literal, you can create file paths like this one:

```
string filename1 = @"c:\documents\files\myFile.txt";
```

that are a lot easier to read. You see string literals used in many examples later in the book.

By the way, all the other data types in this chapter are *value types*. The `string` type, however, is not a value type, as explained in the following section. Chapter 3 of this minibook goes into much more detail about the `string` type.

What's a Value Type?

TECHNICAL STUFF

The variable types described in this chapter are of fixed length — again with the exception of `string`. A fixed-length variable type always occupies the same amount of memory. So if you assign `a = b`, C# can transfer the value of `b` into `a` without taking extra measures designed to handle variable-length types. In addition, these kinds of variables are stored in a special location called the *stack* as actual values. You don't need to worry about the stack; you just need to know that it exists as a location in memory. This characteristic is why these types of variables are called *value types*.

REMEMBER

The types `int`, `double`, and `bool`, and their close derivatives (like unsigned `int`), are intrinsic variable types built right into the processor. The intrinsic variable types plus `decimal` are also known as value types because variables store the actual data. The `string` type is neither an intrinsic nor a value type — because the variable actually stores a sort of "pointer" to the string's data, called a *reference*. The data in the string is actually off in another location. Think of a reference type as you would an address for a house. Knowing the address tells you the location of the house, but you must actually go to the address to find the physical house.

The programmer-defined types explained in Chapter 8 of this minibook, known as reference types, are neither value types nor intrinsic. The `string` type is a reference type, although the C# compiler does accord it some special treatment because `string` types are so widely used.

Comparing string and char

Although strings deal with characters, the `string` type is amazingly different from the `char`. Of course, certain trivial differences exist. You enclose a character with single quotation marks, as in this example:

```
'a'
```

On the other hand, you put double quotation marks around a string:

```
"this is a string"
"a" // So is this -- see the double quotes?
```

The rules concerning strings are not the same as those concerning characters. For one thing, you know right up front that a `char` is a single character, and that's it. For example, the following code makes no sense, either as addition or as concatenation:

```
char c1 = 'a';
char c2 = 'b';
char c3 = c1 + c2;
```

Actually, this bit of code almost compiles — but with a completely different meaning from what was intended. These statements convert `c1` into an `int` consisting of the numeric value of `c1`. C# also converts `c2` into an `int` and then adds the two integers. The error occurs when trying to store the results back into `c3` — numeric data may be lost storing an `int` into the smaller `char`. In any case, the operation makes no sense.

A string, on the other hand, can be any length. So concatenating two strings, as shown here, *does* make sense:

```
string s1 = "a";
string s2 = "b";
string s3 = s1 + s2; // Result is "ab"
```

As part of its library, C# defines an entire suite of string operations. You find these operations described in Chapter 3 of this minibook.

Calculating Leap Years: DateTime

What if you had to write a program that calculates whether this year is a leap year?

The algorithm looks like this:

```
It's a leap year if
  year is evenly divisible by 4
  and, if it happens to be evenly divisible by 100,
    it's also evenly divisible by 400
```

You don't have enough tools yet to tackle that in C#. But you could just ask the `DateTime` type (which is a value type, like `int`):

```
DateTime thisYear = new DateTime(2020, 1, 1);
bool isLeapYear = DateTime.IsLeapYear(thisYear.Year);
```

The result for 2020 is `true`, but for 2021, it's `false`. (For now, don't worry about that first line of code, which uses some things you haven't gotten to yet.)

With the `DateTime` data type, you can do something like 80 different operations, such as pull out just the month; get the day of the week; add days, hours, minutes, seconds, milliseconds, months, or years to a given date; get the number of days in a given month; and subtract two dates.

The following sample lines use a convenient property of `DateTime` called `Now` to capture the present date and time, and one of the numerous `DateTime` methods that let you convert one time into another:

```
DateTime thisMoment = DateTime.Now;
DateTime anHourFromNow = thisMoment.AddHours(1);
```

You can also extract specific parts of a `DateTime`:

```
int year = DateTime.Now.Year;                    // For example, 2021
DayOfWeek dayOfWeek = DateTime.Now.DayOfWeek;   // For example, Sunday
```

If you print that `DayOfWeek` object, it prints something like "Sunday." And you can do other handy manipulations of `DateTimes`:

```
DateTime date = DateTime.Today;                  // Get just the date part.
TimeSpan time = thisMoment.TimeOfDay;            // Get just the time part.
TimeSpan duration = new TimeSpan(3, 0, 0, 0);   // Specify length in days.
DateTime threeDaysFromNow = thisMoment.Add(duration);
```

The first two lines just extract portions of the information in a `DateTime`. The next two lines add a *duration* (length of time) to a `DateTime`. A duration differs from a moment in time; you specify durations with the `TimeSpan` class, and moments with `DateTime`. So the third line sets up a `TimeSpan` of three days, zero hours, zero minutes, and zero seconds. The fourth line adds the three-day duration to the `DateTime` representing right now, resulting in a new `DateTime` whose day component is three greater than the day component for `thisMoment`.

Subtracting a `DateTime` from another `DateTime` (or a `TimeSpan` from a `DateTime`) returns a `DateTime`:

```
TimeSpan duration1 = new TimeSpan(1, 0, 0); // One hour later.
// Since Today gives 12:00:00 AM, the following gives 1:00:00 AM:
DateTime anHourAfterMidnight = DateTime.Today.Add(duration1);
Console.WriteLine("An hour after midnight will be {0}", anHourAfterMidnight);
DateTime midnight = anHourAfterMidnight.Subtract(duration1);
Console.WriteLine("An hour before 1 AM is {0}", midnight);
```

The first line of the preceding code creates a `TimeSpan` of one hour. The next line gets the date (actually, midnight this morning) and adds the one-hour span to it, resulting in a `DateTime` representing 1:00 a.m. today. The next-to-last line subtracts a one-hour duration from 1:00 a.m. to get 12:00 a.m. (midnight).

Declaring Numeric Constants

There are very few absolutes in life; however, C# does have an absolute: Every expression has a value and a type. In a declaration such as `int n`, you can easily see that the variable `n` is an `int`. Further, you can reasonably assume that the type of a calculation `n + 1` is an `int`. However, what type is the constant `1`?

The type of a constant depends on two things: its value and the presence of an optional descriptor letter at the end of the constant. Any integer type between the values of –2,147,483,648 to 2,147,483,647 is assumed to be an `int`. Numbers larger than 2,147,483,647 are assumed to be `long`. Any floating-point number is assumed to be a `double`.

Table 2-4 demonstrates constants that have been declared to be of a particular type. The case of these descriptors is not important; `1U` and `1u` are equivalent.

TABLE 2-4 **Common Constants Declared along with Their Types**

Constant	Type
1	int
1U	unsigned int
1L	long int (avoid lowercase *l*; it's too much like the digit 1)
1.0	double
1.0F	float
1M	decimal
true	bool
false	bool
'a'	char
'\n'	char (the character newline)
'\x123'	char (the character whose numeric value is hex 123)[1]
"a string"	string
""	string (an empty string); same as String.Empty

[1] *"hex" is short for hexadecimal (numbers in base 16 rather than in base 10).*

USING INTERPOLATED CONSTANTS IN C# 10.0

An interpolated string is one in which you use variables and standard text to build up a finalized string. You see interpolated strings used in many examples in this book. For example, you find them used and explained in the "Creating your own interface at home in your spare time" section of Book 2, Chapter 7. An interpolated constant takes the concept of an interpolated string a little further. Here is an example:

```
const string Name = George;
const int Age = 44;
const string GeorgeStat = $"{Name} is {Age} years old.";
```

Like an interpolated string, an interpolated constant begins with a $ and appears within double quotes (""). It relies on the use of constants to fill in information, so Name and Age appear as actual values in the resulting constant that reads:

```
George is 44 years old.
```

To use an interpolated constant, the values must be evaluated at compile time rather than runtime. In addition, you can't declare a static interpolated constant. You can see more details about this new way of creating constants at `https://docs.microsoft.com/en-us/dotnet/csharp/language-reference/keywords/const`.

Changing Types: The Cast

Humans don't treat different types of counting numbers differently. For example, a normal person (as distinguished from a C# programmer) doesn't think about the number 1 as being signed, unsigned, short, or long. Although C# considers these types to be different, even C# realizes that a relationship exists between them. For example, this bit of code converts an `int` into a `long`:

```
int intValue = 10;
long longValue;
longValue = intValue; // This is OK.
```

An `int` variable can be converted into a `long` because any possible value of an `int` can be stored in a `long` — and because they are both counting numbers. C# makes the conversion for you automatically without comment. This is called an *implicit* type conversion.

A conversion in the opposite direction can cause problems, however. For example, this line is illegal:

```
long longValue = 10;
int intValue;
intValue = longValue; // This is illegal.
```

TIP

Some values that you can store in a `long` don't fit in an `int` (4 billion, for example). If you try to shoehorn such a value into an `int`, C# generates an error because data may be lost during the conversion process. This type of bug is difficult to catch.

But what if you know that the conversion is okay? For example, even though `longValue` is a `long`, maybe you know that its value can't exceed 100 in this particular program. In that case, converting the `long` variable `longValue` into the `int` variable `intValue` would be okay.

You can tell C# that you know what you're doing by means of a cast:

```
long longValue = 10;
int intValue;
intValue = (int)longValue; // This is now OK.
```

In a *cast*, you place the name of the type you want in parentheses and put it immediately in front of the value you want to convert. This cast forces C# to convert the `long` named `longValue` into an `int` and assumes that you know what you're doing. In retrospect, the assertion that you know what you're doing may seem overly confident, but it's often valid.

A counting number can be converted into a floating-point number automatically, but converting a floating-point into a counting number requires a cast:

```
double doubleValue = 10.0;
long longValue = (long)doubleValue;
```

All conversions to and from a `decimal` require a cast. In fact, all numeric types can be converted into all other numeric types through the application of a cast. Neither `bool` nor `string` can be converted directly into any other type.

TECHNICAL STUFF

Built-in C# methods can convert a number, character, or Boolean into its string equivalent, so to speak. For example, you can convert the `bool` value `true` into the `string` "true"; however, you cannot consider this change a direct conversion. The `bool true` and the `string "true"` are completely different things. Later in the book, you learn about the `Convert` class that goes a long way toward allowing you to convert anything into anything else, including converting `bool` values into `int` values, but using the `Convert` class isn't the same as performing a cast.

Letting the C# Compiler Infer Data Types

So far in this book — well, so far in this chapter — when you declared a variable, you *always* specified its exact data type, like this:

```
int i = 5;
string s = "Hello C#";
double d = 1.0;
```

You're allowed to offload some of that work onto the C# compiler, using the `var` keyword:

```
var i = 5;
var s = "Hello C# 4.0";
var d = 1.0;
```

Now the compiler *infers* the data type for you — it looks at the stuff on the right side of the assignment to see what type the left side is.

TECHNICAL STUFF

For what it's worth, Chapter 3 of this minibook shows how to calculate the type of an expression like the ones on the right side of the assignments in the preceding example. Not that you need to do that — the compiler mostly does it for you. Suppose, for example, that you have an initializing expression like this:

```
var x = 3.0 + 2 - 1.5;
```

The compiler can figure out that `x` is a `double` value. It looks at `3.0` and `1.5` and sees that they're of type `double`. Then it notices that `2` is an `int`, which the compiler can convert *implicitly* to a `double` for the calculation. All the additional terms in `x`'s initialization expression end up as `double` types. So the *inferred type* of `x` is `double`.

But now, you can simply utter the magic word `var` and supply an initialization expression, and the compiler does the rest:

```
var aVariable = <initialization expression here>;
```

TECHNICAL STUFF

If you've worked with a scripting language such as JavaScript or VBScript, you may have gotten used to all-purpose-in-one data types. VBScript calls them `Variant` data types — and a `Variant` can be anything at all. But does `var` in C# signify a `Variant` type? Not at all. The object you declare with `var` definitely has a C# data type, such as `int`, `string`, or `double`. You just don't have to declare what it is.

What's really lurking in the variables declared in this example with var? Take a look at this:

```
var aString = "Hello C# 3.0";
Console.WriteLine(aString.GetType().ToString());
```

The mumbo jumbo in that WriteLine() statement calls the String.GetType() method on aString to get its C# type. Then it calls the resulting object's ToString() method to display the object's type. Here's what you see in the console window:

```
System.String
```

The output from this code proves that the compiler correctly inferred the type of aString.

TIP

Most of the time, the best practice is to not use var. Save it for when it's necessary. Being explicit about the type of a variable is clearer to anyone reading your code than using var.

You see examples later in which var is definitely called for, and you use it part of the time throughout this book, even sometimes where it's not strictly necessary. You need to see it used, and use it yourself, to internalize it.

TIP

You can see var used in other ways: with arrays and collections of data, in Chapter 6 of this minibook, and with anonymous types, in Book 2. Anonymous? Bet you can't wait.

What's more, the dynamic type takes var a step further. The var type causes the compiler to infer the type of the variable based on the initialization value. The dynamic keyword does this at runtime, using a set of tools called the Dynamic Language Runtime. You can find more about the dynamic type in Chapter 6 of Book 3.

IN THIS CHAPTER

» Pulling and twisting a string with C#

» Matching searching, trimming, splitting, and concatenating strings

» Parsing strings read into the program

» Formatting output strings manually or using `String.Format()`

Chapter 3 Pulling Strings

For many applications, you can treat a `string` like one of the built-in value-type variable types such as `int` or `char`. Certain operations that are otherwise reserved for these intrinsic types are available to strings:

```
int i = 1;          // Declare and initialize an int.
string s = "abc";   // Declare and initialize a string.
```

In other respects, as shown in the following example, a `string` is treated like a user-defined class (Book 2 discusses classes):

```
string s1 = new String();
string s2 = "abcd";
int lengthOfString = s2.Length;
```

Which is it — a value type or a class? In fact, `String` is a class for which C# offers special treatment because strings are so widely used in programs. The keyword `string` is an alias of the `String` class, as shown in this bit of code:

```
String s1 = "abcd"; // Assign a string literal to a String obj.
string s2 = s1;     // Assign a String obj to a string variable.
```

In this example, the two assignments demonstrate that `string` and `String` are the same type, so you can use either. However, by convention, most developers use lowercase `string`. The rest of the chapter covers the `string` type and all the tasks you can accomplish by using them.

REMEMBER

You don't have to type the source code for this chapter manually. In fact, using the downloadable source is a lot easier. You can find the source for this chapter in the `\CSAIO4D2E\BK01\CH03` folder of the downloadable source. See the Introduction for details on how to find these source files.

The Union Is Indivisible, and So Are Strings

You need to know at least one thing that you didn't learn before the sixth grade: You can't change a `string` object after creating it. Even though you may see text that speaks of modifying a string, C# doesn't have an operation that modifies the actual `string` object. Plenty of operations appear to modify the `string` that you're working with, but they always return the modified `string` as a new object instead. The new string contains the modified text and has the same name as the existing string, but it really is a new string. This makes the `string` type *immutable* (unchangeable).

For example, the operation `"His name is " + "Randy"` changes neither of the two strings, but it generates a third string, `"His name is Randy"`. One side effect of this behavior is that you don't have to worry about someone modifying a `string` that you create. Consider the `ModifyString` example program. It starts with a class that simply declares a string like this:

```
class Student
{
    public String Name;
}
```

Book 2 fully discusses classes, but for now, you can see that the `Student` class contains a data variable called `Name`, of type `String`. You can use this class as a replacement for `String` like this:

```
static void Main(string[] args)
{
    // Create a student object.
    Student s1 = new Student();
    s1.Name = "Jenny";

    // Now make a new object with the same name.
    Student s2 = new Student();
    s2.Name = s1.Name;

    // "Changing" the name in the s1 object does not
    // change the object itself because ToUpper() returns
```

```
    // a new string without modifying the original.
    s2.Name = s1.Name.ToUpper();
    Console.WriteLine("s1 - " + s1.Name + ", s2 - " + s2.Name);
    Console.Read();
}
```

The Student objects s1 and s2 are set up so that the student Name data in each points to the same string data. ToUpper() converts the string s1.Name to all uppercase characters. Normally, this would be a problem because both s1 and s2 point to the same object. However, ToUpper() doesn't change Name — it creates a new, independent uppercase string and stores it in the object s2. Now the two Students don't point to the same string data. Here's some sample output from this program:

```
s1 - Jenny, s2 - JENNY
```

TECHNICAL STUFF

The immutability of strings is also important for string constants. A string such as "this is a string" is a form of a string constant, just as 1 is an int constant. A compiler may choose to combine all accesses to the single constant "this is a string". Reusing string constants can reduce the *footprint* of the resulting program (its size on disc or in memory) but would be impossible if anyone could modify the string.

Performing Common Operations on a String

C# programmers perform more operations on strings than Beverly Hills plastic surgeons do on Hollywood hopefuls. Virtually every program uses the addition operator that's used on strings, as shown in this example:

```
string name = "Randy";
Console.WriteLine("His name is " + name); // + means concatenate.
```

The String class provides this special operator. However, the String class also provides other, more direct methods for manipulating strings. You can see the complete list by looking up "String class" in the Visual Studio Help Index, and you'll meet many of the usual suspects in this chapter including:

- Comparing strings — for equality or for tasks like alphabetizing
- Changing and converting strings in various ways: replacing part of a string, changing case, and converting between strings and other things

» Accessing the individual characters in a string
» Finding characters or substrings inside a string
» Performing pattern matching on strings
» Handling input from the command line
» Managing formatted output
» Working efficiently with strings using the `StringBuilder`

Comparing Strings

It's common to need to compare two strings. For example, did the user input the expected value? Or maybe you have a list of strings and need to alphabetize them. Best practice calls for avoiding the standard == and != comparison operators and to use the built-in comparison functions because strings can have nuances of difference between them, and these operators don't always work as expected. In addition, using the comparison functions makes the kind of comparison you want clearer and makes your code easier to maintain. The article at `https://docs.microsoft.com/en-us/dotnet/csharp/how-to/compare-strings` provides some additional details on this issue, but the following sections tell you all you need to know about comparing two strings.

Equality for all strings: The Compare() method

Numerous operations treat a string as a single object — for example, the `Compare()` method. `Compare()`, with the following properties, compares two strings as though they were numbers:

» If the left string is *greater than* the right string, `Compare(left, right)` returns 1.
» If the left string is *less than* the right string, it returns -1.
» If the two strings are equal, it returns 0.

The algorithm works as follows when written in *notational C#* (that is, C# without all the details, also known as *pseudocode*):

```
compare(string s1, string s2)
{
  // Loop through each character of the strings until
  // a character in one string is greater than the
  // corresponding character in the other string.
  foreach character in the shorter string
    if (s1's character > s2's character when treated as a number)
      return 1
    if (s1's character < s2's character)
      return -1
  // Okay, every letter matches, but if the string s1 is longer,
  // then it's greater.
  if s1 has more characters left
    return 1
  // If s2 is longer, it's greater.
  if s2 has more characters left
    return -1
  // If every character matches and the two strings are the same
  // length, then they are "equal."
  return 0
}
```

Thus, `"abcd"` is greater than `"abbd"`, and `"abcde"` is greater than `"abcd"`. More often than not, you don't care whether one string is greater than the other, but only whether the two strings are equal. You *do* want to know which string is bigger when performing a sort.

REMEMBER

The `Compare()` method returns 0 when two strings are identical (as shown by the code in boldface type in the following listing). The following test program, `BuildASentence`, uses the equality feature of `Compare()` to perform a certain operation when the program encounters a particular string or strings. `BuildASentence` prompts the user to enter lines of text. Each line is concatenated to the previous line to build a single sentence. This program ends when the user enters the word *EXIT, exit, QUIT,* or *quit.* (You'll see after the code what the code in bold does.)

```
static void Main(string[] args)
{
    Console.WriteLine("Each line you enter will be "
                    + "added to a sentence until you "
                    + "enter EXIT or QUIT");

    // Ask the user for input; continue concatenating
    // the phrases input until the user enters exit or
    // quit (start with an empty sentence).
    string sentence = "";
```

```
    for (; ; )
    {
        // Get the next line.
        Console.WriteLine("Enter a string ");
        string line = Console.ReadLine();

        // Exit the loop if line is a terminator.
        string[] terms = { "EXIT", "exit", "QUIT", "quit" };

        // Compare the string entered to each of the
        // legal exit commands.
        bool quitting = false;

        foreach (string term in terms)
        {
            // Break out of the for loop if you have a match.
            if (String.Compare(line, term) == 0)
            {
                quitting = true;
            }
        }
        if (quitting == true)
        {
            break;
        }

        // Otherwise, add it to the sentence.
        sentence = String.Concat(sentence, line);

        // Let the user know how she's doing.
        Console.WriteLine("\nyou've entered: " + sentence);
    }

    Console.WriteLine("\ntotal sentence:\n" + sentence);
    Console.Read();
}
```

After prompting the user for what the program expects, the program creates an empty initial sentence string called `sentence`. From there, the program enters an infinite loop.

The `while(true)` and `for(;;)` statements create a loop that loops forever, or at least long enough for some internal `break` or `return` to break you out. The two loops are equivalent, and in practice, you'll see them both. (Looping is covered in Chapter 5 of this minibook.)

BuildASentence prompts the user to enter a line of text, which the program reads using the ReadLine() method. Having read the line, the program checks to see whether it is a terminator by using the code in boldface in the preceding example.

The termination section of the program defines an array of strings called terms and a bool variable quitting, initialized to false. (Book 1, Chapter 6 discusses C# arrays.) Each member of the terms array is one of the strings you're looking for. Any of these strings causes the program to end.

WARNING

The program must include both "EXIT" and "exit" because Compare() considers the two strings to be different by default. (The way the program is written, these are the only two ways to spell *exit*. Strings such as "Exit" and "eXit" aren't recognized as terminators.) You can also use other string operations to check for various spellings of exit. You see how to perform this task in the next section.

The termination section loops through each of the strings in the array of target strings. If Compare() reports a match to any of the terminator phrases, quitting is set to true. If quitting remains false after the termination section and line is not one of the terminator strings, it is concatenated to the end of the sentence using the String.Concat() method. The program outputs the immediate result so that the user can see what's going on. Iterating through an array is a classic way to look for one of various possible values. (The next section shows you another way, and Book 2 gives you an even cooler way.) Here's a sample run of the BuildASentence program:

```
Each line you enter will be added to a
sentence until you enter EXIT or QUIT
Enter a string
Programming with

You've entered: Programming with
Enter a string
 C# is fun

You've entered: Programming with C# is fun
Enter a string
 (more or less)

You've entered: Programming with C# is fun (more or less)
Enter a string
EXIT

Total sentence:
Programming with C# is fun (more or less)
```

Would you like your compares with or without case?

The `Compare()` method used in the previous example considers `"EXIT"` and `"exit"` different strings. However, the `Compare()` method has a second version that includes a third argument. This argument indicates whether the comparison should ignore the letter case. A `true` indicates "ignore."

The following version of the lengthy termination section in the `BuildASentence` example (found in `BuildASentence2`) breaks out of the `for` loop whether the string passed is uppercase, lowercase, or a combination of the two:

```
// Indicate true if passed either exit or quit,
// irrespective of case.
if ((String.Compare("exit", line, true) == 0) ||
    (String.Compare("quit", line, true) == 0))
{
    break;
}
```

This version is much simpler than the previous looping version. This code doesn't need to worry about case, and it can use a single conditional expression because it now has only two options to consider instead of a longer list: any spelling variation of QUIT or EXIT. You can see the difference in BuildASentence2, which requires only 43 lines of code, rather than the 55 lines used by the previous version.

What If I Want to Switch Case?

You may be interested in whether all the characters (or just one) in a string are uppercase or lowercase characters. And you may need to convert from one to the other.

Distinguishing between all-uppercase and all-lowercase strings

You can use the `switch` statement (see Chapter 5 of this minibook) to look for a particular string. Normally, you use the `switch` statement to compare a counting number to some set of possible values; however, `switch` does work on `string` objects as well. This version of the termination section in `BuildASentence` (see `BuildASentence3`) uses the `switch` construct:

```
switch (line)
{
    case "EXIT":
    case "exit":
    case "QUIT":
    case "quit":
        return;
}
```

This approach works because you're comparing only a limited number of strings. Using the caseless Compare() in the previous section gives the program greater flexibility in understanding the user.

Converting a string to upper- or lowercase

Suppose you have a string in lowercase and need to convert it to uppercase. You can use the ToUpper() method:

```
string lowcase = "armadillo";
string upcase = lowcase.ToUpper();  // ARMADILLO.
```

Similarly, you can convert a string to lowercase with ToLower().

What if you want to convert just the first character in a string to uppercase? The following rather convoluted code will do it (but you can see a better way in the last section of this chapter):

```
string name = "chuck";
string properName =
   char.ToUpper(name[0]).ToString() + name.Substring(1, name.Length - 1);
```

The idea in this example is to extract the first char in name (that's name[0]), convert it to uppercase, and then to a one-character string with ToString(), and then tack on the remainder of name after removing the old lowercase first character with Substring().

You can tell whether a string is uppercased or lowercased by using this scary-looking if statement:

```
if (string.Compare(line.ToUpper(CultureInfo.InvariantCulture),
                   line, false) == 0) ...  // True if line is all upper.
```

Here the Compare() method is comparing an uppercase version of line to line itself. There should be no difference if line is already uppercase. The CultureInfo.

InvariantCulture property tells Compare() to perform the comparison without considering culture. You can read more about working with cultures at https://docs.microsoft.com/dotnet/api/system.globalization.cultureinfo.invariantculture. If you want to ensure that the string contains all lowercase characters, stick a not (!) operator in front of the Compare() call. Alternatively, you can use a loop, as described in the next section.

Looping through a String

You can access individual characters of a string in a foreach loop. The following code steps through the characters and writes each to the console — just another (roundabout) way to write out the string:

```
string favoriteFood = "cheeseburgers";
foreach (char c in favoriteFood)
{
  Console.Write(c);  // Could do things to the char here.
}
Console.WriteLine();
```

You can use that loop to solve the problem of deciding whether favoriteFood is all uppercase. (See the previous section for more about case.)

```
bool isUppercase = true;  // Assume that it's uppercase.
foreach (char c in favoriteFood)
{
  if (!char.IsUpper(c))
  {
    isUppercase = false;  // Disproves all uppercase, so get out.
    break;
  }
}
```

At the end of the loop, isUppercase will either be true or false. As shown in the final example in the previous section on switching case, you can also access individual characters in a string by using an array index notation.

REMEMBER

Arrays start with zero, so if you want the first character, you ask for index [0]. If you want the third, you ask for index [2].

```
char thirdChar = favoriteFood[2];   // First 'e' in "cheeseburgers"
```

Searching Strings

What if you need to find a particular word, or a particular character, inside a string? Maybe you need its index so that you can use Substring(), Replace(), Remove(), or some other method on it. In this section, you see how to find individual characters or substrings using favoriteFood from the previous section.

Can I find it?

The simplest task is finding an individual character with IndexOf():

```
int indexOfLetterS = favoriteFood.IndexOf('s');  // 4.
```

Class String also has other methods for finding things, either individual characters or substrings:

- IndexOfAny() takes an array of chars and searches the string for any of them, returning the index of the first one found.

  ```
  char[] charsToLookFor = { 'a', 'b', 'c' };
  int indexOfFirstFound = favoriteFood.IndexOfAny(charsToLookFor);
  ```

  That call is often written more briefly this way:

  ```
  int index = name.IndexOfAny(new char[] { 'a', 'b', 'c' });
  ```

- LastIndexOf() finds not the first occurrence of a character but the last.
- LastIndexOfAny() works like IndexOfAny(), but starting at the end of the string.
- Contains() returns true if a given substring can be found within the target string:

  ```
  if (favoriteFood.Contains("ee")) ...            // True
  ```

- And Substring() returns a part of a string beginning at a certain point in a source string and ending at a certain point in a source string (if it's there), or empty (if not):

  ```
  string sub = favoriteFood.Substring(6, favoriteFood.Length - 6);
  ```

Is my string empty?

How can you tell if a target string is empty ("") or has the value null? (A null value means that the string has nothing assigned to it.) Use the IsNullOrEmpty() method, like this:

```
bool notThere = string.IsNullOrEmpty(favoriteFood);  // False
```

Notice how you call IsNullOrEmpty(): string.IsNullOrEmpty(s). You can set a string to the empty string in these two ways:

```
string name = "";
string name = string.Empty;
```

Using advanced pattern matching

C# 9.0 introduces some enhancements to a method called pattern matching. A *pattern* is something that describes how an object could look, and when you match a pattern, it means that you can see the pattern in the object. Patterns are common in the real world. For example, when making clothing, a person relies on a pattern to cut the material. Likewise, programmers use patterns (Book 2, Chapter 8 discusses the Observer pattern) to create code that behaves in a certain way and is recognizable by other developers. However, the C# 9.0 additions are of a different sort. For example, you can now look for null (as a pattern) in a string like this:

```
if (favoriteFood is not null)
{
    Console.WriteLine(favoriteFood);
}
```

This new form of working with null is clearer than using string.IsNullOrEmpty(), plus it's a lot easier to type.

There is also new support as of C# 9.0 for the use of operators to perform comparisons. The following code is a little complex, but the idea is that you can determine whether a particular expression is correct. In this case, you verify the quantity of a favorite food starting with a special kind of function (you can see this example at work in the CheckFavoriteFood example in the downloadable source):

```
static string Quantity(int burgers) => burgers switch
{
    <= 2 => "too few",
    > 10 => "too many",
    _ => "an acceptable number of",
};
```

This is a newer type of switch that appears as a function. You pass a value to it, the switch decides which case is relevant, and then it outputs the string. So, if the input value, burgers, is less than or equal to 2, you're ordering too few burgers. The => symbol says what to provide as output when a condition is met. The special _ condition simply says that if none of the other conditions is true, C# should use this one.

The main code for this example simply calls the function with various amounts of burgers like this:

```
static void Main(string[] args)
{
    Console.WriteLine("Buying " + Quantity(1) + " burgers.");
    Console.WriteLine("Buying " + Quantity(13) + " burgers.");
    Console.WriteLine("Buying " + Quantity(3) + " burgers.");

    Console.ReadLine();
}
```

This code combines the two strings, `"Buying "` and `" burgers."`, with the amounts passed to `Quantity()`. Here is what you see for output:

```
Buying too few burgers.
Buying too many burgers.
Buying an acceptable number of burgers.
```

REMEMBER

If you try to run this example without adding C# 9.0 support, you'll see an error message. Consequently, you need to add

```
<PropertyGroup>
   <LangVersion>9.0</LangVersion>
</PropertyGroup>
```

to the `CheckFavoriteFood.csproj` file. As the book progresses, you see a number of uses for features that were new as of C# 9.0. If you want to get a preview, check out the C# 9.0 elements in the *Patterns* article at `https://docs.microsoft.com/en-us/dotnet/csharp/language-reference/operators/patterns`.

Getting Input from Users in Console Applications

A common task in console applications is getting the information that the user types when the application prompts for input, such as an interest rate or a name. The console methods provide all input in string format. Sometimes you need to parse the input to extract a number from it. And sometimes you need to process lots of input numbers.

Trimming excess white space

First, consider that in some cases, you don't want to mess with any white space on either end of the string. The term *white space* refers to the characters that don't normally display on the screen — for example, space, newline (or \n), and tab (\t). You may sometimes also encounter the carriage return character, \r. You can use the Trim() method to trim off the edges of the string, like this:

```
// Get rid of any extra spaces on either end of the string.
random = random.Trim();
```

Class String also provides TrimFront() and TrimEnd() methods for getting more specific, and you can pass an array of chars to include in the trimming process. For example, you might trim a leading currency sign, such as '$'. Cleaning up a string can make it easier to parse. The trim methods return a new string.

Parsing numeric input

A program can read from the keyboard one character at a time, but you have to worry about newlines and so on. An easier approach reads a string and then *parses* the characters out of the string. The ReadLine() method used for reading from the console returns a string object. A program that expects numeric input must convert this string. C# provides just the conversion tool you need in the Convert class. This class provides a conversion method from string to each built-in variable type. Thus, this code segment reads a number from the keyboard and stores it in an int variable:

```
string s = Console.ReadLine();  // Keyboard input is string data
int n = Convert.ToInt32(s);     // but you know it's meant to be a number.
```

REMEMBER

The other conversion methods are a bit more obvious: ToDouble(), ToFloat(), and ToBoolean(). ToInt32() refers to a 32-bit, signed integer (32 bits is the size of a normal int), so this is the conversion method for ints. ToInt64() handles the size of a long.

When Convert() encounters an unexpected character type, it can generate unexpected results. Thus, you must know for sure what type of data you're processing and ensure that no extraneous characters are present.

Although you don't know much about methods yet (see Book 2), here's one anyway. The `IsAllDigits()` method (found in the `IsAllDigits` example) returns `true` if the string passed to it consists of only digits. You can call this method prior to converting a string into an integer, assuming that a sequence of nothing but digits is a legal number. Here's the method:

```
public static bool IsAllDigits(string raw)
{
    // First get rid of any benign characters at either end;
    // if there's nothing left, you don't have a number.
    string s = raw.Trim();  // Ignore white space on either side.
    if (s.Length == 0) return false;

    // Loop through the string.
    for (int index = 0; index < s.Length; index++)
    {
        // Minus signs are OK, so go to the next character.
        if (s[index] == '-' && index == 0) continue;

        // A nondigit indicates that the string probably isn't a number.
        if (Char.IsDigit(s[index]) == false) return false;
    }

    // No nondigits found; it's probably okay.
    return true;
}
```

The method `IsAllDigits()` first removes any harmless white space at either end of the string. If nothing is left, the string was blank and could not be an integer. The method then loops through each character in the string.

Notice that the loop looks for a minus sign as the first character so that you can use negative integers. The `&&` specifies that the first character can be a `-` sign and that it must be the first character. The `continue` keyword tells the `for` loop to continue with the next character.

If any of the remaining characters turns out to be a nondigit, the method returns `false`, indicating that the string is probably not a number. If this method returns `true`, the probability is high that you can convert the string into an integer successfully. The following code sample inputs a number from the keyboard and prints it back out to the console.

```
static void Main(string[] args)
{
    // Input a string from the keyboard.
    Console.WriteLine("Enter an integer number");
    string s = Console.ReadLine();
```

```
    // First check to see if this could be a number.
    if (!IsAllDigits(s)) // Call the special method.
    {
        Console.WriteLine("Hey! That isn't a number");
    }
    else
    {
        // Convert the string into an integer.
        int n = Int32.Parse(s);

        // Now write out the number times 2.
        Console.WriteLine("2 * " + n + " = " + (2 * n));
    }

    Console.Read();
}
```

The program reads a line of input from the console keyboard. If `IsAllDigits()` returns `false`, the program alerts the user. If not, the program converts the string into a number using an alternative to `Convert.ToInt32(aString)` — the `Int32.Parse(aString)` call. Finally, the program outputs both the number and two times the number (the latter to prove that the program did, in fact, convert the string as advertised). Here's the output from a sample run of the program:

```
Enter an integer number
1A3
Hey! That isn't a number
```

TIP

You could instead use `Int32.TryParse(s, n)`, which returns `false` if the parse fails or `true` if it succeeds. If it does work, the converted number is found in the second parameter, an `int` named `n`. This method won't throw exceptions. See the next section for an example.

Handling a series of numbers

Often, a program receives a series of numbers in a single line from the keyboard. Using the `String.Split()` method, you can easily break the string into a number of substrings, one for each number, and parse them separately.

The `Split()` method chops a single string into an array of smaller strings using some delimiter. For example, if you tell `Split()` to divide a string using a comma (`,`) as the delimiter, `"1,2,3"` becomes three strings, `"1"`, `"2"`, and `"3"`. (The *delimiter* is whichever character you use to split collections.) The `ParseSequenceWithSplit` example uses the `Split()` method to input a sequence of numbers to be summed. It uses the `IsAllDigits()` function from the previous section as a starting point. The code in bold shows the `Split()` method-specific code.

```
static void Main(string[] args)
{
    // Prompt the user to input a sequence of numbers.
    Console.WriteLine(
    "Input a series of numbers separated by commas:");

    // Read a line of text.
    string input = Console.ReadLine();
    Console.WriteLine();

    // Now convert the line into individual segments
    // based upon either commas or spaces.
    char[] dividers = { ',', ' ' };
    string[] segments = input.Split(dividers);

    // Convert each segment into a number.
    int sum = 0;

    foreach (string s in segments)
    {
        // Skip any empty segments.
        if (s.Length > 0)
        {
            // Skip strings that aren't numbers.
            if (IsAllDigits(s))
            {
                // Convert the string into a 32-bit int.
                int num = 0;
                if (Int32.TryParse(s, out num))
                {
                    Console.WriteLine("Next number = {0}", num);
                    // Add this number into the sum.
                    sum += num;
                }
                // If parse fails, move on to next number.
            }
        }
    }

    // Output the sum.
    Console.WriteLine("Sum = {0}", sum);
    Console.Read();
}
```

The ParseSequenceWithSplit program begins by reading a string from the keyboard. The program passes the dividers array of char to the Split() method to indicate that the comma and the space are the characters used to separate individual numbers. Either character will cause a split there.

The program iterates through each of the smaller subarrays created by Split() using the foreach loop statement. The program skips any zero-length subarrays. (This would result from two dividers in a row.) The program next uses the IsAllDigits() method to make sure that the string contains a number. (It won't if, for instance, you type ,.3 with an extra nondigit, nonseparator character.) Valid numbers are converted into integers and then added to an accumulator, sum. Invalid numbers are ignored. Here's the output of a typical run:

```
Input a series of numbers separated by commas:
1,2,z,,-5,22

Next number = 1
Next number = 2
Next number = -5
Next number = 22
Sum = 20
```

The program splits the list, accepting commas, spaces, or both as separators. It successfully skips over the z to generate the result of 20. In a real-world program, however, you probably don't want to skip over incorrect input without comment. You almost always want to draw the user's attention to garbage in the input stream.

Joining an array of strings into one string

Class String also has a Join() method. If you have an array of strings, you can use Join() to concatenate all the strings. You can even tell it to put a certain character string between each item and the next in the array:

```
string[] brothers = { "Chuck", "Bob", "Steve", "Mike" };
string theBrothers = string.Join(":", brothers);
```

The result in theBrothers is "Chuck:Bob:Steve:Mike", with the names separated by colons. You can put any separator string between the names: ", ", "\t", " ". The first item is a comma and a space. The second is a tab character. The third is a string of two spaces.

Controlling Output Manually

Controlling the output from programs is an important aspect of string manipulation. Face it: The output from the program is what the user sees. No matter how elegant the internal logic of the program may be, the user probably won't be impressed if the output looks shabby.

The `String` class provides help in directly formatting string data for output. The following sections examine the `Pad()`, `PadRight()`, `PadLeft()`, `Substring()`, and `Concat()` methods.

Using the Trim() and Pad() methods

In the "Trimming excess white space" section, you see how to use `Trim()` and its more specialized variants, `TrimFront()` and `TrimEnd()`. This section discusses another common method for formatting output. You can use the `Pad` methods, which add characters to either end of a string to expand the string to some predetermined length. For example, you may add spaces to the left or right of a string to left- or right-justify it, or you can add `"*"` characters to the left of a currency number, and so on. The `AlignOutput` example uses both `Trim()` and `Pad()` to trim up and justify a series of names. However, something to note for this example is that you add the following code to the beginning of the listing:

```
using System.Collections.Generic;
```

This addition lets you use collections. A *collection* is a kind of storage box that you can use to hold multiple variables. Chapter 6 of this minibook tells you all about collections. For now, just think about a collection as a big box partitioned to hold multiple items. The code specific to `Trim()` and `Pad()` appears in bold in the following listing.

```
static void Main(string[] args)
{
    List<string> names = new List<string> {"Christa  ",
                                   "  Sarah",
                                   "Jonathan",
                                   "Sam",
                                   " Schmekowitz "};

    // First output the names as they start out.
    Console.WriteLine("The following names are of "
                  + "different lengths");
```

Pulling Strings

```
    foreach (string s in names)
    {
        Console.WriteLine("This is the name '" + s + "' before");
    }
    Console.WriteLine();

    // This time, fix the strings so they are
    // left justified and all the same length.
    // First, copy the source list into a list that you can manipulate.
    List<string> stringsToAlign = new List<string>();

    // At the same time, remove any unnecessary spaces from either end
    // of the names.
    for (int i = 0; i < names.Count; i++)
    {
        string trimmedName = names[i].Trim();
        stringsToAlign.Add(trimmedName);
    }

    // Now find the length of the longest string so that
    // all other strings line up with that string.
    int maxLength = 0;
    foreach (string s in stringsToAlign)
    {
        if (s.Length > maxLength)
        {
            maxLength = s.Length;
        }
    }

    // Now justify all the strings to the length of the maximum string.
    for (int i = 0; i < stringsToAlign.Count; i++)
    {
        stringsToAlign[i] = stringsToAlign[i].PadRight(maxLength + 1);
    }

    // Finally output the resulting padded, justified strings.
    Console.WriteLine("The following are the same names "
                    + "normalized to the same length");

    foreach (string s in stringsToAlign)
    {
        Console.WriteLine("This is the name '" + s + "' afterwards");
    }

    Console.Read();
}
```

AlignOutput defines a List<string> of names of uneven alignment and length. (You could just as easily write the program to read these names from the console or from a file.) The Main() method first displays the names as they are. Main() then aligns the names using the Trim() and PadRight() methods before redisplaying the resulting trimmed up strings:

```
The following names are of different lengths:
This is the name 'Christa  ' before
This is the name '  Sarah' before
This is the name 'Jonathan' before
This is the name 'Sam' before
This is the name ' Schmekowitz ' before

The following are the same names rationalized to the same length:
This is the name 'Christa     ' afterwards
This is the name 'Sarah       ' afterwards
This is the name 'Jonathan    ' afterwards
This is the name 'Sam         ' afterwards
This is the name 'Schmekowitz ' afterwards
```

The alignment process begins by making a copy of the input names list. The code loops through the list, calling Trim() on each element to remove unneeded white space on either end. The method loops again through the list to find the longest member. The code loops one final time, calling PadRight() to expand each string to match the length of the longest member in the list. Note how the padded names form a neat column in the output.

PadRight(10) expands a string to be at least ten characters long. For example, PadRight(10) adds four spaces to the right of a six-character string. Finally, the code displays the list of trimmed and padded strings for output.

Using the Concatenate() method

You often face the problem of breaking up a string or inserting some substring into the middle of another. Replacing one character with another is most easily handled with the Replace() method, like this:

```
string s = "Danger NoSmoking";
s = s.Replace(' ', '!');
```

This example converts the string into "Danger!NoSmoking". Replacing all appearances of one character (in this case, a space) with another (an exclamation mark) is especially useful when generating comma-separated strings for easier parsing. However, the more common and more difficult case involves breaking a single string into substrings, manipulating them separately, and then recombining them into a single, modified string.

The RemoveWhiteSpace example uses the Replace() method to remove white space (spaces, tabs, and newlines — all instances of a set of special characters) from a string:

```
static void Main(string[] args)
{
    // Define the white space characters.
    char[] whiteSpace = { ' ', '\n', '\t' };

    // Start with a string embedded with white space.
    string s = " this is a\nstring"; // Contains spaces & newline.
    Console.WriteLine("before:" + s);

    // Output the string with the white space missing.
    Console.Write("after:");

    // Start looking for the white space characters.
    for (; ; )
    {
        // Find the offset of the character; exit the loop
        // if there are no more.
        int offset = s.IndexOfAny(whiteSpace);

        if (offset == -1)
        {
            break;
        }

        // Break the string into the part prior to the
        // character and the part after the character.
        string before = s.Substring(0, offset);
        string after = s.Substring(offset + 1);

        // Now put the two substrings back together with the
        // character in the middle missing.
        s = String.Concat(before, after);

        // Loop back up to find next white space char in
        // this modified s.
    }

    Console.WriteLine(s);
    Console.Read();
}
```

The key to this program is the `for` loop. This loop continually refines a string consisting of the input string, `s`, removing every one of a set of characters contained in the array `whiteSpace`.

The loop uses `IndexOfAny()` to find the first occurrence of any of the `char`s in the `whiteSpace` array. It doesn't return until every instance of any of those `chars` has been removed. The `IndexOfAny()` method returns the index within the array of the first white space `char` that it can find. A return value of `-1` indicates that no items in the array were found in the string.

The first pass through the loop removes the leading blank on the target string. `IndexOfAny()` finds the blank at index `0`. The first `Substring()` call returns an empty string, and the second call returns the whole string after the blank. These are then concatenated with `Concat()`, producing a string with the leading blank squeezed out.

The second pass through the loop finds the space after `"this"` and squeezes that out the same way, concatenating the strings `"this"` and `"is a\nstring"`. After this pass, `s` has become `"thisis a\nstring"`.

The third pass finds the `\n` character and squeezes that out. On the fourth pass, `IndexOfAny()` runs out of white space characters to find and returns `-1` (not found). That ends the loop.

`RemoveWhiteSpace` prints out a string containing several forms of white space. The program then strips out white space characters. The output from this program appears as follows:

```
before: this is a
string
after:thisisastring
```

Pulling Strings

Go Ahead and Split() that concatenate program

The `RemoveWhiteSpace` example demonstrates the use of the `Concat()` and `IndexOf()` methods; however, it doesn't use the most efficient approach. As usual, a little examination reveals a more efficient approach using our old friend `Split()`. The method that does the work is shown here (you can see the entire example in `RemoveWhiteSpace2`):

```
// RemoveWhiteSpace -- The RemoveSpecialChars method removes every
//    occurrence of the specified characters from the string.
```

```
public static string RemoveSpecialChars(string input, char[] targets)
{
  // Split the input string up using the target
  // characters as the delimiters.
  string[] subStrings = input.Split(targets);

  // output will contain the eventual output information.
  string output = "";

  // Loop through the substrings originating from the split.
  foreach (string subString in subStrings)
  {
    output = String.Concat(output, subString);
  }
  return output;
}
```

This version uses the `Split()` method to break the input string into a set of substrings, using the characters to be removed as delimiters. The delimiter is not included in the substrings created, which has the effect of removing the character(s). The logic here is much simpler and less error prone.

The `foreach` loop in the second half of the program puts the pieces back together again using `Concat()`. The output from the program is unchanged. Pulling the code out into a method further simplifies it and makes it clearer.

Formatting Your Strings Precisely

C# provides several means of formatting strings. The two most common means are to use `String.Format()` and string interpolation. Both formatting techniques produce approximately the same result, but the techniques differ slightly in their approach. The following sections tell you more.

Using the String.Format() method

The `String` class provides the `Format()` method for formatting output, especially the output of numbers. In its simplest form, `Format()` allows the insertion of string, numeric, or Boolean input in the middle of a format string. For example, consider this call:

```
string myString = String.Format("{0} times {1} equals {2}", 2, 5, 2 * 5);
```

The first argument to Format() is known as the *format string* — the quoted string you see. The {*n*} items in the middle of the format string indicate that the *n*th argument following the format string is to be inserted at that point. {0} refers to the first argument (in this case, the value 2), {1} refers to the next (that is, 5), and so on. This code returns a string, myString. The resulting string is

```
"2 times 5 equals 10"
```

Unless otherwise directed, Format() uses a default output format for each argument type. Format() enables you to affect the output format by including *specifiers* (modifiers or controls) in the placeholders. See Table 3-1 for a listing of some of these specifiers. For example, {0:E6} says, "Output the first number (argument number 0) in exponential form, using six spaces for the fractional part."

TABLE 3-1 **Format Specifiers Using String.Format()**

Control	Example	Result	Notes
C — currency	{0:C} of 123.456	$123.45	The currency sign depends on the Region setting.
	{0:C} of -123.456	($123.45)	Specify Region in Windows control panel.
D — decimal	{0:D5} of 123	00123	Integers only.
E — exponential	{0:E} of 123.45	1.2345E+002	Also known as scientific notation.
F — fixed	{0:F2} of 123.4567	123.46	The number after the F indicates the number of digits after the decimal point.
N — number	{0:N} of 123456.789	123,456.79	Adds commas and rounds off to nearest 100th.
	{0:N1} of 123456.789	123,456.8	Controls the number of digits after the decimal point.
	{0:N0} of 123456.789	123,457	Controls the number of digits after the decimal point.
X — hexadecimal	{0:X} of 123	0x7B	7B hex = 123 decimal (integers only).
{0:0...}	{0:000.00} of 12.3	012.30	Forces a 0 if a digit is not already present.
{0:#...}	{0:###.##} of 12.3	12.3	Forces the space to be left blank; no other field can encroach on the three digits to the left and two digits after the decimal point (useful for maintaining decimal-point alignment).

(continued)

TABLE 3-1 ***(continued)***

Control	Example	Result	Notes
	`{0:##0.0#}` of 0	0.0	Combining the # and zeros forces space to be allocated by the #s and forces at least one digit to appear, even if the number is 0.
`{0:# or 0%}`	`{0:#00.#%}` of 0.1234	12.3%	The % displays the number as a percentage (multiplies by 100 and adds the % sign).
	`{0:#00.#%}` of 0.0234	02.3%	The % displays the number as a percentage (multiplies by 100 and adds the % sign).

TIP

The `Console.WriteLine()` method uses the same placeholder system. The first placeholder, `{0}`, takes the first variable or value listed after the format string part of the statement, and so on. Given the exact same arguments as in the earlier `Format()` call, `Console.WriteLine()` would write the same string to the console. You also have access to the format specifiers. From now on, the examples use the formatted form of `WriteLine()` much of the time, rather than concatenate items to form the final output string with the + operator.

These format specifiers can seem a bit bewildering. You can discover more about format specifiers at `https://docs.microsoft.com/en-us/dotnet/standard/base-types/standard-numeric-format-strings`. To help you wade through these options, the `OutputFormatControls` example enables you to enter a floating-point number followed by a specifier sequence. The program then displays the number, using the specified `Format()` control:

```
static void Main(string[] args)
{
    // Keep looping -- inputting numbers until the user
    // enters a blank line rather than a number.
    for (; ; )
    {
        // First input a number -- terminate when the user
        // inputs nothing but a blank line.
        Console.WriteLine("Enter a double number");
        string numberInput = Console.ReadLine();

        if (numberInput.Length == 0)
        {
            break;
        }
```

```
        double number = Double.Parse(numberInput);

        // Now input the specifier codes; split them
        // using spaces as dividers.
        Console.WriteLine("Enter the format specifiers"
                          + " separated by a blank "
                          + "(Example: C E F1 N0 0000000.00000)");
        char[] separator = { ' ' };
        string formatString = Console.ReadLine();
        string[] formats = formatString.Split(separator);

        // Loop through the list of format specifiers.
        foreach (string s in formats)
        {
            if (s.Length != 0)
            {
                // Create a complete format specifier
                // from the letters entered earlier.
                string formatCommand = "{0:" + s + "}";

                // Output the number entered using the
                // reconstructed format specifier.
                Console.Write(
                     "The format specifier {0} results in ", formatCommand);
                try
                {
                    Console.WriteLine(formatCommand, number);
                }
                catch (Exception)
                {
                    Console.WriteLine("<illegal control>");
                }
                Console.WriteLine();
            }
        }
    }
}
```

`OutputFormatControls` continues to read floating-point numbers into `numberInput` until the user enters a blank line. (Because the input is a bit tricky, the application includes an example for the user to imitate as part of the message asking for input.) Note that the program doesn't include tests to determine whether the input is a legal floating-point number to keep the code simple.

The program then reads a series of specifier strings separated by spaces. Each specifier is then combined with a `"{0}"` string (the number before the colon, which corresponds to the placeholder in the format string) into the variable formatCommand. For example, if you entered **N4**, the program would store the specifier "{0:N4}". The following statement writes the number number using the newly constructed formatCommand. In the case of the lowly N4, the command would be rendered this way:

```
Console.WriteLine("{0:N4}", number);
```

Typical output from the program appears this way:

```
Enter a double number
12345.6789
Enter the specifiers separated by a blank (Example: C E F1 N0 0000000.00000)
C E F1 N0 0000000.00000
The format specifier {0:C} results in $12,345.68

The format specifier {0:E} results in 1.234568E+004

The format specifier {0:F1} results in 12345.7

The format specifier {0:N0} results in 12,346

The format specifier {0:0000000.00000} results in 0012345.67890

Enter a double number
.12345
Enter the specifiers separated by a blank (Example: C E F1 N0 0000000.00000)
00.0%
The format specifier {0:00.0%} results in 12.3%
Enter a double number
```

When applied to the number 12345.6789, the specifier N0 adds commas in the proper place (the N part) and lops off everything after the decimal point (the 0 portion) to render 12,346. (The last digit was rounded off, not truncated.)

Similarly, when applied to 0.12345, the control 00.0% outputs 12.3%. The percent sign multiplies the number by 100 and adds %. The 00.0 indicates that the output should include at least two digits to the left of the decimal point and only one digit after the decimal point. The number 0.01 is displayed as 01.0%, using the same 00.0% specifier.

TECHNICAL STUFF

The mysterious try ... catch catches any errors that spew forth in the event you enter an illegal format command such as a D, which stands for decimal and isn't allowed with double values. (Chapter 9 of this minibook tells you about exceptions.)

Using the interpolation method

Everything you've discovered for `String.Format()` applies to the string interpolation method. The difference is in approach. Instead of specifying placeholders, the string interpolation method places the content directly within the sentence, as shown in the `StringInterpolation` example:

```
static void Main(string[] args)
{
    double MyVar = 123.456;
    Console.WriteLine($"This is the exponential form: {MyVar:E}.");
    Console.WriteLine($"This is the percent form: {MyVar:#.#%}.");
    Console.WriteLine($"This is the zero padded form: {MyVar:0000.0000}.");
}
```

As you can see, you use the same format specifiers as shown in Table 3-1, but the method of working with the variable differs. You place the variable directly in the string. To make this work, you place a dollar sign ($) in front of the string. Here is the output from this example:

```
This is the exponential form: 1.234560E+002.
This is the percent form: 12345.6%.
This is the zero padded form: 0123.4560.
```

TIP

The format specifier is optional when using string interpolation. You need to use a format specifier only when the default formatting won't work for your needs. The article at `https://docs.microsoft.com/en-us/dotnet/csharp/tutorials/string-interpolation` provides more information about string interpolation.

StringBuilder: Manipulating Strings More Efficiently

Building longer strings out of a bunch of shorter strings can cost you an arm and its elbow. Because a string, after it's created, can't be changed; it's immutable, as described at the beginning of this chapter. This example doesn't tack "ly" onto `s1`:

```
string s1 = "rapid";
string s2 = s1 + "ly";                // s2 = rapidly.
```

It creates a new string composed of the combination. (`s1` is unchanged.) Other operations that appear to modify a string, such as `Substring()` and `Replace()`, do the same.

The result is that each operation on a string produces yet another string. Suppose you need to concatenate 1,000 strings into one huge one. You're going to create a new string for each concatenation:

```
string[] listOfNames = ...  // 1000 pet names
string s = string.Empty;
for(int i = 0; i < 1000; i++)
{
  s += listOfNames[i];
}
```

To avoid such costs when you're doing lots of modifications to strings, use the companion class `StringBuilder`. The `UseStringBuilder` example shows how to work with this class. Be sure to add this line at the top of your file, which allows you to use the `StringBuilder` class:

```
using System.Text;
```

REMEMBER

Unlike `String` manipulations, the manipulations you do on a `StringBuilder` directly change the underlying string. Here's an example that results in an output of `"123456"`:

```
StringBuilder builder = new StringBuilder("012");
builder.Append("34");
builder.Append("56");
Console.WriteLine(builder.ToString());
```

You can also create the `StringBuilder` with the capacity you expect it to need, which reduces the overhead of increasing the builder's capacity frequently:

```
StringBuilder builder = new StringBuilder(256); // 256 characters.
```

Use the `Append()` method to add text to the end of the current contents. Use `ToString()` to retrieve the string inside the `StringBuilder` when you finish your modifications. The truly amazing thing about a StringBuilder is that you aren't limited to working with text additions, as shown here (with an output of `5True9.96`):

```
StringBuilder builder2 = new StringBuilder();
builder2.Append(5);
builder2.Append(true);
builder2.Append(9.9);
builder2.Append(2 + 4);
Console.WriteLine(builder2.ToString());
```

Notice that the last addition does math right inside Append(). StringBuilder has a number of other useful string manipulation methods, including Insert(), Remove(), and Replace(). It lacks many of string's methods, though, such as Substring(), CopyTo(), and IndexOf().

Suppose that you want to uppercase just the first character of a string, as in the earlier section "Converting a string to upper- or lowercase." With StringBuilder, it's much cleaner looking than the code provided earlier.

```
StringBuilder sb = new StringBuilder("jones");
sb[0] = char.ToUpper(sb[0]);
Console.WriteLine(sb.ToString());
```

This code puts the lowercase string "jones" into a StringBuilder, accesses the first char in the StringBuilder's underlying string directly with sb[0], uses the char.ToUpper() method to uppercase the character, and reassigns the uppercased character to sb[0]. Finally, it extracts the improved string "Jones" from the StringBuilder.

IN THIS CHAPTER

» Performing a little arithmetic

» Doing some logical arithmetic

» Complicating matters with compound logical operators

Chapter 4

Smooth Operators

Mathematicians create variables and manipulate them in various ways, adding them, multiplying them, and — here's a toughie — even integrating them. Chapter 2 of this minibook describes how to declare and define variables. However, it says little about how to use variables to get anything done after you declare them. This chapter looks at the operations you can perform on variables to do some work. Operations require *operators,* such as `+`, `-`, `=`, `<`, and `&`. This chapter also discusses arithmetic, logical, and other types of operators.

REMEMBER

You don't have to type the source code for this chapter manually. In fact, using the downloadable source is a lot easier. You can find the source for this chapter in the `\CSAIO4D2E\BK01\CH04` folder of the downloadable source. See the Introduction for details on how to find these source files.

Performing Arithmetic

The set of arithmetic operators breaks down into several groups: the simple arithmetic operators, the assignment operators, and a set of special operators unique to programming. After you digest these, you also need to digest a separate set of logical operators. *Bon appétit!*

Simple operators

You most likely learned in elementary school how to use most of the simple operators. Table 4-1 lists them. ***Note:*** Computers use an asterisk (*), not the multiplication sign (×), for multiplication.

TABLE 4-1 **Simple Operators**

Operator	What It Means
- (unary)	Take the negative of
*	Multiply
/	Divide
+	Add
- (binary)	Subtract
%	Modulo

Most of these operators in the table are *binary* operators because they operate on two values: one on the left side of the operator and one on the right side. The lone exception is the unary negative. However, it's just as straightforward as the others, as shown in this example:

```
int n1 = 5;
int n2 = -n1;  // n2 now has the value -5.
```

The modulo operator may not be quite as familiar to you as the others. Modulo is the remainder after division. Thus, `5 % 3` is 2 (5 / 3 = 1, remainder 2), and `25 % 3` is 1 (25 / 3 = 8, remainder 1). Read it as "five modulo three" or simply "five mod three." Even numbers mod 2 are 0: `6 % 2 = 0` (6/2 = 3, remainder 0).

The arithmetic operators other than modulo are defined for all numeric types. The modulo operator isn't defined for floating-point numbers because you have no remainder after the division of floating-point values.

Operating orders

The value of some expressions may not be clear. Consider, for example, the following expression:

```
int n = 5 * 3 + 2;
```

Does the programmer mean "multiply 5 times 3 and then add 2," which is 17, or "multiply 5 times the sum of 3 and 2," which gives you 25?

C# generally executes common operators from left to right and performs multiplication and division before addition and subtraction. So, the preceding example assigns the value 17 to the variable `n`.

C# determines the value of `n` in the following example by first dividing 24 by 6 and then dividing the result of that operation by 2 (as opposed to dividing 24 by the ratio 6 over 2). The result is 2:

```
int n = 24 / 6 / 2;
```

However, the various operators have a *hierarchy*, or order of precedence. C# scans an expression and performs the operations of higher precedence before those of lower precedence. For example, multiplication has higher precedence than addition. Many books take great pains to explain the order of precedence, but, frankly, that's a complete waste of time (and brain cells).

Don't rely on yourself or someone else to know the precedence order. Use parentheses to make your meaning explicit to human readers of the code as well as to the compiler.

The value of the following expression is clear, regardless of the operators' order of precedence:

```
int n = (7 % 3) * (4 + (6 / 3));
```

Parentheses can override the order of precedence by stating exactly how the compiler is to interpret the expression. To find the first expression to evaluate, C# looks for the innermost parentheses, dividing 6 by 3 to yield 2:

```
int n = (7 % 3) * (4 + 2);    // 6 / 3 = 2
```

Then C# works its way outward, evaluating each set of parentheses in turn, from innermost to outermost:

```
int n = 1 * 6;    // (4 + 2) = 6
```

So the final result, and the value of `n`, is 6.

The assignment operator

C# has inherited an interesting concept from C and C++: Assignment is itself a binary operator. The assignment operator has the value of the argument to the right. The assignment has the same type as both arguments, which must match. This view of the assignment operator has no effect on the other expressions described in this chapter:

```
n = 5 * 3;
```

In this example, 5 * 3 is 15 and an `int`. The assignment operator stores the `int` on the right into the `int` on the left and returns the value 15.

The increment operator

Of all the additions that you may perform in programming, adding 1 to a variable is the most common:

```
n = n + 1;  // Increment n by 1.
```

C# extends the simple operators with a set of operators constructed from other binary operators. For example, `n += 1;` is equivalent to `n = n + 1;`. A *compound assignment operator* (one that performs both a math operation and an assignment operation) exists for just about every binary operator: `+=`, `-=`, `*=`, `/=`, `%=`, `&=`, `|=`, `^=`. Look up *C# language, operators* in C# Language Help for full details on them. Yet even `n += 1` is not good enough. C# provides this even shorter version:

```
++n;        // Increment n by 1.
```

All these forms of incrementing a number are equivalent — they all increment `n` by 1.

REMEMBER

The increment operator is strange enough, but believe it or not, C# has two increment operators: `++n` and `n++`. The first one, `++n`, is the *prefix increment* operator, and `n++` is the *postfix increment* operator. The difference is subtle but important. Remember that every expression has a type and a value. In the following code, both `++n` and `n++` are of type `int`:

```
int n;
n = 1;
int p = ++n;
n = 1;
int m = n++;
```

C# has equivalent decrement operators — `n--` and `--n`. They work in exactly the same way as the increment operators.

Performing Logical Comparisons — Is That Logical?

C# provides a set of logical comparison operators, as shown in Table 4-2. These operators are *logical* comparisons because they return either a `true` or a `false` value of type `bool`.

TABLE 4-2 Logical Comparison Operators

Operator	Operator Is True If
a == b	a has the same value as b.
a > b	a is greater than b.
a >= b	a is greater than or equal to b.
a < b	a is less than b.
a <= b	a is less than or equal to b.
a != b	a is not equal to b.

Here's an example that involves a logical comparison:

```
int m = 5;
int n = 6;
bool b = m > n;
```

This example assigns the value `false` to the variable `b` because 5 is *not* greater than 6. The logical comparisons are defined for all numeric types, including `float`, `double`, `decimal`, and `char`. All the following statements are legal:

```
bool b;
b = 3 > 2;        // true
b = 3.0 > 2.0;    // true
b = 'a' > 'b';    // false -- Alphabetically, later = greater.
b = 'A' < 'a';    // true  -- Upper A (value 65) is less than lower a (value 97).
b = 'A' < 'b';    // true  -- All upper are less than all lower.
b = 10M > 12M;    // false
```

The comparison operators always produce results of type bool. The comparison operators other than == and != are not valid for variables of type string. (Not to worry: C# offers other ways to compare strings; see Chapter 3 of this minibook for details.)

Comparing floating-point numbers: Is your float bigger than mine?

Comparing two floating-point values can get dicey, and you need to be careful with these comparisons. Consider the following comparison:

```
float f1;
float f2;
f1 = 10;
f2 = f1 / 3;
bool b1 = (3 * f2) == f1;  // b1 is true if (3 * f2) equals f1.
f1 = 9;
f2 = f1 / 3;
bool b2 = (3 * f2) == f1;
```

Notice that both the fifth and eighth lines in the preceding example contain first an assignment operator (=) and then a logical comparison (==). These are different animals, so don't type = when you mean ==. C# does the logical comparison and then assigns the result to the variable on the left.

The only difference between the calculations of b1 and b2 is the original value of f1. So, what are the values of b1 and b2? The value of b2 is clearly true: 9 / 3 is 3; 3 * 3 is 9; and 9 equals 9. Voilà!

The value of b1 isn't obvious: 10 / 3 is 3.333 . . . and 3.333 . . . * 3 is 9.999. . . . Is 9.999 . . . equal to 10? The manner in which math operations round values can affect comparisons, which means you need to exercise care when making assumptions about the outcome of math operations. Even though you might see two values as potentially equal, the computer won't. Consequently, using the == operator with floating-point values is generally frowned upon because of the potential to introduce errors into your code.

C# does provide some methods around the rounding error issue so that you can use the == operator when appropriate. For example, you can use the system absolute value method to compare f1 and f2:

```
bool compare = Math.Abs(f1 - 3.0 * f2) < .00001; // Use whatever level
   of accuracy.
```

This calculation returns `true` for both cases. You can also use the constant `Double.Epsilon` instead of .00001 to produce the maximum level of accuracy. `Epsilon` is the smallest possible difference between two nonequal `double` variables. For a self-guided tour of the `System.Math` class, where `Abs` and many other useful mathematical functions live, look for *math* in C# Language Help.

Compounding the confusion with compound logical operations

The `bool` variables have another set of operators defined just for them, as shown in Table 4-3.

TABLE 4-3 The Compound Logical Operators

Operator	Operator Is True If
!a	a is false (also known as the "not" operator).
a & b	a and b are true (also known as the "and" operator).
a | b	Either a or b or else both are true (also known as a *and/or* b).
a ^ b	a is true or b is true but not both (also known as *a xor b*, the *exclusive or* operator).
a && b	a is true and b is true with short-circuit evaluation.
a || b	a is true or b is true with short-circuit evaluation. (This section discusses short-circuit evaluation.)

REMEMBER

The `!` operator (NOT) is the logical equivalent of the minus sign. For example, `!a` (read "not a") is true if `a` is false and false if `a` is true. Can that be true?

The next two operators in the table are straightforward. First, `a & b` is true only if both `a` and `b` are true. And `a | b` is true if either `a` or `b` is true (or both are). The exclusive or (xor) operator, or `^`, is sort of an odd beast. An exclusive or is true if either `a` or `b` is true but not if both `a` and `b` are true. It's the sort of operator you use when asking whether someone would like cake or ice cream for dessert, indicating through body language that they can't have both. All three operators produce a logical `bool` value as their result.

TECHNICAL STUFF

The `&`, `|`, and `^` operators also have a *bitwise operator* version. When applied to `int` variables, these operators perform their magic on a bit-by-bit basis. Thus `6 & 3` is 2 (0110_2 & 0011_2 is 0010_2), `6 | 3` is 7 (0110_2 | 0011_2 is 0111_2), and `6 ^ 3` is 5 (0110_2 ^ 0011_2 is 0101_2). Binary arithmetic is cool but beyond the scope of this book. You can read more about it at `https://docs.microsoft.com/en-us/dotnet/csharp/language-reference/operators/bitwise-and-shift-operators`.

The remaining two logical operators are similar to, but subtly different from, the first three. Consider the following example:

```
bool b = (boolExpression1) & (boolExpression2);
```

In this case, C# evaluates `boolExpression1` and `boolExpression2`. It then looks to see whether they both are true before deciding the value of `b`. However, this may be a wasted effort. If one expression is false, there's no reason to evaluate the other. Regardless of the value of the second expression, the result will be false. Nevertheless, `&` goes on to evaluate both expressions. The `&&` operator avoids evaluating both expressions unnecessarily, as shown in the following example:

```
bool b = (boolExpression1) && (boolExpression2);
```

In this case, C# evaluates `boolExpression1`. If it's false, then `b` is set to false and the program continues on its merry way. On the other hand, if `boolExpression1` is true, then C# evaluates `boolExpression2` and stores the result in `b`. The `&&` operator uses this *short-circuit evaluation* because it short-circuits around the second Boolean expression, if necessary.

Most programmers use the doubled forms most of the time. The `||` operator works the same way, as shown in the following expression:

```
bool b = (boolExpression1) || (boolExpression2);
```

If `boolExpression1` is true, there's no point in evaluating `boolExpression2` because the result is always true. You can read these operators as "short-circuit and" and "short-circuit or."

Some programmers do rely on the standard operators for specific tasks. For example, if the expressions perform a task other than provide just a value, it's important not to use the short-circuit operator or C# will never perform the second task when the first task is false. Don't worry about this particular case right now, but file it away as useful information for later. Sometimes, short-circuit operators produce unexpected results when you rely on the code to do more than just provide an evaluation of two values.

Matching Expression Types at TrackDownAMate.com

In calculations, an expression's type is just as important as its value. Consider the following expression:

```
int n;
n = (5 * 5) + 7;
```

My calculator says the resulting value of n is 32. However, that expression also has an overall type based on the types of its parts. Written in "type language," the preceding expression becomes

```
int [=] (int * int) + int;
```

To evaluate the type of an expression, follow the same pattern you use to evaluate the expression's value. Multiplication takes precedence over addition. An int times an int is an int. Addition comes next. An int plus an int is an int. In this way, you can reduce the preceding expression this way:

```
(int * int) + int
int + int
int
```

Calculating the type of an operation

Most operators come in various flavors. For example, the multiplication operator comes in the following forms (the arrow means "produces"):

```
int     * int     --> int
uint    * uint    --> uint
long    * long    --> long
float   * float   --> float
decimal * decimal --> decimal
double  * double  --> double
```

Thus, 2 * 3 uses the int * int version of the * operator to produce the output of int 6.

Implicit type conversion

The * operator works well for multiplying two ints or two floats. But imagine what happens when the left and right arguments aren't of the same type. For example, consider what happens in this case:

```
int anInt = 10;
double aDouble = 5.0;
double result = anInt * aDouble;
```

First, C# doesn't have an int * double operation. C# could just generate an error message and leave it at that; however, it tries to make sense of the programmer's intention. C# has int * int and double * double versions of multiplication and could convert aDouble into its int equivalent, but that would involve losing any fractional part of the number (the digits to the right of the decimal point). Instead, in *implicit promotion,* C# converts the int anInt into a double and uses the double * double operator.

An implicit promotion is implicit because C# does it automatically, and it's a promotion because it involves the natural concept of uphill and downhill. The list of multiplication operators is in promotion order from int to double or from int to decimal — *from narrower type to wider type.* No implicit conversion exists between the floating-point types and decimal. Converting from the more capable type, such as double, to a less capable type, such as int, is known as a *demotion.*

WARNING

Implicit demotions aren't allowed; C# generates an error message.

Explicit type conversion — the cast

Imagine what happens if C# was wrong about implicit conversion and the programmer *wanted* to perform integer multiplication. You can change the type of any value-type variable by using the cast operator. A *cast* consists of a type enclosed in parentheses and placed immediately in front of the variable or expression in question. Thus the following expression uses the int * int operator:

```
int anInt = 10;
double aDouble = 5.0;
int result = anInt * (int)aDouble;
```

The cast of aDouble to an int is known as an *explicit demotion* or *downcast.* The conversion is explicit because of the programmer's explicit declaration of intent.

REMEMBER

You can make an explicit conversion between any two value types, whether it's up or down the promotion ladder.

TIP

Avoid implicit type conversion. Make any changes in value types explicit by using a cast. Doing so reduces the possibility of error and makes code much easier for humans to read.

Leave logical alone

C# offers no type conversion path to or from the `bool` type.

Assigning types

The same matching of types that you find in conversions applies to the assignment operator.

WARNING

Inadvertent type mismatches that generate compiler error messages usually occur in the assignment operator, not at the point of the mismatch. Consider the following multiplication example:

```
int n1 = 10;
int n2 = 5.0 * n1;
```

The second line in this example generates an error message because of a type mismatch, but the error occurs *at the assignment* — not at the multiplication. Here's the horrible tale: To perform the multiplication, C# implicitly converts `n1` to a `double`. C# can then perform `double` multiplication, the result of which is the all-powerful `double`. The type of the right and left operators of the assignment operator must match, but the type of the left operator cannot change. Because C# refuses to demote an expression implicitly, the compiler generates the error message `Cannot implicitly convert type double to int`. C# allows this expression with an explicit cast:

```
int n1 = 10;
int n2 = (int)(5.0 * n1);
```

(The parentheses are necessary because the cast operator has very high precedence.) This example works — *explicit* demotion is okay. The `n1` is promoted to a `double`, the multiplication is performed, and the `double` result is demoted to an `int`. In this case, however, you would worry about the sanity of the programmer because `5 * n1` is so much easier for both the programmer and the C# compiler to read.

Changing how an operator works: Operator overloading

To further complicate matters, the behavior of any operator can be changed with a feature of C# called operator overloading. *Operator overloading* is essentially defining a new function that is run any time you use an operator in the same project where the overload is defined. Operator overloading is actually simpler than it sounds. If you code

```
var x = 2 + 2;
```

you'd expect x to equal 4 right? That's the way + works. Well, this is the twenty-first century, people, and answers are a matter of opinion! To make things interesting, you should give users more than they ask for on any transaction. For that reason, you may want to add a value of 1 to every addition operation.

To add a value of 1 to each addition operation, you need to create a custom class that your overloaded operator can use. This class will have some custom types and a method that you'll use for the overload operation. In short, if you add regular numbers, you'll get a regular answer; if you add the special AddOne numbers, you'll get one added (you can also find this code in the AddOneToNumber example in the downloadable source):

```
public class AddOne
{
    public int x;

    public static AddOne operator +(AddOne a, AddOne b)
    {
        AddOne addone = new AddOne();
        addone.x = a.x + b.x + 1;
        return addone;
    }
}
```

Note that you put class AddOne outside of class Program, but within namespace AddOneToNumber. Book 2 tells you more about how classes work — focus on the operator part of the code for now. After the + operator is overloaded (with the operator tag in the listing), you can use it as usual:

```
static void Main(string[] args)
{
    AddOne foo = new AddOne();
    foo.x = 2;

    AddOne bar = new AddOne();
    bar.x = 3;

    // And 2 + 3 now is 6...
    Console.WriteLine((foo + bar).x.ToString());
    Console.Read();
}
```

The answer, of course, will be 6, not 5. Operator overloading isn't useful for integers unless you're planning to rewrite the laws of mathematics. However, if you genuinely have two entities that you want to be able to add together, this technique may be useful. For instance, if you have a `Product` class, you can redefine the + operator for that class to add the prices.

IN THIS CHAPTER

» Making decisions `if` you can

» Deciding what `else` to do

» Using the `while` and `do ... while` loops

» Using the `for` loop and understanding scope

Chapter 5

Getting into the Program Flow

Consider this simple program:

```
using System;
namespace HelloWorld
{
  public class Program
  {
    // This is where the program starts.
    static void Main(string[] args)
    {
      // Prompt user to enter a name.
      Console.WriteLine("Enter your name, please:");

      // Now read the name entered.
      string name = Console.ReadLine();

      // Greet the user with the entered name.
      Console.WriteLine("Hello, " + name);
```

```
        // Wait for user to acknowledge the results.
        Console.WriteLine("Press Enter to terminate ... ");
        Console.Read();
      }
    }
  }
```

Beyond introducing you to a few fundamentals of C# programming, this program is almost worthless. It simply spits back out whatever you entered. You can imagine more complicated program examples that accept input, perform some type of calculations, generate some type of output (otherwise, why do the calculations?), and then exit at the bottom. However, a program such as this one can be of only limited use.

One key element of any computer processor is its ability to make decisions, which means that the processor sends the flow of execution down one path of instructions if a condition is true or down another path if the condition is false (not true). Any programming language must offer this fundamental capability to control the flow of execution.

The three basic types of *flow control* are the `if` statement, the loop, and the jump. (Chapter 6 of this minibook describes the `foreach` looping control.)

REMEMBER

You don't have to type the source code for this chapter manually. In fact, using the downloadable source is a lot easier. You can find the source for this chapter in the `\CSAIO4D2E\BK01\CH05` folder of the downloadable source. See the Introduction for details on how to find these source files.

Branching Out with if and switch

The basis of all C# decision-making capability is the `if` statement:

```
if (bool-expression)
{
    // Control goes here if the expression is true.
}
// Control passes to this statement whether the expression is true or not.
```

A pair of parentheses immediately following the keyword `if` contains a *conditional expression* of type `bool`. (See Chapter 2 of this minibook for a discussion of `bool` expressions.) Immediately following the expression is a block of code set off by a pair of braces. If the expression is true, the program executes the code within the braces; if the expression is not true, the program skips the code in the braces. (If the program executes the code in braces, it ends just after the closing brace and continues from there.) The `if` statement is easier to understand by looking at a concrete example:

```
// Make sure that a is positive:
// If a is less than 1 ...
if (a < 1)
{
    // ... then assign 1 to it so that it's positive.
    a = 1;
}
```

This segment of code ensures that the variable `a` is non-negative — greater than or equal to 1. The `if` statement says, "If `a` is less than 1, assign 1 to `a`." (In other words, turn `a` into a positive value.)

TECHNICAL STUFF

The braces aren't required if there is only one statement. C# treats `if(bool-expression) statement;` as though it had been written `if(bool-expression) {statement;}`. The general consensus, however, is to always use braces for better clarity. In other words, don't ask — just do it.

Introducing the if statement

Consider a small program that calculates interest. The user enters the principal amount and the interest rate, and the program spits out the resulting value for each year. (This program isn't sophisticated.) The simplistic calculation appears as follows in C#:

```
// Calculate the value of the principal plus interest.
decimal interestPaid;
interestPaid = principal * (interest / 100);

// Now calculate the total.
decimal total = principal + interestPaid;
```

The first equation multiplies the principal `principal` times the interest `interest` to produce the interest to be paid — `interestPaid`. (You divide by `100` because interest is usually calculated by entering a percentage amount.) The interest to be paid is then added back into the principal, resulting in a new principal, which is stored in the variable `total`.

The program must anticipate almost anything when dealing with human input. For example, you don't want your program to accept a negative principal or interest amount (well, maybe a negative interest). The following `CalculateInterest` program includes checks to ensure that neither of these entries happens:

```
static void Main(string[] args)
{
    // Prompt user to enter source principal.
    Console.Write("Enter principal: ");
    string principalInput = Console.ReadLine();
    decimal principal = Convert.ToDecimal(principalInput);

    // Make sure that the principal is not negative.
    if (principal < 0)
    {
        Console.WriteLine("Principal cannot be negative");
        principal = 0;
    }

    // Enter the interest rate.
    Console.Write("Enter interest: ");
    string interestInput = Console.ReadLine();
    decimal interest = Convert.ToDecimal(interestInput);

    // Make sure that the interest is not negative either.
    if (interest < 0)
    {
        Console.WriteLine("Interest cannot be negative");
        interest = 0;
    }

    // Calculate the value of the principal plus interest.
    decimal interestPaid = principal * (interest / 100);

    // Now calculate the total.
    decimal total = principal + interestPaid;

    // Output the result.
    Console.WriteLine();  // Skip a line.
    Console.WriteLine("Principal     = " + principal);
    Console.WriteLine("Interest      = " + interest + "%");
    Console.WriteLine();
    Console.WriteLine("Interest paid = " + interestPaid);
    Console.WriteLine("Total         = " + total);
    Console.Read();
}
```

TIP

The `CalculateInterest` program begins by prompting the user for a principle amount using `Write()` to write a `string` to the console. Tell the user exactly what you want and, if possible, specify the format. Users don't respond well to uninformative prompts, such as `>`.

The sample program uses the `ReadLine()` command to read in whatever the user types; the program returns the value entered, in the form of a `string`, when the user presses Enter. Because the program is looking for the principal in the form of a `decimal`, the input `string` must be converted using the `Convert.ToDecimal()` command. The result is stored in `principalInput`.

REMEMBER

The `ReadLine()`, `WriteLine()`, and `ToDecimal()` commands are all examples of method calls. A *method call* delegates some work to another part of the program, called a method. Book 2 describes method calls in detail. For now, don't worry if you have problems understanding precisely how method calls work.

The next line in the example checks `principal`. If it's negative, the program outputs a polite message indicating that the input is invalid. The program does the same thing for the interest rate, and then it performs the simplistic interest calculation outlined earlier, in the "Introducing the if statement" section, and spits out the result, using a series of `WriteLine()` commands. Here's some example output from the program:

```
Enter principal: 1234
Enter interest: 21

Principal      = 1234
Interest       = 21%

Interest paid = 259.14
Total          = 1493.14
```

Executing the program with illegal input generates the following output:

```
Enter principal: 1234
Enter interest: -12.5
Interest cannot be negative

Principal      = 1234
Interest       = 0%

Interest paid = 0
Total          = 1234
```

TIP

Indent the lines within an `if` statement to enhance readability. This type of indentation is ignored by C# but is helpful to us humans. Most programming editors support autoindenting, whereby the editor automatically indents as soon as you enter the `if` statement. To set autoindenting in Visual Studio, choose Tools ⇨ Options. Then expand the Text Editor node. From there, expand C#. Finally, click Tabs. On this page, enable Smart Indenting and set the number of spaces per indent to your preference. (The book uses four spaces per indent.) Set the tab size to the same value.

Examining the else statement

Sometimes, your code must check for mutually exclusive conditions. For example, the following code segment stores the maximum of two numbers, `a` and `b`, in the variable `max`:

```
// Store the maximum of a and b into the variable max.
int max;

// If a is greater than b ...
if (a > b)
{
    //  ... save a as the maximum.
    max = a;
}

// If a is less than or equal to b ...
if (a <= b)
{
    //  ... save b as the maximum.
    max = b;
}
```

The second `if` statement causes needless processing because the two conditions are mutually exclusive. If `a` is greater than `b`, `a` can't possibly be less than or equal to `b`. C# defines an `else` statement for just this case. The `else` keyword defines a block of code that's executed when the `if` block isn't. The code segment to calculate the maximum now appears this way:

```
// Store the maximum of a and b into the variable max.
int max;

// If a is greater than b ...
if (a > b)
```

```
{
    //  ... save a as the maximum; otherwise ...
    max = a;
}
else
{
    //  ... save b as the maximum.
    max = b;
}
```

If `a` is greater than `b`, the first block is executed; otherwise, the second block is executed. In the end, `max` contains the greater of `a` or `b`.

Avoiding even the else

Sequences of `else` clauses can become confusing. Some programmers like to avoid them when doing so doesn't cause even more confusion. You could write the maximum calculation like this:

```
// Store the maximum of a and b into the variable max.
int max;

// Start by assuming that a is greater than b.
max = a;

// If it is not ...
if (b > a)
{
  //  ... then you can change your mind.
  max = b;
}
```

TIP

Programmers who like to be cool and cryptic often use the *ternary operator*, `?:`, equivalent to an `if/else` on one line:

```
bool informal = true;
string name = informal ? "Chuck" : "Charles";  // Returns "Chuck"
```

This chunk evaluates the expression before the colon. If the expression is true, return the value after the colon but before the question mark. If the expression is false, return the value after the question mark. This process turns an `if...else` into an expression. Best practice advises using ternary only rarely because it truly *is* cryptic.

TECHNICAL STUFF

C# 9.0 and above offers something called a target typed conditional expression. Normally, the data types of the two outputs of the ternary operator must match. However, in C# 9.0 and above, this requirement changes. Consequently, while this code won't compile in earlier versions of C#, you can use it in C# 9.0 and above.

```
int x = 2;
Console.WriteLine(x == 1 ? 1 : "Hello");
```

When x is equal to 1, the output of this conditional expression is the value 1. When x isn't equal to 1, the output of this conditional expression is the string "Hello". There are all sorts of ways in which to use this new typed conditional expression, including within switch statements. You can discover more about them at https://docs.microsoft.com/en-us/dotnet/csharp/language-reference/proposals/csharp-9.0/target-typed-conditional-expression.

Nesting if statements

The CalculateInterest program warns the user of illegal input; however, continuing with the interest calculation, even if one of the values is illogical, doesn't seem quite right. It causes no real harm here because the interest calculation takes little or no time and the user can ignore the results, but some calculations aren't nearly as quick. In addition, why ask the user for an interest rate after entering an invalid value for the principal? The user knows that the results of the calculation will be invalid. (You'd be amazed at how much it infuriates users to require input after they know the calculation will fail.) The program should ask the user for an interest rate only if the principal is reasonable and perform the interest calculation only if both values are valid. To accomplish this, you need two if statements, one within the other.

REMEMBER

An if statement found within the body of another if statement is an *embedded*, or *nested*, statement. The following program, CalculateInterestWithEmbeddedTest, uses embedded if statements to avoid stupid questions if a problem is detected in the input:

```
static void Main(string[] args)
{
    // Define a maximum interest rate.
    int maximumInterest = 50;

    // Prompt user to enter source principal.
    Console.Write("Enter principal: ");
    string principalInput = Console.ReadLine();
    decimal principal = Convert.ToDecimal(principalInput);
```

```
    // If the principal is negative ...
    if (principal < 0)
    {
        // ... generate an error message ...
        Console.WriteLine("Principal cannot be negative");
    }
    else  // Go here only if principal was > 0: thus valid.
    {
        //  ... otherwise, enter the interest rate.
        Console.Write("Enter interest: ");
        string interestInput = Console.ReadLine();
        decimal interest = Convert.ToDecimal(interestInput);

        // If the interest is negative or too large ...
        if (interest < 0 || interest > maximumInterest)
        {
            //  ... generate an error message as well.
            Console.WriteLine("Interest cannot be negative " +
                              "or greater than " + maximumInterest);
            interest = 0;
        }
        else  // Reach this point only if all is well.
        {
            // Both the principal and the interest appear to be legal;
            // calculate the value of the principal plus interest.
            decimal interestPaid;
            interestPaid = principal * (interest / 100);

            // Now calculate the total.
            decimal total = principal + interestPaid;

            // Output the result.
            Console.WriteLine();  // Skip a line.
            Console.WriteLine("Principal     = " + principal);
            Console.WriteLine("Interest      = " + interest + "%");
            Console.WriteLine();
            Console.WriteLine("Interest paid = " + interestPaid);
            Console.WriteLine("Total         = " + total);
        }
    }

    Console.Read();
}
```

The program first reads the principal from the user. If the principal is negative, the program outputs an error message and quits. If the principal is not negative, control passes to the `else` clause, where the program continues executing.

The interest rate test has been improved in this example. Here, the program requires an interest rate that's non-negative (a mathematical law) and less than a maximum rate (a judiciary law). This `if` statement uses the following compound test:

```
if (interest < 0 || interest > maximumInterest)
```

This statement is true if `interest` is less than 0 or greater than `maximumInterest`. Notice the code declares `maximumInterest` as a variable at the top of the program rather than *hard-code* it here. *Hard-coding* refers to using values directly in your code rather than creating a variable to hold them.

TIP

Define important constants at the top of your program. Giving a constant a descriptive name (rather than just a number) makes it easy to find and easier to change. If the constant appears ten times in your code, you still have to make only one change to change all references. Entering a correct principal but a negative interest rate generates this output:

```
Enter principal: 1234
Enter interest: -12.5
Interest cannot be negative or greater than 50.
```

Only when the user enters both a legal principal and a legal interest rate does the program generate the correct calculation:

```
Enter principal: 1234
Enter interest: 12.5

Principal     = 1234
Interest      = 12.5%

Interest paid = 154.250
Total         = 1388.250
```

Running the switchboard

You often want to test a variable for numerous different values. For example, `maritalStatus` may be 0 for unmarried, 1 for married, 2 for divorced, 3 for widowed, or 4 for none of your business. To differentiate among these values, you could use the following series of `if` statements:

```
if (maritalStatus == 0)
{
  // Must be unmarried ...
```

```
  //  ... do something ...
}
else
{
  if (maritalStatus == 1)
  {
    // Must be married ...
    //  ... do something else ...
```

You can see that these repetitive `if` statements grow tiresome quickly. Testing for multiple cases is such a common occurrence that C# provides a special construct to decide between a set of mutually exclusive conditions. This control, the `switch`, works as follows:

```
switch (maritalStatus)
{
  case 0:
       //  ... do the unmarried stuff ...
           break;
  case 1:
       //  ... do the married stuff ...
           break;
  case 2:
       //  ... do the divorced stuff ...
           break;
  case 3:
       //  ... do the widowed stuff ...
           break;
  case 4:
       //  ... get out of my face ...
           break;
  default:
       // Goes here if it fails to pass a case;
       // this is probably an error condition.
           break;
}
```

The expression at the top of the `switch` statement is evaluated. In this case, the expression is simply the variable `maritalStatus`. The value of that expression is then compared against the value of each of the cases. Control passes to the `default` clause if no match is found. The argument to the `switch` statement can also be a `string`:

```
string s = "Davis";
switch(s)
```

```
{
  case "Davis":
          //  ... control will actually pass here ...
          break;
  case "Smith":
          //  ... do Smith stuff ...
          break;
  case "Jones":
          //  ... do Jones stuff ...
          break;
  case "Hvidsten":
          //  ... do Hvidsten stuff ...
          break;
  default:
          // Goes here if it doesn't pass any cases.
          break;
}
```

REMEMBER

Using the `switch` statement involves these restrictions:

- The argument to the `switch()` must be one of the counting types (including `char`) or a `string` when using older versions of C#. Starting with C# 7.0, you can use any non-null value.
- The various `case` values must refer to values of the same type as the `switch` expression.
- The `case` values must be constant in the sense that their value must be known at compile time. (A statement such as `case x` isn't legal unless `x` is a type of constant.)
- Each clause must end in a `break` statement (or another exit command, such as `return`). The `break` statement passes control out of the `switch`.

  You can omit a break statement if two cases lead to the same actions: A single `case` clause may have more than one `case` label, as in this example:

  ```
  string s = "Davis";
  switch(s)
  {
    case "Davis":
    case "Hvidsten":
            // Do the same thing whether s is Davis or Hvidsten
            // since they're related.
            break;
    case "Smith":
            //  ... do Smith stuff ...
            break;
  ```

```
    default:
        // Goes here if it doesn't pass any cases.
        break;
}
```

This approach enables the program to perform the same operation, whether the input is Davis or Hvidsten.

Working with switch expressions

Starting with C# 8.0 and above, you can use a new type of `switch` called a *switch expression*. This kind of `switch` allows you to use expressions as part of a `switch` statement. An *expression* is a construction that consists of operators and operands. For example, `x > y` is an expression. The best way to understand switch expressions is to see one in action, as shown in the `SwitchExpression` example.

```
public enum Greetings
{
    Morning,
    Afternoon,
    Evening,
    Night
}

public static string GreetString(Greetings value) => value switch
{
    Greetings.Morning => "Good Morning!",
    Greetings.Afternoon => "Good Afternoon!",
    Greetings.Evening => "See you tomorrow!",
    Greetings.Night => "Are you still here?",

    // Added solely to cover all cases.
    _ => "Not sure what time it is!"
};

static void Main(string[] args)
{
    Console.WriteLine(GreetString(Greetings.Morning));
    Console.WriteLine(GreetString(Greetings.Afternoon));
    Console.WriteLine(GreetString(Greetings.Evening));
    Console.WriteLine(GreetString(Greetings.Night));
    Console.ReadLine();
}
```

The example begins by creating the `Greetings enum` (or enumeration). An *enumeration* is simply a list of value names you want to use. Don't worry about enumerations too much now because you see them demonstrated in Chapter 10 of this minibook. In this case, the enumeration specifies the kinds of greetings that someone can use.

The `switch` expression comes next. It works similarly to a regular `switch` in that you start with a variable, `value`, that you compare to a series of cases. The difference is that `value` is of type `Greetings` in this case. When a particular `Greetings` value matches, the `switch` expression outputs a `string`.

TECHNICAL STUFF

Notice that there is a special value, _, that indicates what the `switch` should do when none of the other values match. This is a default value. If you don't include the default value, Visual Studio displays a warning message stating that you didn't cover all contingencies. In this case, you could leave it out because using an enumeration prevents someone from providing an unanticipated value that would require a default value.

Testing the `switch` expression comes next. The code in `Main()` tests every combination of Greetings. You see this output:

```
Good Morning!
Good Afternoon!
See you tomorrow!
Are you still here?
```

REMEMBER

Because this is a C# 8.0 and above feature, you still need to tell the IDE to use a different language version than the default. Make sure to add the following entry to `SwitchExpression.csproj`.

```
<PropertyGroup>
   <LangVersion>8.0</LangVersion>
</PropertyGroup>
```

Using pattern matching

C# 9.0 made it possible to extend the `switch` expression even further by using pattern matching. A pattern can be just about anything that you can recognize as representing a group of related values, even if the values aren't necessarily contiguous or of the same type. For example, a telephone number is a pattern because you recognize its structure. The `SwitchPattern` example uses an easier to recognize pattern, those of letters, numbers, and special characters.

A QUICK OVERVIEW OF THE LAMBDA EXPRESSION

You may wonder about the funny arrow, `=>`, in the `switch` expression code. The *lambda operator*, `=>`, is part of creating a lambda expression, which is a kind of shorthand for what is known as an anonymous function. (Just like the horse with no name, these functions don't have a name, either.) This book uses lambda expressions from time to time to help you create useful applications with less code, but it doesn't explain them in any detail because lambda expressions can become quite complex. (To give you some idea of just how complex, *Functional Programming For Dummies,* by John Paul Mueller [Wiley], is an entire book that goes into them in considerably more detail.)

This book keeps things simple so that you can enjoy using lambda expressions without going a bit mad first. For the purpose of creating a `switch` expression in this book, each lambda expression simply states that if the user inputs this, such as `Greetings.Morning`, the `switch` should output that, such as the `"Good Morning!"` string. Lambda expressions are significantly more useful than the coverage you see offered in this book. The Microsoft documentation for them appears at `https://docs.microsoft.com/en-us/dotnet/csharp/language-reference/operators/lambda-expressions`. The article at `https://csharp.christiannagel.com/2019/08/14/moving-from-the-switch-statement-to-switch-expressions-c-8/` provides a more detailed example than the one shown in this book for `switch` expressions. It gives you an idea of just how flexible using lambda expressions can be. However, don't be frightened away by lambda expressions; it's a topic you should explore in more detail.

```
public static string LetterType(char letter) => letter switch
{
    >= 'a' and <= 'z' => "lowercase letter",
    >= 'A' and <= 'Z' => "uppercase letter",
    >= '1' and <= '9' => "number",
    >= ' ' and <= '/' or
    >= ':' and <= '@' or
    >= '[' and <= '`' or
    >= '{' and <= '~' => "special character",
    _ => "Unknown letter type"
};

static void Main(string[] args)
{
    Console.WriteLine("a is a " + LetterType('a') + ".");
    Console.WriteLine("B is an " + LetterType('B') + ".");
    Console.WriteLine("3 is a " + LetterType('3') + ".");
```

```
    Console.WriteLine("? is a " + LetterType('?') + ".");
    Console.WriteLine("À is a " + LetterType('À') + ".");
    Console.ReadLine();
}
```

In this case, the switch uses logical patterns to define letter types based on the content of an input. Notice how you can combine and and or values to create the pattern. The final entry provides a default response in case the input character isn't recognized as part of the pattern. You can see more pattern types supported by C# at https://docs.microsoft.com/en-us/dotnet/csharp/language-reference/operators/patterns.

The testing coding in Main() goes through all the various expected character types. It then provides an uppercase *A* with a grave accent as input, which isn't part of the pattern. Here's the output from the example.

```
a is a lowercase letter.
B is an uppercase letter.
3 is a number.
? is a special character.
A is an Unknown letter type.
```

REMEMBER

Because this is a C# 9.0 and above feature, you still need to tell the IDE to use a different language version than the default. Make sure to add the following entry to SwitchPattern.csproj.

```
<PropertyGroup>
   <LangVersion>9.0</LangVersion>
</PropertyGroup>
```

Here We Go Loop-the-Loop

The if statement enables a program to take different paths through the code being executed, depending on the results of a bool expression. This statement provides for drastically more interesting programs than programs without decision-making capability. Adding the ability to execute a set of instructions *repeatedly* adds another quantum jump in capability.

Consider the CalculateInterest program from the section "Introducing the if statement," earlier in this chapter. Performing this simple interest calculation by using a calculator (or by hand, using a piece of paper) would be much easier than writing and executing a program.

If you could calculate the amount of principal for each of several succeeding years, that would be even more useful. What you need is a way for the computer to execute the same short sequence of instructions multiple times — known as a *loop.*

Looping for a while

The C# keyword `while` introduces the most basic form of execution loop:

```
while (bool-expression)
{
    // ... repeatedly executed as long as the expression is true.
}
```

When the `while` loop is first encountered, the `bool` expression is evaluated. If the expression is true, the code within the block is executed. When the block of code reaches the closed brace, control returns to the top, and the whole process starts over again. Control passes beyond the closed brace the first time the `bool` expression is evaluated and turns out to be false.

REMEMBER

If the condition is not true the first time the `while` loop is encountered, the set of commands within the braces is never executed.

WARNING

It's easy to become confused about how a `while` loop executes. You may feel that a loop executes until a condition is false, which implies that control passes outside the loop — no matter where the program happens to be executing — as soon as the condition becomes false. This definitely isn't the case. The program doesn't check whether the condition is still true until control specifically passes back to the top of the loop.

You can use the `while` loop to create the `CalculateInterestTable` program, a looping version of the `CalculateInterest` program. `CalculateInterestTable` calculates a table of principals showing accumulated annual payments:

```
static void Main(string[] args)
{
    // Define a maximum interest rate.
    int maximumInterest = 50;

    // Prompt user to enter source principal.
    Console.Write("Enter principal: ");
    string principalInput = Console.ReadLine();
    decimal principal = Convert.ToDecimal(principalInput);

    // If the principal is negative ...
    if (principal < 0)
```

```
{
    // ... generate an error message ...
    Console.WriteLine("Principal cannot be negative");
}
else  // Go here only if principal was > 0: thus valid.
{
    //  ... otherwise, enter the interest rate.
    Console.Write("Enter interest: ");
    string interestInput = Console.ReadLine();
    decimal interest = Convert.ToDecimal(interestInput);

    // If the interest is negative or too large ...
    if (interest < 0 || interest > maximumInterest)
    {
        //  ... generate an error message as well.
        Console.WriteLine("Interest cannot be negative " +
                          "or greater than " + maximumInterest);
        interest = 0;
    }
    else  // Reach this point only if all is well.
    {
        // Both the principal and the interest appear to be
        // legal; finally, input the number of years.
        Console.Write("Enter number of years: ");
        string durationInput = Console.ReadLine();
        int duration = Convert.ToInt32(durationInput);

        // Verify the input.
        Console.WriteLine();  // Skip a line.
        Console.WriteLine("Principal     = " + principal);
        Console.WriteLine("Interest      = " + interest + "%");
        Console.WriteLine("Duration      = " + duration + " years");
        Console.WriteLine();

        // Now loop through the specified number of years.
        int year = 1;
        while (year <= duration)
        {
            // Calculate the value of the principal plus interest.
            decimal interestPaid;
            interestPaid = principal * (interest / 100);

            // Now calculate the new principal by adding
            // the interest to the previous principal amount.
            principal = principal + interestPaid;

            // Round off the principal to the nearest cent.
            principal = decimal.Round(principal, 2);
```

```
                // Output the result.
                Console.WriteLine(year + "-" + principal);

                // Skip over to next year.
                year = year + 1;
            }
        }
    }

    Console.Read();
}
```

The output from a trial run of `CalculateInterestTable` appears this way:

```
Enter principal: 10000
Enter interest: 5.5
Enter number of years: 5

Principal     = 10000
Interest      = 5.5%
Duration      = 5 years

1-10550.00
2-11130.25
3-11742.41
4-12388.24
5-13069.59
```

Each value represents the total principal after the number of years elapsed, assuming simple interest compounded annually. For example, the value of $10,000 at 5.5 percent is $13,069.59 after five years.

The `CalculateInterestTable` program begins by reading the principal and interest values from the user and checking to make sure that they're valid. `CalculateInterestTable` then reads the number of years over which to iterate and stores this value in the variable `duration`.

Before entering the `while` loop, the program declares a variable `year`, which it initializes to `1`. This will be the "current year" — that is, this number changes "each year" as the program loops. If the year number contained in `year` is less than the total duration contained in `duration`, the principal for "this year" is recalculated by calculating the interest based on the "previous year." The calculated principal is output along with the current-year offset.

TECHNICAL STUFF

The statement `decimal.Round()` rounds the calculated value to the nearest fraction of a cent.

The key to the program lies in the last line within the block. The statement `year = year + 1;` increments `year` by 1. If `year` begins with the value `3`, its value will be `4` after this expression. This incrementing moves the calculations along from one year to the next.

After the year has been incremented, control returns to the top of the loop, where the value `year` is compared to the requested duration. In the sample run, if the current year is less than 5, the calculation continues. After being incremented five times, the value of `year` becomes 6, which is greater than 5, and program control passes to the first statement after the `while` loop — the program stops looping.

The counting variable `year` in `CalculateInterestTable` must be declared and initialized before the `while` loop in which it is used. In addition, the `year` variable must be incremented, usually as the last statement within the loop. As this example demonstrates, you have to look ahead to see which variables you need. This pattern is easier to use after you've written a few thousand `while` loops.

WARNING

When writing `while` loops, don't forget to increment the counting variable, as shown in this example:

```
int nYear = 1;
while (nYear < 10)
{
    //  ... whatever ...
}
```

This example doesn't increment `nYear`. Without the increment, `nYear` is always `1` and the program loops forever. The only way to exit this *infinite loop* is to terminate the program by pressing Ctrl+C. (So nothing is truly infinite, with the possible exception of a particle passing through the event horizon of a black hole.)

REMEMBER

Make sure that the terminating condition can be satisfied. Usually, this means your counting variable is being incremented properly. Otherwise, you're looking at an infinite loop, an angry user, bad press, and 50 years of drought. Infinite loops are a common mistake, so don't be embarrassed when you get caught in one.

Doing the do . . . while loop

A variation of the `while` loop is the `do ... while` loop. In this example, the condition isn't checked until the *end* of the loop:

```
int year = 1;
do
{
    //  ... some calculation ...
    year = year + 1;
} while (year < duration);
```

In contrast to the `while` loop, the `do ... while` loop is executed at least once, regardless of the value of `duration`.

Breaking up is easy to do

You can use two special commands to change how a loop executes: `break` and `continue`. Executing the `break` statement causes control to pass to the first expression immediately following the loop. The similar `continue` statement passes control straight back up to the conditional expression at the top of the loop to start over and get it right this time.

Suppose that you want to take your money out of the bank as soon as the principal exceeds a certain number of times the original amount, irrespective of the duration in years. You could easily accommodate this amount by adding the following code (in bold) within the loop:

```
// Now loop through the specified number of years.
int year = 1;
while (year <= duration)
{
  // Calculate the value of the principal plus interest.
  decimal interestPaid;
  interestPaid = principal * (interest / 100);

  // Now calculate the new principal by adding
  // the interest to the previous principal amount.
  principal = principal + interestPaid;

  // Round off the principal to the nearest cent.
  principal = decimal.Round(principal, 2);

  // Output the result.
  Console.WriteLine(year + "-" + principal);

  // Skip over to next year.
  year = year + 1;
```

```
    // Determine whether we have reached our goal.
    if (principal > (maxPower * originalPrincipal))
    {
      break;
    }
  }
```

The break statement isn't executed until the condition within the if comparison is true — in this case, until the calculated principal is maxPower times the original principal or more. Executing the break statement passes control outside the while(year <= duration) statement, and the program resumes execution immediately after the loop.

Looping until you get it right

The CalculateInterestTable program is smart enough to terminate in the event that the user enters an invalid balance or interest amount. However, jumping immediately out of the program just because the user mistypes something seems harsh. A combination of while and break enables the program to be a little more flexible. The CalculateInterestTableMoreForgiving program demonstrates the principle this way:

```
static void Main(string[] args)
{
    // Define a maximum interest rate.
    int maximumInterest = 50;

    // Prompt user to enter source principal; keep prompting
    // until the correct value is entered.
    decimal principal;
    while (true)
    {
        Console.Write("Enter principal: ");
        string principalInput = Console.ReadLine();
        principal = Convert.ToDecimal(principalInput);

        // Exit if the value entered is correct.
        if (principal >= 0)
        {
            break;
        }

        // Generate an error on incorrect input.
        Console.WriteLine("Principal cannot be negative");
        Console.WriteLine("Try again");
        Console.WriteLine();
    }
```

```
// Now enter the interest rate.
decimal interest;
while (true)
{
    Console.Write("Enter interest: ");
    string interestInput = Console.ReadLine();
    interest = Convert.ToDecimal(interestInput);

    // Don't accept interest that is negative or too large ...
    if (interest >= 0 && interest <= maximumInterest)
    {
        break;
    }

    //  ... generate an error message as well.
    Console.WriteLine("Interest cannot be negative " +
                      "or greater than " + maximumInterest);
    Console.WriteLine("Try again");
    Console.WriteLine();
}

// Both the principal and the interest appear to be
// legal; finally, input the number of years.
Console.Write("Enter number of years: ");
string durationInput = Console.ReadLine();
int duration = Convert.ToInt32(durationInput);

// Verify the input.
Console.WriteLine();  // Skip a line.
Console.WriteLine("Principal     = " + principal);
Console.WriteLine("Interest      = " + interest + "%");
Console.WriteLine("Duration      = " + duration + " years");
Console.WriteLine();

// Now loop through the specified number of years.
int year = 1;
while (year <= duration)
{
    // Calculate the value of the principal plus interest.
    decimal interestPaid;
    interestPaid = principal * (interest / 100);

    // Now calculate the new principal by adding
    // the interest to the previous principal.
    principal = principal + interestPaid;

    // Round off the principal to the nearest cent.
    principal = decimal.Round(principal, 2);
```

```
        // Output the result.
        Console.WriteLine(year + "-" + principal);

        // Skip over to next year.
        year = year + 1;
      }

    Console.Read();
  }
```

This program works largely the same way as do the examples in previous sections of this chapter, except in the area of user input. This time, a `while` loop replaces the `if` statement used in earlier examples to detect invalid input (you would use the same sort of loop to obtain the number of years, but it has been omitted to save space):

```
decimal principal;
while (true)
{
  Console.Write("Enter principal: ");
  string principalInput = Console.ReadLine();
  principal = Convert.ToDecimal(principalInput);

  // Exit when the value entered is correct.
  if (principal >= 0)
  {
    break;
  }

  // Generate an error on incorrect input.
  Console.WriteLine("Principal cannot be negative");
  Console.WriteLine("Try again");
  Console.WriteLine();
}
```

This section of code inputs a value from the user within a loop. If the value of the text is okay, the program exits the input loop and continues. However, if the input has an error, the user sees an error message and control passes back to the program flow to start over.

REMEMBER

The program continues to loop until the user enters the correct input. (In the worst case, the program could loop until an obtuse user dies of old age.)

Notice that the conditionals have been reversed because the question is no longer whether illegal input should generate an error message, but rather whether the correct input should exit the loop. In the interest section, for example, consider this test:

```
principal < 0 || principal > maximumInterest
```

This test changes to this:

```
interest >= 0 && interest <= maximumInterest
```

Clearly, `interest >= 0` is the opposite of `interest < 0`. What may not be as obvious is that the OR (`||`) operator is replaced with an AND (`&&`) operator. It says, "Exit the loop if the interest is greater than zero AND less than the maximum amount (in other words, if it is correct)." Note that the `principal` variable must be declared outside the loop because of scope rules, which is explained in the next section.

WARNING

It may sound obvious, but the expression `true` evaluates to `true`. Therefore, `while (true)` is your archetypical infinite loop. It's the embedded `break` statement that exits the loop. Therefore, if you use the `while (true)` loop, make sure that your break condition can occur. The output from a sample execution of this program appears this way:

```
Enter principal: -1000
Principal cannot be negative
Try again

Enter principal: 1000
Enter interest: -10
Interest cannot be negative or greater than 50
Try again

Enter interest: 10
Enter number of years: 5

Principal      = 1000
Interest       = 10%
Duration       = 5 years

1-1100.0
2-1210.00
3-1331.00
4-1464.10
5-1610.51
Press Enter to terminate ...
```

The program refuses to accept a negative principal or interest amount and patiently explains the mistake on each loop. However, you'd still need to add code to handle situations in which the user entered a blank input or a string value, such as seven.

WARNING

Explain exactly what the user did wrong before looping back for further input or else that person will become extremely confused. Showing an example may also help, especially for formatting problems. A little diplomacy can't hurt, either, as Grandma may have pointed out.

Focusing on scope rules

A variable declared within the body of a loop is *defined only within* that loop. Consider this code snippet:

```
int days = 1;
while (days < duration)
{
    int average = value / days;
    //  ... some series of commands ...
    days = days + 1;
}
```

TECHNICAL STUFF

The variable `average` isn't defined outside the `while` loop. Various reasons for this exist, but consider this one: The first time the loop executes, the program encounters the declaration `int average` and the variable is defined. On the second loop, the program again encounters the declaration for `average`, and were it not for scope rules, it would be an error because the variable is already defined. Suffice it to say that the variable `average` goes away, as far as C# is concerned, as soon as the program reaches the closed brace — and is redefined each time through the loop.

TIP

Experienced programmers say that the *scope* of the variable `average` is limited to the `while` loop.

Looping a Specified Number of Times with for

The `while` loop is the simplest and second most commonly used looping structure in C#. Compared to the `for` loop, however, the `while` loop is used about as often as metric tools in an American machine shop. The `for` loop has this structure:

```
for (initExpression; condition; incrementExpression)
{
    // ... body of code ...
}
```

When the for loop is encountered, the program first executes the initExpression expression and then tests the condition. If the condition expression is true, the program executes the body of the loop, which is surrounded by the braces immediately following the for command. When the program reaches the closed brace, control passes to incrementExpression and then back to condition, where the next pass through the loop begins. In fact, the definition of a for loop can be converted into this while loop:

```
initExpression;
while(condition)
{
    //  ... body of code ...
    incrementExpression;
}
```

A for loop example

You can better see how the for loop works in this example:

```
// Here is one C# expression or another.
a = 1;

// Now loop for awhile.
for (int year = 1; year <= duration; year = year + 1)
{
    //  ... body of code ...
}

// The program continues here.
a = 2;
```

Assume that the program has just executed the a = 1; expression. Next, the program declares the variable year and initializes it to 1. Then the program compares year to duration. If year is less than duration, the body of code within the braces is executed. After encountering the closed brace, the program jumps back to the top and executes the year = year + 1 clause before sliding back over to the year < duration comparison.

WARNING

The `year` variable is undefined outside the scope of the `for` loop. The loop's scope includes the loop's heading as well as its body.

Why do you need another loop?

Why do you need the `for` loop if C# has an equivalent `while` loop? The short answer is that you don't — the `for` loop doesn't bring anything to the table that the `while` loop can't already do.

However, the sections of the `for` loop exist for convenience — and to clearly establish the three parts that every loop should have: the setup, exit criteria, and increment. Not only is this arrangement easier to read, it's also easier to get right. (Remember that the most common mistakes in a `while` loop are forgetting to increment the counting variable and failing to provide the proper exit criteria.) The most important reason to understand the `for` loop is that it's the loop everyone uses — and it (along with its cousin, `foreach`) is the one you see 90 percent of the time when you're reading other people's code.

TECHNICAL STUFF

The `for` loop is designed so that the first expression initializes a counting variable and the last section increments it; however, the C# language doesn't enforce any such rule. You can do anything you want in these two sections; however, you would be ill advised to do anything *but* initialize and increment the counting variable.

The increment operator is particularly popular when writing `for` loops. (Chapter 4 of this minibook describes the increment operator along with other operators.) The previous `for` loop is usually written this way:

```
for (int year = 1; year <= nDuration; year++)
{
    // ... body of code ...
}
```

TIP

You almost always see the postincrement operator used in a `for` loop instead of the preincrement operator, although the effect in this case is the same. There's no reason other than habit and the fact that it looks cooler. (The next time you want to break the ice, just haul out your C# listing full of postincrement operators to show how cool you are. It almost never works, but it's worth a try.)

The `for` loop has one variation that you may find hard to understand. If the logical condition expression is missing, it's assumed to be `true`. Thus `for (;;)` is an infinite loop. You see `for (;;)` used as an infinite loop more often than `while (true)`.

Nesting loops

An inner loop can appear within an outer loop, this way:

```
for ( ...some condition ...)
{
  for ( ...some other condition ...)
  {
    // ... do whatever ...
  }
}
```

The inner loop is executed to completion during each pass through the outer loop. The loop variable (such as `year`) used in the inner `for` loop isn't defined outside the inner loop's scope.

REMEMBER

A loop contained within another loop is a *nested* loop. Nested loops cannot "cross." For example, the following code won't work:

```
do                // Start a do..while loop.
{
  for( ...)       // Start some for loop.
  {
  } while( ...)   // End do..while loop.
}                 // End for loop.
```

REMEMBER

A `break` statement within a nested loop breaks out of the inner loop only. In the following example, the `break` statement exits loop B and goes back into loop A:

```
// for loop A
for( ...some condition ...)
{
  // for loop B
  for( ...some other condition ...)
  {
    // ... do whatever ...
    if (something is true)
    {
      break;          // Breaks out of loop B and not loop A
    }
  }
}
```

C# doesn't have a `break` statement that exits both loops simultaneously. You must use two separate `break` statements, one for each loop.

Having to use two `break` statements isn't as big a limitation as it sounds. In practice, the often-complex logic contained within such nested loops is better encapsulated in a method. Executing a `return` from within any of the loops exits the method, thereby bailing out of all loops, no matter how nested they are. Book 2 Chapter 2 of this minibook describes methods and the `return` statement.

IN THIS CHAPTER

» Creating variables that contain multiple items of data: Arrays

» Going arrays one better with flexible collections

» Looking at array and collection initializers and set-type collections

Chapter 6
Lining Up Your Ducks with Collections

Simple one-value variables of the sort you may encounter in this book fall a bit short in dealing with lots of items of the same kind: ten ducks instead of just one, for example. C# fills the gap with two kinds of variables that store multiple items, generally called *collections.* The two species of collection are the *array* and the more general-purpose *collection class.*

This book specifically uses the term *array* when discussing arrays. When working with the collection class, the book uses the term *collection class.* If the book refers to a *collection* or a *list,* the object in question can be either an array or a collection class.

An *array* is a data type that holds a list of objects of the same type. You can't create a single array that contains both `int` and `double` objects, for example. Every object must be of the same type.

C# gives you quite a collection of collection classes, and they come in various shapes, such as flexible lists (like strings of beads), queues (like the line at the bank), stacks (like a stack of pancakes), and more. Most collection classes are like arrays in that they can hold just apples or just oranges. But C# also gives you a few collection classes that can hold both apples and oranges at the same time — which is useful only rarely. (And you have much better ways to manage the feat than using these elderly collections.)

For now, if you can master arrays and the `List` collection, you'll do fine throughout most of this book. But circle back here later if you want to pump up your collection repertoire. This chapter does introduce two other collection types.

REMEMBER

You don't have to type the source code for this chapter manually. In fact, using the downloadable source is a lot easier. You can find the source for this chapter in the `\CSAIO4D2E\BK01\CH06` folder of the downloadable source. See the Introduction for details on how to find these source files.

The C# Array

Variables that contain single values are plenty useful. Even class structures that can describe compound objects made up of parts (such as a vehicle with its engine and transmission) are critical. But you also need a construct for holding a bunch of objects, such as Nick Mason's extensive collection of Italian super sport cars (see the largest collections of cars at `http://www.collectiblewheels.com/news/2018/4/19/the-10-biggest-car-collectors-in-the-world`) or a list of tunes in a music collection. The built-in class `Array` is a structure that can contain a series of elements of the same type (all `int` values and all `double` values, for example, or all `Vehicle` objects and `Motor` objects; you meet these latter sorts of objects in Book 2 Chapter 1).

The argument for the array

Consider the problem of averaging a set of six floating-point numbers. Each of the six numbers requires its own `double` storage:

```
double d0 = 5;
double d1 = 2;
double d2 = 7;
double d3 = 3.5;
double d4 = 6.5;
double d5 = 8;
```

Computing the average of those variables might look like this (remember that averaging `int` variables can result in rounding errors, as described in Chapter 2 of this minibook):

```
double sum = d0 + d1 + d2 + d3 + d4 + d5;
double average = sum / 6;
```

Listing each element by name is tedious. Okay, maybe it's not so tedious when you have only 6 numbers to average, but imagine averaging 600 (or even 6 million) floating-point values.

The fixed-value array

Fortunately, you don't need to name each element separately. C# provides the array structure that can store a sequence of values. Using an array, you can put all your `doubles` into one variable, like this:

```
double[] doublesArray = {5, 2, 7, 3.5, 6.5, 8, 1, 9, 1, 3};
```

You can also declare an empty array without initializing it:

```
double[] doublesArray = new double[6];
```

This line allocates space for six `doubles` but doesn't initialize them.

REMEMBER

The `Array` class, on which all C# arrays are based, provides a special syntax that makes it more convenient to use. The paired brackets `[]` refer to the way you access individual elements in the array:

```
doublesArray[0] // Corresponds to 5
doublesArray[1] // Corresponds to 2
...
```

The 1st element of the array corresponds to a value of 5, the 2nd element to a value of 2, the 3rd element to a value of 7, and so on. Programmers call arrays that begin counting their elements at 0 *zero-based*. Some languages, such as Fortran and COBOL, use *one-based* arrays, which begin counting elements at 1. The array's element numbers — 0, 1, 2, . . . — are known as the *index*. A particular array element, such as `doublesArray[0]`, is called a *subarray* because it's part of a larger array.

SPECIALIZED ARRAY SUPPORT IN SOME C# ENVIRONMENTS

Starting with C# 8.0, you can also access more than one element as a subarray by adding two periods and the second value, such as `doublesArray[0..3]`, which would refer to the numbers: 5, 2, and 7. Using this syntax relies on the use of a *range,* a starting and ending index. Notice that the ending index, 3, isn't included in the output. However, to get this support (and the other goodies listed in this sidebar) you normally use the .NET Core 3.*x*, rather than .NET standard. When you access a range, what you get is another array that contains just the elements you requested, so you still need to use a `foreach` loop (discussed in the "Processing Arrays by Using foreach" section, later in this chapter) to access the individual members.

You also don't have to access `doublesArray` from the beginning; you can do it from the end instead using `doublesArray[^1]`, which equates to the number 3. Note that index 0 is ignored when you use the end-of-array addressing, so `doublesArray[^0]` would display an index-out-of-range exception. In addition, you can create ranges that begin at the end, such as `doublesArray[^3..^0]`, which equates to the numbers: 9, 1, and 3. Notice that a range that works with the end of an array starts with the higher index number and ends with the lower index numbers. You can read more about these specialized indexes and ranges at `https://docs.microsoft.com/en-us/dotnet/csharp/whats-new/tutorials/ranges-indexes`.

Fortunately, you can add support for these specialized indexing and range features to a standard .NET application using the technique described at `https://www.meziantou.net/how-to-use-csharp-8-indices-and-ranges-in-dotnet-standard-2-0-and-dotn.htm`. Modify the project file after you close the solution to include:

```
<PropertyGroup>
  <LangVersion>8.0</LangVersion>
</PropertyGroup>
```

You must then download the `Range.cs` file from the website and place it in the same folder as your `Program.cs` file for your project. Reopen your solution and choose Show All Files in the Solution Explorer. Right-click `Range.cs` when you see it, and choose Include in Project from the context menu. You can now use this support in your project. (You can see an example of it in the `Special`IndexAndRange project included in the downloadable source code.)

The doublesArray variable wouldn't be much of an improvement were it not for the possibility that the index of the array is a variable. Using a for loop is easier than writing each element manually, as the FixedArrayAverage program demonstrates:

```
static void Main(string[] args)
{
    double[] doublesArray = { 5, 2, 7, 3.5, 6.5, 8, 1, 9, 1, 3 };

    // Accumulate the values in the array into the variable sum.
    double sum = 0;
    for (int i = 0; i < doublesArray.Length; i++)
    {
        sum = sum + doublesArray[i];
    }

    // Now calculate the average.
    double average = sum / doublesArray.Length;
    Console.WriteLine(average);
    Console.Read();
}
```


The program begins by initializing a variable sum to 0. Then it loops through the values stored in doublesArray, adding each one to sum. By the end of the loop, sum has accumulated the sum of all values in the array. The resulting sum is divided by the number of elements to create the average. The output from executing this program is the expected 4.6. (You can check it with your calculator.)

TIP

Notice how the code automatically obtains the correct ending point by using doublesArray.Length. Yes, you could have simply used the value 10, but then you couldn't be sure that the value is correct. If the array length changes for some reason, you might not get the correct average, or the code could generate a System.IndexOutOfRangeException. When working with arrays, always assume that you don't know the array length and use the array's Length property to obtain it.

The variable-length array

The array used in the FixedArrayAverage program example suffers from these two serious problems:

- » The size of the array is fixed at ten elements.
- » Worse, the elements' values are specified directly in the program.

A program that could read in a variable number of values, perhaps determined by the user during execution, would be much more flexible. It would work not only for the ten values specified in `FixedArrayAverage` but also for any other set of values, regardless of their number. The format for declaring a variable-size array differs slightly from that of a fixed-size, fixed-value array:

```
double[] doublesArrayVariable = new double[N];  // Variable, versus ...
double[] doublesArrayFixed = new double[10];    // Fixed
```

Here, `N` represents the number of elements to allocate. The updated program `VariableArrayAverage` enables the user to specify the number of values to enter. (`N` has to come from somewhere.) Because the program retains the values entered, not only does it calculate the average, it also displays the results in a pleasant format, as shown here:

```
static void Main(string[] args)
{
    // First read in the number of doubles the user intends to enter.
    Console.Write("Enter the number of values to average: ");
    string numElementsInput = Console.ReadLine();
    int numElements = Convert.ToInt32(numElementsInput);
    Console.WriteLine();

    // Now declare an array of that size.
    double[] doublesArray = new double[numElements]; // Here's the 'N'.

    // Accumulate the values into an array.
    for (int i = 0; i < numElements; i++)
    {
        // Prompt the user for another double.
        Console.Write("enter double #" + (i + 1) + ": ");
        string val = Console.ReadLine();
        double value;
        if (Double.TryParse(val, out value))
        {
            // Add this to the array using bracket notation.
            doublesArray[i] = value;
        }
        else
        {
            Console.WriteLine($"Attempted to input {val}, using 0 instead.");
            doublesArray[i] = 0;
        }
    }

    // Accumulate the array values in the variable sum.
    double sum = 0;
```

```
    for (int i = 0; i < doublesArray.Length; i++)
    {
        sum = sum + doublesArray[i];
    }

    // Now calculate the average.
    double average = sum / numElements;

    // Output the results in an attractive format.
    Console.WriteLine();
    Console.Write(average + " is the average of (" + doublesArray[0]);
    for (int i = 1; i < doublesArray.Length; i++)
    {
        Console.Write(" + " + doublesArray[i]);
    }
    Console.WriteLine(") / " + doublesArray.Length);

    // Wait for user to acknowledge the results.
    Console.Read();
}
```


The VariableArrayAverage program begins by prompting the user for the number of values to average. The result is stored in the int variable numElements.

The program continues by allocating an array doublesArray with the specified number of elements. The program loops the number of times specified by numElements, reading a new value from the user each time. After the last value, the program calculates the average.

This example adds a couple of improvements to the data entry techniques in previous examples that you should note. The first is to use Double.TryParse() to determine whether an input value is correct. Given that this is a manual input scenario, you could also use a loop to keep asking the user for the correct input until you beat them into submission, but this approach works for situations where you can't ask for a retry. For example, if you're reading values from a database, you can't ask for a retry and must assume some value rather than just allowing the application to die gracelessly after displaying an exception that the user won't understand.

The second improvement is that the code assigns a 0 to bad values. You could also use the current average of the other values or some other default. Note that the code displays a message telling the user about the substitution, which is always a good idea, even if you're processing data from another source.

TIP

Getting console output just right, as in this example, is a little tricky. Follow each statement in `VariableArrayAverage` carefully as the program outputs open parentheses, equals signs, plus signs, and each of the numbers in the sequence, and compare it with the output.

The `VariableArrayAverage` program probably doesn't completely satisfy your thirst for flexibility. You don't want to have to tell the program how many numbers you want to average. What you really want is to enter numbers to average as long as you want — and then tell the program to average what you entered. That's where the C# collections come in. They give you a powerful, flexible alternative to arrays. Getting input directly from the user isn't the only way to fill up your array or another collection, either.

Look at the following output of a sample run in which you enter five sequential values, 1 through 5, and the program calculates the average to be 3.2:

```
Enter the number of values to average: 5

enter double #1: X
Attempted to input X, using 0 instead.
enter double #2: 5
enter double #3: 2
enter double #4: !
Attempted to input !, using 0 instead.
enter double #5: 9

3.2 is the average of (0 + 5 + 2 + 0 + 9) / 5
```

Initializing an array

The following lines show an array with its initializer and then one that allocates space but doesn't initialize the elements' values:

```
double[] initializedArray = {5, 2, 7, 3.5, 6.5, 8, 1, 9, 1, 3};
double[] blankArray = new double[10];
```

REMEMBER

Even though `blankArray` allocates space for the elements, you must still initialize its values. You could use a `for` loop to perform this task by assigning a value to each indexed element in turn or relying on the code shown for `initializedArray`.

Processing Arrays by Using foreach

Even if you use all the correct techniques, using a `for` loop to process arrays and collections is error prone. There are just too many places where you can enter the wrong information and expose your user to exceptions that will ruin everyone's day. The `foreach` loop fixes these problems by getting rid of the guesswork, as you see in the sections that follow.

Working with foreach loops in a standard way

Given an array of strings, the following loop found in the `UsingForeach` example averages their lengths:

```
static void Main(string[] args)
{
    string[] myStrings = { "Hello", "Goodbye", "Today", "Tomorrow" };

    int sum = 0;
    foreach (string thisString in myStrings)
    {
        Console.WriteLine($"The current string is: {thisString}.");
        Console.WriteLine($"It's {thisString.Length} characters long.");
        sum += thisString.Length;
    }

    double average = (double)sum / myStrings.Length;
    Console.WriteLine($"The average character length is: {average}.");
    Console.ReadLine();
}
```

This example begins by defining the `myStrings` array using the same approach you did when defining `doublesArray`. The code then uses a `foreach` loop to process `myStrings` without any regard to the array length or a specific index. What the loop expression basically says is that C# should take one `string`, `thisString`, from the `myStrings` array and do something with it. When you need to process all the elements in an array or collection, using `foreach` requires a lot less labor on your part and produces far fewer errors for the user. When you run this application, you see the following output:

```
The current string is: Hello.
It's 5 characters long.
The current string is: Goodbye.
It's 7 characters long.
```

```
The current string is: Today.
It's 5 characters long.
The current string is: Tomorrow.
It's 8 characters long.
The average character length is: 6.25.
```

TECHNICAL STUFF

The foreach loop is even more powerful than it would seem from the example. This statement works on other collection types in addition to arrays. In addition, foreach handles *multidimensional* arrays (arrays of arrays, in effect), a topic not described in this book. You can find out more about multidimensional arrays at https://www.tutorialspoint.com/csharp/csharp_multi_dimensional_arrays.htm.

Relying on GetEnumerator support

TECHNICAL STUFF

An enumerator depends on the IEnumerator interface that you can add to a class. Here's what an enumerator does for you:

- Lets you iterate a collection without knowing anything about how to iterate it. For example, you don't need to know whether the collection provides an index.
- Allows iteration of part of a collection, rather than all of it. For example, you could look for a particular word in an array and then start to iterate from that point.
- Performs late execution of the iteration. You may not actually need to iterate an array unless the user plans to do something with it. Using an enumerator with certain C# techniques (such as Language Integrated Query, LINQ, https://www.tutorialspoint.com/linq/index.htm) enables you to ignore the iteration until later — making your code run faster.

C# 9.0 made it possible to use an enumerator with a foreach loop, rather than work with the object itself. The UsingEnumeratedForeach example shows how to perform this task. You must add C# 9.0 or above support to the application to use this example. This first part of the example adds an extension that you need to access the GetEnumerator() method.

```
public static class Extensions
{
    public static IEnumerator<T> GetEnumerator<T>(this
        IEnumerator<T> enumerator) => enumerator;
}
```

Don't worry too much about this code for now. All you need to know is that it makes GetEnumerator() accessible to the code that follows here:

```
static void Main(string[] args)
{
    String[] myStrings = { "Hello", "Goodbye", "Today", "Tomorrow" };
    IEnumerator<string> stringEnum = (IEnumerator<string>)new
        List<string>(myStrings).GetEnumerator();

    while ((string)stringEnum.Current != "Hello")
        stringEnum.MoveNext();

    int sum = 0;
    int count = 0;
    foreach (var thisString in stringEnum)
    {
        Console.WriteLine($"The current string is: {thisString}.");
        Console.WriteLine($"It's {thisString.Length} characters long.");
        sum += thisString.Length;
        count++;
    }

    double average = (double)sum / count;
    Console.WriteLine($"The average character length is: {average}.");
    Console.ReadLine();
}
```

The example starts with array of strings. However, arrays are special in that they can't use the public version of GetEnumerator(), so you must convert the array to a List, which means adding this using statement to the beginning of the file:

```
using System.Collections.Generic;
```

The second line of the example code creates the stringEnum enumerator from a List that contains the converted myStrings by calling GetEnumerator().You end up with an enumerator that has a public GetEnumerator() member that is used as part of the foreach loop later.

Before the code attempts to list the members of myStrings using stringEnum, it looks for a particular member using a while loop. If stringEnum.Current doesn't contain the string "Hello", the code calls stringEnum.MoveNext() to move onto the next entry. When the code finds "Hello", the while loop exits and the foreach loop begins.

The `foreach` loop is just like the `foreach` loop in the `UsingForeach` example, except that it relies on an enumerator. However, it starts at the element after the current element, so the first entry processed is actually `"Goodbye"`. Here's what you see when you run the example.

```
The current string is: Goodbye.
It's 7 characters long.
The current string is: Today.
It's 5 characters long.
The current string is: Tomorrow.
It's 8 characters long.
The average character length is: 6.66666666666667.
```

Sorting Arrays of Data

A common programming challenge is the need to sort the elements within an array. Just because an array cannot grow or shrink doesn't mean that the elements within it cannot be moved, removed, or added. For example, the following code snippet swaps the location of two `string` elements within the array `strings`:

```
string temp = strings[i]; // Save the i'th string.
strings[i] = strings[k];  // Replace it with the kth.
strings[k] = temp;        // Replace kth with temp.
```

In this example, the object reference in the *i*th location in the `strings` array is saved so that it isn't lost when the second statement replaces it with another element. Finally, the `temp` variable is saved back into the *k*th location. Pictorially, this process looks like Figure 6-1.

TIP

The data collections discussed in the rest of this chapter are more versatile than the array for adding and removing elements. The following program demonstrates how to use the ability to manipulate elements within an array as part of a sort. This particular sorting algorithm is the *bubble sort*. Though it's not so great on large arrays with thousands of elements, it's simple and effective on small arrays, as shown in the `BubbleSortArray` example:

```
static void Main(string[] args)
{
    Console.WriteLine("The 5 planets closest to the sun, in order: ");
    string[] planets =
      new string[] { "Mercury", "Venus", "Earth", "Mars", "Jupiter" };
```

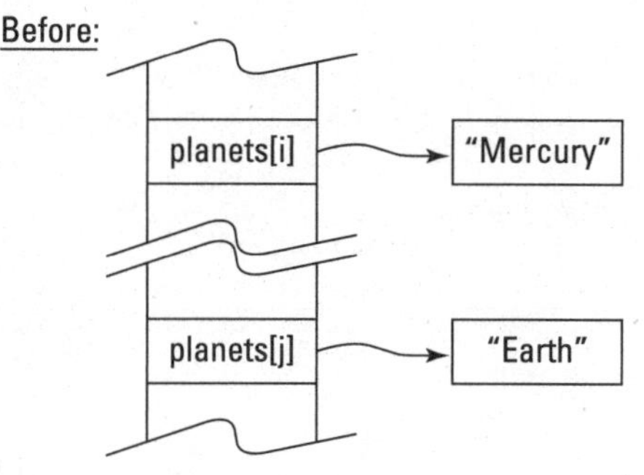

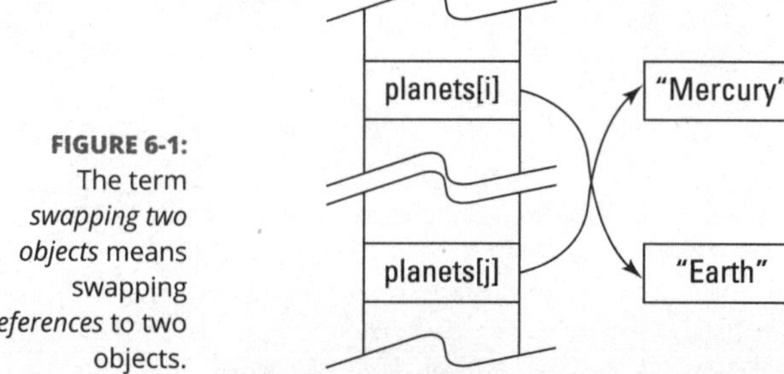

FIGURE 6-1: The term *swapping two objects* means swapping *references* to two objects.


```
foreach (string planet in planets)
{
    // Use the special char \t to insert a tab in the printed line.
    Console.WriteLine("\t" + planet);
}

Console.WriteLine("\nNow listed alphabetically: ");

// Array.Sort() is a method on the Array class.
// Array.Sort() does its work in-place in the planets array,
// which leaves you without a copy of the original array. The
// solution is to copy the old array to a new one and sort it.
string[] sortedNames = planets;
Array.Sort(sortedNames);

// This demonstrates that (a) sortedNames contains the same
// strings as planets and (b) that they're now sorted.
foreach (string planet in sortedNames)
{
    Console.WriteLine("\t" + planet);
}

Console.WriteLine("\nList by name length - shortest first: ");

// This algorithm is called "Bubble Sort": It's the simplest
// but worst-performing sort. The Array.Sort() method is much
```

```
        // more efficient, but you can't use it directly to sort the
        // planets in order of name length because it sorts strings,
        // not their lengths.
        int outer;  // Index of the outer loop
        int inner;  // Index of the inner loop

        // Loop DOWN from last index to first: planets[4] to planets[0].
        for (outer = planets.Length - 1; outer >= 0; outer--)
        {

            // On each outer loop, loop through all elements BEYOND the
            // current outer element. This loop goes up, from planets[1]
            // to planets[4]. Using the for loop, you can traverse the
            // array in either direction.
            for (inner = 1; inner <= outer; inner++)
            {

                // Compare adjacent elements. If the earlier one is longer
                // than the later one, swap them. This shows how you can
                // swap one array element with another when they're out of
                // order.
                if (planets[inner - 1].Length > planets[inner].Length)
                {
                    // Temporarily store one planet.
                    string temp = planets[inner - 1];

                    // Now overwrite that planet with the other one.
                    planets[inner - 1] = planets[inner];

                    // Finally, reclaim the planet stored in temp and put
                    // it in place of the other.
                    planets[inner] = temp;
                }
            }
        }

        foreach (string planet in planets)
        {
            Console.WriteLine("\t" + planet);
        }

        Console.Read();
    }
```

The program begins with an array containing the names of the first five planets closest to the sun. (The example excludes the outer planets to keep the figures small.) The program then invokes the array's own Sort() method. The built-in Sort() method for arrays (and other collections) is, without a doubt, more efficient than the custom bubble sort. Don't roll your own unless you have good reason to.

After sorting with the built-in `Sort()` method on the `Array` class, the program sorts the lengths of the planets' names using a custom sort to show one technique of addressing needs (such as sorting by name length) that the standard sorts don't address. The algorithm for the second sort works by continuously looping through the list of strings until the list is sorted. On each pass through the `sortedNames` array, the program compares each string to its neighbor. If the two are found to be out of order, the method swaps them and then flags the list as not sorted.

Eventually, shorter planet names "bubble" their way to the top of the list; hence the name *bubble sort.* Here's the output you see from this example:

```
The 5 planets closest to the sun, in order:
        Mercury
        Venus
        Earth
        Mars
        Jupiter

Now listed alphabetically:
        Earth
        Jupiter
        Mars
        Mercury
        Venus

List by name length - shortest first:
        Mars
        Earth
        Venus
        Jupiter
        Mercury
```


Using var for Arrays

Traditionally, you used one of the following forms (which are as old as C#) to initialize an array:

```
int[] numbers = new int[3];            // Size but no initializer, or ...
int[] numbers = new int[] { 1, 2, 3 }; // Initializer but no size, or ...
int[] numbers = new int[3] { 1, 2, 3 };// Size and initializer, or ...
int[] numbers = { 1, 2, 3 };           // No 'new' keyword -- short form.
```

Chapter 2 of this minibook introduces the var keyword, which tells the C# compiler, "Determine the variable type from the initializer expression." Happily, var works with arrays, too:

```
// myArray is an int[] with 6 elements.
var myArray = new [] { 2, 3, 5, 7, 11, 13 };  // Initializer required!
```

The new syntax has only two changes:

- var is used instead of the explicit type information for the numbers array on the left side of the assignment.
- The int keyword is omitted before the brackets on the right side of the assignment. It's the part that the compiler can infer.

REMEMBER

In the var version, the initializer is required. The compiler uses it to infer the type of the array elements without the int keyword. Here are a few more examples:

```
var names = new [] { "John", "Paul", "George", "Ringo" };          // Strings
var averages = new [] { 3.0, 3.34, 4.0, 2.0, 1.8 };                // Doubles
var prez = new [] {new President("FDR"), new President("JFK")};  // Presidents
```

REMEMBER

You can't use the short form for initializing an array when you use var. The following line doesn't compile:

```
var names = { "John", "Paul", "George", "Ringo" };  // Needs 'new []'
```

The var way is less concise, but when used in some other situations not involving arrays, it truly shines and in some cases is mandatory.

Loosening Up with C# Collections

Often an array is the simplest, most straightforward way to deal with a list of doubles. You also encounter many places in the .NET Framework class library that require the use of arrays. But arrays have a couple of fairly serious limitations that sometimes get in your way. At such times, you'll appreciate the extensive C# repertoire of more flexible collection classes. Although arrays have the advantage of simplicity and can have multiple dimensions, they suffer from two important limitations:

- **A program must declare the size of an array when it's created.** Unlike Visual Basic, C# doesn't let you change the size of an array after it's defined. For example, you might not know up front how big the array needs to be.
- **Inserting or removing an element in the middle of an array is wildly inefficient.** You have to move around all the elements to make room. In a big array, that can be a huge, time-consuming job.

Most collections, on the other hand, make it much easier to add, insert, or remove elements, and you can resize them as needed, right in midstream. In fact, most collections usually take care of resizing automatically.

TIP

If you need a multidimensional data structure, use an array. No collection allows multiple dimensions (although you can create some elaborate data structures, such as collections of arrays or collections of collections). Arrays and collections have some characteristics in common:

- Each can contain elements of only one type. You must specify that type in your code, at compile time, and after you declare the type, it can't change.
- As with arrays, you can access most collections with array-like syntax using square brackets to specify an index: `myList[3] = "Joe"`.
- Both collections and arrays have methods and properties. Thus, to find the number of elements in the following `smallPrimeNumbers` array, you call its `Length` property:

```
var smallPrimeNumbers = new [] { 2, 3, 5, 7, 11, 13 };
int numElements = smallPrimeNumbers.Length;  // Result is 6.
```

  With a collection, you call its `Count` property:

```
List<int> smallPrimes = new List<int> { 2, 3, 5, 7, 11, 13 };

// Collections have a Count property.
int numElements = smallPrimes.Count;
```

Understanding Collection Syntax

In this section, you discover collection syntax and see the most important and most frequently used collection classes. Table 6-1 lists the main collection classes in C#. It's useful to think of collections as having various *shapes* — how C# views the collection and how you can interact with it.

TABLE 6-1 The Most Common Collection "Shapes"

Class	Description
List<T>	This dynamic array contains objects of type T.
LinkedList<T>	This is a linked list of objects of type T.
Queue<T>	Start at the back end of the line and end up at the front.
Stack<T>	Always add or delete items at the "top" of the list, like a stack of cafeteria trays.
Dictionary<TKey, TValue>	This structure works like a dictionary. Look up a key (a word, for example) and retrieve its corresponding value (for example, definition).
HashSet<T>	This structure resembles a mathematical set, with no duplicate items. It works much like a list but provides mathematical set operations, such as union and intersection.

Figuring out <T>

In the mysterious-looking `<T>` notation you see in Table 6-1, `<T>` is a placeholder for a particular data type. To bring this symbolic object to life, *instantiate* it by inserting a real type, like this:

```
List<int> intList = new List<int>(); // Instantiating for int
```

REMEMBER

Instantiate is geekspeak for creating an object (instance) of this type. For example, you might create different `List<T>` instantiations for types `int` or `string`. By the way, `T` isn't a sacred name. You can use anything you like — for instance, `<dummy>` or `<aType>`. It's common to use `T`, `U`, `V`, and so on.

Notice how Table 6-1 shows the `Dictionary<TKey, TValue>` collection. Here, two types are needed: one for the dictionary's keys and one for the values associated with the keys. The "Using Dictionaries" section, later in this chapter, describes how to use dictionaries.

Going generic

These modern collections are known as *generic* collections, in the sense that you can fill in a blank template, of sorts, with a type (or types) in order to create a custom collection. If the generic `List<T>` seems puzzling, check out Chapter 8 in this minibook. That chapter discusses the generic C# facilities in more detail.

Using Lists

Suppose you need to store a list of MP3 objects, each of which represents one item in your MP3 music collection. As an array, it might look like this:

```
MP3[] myMP3s = new MP3[50];         // Start with an empty array.
myMP3s[0] = new MP3("Norah Jones"); // Create and add an MP3 to the array.
// ... and so on.
```

With a list collection, it looks like this:

```
List<MP3> myMP3s = new List<MP3>();   // An empty list
myMP3s.Add(new MP3("Avril Lavigne")); // Add an MP3 to the list.
// ... and so on.
```

These examples look similar, and the list doesn't appear to provide any advantage over the array. But what happens when you add the 50th MP3 to the array and then want to add a 51st? You're out of room. Your only course is to declare a new, larger array and then copy all MP3s from the old array into the new one. Also, if you remove an MP3 from the array, your array is left with a gaping hole. What do you put into that empty slot to take the place of the MP3 you ditched? The value null (essentially a value of nothing, as with strings in Chapters 2 and 3 of this minibook), maybe?

The list collection sails happily on, in the face of those same obstacles. Want to add MP3 number 51? No problem. Want to junk your old MP3s? No problem. The list takes care of healing itself after you delete them.

WARNING

If your list (or array, for that matter) can contain null items, be sure to check for null when you're looping through with for or foreach. You don't want to call the Play() method on a null MP3 item. It results in an error. The following sections show how to deal with various situations using lists.

Instantiating an empty list

The following code shows how to instantiate a new, empty list for the string type. In other words, this list can hold only strings:

```
// List<T>: note angle brackets plus parentheses in
// List<T> declaration; T is a "type parameter",
// List<T> is a "parameterized type."
// Instantiate for string type.
List<string> nameList = new List<string>();
```

```
nameList.Add("one");
nameList.Add(3);                              // Compiler error here!
nameList.Add(true);                           // Compiler error here!
```

You add items to a List<T> by using its Add() method. The preceding code snippet successfully adds one string to the list, but then it runs into trouble trying to add first an integer and then a bool. The list was instantiated for strings, so the compiler rejects both attempts.

Creating a list of type int

The following code fragment instantiates a new list for type int and then adds two int values to the list. Afterward, the foreach loop iterates the int list, printing out the ints:

```
// Instantiate for int.
List<int> intList = new List<int>();
intList.Add(3);                              // Fine.
intList.Add(4);
Console.WriteLine("Printing intList:");
foreach (int i in intList)  // foreach just works for all collections.
{
  Console.WriteLine("int i = " + i);
}
```

Converting between lists and arrays

You can easily convert lists to arrays and vice versa. To put an array into a list, use the list's AddRange() method as shown in the following code. To convert a list to an array, call the list's ToArray() method.

```
string[] myStrings = { "Hello", "Goodbye", "Today", "Tomorrow" };
List<string> myStringList = new List<string>();
myStringList.AddRange(myStrings);
string[] newStringArray = myStringList.ToArray();
```

Searching lists

There are several ways to search a list: IndexOf() returns the array-style index of an item within the list, if found, or -1 if not found. The following code also demonstrates accessing an item with array-style indexing and via the Contains() method. Other searching methods include BinarySearch() (which works only when the list is sorted), not shown:

```
List<string> myStringList = new List<string>()
    { "Hello", "Goodbye", "Today", "Tomorrow" };
Console.WriteLine($"Greeting at: {myStringList[3]}");
if (myStringList.Contains("Goodbye"))
{
    Console.WriteLine("Goodbye appears in the list.");
}
```

Performing other list tasks

The code in this section demonstrates several more `List<T>` operations, including sorting, inserting, and removing items:

```
myStringList.Sort();
myStringList.Insert(3, "Yellow");
myStringList.RemoveAt(3);
```

That's only a sampling of the `List<T>` methods. You can look up the full list at `https://docs.microsoft.com/en-us/dotnet/api/system.collections.generic.list-1?view=net-5.0#methods`.

Using Dictionaries

You've no doubt used *Webster's* or another dictionary. It's organized as a bunch of words in alphabetical order. Associated with each word is a body of information including pronunciations, definitions, and other information. To use a dictionary, you look up a word and retrieve its information.

In C#, a dictionary differs from a list. Dictionaries are represented by the `Dictionary<TKey, TValue>` class. `TKey` represents the data type used for the dictionary's *keys* (similar to the words in a standard dictionary or the terms you look up). `TValue` represents the data type used to store the information or data associated with a key (similar to the word's definitions in *Webster's*). The following sections demonstrate how to work with dictionaries.

Creating a dictionary

The first piece of the code just creates a new `Dictionary` object that has `string` keys and `string` values. You aren't limited to strings, though. Either the key or the value, or both, can be any type. Note that the Add() method requires both a key and a value.

```
Dictionary<string, string> dict = new Dictionary<string, string>();
//  Add(key, value).
dict.Add("C#", "cool");
dict.Add("C++", "like writing Sanskrit poetry in Morse code");
dict.Add("VB", "a simple but wordy language");
dict.Add("Java", "good, but not C#");
dict.Add("Fortran", "ancient");
dict.Add("Cobol", "even wordier and more verbose than VB");
```

Searching a dictionary

The ContainsKey() method tells you whether the dictionary contains a particular key. There's a corresponding ContainsValue() method, too:

```
// See if the dictionary contains a particular key.
Console.WriteLine("Contains C# " + dict.ContainsKey("C#"));      // True
Console.WriteLine("Contains Ruby " + dict.ContainsKey("Ruby")); // False
```

Dictionary pairs are in no particular order, and you can't sort a dictionary. It really is just like a bunch of buckets spread around the floor.

Iterating a dictionary

You can, of course, iterate the dictionary in a loop just as you can in any collection. But keep in mind that the dictionary is like a list of *pairs* of items. Think of each pair as an object that contains both the key and the value. So to iterate the whole dictionary with foreach, you need to retrieve one of the *pairs* each time through the loop. The pairs are objects of type KeyValuePair<TKey, TValue>. This WriteLine() call uses the pair's Key and Value properties to extract the items. Here's what it looks like:

```
// Iterate the dictionary's contents with foreach.
// Note that you're iterating pairs of keys and values.
Console.WriteLine("\nContents of the dictionary:");
foreach (KeyValuePair<string, string> pair in dict)
{
  // Because the key happens to be a string, we can call string methods on it.
  Console.WriteLine("Key: " + pair.Key.PadRight(8) + "Value: " + pair.Value);
}
```

The following code snippet shows how to iterate just the keys or just the values. The dictionary's Keys property returns another collection: a list-shaped collection of type Dictionary<TKey, TValue>.KeyCollection. Because the keys happen to be strings, you can iterate the keys as strings and call string methods on them. The Values property is similar. The final bit of code uses the dictionary's Count property to see how many key/value pairs it contains.

```
// List the keys, which are in no particular order.
Console.WriteLine("\nJust the keys:");

// Dictionary<TKey, TValue>.KeyCollection is a collection of just the
// keys,in this case strings. So here's how to retrieve the keys:
Dictionary<string, string>.KeyCollection keys = dict.Keys;
foreach (string key in keys)
{
  Console.WriteLine("Key: " + key);
}

// List the values, which are in same order as key collection above.
Console.WriteLine("\nJust the values:");
Dictionary<string, string>.ValueCollection values = dict.Values;
foreach (string value in values)
{
  Console.WriteLine("Value: " + value);
}

Console.Write("\nNumber of items in the dictionary: " + dict.Count);
```

Of course, that doesn't exhaust the possibilities for working with dictionaries. You can find a complete list of dictionary methods at https://docs.microsoft.com/en-us/dotnet/api/system.collections.generic.dictionary-2?view=net-5.0#methods.

Array and Collection Initializers

This section summarizes initialization techniques for both arrays and collections — both old-style and new. You may want to bend the page corner.

Initializing arrays

REMEMBER

As a reminder, given the var syntax covered in the section "Using var for Arrays," earlier in this chapter, an array declaration can look like either of these examples:

```
int[] numbers = { 1, 2, 3 };            // Shorter form -- can't use var.
var numbers = new [] { 1, 2, 3 };       // Full initializer mandatory with var.
```

Initializing collections

Meanwhile, the traditional way to initialize a collection, such as a `List<T>` — or a `Queue<T>` or `Stack<T>` was this:

```
List<int> numList = new List<int>();         // New empty list.
numbers.Add(1);                              // Add elements one at a time.
numbers.Add(2);
numbers.Add(3);                              // ...tedious!
```

Or, if you had the numbers in an array or another collection already, it went like this:

```
List<int> numList = new List<int>(numbers); // Initializing from an array or...
List<int> numList2 = new List<int>(numList);// from another collection or...
numList.AddRange(numbers);                  // using AddRange
```

REMEMBER

Since C# 3.0, collection initializers resemble array initializers and are much easier to use than most of the earlier forms. They look like this:

```
List<int> numList = new List<int> { 1, 2, 3 };  // List
int[] intArray = { 1, 2, 3 };                   // Array
```

The key difference between the new array and collection initializers is that you still must spell out the type for collections — which means giving `List<int>` after the new keyword (see the boldface in the preceding example).

REMEMBER

Of course, you can also use the var keyword with collections:

```
var list = new List<string> { "Head", "Heart", "Hands", "Health" };
```

You can also use the dynamic keyword:

```
dynamic list = new List<string> { "Head", "Heart", "Hands", "Health" };
```

Dynamic objects are still static, but they bypass static type checking during compilation. They expose their properties and methods during runtime rather than compile time. This makes `dynamic` objects different from `var` objects because `var` object types are inferred during compilation. You can read a more thorough comparison at `https://www.c-sharpcorner.com/UploadFile/b1df45/var-vs-dynamic-keywords-in-C-Sharp/`. Initializing dictionaries can look like this:

```
Dictionary<int, string> dict =
  new Dictionary<int, string> { { 1, "Sam" }, { 2, "Joe" } };
```

Outwardly, this example looks the same as for `List<T>`, but inside the outer curly braces, you see a second level of curly-brace-enclosed items, one per entry in the dictionary. Because this dictionary `dict` has integer keys and string values, each inner pair of curly braces contains one of each, separated by a comma. The key/value pairs are separated by commas as well.

Initializing sets (see the next section) is much like initializing lists:

```
HashSet<int> biggerPrimes = new HashSet<int> { 19, 23, 29, 31, 37, 41 };
```


Using Sets

C# 3.0 added the collection type `HashSet<T>`. A *set* is an unordered collection with no duplicate items. The set concept comes from mathematics. Think of a set of odd numbers like `{1, 3, 5, 7, 9}`, the set of days in a week, or the set of variations on the triangle (isosceles, equilateral, scalene, right, obtuse). Unlike math sets, C# sets can't be infinite, though they can be as large as available memory. The following sections tell you more about working with sets.

Performing special set tasks

You can do things to a set in common with other collections, such as add, delete, and find items. But you can also perform several specifically setlike operations, such as union and intersection that are good for combining and eliminating items (you can read more about set operations at `https://www.probabilitycourse.com/chapter1/1_2_2_set_operations.php`).

- **Union:** Joins the members of two sets into one
- **Intersection:** Finds the overlap between two sets and results in a set containing only the overlapping members
- **Difference:** Determines which elements of one set do not appear in a second set

When would you use HashSet<T>? Anytime you're working with two or more collections and you want to find such items as the overlap (or create a collection that contains two other collections or exclude a group of items from a collection), sets can be useful. Many of the HashSet<T> methods can relate sets and other collection classes. You can read more about HashSets at https://docs.microsoft.com/en-us/dotnet/api/system.collections.generic.hashset-1?view=net-5.0.

Creating a set

To create a HashSet<T>, you can do this:

```
HashSet<int> smallPrimeNumbers = new HashSet<int>();
smallPrimeNumbers.Add(2);
smallPrimeNumbers.Add(3);
```

Or, more conveniently, you can use a collection initializer:

```
HashSet<int> smallPrimeNumbers = new HashSet<int> { 2, 3, 5, 7, 11, 13 };
```

Or create the set from an existing collection of any listlike kind, including arrays:

```
List<int> intList = new List<int> { 0, 1, 2, 3, 4, 5, 6, 7 };
HashSet<int> numbers = new HashSet<int>(intList);
```

Adding items to a set

If you attempt to add to a HashSet an item that the set already contains, as in this example:

```
smallPrimeNumbers.Add(2);
```

the compiler doesn't treat the duplication as an error (and doesn't change the HashSet, which can't have duplicates). Actually, Add() returns true if the addition occurred and false if it didn't. You don't have to use that fact, but it can be useful if you want to do something when an attempt is made to add a duplicate:

```
bool successful = smallPrimeNumbers.Add(2);
if (successful)
{
  // 2 was added, now do something useful.
}
// If successful is false, not added because it was already there
```

Performing a union

The following example shows off several HashSet<T> methods but, more important, demonstrates using a HashSet<T> as a tool for working with other collections. You can do strictly mathematical operations with HashSet<T>, but its capability to combine collections in various ways is quite handy.

To begin, the example starts with a List<string> and an array. Each contains color names. Though you could combine the two by simply calling the list's AddRange() method:

```
colors.AddRange(moreColors);
```

the resulting list contains some duplicates (yellow, orange). By using a HashSet<T> and the UnionWith() method, on the other hand, you can combine two collections and eliminate any duplicates in one shot, as the following example shows:

```
Console.WriteLine("Combining two collections with no duplicates:");

List<string> colors = new List<string> { "red", "orange", "yellow" };
string[] moreColors = { "orange", "yellow", "green", "blue", "violet" };

// Want to combine but without any duplicates.
// Following is just the first stage ...
HashSet<string> combined = new HashSet<string>(colors);

// ... now for the second stage.
// UnionWith() collects items in both lists that aren't duplicated,
// resulting in a combined collection whose members are all unique.
combined.UnionWith(moreColors);

foreach (string color in combined)
{
  Console.WriteLine(color);
}
```

The result given here contains "red", "orange", "yellow", "green", "blue", and "violet". The first stage uses the colors list to initialize a new HashSet<T>. The second stage then calls the set's UnionWith() method to add in the moreColors array — but only the colors that aren't already in the set. The set ends up containing just the colors in either of the original lists. Green, blue, and violet come from the second list; red, orange, and yellow come from the first. The moreColors array's orange and yellow would duplicate the ones already in the set, so they're screened out.

But suppose that you want to end up with a `List<T>` containing those colors, not a `HashSet<T>`. The next segment shows how to create a new `List<T>` initialized with the `combined` set:

```
Console.WriteLine("\nConverting the combined set to a list:");
// Initialize a new List from the combined set above.
List<string> spectrum = new List<string>(combined);
foreach (string color in spectrum)
{
  Console.WriteLine(color);
}
```

Performing an intersection

Imagine that you need to work with data from a presidential campaign with about ten early candidates in each major party. A good many of those candidates are also members of the U.S. Senate. How can you produce a list of just the candidates who are also in the Senate? The `HashSet<T> IntersectWith()` method gives you the overlapping items between the candidate list and the Senate list — items in both lists, but only those items:

```
Console.WriteLine("\nFinding the overlap in two lists:");
List<string> presidentialCandidates =
  new List<string> { "Clinton", "Edwards", "Giuliani", "McCain", "Obama",
   "Romney" };
List<string> senators = new List<string> { "Alexander", "Boxer", "Clinton",
   "McCain", "Obama", "Snowe" };
HashSet<string> senatorsRunning = new HashSet<string>(presidentialCandidates);
// IntersectWith() collects items that appear in both lists, eliminates others.
senatorsRunning.IntersectWith(senators);
foreach (string senator in senatorsRunning)
{
  Console.WriteLine(senator);
}
```

The result is `"Clinton"`, `"McCain"`, and `"Obama"` because those are the only ones in both lists.

The following code segment uses the `SymmetricExceptWith()` method to create the opposite result from `IntersectWith()`. Whereas intersection gives you the overlapping items, `SymmetricExceptWith()` gives you the items in both lists that don't overlap. The `uniqueToOne` set ends up containing just 5, 3, 1, 12, and 10:

```
Console.WriteLine("\nFinding just the non-overlapping items in two lists:");
Stack<int> stackOne = new Stack<int>(new int[] { 1, 2, 3, 4, 5, 6, 7, 8 });
```

```
Stack<int> stackTwo = new Stack<int>(new int[] { 2, 4, 6, 7, 8, 10, 12 });
HashSet<int> nonoverlapping = new HashSet<int>(stackOne);
// SymmetricExceptWith() collects items that are in one collection but not
// the other: the items that don't overlap.
nonoverlapping.SymmetricExceptWith(stackTwo);
foreach (int n in nonoverlapping)
{
  Console.WriteLine(n.ToString());
}
Console.WriteLine("Press Enter to terminate...");
Console.Read();
```

The use of stacks here is a bit unorthodox because the code adds all members at one time rather than *pushes* each one individually, and removes a bunch at a time rather than *pops* each one individually. Those operations — pushing and popping — are the correct ways to interact with a stack.

TECHNICAL STUFF

Notice that all the `HashSet<T>` methods demonstrated in this chapter are `void` methods; they don't return a value. Thus the results are reflected directly in the hash set on which you call these methods: `nonoverlapping` in the preceding code example.

Performing a difference

The opposite trick is to remove any items that appear in both of two lists so that you end up with just the items in your target list that aren't duplicated in the other list. This calls for the `HashSet<T>` method `ExceptWith()`:

```
Console.WriteLine("\nExcluding items from a list:");
Queue<int> queue =
  new Queue<int>(new int[] { 0, 1, 2, 3, 4, 5, 6, 7, 8, 9, 17 });
HashSet<int> unique = new HashSet<int> { 1, 3, 5, 7, 9, 11, 13, 15 };
// ExceptWith() removes items in unique that are also in queue: 1, 3, 5, 7.
unique.ExceptWith(queue);
foreach (int n in unique)
{
  Console.WriteLine(n.ToString());
}
```

After this code, `unique` excludes its own items that duplicate items in `queue` (1, 3, 5, 7, and 9) and also excludes items in `queue` that aren't in `unique` (0, 2, 4, 6, 8, and 17). You end up with 11, 13, and 15 in `unique`.

IN THIS CHAPTER

» Working with directories and files as collections

» Enumerating a collection

» Implementing an indexer for easy access to collection objects

» Looping through a collection by using C# iterator blocks

Chapter 7
Stepping through Collections

Chapter 6 in this minibook explores the *collection classes* provided by the .NET Framework class library for use with C# and other .NET languages. Collection classes are constructs in .NET that can be instantiated to hold groups of items (see Chapter 6).

The first part of this chapter extends the notion of *collections* a bit. For instance, consider the following collections: a file as a collection of lines or records of data, and a directory as a collection of files. Thus, this chapter builds on both the collection material in Chapter 6 of this minibook and the file material in Book 3.

However, the focus in this chapter is on several ways to step through, or *iterate*, all sorts of collections, from file directories to arrays and lists of all sorts.

REMEMBER

You don't have to type the source code for this chapter manually. In fact, using the downloadable source is a lot easier. You can find the source for this chapter in the `\CSAIO4D2E\BK01\CH07` folder of the downloadable source. See the Introduction for details on how to find these source files.

Iterating through a Directory of Files

Sometimes you want to skim a directory of files, looking for something. The following `LoopThroughFiles` program looks at all files in a given directory, reading each file and dumping its contents in hexadecimal format to the console. That may sound like a silly thing to do, but this program also demonstrates how to write out a file in a format other than just `string` types. (You can find a description of hexadecimal format in the "Getting hexed" sidebar.)

Using the LoopThroughFiles program

From the command line, the user specifies the directory to use as an argument to the program. The following command "hex-dumps" each file in the `temp` directory (including binary files as well as text files):

```
loopthroughfiles c:\temp
```

If you don't enter a directory name, the program uses the current directory by default. (A *hex dump* displays the output as numbers in the hexadecimal — base 16 — system. See the nearby sidebar "Getting hexed.")

WARNING

If you run this program in a directory with lots of files, the hex dump can take a while. Also, long files take a while to loop through. Either pick a directory with few files or stop a lengthy program run by pressing Ctrl+C. This command interrupts a program running in any console window.

GETTING HEXED

Like binary numbers (0 and 1), hexadecimal, or "hex," numbers are fundamental to computer programming. In base 16, the digits are 0 through 9 and then A, B, C, D, E, F — where A=10, B=11 . . . F=15. To illustrate (using the zero-x prefix to indicate hex):

```
0xD = 13 decimal
0x10 = 16 decimal: 1*16 + 0*1
0x2A = 42 decimal: 2*16 + A*1 (where A*1 = 10*1)
```

The alphabetic digits can be uppercase or lowercase: *C* is the same as *c*. It's weird, but quite useful, especially when you're debugging or working close to the metal with memory contents.

The following example shows what happens when the user specifies the invalid directory x:

```
Directory "x" invalid
Could not find a part of the path "C:\C#Programs\LoopThroughFiles\bin\Debug\x".

No files left
```

Getting started

As with all examples in this book, you begin with a basic program structure, as shown in the following code. Note that you must include a separate using statement for the System.IO namespace. To this basic structure, you add the individual functions described in the sections that follow.

```
using System;
using System.IO;

// LoopThroughFiles -- Loop through all files contained in a directory;
//   this time perform a hex dump, though it could have been anything.
namespace LoopThroughFiles
{
  public class Program
  {
  }
}
```


Obtaining the initial input

Every console application begins with a Main() function, as previous chapters indicate. Don't worry for now if you don't quite understand how the Main() function is supposed to work as part of the console application. For now, just know that the first function that C# calls is the Main() function of your console application, as shown in the following code:

```
    public static void Main(string[] args)
    {
      // If no directory name provided...
      string directoryName;
      if (args.Length == 0)
      {
        // ...get the name of the current directory...
        directoryName = Directory.GetCurrentDirectory();
      }
      else
```

```
    {
      // ...otherwise, assume that the first argument
      // is the name of the directory to use.
      directoryName = args[0];
    }
    Console.WriteLine(directoryName);

    // Get a list of all files in that directory.
    FileInfo[] files = GetFileList(directoryName);

    // Now iterate through the files in that list,
    // performing a hex dump of each file.
    foreach (FileInfo file in files)
    {
      // Write the name of the file.
      Console.WriteLine("\n\nhex dump of file {0}:", file.FullName);

      // Now "dump" the file to the console.
      DumpHex(file);

      // Wait before outputting next file.
      Console.WriteLine("\nPress Enter to continue to next file");
      Console.ReadLine();
    }

    // That's it!
    Console.WriteLine("\nNo files left");
    Console.Read();
  }
```

The first line in `LoopThroughFiles` looks for a program argument. If the argument list is empty (`args.Length` is zero), the program calls `Directory.GetCurrentDirectory()`. If you run inside Visual Studio rather than from the command line, that value defaults to the `bin\Debug` subdirectory of your `LoopThroughFiles` project directory.

TIP

The `Directory` class gives the user a set of methods for manipulating directories. The `FileInfo` class provides methods for moving, copying, and deleting files, among other tasks.

The program then creates a list of all files in the specified directory by calling `GetFileList()`. This method returns an array of `FileInfo` objects. Each `FileInfo` object contains information about a file — for example, the filename (with the full path to the file, `FullName`, or without the path, `Name`), the creation date, and the last modified date. `Main()` iterates through the list of files using your old friend, the `foreach` statement. It displays the name of each file and then passes off the file to the DumpHex() method for display to the console. At the end of the loop, it pauses to allow the programmer a chance to gaze on the output from DumpHex().

Creating a list of files

Before you can process a list of files, you need to create one. The GetFileList() method begins by creating an empty FileInfo array and then filling it with a list of files. Here's the required code.

```
// GetFileList -- Get a list of all files in a specified directory.
public static FileInfo[] GetFileList(string directoryName)
{
  // Start with an empty list.
  FileInfo[] files = new FileInfo[0];
  try
  {
    // Get directory information.
    DirectoryInfo di = new DirectoryInfo(directoryName);

    // That information object has a list of the contents.
    files = di.GetFiles();
  }
  catch(Exception e)
  {
    Console.WriteLine("Directory \"{0}\" invalid", directoryName);
    Console.WriteLine(e.Message);
  }
  return files;
}
```

GetFileList() then creates a DirectoryInfo object. Just as its name implies, a DirectoryInfo object contains the same type of information about a directory that a FileInfo object does about a file: name, rank, and serial-number-type stuff. However, the DirectoryInfo object has access to one thing that a FileInfo doesn't: a list of the files in the directory, in the form of a FileInfo array.

To help trap errors, GetFileList() wraps the directory- and file-related code in a big try block. (For an explanation of try and catch, see Chapter 9 in this minibook.) The catch at the end traps any errors that are generated. Just to embarrass you further, the catch block flaunts the name of the directory (which probably doesn't exist, because you entered it incorrectly).

WARNING

The final step is to return files, which contains the list of files in the code collection. Be careful about returning a reference to an object. For instance, don't return a reference to one of the underlying queues wrapped up in the PriorityQueue class, described in Chapter 8 of this minibook — unless you want to invite folks to mess with those queues through the reference instead of through your class methods, that is. That's a sure ticket to a corrupt, unpredictable queue. But `GetFileList()` doesn't expose the innards of one of your classes here, so it's okay.

Formatting the output lines

You can do anything you want with the list of files you collect. This example displays the content of each file in hexadecimal format, which can be useful in certain circumstances, such as when you need to know how files are actually put together. Before you can create a line of hexadecimal output, however, you need to create individual output lines. The `DumpHex()` method, shown here, is a little tricky only because of the difficulties in formatting the output just right.

```
// DumpHex -- Given a file, dump the file contents to the console.
public static void DumpHex(FileInfo file)
{
  // Open the file.
  FileStream fs;
  BinaryReader reader;
  try
  {
    fs = file.OpenRead();
    // Wrap the file stream in a BinaryReader.
    reader = new BinaryReader(fs);
  }
  catch (Exception e)
  {
    Console.WriteLine("\ncan't read from \"{0}\"", file.FullName);
    Console.WriteLine(e.Message);
    return;
  }

  // Iterate through the contents of the file one line at a time.
  for (int line = 1; true; line++)
  {
    // Read another 10 bytes across (all that will fit on a single
    // line) -- return when no data remains.
    byte[] buffer = new byte[10];
    // Use the BinaryReader to read bytes.
    // Note: Using FileStream is just as easy in this case.
    int numBytes = reader.Read(buffer, 0, buffer.Length);
    if (numBytes == 0)
    {
      return;
    }
```

```
            // Write the data in a single line preceded by line number.
            Console.Write("{0:D3} - ", line);
            DumpBuffer(buffer, numBytes);

            // Stop every 20 lines so that the data doesn't scroll
            // off the top of the Console screen.
            if ((line % 20) == 0)
            {
                Console.WriteLine("Press Enter to continue another 20 lines" +
                    " or type Q to go to the next file.");
                string Input = Console.ReadLine();
                if (Input.ToUpper() == "Q")
                    break;
            }
        }
    }
```

`DumpHex()` starts by opening `file`. A `FileInfo` object contains information about the file — it doesn't open the file. `DumpHex()` gets the full name of the file, including the path, and then opens a `FileStream` in read-only mode using that name. The `catch` block throws an exception if `FileStream` can't read the file for some reason.

`DumpHex()` then reads through the file, 10 bytes at a time. It displays every 10 bytes in hexadecimal format as a single line. Every 20 lines, it pauses until the user presses Enter. The code uses the modulo operator, `%`, to accomplish that task.

TIP

Vertically, a console window has room for 25 lines by default. (The user can change the window's size, of course, allowing more or fewer lines.) That means you have to pause every 20 lines or so. Otherwise, the data just streams off the top of the screen before the user can read it.

The modulo operator (`%`) returns the remainder after division. Thus `(line % 20) == 0` is true when `line` equals 20, 40, 60, 80 — you get the idea. This trick is valuable, useful in all sorts of looping situations where you want to perform an operation only so often.

Displaying the hexadecimal output

After you have a single line of output to display, you can output it in hexadecimal form. `DumpBuffer()` writes each member of a byte array using the X2 format control. Although X2 sounds like the name of a secret military experiment, it *simply* means "display a number as two hexadecimal digits."

```
// DumpBuffer -- Write a buffer of characters as a single line in
// hex format.
public static void DumpBuffer(byte[] buffer, int numBytes)
{
  for(int index = 0; index < numBytes; index++)
  {
    byte b = buffer[index];
    Console.Write("{0:X2}, ", b);
  }
  Console.WriteLine();
}
```

The range of a `byte` is 0 to 255, or 0xFF — two hex digits per byte. Here are the first 20 lines of an example file:

```
Hex dump of file C:\Temp\output.txt:
001 - 53, 74, 72, 65, 61, 6D, 20, 28, 70, 72,
002 - 6F, 74, 65, 63, 74, 65, 64, 29, 0D, 0A,
003 - 20, 20, 46, 69, 6C, 65, 53, 74, 72, 65,
004 - 61, 6D, 28, 73, 74, 72, 69, 6E, 67, 2C,
005 - 20, 46, 69, 6C, 65, 4D, 6F, 64, 65, 2C,
006 - 20, 46, 69, 6C, 65, 41, 63, 63, 65, 73,
007 - 73, 29, 0D, 0A, 20, 20, 4D, 65, 6D, 6F,
008 - 72, 79, 53, 74, 72, 65, 61, 6D, 28, 29,
009 - 3B, 0D, 0A, 20, 20, 4E, 65, 74, 77, 6F,
010 - 72, 6B, 53, 74, 72, 65, 61, 6D, 0D, 0A,
011 - 20, 20, 42, 75, 66, 66, 65, 72, 53, 74,
012 - 72, 65, 61, 6D, 20, 2D, 20, 62, 75, 66,
013 - 66, 65, 72, 73, 20, 61, 6E, 20, 65, 78,
014 - 69, 73, 74, 69, 6E, 67, 20, 73, 74, 72,
015 - 65, 61, 6D, 20, 6F, 62, 6A, 65, 63, 74,
016 - 0D, 0A, 0D, 0A, 42, 69, 6E, 61, 72, 79,
017 - 52, 65, 61, 64, 65, 72, 20, 2D, 20, 72,
018 - 65, 61, 64, 20, 69, 6E, 20, 76, 61, 72,
019 - 69, 6F, 75, 73, 20, 74, 79, 70, 65, 73,
020 - 20, 28, 43, 68, 61, 72, 2C, 20, 49, 6E,
Enter return to continue another 20 lines
```

TECHNICAL STUFF

You could reconstruct the file as a `string` from the hex display. The 0x61 value is the numeric equivalent of the character *a*. The letters of the alphabet are arranged in order, so 0x65 should be the character *e*; 0x20 is a space. The first line in this example (after the line number) is `s)\n\r Nemo`, where `\n` is a newline and `\r` is a carriage return. Intriguing, eh? You can find a complete ASCII table at `https://www.asciitable.com/`.

The output codes are also valid for the lower part of the much vaster Unicode character set, which C# uses by default. (The site at `http://www.i18nguy.com/unicode/codepages.html` provides you with listings of character sets of all kinds and is very useful if you have to deal with input from devices like mainframes.)

Running from inside Visual Studio

To run LoopThroughFiles, you need to do one of the following:

- Start it from the command line by opening a Developer Command Prompt for VS 2022 found in the Start⇨Visual Studio 2022 folder
- Supply command-line arguments in Visual Studio
- Execute it without command-line arguments at the command line or within Visual Studio

The second option in the preceding list, that of supplying a command-line argument in Visual Studio, requires a little special setting up on your part by following these steps:

1. **Choose Project⇨LoopThroughFiles Properties.**

   You see a Properties dialog box for the application.

2. **Select Debug in the left pane.**

   You see the debug options shown in Figure 7-1.

3. **Type the path you want to use, such as `C:\Temp`, in the Command Line Arguments field.**

   The path you type will work within Visual Studio whether you're in debug mode or not.

4. **Choose File⇨Save All.**

   Visual Studio saves the new path to disk.

5. **Choose Debug⇨Start Debugging or Debug⇨Start Without Debugging.**

   You see the program execute in the path that you chose.

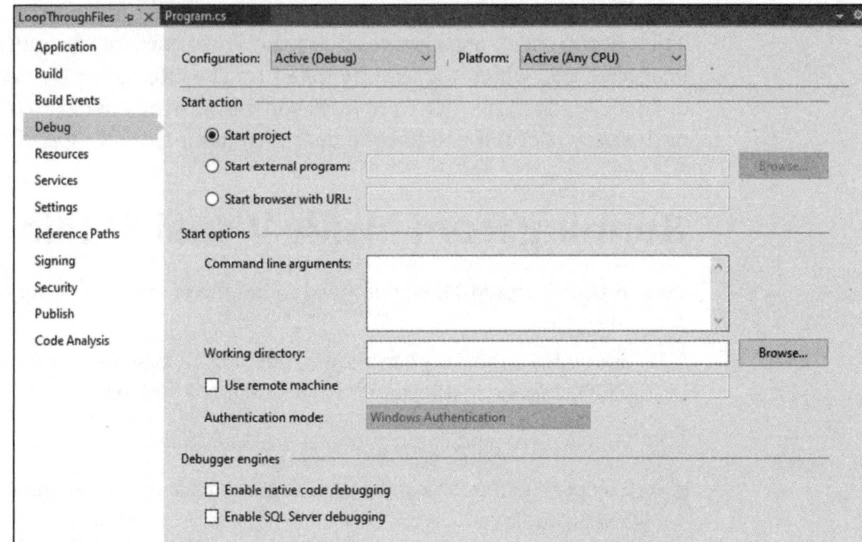

FIGURE 7-1: Adding a path for the files to list.

Iterating foreach Collections: Iterators

In the rest of this chapter, you see three different approaches to the general problem of iterating a collection. This section continues discussing the most traditional approach (at least for C# programmers), the iterator class, or enumerator, which implements the `IEnumerator` interface.

TIP

The terms *iterator* and *enumerator* are synonymous for the purposes of this discussion (there are technical differences, but in both cases you receive individual values from the collection). The term *iterator* is more common despite the name of the interface (see `https://docs.microsoft.com/en-us/dotnet/csharp/iterators` for details on iterators), but *enumerator* has also been popular at Microsoft. Verb forms of these two nouns are also available: You iterate or enumerate through a container or collection. Note that the indexers and the new iterator blocks discussed later in this chapter are other approaches to the same problem.

Accessing a collection: The general problem

Different collection types may have different accessing schemes. Not all types of collections can be accessed efficiently with an index like an array's — the linked list, for example. A linked list just contains a reference to the next item in the list and is made to be consecutively — not randomly — accessed. Differences between collection types make it impossible to write a method such as the following without special provisions:

```
// Pass in any kind of collection:
void MyClearMethod(Collection aColl, int index)
{
  aColl[index] = 0; // Indexing doesn't work for all types of collections.
  // ...continues...
}
```

Each collection type can (and does) define its own access methods. You decide on which access method to use based on the task requirements. The CollectionMoveNext example, shown here, demonstrates three access methods for a `List<string>` **object,** `Colors`:

```
static void Main(string[] args)
{
    List<string> Colors = new List<string> {
        "Red", "Yellow", "Green", "Blue" };

    Console.WriteLine("Using a delegate.");
    Colors.ForEach(delegate (string value)
    {
        Console.WriteLine(value);
    });

    Console.WriteLine("\r\nUsing a foreach.");
    foreach (string col in Colors)
        Console.WriteLine(col);

    Console.WriteLine("\r\nUsing an enumerator.");
    var colEnum = Colors.GetEnumerator();
    while (colEnum.MoveNext())
        Console.WriteLine(colEnum.Current);
    Console.ReadLine();
}
```

This example shows how to use a delegate (described in detail in Book 2 Chapter 8 of this minibook), a `foreach` loop (described in Chapter 6 of this minibook), and an enumerator (which Microsoft tends to confuse with iterators). The `Colors.ForEach()` approach has an advantage in that you can use lambda expressions with it and it's extremely flexible, but sometimes it's hard to read. The `foreach` loop method is easy to read and quite common, but it lacks flexibility. The call to `GetEnumerator()` obtains a special object that knows how to move between entries in a `List<string>`. This is the best approach when you need to perform additional levels of processing and want strict control over when the `Current` property value changes. The iterator (enumerator) approach offers these advantages:

- Each collection class can define its own iteration class. Because the iteration class implements the standard `IEnumerator` interface, it's usually straightforward to code.
- The application code doesn't need to know how the collection code works. As long as the programmer understands how to use the iterator, the iteration class can handle the details. That's good encapsulation.
- The application code can create multiple independent iterator objects for the same collection. Because the iterator contains its own state information ("knows where it is," in the iteration), each iterator can navigate through the collection independently. You can have several iterations going at one time, each one at a different location in the collection.

To make the `foreach` loop possible, the `IEnumerator` interface must support all different types of collections, from arrays to linked lists. Consequently, its methods must be as general as possible. For example, you can't use the iterator to access locations within the collection class randomly because most collections don't provide random access. (You'd need to invent a different enumeration interface with that capability, but it wouldn't work with `foreach`.) `IEnumerator` provides these three features:

- `Reset()`: Sets the enumerator to point to the beginning of the collection. ***Note:*** The generic version of `IEnumerator`, `IEnumerator<T>`, doesn't provide a `Reset()` method. With .NET's generic `LinkedList`, for example, just begin with a call to `MoveNext()`. That generic `LinkedList` is found in `System.Collections.Generic`.
- `MoveNext()`: Moves the enumerator from the current object in the collection to the next one.
- `Current`: A property, rather than a method, that retrieves the data object stored at the current position of the enumerator.

The following method demonstrates this principle. The programmer of the `MyCollection` class (not shown) creates a corresponding iterator class — say, `IteratorMyCollection`. The application programmer stores `ContainedDataObjects` in `MyCollection`. The following code segment uses the three standard `IEnumerator` methods to read these objects:

```
// The MyCollection class holds ContainedDataObject type objects as data.
void MyMethod(MyCollection myColl)
{
```

```
  // The programmer who created the MyCollection class also
  // creates an iterator class IteratorMyCollection;
  // the application program creates an iterator object
  // in order to navigate through the myColl object.
  IEnumerator iterator = new IteratorMyCollection(myColl);

  // Move the enumerator to the "next location" within the collection.
  while (iterator.MoveNext())
  {
    // Fetch a reference to the data object at the current location
    // in the collection.
    ContainedDataObject contained;  // Data
    contained = (ContainedDataObject)iterator.Current;

    // ...use the contained data object...
  }
}
```

The method `MyMethod()` accepts as its argument the collection of `Contained-DataObjects`. It begins by creating an `iterator` of class `IteratorMyCollection`. The method starts a loop by calling `MoveNext()`. On this first call, `MoveNext()` moves the iterator to the first element in the collection. On each subsequent call, `MoveNext()` moves the pointer to the next position. `MoveNext()` returns `false` when the collection is exhausted and the iterator cannot be moved any farther.

The `Current` property returns a reference to the data object at the current location of the iterator. The program converts the object returned into a `Contained-DataObject` before assigning it to `contained`. Calls to `Current` are invalid if the `MoveNext()` method didn't return `true` on the previous call or if `MoveNext()` hasn't yet been called.

Stepping through Collections

Letting C# access data foreach container

The `IEnumerator` methods are standard enough that C# uses them automatically to implement the `foreach` statement. The `foreach` statement can access any class that implements `IEnumerable` or `IEnumerable<T>`. This section discusses `foreach` in terms of `IEnumerable<T>` as shown in this general method that is capable of processing any such class, from arrays to linked lists to stacks and queues:

```
void MyMethod(IEnumerable<T> containerOfThings)
{
  foreach (string s in containerOfThings)
  {
    Console.WriteLine("The next thing is {0}", s);
  }
}
```

A class implements `IEnumerable<T>` by defining the method `GetEnumerator()`, which returns an instance of `IEnumerator<T>`. Under the hood, `foreach` invokes the `GetEnumerator()` method to retrieve an iterator. It uses this iterator to make its way through the collection. Each element it retrieves has been cast appropriately before continuing into the block of code contained within the braces. Note that `IEnumerable<T>` and `IEnumerator<T>` are different, but related, interfaces. C# provides nongeneric versions of both as well, but you should prefer the generic versions for their increased type safety. `IEnumerable<T>` looks like this:

```
interface IEnumerable<T>
{
  IEnumerator<T> GetEnumerator();
}
```

while `IEnumerator<T>` looks like this:

```
interface IEnumerator<T>
{
  bool MoveNext();
  T Current { get; }
}
```

The nongeneric `IEnumerator` interface adds a `Reset()` method that moves the iterator back to the beginning of the collection, and its `Current` property returns type `Object`. Note that `IEnumerator<T>` inherits from `IEnumerator` (Interface inheritance, covered in Book 2, Chapter 7, is different from normal object inheritance).

C# arrays (embodied in the `Array` class they're based on) and all the .NET collection classes already implement both interfaces. So it's only when you're writing your own custom collection class that you need to take care of implementing these interfaces. For built-in collections, you can just use them. See the `System.Collections.Generic namespace` topic at `https://docs.microsoft.com/en-us/dotnet/api/system.collections.generic?view=net-5.0` for details. Thus you can write the `foreach` loop this way:

```
foreach(int nValue in myCollection)
{
  // ...
}
```

Accessing Collections the Array Way: Indexers

Accessing the elements of an array is simple: The statement `container[n]` accesses the *n*th element of the `container` array. The value in brackets is an index, while the `[]` are called the *subscript operator*. If only indexing into other types of collections were so simple.

C# enables you to write your own implementation of the index operation. You can provide an index feature for collections that wouldn't otherwise enjoy such a feature. In addition, you can index on subscript types other than the simple integers to which C# arrays are limited. For example, by writing your own index feature, you can interact with `string` types. As another example, you could create an index feature for a programming construct like `container["Joe"]`. (The "Indexers" section of Book 2, Chapter 11 shows how to add an indexer to a `struct`.)

Indexer format

The indexer looks much like an ordinary `get/set` property (Book 2 Chapter 3 describes accessors in more detail), except for the appearance of the keyword `this` and the subscript operator `[]` instead of the property name, as shown in this bit of code:

```
class MyArray
{
  public string this[int index]   // Notice the "this" keyword.
  {
    get => MyArray[index];
    set => MyArray[index] = value;
  }
}
```

The example shows a short form of an indexer that you use when you don't need to do anything except get and set values. The "Working with indexers" section, later in this chapter, shows a longer version. Under the hood, the expression `s = myArray[i];` invokes the `get` accessor method, passing it the value of `i` as the index. In addition, the expression `myArray[i] = "some string";` invokes the `set` accessor method, passing it the same index `i` and `"some string"` as `value`.

An indexer program example

The index type isn't limited to int. You may choose to index a collection of houses by their owners' names, by house address, or by any number of other indices. In addition, the indexer property can be overloaded with multiple index types, so you can index on a variety of elements in the same collection. The following sections discuss the Indexer program, which generates the virtual array class KeyedArray. This virtual array looks and acts like an array except that it uses a string value as the index. (Note that you could replicate the functionality found in this example by using a C# Dictionary, as described at https://docs.microsoft.com/en-us/dotnet/api/system.collections.generic.dictionary-2.)

Performing the required class setup

The Indexer example relies on a special class, which means you must create a class framework for it. (Don't worry if some of the terms for this example seem strange; you discover a lot more about classes and other Object Oriented Programming, or OOP, techniques in Book 2.) Here is the framework used to hold the class methods discussed in sections that follow.

```
public class KeyedArray
{
    // The following string provides the "key" into the array --
    // the key is the string used to identify an element.
    private string[] _keys;

    // The object is the actual data associated with that key.
    private object[] _arrayElements;

    // KeyedArray -- Create a fixed-size KeyedArray.
    public KeyedArray(int size)
    {
        _keys = new string[size];
        _arrayElements = new object[size];
    }
}
```

The class KeyedArray holds two ordinary arrays. The _arrayElements array of objects contains the actual KeyedArray data. The string types that inhabit the _keys array act as identifiers for the object array. The *i*th element of _keys corresponds to the *i*th entry of _arrayElements. The application program can then index KeyedArray via string identifiers that have meaning to the application. A noninteger index is referred to as a *key*.

The line that reads `public KeyedArray(int size)` is the start of a special kind of function called a *constructor*. Think of a constructor as an instruction to build an instance of the class. You don't need to worry about it for now, but the constructor actually assigns values to `_keys` and `_arrayElements`.

Working with indexers

At this point, you need to define an indexer to make your code work, as shown in the following code. The indexer, `public object this[string key]`, requires the use of two functions, `Find()` and `FindEmpty()`. Note that you add this code to the end of the `KeyedArray` class.

```
// Find -- Find the index of the element corresponding to the
//    string targetKey (return a negative if it can't be found).
private int Find(string targetKey)
{
  for (int i = 0; i < _keys.Length; i++)
  {
    if (String.Compare(_keys[i], targetKey) == 0)
    {
      return i;
    }
  }
  return -1;
}

// FindEmpty -- Find room in the array for a new entry.
private int FindEmpty()
{
  for (int i = 0; i < _keys.Length; i++)
  {
    if (_keys[i] == null)
    {
      return i;
    }
  }

  throw new Exception("Array is full");
}

// Look up contents by string key -- this is the indexer.
public object this[string key]
{
  set
  {
    // See if the string is already there.
    int index = Find(key);
    if (index < 0)
```

```
    {
      // It isn't -- find a new spot.
      index = FindEmpty();
      _keys[index] = key;
    }

    // Save the object in the corresponding spot.
    _arrayElements[index] = value;
  }

  get
  {
    int index = Find(key);
    if (index < 0)
    {
      return null;
    }
    return _arrayElements[index];
  }
}
```

The set[string] indexer starts by checking to see whether the specified key already exists by calling the method Find(). If Find() returns an index, set[] stores the new data object into the corresponding index in _arrayElements. If Find() can't find the key, set[] calls FindEmpty() to return an empty slot in which to store the object provided.

The get[] side of the indexer follows similar logic. It first searches for the specified key using the Find() method. If Find() returns a non-negative index, get[] returns the corresponding member of _arrayElements where the data is stored. If Find() returns -1, get[] returns null, indicating that it can't find the provided key anywhere in the list.

The Find() method loops through the members of _keys to look for the element with the same value as the string targetKey passed in. Find() returns the index of the found element (or -1 if none was found). FindEmpty() returns the index of the first element that has no key element.

Testing your new class

The Main() method, which is part of the Indexer program and not part of the class, demonstrates the KeyedArray class in a trivial way:

```
static void Main(string[] args)
{
    // Create an array with enough room.
    KeyedArray ma = new KeyedArray(100);

    // Save the ages of the Simpson kids.
    ma["Bart"] = 10;
    ma["Lisa"] = 8;
    ma["Maggie"] = 2;

    // Look up the age of Lisa.
    Console.WriteLine("Let's find Lisa's age");
    int age = (int)ma["Lisa"];
    Console.WriteLine("Lisa is {0}", age);
    Console.Read();
}
```

The program creates a `KeyedArray` object `ma` of length 100 (that is, with 100 free elements). It continues by storing the ages of the children in *The Simpsons* TV show, indexed by each child's name. Finally, the program retrieves Lisa's age using the expression `(int)ma["Lisa"]` and displays the result.

Notice that the program has to cast the value returned from `ma[]` because `KeyedArray` is written to hold any type of object. The cast wouldn't be necessary if the indexer were written to handle only `int` values — or if the `KeyedArray` were generic. (For more information about generics, see Chapter 8 in this minibook.) The output of the program is simple yet elegant:

```
Let's find Lisa's age
Lisa is 8
```


Looping Around the Iterator Block

In previous versions of C#, the techniques associated with linked lists discussed in the section "Accessing Collections the Array Way: Indexers," earlier in this chapter, was the primary practice for moving through collections, just as it was done in C++ and C before this. Although that solution does work, it turns out that C# versions 2.0 and above have simplified this process so that

- You don't have to call `GetEnumerator()` (and cast the results).
- You don't have to call `MoveNext()`.

» You don't have to call `Current` and cast its return value.

» You can simply use `foreach` to iterate the collection. (C# does the rest for you under the hood — it even writes the enumerator class.)

Rather than implement all those interface methods in collection classes that you write, you can provide an iterator block as shown in the `IteratorBlocks` example — and you don't have to write your own iterator class to support the collection. You can use iterator blocks for a host of other chores, too, as shown in the next example.

Creating the required iterator block framework

The best approach to iteration uses iterator blocks. When you write a collection class — and the need still exists for custom collection classes such as `KeyedList` and `PriorityQueue` — you implement an iterator block in its code rather than implement the `IEnumerator` interface. Then users of that class can simply iterate the collection with `foreach`. Here is the basic framework used for this example, which contains the functions that follow in the upcoming sections:

```
static void Main(string[] args)
{
    // Instantiate a MonthDays "collection" class.
    MonthDays md = new MonthDays();

    // Iterate it.
    Console.WriteLine("Stream of months:\n");
    foreach (string month in md)
    {
        Console.WriteLine(month);
    }

    // Instantiate a StringChunks "collection" class.
    StringChunks sc = new StringChunks();

    // Iterate it: prints pieces of text.
    // This iteration puts each chunk on its own line.
    Console.WriteLine("\nstream of string chunks:\n");
    foreach (string chunk in sc)
    {
        Console.WriteLine(chunk);
    }
```

```
    // And this iteration puts it all on one line.
    Console.WriteLine("\nstream of string chunks on one line:\n");
    foreach (string chunk in sc)
    {
        Console.Write(chunk);
    }
    Console.WriteLine();

    // Instantiate a YieldBreakEx "collection" class.
    YieldBreakEx yb = new YieldBreakEx();

    // Iterate it, but stop after 13.
    Console.WriteLine("\nstream of primes:\n");
    foreach (int prime in yb)
    {
        Console.WriteLine(prime);
    }

    // Instantiate an EvenNumbers "collection" class.
    EvenNumbers en = new EvenNumbers();

    // Iterate it: prints even numbers from 10 down to 4.
    Console.WriteLine("\nstream of descending evens :\n");
    foreach (int even in en.DescendingEvens(11, 3))
    {
        Console.WriteLine(even);
    }

    // Instantiate a PropertyIterator "collection" class.
    PropertyIterator prop = new PropertyIterator();

    // Iterate it: produces one double at a time.
    Console.WriteLine("\nstream of double values:\n");
    foreach (double db in prop.DoubleProp)
    {
        Console.WriteLine(db);
    }
    Console.Read();
}
```

The `Main()` method shown provides basic testing functions for the iterator block code. Each of the sections that follow tell you how the code in the `Main()` method interacts with the iterator block. In other words, the example won't compile until you add the code from the upcoming sections. For now, just know that the `Main()` method is just one function, and the following sections break it apart so that you can understand it better.

Iterating days of the month: A first example

The following class provides an iterator (shown in bold) that steps through the months of the year:

```
//MonthDays -- Define an iterator that returns the months
//   and their lengths in days -- sort of a "collection" class.
class MonthDays
{
  // Here's the "collection."
  string[] months =
          { "January 31", "February 28", "March 31",
            "April 30", "May 31", "June 30", "July 31",
            "August 31", "September 30", "October 31",
            "November 30", "December 31" };

  //GetEnumerator -- Here's the iterator. See how it's invoked
  //   in Main() with foreach.
  public System.Collections.IEnumerator GetEnumerator()
  {
    foreach (string month in months)
    {
      // Return one month per iteration.
      yield return month;
    }
  }
}
```

Here's part of a `Main()` method that iterates this collection using a `foreach` loop:

```
// Instantiate a MonthDays "collection" class.
MonthDays md = new MonthDays();

// Iterate it.
foreach (string month in md)
{
  Console.WriteLine(month);
}
```

This collection class is based on an array, as `KeyedArray` is. The class contains an array whose items are `string` types. When a client iterates this collection, the collection's iterator block delivers `string` types one by one. Each `string` contains the name of a month (in sequence), with the number of days in the month tacked on to the `string`.

The class defines its own iterator block, in this case as a method named `GetEnumerator()`, which returns an object of type `System.Collections.IEnumerator`.

Now, it's true that you had to write such a method before, but you also had to write your own enumerator class to support your custom collection class. Here, you just write a fairly simple method to return an enumerator based on the new `yield return` keywords. C# does the rest for you: It creates the underlying enumerator class and takes care of calling `MoveNext()` to iterate the array. You get away with much less work and much simpler code.

REMEMBER

Your class containing the `GetEnumerator()` method no longer needs to implement the `IEnumerator` interface. In fact, you don't want it to. In the following sections, you discover several varieties of iterator blocks:

- Ordinary iterators
- Named iterators
- Class properties implemented as iterators

Note that class `MonthDays`' `GetEnumerator()` method contains a `foreach` loop to yield the `string` types in its inner array. Iterator blocks often use a loop of some kind to do this, as you can see in several later examples. In effect, you have in your own calling code an inner `foreach` loop serving up item after item that can be iterated in another `foreach` loop outside `GetEnumerator()`.

What a collection is, really

Take a moment to compare the little collection in this example with an elaborate `LinkedList` collection. Whereas `LinkedList` has a complex structure of nodes connected by pointers, this little `months` collection is based on a simple array — with canned content, at that. The example expands the *collection* notion a bit and then develops it even more before this chapter concludes.

Your collection class may not contain canned content — most collections are designed to hold things you put into them via `Add()` methods and the like. The `KeyedArray` class in the earlier section "Accessing Collections the Array Way: Indexers," for example, uses the `[]` subscript operator to add items. Your collection could also provide an `Add()` method as well as add an iterator block so that it can work with `foreach`.

The point of a collection, in the most general sense, is to store multiple objects and to allow you to iterate those objects, retrieving them one at a time sequentially — and sometimes randomly, or apparently randomly, as well, as in the `Indexer` example. (Of course, an array can do that, even without the extra apparatus of a class such as `MonthDays`, but iterators go well beyond the `MonthDays` example.)

More generally, regardless of what an iterable collection does under the hood, it produces a "stream" of values, which you get at with foreach. To drive home the point, here's another simple collection class from IteratorBlocks, one that stretches the idea of a collection about as far as possible (you may think):

```
//StringChunks -- Define an iterator that returns chunks of text,
//   one per iteration -- another oddball "collection" class.
class StringChunks
{
  //GetEnumerator -- This is an iterator; see how it's invoked
  //   (twice) in Main.
  public System.Collections.IEnumerator GetEnumerator()
  {
    // Return a different chunk of text on each iteration.
    yield return "Using iterator ";
    yield return "blocks ";
    yield return "isn't all ";
    yield return "that hard";
    yield return ".";
  }
}
```

Oddly, the StringChunks collection *stores* nothing in the usual sense. It doesn't even contain an array. So where's the collection? It's in that sequence of yield return calls, which use a special syntax to return one item at a time until all have been returned. The collection "contains" five objects, each a simple string much like the ones stored in an array in the previous MonthDays example. And, from outside the class, in Main(), you can iterate those objects with a simple foreach loop because the yield return statements deliver one string at a time, in sequence. Here's part of a simple Main() method that iterates a StringChunks collection:

```
// Instantiate a StringChunks "collection" class.
StringChunks sc = new StringChunks();

// Iterate it: prints pieces of text.
foreach (string chunk in sc)
{
  Console.WriteLine(chunk);
}
```

Iterator syntax gives up so easily

The sections that follow focus on two useful statements: yield return and yield break. The yield return statement resembles the combination of MoveNext()

and Current for retrieving the next item in a collection. The yield break statement resembles the C# break statement, which lets you break out of a loop or switch statement.

Yield return: Okay, I give up

The yield return syntax works this way:

1. The first time it's called, it returns the first value in the collection.
2. The next time it's called, it returns the second value.
3. And so on....

Using yield is much like calling the MoveNext() method explicitly, as in a LinkedList. Each MoveNext() call produces a new item from the collection. But here you don't need to call MoveNext(). (You can bet, though, that it's being done for you somewhere behind that yield return syntax.)

You might wonder what's meant by "the next time it's called." Here again, the foreach loop is used to iterate the StringChunks collection:

```
foreach (string chunk in sc)
{
  Console.WriteLine(chunk);
}
```

Each time the loop obtains a new chunk from the iterator (on each pass through the loop), the iterator stores the position it has reached in the collection (as all iterators do). On the next pass through the foreach loop, the iterator returns the next value in the collection, and so on.

Yield break: I want out of here!

You need to understand an interesting bit of syntax related to yield. You can stop the progress of the iterator at some point by specifying the yield break statement in the iterator. Say that a threshold is reached after testing a condition in the collection class's iterator block, and you want to stop the iteration at that point. Here's a brief example of an iterator block that uses yield break in just that way:

```
//YieldBreakEx -- Another example of the yield break keyword
class YieldBreakEx
{
  int[] primes = { 2, 3, 5, 7, 11, 13, 17, 19, 23 };

  //GetEnumerator -- Returns a sequence of prime numbers
```

```
  // Demonstrates yield return and yield break
  public System.Collections.IEnumerator GetEnumerator()
  {
    foreach (int prime in primes)
    {
      if (prime > 13) yield break;
      yield return prime;
    }
  }
}
```

In this case, the iterator block contains an `if` statement that checks each prime number as the iterator reaches it in the collection (using another `foreach` inside the iterator, by the way). If the prime number is greater than 13, the block invokes `yield break` to stop producing primes. Otherwise, it continues — with each `yield return` giving up another prime number until the collection is exhausted.

TIP

Besides using iterator blocks in formal collection classes, using them to implement enumerators, you could simply write any of the iterator blocks in this chapter as, say, static methods parallel to `Main()` in the `Program` class. In cases such as many of the examples in this chapter, the collection is inside the method. Such special-purpose collections can have many uses, and they're typically quick and easy to write.

TIP

You can also write an *extension method* on a class (or another type) that behaves as an iterator block. That can be quite useful when you have a class that can be thought of in some sense as a collection. Book 2 covers extension methods.

Iterator blocks of all shapes and sizes

In earlier examples in this chapter, iterator blocks have looked like this:

```
public System.Collections.IEnumerator GetEnumerator()
{
  yield return something;
}
```

But iterator blocks can also take a couple of other forms:

- Named iterators
- Class properties

An iterator named Fred

Rather than always write an iterator block presented as a method named `GetEnumerator()`, you can write a *named iterator* — a method that returns the `System.Collections.IEnumerable` interface instead of `IEnumerator` and that you don't have to name `GetEnumerator()` — you can name it something like `MyMethod()` instead. For example, you can use this simple method to iterate the even numbers from a top value that you specify down to a stop value — yes, in *descending* order. Iterators can do just about anything:

```
//EvenNumbers -- Define a named iterator that returns even numbers
//   from the "top" value you pass in DOWN to the "stop" value.
//   Another oddball "collection" class
class EvenNumbers
{
  //DescendingEvens -- This is a "named iterator."
  //   Also demonstrates the yield break keyword
  //   See how it's invoked in Main() with foreach.
  public System.Collections.IEnumerable DescendingEvens(int top,
                                                        int stop)
  {
    // Start top at nearest lower even number.
    if (top % 2 != 0) // If remainder after top / 2 isn't 0.
      top -= 1;

    // Iterate from top down to nearest even above stop.
    for (int i = top; i >= stop; i -= 2)
    {
      if (i < stop)
        yield break;

      // Return the next even number on each iteration.
      yield return i;
    }
  }
}
```

The `DescendingEvens()` method takes two parameters (a handy addition), which set the upper limit of even numbers that you want to start from and the lower limit where you want to stop. The first even number that's generated will equal the top parameter or, if `top` is odd, the nearest even number below it. The last even number generated will equal the value of the `stop` parameter (or if `stop` is odd, the nearest even number above it). The method doesn't return an `int` itself, however; it returns the `IEnumerable` interface. But it still contains a `yield return` statement to return one even number and then waits until the next time it's invoked from a `foreach` loop. That's where the `int` is yielded up.

REMEMBER

This example shows another collection with no underlying collection — such as `StringChunks`, mentioned earlier in this chapter. Note that this one is *computed* — the method "yield returns" a computed value rather than a stored or hard-coded value. That's another way to implement a collectionless collection. (You can also retrieve items from a data source or web service.) And, finally, the example shows that you can iterate a collection pretty much any way you like: down instead of up or by steps of two instead of one, for example.

TIP

An iterator needn't be finite, either. Consider the following iterator, which delivers a new number as long as you care to request them:

```
public System.Collections.IEnumerable PositiveIntegers()
{
  for (int i = 0; ; i++)
  {
    yield return i;
  }
}
```

WARNING

This example is, in effect, an infinite loop. You might want to pass a value used to stop the iteration. Here's how you would call `DescendingEvens()` from a `foreach` loop in `Main()`. (Calling `PositiveIntegers()` in the preceding example would work similarly.) This example demonstrates what happens if you pass odd numbers as the limit values, too — another use of the `%` operator:

```
// Instantiate an EvenNumbers "collection" class.
EvenNumbers en = new EvenNumbers();

// Iterate it: prints even numbers from 10 down to 4.
Console.WriteLine("\nstream of descending evens :\n");
foreach (int even in en.DescendingEvens(11, 3))
{
  Console.WriteLine(even);
}
```

This call produces a list of even-numbered integers from 10 down through 4. Notice also how the `foreach` is specified. You have to instantiate an `EvenNumbers` object (the collection class). Then, in the `foreach` statement, you invoke the named iterator method through that object:

```
EvenNumbers en = new EvenNumbers();
foreach (int even in en.DescendingEvens(nTop, nStop)) ...
```

TIP

If DescendingEvens() were static, you wouldn't even need the class instance. You would call it through the class itself, as usual:

```
foreach(int even in EvenNumbers.DescendingEvens(nTop, nStop)) ...
```

It's a regular wetland out there!

If you can produce a "stream" of even numbers with a foreach statement, think of all the other useful things you may produce with special-purpose collections like these: streams of powers of two or of terms in a mathematical series such as prime numbers or squares — or even something exotic such as Fibonacci numbers. Or, how about a stream of random numbers (that's what the Random class already does) or of randomly generated objects?

Iterated property doesn't mean "a house that keeps getting sold"

You can also implement an iterator block as a *property* of a class — specifically in the get() accessor for the property. In this simple class with a DoubleProp property, the property's get() accessor acts as an iterator block to return a stream of double values:

```
//PropertyIterator -- Demonstrate implementing a class
//   property's get accessor as an iterator block.
class PropertyIterator
{
  double[] doubles = { 1.0, 2.0, 3.5, 4.67 };

  // DoubleProp -- A "get" property with an iterator block
  public System.Collections.IEnumerable DoubleProp
  {
    get
    {
      foreach (double db in doubles)
      {
        yield return db;
      }
    }
  }
}
```

You write the DoubleProp header in much the same way as you write the DescendingEvens() method's header in the named iterators example. The header returns an IEnumerable interface, but as a property it has no parentheses after the property name and it has a get() accessor — though no set(). The get()

accessor is implemented as a `foreach` loop that iterates the collection and uses the standard `yield return` to yield up, in turn, each item in the collection of `doubles`. Here's the way the property is accessed in `Main()`:

```
// Instantiate a PropertyIterator "collection" class.
PropertyIterator prop = new PropertyIterator();

// Iterate it: produces one double at a time.
Console.WriteLine("\nstream of double values:\n");
foreach (double db in prop.DoubleProp)
{
  Console.WriteLine(db);
}
```

TIP

You can also have a generic iterator. The help documentation at `https://docs.microsoft.com/en-us/dotnet/csharp/programming-guide/concepts/iterators` provides additional details. Now that the application is complete, you can run it and see the output that follows:

```
Stream of months:

January 31
February 28
March 31
April 30
May 31
June 30
July 31
August 31
September 30
October 31
November 30
December 31

Stream of string chunks:

Using iterator
blocks
isn't all
that hard
.

stream of string chunks on one line:

Using iterator blocks isn't all that hard.

stream of primes:
```

```
2
3
5
7
11
13

stream of descending evens :

10
8
6
4

stream of double values:

1
2
3.5
4.67
```

IN THIS CHAPTER

» **Making your code generic — and truly powerful**

» **Writing your own generic class**

» **Writing generic methods**

» **Using generic interfaces and delegates**

Chapter 8 Buying Generic

The problem with collections is that you need to know exactly what you're sending to them. Can you imagine a recipe that accepts only the exact listed ingredients and no others? No substitutions — nothing even named differently? That's how most collections treat you, but not generics.

As with prescriptions at your local pharmacy, you can save big by opting for the generic version. *Generics* are fill-in-the-blanks classes, methods, interfaces, and delegates. For example, the `List<T>` class defines a generic array-like list that's quite comparable to the older, nongeneric `ArrayList` — but better! When you pull `List<T>` off the shelf to instantiate your own list of, say, `int`s, you replace `T` with `int`:

```
List<int> myList = new List<int>();  // A list limited to ints
```

The versatile part is that you can instantiate `List<T>` for *any single* data type (`string`, `Student`, `BankAccount`, `CorduroyPants` — whatever), and it's still type-safe like an array, without nongeneric costs. It's the superarray. (This chapter explains type-safety and the costs of using nongeneric collections before you discover how to create a generic class because knowing what these terms mean is essential.)

Generics come in two flavors in C#: the built-in generics, such as `List<T>`, and a variety of roll-your-own items. After a quick tour of generic concepts, this chapter covers roll-your-own generic classes, generic methods, and generic interfaces and delegates.

REMEMBER

You don't have to type the source code for this chapter manually. In fact, using the downloadable source is a lot easier. You can find the source for this chapter in the \CSAIO4D2E\BK01\CH08 folder of the downloadable source. See the Introduction for details on how to find these source files.

Writing a New Prescription: Generics

What's so hot about generics? They excel for two reasons: safety and performance.

Generics are type-safe

REMEMBER

When you declare an array, you must specify the exact type of data it can hold. If you specify `int`, the array can't hold anything other than `int`s or other numeric types that C# can convert implicitly to `int`. You see compiler errors at build-time if you try to put the wrong kind of data into an array. Thus the compiler enforces *type-safety*, enabling you to fix a problem before it ever gets out the door. A compiler error beats the heck out of a runtime error. Compiler errors are useful because they help you spot problems now.

REMEMBER

The old-fashioned nongeneric collections aren't type-safe. In C#, everything IS_A `Object` because `Object` is the base type for all other types, both value types and reference types. (Don't worry if you don't understand IS_A — it's explained in the "IS_A versus HAS_A — I'm So Confused_A" section of Book 2, Chapter 5.) But when you store *value types* (numbers, `char`s, `bool`s, and `struct`s) in a collection, they must be *boxed* going in and *unboxed* coming back out. It's as though you're putting items in an egg to place them inside an egg carton and then breaking the eggshells after removing them from the egg carton to get the items back out. (Reference types such as `string`, `Student`, and `BankAccount` don't undergo boxing.)

The first consequence of nongenerics lacking type-safety is that you need a cast, as shown in the following code, to get the original object out of the `ArrayList` because it's hidden inside an `Object`:

```
ArrayList aList = new ArrayList();
// Add five or six items, then ...
string myString = (string)aList[4];  // Cast to string.
```

WARNING

Fine, but the second consequence is this: You can put eggs in the carton, sure. But you can also add marbles, rocks, diamonds, fudge — you name it. An `ArrayList` can hold many *different types* of objects *at the same time*. So it's legal to write this:

```
ArrayList aList = new ArrayList();
aList.Add("a string");       // string -- OK
aList.Add(3);                // int -- OK
aList.Add(aStudent);         // Student -- OK
```

However, if you put a mixture of incompatible types into an `ArrayList` (or another nongeneric collection), how do you know what type is in, say, `aList[3]`? If it's `aStudent` and you try to cast it to `string`, you get a runtime error. It's just like Harry Potter reaching into a box of Bertie Botts's Every Flavor Beans: He doesn't know whether he'll grab raspberry beans or earwax.

TECHNICAL STUFF

To be safe, you have to resort to using the `is` operator (discussed in Book 2) or the alternative, the `as` operator:

```
// See if the object is the right type, then cast it ...
if (aList[i] is Student)                    // Is the object there a Student?
{
  Student theStudent = (Student)aList[i]; // Yes, so it's safe to cast.
}
// Or do the conversion and see if it went well...
Student aStudent = aList[i] as Student;   // Extract a Student, if present;
if (aStudent != null)                       // if not, "as" returns null.
{
  // OK to use aStudent; "as" operator worked.
}
```

You can avoid all this extra work by using generics. Generic collections work like arrays: You specify the one and only type they can hold when you declare them.

Generics are efficient

Polymorphism allows the type `Object` to hold any other type, as with the egg carton analogy in the previous section. But you can incur a penalty by putting in value-type objects — numeric, `char`, and `bool` types and `structs` — and taking them out. That's because value-type objects that you add have to be boxed. (See Book 2 for more on polymorphism.)

Boxing isn't worrisome unless your collection is big (although the amount of boxing going on can startle you and be more costly than you imagined). If you're stuffing a thousand, or a million, `ints` into a nongeneric collection, it takes about 20 times as long, plus extra space on the memory heap, where reference-type objects are stored. Boxing can also lead to subtle errors that will have you tearing your hair out. Generic collections eliminate boxing and unboxing.

Classy Generics: Writing Your Own

Besides the built-in generic collection classes, C# lets you write your own generic classes, regardless of whether they're collections. The point is that you can create generic versions of classes that *you* design.

Picture a class definition full of `<T>` notations. When you instantiate such a class, you specify a type to replace its generic placeholders, just as you do with the generic collections. Note how similar these declarations are:

```
LinkedList<int> aList = new LinkedList<int>(); // Built-in LinkedList class
MyClass<int> aClass = new MyClass<int>();      // Custom class
```

Both are instantiations of classes — one built-in and one programmer-defined. Not every class makes sense as a generic; in the section "Writing generic code the easy way," later in this chapter, you see an example of one that does.

REMEMBER

Classes that logically could do the same things for different types of data make the best generic classes. Collections of one sort or another are the prime example. If you find yourself mumbling, "I'll probably have to write a version of this for `Student` objects, too," it's probably a good candidate for generics.

To show you how to write your own generic class, the `PriorityQueue` example develops a special kind of queue collection class, a priority queue.

Shipping packages at OOPs

Here's the scene for an example: a busy shipping warehouse similar to UPS or FedEx. Packages stream in the front door at OOPs, Inc., and are shipped out the back as soon as they can be processed. Some packages need to be delivered by way of superfast, next-day teleportation; others can travel a tiny bit slower, by second-day cargo pigeon; and most can take the snail route: ground delivery in your cousin Fred's '82 Volvo.

But the packages don't arrive at the warehouse in any particular order, so as they come in, you need to expedite some of them as next-day or second-day. Because some packages are more equal than others, they are prioritized, and the folks in the warehouse give the high-priority packages special treatment.

Except for the priority aspect, this situation is tailor-made for a queue data structure. A queue is perfect for anything that involves turn-taking. You've stood (or driven) in thousands of queues in your life, waiting for your turn to buy Twinkies or pay too much for prescription medicines. You know the drill.

The shipping warehouse scenario is similar: New packages arrive and go to the back of the line — normally. But because some have higher priorities, they're privileged characters, like those Premium Class folks at the airport ticket counter. They get to jump ahead, either to the front of the line or not far from the front.

Queuing at OOPs: PriorityQueue

The shipping queue at OOPs deals with high-, medium-, and low-priority packages coming in. Here are the queuing rules:

- **High-priority packages** (next-day) go to the front of the queue — but behind any other high-priority packages that are already there.
- **Medium-priority packages** (second-day) go as far forward as possible — but behind all the high-priority packages, even the ones that a laggard will drop off later, and also behind other medium-priority packages that are already in the queue.
- **Low-priority ground-pounders** must join at the back of the queue. They get to watch all the high priorities sail by to cut in front of them — sometimes, *way* in front of them.

C# comes with built-in queues, even generic ones. But older versions don't come with a priority queue, so you have to build your own. How? A common approach is to embed several actual queues within a wrapper class, sort of like this:

```
class Wrapper       // Or PriorityQueue
{
  Queue queueHigh   = new Queue ();
  Queue queueMedium = new Queue ();
  Queue queueLow    = new Queue ();
  // Methods to manipulate the underlying queues...
```

Wrappers are classes (or methods) that encapsulate complexity. A wrapper may have an interface quite different from the interfaces of what's inside it — that's an *adapter*.

The wrapper encapsulates three actual queues here (they could be generic), and the wrapper must manage what goes into which underlying queue and how. The standard interface to the `Queue` class, as implemented in C#, includes these two key methods:

- `Enqueue()` (pronounced "N-Q") inserts items into a queue *at the back*.
- `Dequeue()` (pronounced "D-Q") removes items from the queue *at the front*.

TECHNICAL STUFF

For the shipping-priority queue, the wrapper provides the same interface as a normal queue, thus pretending to be a normal queue itself. It implements an `Enqueue()` method that determines an incoming package's priority and decides which underlying queue it gets to join. The wrapper's `Dequeue()` method finds the highest-priority `Package` in any of the underlying queues. The formal name of this wrapper class is `PriorityQueue`.

TIP

The example relies on a random-number generator that you can set in both `Main()` and the `CreatePackage()` method of the `PackageFactory`. The call to `Random(2)` uses a *seed value* (the number used as a starting point for the random-number calculation) so that you get the same results every time. This approach allows for reproducible testing results, which is a common practice with developers who don't want to deal with number differences between application runs. Of course, you could use `Random()` by itself, which would allow the seed to change automatically, so you can see a more realistic presentation of application output, but you'll need to make this change yourself. Using the default `Random(2)`, you see the following output:

```
Add a random number (0 - 20) of random packages to queue:
        Creating 15 packages:
                Generating and adding random package 0 with priority High
                Generating and adding random package 1 with priority Medium
                Generating and adding random package 2 with priority Low
                Generating and adding random package 3 with priority High
                Generating and adding random package 4 with priority Low
                Generating and adding random package 5 with priority Low
                Generating and adding random package 6 with priority High
                Generating and adding random package 7 with priority Medium
                Generating and adding random package 8 with priority Low
                Generating and adding random package 9 with priority Low
                Generating and adding random package 10 with priority High
                Generating and adding random package 11 with priority Low
                Generating and adding random package 12 with priority Low
                Generating and adding random package 13 with priority Medium
                Generating and adding random package 14 with priority Medium
See what we got:
Packages received: 15
Remove a random number of packages (0-20):
        Removing up to 8 packages
                Shipped package with priority High
                Shipped package with priority High
                Shipped package with priority High
                Shipped package with priority High
                Shipped package with priority Medium
                Shipped package with priority Medium
                Shipped package with priority Medium
                Shipped package with priority Medium
```

USING THE C# 10.0 PriorityQueue

C# 10.0 and the associated .NET 6 do come with a priority queue in the form of the PriorityQueue<> class. To use it, you must create a .NET Core project so that you can access .NET 6. The ColorsPriorityQueue example shows how to create a simple priority queue, as shown here:

```
// Define the preference levels.
enum Preference
{
    First, Second, Third
}

static void Main(string[] args)
{
    // Create a priority queue.
    PriorityQueue<string, Preference> colors =
        new PriorityQueue<string, Preference>();

    // Add some colors and their preference to it.
    colors.Enqueue("Red", Preference.First);
    colors.Enqueue("Orange", Preference.Third);
    colors.Enqueue("Yellow", Preference.First);
    colors.Enqueue("Green", Preference.Second);
    colors.Enqueue("Blue", Preference.Second);
    colors.Enqueue("Purple", Preference.First);
    colors.Enqueue("White", Preference.Third);
    colors.Enqueue("Black", Preference.Third);

    // Display the list by priority on screen.
    while (colors.TryDequeue(out var Color, out var Pref))
        Console.WriteLine($"{Color} is {Pref} preference.");
}
```

This example relies on the Preference enumeration to provide the priority levels. The code creates a PriorityQueue, colors, using a string value and a Preference as input. The call to colors.Enqueue() adds a new entry to the priority queue. To display the content onscreen in the proper priority, the example uses a while loop in which a call to colors.TryDequeue() continues the loop until there are no more entries to process. Here is the output you see when you run this example:

```
Red is First preference.
Purple is First preference.
```

(continued)

(continued)

```
Yellow is First preference.
Green is Second preference.
Blue is Second preference.
Orange is Third preference.
White is Third preference.
Black is Third preference.
```

Unwrapping the package

This example relies on a simplified example package. Class `Package` focuses on the priority part, although a real `Package` object would include other members. Here's the code for `class Package`:

```
class Package : IPrioritizable
{
    private Priority _priority;

    //Constructor
    public Package(Priority priority) => _priority = priority;

    //Priority -- Return package priority -- read-only.
    public Priority Priority
    {
        get => _priority;
    }

    // Plus ToAddress, FromAddress, Insurance, etc.
}
```

All that `Package` needs for the example are

- » A private data member to store its priority
- » A constructor to create a package with a specific priority (Because there is only one variable to initialize, you can use the expression body constructor version, which is explained in the "Using Expression-Bodied Members" section of Book 2, Chapter 4.)
- » A method (implemented as a read-only property here) to return the priority (Because there is no special code in this property, you can use the expression body version.)

Two aspects of class Package require some explanation: the Priority type and the IPrioritizable interface that Package implements.

Specifying the possible priorities

Priorities are measured with an enumerated type, or enum, named Priority. The Priority enum looks like this:

```
enum Priority
{
  Low, Medium, High
}
```

Implementing the IPrioritizable interface

Any object going into the PriorityQueue must "know" its own priority. (A general object-oriented principle states that objects should be responsible for themselves.)

TIP

You can informally "promise" that class Package has a member to retrieve its priority, but you should make it a requirement that the compiler can enforce. You require any object placed in the PriorityQueue to have such a member. One way to enforce this requirement is to insist that all shippable objects implement the IPrioritizable interface, which follows:

```
interface IPrioritizable
{
    Priority Priority { get; } // Example of a property in an interface
}
```

The notation { get; } is how to write a property in an interface declaration (as described in Book 2, Chapter 7. Class Package implements the interface by providing a fleshed-out implementation for the Priority property:

```
public Priority Priority
{
    get => _priority;
}
```

You encounter the other side of this enforceable requirement in the declaration of class PriorityQueue, in the later section "Saving PriorityQueue for last."

Buying Generic

Touring Main()

Before you spelunk the `PriorityQueue` class, it's useful to get an overview of how it works in practice at OOPs, Inc. Here's the `Main()` method for the `PriorityQueue` example:

```
static void Main(string[] args)
{
    Console.WriteLine("Create a priority queue:");
    PriorityQueue<Package> pq = new PriorityQueue<Package>();
    Console.WriteLine(
      "Add a random number (0 - 20) of random packages to queue:");
    Package pack;
    PackageFactory fact = new PackageFactory();

    // You want a random number less than 20.
    Random rand = new Random(2);
    int numToCreate = rand.Next(20); // Random int from 0 - 20
    Console.WriteLine("\tCreating {0} packages: ", numToCreate);

    for (int i = 0; i < numToCreate; i++)
    {
        Console.Write("\t\tGenerating and adding random package {0}", i);
        pack = fact.CreatePackage();
        Console.WriteLine(" with priority {0}", pack.Priority);
        pq.Enqueue(pack);
    }

    Console.WriteLine("See what we got:");
    int total = pq.Count;
    Console.WriteLine("Packages received: {0}", total);

    Console.WriteLine("Remove a random number of packages (0-20): ");
    int numToRemove = rand.Next(20);
    Console.WriteLine("\tRemoving up to {0} packages", numToRemove);

    for (int i = 0; i < numToRemove; i++)
    {
        pack = pq.Dequeue();
        if (pack != null)
        {
            Console.WriteLine("\t\tShipped package with priority {0}",
                pack.Priority);
        }
    }

    Console.Read();
}
```

Here's what happens in `Main()`:

1. **Instantiate a** `PriorityQueue` **object for type** `Package`.
2. **Create a** `PackageFactory` **object whose job is to create new packages with randomly selected priorities, on demand.**

   A *factory* is a class or method that creates objects for you. You tour `PackageFactory` in the section "Using a (nongeneric) Simple Factory class," later in this chapter.
3. **Use the .NET library class** `Random` **to generate a random number and then call** `PackageFactory` **to create that number of new** `Package` **objects with random priorities.**
4. **Add each package to the** `PriorityQueue` **by using** `pq.Enqueue(pack)`.
5. **Write the number of packages created and then randomly remove some of them from the** `PriorityQueue` **by using** `pq.Dequeue()`.
6. **End after displaying the number of packages removed.**

Writing generic code the easy way

Now you have to figure out how to write a generic class, with all those `<T>`s. Looks confusing, doesn't it? Well, it's not so hard, as this section demonstrates.

TIP

The simple way to write a generic class is to write a nongeneric version first and then substitute the `<T>`s. For example, you can write the `PriorityQueue` class for `Package` objects, test it, and then "genericize" it. Here's a small piece of a non-generic `PriorityQueue` to illustrate (don't add this code to the current example; it won't compile):

```
class PriorityQueue<T> where T : IPrioritizable
{
    //Queues -- the three underlying queues: all generic!
    private Queue<T> _queueHigh = new Queue<T>();
    private Queue<T> _queueMedium = new Queue<T>();
    private Queue<T> _queueLow = new Queue<T>();

    //Enqueue -- Prioritize T and add an item of type T to correct queue.
    //   The item must know its own priority.
    public void Enqueue(T item)
    {
        switch (item.Priority) // Require IPrioritizable for this property.
        {
            case Priority.High:
                _queueHigh.Enqueue(item);
```

```
                break;
            case Priority.Medium:
                _queueMedium.Enqueue(item);
                break;
            case Priority.Low:
                _queueLow.Enqueue(item);
                break;
            default:
                throw new ArgumentOutOfRangeException(
                  item.Priority.ToString(),
                  "bad priority in PriorityQueue.Enqueue");
        }
    }
// And so on ...
```

Testing the logic of the class is easier when you write the class nongenerically first. When all the logic is straight, you can use find-and-replace to replace the name Package with T.

Saving PriorityQueue for last

Why would a priority queue be last? It may seem a little backward, but you've seen the code that relies on the priority queue to perform tasks. Now it's time to examine the PriorityQueue class. This section shows the code and then walks you through it so that you see how to deal with a couple of small issues. Take it a piece at a time.

The underlying queues

PriorityQueue is a wrapper class that hides three ordinary Queue<T> objects, one for each priority level. Here's the first part of PriorityQueue, showing the three underlying queues (now generic):

```
private Queue<T> _queueHigh = new Queue<T>();
private Queue<T> _queueMedium = new Queue<T>();
private Queue<T> _queueLow = new Queue<T>();
```

The lines declare three private data members of type Queue<T> and initialize them by creating the Queue<T> objects. The T (type) used for the three queues must implement the IPrioritizable interface. Otherwise, the compiler raises an error during compilation. Consequently, you can't try to create a Queue<T> of type int (as an example) because int lacks the IPrioritizable interface. The "Understanding constraints" section, later in the chapter, explains the use of this feature in more detail.

The Enqueue() method

Enqueue() adds an item of type T to the PriorityQueue. This method's job is to look at the item's priority and put it into the correct underlying queue. In the first line, it gets the item's Priority property and switches based on that value. To add the item to the high-priority queue, for example, Enqueue() turns around and enqueues the item in the underlying _queueHigh. Here's PriorityQueue's Enqueue() method:

```
public void Enqueue(T item)
{
    switch (item.Priority) // Require IPrioritizable for this property.
    {
        case Priority.High:
            _queueHigh.Enqueue(item);
            break;
        case Priority.Medium:
            _queueMedium.Enqueue(item);
            break;
        case Priority.Low:
            _queueLow.Enqueue(item);
            break;
        default:
            throw new ArgumentOutOfRangeException(
              item.Priority.ToString(),
              "bad priority in PriorityQueue.Enqueue");
    }
}
```

The Dequeue() method

Dequeue()'s job is a bit trickier than Enqueue()'s: It must locate the highest-priority underlying queue that has contents and then retrieve the front item from that sub-queue. Dequeue() delegates the first part of the task, finding the highest-priority queue that isn't empty, to a private TopQueue() method (described in the next section). Then Dequeue() calls the underlying queue's Dequeue() method to retrieve the frontmost object, which it returns. Here's how Dequeue() works:

```
public T Dequeue()
{
    // Find highest-priority queue with items.
    Queue<T> queueTop = TopQueue();

    // If a non-empty queue is found.
    if (queueTop != null && queueTop.Count > 0)
    {
        return queueTop.Dequeue(); // Return its front item.
    }
```

Buying Generic

```
        // If all queues empty, return null (you could throw exception).
        return default(T); // What's this? See discussion.
    }
```

A difficulty arises only if none of the underlying queues have any packages — in other words, the whole PriorityQueue is empty. What do you return in that case? It's that odd duck, default(T), at the end. The later "Determining the null value for type T: default(T)" section deals with default(T).

The TopQueue() utility method

Dequeue() relies on the private method TopQueue() to find the highest-priority, non-empty underlying queue. TopQueue() just starts with _queueHigh and asks for its Count property. If it's greater than zero, the queue contains items, so TopQueue() returns a reference to the whole underlying queue that it found. (The TopQueue() return type is Queue<T>.) On the other hand, if _queueHigh is empty, TopQueue() tries _queueMedium and then _queueLow. What happens if all subqueues are empty? TopQueue() returns null. TopQueue() works like this:

```
private Queue<T> TopQueue()
{
    if (_queueHigh.Count > 0)    // Anything in high-priority queue?
        return _queueHigh;
    if (_queueMedium.Count > 0) // Anything in medium-priority queue?
        return _queueMedium;
    if (_queueLow.Count > 0)    // Anything in low-priority queue?
        return _queueLow;
    return null;                // All empty, so return null.
}
```

The remaining PriorityQueue members

PriorityQueue is useful because it knows how many items it contains. (An object should be responsible for itself.) Look at PriorityQueue's Count property. You might also find it useful to include methods that return the number of items in each of the underlying queues. *Be careful:* Doing so may reveal too much about how the priority queue is implemented. Keep your implementation private. Here is the code used for Count():

```
public int Count  // Implement this one as a read-only property.
{
    get
    {
        return _queueHigh.Count + _queueMedium.Count +
```

```
                _queueLow.Count;
    }
}
```

Using a (nongeneric) Simple Factory class

The "Saving PriorityQueue for last" section, earlier in this chapter, uses a simple factory object to generate an endless stream of Package objects with randomized priority levels. At long last, that simple class can be revealed:

```
class PackageFactory
{
    //A random-number generator
    Random _randGen = new Random(2);

    //CreatePackage -- The factory method selects a random priority,
    //   then creates a package with that priority.
    //   Could implement this as iterator block.
    public Package CreatePackage()
    {
        // Return a randomly selected package priority.
        // Need a 0, 1, or 2 (values less than 3).
        int rand = _randGen.Next(3);

        // Use that to generate a new package.
        // Casting int to enum is clunky, but it saves
        // having to use ifs or a switch statement.
        return new Package((Priority)rand);
    }
}
```

Class PackageFactory has one data member and one method. (You can just as easily implement a simple factory as a method rather than as a class — for example, a method in class Program.) When you instantiate a PackageFactory object, it creates an object of class Random() and stores it in the data member _randGen. To obtain a value between 0 and 2 to store in rand as a priority, the code calls _randGen.Next(3). A value of 0 represents a high-priority item.

Using PackageFactory

To generate a randomly prioritized Package object, you call your factory object's CreatePackage() method like this in Main():

```
Package pack;
PackageFactory fact = new PackageFactory();
... Additional setup code ...
```

```
for (int i = 0; i < numToCreate; i++)
{
    Console.Write("\t\tGenerating and adding random package {0}", i);
    pack = fact.CreatePackage();
    Console.WriteLine(" with priority {0}", pack.Priority);
    pq.Enqueue(pack);
}
```

`CreatePackage()` tells its random-number generator to generate a number from 0 to 2 (inclusive) and uses the number to set the priority of a new `Package`, which the method returns (to a `Package` variable). The resulting `Package` is then queued to the `PriorityQueue`, `pq`.

More about factories

REMEMBER

Factories are helpful for generating lots of test data. (A factory needn't use random numbers — that's just what was needed for the `PriorityQueue` example.) Factories improve programs by isolating object creation. Every time you mention a specific class by name in your code, you create a *dependency* on that class. The more such dependencies you have, the more *tightly coupled* (bound together) your classes become.

Programmers have long known that they should avoid tight coupling. (One of the more *decoupled* approaches is to use the factory indirectly via an interface, such as `IPrioritizable`, rather than a concrete class, such as `Package`.) Programmers still create objects directly all the time, using the `new` operator, and that's fine. But factories can make code less coupled — and therefore more flexible. Here's a version of the code from the "Using PackageFactory" section that relies on `IPrioritizable` (note the need for a cast during queuing):

```
IPrioritizable pack;
PackageFactory fact = new PackageFactory();
... Additional setup code ...
for (int i = 0; i < numToCreate; i++)
{
    Console.Write("\t\tGenerating and adding random package {0}", i);
    pack = fact.CreatePackage();
    Console.WriteLine(" with priority {0}", pack.Priority);
    pq.Enqueue((Package)pack);
}
```

Understanding constraints

`PriorityQueue` must be able to ask an object what its priority is. To make it work, all classes that are storable in `PriorityQueue` must implement the `IPrioritizable` interface, as Package does. Package lists IPrioritizable in its class declaration heading, like this:

```
class Package : IPrioritizable
```

Then it implements IPrioritizable's Priority property.

REMEMBER

A matching limitation is needed for PriorityQueue. You want the compiler to squawk if you try to instantiate for a type that doesn't implement IPrioritizable. In the nongeneric form of PriorityQueue (written specifically for type Package, say), the compiler squeals automatically when one of your priority queue methods tries to call a method that Package doesn't have. But, for generic classes, you can go to the next level with an explicit *constraint*. Because you could instantiate the generic class with literally any type, you need a way to tell the compiler which types are acceptable — because they're guaranteed to have the right methods.

REMEMBER

You add the constraint by specifying IPrioritizable in the heading for PriorityQueue, like this:

```
class PriorityQueue<T> where T : IPrioritizable
```

Did you notice the where clause earlier? This boldfaced where clause specifies that T must implement IPrioritizable. That's the enforcer. It means, "Make sure that T implements the IPrioritizable interface — or else!"

REMEMBER

You specify constraints by listing one or more of the following elements (separated by commas) in a where clause:

- The name of a required base class that T must derive from (or be).
- The name of an interface that T must implement, as shown in the previous example.
- You can see more; Table 8-1 has the complete list. The documentation at https://docs.microsoft.com/en-us/dotnet/csharp/programming-guide/generics/constraints-on-type-parameters provides more details.

Note the struct and class options in particular. Specifying struct means that T can be any value type: a numeric type, a char, a bool, or any object declared with the struct keyword. Specifying class means that T can be any reference type: any *class* type.

TABLE 8-1 **Generic Constraint Options**

Constraint	Meaning	Example
MyBaseClass	T must be, or extend, MyBaseClass.	where T: MyBaseClass
IMyInterface	T must implement IMyInterface.	where T: IMyInterface
struct	T must be any value type.	where T: struct
class	T must be any reference type.	where T: class
new()	T must have a parameterless constructor.	where T: new()

These constraint options give you quite a bit of flexibility for making your new generic class behave just as you want. And a well-behaved class is a pearl beyond price. You aren't limited to just one constraint, either. Here's an example of a hypothetical generic class declared with multiple constraints on `T`:

```
class MyClass<T> : where T: class, IPrioritizable, new()
{ ... }
```

In this line, `T` must be a class, not a value type; it must implement `IPrioritizable`; and it must contain a constructor without parameters. Strict!

TECHNICAL STUFF

You might have two generic parameters, and both need to be constrained. (Yes, you can have more than one generic parameter — think of `Dictionary<TKey, TValue>`.) Here's how to use two `where` clauses:

```
class MyClass<T, U> : where T: IPrioritizable, where U: new()
```

You see two `where` clauses, separated by a comma. The first constrains `T` to any object that implements the `IPrioritizable` interface. The second constrains `U` to any object that has a default (parameterless) constructor.

Determining the null value for type T: default(T)

In C#, variables have a default value that signifies "nothing" for that type. For `int`s, `double`s, and other types of numbers, it's `0` (or `0.0`). For `bool`, it's `false`. And, for all reference types, such as `Package`, it's `null`. As with all reference types, the default for `string` is `null`.

But because a generic class such as `PriorityQueue` can be instantiated for almost any data type, C# can't predict the proper `null` value to use in the generic class's code. For example, if you use the `Dequeue()` method of `PriorityQueue`, you may face this situation: You call Dequeue() to get a package, but none is available. What do you return to signify "nothing"? Because Package is a class type, it should return null. That signals the caller of Dequeue() that there was nothing to return (and the caller must check for a null return value).

REMEMBER

The compiler can't make sense of the null keyword in a generic class because the class may be instantiated for all sorts of data types. That's why Dequeue() uses this line instead:

```
return default(T);  // Return the right null for whatever T is.
```

This line tells the compiler to look at T and return the right kind of null value for that type. In the case of Package, which as a class is a reference type, the right null to return is, well, null. But, for some other T, it may be different, and the compiler can figure out what to use.

Understanding Variance in Generics

All fourth-generation languages support some kind of variance. *Variance* has to do with types of parameters and return values:

- *Covariance* means that an instance of a subclass can be used when an instance of a parent class is expected.
- *Contravariance* means that an instance of a superclass can be used when an instance of a subclass is expected.
- *Invariance* means that it's not possible to use either covariance or contravariance.

If you look at a method like the following one:

```
public static void WriteMessages()
{
    List<string> someMessages = new List<string>();
    someMessages.Add("The first message");
    someMessages.Add("The second message");
    MessagesToYou(someMessages);
}
```

and then you try to call MessagesToYou() as you did earlier in this chapter with a string type

```
public static void MessagesToYou(IEnumerable<object> theMessages)
{
    foreach (var item in theMessages)
        Console.WriteLine(item);
}
```

This code compiles because IEnumerable<T> is covariant — you can use a more derived type as a substitute for a higher-order type. The next section shows a real example.

Contravariance

A scheduling application could have Events, which have a date, and then a set of subclasses, one of which is Course. A Course is an Event. Each course knows its own number of students and the methods used to interact with them. One of these methods is MakeCalendar():

```
public void MakeCalendar(IEnumerable<Event> theEvents)
{
    foreach (Event item in theEvents)
    {
        Console.WriteLine(item.WhenItIs.ToString());
    }
}
```

Pretend that it makes a calendar. For now, all it does is print the date to the console. MakeCalendar is system-wide, so it expects some enumerable list of events.

The application also has an EventSorter class that you can pass into a list's Sort() method. That method then uses the EventSorter object's Compare() method to decide which item should come first in the sorted list. Here is the EventSorter class:

```
class EventSorter : IComparer<Event>
{
    public int Compare(Event x, Event y)
    {
        return x.WhenItIs.CompareTo(y.WhenItIs);
    }
}
```

The event manager makes a list of courses, sorts them, and then makes a calendar. ScheduleCourses creates the list of courses and then calls courses.Sort() with an EventSorter as an argument, as shown here:

```
public void ScheduleCourses()
{
    List<Course> courses = new List<Course>()
    {
        new Course(){NumberOfStudents=20,
                    WhenItIs = new DateTime(2021, 2, 1)},
        new Course(){NumberOfStudents=14,
                    WhenItIs = new DateTime(2021, 3, 1)},
        new Course(){NumberOfStudents=24,
                    WhenItIs = new DateTime(2021, 4, 1)},
    };

    // Pass an ICompare<Event> class to the List<Course> collection.
    // It should be an ICompare<Course>, but it can use ICompare<Event>
    // because of contravariance
    courses.Sort(new EventSorter());


    // Pass a List of courses, where a List of Events was expected.
    // We can do this because generic parameters are covariant
    MakeCalendar(courses);
}
```

But wait, this is a list of courses that calls Sort(), not a list of events. Doesn't matter — IComparer<Event> is a contravariant generic for T (its return type) as compared to IComparer<Course>, so it's still possible to use the algorithm.

Now the application passes a list into the MakeSchedule method, but that method expects an enumerable collection of Events. Parameters are covariant for generics, so it's possible to pass in a List of courses because Course is covariant to Event.

There is another example of contravariance, using parameters rather than return values. If you have a method that returns a generic list of courses, you can call that method expecting a list of Events, because Event is a superclass of Course.

You know how you can have a method that returns a String and assign the return value to a variable that you have declared an object? Now you can do that with a generic collection, too.

In general, the C# compiler makes assumptions about the generic type conversion. As long as you're working up the chain for parameters or down the chain for return types, C# will just magically figure the type out.

Covariance

The application now passes the list into the `MakeSchedule` method, but that method expects an enumerable collection of `Events`. Parameters are covariant for generics, so it's possible to pass in a `List` of `courses` because `Course` is covariant to `Event`. This is covariance for parameters. You can read more about covariance and contravariance for generic types at `https://docs.microsoft.com/en-us/dotnet/standard/generics/covariance-and-contravariance`.

IN THIS CHAPTER

» **Handling errors via return codes**

» **Using the exception mechanism instead of return codes**

» **Plotting your exception-handling strategy**

Chapter 9 Some Exceptional Exceptions

It's difficult to accept, but occasionally application code doesn't do what it's supposed to do, which results in an error. Users are notoriously unreliable as well. No sooner do you ask for an `int` than a user inputs a `double`, which also results in an error. Sometimes the code goes merrily along, blissfully ignorant that it is spewing out garbage. However, good programmers write their code to anticipate problems and report them as they occur.

This chapter discusses runtime errors, not compile-time errors, which C# spits out when you try to build your program. *Runtime errors* occur when the program is running, not at compile time.

The C# *exception mechanism* is a means for reporting these errors in a way that the calling method can best understand and use to handle the problem. This mechanism has a lot of advantages over the ways that programmers handled errors in the, uh, good old days. This chapter walks you through the fundamentals of exception handling. You have a lot to digest here, so lean back in your old, beat-up recliner.

You don't have to type the source code for this chapter manually. In fact, using the downloadable source is a lot easier. You can find the source for this chapter in the `\CSAIO4D2E\BK01\CH09` folder of the downloadable source. See the Introduction for details on how to find these source files.

Using an Exceptional Error-Reporting Mechanism

C# provides a specific mechanism for capturing and handling errors: the *exception.* This mechanism is based on the keywords `try`, `catch`, `throw`, and `finally`. In outline form, it works like this: A method will `try` to execute a piece of code. If the code detects a problem, it will `throw` an error indication, which your code can `catch`, and no matter what happens, it `finally` executes a special block of code at the end, as shown in this snippet:

```
public class MyClass
{
  public void SomeMethod()
  {
    // Set up to catch an error.
    try
    {
      // Call a method or do something that could throw an exception.
      SomeOtherMethod();
      // ... make whatever other calls you want ...
    }
    catch (Exception e)
    {
      // Control passes here in the event of an error anywhere
      // within the try block.
      // The Exception object e describes the error in detail.
    }
    finally
    {
      // Clean up here: close files, release resources, etc.
      // This block runs even if an exception was caught.
    }
  }
  public void SomeOtherMethod()
  {
    // ... error occurs somewhere within this method ...
    // ... and the exception bubbles up the call chain.
    throw new Exception("Description of error");
    // ... method continues if throw didn't happen ...
  }
}
```

REMEMBER

The combination of `try`, `catch`, and (possibly) `finally` is an *exception handler.* The `SomeMethod()` method surrounds a section of code in a block labeled with the keyword `try`. Any method called within the call tree within the block is part of the `try` block. If you have a `try` block, you must have either a `catch` block or a `finally` block, or both.

WARNING

A variable declared inside a try, catch, or finally block isn't accessible from outside the block. If you need access, declare the variable outside, before the block:

```
int aVariable;  // Declare aVariable outside the block.

try
{
  aVariable = 1;
  // Declare aString inside the block.
  string aString = aVariable.ToString(); // Use aVariable in block.
}
catch (Exception e)
{
  // Exception processing code.
}

// aVariable is visible here; aString is not.
```

About try blocks

Think of using the try block as putting the C# runtime on alert. The keyword is basically saying that the runtime should try to execute the code with the idea that it might not work. Exceptions bubble up through the code until the exception encounters a catch block or the application ends.

TIP

When working with a try block, make the code within it specific to a particular task or exception. Keep the try block as short as possible to reduce debugging time and to make it more likely that the code can recover from the exception. Use multiple short try blocks rather than trying to encompass all the code that could generate an exception within a single try block. Using a single large try block is akin to trying to eat an entire hero sandwich in a single bite: You might succeed, but you won't enjoy it, and there is always a mess to clean up later.

About catch blocks

A try block is usually followed immediately by the keyword catch, which is followed by the catch keyword's block. Control passes to the catch block in the event of an error anywhere within the try block. The argument to the catch block is an object of class Exception or, more likely, a subclass of Exception as shown here:

```
catch (Exception e)
{
  // Display the error
  Console.WriteLine(e.ToString());
}
```

If your catch doesn't need to access any information from the exception object it catches, you can specify only the exception type:

```
catch (SomeException)  // No object specified here (no "Exception e")
{
  // Do something that doesn't require access to exception object.
}
```

However, a catch block doesn't have to have arguments: A bare catch catches any exception, equivalent to catch(Exception):

```
catch
{
}
```

TIP

Make catch blocks as specific as possible to reduce the work required to handle them and to make recovery more likely. In addition, you can stack catch blocks to enable you to handle exceptions as specifically as possible, with the most specific exception listed first. For example, in the following catch blocks, the ArgumentOutOfRangeException is the most specific exception, followed by ArgumentException, and finally the generic Exception:

```
catch (ArgumentOutOfRangeException e)
{
    ...Some remediation code to try.
}
catch (ArgumentException e)
{
    ...Some more remediation code to try.
}
catch (Exception e)
{
    ...Some last ditch remediation code to try.
}
```

After C# finds an exception handler that will address the exception, it ignores the other catch blocks, which is why you need the most specific exception listed first.

About finally blocks

A finally block, if you supply one, runs regardless of the following:

- Whether the try block throws an exception
- The code uses a break or continue to jump out of the block
- There is a return statement to exit the method containing the block

The `finally` block is called after a successful `try` or after a `catch`. You can use `finally` even if you don't have a `catch`. For example, you use the `finally` block to clean up before moving on so that files aren't left open. A common use of `finally` is to clean up after the code in the `try` block, regardless of whether an exception occurs. So you often see code that looks like this:

```
try
{
  ...
}
finally
{
  // Clean up code, such as close a file opened in the try block.
}
```

In fact, you should use `finally` blocks liberally — only one per `try`. A `finally` block won't execute under these conditions:

- The program terminates because a fatal exception isn't handled.
- The `try` block encounters a `StackOverflowException`, `OutOfMemoryException`, or `ExecutingEngineException`.
- An external application kills the process in which the `finally` block appears.

TECHNICAL STUFF

A method can have multiple `try...catch` handlers. You can even nest a `try...catch` inside a `try`, a `try...catch` inside a `catch`, or a `try...catch` inside a `finally` — or all the above. (And you can substitute `try/finally` for all the above.)

What happens when an exception is thrown

When an exception occurs, a variation of this sequence of events takes place:

1. **An exception is thrown.**

   Somewhere deep in the bowels of `SomeOtherMethod()`, an error occurs. Always at the ready, the method reports a runtime error with the `throw` of an `Exception` object back to the first block that knows enough to `catch` and handle it.

   Note that because an exception is a *runtime error,* not a compile error, it occurs as the program executes. So an error can occur after you release your masterpiece to the public. Oops!

2. **C# "unwinds the call stack," looking for a `catch` block.**

   The exception works its way back to the calling method, and then to the method that called that method, and so on, even all the way to the top of the program in `Main()` if no `catch` block is found to handle the exception. Figure 9-1 shows the path that's followed as C# searches for an exception handler.

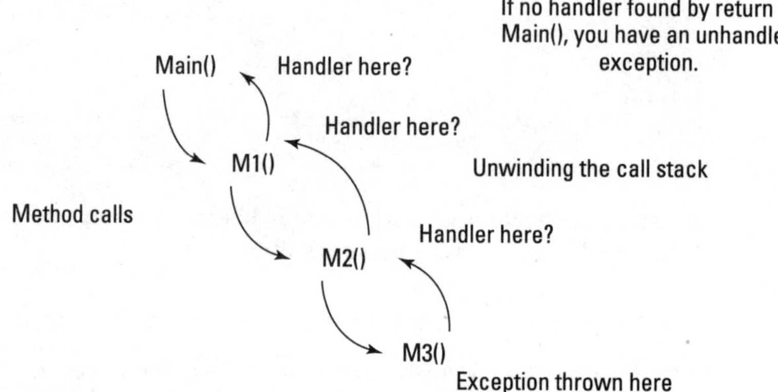

FIGURE 9-1: Where, oh where can a handler be found?

3. **If an appropriate `catch` block is found, it executes.**

   An *appropriate* `catch` block is one that's looking for the right exception class (or any of its derived classes — `Exception` will handle any exception, but `ArgumentOutOfRangeException` will handle exceptions only when the argument is out of range). This `catch` block might do any of a number of things. As the stack unwinds, if a given method doesn't have enough context — that is, doesn't know enough — to correct the exceptional condition, it simply doesn't provide a `catch` block for that exception. The right `catch` may be higher up the stack.

4. **If a `finally` block accompanies the `try` block, it executes, whether an exception was caught or not.**

   The `finally` is called before the stack unwinds to the next-higher method in the call chain. All `finally` blocks anywhere up the call chain also execute.

5. **If no appropriate `catch` block is found anywhere, the program generally crashes.**

   If C# gets to `Main()` and doesn't find a `catch` block there, the user sees an "unhandled exception" message, and the program normally exits unless the underlying operating system can supply a fix (which is rare). This is a *crash.* However, you can deal with exceptions not caught elsewhere by using an exception handler in `Main()`. See the section "Grabbing Your Last Chance to Catch an Exception," later in this chapter.

The exception mechanism provides you with these benefits:

- Exceptions provide an expressive model — one that lets you express a wide variety of error-handling strategies.
- An exception object carries a lot of information with it, thus aiding in debugging.
- Exceptions lead to more readable code because you can see what could go wrong at a glance — and less code because you spend less time trying to figure out how to fix errors.
- Exceptions are consistent, and a consistent model promotes understanding.

TECHNICAL STUFF

C# provides mechanisms to support other error-handling methods that you will encounter when working with the underlying operating system directly. This book doesn't discuss such techniques, so you see exception handling as the only error-handling method. However, you can read more about interacting with the underlying Win32 API at `https://docs.microsoft.com/en-us/windows/apps/desktop/modernize/desktop-to-uwp-enhance`, which is an advanced programming technique best left to people with a desire to slowly drive themselves nuts in pursuit of they know not what.

Throwing Exceptions Yourself

If code supplied with C# can throw exceptions, so can you. To throw an exception when you detect an error worthy of an exception, use the `throw` keyword:

```
throw new ArgumentException("Don't argue with me!");
```

You have as much right to throw things as anybody. Because C# has no awareness of your custom `BadHairDayException`, who will throw it but you?

TIP

If one of the .NET predefined exceptions fits your situation, throw it. Using a standard exception is always preferred because .NET already provides documentation for it and developers are used to using it. But if none fits, you can invent your own custom exception class.

TECHNICAL STUFF

.NET has some exception types that you should never catch: `StackOverflowException`, `OutOfMemoryException`, `ExecutionEngineException`, and a few more advanced items related to working with non-.NET code. These exceptions represent a kind of ultimate failure. For example, if you're out of stack space, as indicated by `StackOverflowException`, you simply don't have any memory to continue executing the program. Given that exception handling occurs on the stack, you don't even have enough memory to continue with the exception handling. Likewise, the `OutOfMemoryException` defines a condition in which your application is out of heap space (used for reference variables). And if the exception engine, `ExecutionEngineException`, isn't working at all, there isn't any point in continuing because you have no way to handle this error.

Can I Get an Exceptional Example?

It's helpful to see exceptions at work, so this section shows you how to create a basic application that exercises them. A factorial calculation (`https://www.mathsisfun.com/numbers/factorial.html`) performs a whole number calculation starting with the highest number down to 1, such as 4 * 3 * 2 * 1, for an output of 24, which would be 4! (or four factorial). The `FactorialException` program begins with the `MyMathFunctions` class shown here that contains the `Factorial()` function, which calculates the factorial of the number you provide:

```
public class MyMathFunctions
{
    // Factorial -- Return the factorial of the provided value.
    public static int Factorial(int value)
    {
        // Don't allow negative numbers.
        if (value < 0)
        {
            // Report negative argument.
            string s = String.Format(
                "Illegal negative argument to Factorial {0}", value);

            throw new ArgumentOutOfRangeException(s);
        }

        // Check specifically for 0.
        if (value == 0)
            return 1;

        // Begin with an "accumulator" of 1.
        int factorial = 1;

        // Loop from value down to 1, each time multiplying
        // the previous accumulator value by the result.
        do
        {
            factorial *= value;
```

```
            // Check for an overflow.
            if (factorial == 0)
            {
                string s = String.Format(
                     "Input Number {0} Too Large!", value);
                throw new OverflowException(s);
            }
        } while (--value > 1);

        // Return the accumulated value.
        return factorial;
    }
}
```

The code you see doesn't catch every possible error, but it does look for negative numbers as bad inputs. If it sees such an error, it throws the `ArgumentOutOfRangeException`. This exception is specific to this particular error because negative numbers are not within the numeric range of 0 and above (0! has a value of 1, so there is a special check for it). You use this exception rather than `ArgumentException` because `ArgumentOutOfRangeException` is more specific than `ArgumentException`, which could refer to anything.

In addition, it's entirely possible that the user could enter a correct value but the `Factorial()` function won't be able to handle it. In this case, the correct response is an `OverflowException`. The following code calls the `Factorial()` function:

```
static void Main(string[] args)
{
    string Input = string.Empty;

    while (Input.ToLower() != "quit")
    {
        // Get input from the user and check for Quit.
        Console.WriteLine("Enter a positive number or Quit: ");
        Input = Console.ReadLine();
        if (Input.ToLower() == "quit")
            continue;

        // Make sure the input is an integer number.
        int Value = 0;
        if (!Int32.TryParse(Input, out Value))
        {
            Console.WriteLine("Please enter an integer number or Quit!");
            continue;
        }
```

```
        // Here's the exception handler.
        int Factorial = 0;
        try
        {
            // Calculate the factorial of the number.
            Factorial = MyMathFunctions.Factorial(Value);
        }
        catch (ArgumentOutOfRangeException e)
        {
            // Tell the user about the problem.
            Console.WriteLine("You must enter a positive number!");

            // Fix the problem by trying again.
            continue;
        }
        catch (OverflowException e)
        {
            // Tell the user about the problem.
            Console.WriteLine("The number supplied is too large!");

            // Fix the problem by trying again.
            continue;
        }
        catch (Exception e)
        {
            // OK, now we have no idea of what's wrong.
            Console.WriteLine("An unexplainable error has happened!");

            // Output the error information so someone can learn more.
            Console.WriteLine(e.ToString());

            // Exit the application gracefully with an error code.
            System.Environment.Exit(-1);
        }
        finally
        {
            Console.WriteLine("Thank you for testing the application!");
        }
        Console.WriteLine($"The factorial of {Value} is {Factorial}.");
    }

    Console.Read();
}
```

This example takes a reasonable number of precautions. First, it checks to verify that the input is indeed an integer number or the special string `quit` (the capitalization is unimportant). Entering a character or floating-point value won't do the trick. So, the application won't even call `factorial()` unless there is a good chance of success.

Notice that the `try...catch` block is short and focuses on the call to `Factorial()`. The output doesn't appear until the `try...catch` block is satisfied. After the example calls `Factorial()`, it provides three levels of exception handling (in the following order):

1. Display an error message because there is something wrong with the input, and give the user another chance to perform the task correctly.
2. Handle the situation where the input is correct but the number is too high for `Factorial()` to handle.
3. Do something when the unexplained happens to allow a graceful exit.

Because it's more likely that the user will provide incorrect input, rather than that `Factorial()` will receive too large a number, you check the incorrect input first. It's a small but helpful way to improve application performance when an exception occurs. Here is a sample run of the code:

```
Enter a positive number or Quit:
s
Please enter an integer number or Quit!
Enter a positive number or Quit:
2.2
Please enter an integer number or Quit!
Enter a positive number or Quit:
-5
You must enter a positive number!
Thank you for testing the application!
Enter a positive number or Quit:
99
The number supplied is too large!
Thank you for testing the application!
Enter a positive number or Quit:
5
Thank you for testing the application!
The factorial of 5 is 120.
Enter a positive number or Quit:
quit
```

Working with Custom Exceptions

Earlier in the chapter, you learn that you can define your own custom exception types. Suppose that you want to define a CustomException class. The class might look something like this:

```
public class CustomException : System.Exception
{
   // Default constructor
   public CustomException() : base()
   {
   }

   // Argument constructor
   public CustomException(String message) : base(message)
   {
   }

   // Argument constructor with inner exception
   public CustomException(String message, Exception innerException) :
      base(message, innerException)
   {
   }

   // Argument constructor with serialization support
   protected CustomException(
      SerializationInfo info, StreamingContext context) :
      base(info, context)
   {
   }
}
```

You can use this basic setup for any custom exception that you want to create. There is no special code (unless you want to add it) because the base() entries mean that the code relies on the code found in System.Exception. What you're seeing here is the work of inheritance, something you see quite a lot in Book 2. In other words, for now, you don't have to worry too much about how this custom exception works.

Planning Your Exception-Handling Strategy

It makes sense to have a plan for how your program will deal with errors, as described in the following sections.

Some questions to guide your planning

Several questions should be on your mind as you develop your program:

- **What could go wrong?** Ask this question about each bit of code you write.
- **If it does go wrong, can I fix it?** If so, you may be able to recover from the problem, and the program may be able to continue.
- **Does the problem put user data at risk?** If so, you must do everything in your power to keep from losing or damaging that data. Knowingly releasing code that can mangle user data is akin to software malpractice.
- **Where should I put my exception handler for this problem?** Trying to handle an exception in the method where it occurs may not be the best approach. Often, another method higher up in the chain of method calls has better information and may be able to do something more intelligent and useful with the exception. Put your `try...catch` there so that the `try` block surrounds the call that leads to the place where the exception can occur.
- **Which exceptions should I handle?** The answer is simple, all of them. There is never a good reason to leave exceptions unhandled in a way that leaves the user with one of those terrifying dialog boxes to gape at. If you can't provide a specific fix, at least exit from the application gracefully.
- **What about exceptions that slip through the cracks and elude my handlers?** Testing, testing, and more testing is the word of the day! Exceptions should never just sort of happen to anyone.
- **What sort of input errors might my application see?** Input errors happen from a wide range of sources, not just users. A file may contain bad data, or it might simply be missing or locked. Equipment, such as a network, used to retrieve data can malfunction. So, it's not even enough to check for range and data type; you also need to check for issues such as missing sources.
- **How robust (unbreakable) does my code need to be?** You never know where your code is going to end up. You might have designed it as a simple utility, but if it does something useful, it could end up in an air-traffic-control system. With this need in mind, you need to make your code as bulletproof as possible every time you write code.

Guidelines for code that handles errors well

You should keep the questions in the previous section in mind as you work. These guidelines may help, too:

- **Protect the user's data at all costs.** This is the Top Dog guideline. See the next bullet item.
- **Don't crash.** Recover if you can, but be prepared to go down as gracefully as possible. Don't let your program just squeak out a cryptic, geeky message and go belly up. *Gracefully* means that you provide clear messages containing as much helpful information as possible before shutting down. Users truly hate crashes. But you probably knew that.
- **Don't let your program continue running if you can't recover from a problem.** The program could be unstable or the user's data left in an inconsistent state. When all is most certainly lost, you can display a message and call `System.Environment.FailFast()` to terminate the program immediately rather than throw an exception. It isn't a crash — it's deliberate.
- **Treat class libraries differently from applications.** In *class libraries,* let exceptions reach the caller, which is best equipped to decide how to deal with the problem. Don't keep the caller in the dark about problems. But in *applications,* handle any exceptions you can. Your goal is to keep the code running if possible and protect the user's data without putting a lot of inconsequential messages in the user's face.
- **Throw exceptions when, for any reason, a method can't complete its task.** The caller needs to know about the problem. (The caller may be a method higher up the call stack in your code or a method in code by another developer using your code.) If you check input values for validity before using them and they aren't valid — such as an unexpected `null` value — fix them and continue if you can. Otherwise, throw an exception.

  Try to write code that doesn't need to throw exceptions — and correct bugs when you find them — rather than rely on exceptions to patch up the code. But use exceptions as your main method of reporting and handling errors.
- **In most cases, don't catch exceptions in a particular method unless you can handle them in a useful way, preferably by recovering from the error.** Catching an exception that you can't handle is like catching a wasp in your bare hand. Now what? Most methods don't contain exception handlers.
- **Test your code thoroughly,** especially for any category of bad input you can think of. Can your method handle negative input? Zero? A very large value? An empty string? A `null` value? What could the user do to cause an exception? What fallible resources, such as files, databases, or URLs, does your code use? See the two previous bullet paragraphs.

- **Catch the most specific exception you can.** Don't write many `catch` blocks for high-level exception classes such as `Exception` or `ApplicationException`.
- **Always put a last-chance exception handler block in `Main()`** — or wherever the "top" of your program is (except in reusable class libraries). You can catch type `Exception` in this block. Catch and handle the ones you can and let the last-chance exception handler pick up any stragglers. (The upcoming "Grabbing Your Last Chance to Catch an Exception" section explains last-chance handlers.)
- **Don't use exceptions as part of the normal flow of execution.** For example, don't throw an exception as a way to get out of a loop or exit a method.
- **Consider writing your own custom exception classes** if they bring something to the table — such as more information to help in debugging or more meaningful error messages for users. You can also use custom exception classes to catch a less informational exception, such as `DivideByZero`, and provide a more informational exception, such as `InvalidSalesTaxRate`, to pass to the caller.

The rest of this chapter gives you the tools needed to follow these guidelines. For more information check out `https://docs.microsoft.com/en-us/dotnet/csharp/fundamentals/exceptions/`.

REMEMBER

If a public method throws any exceptions that the caller may need to catch, those exceptions are part of your class's public interface. You need to document them, preferably with the "How to find out which methods throw which exceptions" section of Book 1, Chapter 9.

How to find out which methods throw which exceptions

TIP

To find out whether calling a particular method in the .NET class libraries, such as `String.IndexOf()` — or even one of your own methods — can throw an exception, consider these guidelines:

- **Visual Studio provides immediate help with tooltips.** When you hover the mouse pointer over a method name in the Visual Studio editor, a tooltip window lists not only the method's parameters and return type but also the exceptions it can throw. If you need additional information, right-click the method name and choose Peek Definition from the context menu to see more specifics in a separate window.

» **If you have used XML comments to comment your own methods,** Visual Studio shows the information in those comments in its IntelliSense tooltips just as it does for .NET methods. If you documented the exceptions your method can throw (see the previous section), you see them in a tooltip, as part of autocomplete, and in the Object Browser. Place the `<exception>` line below your `<summary>` comment to make it show in the tooltip (see `https://docs.microsoft.com/en-us/dotnet/csharp/codedoc` for more details). Here is an example of XML comments for the `Factorial()` method in the `FactorialException` example:

```
/// <summary>
///   public static int Factorial(int value)
///   <para>Return the factorial of the provided value.</para>
///   <example>
///     This shows a basic call.
///     <code>
///       input = 5;
///       int output = Factorial(input);
///     </code>
///   </example>
/// </summary>
/// <param name="value">The x! to find.</param>
/// <returns>Factorial value as int.</returns>
/// <exception cref="ArgumentOutOfRangeException">
///   The value must be greater than 0.
/// </exception>
/// <exception cref="OverflowException">
///   The x! is too large to compute.
/// </exception>
```

When you hover your mouse over `Factorial = MyMathFunctions.Factorial(Value);`, you see the output shown in Figure 9-2.

» **The C# Language Help files provide even more.** When you look up a .NET method in C# Language Help, you find a list of exceptions that the method can throw, along with additional descriptions not provided via the yellow Visual Studio tooltip. To open the C# Language Help page for a given method, click the method name in your code and press F1. You can also supply similar help for your own classes and methods.

You should look at each of the exceptions you see listed, decide how likely it is to occur, and (if warranted for your program) guard against it using the techniques covered in the rest of this chapter.

int MyMathFunctions.Factorial(int value)
public static int Factorial(int value)

Return the factorial of the provided value.

This shows a basic call.

```
input = 5;
int output = Factorial(input);
```

Returns:
Factorial value as int.

Exceptions:
ArgumentOutOfRangeException
OverflowException

FIGURE 9-2: Providing XML comments for your methods.

Grabbing Your Last Chance to Catch an Exception

Most applications benefit when you sandwich the contents of `Main()` in a `try` block because `Main()` is the starting point for the program and thus the ending point as well. Any exception not caught somewhere else percolates up to `Main()`. This is your last opportunity to grab the error before it ends up back in Windows, where the error message is much harder to interpret and may frustrate — or scare the bejabbers out of — the program's user.

All the serious code in `FactorialException`'s `Main()` is inside a `try` block. The associated `catch` blocks catch any exception whatsoever and output a message to the console. In most cases, the application recovers from the error and gives the user another chance.

This `catch` block serves to prevent hard crashes by intercepting all exceptions not handled elsewhere. And it's your chance to explain why the application is quitting. To see why you need this last-chance handler, deliberately throw an exception in a little program without handling it. You see what the user would see without your efforts to make the landing a bit softer.

REMEMBER

During development, you want to see exceptions that occur as you test the code, in their natural habitat — so you want all the geekspeak. In the version you release, convert the programmerish details to normal English, display the message to the user, including, if possible, what the user might do to run successfully next time, and exit stage right. Make this plain-English version of the exception handler one of the last chores you complete before you release your program into the wild. Your last-chance handler should certainly log the exception information somehow, for later forensic analysis.

Throwing Expressions

C# versions prior to 7.0 have certain limits when it comes to throwing an exception as part of an expression. In these previous versions, you essentially had two choices. The first choice was to complete the expression and then check for a result, as shown here:

```
var myStrings = "One,Two,Three".Split(',');
var numbers = (myStrings.Length > 0) ? myStrings : null;
if (numbers == null){ throw new Exception("There are no numbers!"); }
```

The second option was to make throwing the exception part of the expression, as shown here:

```
var numbers = (myStrings.Length > 0) ?
   myStrings :
   new Func<string[]>(() => {
      throw new Exception("There are no numbers!"); })();
```

C# 7.0 and above includes a new null-coalescing operator, ?? (two question marks). Consequently, you can compress the two previous examples so that they look like this:

```
var numbers = myStrings ?? throw new Exception("There are no numbers!");
```

In this case, if `myStrings` is `null`, the code automatically throws an exception. You can also use this technique within a conditional operator (like the second example):

```
var numbers = (myStrings.Length > 0) ? myStrings :
  throw new Exception("There are no numbers!");
```

The capability to throw expressions also exists with expression-bodied members. You might have seen these members in one of the two following forms (if not, you find them covered completely in Book 2, so don't worry too much about the specifics for now):

```
public string getMyString()
{
  return " One,Two,Three ";
}
```

or

```
public string getMyString() => "One,Two,Three";
```

However, say that you don't know what content to provide. In this case, you had these two options before version 7.0:

```
public string getMyString() => return null;
```

or

```
public string getMyString() { throw new NotImplementedException(); }
```

Both of these versions have problems. The first example leaves the caller without a positive idea of whether the method failed — a `null` return might be the expected value. The second version is cumbersome because you need to create a standard function just to throw the exception. Because of the new additions to C# 7.0 and above, it's now possible to throw an expression in an expression-bodied method. The previous lines become

```
public string getMyString() => throw new NotImplementedException();
```

IN THIS CHAPTER

» Finding real-world examples of enumerations

» Creating and using enumerations

» Using enumerations to define flags

» Using enumerations as parts of switches

Chapter 10

Creating Lists of Items with Enumerations

To *enumerate* means to specify individual items, as in a list. For example, you might create an enumeration of colors and then list individual colors, such as red, blue, green, and so on. Using enumerations in programming makes sense because you can list individual items as part of a common collection. For example, `Colors.Blue` would indicate the color blue, and `Colors.Red` would indicate the color red. Because enumerations are so handy, you see them used all the time in the actual world, which is why you also see them in applications. Code should model the real world to provide useful functionality in an easy-to-understand form.

The `enum` keyword lets you create enumerations in C#. This chapter begins by discussing basic `enum` usage but then moves on to some interesting additions you can make. For example, you can use *initializers* to determine the initial value of each enumeration element.

Flags give you a compact way to track small configuration options — normally on or off, but you can make them more complicated than that. You see them used a lot in older applications because they make memory usage significantly more efficient. C# applications use flags to group like options and make them easier to find and work with. You can use a single flag variable to determine precisely how some objects work.

Enumerations also see use as part of C# switches. Book 1, Chapter 5 introduces you to the `switch` statement, but this chapter takes you a little further by demonstrating how using enumerations can make your `switch` statements even easier to read and understand.

REMEMBER

You don't have to type the source code for this chapter manually. In fact, using the downloadable source is a lot easier. You can find the source for this chapter in the `\CSAIO4D2E\BK01\CH10` folder of the downloadable source. See the Introduction for details on how to find these source files.

Seeing Enumerations in the Real World

A problem with many programming constructs is relating them to the real world, and such can be the case with enumerations. An enumeration is any permanent collection of items. As previously mentioned, colors are one of the more common enumerations, and you use them often in the real world. However, if you were to look up color enumerations online, you'd find a stack of programming-specific references and not a single real-world reference. Instead of a color enumeration, look for a color wheel; that's how people in the real world enumerate colors and create collections of color types. People often organize the color sets by their position on the color wheel, such as complementary or analogous colors. (See `https://www.sessions.edu/color-calculator/` for a color calculator and description of the color wheel.)

Collections take many forms, and you may not even realize that you've created one. For example, the site at `https://www.iberdrola.com/sustainability/biology-kingdoms-living-things-classification` tells you about the classification of living organisms. Because these classifications follow a pattern and tend not to change much, you could express them as an enumeration within an application. For example, the list of five kingdoms is unlikely to ever change. Even the list of phylums within each kingdom is unlikely to change, so you could express them as enumerations as well.

Practical, everyday uses for enumerations include lists of items or information that everyone needs. For example, you can't mail something without knowing which state the package is supposed to go to. An enumeration of states within an application saves everyone time and ensures that the address appears without errors. You use enumerations to represent actual objects correctly. People make mistakes, and enumerations reduce errors; also, because they save time, people really want to use them.

REMEMBER

Enumerations work only under certain circumstances. In fact, situations arise in which you should most definitely not use an enumeration. The following list offers some rules of thumb to use when deciding whether to create an enumeration:

- **Collection stability:** The collection must present a stable, unchanging list of members. A list of states is stable and unlikely to change frequently. A list of the top-ten songs on the Billboard chart isn't stable and can change almost daily.
- **Member stability:** Each member within the collection must also remain stable and present a recognizable, consistent value. A list of area codes, even though quite large, is also consistent and recognizable, so you could create such an enumeration, should you decide to do so. A list of people's first names is a bad idea because people change the spelling of names constantly and add new names at the drop of a hat.
- **Consistent value:** Enumerations exchange numeric values that a program can understand for word values that a human can understand. If the numeric value associated with a particular word changes, the enumeration won't work because you can't rely on a dependable association between the numeric value and the word used to represent it.

Working with Enumerations

The basic idea behind enumerations is relatively simple. All you really need to do is create a list of names and assign the collection a name. However, you can make additions to a basic enumeration that enhances flexibility and your ability to use enumerations in a wide range of scenarios. The following sections use the `Enumerations` example to describe how to create various kinds of enumerations.

Using the enum keyword

You use the `enum` keyword to create an enumeration. For example, the following code creates an enumeration named `Colors`.

```
enum Colors {Red, Orange, Yellow, Green, Blue, Purple};
```

REMEMBER

C# offers multiple ways to access the enumeration. If you need just a single value, you can use the color name. The output you get depends on how you access the value, as shown here:

```
// Display the color name.
Console.WriteLine($"Color Name: {Colors.Blue}.");

// Display the color value.
Console.WriteLine($"Color Value: {(int)Colors.Blue}.");
```

If you were to execute this code, you'd see `Blue` as the output for the first line and `4` for the output of the second line. When creating a default enumeration setup, the values begin at 0 and proceed sequentially from there. Because `Blue` is the fifth element of `Colors`, its value is `4`. (Initializers, discussed in the next section, allow you to change the value default.)

You might need to access the entire list of enumerated values at some point. To perform this task, you use a `foreach` statement, like this:

```
// Display all the elements starting with names.
Console.WriteLine("\r\nAll Color Names:");
foreach (String Item in Enum.GetNames(typeof(Colors)))
    Console.WriteLine(Item);

// Display the values too.
Console.WriteLine("\r\nAll Color Values:");
foreach (Colors Item in Enum.GetValues(typeof(Colors)))
    Console.WriteLine($"{Item} = {(int)Item}");
```

However, you might actually need only a range of values. In this case, you could also use a `for` statement, like this:

```
// Display a range of names.
for (Colors Item = Colors.Orange; Item <= Colors.Blue; Item++)
    Console.WriteLine("{0} = {1}", Item, (int)Item);
```

In this case, you see only a range of the values that `Colors` provides. The output is

```
Orange = 1
Yellow = 2
Green = 3
Blue = 4
```

Creating enumerations with initializers

Using the default values that the enum keyword provides works fine in most cases because you don't really care about the value — you care about the human-readable form of the value. However, sometimes you really do need to assign specific values to each of the enumeration elements. In this case, you need an initializer. An *initializer* simply specifies the specific value assigned to each element member, like this:

```
enum Colors2
{
    Red = 5,
    Orange = 10,
    Yellow = Orange + 5,
    Green = 5 * 4,
    Blue = 0x19,
    Purple = Orange | Green
}
```


To assign a value to each element, just add an equals sign, followed by a value. You must provide a numeric value. For example, you can't assign a value of "Hello" to one of the elements.

REMEMBER

You might be thinking to yourself that those last four initializers look strange. The fact is that an initializer can equate to anything that ends up being an integer. In the first case, you add 5 to the value of Orange to initialize Yellow. Green is the result of a math equation. Meanwhile, Blue uses hexadecimal format instead of decimal. Finally, Purple is the result of performing a logical or of Orange and Green. You use the same techniques as before to enumerate an enum that uses initializers:

```
// Display Colors2.
Console.WriteLine("\r\nDisplay Colors with a Specific Value:");
foreach (Colors2 Item in Enum.GetValues(typeof(Colors2)))
    Console.WriteLine($"{Item} = {(int)Item}");
```

Here are the results:

```
Red = 5
Orange = 10
Yellow = 15
Green = 20
Blue = 25
Purple = 30
```

FLOAT OR DOUBLE FOR ENUM?

Many people ask about using a `float` or a `double` for an enum type. C# doesn't allow the use of `float`, `double`, or `decimal` for enums. The Common Language Runtime (CLR) apparently doesn't allow it according to posts like `https://stackoverflow.com/questions/8371319/how-to-somehow-define-enum-type-as-float-or-double-in-c-sharp`. And you can still see those in the know discussing odd C# behaviors with regard to the use of the `float` or `double` types, like the one at `https://github.com/dotnet/runtime/issues/29266`. Just remember that C# doesn't allow the use of the `float`, `double`, or `decimal` type for an enum and you'll be fine; chanting helps. However, there are some workarounds you can find online, such as those found in the discussion at `https://stackoverflow.com/questions/65452203/unity-enum-dropdown-with-float-values`. The conversation actually contains an interesting use case for enums that use the `float` type.

Specifying an enumeration data type

The default enumeration data type is `int`. However, you might not want to use an `int`; you might need some other value, such as a `long` or a `short`. You can, in fact, use the `byte`, `sbyte`, `short`, `ushort`, `int`, `uint`, `long`, and `ulong` types to create an enumeration. The type you choose depends on how you plan to use the `enum` and how many values you plan to store in it.

To define an `enum` data type, you add a colon and type name after the enumeration name. Here's an example:

```
enum Colors3: byte {Red, Orange, Yellow, Green, Blue, Purple};
```

The `Colors3` enumeration is supposedly of type `byte`. Of course, you don't know for certain that it is until you test it. The following code shows how to perform the testing:

```
// Display Colors3.
Console.WriteLine("\r\nDisplay Byte-sized Colors:");
foreach (Colors3 Item in Enum.GetValues(typeof(Colors3)))
    Console.WriteLine($"{Item} is {Item.GetTypeCode()} = {(int)Item}");
```

REMEMBER

Note that you must use the `Item.GetTypeCode()` method, not the `Item.GetType()` method, to obtain the underlying enumeration type. If you use `Item.GetType()` instead, C# tells you that `Item` is of type `Colors3`. Here's the output from this example:

```
Red is Byte = 0
Orange is Byte = 1
Yellow is Byte = 2
Green is Byte = 3
Blue is Byte = 4
Purple is Byte = 5
```

Creating Enumerated Flags

Flags provide an interesting way to work with data. You can use them in various ways to perform tasks such as defining options that aren't exclusive. For example, you can buy a car that has air conditioning, GPS, Bluetooth, and a number of other features. Each of these features is an addition, but they all fall within the category of optional accessories.

REMEMBER

When working with flags, you must think in terms of bits. For example, most people would think of a `byte` as being able to hold values up to 256, or they might think of a byte as being eight bits long. However, what you need to think about when working with flags is that the `byte` can hold eight individual bit values. So, a value of 1 might indicate that the person wants air conditioning. A value of 2 might indicate a desire for GPS. Likewise, a value of 4 might indicate a need for Bluetooth — with all using bit positions, as shown here:

```
0000 0001 Air Conditioning
0000 0010 GPS
0000 0100 Bluetooth
```

By reserving bit positions and associating them each with a particular option, you can start to perform bit manipulation using and (`&`), or (`|`), and exclusive or (`^`). For example, a value of 3, which equates to 0000 0011, would tell someone that a buyer needs both air conditioning and GPS.

REMEMBER

The most common way to work with bit values is using hexadecimal (although, you can also use binary), which can represent 16 different values directly, which equates to four bit positions. Consequently, 0x11 would appear as 0001 0001 in bit form. Hexadecimal values range from 0 through F, where A = 10, B = 11, C = 12, D = 13, E = 14, and F = 15 in decimal form. Here's an example of an enumerated flag:

```
[Flags]
enum Colors4
{
    Red = 0x01,
    Orange = 0x02,
```

```
    Yellow = 0x04,
    Green = 0x08,
    Blue = 0x10,
    Purple = 0x20
}
```

Note the [Flags] attribute that appears immediately before the enum keyword. An *attribute* tells the C# compiler how to react to a common structure in a special way. In this case, you tell the C# compiler that this isn't a standard enumeration; this enumeration defines flag values.

TIP

You should also see that the individual elements rely on hexadecimal initializers (see the "Creating enumerations with initializers" section, earlier in this chapter, for details). C# doesn't require that you use hexadecimal initializers, but doing so makes your code significantly easier to read. The following code shows how an enumerated flag might work:

```
// Create a variable containing three color options.
Colors4 myColors = Colors4.Red | Colors4.Green | Colors4.Purple;

// Display the result.
Console.WriteLine("\r\nWork with Color Flags:");
Console.WriteLine(myColors);
Console.WriteLine("0x{0:X2}", (int)myColors);
```

The code begins by creating myColors, which contains three options, Colors4.Red, Colors4.Green, and Colors4.Purple. To create an additive option list, you always or the values together using the | operator. Normally, myColors would contain a value of 41. However, the next two lines of code show the effects of the [Flags] attribute:

```
Red, Green, Purple
0x29
```

The output shows the individual options when you display myColors. Because myColors represents flag values, the example also outputs the myColors value of 41 as a hexadecimal value of 0x29. The addition of the X2 format string to the format argument outputs the value in hexadecimal, rather than decimal form with two significant digits. The format argument and the format string are separated with a colon (:). You can read more about format types (which include format strings) at https://docs.microsoft.com/en-us/dotnet/standard/base-types/standard-numeric-format-strings.

Defining Enumerated Switches

When working with a `switch` statement, the reason for a decision can be quite unclear if you use a numeric value. For example, the following code doesn't really tell you much about the decision-making process:

```
// Create an ambiguous switch statement.
int mySelection = 2;
switch (mySelection)
{
    case 0:
        Console.WriteLine("You chose red.");
        break;
    case 1:
        Console.WriteLine("You chose orange.");
        break;
    case 2:
        Console.WriteLine("You chose yellow.");
        break;
    case 3:
        Console.WriteLine("You chose green.");
        break;
    case 4:
        Console.WriteLine("You chose blue.");
        break;
    case 5:
        Console.WriteLine("You chose purple.");
        break;
}
```

This code leaves you wondering why `mySelection` has a value of `2` assigned to it and what those output statements are all about. The code works, but the reasoning behind it is muddled. This is also a good way to create a hard to find bug. To make this code more readable, you can use an enumerated switch, like this:

```
// Create a readable switch statement.
Colors myColorSelection = Colors.Yellow;
switch (myColorSelection)
{
    case Colors.Red:
        Console.WriteLine("You chose red.");
        break;
    case Colors.Orange:
        Console.WriteLine("You chose orange.");
        break;
```

```
    case Colors.Yellow:
        Console.WriteLine("You chose yellow.");
        break;
    case Colors.Green:
        Console.WriteLine("You chose green.");
        break;
    case Colors.Blue:
        Console.WriteLine("You chose blue.");
        break;
    case Colors.Purple:
        Console.WriteLine("You chose purple.");
        break;
}
```

The output is the same in both cases: "You chose yellow." However, in the second case, the code is infinitely more readable. Simply by looking at the code, you know that `myColorSelection` has a color value assigned to it. In addition, the use of a `Colors` member for each `case` statement makes the choice clear. You understand why the code takes a particular path.

Working with Enumeration Methods

It's possible to extend enumeration functionality using methods. For example, you might want to create a special formatting of a `Colors` enumeration like this:

```
public enum Colors { Red, Orange, Yellow, Green, Blue, Purple};

public static class Extensions
{
    public static string GetNameValue(this Colors color)
    {
        return $"{color} is {color.GetTypeCode()} = {((long)color)}";
    }
}
```

The `Extensions` class contains the `GetNameValue()` method that accepts a `Colors` object as input and outputs a specially formatting `string`. The code should look somewhat familiar because it's based on the code found in the "Specifying an enumeration data type" section, earlier in this chapter. However, the use of the `Extensions` class changes how you work with `Colors`. You can list the colors in the enumeration like this now:

```
static void Main(string[] args)
{
    // Display each of the colors in turn.
    foreach (Colors color in Enum.GetValues(typeof(Colors)))
        Console.WriteLine(color.GetNameValue());
}
```

REMEMBER

As you can see, the use of `GetNameValue()` is straightforward and makes working with the enumeration easier. Notice that you don't supply a value to `GetNameValue()`, though, and that's because the input argument is defined at `this Colors color`, which means to use the object itself as the input. Book 2, Chapter 3 tells you all about working with `this`.

2

Object-Oriented C# Programming

Contents at a Glance

IN THIS CHAPTER

» Introducing and using the C# class

» Assigning and using object references

» Examining classes that contain classes

» Identifying static and instance class members

Chapter 1
Showing Some Class

You can freely declare and use all the intrinsic data types — such as `int`, `double`, and `bool` — to store the information necessary to make your program the best it can be. For some programs, these simple variables are enough. However, most programs need a way to bundle related data into a neat package.

As shown in Book 1, C# provides arrays and other collections for gathering into one structure groups of *like-typed* variables, such as `string` or `int`. A hypothetical college, for example, might track its students by using an array. But a student is much more than just a name — how should this type of program represent a student?

Some programs need to bundle pieces of data that logically belong together but aren't of the same type. A college enrollment application handles students, each of whom has a name, rank (grade-point average), and serial number. Logically, the student's name may be a `string`; the grade-point average, a `double`; and the serial number, a `long`. That type of program needs a way to bundle these three different types of variables into a single structure named `Student`. Fortunately, C# provides a structure known as the *class* for accommodating groupings of unlike-typed variables.

REMEMBER

You don't have to type the source code for this chapter manually. In fact, using the downloadable source is a lot easier. You can find the source for this chapter in the `\CSAIO4D2E\BK02\CH01` folder of the downloadable source. See the Introduction for details on how to find these source files.

A Quick Overview of Object-Oriented Programming

There are many ways to write applications, and Object-Oriented Programming (OOP) is one of them. You've already seen procedural programming techniques in minibook 1, so minibook 2 is your foray into OOP. The purpose of OOP is to make it easier to model the real world using code. So, when you see a `Student` class, what you see is a model of a real-world student in the form of code. Of course, this model is limited to what you need to do with the student in specific circumstances. For example, the model wouldn't include the student's eating preferences, unless that's what you're modeling. The following sections provide you with a quick overview of OOP that the rest of Book 2 develops further.

Considering OOP basics

OOP relies on the class to create a container for the `Student` model, so developers call the result the `Student` class. When you work with `Student`, your focus is on a real-world student, so you don't care about the underlying code details. The first principle of OOP then is *abstraction* — the ability to focus on what is needed in the real world, rather than what is needed to program the underlying details. By changing the focus of programming, the development process becomes easier and less error prone.

Keeping data and code together so that everything you need is in one place is another principle of OOP that developers call *encapsulation.* A class is self-contained in that it has everything needed to model a particular kind of object.

Because of the manner in which classes are put together, after you create a class, you can reuse it for every object that fits within that class' model. *Reuse* makes it possible to write a class once and then use it everywhere that the class fits. Many people use the phase Don't Repeat Yourself (DRY) to emphasize this part of OOP.

Extending classes to meet other needs

An extension of DRY is the idea that you can create a class hierarchy. For example, you could create a class called `Vehicle`. Vehicles come in many forms, such as `Car`, `Truck`, and `Bus`. Each of these subclasses of `Vehicle` would inherit (derive and use) the features that `Vehicle` provides and add specifics of their own with regard to that particular kind of vehicle. The `Car` class might be further broken down into the `Coup`, `Sedan`, and `Racer` classes. *Inheritance* makes it possible to start with a general kind of object and then become very specific.

REMEMBER

Inheriting characteristics of a parent class may not be enough to fully define a child class. For example, all vehicles have a roof, even if that roof is a temporary structure, as it would be in a convertible. So, you define the `Roof` property in `Vehicle`, but further define it in `Car`, and then provide additional specifics by `Car` type. This ability to further define classes in subclasses is *polymorphism*. It's easier to look at polymorphism as saying that one thing is like another thing, but with these changes. People use this form of explanation all the time in the real world, so it shouldn't be surprising that OOP uses it, too.

Keeping objects safe

Trying to keep the focus on the object and not the underlying code is one reason that OOP classes employ *access modifiers*, which are indicators of what is and isn't accessible to users of a class. The use of access modifiers keeps code private so that users don't worry about implementation details. It also provides the developer with the flexibility to make code changes that don't modify the class interface.

TECHNICAL STUFF

The use of access modifiers differs by programming language. In C#, you have these access modifiers:

- `public`: The code used to create a particular parent class element is accessible by any other class, even if that class hasn't inherited from the parent class.
- `protected`: The code is accessible by members of the same class and any child classes. So, this code would be accessible by members of the `Vehicle` class and the `Car` class, but not accessible by members of the Road class, which doesn't inherit from the `Vehicle` class.
- `private`: The code is accessible only by members of the same class. For example, the code is accessible by any member of the `Vehicle` class, but not accessible by members of the `Car` class.
- `internal`: This is the super-secret code that is accessible only from within a given assembly, but not within any other assembly. It means that you can create code that is only accessible from your application and not any other application, even if the other application uses classes from your application.

TIP

You can also find odd combinations of the four basic access modifiers in use such as `protected internal`. This book doesn't cover the odd assorted access modifier combinations, but you can read about them online in places like `https://www.c-sharpcorner.com/uploadfile/puranindia/what-are-access-modifiers-in-C-Sharp/`.

Working with objects

Classes represent blueprints for real-world objects. When you create a `Student` class, what you really have is a blueprint for creating a student object. To create an object, you *instantiate* the class. Perhaps you might create the `Mike` and `Sally` objects, both of which are instances of the `Student` class. Both objects would have the same structure, but the details would differ. For example, one object would have a `Name` value of `"Mike"` and the other a `Name` value of `"Sally"`.

REMEMBER

This idea of objects being instances of classes brings up the final consideration for this section, which is the structure of a class and therefore an object. A class contains these elements:

- **Methods:** Defines what you can do with the object, such as changing a name or a grade-point average. Methods make it possible to interact with objects in a consistent manner.
- **Properties:** Determines the characteristics of the object, such as name or grade-point average. Properties ensure that every object has the same characteristics, even though the specifics of those characteristics differ between objects. Also, properties make data types easier to deal with. Instead of thinking about a `string` data type for a student's identifier, you think about a `Name` property.
- **Events:** Alerts anyone who is listening for the event that something has changed within the object. Perhaps someone has spoken to the `Student` or changed their grade-point average. Events make it possible to monitor objects.

Defining a Class and an Object

A *class* is a bundling of unlike data and functions that logically belong together into one tidy package. C# gives you the freedom to foul up your classes any way you want, but good classes are designed to represent *concepts.*

Computer science models the world via structures that represent concepts or things in the world, such as bank accounts, tic-tac-toe games, customers, game boards, documents, and products. Analysts say that "a class maps concepts from the problem into the program." For example, your problem might be to build a traffic simulator that models traffic patterns for the purpose of building streets, intersections, and highways.

Any description of a problem concerning traffic would include the term *vehicle* in its solution. Vehicles have a top speed that must be figured into the equation. They also have a weight, and some of them are clunkers. In addition, vehicles stop and vehicles go. Thus, as a concept, *vehicle* is part of the problem domain.

A good C# traffic-simulator program would necessarily include the class `Vehicle`, which describes the relevant properties of a vehicle. The C# `Vehicle` class would have properties such as `topSpeed`, `weight`, and `isClunker`.

Because the class is central to C# programming, the rest of minibook 2 discusses the ins and outs of classes in much more detail. This chapter gets you started.

Defining a class

This section begins with a class declaration for the `VehicleData` example. An example of the class `Vehicle` may appear this way (you put this class definition before `class Program` in the file):

```
public class Vehicle
{
    public string model { get; set; }         // Name of the model
    public string manufacturer { get; set; }  // Name of the manufacturer
    public int numOfDoors { get; set; }       // Number of vehicle doors
    public int numOfWheels { get; set; }      // You get the idea.
}
```

A class definition begins with the words `public` (the access modifier) and `class` (the kind of structure you're creating), followed by the name of the class — in this case, `Vehicle`. Like all names in C#, the name of the class is case sensitive. C# doesn't enforce any rules concerning class names, but an unofficial rule holds that the name of a class starts with a capital letter.

The class name is followed by a pair of open and closed braces. Within the braces, you have zero or more *members*. The members of a class are items that make up the parts of the class. In this example, class `Vehicle` starts with the member `model` of type `string`, which contains the name of the model of the vehicle. If the vehicle were a car, its model name could be Trooper II. The second member of this `Vehicle` class example is `manufacturer` of type `string`. The other two properties are the number of doors and the number of wheels on the vehicle, both of which are type `int`.

TIP

As with any variable, make the names of the members as descriptive as possible. A good variable name usually says it all. However, adding comments, as shown in this example, can make the purpose and usage of the members clearer.

PROPERTIES VERSUS FIELDS

You see a lot of examples online that supposedly use C# properties, but they actually use fields. There is a difference. To create the `Vehicle` class using fields, you'd use code like this:

```
public class Vehicle
{
  public string model;          // Name of the model
  public string manufacturer;   // Name of the manufacturer
  public int numOfDoors;        // Number of vehicle doors
  public int numOfWheels;       // You get the idea.
}
```

Using fields breaks one of the OOP rules of abstraction because you expose the class implementation. Using properties keeps the underlying variables safe by controlling access to them. In addition, unlike fields, using properties allows you to validate input and modify it as needed. Likewise, you can format output to meet specific needs. Consequently, properties provide great control; fields do not. Avoid using fields in your applications because fields come with all sorts of risks, and using properties doesn't require more than a few extra keystrokes.

There is one additional benefit to using properties, and it appears in the C# IDE. If you use fields, you can't track the number of code references to the field. However, the IDE does tell you how many references there are to a property as shown here:

```
2 references
public class Vehicle
{
    2 references
    public string model { get; set; }          // Name of the model
    2 references
    public string manufacturer { get; set; }   // Name of the manufacturer
    2 references
    public int numOfDoors { get; set; }        // Number of vehicle doors
    2 references
    public int numOfWheels { get; set; }       // You get the idea.
}
```

The `public` modifier in front of the class name makes the class universally accessible throughout the program. Similarly, the `public` modifier in front of the member names makes them accessible to everything else in the program. Other modifiers are possible. (Chapter 4 in this minibook covers the topic of accessibility in more detail and shows how you can hide some members.)

The class definition should describe the properties of the object that are salient to the problem at hand. That's a little hard to do right now because you don't know what the problem is, but it becomes clearer as you work through the problem.

What's the object?

Defining a `Vehicle` design isn't the same task as building a car. Someone has to cut some sheet metal and turn some bolts before anyone can drive an actual car. A class object is declared in a similar (but not identical) fashion to declaring an intrinsic object such as an `int`.

The term *object* is used universally to mean a "thing." Okay, that isn't helpful. An `int` variable is an `int` object. A `car` is a `Vehicle` object. The following code segment creates a car of class `Vehicle`:

```
Vehicle myCar;
myCar = new Vehicle();
```

The first line declares a variable `myCar` of type `Vehicle`, just as you can declare a `somethingOrOther` of class `int`. (Yes, a class is a type, and all C# objects are defined as classes.) The `new Vehicle()` call instantiates (creates) a specific object of type `Vehicle` (the blueprint or class) and stores the location in memory of that object into the variable `myCar` (the instance). The `new` keyword has nothing to do with the age of `myCar`. (My car could qualify for an antique license plate if it weren't so ugly.) The `new` operator creates a new block of memory in which your program can store the properties of `myCar`.

The intrinsic `num` and the object `myCar` are stored differently in memory. The first uses the *stack* (linear memory that is part of the program itself) and the second uses the *heap* (hierarchical memory that is taken from the system). (If you want a really detailed description of the difference, check out the article at `https://www.guru99.com/stack-vs-heap.html`.) The variable `num` actually contains the value `1` (as an example) rather than a memory location. The `new Vehicle()` expression allocates the memory necessary on the heap. The variable `myCar` contains a memory reference (a pointer to the memory) rather than the actual values used to describe a `Vehicle`.

Accessing the Members of an Object

Each object of class `Vehicle` has its own set of members. The following expression stores the number 1 into the `numberOfDoors` member of the object referenced by `myCar`:

```
myCar.numberOfDoors = 1;
```

TECHNICAL STUFF

Every C# operation must be evaluated by type as well as by value. The object `myCar` is an object of type `Vehicle`. The variable `Vehicle.numberOfDoors` is of type `int`. (Look again at the definition of the `Vehicle` class.) The constant `5` is also of type `int`, so the type of the variable on the right side of the assignment operator matches the type of the variable on the left. Similarly, the following code stores a reference to the `strings` describing the model and manufacturer name of `myCar`:

```
myCar.manufacturer = "BMW";       // Don't get your hopes up.
myCar.model = "Isetta";           // The Urkel-mobile
```

The Isetta was a small car built during the 1950s with a single door that opened the entire front of the car. Check it out at `https://www.motortrend.com/vehicle-genres/1956-1962-bmw-isetta-300-collectible-classic/`.

Working with Object-Based Code

The "Defining a class" section of this chapter tells you how to declare a class to use within an application. Starting with C# 9.0, you have a number of ways to interact with this class. The following sections show two of these techniques. The traditional approach in the first section that follows uses the `Vehicle` class in a manner that works with older versions of C#, and you should use it for compatibility purposes with existing code that uses the same approach. It requires 52 lines of code to get the job done. The C# 9.0 approach in the second section that follows is easier to read and uses only 47 lines of code. That's not much of a difference until you start looking at the number of lines saved in a larger program.

Using the traditional approach

The simple `VehicleData` program performs these tasks:

- Define the class `Vehicle`.
- Create an object `myCar`.

» Assign properties to myCar.

» Retrieve those values from the object for display.

Here's the code for the VehicleData program:

```
static void Main(string[] args)
{
    // Prompt user to enter a name.
    Console.WriteLine("Enter the properties of your vehicle");

    // Create an instance of Vehicle.
    Vehicle myCar = new Vehicle();

    // Populate a data member via a temporary variable.
    Console.Write("Model name = ");
    string s = Console.ReadLine();
    myCar.model = s;

    // Or you can populate the data member directly.
    Console.Write("Manufacturer name = ");
    myCar.manufacturer = Console.ReadLine();

    // Enter the remainder of the data.
    // A temp variable, s, is useful for reading ints.
    Console.Write("Number of doors = ");
    s = Console.ReadLine();
    myCar.numOfDoors = Convert.ToInt32(s);
    Console.Write("Number of wheels = ");
    s = Console.ReadLine();
    myCar.numOfWheels = Convert.ToInt32(s);

    // Now display the results.
    Console.WriteLine("\nYour vehicle is a ");
    Console.WriteLine(myCar.manufacturer + " " + myCar.model);
    Console.WriteLine("with " + myCar.numOfDoors + " doors, "
                      + "riding on " + myCar.numOfWheels
                      + " wheels.");

    Console.Read();
}
```

The program creates an object myCar of class Vehicle and then populates each field by reading the appropriate data from the keyboard. (The input data isn't — but should be — checked for legality.) The program then writes myCar's properties in a slightly different format. Here's some example output from executing this program:

```
Enter the properties of your vehicle
Model name = Metropolitan
Manufacturer name = Nash
Number of doors = 2
Number of wheels = 4

Your vehicle is a
Nash Metropolitan
with 2 doors, riding on 4 wheels
```

TIP

The calls to `Write()` as opposed to `WriteLine()` leave the cursor directly after the output string, which makes the user's input appear on the same line as the prompt. In addition, inserting the newline character `'\n'` in a write generates a blank line without the need to execute `WriteLine()` separately.

Using the C# 9.0 approach

The C# 9.0 approach to this example appears in the `VehicleData2` example. The `Main()` method is different in arrangement, as shown here.

```
static void Main(string[] args)
{
    // Prompt user to enter a name.
    Console.WriteLine("Enter the properties of your vehicle");

    // Obtain the data needed to create myCar.
    Console.Write("Model name = ");
    string s = Console.ReadLine();

    Console.Write("Manufacturer name = ");
    string mfg = Console.ReadLine();

    Console.Write("Number of doors = ");
    int doors = Convert.ToInt32(Console.ReadLine());

    Console.Write("Number of wheels = ");
    int wheels = Convert.ToInt32(Console.ReadLine());

    // Create an instance of Vehicle.
    Vehicle myCar = new()
    {
        model = s,
        manufacturer = mfg,
```

```
        numOfDoors = doors,
        numOfWheels = wheels
    };

    // Now display the results.
    Console.WriteLine($"\nYour vehicle is a {myCar.manufacturer} " +
        $"{myCar.model} with {myCar.numOfDoors} doors riding on " +
        $"{myCar.numOfWheels} wheels");

    Console.Read();
}
```

The example is much more structured because it collects all of the data needed to create `myCar` first. It then instantiates the `myCar` object using `Vehicle` with two changes. First, you don't declare the object type when calling `new()`. The compiler deduces the object type based on the type you provide for the object. Second, you set the properties individually, which means that you set them as part of a list after `new()`. Using this approach is significantly clearer because you know precisely where the values in `myCar` come from and have to look in only one place to see them. The output of this version is the same as before.

Discriminating between Objects

Detroit car manufacturers can track every car they make without getting the cars confused. Similarly, a program can create numerous objects of the same class, as shown in this example:

```
Vehicle car1 = new() {manufacturer = "Studebaker", model = "Avanti"};

// The following has no effect on car1.
Vehicle car2 = new() {manufacturer = "Hudson", model = "Hornet"};
```

Creating an object `car2` and assigning it the manufacturer name `Hudson` has no effect on the `car1` object (with the manufacturer name `Studebaker`). That's because `car1` and `car2` appear in totally separate memory locations. In part, the ability to discriminate between objects is the real power of the class construct. The object associated with the Hudson Hornet can be created, manipulated, and dispensed with as a single entity, separate from other objects, including the Avanti. (Both are classic automobiles, especially the latter.)

Can You Give Me References?

The dot operator and the assignment operator are the only two operators defined on reference types:

```
// Create a null reference.
Vehicle yourCar;

// Assign the reference a value.
yourCar = new Vehicle();

// Use dot to access a member.
yourCar.manufacturer = "Rambler";

// Create a new reference and point it to the same object.
Vehicle yourSpousalCar = yourCar;
```

The first line creates an object yourCar without assigning it a value. A reference that hasn't been initialized is said to point to the *null object.* Any attempt to use an uninitialized (null) reference generates an immediate error that terminates the program.

TECHNICAL STUFF

The C# compiler can catch most attempts to use an uninitialized reference and generate a warning at build-time. If you somehow slip one past the compiler, accessing an uninitialized reference terminates the program immediately.

The second statement creates a new Vehicle object and assigns it to yourCar. The last statement in this code snippet assigns the reference yourSpousalCar to the reference yourCar. This action causes yourSpousalCar to refer to the same object as yourCar. This relationship is shown in Figure 1-1.

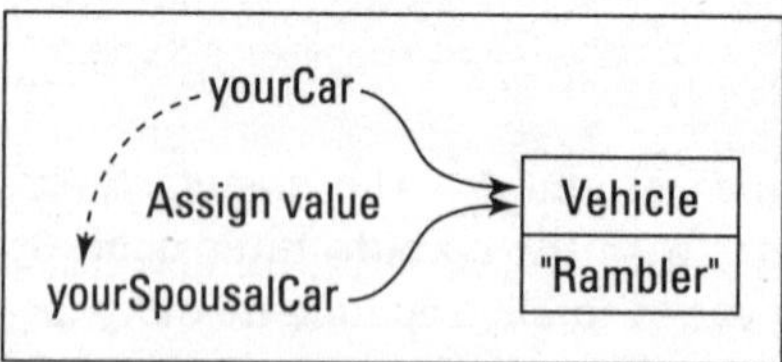

FIGURE 1-1: Two references to the same object.

The following two calls that set the car's model in the following code have the same effect:

```
// Build your car.
Vehicle yourCar = new Vehicle();
yourCar.model = "Kaiser";
```

```
// It also belongs to your spouse.
Vehicle yourSpousalCar = yourCar;

// Changing one changes the other.
yourSpousalCar.model = "Henry J";
Console.WriteLine("Your car is a " + yourCar.model);
```

Executing this program would output `Henry J` and not `Kaiser`. Notice that `yourSpousalCar` doesn't point to `yourCar`; rather, both `yourCar` and `yourSpousalCar` refer to the same vehicle (the same memory location). In addition, the reference `yourSpousalCar` would still be valid, even if the variable `yourCar` were somehow "lost" (if it went out of scope, for example), as shown in this chunk of code:

```
// Build your car.
Vehicle yourCar = new Vehicle();
yourCar.model = "Kaiser";

// It also belongs to your spouse.
Vehicle yourSpousalCar = yourCar;

// When your spouse takes your car away ...
yourCar = null;          // yourCar now references the "null object."

//  ...yourSpousalCar still references the same vehicle
Console.WriteLine("your car was a " + yourSpousalCar.model);
```


Executing this program generates the output `Your car was a Kaiser`, even though the reference `yourCar` is no longer valid. The object is no longer *reachable* from the reference `yourCar` because `yourCar` no longer contains a reference to the required memory location. The object doesn't become completely unreachable until both `yourCar` and `yourSpousalCar` are "lost" or nulled out.

At some point, the C# *garbage collector* steps in and returns the space formerly used by that particular `Vehicle` object to the pool of space available for allocating more `Vehicles` (or `Students`, for that matter). The garbage collector only runs after all the references to an object are lost. (The "Garbage Collection and the C# Destructor" sidebar at the end of Chapter 5 of this minibook says more about garbage collection.)

TIP

Making one *object variable* (a variable of a reference type, such as `Vehicle` or `Student`, rather than one of a simple type such as `int` or `double`) point to a different object — as shown here — makes storing and manipulating reference objects in arrays and collections quite efficient. Each element of the array stores a reference to an object, and when you swap elements within the array, you're just moving references, not the objects themselves. References have a fixed size in memory, unlike the objects they refer to.

Classes That Contain Classes Are the Happiest Classes in the World

The members of a class can themselves be references to other classes, as shown in the VehicleData3 example, which uses the VehicleData2 example as a starting point. For example, vehicles have motors, which have power and efficiency factors, including displacement. You could throw these factors directly into the class this way:

```
public class Vehicle
{
  public string model;          // Name of the model
  public string manufacturer;   // Ditto
  public int numOfDoors;        // The number of doors on the vehicle
  public int numOfWheels;       // You get the idea.

  // New stuff:
  public int power;             // Power of the motor [horsepower]
  public double displacement;   // Engine displacement [liter]
}
```

However, power and engine displacement aren't properties of the car. For example, your friend's Jeep might be supplied with two different motor options that have drastically different levels of horsepower. The 2.4-liter Jeep is a snail, and the same car outfitted with the 4.0-liter engine is quite peppy. The motor is a concept of its own and deserves its own class:

```
public class Motor
{
    public int power;             // Power [horsepower]
    public double displacement;   // Engine displacement [liter]
}
```

You can combine this class into the Vehicle (see boldfaced text):

```
public class Vehicle
{
    public string model { get; set; }          // Name of the model
    public string manufacturer { get; set; }  // Name of the manufacturer
    public int numOfDoors { get; set; }        // Number of vehicle doors
    public int numOfWheels { get; set; }       // You get the idea.
    public Motor motor { get; set; }           // Type of engine.
}
```

Creating myCar now appears this way (instead of asking for input, this version simply provides the required values in the interest of space):

```
static void Main(string[] args)
{
    // Create an instance of Vehicle.
    Vehicle myCar = new()
    {
        model = "Cherokee Sport",
        manufacturer = "Jeep",
        numOfDoors = 2,
        numOfWheels = 4,
        motor = new()
        {
            power = 230,
            displacement = 4.0
        }
    };

    // Now display the results.
    Console.WriteLine($"\nYour vehicle is a {myCar.manufacturer} " +
        $"{myCar.model} with {myCar.numOfDoors} doors riding on " +
        $"{myCar.numOfWheels} wheels using a {myCar.motor.displacement}" +
        $" liter engine producing {myCar.motor.power} hp.");

    Console.Read();
}
```

Notice how you can place new() statements within new() statements to define an entire hierarchy in a manner that is very easy to follow. Earlier versions of C# would require that you instantiate motor first and then add it to myCar. Everything is self-contained within a single hierarchical declaration now so that the opportunities for errors are fewer. Notice that you access the power and displacement values using a dot hierarchy as well: myCar.motor.power and myCar.motor.displacement.

Generating Static in Class Members

Most data members of a class are specific to their containing object, not to any other objects. Consider the Car class:

```
public class Car
{
  public string licensePlate;       // The license plate ID
}
```

Because the license plate ID is an *object property*, it describes each object of class Car uniquely. For example, your spouse's car will have a different license plate from your car, as shown here:

```
Car spouseCar = new Car();
spouseCar.licensePlate = "XYZ123";

Car yourCar = new Car();
yourCar.licensePlate = "ABC789";
```

However, some properties exist that all cars share. For example, the number of cars built is a property of the class Car but not of any single object. These *class properties* are flagged in C# with the keyword static:

```
public class Car
{
  public static int numberOfCars; // The number of cars built
  public string licensePlate;     // The license plate ID
}
```

REMEMBER

Static members aren't accessed through the object. Instead, you access them by way of the class itself, as this code snippet demonstrates:

```
// Create a new object of class Car.
Car newCar = new Car();
newCar.licensePlate = "ABC123";

// Now increment the count of cars to reflect the new one.
Car.numberOfCars++;
```

The object member newCar.licensePlate is accessed through the object newCar, and the class (static) member Car.numberOfCars is accessed through the class Car. All Cars share the same numberOfCars member, so each car contains exactly the same value as all other cars.

REMEMBER

Class members are static members. Non-static members are specific to each "instance" (each individual object) and are *instance members*. The italicized phrases you see here are the generic way to refer to these types of members.

Defining const and readonly Data Members

One special type of static member is the const data member, which represents a constant. You must establish the value of a const variable in the declaration, and you cannot change it anywhere within the program, as shown here:

```
class Program
{
  // Number of days in the year (including leap day)
  public const int daysInYear = 366;  // Must have initializer.

  public static void Main(string[] args)
  {
    // This is an array, covered later in this chapter.
    int[] maxTemperatures = new int[daysInYear];
    for(int index = 0; index < daysInYear; index++)
    {
      // ...accumulate the maximum temperature for each
      // day of the year ...
    }
  }
}
```

You can use the constant daysInYear in place of the value 366 anywhere within your program. The const variable is useful because it can replace a mysterious number such as 366 with the descriptive name daysInYear to enhance the readability of your program. C# provides another way to declare constants — you can preface a variable declaration with the readonly modifier, like so:

```
public readonly int daysInYear = 366; // This could also be static.
```

As with const, after you assign the initial value, it can't be changed. Although the reasons are too technical for this book, the readonly approach to declaring constants is usually preferable to const.

You can use const with class data members like those you might have seen in this chapter and inside class methods. But readonly isn't allowed in a method. Chapter 2 of this minibook dives into methods.

An alternative convention also exists for naming constants. Rather than name them like variables (as in daysInYear), many programmers prefer to use uppercase letters separated by underscores, as in DAYS_IN_YEAR. This convention separates constants clearly from ordinary read-write variables.

IN THIS CHAPTER

» **Defining a method**

» **Passing arguments to a method**

» **Getting results back**

» **Reviewing the `WriteLine()` method**

Chapter 2

We Have Our Methods

Programmers need to be able to break large programs into smaller chunks that are easy to handle. For example, some programs contained in previous chapters of this minibook reach the limit of the amount of programming information a person can digest at one time. Many developers use rules like being able to see all the code for a particular task on a single monitor screen or printed piece of paper. The idea is that it's hard to keep scrolling back and forth to see what a particular piece of code does.

This chapter looks at *methods,* which is one way to split code into smaller pieces. C# lets you divide your class code into methods. A method is equivalent to a function, procedure, or subroutine. C# 7.0 and above supports something called a *local function,* which is really a method in disguise, but it lurks inside another method (the terminology appears to just confuse matters — that's right, take a deep breath and move on). The difference is that a method is always part of a class. Properly designed and implemented methods can greatly simplify the job of writing complex programs.

REMEMBER

You don't have to type the source code for this chapter manually. In fact, using the downloadable source is a lot easier. You can find the source for this chapter in the `\CSAIO4D2E\BK02\CH02` folder of the downloadable source. See the Introduction for details on how to find these source files.

Defining and Using a Method

Consider the following code (found in the `Example` application):

```
class Example
{
  public int anInt;                   // Instance
  public static int staticInt;        // Static

  public void InstanceMethod()        // Instance
  {
    Console.WriteLine("this is an instance method");
  }

  public static void ClassMethod()   // Static
  {
    Console.WriteLine("this is a static method");
  }
}
```

Look at the fields first. The `anInt` field is non-static, or an *instance field*, which means that you must create an instance of the `Example` class to use it. However, `staticInt` is a *static field*, which means that you can access it without creating an instance of the `Example` class, such as `Example.staticInt`. The "Generating Static in Class Members" section of Chapter 1 of this minibook tells you about these differences. Here is some sample code that shows the difference in static and instance field use:

```
Example fieldInstance = new Example();  // Create an instance of class Example.
fieldInstance.anInt = 1;                // Initialize instance member.
Example.staticInt = 2;                  // Initialize class member.
```

The same distinction between fields and properties also extends to methods. `InstanceMethod()` is known as an *instance method*, which is a set of C# statements that you can execute by referencing an instance of the `Example` class. On the other hand, `ClassMethod()` is a *static method* that you access using the method's name as part of the class, such as `Example.ClassMethod()`. You find a lot of static methods used in C#. For example, when writing `Console.WriteLine()`, `Console` is the class name (see `https://docs.microsoft.com/en-us/dotnet/api/system.console`) and `WriteLine()` is the static method name. The following snippet defines and accesses `InstanceMethod()` and `ClassMethod()` in almost the same way as the fields:

```
// These lines will compile.
Example thisInstance = new Example(); // Create an instance.
```

```
thisInstance.InstanceMethod();        // Invoke the instance method.
Example.ClassMethod();                // Invoke the class method.

// The following lines won't compile.
thisInstance.ClassMethod();           // No class method access via instance.
Example.InstanceMethod();             // No instance method access via a class.

Console.ReadLine();
```

REMEMBER

Every instance of a class has its own, private copy of any instance members. But all instances of the same class share the same static members — both data members and methods — and their values.

The expression `thisInstance.InstanceMethod()` passes control to the code contained within the method. C# follows an almost identical process for `Example.ClassMethod()`. Executing the lines just shown (after commenting out the last two lines, which don't compile) generates this output:

```
this is an instance method
this is a static method
```

REMEMBER

After a method completes execution, it returns control to the point where it was called. That is, control moves to the next statement after the call.

The bit of C# code given in the two sample methods does nothing more than write a silly `string` to the console, but methods generally perform useful (and sometimes complex) operations such as calculate sines, concatenate two `strings`, or sort an array of students. A method can be as large and complex as you want, but try to strive for shorter methods, using the approach described next.

TIP

This book includes the parentheses when describing methods in text — as in `InstanceMethod()` — to make them a little easier to recognize. Otherwise, you might become confused in trying to understand the text.

Method Examples for Your Files

The idea behind methods is to break your code into small sections. C# allows many different ways to accomplish this task. The following sections show how to break a monolithic application into a much easier-to-understand application employing methods.

Understanding the problem

The monolithic `CalculateInterestTable` program from Book 1, Chapter 5 is a little difficult to read, so breaking it into several reasonable methods is important. The demonstrations in the sections that follow show how the proper definition of methods can help make a program easier to write and understand. The process of dividing working code this way is known as *refactoring*, and versions of Visual Studio 2012 and above provide a handy Refactor menu that automates the most common refactorings. When working with Visual Studio 2017 and above, you choose Edit ⇨ Refactor to access the refactoring options.

REMEMBER

You find the exact details of method definitions and method calls in later sections of this chapter. This example simply gives an overview. In outline form, the `CalculateInterestTable` program appears this way:

```
public static void Main(string[] args)
{
  // Prompt user to enter source principal.
  // If the principal is negative, generate an error message.
  // Prompt user to enter the interest rate.
  // If the interest is negative, generate an error message.
  // Finally, prompt user to input the number of years.
  //
  // Display the input back to the user.
  //
  // Now loop through the specified number of years.
  while (year <= duration)
  {
    // Calculate the value of the principal plus interest.
    // Output the result.
  }
}
```

USING COMMENTS

By reading the comments *with the C# code removed*, you should be able to get a good idea of a program's intention. If you can't, you aren't commenting properly. Conversely, if you can't strip out most comments and still understand the intention from the method and variable names, you aren't naming your methods clearly enough or aren't making them small enough (or both). Smaller methods are preferable, and using good method names beats using comments. (That's why real-world code has far fewer comments than the code examples in this book. The book's code uses heavy commenting to explain more.)

This bit of code illustrates a good technique for planning a method. If you stand back and study the program from a distance, you can see that it's divided into these three sections:

- An initial input section in which the user inputs the principal, interest, and duration information
- A section mirroring the input data so that the user can verify the entry of the correct data
- A section that creates and outputs the table

Use this list to start looking for ways to refactor the program. In fact, if you further examine the input section of that program, you can see that the same basic code is used to input these amounts:

- Principal
- Interest
- Duration

Working with standard coding methods

Your observation gives you another good place to look. Alternatively, you can write empty methods for some of those comments and then fill them in one by one. That's *programming by intention.* You can use these techniques to plan an approach to create the `CalculateInterestTableWithMethods` program. You can begin with Section 1, as shown here:

```
// InputInterestData -- Retrieve from the keyboard the
//    principal, interest, and duration information needed
//    to create the future value table. (Implements Section 1.)
public static void InputInterestData(
    ref decimal principal, ref decimal interest, ref decimal duration)
{
    // 1a -- Retrieve the principal.
    principal = InputPositiveDecimal("principal");

    // 1b -- Now enter the interest rate.
    interest = InputPositiveDecimal("interest");

    // 1c -- Finally, the duration
    duration = InputPositiveDecimal("duration");
}
```

```
// InputPositiveDecimal -- Return a positive decimal number
//    from the keyboard.
public static decimal InputPositiveDecimal(string prompt)
{
    // Keep trying until the user gets it right.
    while (true)
    {
        // Prompt the user for input.
        Console.Write("Enter " + prompt + ": ");

        // Retrieve a decimal value from the keyboard.
        string input = Console.ReadLine();
        decimal value = Convert.ToDecimal(input);

        // Exit the loop if the value that's entered is correct.
        if (value >= 0)
        {
            // Return the valid decimal value entered by the user.
            return value;
        }

        // Otherwise, generate an error on incorrect input.
        Console.WriteLine(prompt + " cannot be negative");
        Console.WriteLine("Try again");
        Console.WriteLine();
    }
}
```

This code lets the user input data values for principle, interest, and loan duration. It relies on a helper method named `InputPositiveDecimal()` that reduces the amount of code needed to obtain the correct information from the user. Instead of writing the same input code three times, you write it only once, making the code easier to understand, debug, and update. Here's the final step of the process:

```
// OutputInterestTable -- Given the principal and interest,
//    generate a future value table for the number of periods
//    indicated in duration. (Implements Section 3.)
public static void OutputInterestTable(decimal principal,
                                       decimal interest,
                                       decimal duration)
{
    for (int year = 1; year <= duration; year++)
    {
        // Calculate the value of the principal plus interest.
        decimal interestPaid;
        interestPaid = principal * (interest / 100);
```

```
        // Now calculate the new principal by adding
        // the interest to the previous principal.
        principal = principal + interestPaid;

        // Round off the principal to the nearest cent.
        principal = decimal.Round(principal, 2);

        // Output the result.
        Console.WriteLine(year + "-" + principal);
    }
}
```

This code makes it possible to output the results of the calculations you perform. It performs the calculations period-by-period until it reaches the end of the loan duration. The `OutputInterestTable()` method contains an output loop with the interest rate calculations. This loop is the same one used in the inline, nonmethod `CalculateInterestTable` program. The advantage of this version, however, is that when writing this section of code, you don't need to concern yourself with any details of inputting or verifying data. When writing this method, think of it this way: "Given the three numbers — `principal`, `interest`, and `duration` — output an interest table," and that's it. After you're done, you can return to the line that called the `OutputInterestTable()` method and continue from there. The final step is to put everything together in the `Main()` method shown here:

```
static void Main(string[] args)
{
    // Section 1 -- Input the data you need to create the table.
    decimal principal = 0M;
    decimal interest = 0M;
    decimal duration = 0M;
    InputInterestData(ref principal, ref interest, ref duration);

    // Section 2 -- Verify the data by mirroring it back to the user.
    Console.WriteLine();  // Skip a line.
    Console.WriteLine("Principal     = " + principal);
    Console.WriteLine("Interest      = " + interest + "%");
    Console.WriteLine("Duration      = " + duration + " years");
    Console.WriteLine();

    // Section 3 -- Finally, output the interest table.
    OutputInterestTable(principal, interest, duration);
    Console.ReadLine();
}
```

The example divides `Main()` into three clearly distinguishable parts, each marked with comments:

- Part 1 calls the method `InputInterestData()` to input the three variables the program needs in order to create the table: `principal`, `interest`, and `duration`.
- Part 2 displays these three values for verification just as earlier versions of the program do.
- Part 3 outputs the table via the method `OutputInterestTable()`.

When you run this application, you see the same prompts and same results as in Book 1, Chapter 5. Here's an example:

```
Enter Principle: 1000
Enter Interest: 5.5
Enter number of years: 5

Principal      = 1000
Interest       = 5.5%
Duration       = 5 years

1-1055.00
2-1113.02
3-1174.24
4-1238.82
5-1306.96
```

Applying a refactoring approach

Refactoring offers a method of cleaning up code that may not be the easiest to read or that doesn't follow the usual requirements for your organization. In this section, you start with the code found in the `CalculateInterestTableMoreForgiving` example in Book 1, Chapter 5 to produce the `CalculateInterestTableWithRefactoring` program.

Obtaining a copy of the Program.cs file

The following steps begin by obtaining a copy of the programming code for use in the new program.

1. **After creating the** `CalculateInterestTableWithRefactoring`**, right-click** `Program.cs` **in Solution Explorer and choose Delete from the context menu.**

You see a dialog box telling you that this action will delete `Program.cs` permanently. Click OK to close it. The copy of `Program.cs` in Solution Explorer disappears.

2. **Right-click the project entry in Solution Explorer and choose Add ➪ Existing Item from the context menu.**

   You see an Add Existing Item dialog box like the one shown in Figure 2-1. Note that this screenshot shows the required `Program.cs` file already selected.

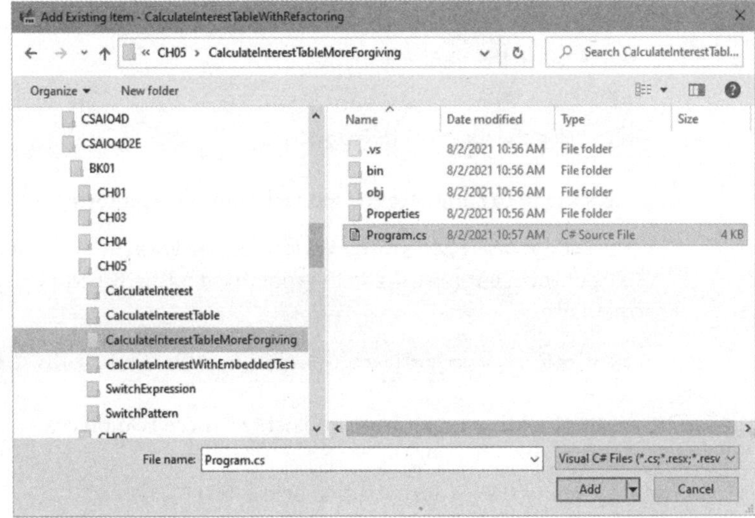

FIGURE 2-1: Obtaining a copy of `Program.cs` from the `CalculateInterestTableMoreForgiving` example.

3. **Locate and highlight the** `Program.cs` **file in the** `\CSAIO4D2E\BK01\CH05\CalculateInterestTableMoreForgiving` **folder. Click Add.**

   A copy of the `Program.cs` file appears in Solution Explorer.

4. **Open** `Program.cs`**.**

   You see the code from Book 1, Chapter 5.

Performing the refactoring

Now that you have a copy of the required `Program.cs` file to use, you can begin refactoring it using the following steps.

1. **Using the example from Book 1, Chapter 5 as a starting point, select the code from the declaration of the** `year` **variable through the end of the** `while` **loop:**

```
int year = 1;                // You grab the loop variable
while (year <= duration)     // and the entire while loop.
```

```
{
  //...
}
```

2. **Choose Edit ➪ Refactor ➪ Extract Method.**

3. **When you see the Rename: New Method dialog box, type OutputInterestTable in the highlighted part of the editing area.**

   Notice that every location where the new method is referenced automatically changes as you type. The proposed signature for the new method begins with the `private static` keywords and includes `principal`, `interest`, and `duration` in parentheses.

```
private static decimal OutputInterestTable(decimal principal,
  decimal interest, int duration)
```

4. **Click Apply to complete the Extract Method refactoring.**

   The code you selected in Step 1 is located below `Main()` and named `OutputInterestTable()`. In the spot that it formerly occupied, you see this method call:

```
principal = OuputInterestTable(principal, interest, duration);
```

The result of all this refactoring consists of these two pieces:

- A new `private static` method below `Main()`, named `OutputInterestTable()`
- The following line of code within `Main()` where the extracted code was:

```
principal = OutputInterestTable(principal, interest, duration);
```

TIP

You can perform additional refactoring to obtain a program appearance much like that found in the previous section. The following steps begin by eliminating redundant code used to enter information. If you look at the original code, you see that there are actually three looping sections for principle, interest, and duration that are duplicates of each other except for prompts, so this is a good place to start refactoring. You can then simplify the input process much as it appears in the previous section. Use these steps to accomplish the task:

1. **Highlight the first `while` loop in the `Main()` method (the one immediately after `decimal principal;`) and choose Edit ➪ Refactor ➪ Extract Method.**

   You see the same Rename: New Method dialog box as before.

2. **Type** InputPositiveDecimal **to create the new method and click Apply.**

   The only problem with this new method is that it's currently specific to the principal variable, which won't save any code.

3. **Choose Edit ⇨ Refactor ⇨ Reorder Parameters.**

   You see the Change Signature dialog box. This dialog box lets you do more than simply change the order of parameters by highlighting a parameter and clicking the up and down arrows. You can also add and remove parameters using it.

4. **Click Add.**

   You see the Add Parameter dialog box.

5. **Type** string **in the Type Name field,** prompt **in the Parameter Name field, and** "Principal" **in the Value field; then click OK.**

   You have created an input parameter of type string, with a name of prompt that has a value of `"Principal"` for this call. More important, the new method is now closer to becoming generic.

6. **Change the first** `Console.write()` **call in** `InputPositiveDecimal()` **to read:** `Console.Write($"Enter {prompt}: ");`**.**

7. **Change the first line of the error message to read:** `Console.WriteLine($"{prompt} cannot be negative");`**.**

   The prompts in the function are now generic. They will work for any of the input variables.

8. **Right-click the** `principal` **variable declaration in** `InputPositiveDecimal()`**, and choose Rename from the context menu. Type** value **and click Apply.**

   The variable used to obtain information from the user prompt is now more generic as well. At this point, you have recreated a form of `InputPositiveDecimal()` from the previous section using refactoring. Even though it doesn't match the hand-coded version perfectly, it's very close.

9. **Replace the second** `while` **loop in** `Main()` **with:** `interest = InputPositiveDecimal("Interest");`**.**

   Make sure you remove the second loop. At this point, you can build and run the application and the results will be the same as before.

Working with local functions

Security is increasingly more difficult to handle in most applications because developers don't really batten things down as they should. For example, if you don't really need to make a method public, keep it private or possibly protected. Starting with C# 7.0, one way to make code more secure is to use local functions. If only one method calls another method, placing the called method inside the calling method will improve security because no one will even see the local function. The `CalculateInterestTableWithLocalMethods` program demonstrates how to perform this task with no loss in functionality.

Begin by using the technique shown in the "Obtaining a copy of the Program.cs file" section, earlier in this chapter, to obtain a copy of the `Program.cs` file from the `CalculateInterestTableWithMethods` program. Open the `Program.cs` file when you're done.

The first change you want to make is to move the `InputPositiveDecimal()` method into the end of the `InputInterestData()` method. Remove `public static` from in front of the `InputPositiveDecimal()` method. Local functions don't normally include these keywords because they're generally private and they follow the host method's static or instance functionality. The updated code will look like this:

```
public static void InputInterestData(ref decimal principal,
                                     ref decimal interest,
                                     ref decimal duration)
{
    // 1a -- Retrieve the principal.
    principal = InputPositiveDecimal("principal");

    // 1b -- Now enter the interest rate.
    interest = InputPositiveDecimal("interest");

    // 1c -- Finally, the duration
    duration = InputPositiveDecimal("duration");

    // InputPositiveDecimal -- Return a positive decimal number
    //    from the keyboard.

    decimal InputPositiveDecimal(string prompt)
    {
        // Keep trying until the user gets it right.
        while (true)
        {
            // Prompt the user for input.
            Console.Write("Enter " + prompt + ":");

            // Retrieve a decimal value from the keyboard.
            string input = Console.ReadLine();
            decimal value = Convert.ToDecimal(input);
```

```
            // Exit the loop if the value that's entered is correct.
            if (value >= 0)
            {
                // Return the valid decimal value entered by the user.
                return value;
            }

            // Otherwise, generate an error on incorrect input.
            Console.WriteLine(prompt + " cannot be negative");
            Console.WriteLine("Try again");
            Console.WriteLine();
        }
    }
}
```

The second change you want to make is to set `public` to `private` for both the `InputInterestData()` and `OutputInterestTable()` methods. You're ready to give the updated program a try. The program will run precisely as before, but now it's a lot more secure.

Having Arguments with Methods

A method such as the following example is about as useful as a snow shovel in July because no data passes into or out of the method:

```
public static void Output()
{
  Console.WriteLine("this is a method");
}
```

Compare this example to real-world methods that *do* something. For example, the mathematical sine operation requires some type of input — after all, you have to calculate the sine of something. Similarly, to concatenate two `strings`, you need two `strings`. So the `Concatenate()` method requires at least two `strings` as input. You need to find a way to move data into and out of a method.

Passing an argument to a method

The values you input to a method are *arguments*. The inputs to a method are *parameters*. Parameters are a complete listing of inputs, some of which can be optional, so the arguments you provide to a method may not match the method's parameter list. Most methods require some type of arguments if they're going to do something. You pass arguments to a method by listing them in the parentheses that follow the method name. Consider this small addition to the earlier Example class provided as the Example2 program:

```
public class Example
{
  ... Other Methods ...

  public static void Output(string someString)
  {
    Console.WriteLine("Output() was passed the argument: " + someString);
  }
}
```

You could invoke this method from within the same class by adding code to Main(), like this:

```
Example.Output("Hello");
```

You'd then see this not-too-exciting output:

```
Output() was passed the argument: Hello
```

The program passes to the method Output() a reference to the string "Hello". The method receives the reference and assigns it the name someString. The Output() method can use someString within the method just as it would use any other string variable. Try adding this code to the end of the code in Main():

```
string myString = "Hello";
Example.Output(myString);
```

This code snippet assigns the variable myString to reference the string "Hello". The call Output(myString) passes the object referenced by myString, which is your old friend "Hello". From there, the effect is the same as before.

A similar idea is passing arguments to a program. For example, you may have noticed that Main() usually takes an array argument.

Passing multiple arguments to methods

You can define a method with multiple arguments of varying types. Consider the following sample method AverageAndDisplay() from the AverageAndDisplay program:

```
// AverageAndDisplay -- Average two numbers with their
//    labels and display the results.
private static void AverageAndDisplay(string s1, double d1,
                                      string s2, double d2)
{
    double average = (d1 + d2) / 2;
    Console.WriteLine($"The average of {s1}"
        + $" whose value is {d1} and {s2}"
        + $" whose value is {d2} is {average}.");
}
```

You call it from `Main()` using this code:

```
static void Main(string[] args)
{
    // Access the member method.
    AverageAndDisplay("grade 1", 3.5, "grade 2", 4.0);
    Console.Read();
}
```

Executing this simple program generates this output:

```
The average of grade 1 whose value is 3.5 and grade 2 whose value is 4 is 3.75.
```

The method `AverageAndDisplay()` is declared with several parameters in the order in which arguments are to be passed to them.

As usual, execution of the sample program begins with the first statement after `Main()`. The first noncomment line in `Main()` invokes the method `AverageAndDisplay()`, passing the two `strings` `"grade 1"` and `"grade 2"` and the two `double` values `3.5` and `4.0`.

The method `AverageAndDisplay()` calculates the average of the two `double` values, `d1` and `d2`, passed to it along with their names contained in `s1` and `s2`, and the calculated average is stored in `average`.

TIP

Changing the value of an argument inside the method can lead to confusion and errors, so be wise and assign the value to a temporary variable and modify it instead.

Matching argument definitions with usage

Each argument in a method call must match the method definition in both type *and order* if you call them without naming them. The following (illegal) version of `Main()` found in `AverageWithCompilerError` generates two build-time errors:

```
static void Main(string[] args)
{
    // Access the member method.
    AverageAndDisplay("grade 1", "grade 2", 3.5, 4.0);
    Console.Read();
}
```

C# can't match the type of each argument in the call to `AverageAndDisplay()` with the corresponding argument in the method definition. The `string`, `"grade 1"`, matches the first `string` in the method definition; however, the method definition calls for a `double` as its second argument rather than the `string` that's passed. Figure 2-2 shows the errors you see when you choose View⇨Error List.

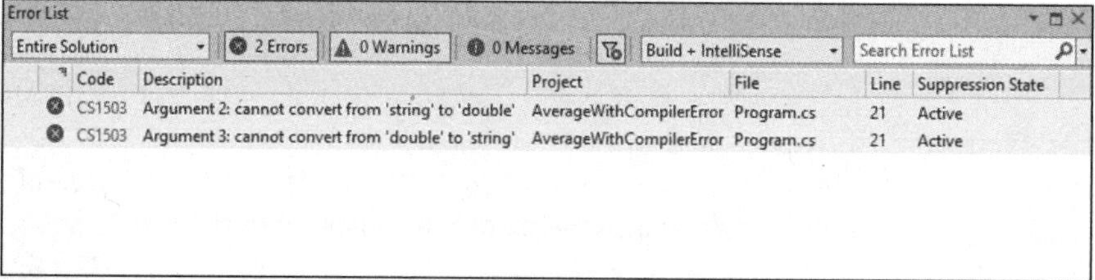

FIGURE 2-2: The IDE will tell you what is wrong with the passing of arguments.

You can easily see that the code transposes the second and third arguments. To fix the problem, swap the second and third arguments.

TIP

Double-clicking an error entry takes you directly to that error in the code. Notice the CS1503 error-code links in Figure 2-2. You can click these links to get additional information about the errors.

Overloading a method doesn't mean giving it too much to do

TIP

You can give two methods within a given class the same name — known as *overloading* the method name — as long as their required parameters differ by type or number. (They can't simply differ in the type or number of optional parameters because the compiler wouldn't be able to tell calls apart.) These two methods in the `AverageAndDisplayOverloaded` example demonstrate overloading:

```
private static void AverageAndDisplay(string s1, double d1,
                                      string s2, double d2)
{
    double average = (d1 + d2) / 2;
    Console.WriteLine($"The average of {s1}"
        + $" whose value is {d1} and\r\n {s2}"
        + $" whose value is {d2} is {average}.\r\n");
}

private static void AverageAndDisplay(double d1, double d2)
{
    double average = (d1 + d2) / 2;
    Console.WriteLine($"The average of {d1} and {d2}"
                + $" is {average}.");
}
```

This program defines two versions of `AverageAndDisplay()`. Notice that the first version uses the `\r\n` escape sequence to create new lines between the outputs, so the outputs are easier to read. You see other escape sequences used in examples throughout the book. The program invokes one and then the other by passing the proper arguments, as shown here:

```
static void Main(string[] args)
{
    // Access the first version of the method.
    AverageAndDisplay("my GPA", 3.5, "your GPA", 4.0);

    // Access the second version of the method.
    AverageAndDisplay(3.5, 4.0);
    Console.Read();
}
```

C# can tell which method the program wants by comparing the call with the definition. The program compiles properly and generates this output when executed:

```
The average of my GPA whose value is 3.5 and
 your GPA whose value is 4 is 3.75.

The average of 3.5 and 4 is 3.75.
```

REMEMBER

C# doesn't allow two methods in the same class to have the same name unless the number or type of the methods' arguments differs (or if both differ). Thus C# differentiates between these two methods:

- » `AverageAndDisplay(string, double, string, double)`
- » `AverageAndDisplay(double, double)`

When you see it that way, it's clear that the two methods are different.

Implementing default arguments

In some cases, a method needs a *default argument*, a predefined value, to make it easier to use. If most of the developers using the method require a particular value, a default value makes sense. Providing a value for the argument then becomes one of flexibility so that developers who need other values still have the option of supplying one. Developers take two common routes:

- » **Method overloading:** The technique shown in the previous section would allow you to create a default argument. You would set the value of the argument that isn't supplied within the body of the method. The problems with this approach are that:
  - It's confusing to anyone reading the code because the purpose for overloading the method is unclear.
  - It's error prone because now you have two or more versions of the same method to maintain.
- » **Default parameters:** C# provides the means to set default arguments as part of the method's parameter list. This technique is clear because anyone looking at the code will see the defaults as part of the method declaration — there is no need to dig into the method code.

Because of the complexity and error-prone nature of using method overloading as a means of handling default arguments, this book always uses the default parameter approach, as shown in the `DisplayRoundedDecimal()` method in the `MethodsWithDefaultArguments` program:

```
static private string DisplayRoundedDecimal(
    decimal value = 0,
    int numberOfSignificantDigits = 2)
{
    // First round off the number to the specified number
    // of significant digits.
```

```
    decimal roundedValue = decimal.Round(
        value, numberOfSignificantDigits);

    // Convert that to a string.
    string s = Convert.ToString(roundedValue);
    return s;
}
```

The `DisplayRoundedDecimal(decimal, int)` method converts the `decimal` value that's provided into a `string` with the specified number of digits after the decimal point using a combination of the `Round()` and `ToString()` methods. Because decimals are often used to display monetary values, the most common choice is to place two digits after the decimal point. Notice the use of the equals sign (=) after each parameter to provide the default values. The default value for `value` is `0`, and the default value for `numberOfSignificantDigits` is `2`. You now have three ways in which to call `DisplayRoundedDecimal()` by employing the default values as shown here:

```
static void Main(string[] args)
{
    // Don't supply any values.
    Console.WriteLine(DisplayRoundedDecimal());

    // Supply just the first value.
    Console.WriteLine(DisplayRoundedDecimal(12.345678M));

    // Provide both values.
    Console.WriteLine(DisplayRoundedDecimal(12.345678M, 3));
    Console.ReadLine();
}
```

The third call is the only one that actually supplies both values, which demonstrates the usefulness of default values. When you hover your cursor over a method with default values, you see these values as part of the pop-up help, as shown in Figure 2-3.

```
string Program.DisplayRoundedDecimal([decimal value = 0], [int numberOfSignificantDigits = 2])
```

FIGURE 2-3: Visual Studio tells you about the default method parameter values.

Here's the output from this example:

```
0
12.35
12.346
```

Using the Call-by-Reference Feature

Many real-world operations create values to return to the caller. For example, `Sin()` accepts an argument and returns the trigonometric sine. A method can return a value to the caller in two ways:

- Using the `return` statement
- Using the *call-by-reference* feature

Most of the preceding examples in the chapter demonstrate the `return` statement approach, so you already know how this approach works. The `Average()` method of the `CallByReference` program demonstrates the call-by-reference feature, as shown here:

```
private static void Average(
    ref double Result,
    double Input1 = 1.0,
    double Input2 = 2.0)
{
    Result = (Input1 + Input2) / 2;
}
```

Notice the addition of the `ref` keyword to this example. When you supply a reference to a variable, rather than the variable's value, the method can change the value of the variable as it appears to the caller. The most common use for a reference variable in this book will be to pass complex variables like structures. However, you can use this technique in situations in which you need to call the Windows API or create complex applications. The discussion at `https://docs.microsoft.com/en-us/dotnet/csharp/language-reference/keywords/ref` tells you more about these advanced topics that aren't covered in the book.

WARNING

A reference variable must always appear as the first variable when you use variables with default values. Otherwise, the compiler will complain. Here is a version of `Main()` that shows how to work with `Average()`:

```
static void Main(string[] args)
{
    // Initialize Result and show it.
    double Result = 0;
    Console.WriteLine(Result);

    // Make the call.
    Average(ref Result, 4.0, 3.0);
```

```
    // Show the change.
    Console.WriteLine(Result);
    Console.ReadLine();
}
```

The code begins by initializing the `Main()` version of `Result` to `0` and then displaying this value on screen. Notice again the use of the `ref` keyword when calling `Average()`. This example supplies two values, but you really don't need to in this case. After the call, `Result` now contains a value of `3.5`, the average of `4.0` and `3.0`. The `Average()` method was able to change `Result` because you passed it by reference.

Defining a Method with No Return Value

Some methods don't need to return a value to the caller. An earlier method, `AverageAndDisplay()`, displays the average of its input arguments but doesn't return that average to the caller. Rather than leave the return type blank, you declare a method such as `AverageAndDisplay()` this way:

```
private void AverageAndDisplay(double, double)
```

The keyword `void`, where the return type is normally used, means *nontype*. That is, the declaration `void` indicates that the `AverageAndDisplay()` method returns no value to the caller. (Regardless, every method declaration specifies a return type, even if it's `void`.)

REMEMBER

A *void method* returns no value. This definition doesn't mean that the method is empty or that it's used for medical or astronautical purposes; it simply refers to the initial keyword. By comparison, a method that returns a value is a *nonvoid method.*

A nonvoid method must pass control back to the caller by executing a `return` followed by the value to return to the caller. A `void` method has no value to return. A `void` method returns when it encounters a `return` with no value attached. Or, by default (if no `return` exists), a `void` method exits automatically when control reaches the closing brace of the method. Consider this `DisplayRatio()` method found in the `VoidMethods` program:

```
private static void DisplayRatio(double numerator,
                                 double denominator)
{
    // If the denominator is zero ...
    if (denominator == 0.0)
```

```
    {
        //  ...output an error message and ...
        Console.WriteLine("The denominator of a ratio cannot be 0");

        //  ...return to the caller.
        return;  // An early return due to the error
    }

    // This code is executed only if denominator is nonzero.
    double ratio = numerator / denominator;
    Console.WriteLine($"The ratio of {numerator}" +
        $" over {denominator} is {ratio}.");
} // If the denominator isn't zero, the method exits here.
```

The `DisplayRatio()` method checks whether the `denominator` value is zero:

- **If the value is zero:** The program displays an error message and returns to the caller without attempting to calculate a ratio. Nothing terrible will happen if you perform the calculation; the result will simply be infinity. However, it's good practice not to provide the user with infinite values when you can help it.
- **If the value is nonzero:** The program displays the ratio. The closed brace immediately following `WriteLine()` is the closed brace of the method `DisplayRatio()` and therefore acts as the return point for the program.

Returning Multiple Values Using Tuples

In versions of C# prior to C# 7.0, every return value was a single object. It could be a really complex object, but it was still a single object. In C# 7.0, you can actually return multiple values using tuples. A tuple is a kind of dynamic array nominally containing two items that you can interpret as a key and value pair (but it isn't strictly required). In C#, you can also create tuples containing more than two items. Many languages, such as Python, use tuples to simplify coding and to make interacting with values considerably easier.

C# 4.*x* actually introduced the concept of a tuple as part of dynamic programming techniques. However, C# 7.0 advances the use of tuples to allow returning multiple values rather than just one object. This book doesn't provide extensive coverage of tuples, but they work so well in returning complex data that you definitely need to know something about this use of tuples.

Using a tuple

A tuple relies on the Tuple data type, which can accept up to seven generic parameters, with the potential for an eighth. The best way to work with tuples is to provide the data types of the variables you plan to provide as part of the declaration. Here's an example of a method that returns a tuple, as found in the UseTuples program:

```
private static Tuple<string, int> getTuple()
{
    // Return a single value using the tuple.
    return new Tuple<string, int>("Hello", 123);
}
```

The code begins by specifying that getTuple() returns a Tuple consisting of two items, a string and an int. You use the new keyword to create an instance of Tuple, specify the data types in angle brackets, <string, int>, and then provide the data values. The getTuple() method effectively returns two values that you can manipulate individually, as shown here:

```
// This is where your program starts.
static void Main(string[] args)
{
    // Obtain a single entry tuple.
    Console.WriteLine(
        getTuple().Item1 + " " + getTuple().Item2);
    Console.Read();
}
```

To access a tuple like this one, you call getTuple(), add a period, and then specify which item to use, Item1 or Item2. This example just demonstrates how tuples work, so it's simple. The output looks like this:

```
Hello 123
```

TIP

Using a tuple lets you return two values without resorting to complex data types or other odd structures. It makes your code simpler when the output requirements fit within the confines of a tuple. For example, when performing certain math operations, you need to return a result and a remainder or the real part and the imaginary part of a complex number.

Relying on the Create() method

An alternative way to create a tuple is to rely on the `Create()` method. The result is the same as when working with the method found in the previous section. Here's an example of using the `Create()` method, as found in the `CreateTuples` program:

```
// Use the Create() method.
var myTuple = Tuple.Create<string, int>("Hello", 123);
Console.WriteLine(myTuple.Item1 + "\t" + myTuple.Item2);
```

This approach isn't quite as safe as using the method shown in the previous section because `myTuple` could end up with anything inside because of the use of `var`. You could further eliminate the `<string, int>` portion of the constructor to force the compiler to ascertain what `myTuple` should receive as input. You can also rely on this shorthand method of creating a tuple (specifically a `ValueTuple`) when using the .NET Framework version 4.7 or above:

```
(string, int) t1 = ("Hello", 123);
Console.WriteLine($"{t1.Item1}\t{t1.Item2}");
```

Creating tuples with more than two items

Tuples can have one to eight items in most cases (see `https://docs.microsoft.com/en-us/dotnet/api/system.tuple-8?view=net-5.0` for details). If you want more than eight items, the eighth item must contain another tuple. Nesting tuples enables you to return an almost infinite number of items, but at some point you really do need to look at the complexity of your code and see whether you can keep the number of return items down. Otherwise, you find that your application executes slowly and uses a lot of resources. Here is an example that uses three Tuples holding three items, each enclosed in an array of Tuples (shown in the `LotsOfTupleItems` program):

```
static Tuple<string, int, bool>[] getTuple()
{
    // Create a new tuple.
    Tuple<string, int, bool>[] aTuple =
    {
        new Tuple<string, int, bool>("One", 1, true),
        new Tuple<string, int, bool>("Two", 2, false),
        new Tuple<string, int, bool>("Three", 3, true)
    };
```

```
    // Return a list of values using the tuple.
    return aTuple;
}
```

The technique follows the same pattern as before. The only difference is that you provide more values for each tuple. It also doesn't matter whether you create a single tuple or a tuple array used as a dataset. Either choice allows you to use up to eight items per tuple. However, there is another option. Here is a version of a tuple available in the .NET Framework version 4.7 and above that contains a lot more than just eight items:

```
var myTuple2 = (1, 2, 3, 4, 5, 6, 7, 8, 9, 10, 11, 12, 13, 14);
Console.WriteLine(myTuple2.Item11);
foreach (var Item in myTuple2.ToString().Split(','))
{
    Console.WriteLine(Item);
}
```

This form of tuple is the `ValueTuple`, and it offers quite a bit of flexibility when you need to return a lot of values from a method. You can't use a `ValueTuple` directly with a `foreach` statement, but you can use a little trickery to make things work by converting it to a string first. In addition, it's a faster way to return data than using a standard tuple. You won't find the `ValueTuple` used in this book, but you can find out more about it at `https://www.dotnetperls.com/valuetuple`. This is just an overview of the `Tuple` type; you can find more information about these types at `https://docs.microsoft.com/en-us/dotnet/csharp/language-reference/builtin-types/value-tuples`.

IN THIS CHAPTER

» Passing an object to a method

» Comparing class and instance methods

» Understanding `this`

» Working with local functions

Chapter 3
Let Me Say This about this

This chapter moves from the static methods emphasized in Chapter 2 in this minibook to the instance methods of a class. Static methods belong to the whole class, and instance methods belong to each instance created from the class. Important differences exist between static and instance class members, such as the passing of objects (no, it's not a matter of objectifying anything — it's just the term used for all sorts of real-world entities, none of which are degraded by the code in this chapter).

You also discover that the keyword `this` identifies the instance, rather than the class as a whole, or properties defined as part of the method or passed to the method. The `this` keyword lets you do all sorts of amazing things.

Chapter 2 also discusses local functions as part of the refactoring process used to make your code more readable. However, you don't have to wait until you refactor your code to use a local function. This chapter discusses their use as part of the code planning process.

REMEMBER

You don't have to type the source code for this chapter manually. In fact, using the downloadable source is a lot easier. You can find the source for this chapter in the `\CSAIO4D2E\BK02\CH03` folder of the downloadable source. See the Introduction for details on how to find these source files.

Passing an Object to a Method

You pass object references as arguments to methods in the same way as you pass value-type variables, with one difference: You always pass objects by reference. The Student class of the PassObject program shows the very simple class used for this example:

```
internal class Student
{
    internal string Name { get; set; }
}
```

TIP

Notice that the Student class is marked as internal. The internal scope allows anything inside the current *assembly* (essentially a package used to deploy code) to see the Student class (such as the Program class where Main() resides), but nothing outside the current assembly can see it. Using this scope makes your code substantially more secure. The "Restricting Access to Class Members" section of Chapter 4 of this minibook tells you more about scope, but it's important to keep security in mind as you create more applications. Otherwise, the Student class is unremarkable — it contains only the auto-implemented Name property.

This example uses two methods to interact with the Student class in addition to Main(), which serves to coordinate activities. Here they are:

```
// OutputName -- Output the student's name.
private static void OutputName(Student student)
{
    // Output current student's name.
    Console.WriteLine($"Student's name is {student.Name}.");
}

// SetName -- Modify the student object's name.
private static void SetName(Student student, string name)
{
    if (name.Length > 1)
        student.Name = name;
    else
        throw new ArgumentException("Blank names not allowed!", "name");
}
```

The OutputName() method displays the Name property using specific formatting. It's common to separate output functionality from flow-control functionality in programs. Using this approach makes it possible to provide multiple output techniques without having to constantly modify the flow-control code. Rewriting less code is better. Notice that both methods rely on the private scope, which is appropriate because nothing outside the Program class needs to see these methods.

REMEMBER

Normally, when you want to change a property value, you simply set it as needed. The SetName() method enforces a particular approach to updating the Name property. The Student class doesn't care if someone provides a blank name, but the SetName() method does. You could perform all sorts of checks this way, such as looking for non-alpha characters in the input that would be associated with certain code exploits. This example simply ensures that the caller provides something other than a blank name. If it detects a blank name, it throws an exception with a helpful message and the name of the bad argument. It's time to look at Main():

```
static void Main(string[] args)
{
    Student student = new Student();

    // Set the name by accessing it directly.
    Console.WriteLine("The first time:");
    student.Name = "Madeleine";
    OutputName(student);

    // Try to supply a bad name.
    Console.WriteLine("\r\nTrying a bad value:");
    try
    {
        SetName(student, "");
        OutputName(student);
    }
    catch (ArgumentException e)
    {
        Console.WriteLine(e.Message);
        Console.WriteLine($"Sent {e.ParamName} \"\" value.");
    }

    // Change the name using a method.
    Console.WriteLine("\r\nAfter being modified:");
    try
    {
        SetName(student, "Willa");
        OutputName(student);
    }
    catch (ArgumentException e)
    {
        Console.WriteLine(e.Message);
        Console.WriteLine($"Sent {e.ParamName} \"\" value.");
    }
    Console.Read();
}
```

The program creates a `student` object. The program first sets the name of the `student` directly and passes the *student object* to the output method `OutputName()`. `OutputName()` displays the name of any `Student` object it receives.

The program then attempts to update the name of the `student` by calling `SetName()` with a blank value. This action causes an exception, which the code then handles. Notice the use of the escaped double quotes (`\"\"`) to provide double quotes in the output. `OutputName()` isn't called in this case because the exception occurs before the call.

The second call to `SetName()` is more successful because the code provides something other than a blank value. Because all reference-type objects are passed by reference in C#, the changes made to `student` are retained in the calling method. When `Main()` outputs the `student` object again, the name has changed, as shown in this bit of code:

```
The first time:
Student's name is Madeleine.

Trying a bad value:
Blank names not allowed!
Parameter name: name
Sent name "" value.

After being modified:
Student's name is Willa.
```

Comparing Static and Instance Methods

A class is supposed to collect the elements that describe a real-world object or concept. For example, a `Vehicle` class may contain vehicle-specific attributes for maximum velocity, weight, and carrying capacity. These kinds of attributes normally appear as instance properties or instance methods. However, a `Vehicle` also has attributes that affect every kind of vehicle: the capability to start and stop and the like. These global attributes normally appear as static properties or methods. The following sections tell how to mix static and instance methods to create better object descriptions.

Employing static properties and methods effectively

Normally, you keep data and behaviors that reflect an object within the class definition. In the previous example, OutputName() and SetName() appeared as part of the Program class, which definitely breaks the Object-Oriented Programming (OOP) encapsulation rules. You could rewrite the Student class from the previous section in a better way, as shown in the StudentClass1 program:

```
internal class Student
{
    private static int _numStudents = 1;

    internal string Name { get; set; }

    internal static void OutputName(Student student)
    {
        Console.WriteLine($"Student's name is {student.Name}.");
    }

    internal static int NumStudents { get => _numStudents; }

    internal static void SetNumStudents(int NumStudents)
    {
        if (NumStudents > 0)
            _numStudents = NumStudents;
        else
            throw new ArgumentOutOfRangeException(
                "Value must be greater than 0", "NumStudents");
    }

    internal static void OutputNumStudents()
    {
        Console.WriteLine($"The number of students is: {_numStudents}.");
    }
}
```

This version of the class focuses on moving OutputName(), which is implemented as a static method, to the class. It directly accesses the instance property Name. The reason you create OutputName() as a static method is that it works just fine for any instance. One instance won't use one version of OutputName(), while another instance uses a completely different version. The resulting confusion of such a scenario would boggle anyone's mind. So, you can combine static methods and instance properties as needed within your application.

You also see a new static property member, NumStudents. The reason you implement NumStudents as a static property, rather than an instance property, is that the number of students at a school will apply to every student equally. Unless some funny stuff is going on, every student will see the same number of students at the school, rather than see some invisible students that only they can see. Accessing _numStudents, which is the field that holds the NumStudents property value, requires a somewhat different form of get accessor because you now have an actual named field. Also notice that _numStudents has a private scope because nothing outside the class needs to access it. Normally, static properties are get-only, so this example provides a specific SetNumStudents() static method to change the value. Notice that this set accessor provides error trapping in the form of an ArgumentOutOfRangeException. Finally, the OutputNumStudents() method outputs the current number of students in a formatted manner. In general, you don't combine static properties with instance methods; you use static methods to access static properties.

The Main() method is changed from the previous example in that it provides access to the new static property. However, this version of Main() is also broken because Name no longer provides any error trapping. Don't worry, this problem gets fixed in the next section. Here is the current Main() code.

```
static void Main(string[] args)
{
    Student student = new Student();

    // Set the number of students.
    try
    {
        Student.SetNumStudents(2);

        // Display the number of students.
        Student.OutputNumStudents();
        Console.WriteLine($"The Number of Students is: " +
            $"{Student.NumStudents}.");
    }
    catch (ArgumentOutOfRangeException e)
    {
        Console.WriteLine(e.Message);
    }

    // Try to supply a bad name.
    Console.WriteLine("\r\nTrying a bad value:");
    try
    {
        student.Name = "";
        Student.OutputName(student);
    }
```

```
        catch (ArgumentException e)
        {
            Console.WriteLine(e.Message);
            Console.WriteLine($"Sent {e.ParamName} \"\" value.");
        }

        // Change the name using a method.
        Console.WriteLine("\r\nAfter being modified:");
        try
        {
            student.Name = "Sally";
            Student.OutputName(student);
        }
        catch (ArgumentException e)
        {
            Console.WriteLine(e.Message);
            Console.WriteLine($"Sent {e.ParamName} \"\" value.");
        }
        Console.Read();
    }
```

This version of `Main()` will form most of the basis for the code in the next section, where you'll see the current problems fixed. For now, supplying a blank name doesn't trigger an error message, as shown here:

```
The number of students is: 2.
The Number of Students is: 2.

Trying a bad value:
Student's name is .

After being modified:
Student's name is Sally.
```

Employing instance properties and methods effectively

Instance properties and methods tend to focus on object elements that differ between instances or are somehow instance-specific. The updated version of the `Student` class found in the `StudentClass2` program shows some interesting changes that make the class work a lot better than the version in the previous section.

```
internal class Student
{
```

```
    private string _name = "";
    private static int _numStudents = 1;

    internal string Name
    {
        get => _name;
        set
        {
            if (value.Length > 1)
                _name = value;
            else
                throw new ArgumentException("Blank names not allowed!",
                    "Name");
        }
    }

    internal static void OutputName(Student student)
    {
        Console.WriteLine($"Student's name is {student.Name}.");
    }

    public override string ToString()
    {
        // Output current student's name.
        return $"Student's name is {Name}.";
    }

    internal static int NumStudents { get => _numStudents; }

    internal static void SetNumStudents(int NumStudents)
    {
        if (NumStudents > 0)
            _numStudents = NumStudents;
        else
            throw new ArgumentOutOfRangeException(
                "Value must be greater than 0", "NumStudents");
    }

    internal static void OutputNumStudents()
    {
        Console.WriteLine($"The number of students is: {_numStudents}.");
    }
}
```

The first thing to notice is that the Name property now uses a field, just as NumStudents does. It's likewise set to have a private scope for reasons of security. The Name property code now includes the same kind of security features as the SetName() method did in the first example, but now it's part of the actual property code, where it belongs. Because of the addition of the _name field, the get accessor also needs to change as shown.

TIP

As you're looking down the list of methods, you notice a law breaker, the ToString() method. The standard ToString() method, which is provided by default with every class, outputs StudentClass.Student, which is singularly uninformative. So, this version of the class defines a new ToString() method by overriding the default version using the override keyword. Because you're overriding an existing method, you must use the same scope that it uses for your override. This is an instance method because you want the string value of the current class instance, rather than the class as a whole. Using this version of ToString(), you can replace Student.OutputName(student); with Console.WriteLine(student.ToString()); in Main(). Using the ToString() approach offers significant advantages, such as being able to modify the string as needed for a specific requirement. Now that the Student class is fixed, you see this output:

```
The number of students is: 2.
The Number of Students is: 2.

Trying a bad value:
Blank names not allowed!
Parameter name: Name
Sent Name "" value.

After being modified:
Student's name is Sally.
Student's name is Sally.
```

Expanding a method's full name

A subtle but important problem exists with the method names found in some applications. To see the problem, consider this sample code snippet:

```
public class Person
{
  public void Address()
  {
    Console.WriteLine("Hi");
  }
}

public class Letter
{
  string address;
```

```
    // Store the address.
    public void Address(string newAddress)
    {
      address = newAddress;
    }
  }
```

Any subsequent discussion of the Address() method is now ambiguous. The Address() method within Person has nothing to do with the Address() method in Letter. If an application needs to access the Address() method, which Address() does it access? The problem lies not with the methods themselves, but rather with the description. In fact, no Address() method exists as an independent entity — only a Person.Address() and a Letter.Address() method. Attaching the class name to the beginning of the method name clearly indicates which method is intended.

This description is quite similar to people's names. At home, you might not ever experience any ambiguity because you're the only person who has your name. However, at work, you might respond to a yell when someone means to attract the attention of another person with the same name as yours. Of course, this is the reason that people resort to using last names. Thus, you can consider Address() to be the first name of a method, with its class as the family name.

Accessing the Current Object

Consider the following Student.SetName() method found in the CurrentObject program:

```
internal class Student
{
    // The name information to describe a student
    private string firstName;
    private string lastName;

    // SetName -- Save name information.
    internal void SetName(string FirstName, string LastName)
    {
        firstName = FirstName;
        lastName = LastName;
    }
```

```
    public override string ToString()
    {
        return $"{firstName} {lastName}";
    }
}

class Program
{
    static void Main(string[] args)
    {
        Student student1 = new Student();
        student1.SetName("Joseph", "Smith");

        Student student2 = new Student();
        student2.SetName("John", "Davis");

        // Show that the students are separate.
        Console.WriteLine(student1.ToString());
        Console.WriteLine(student2.ToString());
        Console.ReadLine();
    }
}
```

The method `Main()` uses the `SetName()` method to update first `student1` and then `student2`. But you don't see a reference to either `Student` object within `SetName()` itself. In fact, no reference to a `Student` object exists. An instance method is said to operate on the *current object* (the one in use now) in this case. How does a method know which one is the current object? Will the real current object please stand up? The answer is simple. The current object is passed as an implicit argument in the call to a method. For example:

```
student1.SetName("Joseph", "Smith");
```

This call is equivalent to the following:

```
Student.SetName(student1, "Joseph", "Smith"); // Equivalent call,
                                              // (but this won't build properly).
```

The example isn't saying that you can invoke `SetName()` in two different ways; just that the two calls are semantically equivalent. The object identifying the current object — the hidden first argument — is passed to the method, just as other arguments are. Leave that task to the compiler.

Passing an object implicitly is easy to swallow, but what about a reference from one method to another? The following code snippet (found in `CurrentObject2`) illustrates calling one method from another:

```
internal class Student
{
    // The name information to describe a student
    private string firstName;
    private string lastName;

    // SetName -- Save name information.
    internal void SetName(string FirstName, string LastName)
    {
        SetFirstName(FirstName);
        SetLastName(LastName);
    }

    private void SetFirstName(string FirstName)
    {
        firstName = FirstName;
    }

    private void SetLastName(string LastName)
    {
        lastName = LastName;
    }

    public override string ToString()
    {
        return $"{firstName} {lastName}";
    }
}
```

No object appears in the call to `SetFirstName()`. The current object continues to be passed along silently from one method call to the next. An access to any member from within an object method is assumed to be with respect to the current object. The upshot is that a method knows which object it belongs to. *Current object* (or *current instance*) means something like *me*.

What is the this keyword?

Unlike most arguments, the current object doesn't appear in the method argument list, so it isn't assigned a name by the programmer. Instead, C# assigns this object the less-than-imaginative name `this`, which is useful in the few situations in which you need to refer directly to the current object. Thus you could write the previous example this way (as shown in `CurrentObject3`):

```
internal class Student
{
    // The name information to describe a student
    private string firstName;
    private string lastName;

    // SetName -- Save name information.
    internal void SetName(string FirstName, string LastName)
    {
        this.SetFirstName(FirstName);
        this.SetLastName(LastName);
    }

    private void SetFirstName(string FirstName)
    {
        this.firstName = FirstName;
    }

    private void SetLastName(string LastName)
    {
        this.lastName = LastName;
    }

    public override string ToString()
    {
        return $"{firstName} {lastName}";
    }
}
```

Notice the explicit addition of the keyword `this`. Adding it to the member references doesn't add anything because `this` is assumed. However, when `Main()` makes the following call, `this` references `student1` throughout `SetName()` and any other method it may call:

```
student1.SetName("John", "Smith");
```

When is the this keyword explicit?

You don't normally need to refer to `this` explicitly because it is understood where necessary by the compiler. However, two common cases require `this`. You may need it when initializing data members, as in this example:

```
internal class Person
{
  private string name;  // This is this.name below.
  private int id;       // And this is this.id below.
```

```
    internal void Init(string name, int id)  // These are method arguments.
    {
      this.name = name;  // Argument names same as data member names
      this.id = id;
    }
  }
```

The parameters in the `Init()` method declaration are named `name` and `id`, which match the names of the corresponding data members. The method is then easy to read because you know immediately which argument is stored where. The only problem is that the name `name` in the argument list obscures the name of the data member. The compiler complains about it.

REMEMBER

The addition of `this` clarifies which `name` is intended. Within `Init()`, the variable `name` refers to the method parameter, but `this.name` refers to the `name` field. Of course, the best way to avoid needing to use `this` in this example is to ensure that the field name differs from the parameter name, which is considered good coding practice now. Using `this` is likely not required in most instances where a developer uses good variable name choices and proper scoping.

Using Local Functions

Even with all the methods of making code smaller and easier to work with that you have seen so far, sometimes a method might prove complex and hard to read anyway. A local function enables you to declare a function within the scope of a method to help promote further encapsulation. You use this approach when you need to perform a task a number of times within a method, but no other method within the application performs this particular task. The "Working with local functions" section of Chapter 2 of this minibook provides a refactored view of local functions. The following sections tell you more about local functions as part of an original code design.

Creating a basic local function

Here's a simple example of a local function that you can also find in `BasicLocalFunction`:

```
static void Main(string[] args)
{
   //Create a local function
   int Sum(int x, int y) { return x + y; }
```

```
    // Use the local function to output some sums.
    Console.WriteLine(Sum(1, 2));
    Console.WriteLine(Sum(5, 6));
    Console.Read();
}
```

The `Sum()` method is relatively simple, but it demonstrates how a local function could work. The function encapsulates some code that only `Main()` uses. Because `Main()` performs the required task more than once, using `Sum()` makes sense to make the code more readable, easier to understand, and easier to maintain.

TIP

Local functions have all the functionality of any method except that you can't declare them as static in most cases (you have the option of declaring them static when using C# 8.0 or later—the article at `https://www.telerik.com/blogs/c-8-static-local-functions-and-using-declarations` provides some additional information on this topic). A local function has access to all the variables found within the enclosing method, so if you need a variable found in `Main()`, you can access it from `Sum()`.

Using attributes with local functions

C# 9.0 introduces the ability to use attributes with local functions. An *attribute* is a special code decorator that defines how and when a particular piece of code should interact with the rest of the application. This section discusses a couple of simple examples using the `LocalFunctionWithAttributes` program. Before you move forward, however, make sure to add the required C# 9.0 to your `.csproj` file when writing the code on your own, rather than using the downloadable source (which already has all of the required additions for you). You also add this `using` statement to the top of the `Program.cs` file:

```
using System.Diagnostics;
```

The example uses two attributes, as shown in the following code:

```
class Program
{
    static void Main(string[] args)
    {
        //Create a debug local function
        [Obsolete]
        [Conditional("DEBUG")]
        static void DebugInfo(int x, int y)
        {
            Console.WriteLine($"Input x: {x}\r\nInput y: {y}");
        }
```

```
        static int Sum(int x, int y) { return x + y; }

        // Use the local function to output some sums.
        Console.WriteLine(Sum(1, 2));
        DebugInfo(1, 2);
        Console.WriteLine(Sum(5, 6));
        DebugInfo(5, 6);
        Console.Read();
    }
}
```

The `[Obsolete]` attribute tells the compiler that this particular function is still included in the code, but that the developer plans to deprecate it at some point. When the user compiles the code, the following warning appears in the Error List window for each use of the local function:

```
Warning   CS0612   'DebugInfo(int, int)' is obsolete
```

The `[Conditional("DEBUG")]` attribute tells the compiler to add the function into the debug builds of the application only. Both the function and the call to the function are removed from the release version of the application. Consequently, when in debug mode, you see this output:

```
3
Input x: 1
Input y: 2
11
Input x: 5
Input y: 6
```

REMEMBER

There are special requirements for using the `[Conditional]` attribute (`https://docs.microsoft.com/en-us/dotnet/api/system.diagnostics.conditionalattribute`) on local functions:

- You must declare the function as static.
- The function can't return a value.
- You must be using C# 9.0 or later.

Different attributes will have different requirements for use, so it pays to spend some time determining just how you plan to use the attribute. For example, the `[Obsolete]` attribute works on any local function, so you don't need to do anything special to use it. The [Obsolete] attribute provides considerable additional functionality, which you can read about at `https://docs.microsoft.com/en-us/dotnet/api/system.obsoleteattribute`.

IN THIS CHAPTER

» Protecting a class

» Working with class constructors

» Constructing static or class members

» Working with expression-bodied members

Chapter 4
Holding a Class Responsible

A class must be held responsible for its actions. Just as a microwave oven shouldn't burst into flames if you press the wrong key, so a class shouldn't allow itself to roll over and die when presented with incorrect data.

To be held responsible for its actions, a class must ensure that its initial state is correct and then control its subsequent state so that it remains valid. C# provides both these capabilities. This chapter discusses how to make your classes responsible members of the code community. After all, you wouldn't want to design a renegade class that runs amok and creates chaos.

REMEMBER

You don't have to type the source code for this chapter manually. In fact, using the downloadable source is a lot easier. You can find the source for this chapter in the `\CSAIO4D2E\BK02\CH04` folder of the downloadable source. See the Introduction for details on how to find these source files.

Restricting Access to Class Members

As you saw in previous chapters of this minibook, best practice for defining classes is to ensure that each member only provides the level of visibility absolutely required by other class members. Making everything private is the best idea when you can achieve this level of hiding (which definitely isn't always possible). Consider a BankAccount program that maintains a balance data member to retain the balance in each account. Making that data member public puts everyone on the honor system.

Most banks aren't nearly so forthcoming as to leave a pile of money and a register for you to mark down every time you add money to or take money away from the pile. After all, you may forget to mark your withdrawals in the register. Controlling access avoids little mistakes, such as forgetting to mark a withdrawal here or there, and manages to avoid some truly big mistakes with withdrawals. The following sections provide you with techniques for maintaining control over how other developers interact with the classes you create.

A public example of public BankAccount

The BankAccount example declares all its methods public but declares its data members, including _accountNumber and _balance, as private. The example leaves the variables in an incorrect state to make a point. The following code contains the BankAccount class uses for the example:

```
// BankAccount -- Define a class that represents a simple account.
public class BankAccount
{
    private static int _nextAccountNumber = 1000;
    private int _accountNumber;

    // Maintain the balance as a double variable.
    private double _balance;

    // Init -- Initialize a bank account with the next
    //    account id and a balance of 0.
    public void InitBankAccount()
    {
        _accountNumber = ++_nextAccountNumber;
        _balance = 0.0;
    }

    // Balance property only obtains a balance.
    public double Balance
        { get => _balance; }

    // AccountNumber property
    public int AccountNumber
        { get => _accountNumber; set => _accountNumber = value; }
```

```
    // Deposit -- Any positive deposit is allowed.
    public void Deposit(double amount)
    {
        if (amount > 0.0)
        {
            _balance += amount;
        }
    }

    // Withdraw -- You can withdraw any amount up to the
    //    balance; return the amount withdrawn.
    public double Withdraw(double withdrawal)
    {
        if (_balance <= withdrawal)
        {
            withdrawal = _balance;
        }
        _balance -= withdrawal;
        return withdrawal;
    }

    // Return the account data as a string.
    public override string ToString()
    {
        return $"{AccountNumber} = {Balance:C}";
    }
}
```

The BankAccount class provides an InitBankAccount() method to initialize the members of the class, a Deposit() method to handle deposits, and a Withdraw() method to perform withdrawals. The Deposit() and Withdraw() methods even provide some rudimentary rules, such as "You can't deposit a negative number" and "You can't withdraw more than you have in your account" (both good rules for a bank, as I'm sure you'll agree). However, everyone would be on the honor system if _balance were accessible to external methods, which is why you make it private. (In this context, *external* means external to the class but within the same program.) The honor system can be a problem on big programs written by teams of programmers. It can even be a problem for you (and me), given general human fallibility. Here's the Main() method, which exercises this code:

```
static void Main(string[] args)
{
    Console.WriteLine("This program doesn't compile.");

    // Open a bank account.
    Console.WriteLine("Create a bank account object");
    BankAccount ba = new BankAccount();
    ba.InitBankAccount();
```

Holding a Class Responsible

```
    // Accessing the balance via the Deposit() method is okay --
    // Deposit() has access to all the data members.
    ba.Deposit(10);

    // Accessing the data member directly is a compile-time error.
    Console.WriteLine("Just in case you get this far the following is "
                + "supposed to generate a compile error");
    ba._balance += 10;
    Console.Read();
}
```

All that Main() does is create a new bank account, initialize it, then add money to it. Notice the attempt to access `_balance` directly using `ba._balance += 10;`.

REMEMBER

Well-written code with rules that the compiler can enforce saves everyone from the occasional bullet to the big toe. Before you get too excited, however, notice that the program doesn't build. Attempts to do so generate this error message:

```
'BankAccount.BankAccount._balance' is inaccessible due to its protection level.
```

The error message seems a bit hard to understand because that's how error messages are, for the most part (writing a truly understandable error message is incredibly tough). The crux of the problem is that `_balance` is private, which means no one can see it. The statement `ba._balance += 10;` is illegal because `_balance` isn't accessible to `Main()`, a method outside the `BankAccount` class. Replacing this line with `ba.Deposit(10);` solves the problem. The `BankAccount.Deposit()` method is public and therefore accessible to `Main()` and other parts of your program.

REMEMBER

The default access type is `private`. Not declaring a class member's access type explicitly is the same as declaring it `private`. However, you should include the `private` keyword to remove any doubt. Good programmers make their intentions explicit, which is another way to reduce errors.

Jumping ahead — other levels of security

WARNING

Understanding this section depends on your having some knowledge of inheritance (see Chapter 6 in this minibook) and namespaces (see Chapter 9 in this minibook). You can skip this section for now if you want, but just know that it's here when you need it. C# provides these levels of security:

- A `public` member is accessible to any class in the program.
- A `private` member is accessible only from the current class.

» A `protected` member is accessible from the current class and any of its subclasses.

» An `internal` member is accessible from any class within the same program module or assembly.

A C# *module*, or *assembly*, is a separately compiled piece of code, either an executable program in an `.EXE` file or a supporting library module in a `.DLL` file. A single namespace can extend across multiple assemblies. (Chapter 9 in this minibook explains C# assemblies and namespaces and discusses access levels other than `public` and `private`.)

» An `internal protected` member is accessible from the current class and any subclass, and from classes within the same module.

» A `private protected` member is accessible by code in the same assembly by code in the same class or by a type that is derived from that class.

Keeping a member hidden by declaring it `private` offers the maximum amount of security. However, in many cases, you don't need that level of security. After all, the members of a subclass already depend on the members of the base class, so `protected` offers a comfortable level of security.

Why You Should Worry about Access Control

Declaring the internal members of a class `public` is a bad idea for at least these reasons:

» **With all data members `public`, you can't easily determine when and how data members are being modified.** Why bother building safety checks into the `Deposit()` and `Withdraw()` methods? In fact, why even bother with these methods? Any method of any class can modify these elements at any time. If other methods can access these data members, they almost certainly will.

Your `BankAccount` program may execute for an hour or so before you notice that one of the accounts has a negative balance. The `Withdraw()` method would have ensured that this situation didn't happen, so obviously another method accessed the balance without going through `Withdraw()`. Figuring out which method is responsible and under which conditions is a difficult problem.

» **Exposing all data members of the class makes the interface too complicated.** As a programmer using the `BankAccount` class, you don't want to know about the internal workings of the class. You just need to know that you can deposit and withdraw funds. It's like a candy machine that has 50 buttons versus one with just a few buttons — the ones you need.

» **Exposing internal elements leads to a distribution of the class rules.** For example, my `BankAccount` class doesn't allow the balance to be negative under any circumstances. That required business rule should be isolated within the `Withdraw()` method. Otherwise, you have to add this check everywhere the balance is updated.

  Sometimes a bank decides to change the rules so that valued customers are allowed to carry slightly negative balances for a short period, to avoid unintended overdrafts. Then you have to search through the program to update every section of code that accesses the balance, to ensure that the safety checks are changed.

TIP

Make your classes and methods no more accessible than necessary. This advice isn't meant to cause paranoia about snoopy hackers so much as it is to suggest a prudent step that helps reduce errors as you code. Use `private`, if possible, and then escalate to `protected`, `private protected`, `internal`, `internal protected`, or `public` as necessary.

Accessor methods

If you look more carefully at the `BankAccount` class, you see a few other methods. One, `ToString()`, returns a `string` version of the account fit for presentation to any `Console.WriteLine()` for display. However, displaying the contents of a `BankAccount` object may be difficult if its contents are inaccessible. The class should have the right to decide how it is displayed.

In addition, you see two *getter* methods and one *setter* method in the form of the `Balance` and `AccountNumber` properties. You may wonder why it's important to declare a data member such as `_balance` as `private`, but to provide a `public Balance` property to return its value:

» `Balance` **doesn't provide a way to modify `_balance` — it merely returns its value.** The balance is read-only. To use the analogy of an actual bank, you can look at your balance any time you want; you just can't withdraw money from your account without using the bank's withdrawal mechanism.

» `Balance` **hides the internal format of the class from external methods.** `Balance` may perform an extensive calculation by reading receipts, adding account charges, and accounting for any other amounts your bank may want to subtract from your balance. External methods don't know and don't care. Of course, you care which fees are being charged — you just can't do anything about them, short of changing banks.

Finally, `Balance` provides a mechanism for making internal changes to the class without the need to change the interface seen by users of `BankAccount`. If the Federal Deposit Insurance Corporation (FDIC) mandates that your bank store deposits differently, the mandate shouldn't change the way you access your account.

Working with init-only setters

C# 9.0 introduces a new technique for working with properties where you can set the property only once, but then the property becomes *immutable* (unchangeable). Having immutable properties is good when you don't want to allow changes beyond that initial setup, such as the identification numbers of club members. The member receives an identifier once, but then retains that identifier permanently. The `CreditMember` class in the `InitOnly` example shows how a class for quickly identifying the credit limit of a club member might work.

```
internal class CreditMember
{
    internal int Id { get; init; }
    internal string Name { get; set; }
    internal decimal Limit { get; set; }

    public override string ToString()
    {
        return $"{Name}, member ID {Id}, has a " +
            $"limit of {Limit:C}";
    }

    internal protected CreditMember(int MemberId)
    {
        Id = MemberId;
    }
}
```

The code shows three properties, an override for `ToString()`, and something new, a constructor. A *constructor* builds an object based on the blueprint provided by the class description. You find out more about them in the "Getting Your Objects Off to a Good Start — Constructors" section of this chapter. The constructor has an access level of `internal protected` so that any class that inherits this class also inherits the constructor.

REMEMBER

Notice also that the `Id` property has a substitution for `set;` in the form of `init;`. This entry means that you can set the property once during initialization, but not afterward. This is the reason that the constructor sets the `Id` property value. To make the functionality work from a standard Windows console application, you must add the following code right after the `using` statements in the application, but before the `namespace InitOnly` declaration:

```
namespace System.Runtime.CompilerServices
{
    internal static class IsExternalInit { }
}
```

The code that appears here doesn't actually do anything — it simply gets rid of the compiler error message. An alternative solution to including this code is to create a .NET Core application, instead of a .NET Framework console application, as shown in the `InitOnly2` program. Note that you must select .NET 6.0 (Current) in the Target Framework field of the Console Application Wizard. Book 5 Chapter 5 tells you more about .NET Core applications.

The `Main()` method instantiates the `CreditMember` object, `Sam`, and then sets values in it. Afterward, it prints out the `Sam` object information. Here's the short code to test the `InitOnly` program.

```
static void Main(string[] args)
{
    CreditMember Sam = new CreditMember(1);
    Sam.Name = "Sam Jones";
    Sam.Limit = 5000;

    Console.WriteLine(Sam.ToString());
    Console.ReadLine();
}
```

If you were to attempt to set Id at this point, you'd see an error message telling you that you can't. Since this is a C# 9.0 example, you must add the following entry to the `InitOnly.csproj` file:

```
<PropertyGroup>
   <LangVersion>9.0</LangVersion>
</PropertyGroup>
```

When you run this program, you see this output:

```
Sam Jones, member ID 1, has a limit of $5,000.00
```

Access control to the rescue — an example

The following DoubleBankAccount program demonstrates a potential flaw in the BankAccount program. The following listing shows Main() — the only portion of the program that differs from the earlier BankAccount program:

```
static void Main(string[] args)
{
    // Open a bank account.
    Console.WriteLine("Create a bank account object");
    BankAccount ba = new BankAccount();
    ba.InitBankAccount();

    // Make a deposit.
    double deposit = 123.454;
    Console.WriteLine($"Depositing {deposit:C}");
    ba.Deposit(deposit);

    // Account balance
    Console.WriteLine(ba.ToString());

    // Here's the problem.
    double fractionalAddition = 0.002;
    Console.WriteLine($"Adding {fractionalAddition:C}");
    ba.Deposit(fractionalAddition);

    // Resulting balance
    Console.WriteLine(ba.ToString());
    Console.Read();
}
```

The Main() method creates a bank account and then deposits $123.454, an amount that contains a fractional number of cents. Main() then deposits a small fraction of a cent to the balance and displays the resulting balance. The output from this program appears this way:

```
Create a bank account object
Depositing $123.45
Account = #1001 = $123.45
Adding $0.00
Resulting account = #1001 = $123.46
```

Users start to complain: "I just can't reconcile my checkbook with my bank statement." Apparently, the program has a bug.

The problem, of course, is that $123.454 shows up as $123.45. To avoid the problem, the bank decides to round deposits and withdrawals to the nearest cent.

Deposit $123.454 and the bank takes that extra 0.4 cent. On the other side, the bank gives up enough 0.4 amounts that everything balances out in the long run. Well, in theory, it does.

The easiest way to solve the rounding problem is by converting the bank accounts to `decimal` and using the `Decimal.Round()` method, as shown in `BankAccount` class of the `DecimalBankAccount` program:

```
// BankAccount -- Define a class that represents a simple account.
internal class BankAccount
{
    private static int _nextAccountNumber = 1000;
    private int _accountNumber;

    // Maintain the balance as a double variable.
    private decimal _balance;

    // Init -- Initialize a bank account with the next
    //    account id and a balance of 0.
    internal protected void InitBankAccount()
    {
        _accountNumber = ++_nextAccountNumber;
        _balance = 0.0M;
    }

    // Balance property only obtains a balance.
    internal decimal Balance
        { get => _balance; }

    // AccountNumber property
    internal int AccountNumber
        { get => _accountNumber; set => _accountNumber = value; }

    // Deposit -- Any positive deposit is allowed.
    internal void Deposit(decimal amount)
    {
        if (amount > 0.0M)
        {
            // Round off the double to the nearest cent before depositing.
            decimal temp = amount;
            temp = Decimal.Round(temp, 2);

            _balance += temp;
        }
    }

    // Withdraw -- You can withdraw any amount up to the
    //    balance; return the amount withdrawn.
    internal decimal Withdraw(decimal withdrawal)
```

```
    {
        decimal temp = withdrawal;
        temp = Decimal.Round(temp, 2);

        if (_balance <= temp)
        {
            temp = _balance;
        }
        _balance -= temp;
        return temp;
    }

    // Return the account data as a string.
    public override string ToString()
    {
        return $"{AccountNumber} = {Balance:C}";
    }
}
```

This version of the example changes all internal representations to `decimal` values, a type better adapted to handling bank account balances than `double` in any case. The `Deposit()` and `Withdrawal()` methods now use the `Decimal.Round()` method to round the deposit amount to the nearest cent before making the deposit. Notice that the access levels are now appropriately set for this class. Note that you must also change `Main()` to use the correct data types, but the compiler will warn you about that issue. The output from the program is now as expected:

```
Create a bank account object
Depositing $123.45
Account = #1001 = $123.45
Adding $0.00
Resulting account = #1001 = $123.45
```

Defining Class Properties

C# defines a construct known as a *property*, a method-like construction that allows safe access to data fields within a class. The field contains the actual variable; the property provides access to that variable. You have already seen properties used in the `BankAccount` class examples in this chapter and in other examples in previous chapters. C# supports a number of property constructions that include:

- **Backing fields:** This is an older style of property that doesn't use any shortcuts. It actually provides a getter and/or setter method that interacts with the underlying field directly such as:

  ```
  private int _myProp = 0;
  internal int MyProp
  {
      get { return _myProp; }
      set { _myProp = value; }
  }
  ```

  This form of property is useful when you need to perform data manipulations as part of working with the underlying field. For example, the property might handle time values in hours, but represent them internally as milliseconds, so you need to modify the values during the setting and getting process.

- **Expression body:** You can use this form to assign an expression to the getter and setter. This shortcut method works well for many purposes. It uses the => operator to define the division between the getter or setter and the expression. You usually see it used something like this:

  ```
  private int _myProp = 0;
  internal int MyProp
      { get => _myProp; set => _myProp = value; }
  ```

  When using this form, the expression can be more complex than just a variable and the getter need not be specifically included if the property has only a setter, such as this form:

  ```
  private string _firstName = "John";
  private string _lastName = "Smith";
  internal string Name => $"{_firstName} {_lastName}";
  ```

- **Auto-implemented:** This is the shortest way to create a property, but also allows the least flexibility. You don't even have to provide a private variable to use it. This version looks like this:

  ```
  internal int MyProp
      { get; set; }
  ```

TIP

By convention, the name of a property begins with a capital letter. Note that properties don't have parentheses: It's `Balance`, not `Balance()`.

TECHNICAL STUFF

Properties aren't necessarily inefficient. The C# compiler can optimize a simple accessor to the point that it generates no more machine code than accessing the data member directly does. This concept is important, not only to an application program but also to C# itself. The C# library uses properties throughout, and you should, too. Use properties to access class data members, even from methods in the same class.

Static properties

A static (class) data member may be exposed through a static property, as shown in this simplistic example (note its compact layout):

```
public class BankAccount
{
  private static int _nextAccountNumber = 1000;
  public static int NextAccountNumber { get {return _nextAccountNumber += 1; }}
  // ...
}
```

The `NextAccountNumber` property is accessed through the class as follows because it isn't an instance property (it's declared static):

```
// Read the account number property.
int value = BankAccount.NextAccountNumber;
```

(In this example, `value` is outside the context of a property, so it isn't a reserved word.)

Properties with side effects

A `get` operation can perform extra work other than simply retrieving the associated property, as shown here:

```
public static int AccountNumber
{
  // Retrieve the property and set it up for the
  // next retrieval by incrementing it.
  get { return ++_nextAccountNumber; }
}
```

This property increments the static account number member before returning the result. This action probably isn't a good idea, however, because the user of the property receives no clue that anything is happening other than the actual reading of the property. Incrementing `_nextAccountNumber` is a side effect.

REMEMBER

Like the accessor methods that they mimic, properties shouldn't change the state of the class other than, say, setting a data member's value. Both properties and methods generally should avoid side effects because they can lead to subtle bugs. Change a class as directly and explicitly as possible.

Accessors with access levels

It's usually a good idea to declare properties (when possible) as something other than `public`. You can declare them at any appropriate level, even `private`, if the accessor is used only inside its class. (The upcoming example marks the `Name` property `internal`, which is the best option for classes that aren't part of a library or API and only used within the host application.)

You can even adjust the access levels of the `get` and `set` portions of an accessor individually. Suppose that you don't want to expose the `set` accessor outside your class — it's for internal use only. You can write the property like this:

```
internal string Name { get; private set; }
```

Using Target Typing for Your Convenience

Target typing refers to the ability of the compiler to derive the appropriate type for a variable based on context, rather than actual code. You see it used relatively often, but C# 9.0 provides two new ways to use target typing. The first way is when you declare variables, such as in a list. It's no longer necessary to work your fingers to the bone; let the compiler do the heavy lifting. The following class and enumeration appear in the `TargetType1` program and provide the means for testing what target typing means in this case (note that you must configure the application to use C# 9.0 by modifying the `.csproj` file):

```
internal enum FoodGroups
{
    Meat,
    Vegetables,
    Fruit,
    Grain,
    Dairy
}

internal class MyFavorteFoods
{
    internal int Rank { get; set; }
```

```
    internal string Name { get; set; }
    internal FoodGroups Group { get; set; }

    public MyFavorteFoods(int Position,
        string Food, FoodGroups Category)
    {
        Rank = Position;
        Name = Food;
        Group = Category;
    }
}
```

The example class is simple—it provides three properties, one of which relies on the `FoodGroups` enumeration, and a constructor to instantiate objects. Notice that the constructor is `public` to ensure proper access. Here's the `Main()` code used to work with the class:

```
static void Main(string[] args)
{
    var Foods = new List<MyFavorteFoods>
    {
        new (1, "Apples", FoodGroups.Fruit),
        new (2, "Steaks", FoodGroups.Meat),
        new (3, "Asparagus", FoodGroups.Vegetables)
    };

    foreach (MyFavorteFoods Item in Foods)
        Console.WriteLine($"Food #{Item.Rank} is {Item.Name} " +
            $"of {Item.Group} food category.");
    Console.ReadLine();
}
```

The most important thing you should notice is that the `Foods` list construction doesn't require any type information. The compiler automatically provides the correct type. When you run this application, you see the following output:

```
Food #1 is Apples of Fruit food category.
Food #2 is Steaks of Meat food category.
Food #3 is Asparagus of Vegetables food category.
```

The second case is with conditional compilation situations. Again, the easiest way to understand how this works is to see an example. The `TargetType2` example begins with the `MyFavorteFoods` class found in the `TargetType1` example. To see how things work, you create two derived classes as shown here (again, ensuring your project supports C# 9.0):

```
internal class MyLuxuryFoods : MyFavorteFoods
{
    internal decimal HowMuch { get; set; }

    public MyLuxuryFoods(int Position,
        string Food, FoodGroups Category, decimal Cost) :
        base(Position, Food, Category)
    {
        HowMuch = Cost;
    }
}

internal class MyComfortFoods: MyFavorteFoods
{
    internal string HowOften { get; set; }
    public MyComfortFoods(int Position,
        string Food, FoodGroups Category, string Time) :
        base(Position, Food, Category)
    {
        HowOften = Time;
    }
}
```

Both subclasses rely on `MyFavorteFoods` as a starting point. However, they both add something different. Generally, you couldn't use these two classes with the `??` null-coalescing operator. However, the following code does work with C# 9.0:

```
static void Main(string[] args)
{
    MyLuxuryFoods GreatFood = new MyLuxuryFoods(
        1, "Salmon", FoodGroups.Meat, 35.95M);
    MyComfortFoods SatisfyingFood = new MyComfortFoods(
        1, "Oatmeal", FoodGroups.Grain, "Weekly");
    MyFavorteFoods Choice = GreatFood ?? SatisfyingFood;
    Console.WriteLine(Choice.Name);
    Console.ReadLine();
}
```

So, you might wonder what `MyFavorteFoods Choice = GreatFood ?? SatisfyingFood;` actually means. If `GreatFood` is available, then eat it, otherwise, eat `SatisfyingFood`. So, if you were to add `GreatFood = null;` before instantiating `Choice`, the output would be `Oatmeal` instead of `Salmon`.

Dealing with Covariant Return Types

A *covariant return type* is one in which you can return a type that is more detailed (at a lower level in the class hierarchy) than the type that would normally be returned. This particular feature only works if you use the .NET Core version of the Console Application template and select .NET 6.0 in the Target Framework field of the wizard. The best way to understand how this feature works is to look at an example. The CovariantReturn program provides a basic example that focuses on the C# record type (https://docs.microsoft.com/en-us/dotnet/csharp/whats-new/tutorials/records). The following code shows the class hierarchy:

```
public abstract record Number
    { public int Value { get; set; } }

public abstract record BadgeNumber
    { public virtual Number Id { get; } }

public record EmployeeID : Number
    { public string FullName { get; set; } }

public record ThisPerson : BadgeNumber
{
    public ThisPerson(int Identifier, string Name)
    {
        Id = new EmployeeID
        {
            FullName = Name,
            Value = Identifier
        };
    }

    public override Number Id { get; }
}
```

The example begins with a base type, Number, which contains a single property, Value, of type int. The second base type, BadgeNumber, also contains a single property, but this one is virtual and it uses Number as its type. Both of these base types are abstract (https://docs.microsoft.com/en-us/dotnet/csharp/language-reference/keywords/abstract), which means you can't instantiate them.

The next two types are derived from Number and BadgeNumber. EmployeeID adds a new property, FullName, of type string. This means that EmployeeID contains two properties: Value and FullName.

The magic of covariant return types makes its appearance in `ThisPerson`. Notice that `ThisPerson` has a constructor and initializes the `Id` property found in `BadgeNumber` to an `EmployeeID`, rather than to an `int`. So, `Id` now contains a more detailed type than originally expected. The `ThisPerson` record also contains a property that returns `Id` as type `Number`, rather than type `int`, as you might expect. So, how does this all work? Is it mumbo jumbo or real code? The `Main()` method demonstrates it does work in C# 9.0 when using the .NET 6.0 framework:

```
static void Main(string[] args)
{
    var Josh = new ThisPerson(22, "Josh");
    Console.WriteLine(Josh);
    Console.WriteLine(Josh.GetType());

    BadgeNumber ThisNumber = Josh;
    Console.WriteLine(ThisNumber);
    Console.WriteLine(ThisNumber.GetType());
}
```

The code begins by creating a new `ThisPerson`, `Josh`, who has badge number `22` and a name of, well, `Josh`. The code then creates another object, `ThisNumber`, of type `BadgeNumber`, and tries to assign `Josh` to it. You might think that this code really shouldn't work, but when you run it you see this output that demonstrates that the compiler assigns the proper object of the proper type to `ThisNumber`, even though it's supposedly of type `BadgeNumber`.

```
ThisPerson { Id = EmployeeID { Value = 22, FullName = Josh } }
CovariantReturn.ThisPerson
ThisPerson { Id = EmployeeID { Value = 22, FullName = Josh } }
CovariantReturn.ThisPerson
```

Getting Your Objects Off to a Good Start — Constructors

REMEMBER

Controlling class access is only half the problem: An object needs a good start in life if it is to grow. A class can supply an initialization method that the application calls to get things started, but the application could forget to call the method. The class starts out with garbage, and the situation gets no better after that. If you want to hold the class accountable, you have to ensure that it has a chance to start out correctly. C# solves that problem by calling the initialization method for you — for example:

```
MyObject mo = new MyObject();
```

REMEMBER

In other words, this statement not only grabs an object from a special memory area but also initializes that object's members. Keep the terms class and object separate in your mind. Cat is a class. An instance of Cat named Striper is an object of class Cat.

The C#-Provided Constructor

C# keeps track of whether a variable has been initialized and doesn't allow you to use an uninitialized variable. For example, the following code chunk generates a compile-time error:

```
public static void Main(string[] args)
{
  int n;
  double d;
  double calculatedValue = n + d;
}
```

C# tracks the fact that the local variables n and d haven't been assigned a value and doesn't allow them to be used in the expression. Compiling this tiny program generates these compiler errors:

```
Use of unassigned local variable 'n'
Use of unassigned local variable 'd'
```

By comparison, C# provides a default constructor that initializes the data members of an object to

- 0 for numbers
- false for Booleans
- null for object references

Consider the MyObject class from the UseConstructor program example:

```
internal class MyObject
{
    internal int n;
    internal MyObject nextObject;
}
```

You can work with it using the following code:

```
static void Main(string[] args)
{
    // First create an object.
    MyObject localObject = new MyObject();
    Console.WriteLine("localObject.n is {0}", localObject.n);

    if (localObject.nextObject == null)
    {
        Console.WriteLine("localObject.nextObject is null");
    }
    Console.Read();
}
```

This program defines a class MyObject, which contains both a simple data member n of type int and a reference to an object, nextObject (both declared internal). The Main() method creates a MyObject and then displays the initial contents of n and nextObject. The output from executing the program appears this way:

```
localObject.n is 0
localObject.nextObject is null
```

When the object is created, C# executes a small piece of code that the compiler provides to initialize the object and its members. Left to their own devices, the data members localObject.n and nextObject would contain random, garbage values.

REMEMBER

The code that initializes values when they're created is the default constructor. It constructs the class, in the sense of initializing its members. Thus C# ensures that an object starts life in a known state: all zeros, nulls, or false values, depending on type. This concept affects only data members of the class, not local variables in a method.

Replacing the Default Constructor

Although the compiler automatically initializes all instance variables to the appropriate values, for many classes (probably most classes), the default value isn't a valid state. Consider the following BankAccount class from earlier in this chapter:

```
internal class BankAccount
{
  private int _accountNumber;
  private double _balance;
  // ...other members
}
```

Although an initial balance of 0 is probably okay, an account number of 0 definitely isn't the hallmark of a valid bank account.

At this point in the chapter, the BankAccount class includes the InitBankAccount() method to initialize the object. However, this approach puts too much responsibility on the application software using the class. If the application fails to invoke the InitBankAccount() method, the bank account methods may not work, through no fault of their own.

REMEMBER

A class shouldn't rely on methods such as InitBankAccount() to start the object in a valid state. To work around this problem, you can have your class provide its own explicit *class constructor* that C# calls automatically when the object is created. The constructor could have been named Init(), Start(), or Create(), but C# requires the constructor to carry the name of the class. Thus a constructor for the BankAccount class appears this way:


```
public void Main(string[] args)
{
  BankAccount ba = new BankAccount();  // This invokes the constructor.
}

public class BankAccount
{
  // Bank accounts start at 1000 and increase sequentially.
  private static int _nextAccountNumber = 1000;

  // Maintain the account number and balance for each object.
  private int _accountNumber;
  private double _balance;

  // BankAccount constructor -- Here it is -- ta-da!
  // Parentheses, possible arguments, no return type
  public BankAccount()
  {
    _accountNumber = ++_nextAccountNumber;
    _balance = 0.0;
  }

  // ... other members ...
}
```

The contents of the BankAccount constructor are the same as those of the original Init...() method. However, the way you declare and use the constructor differs:

- The constructor always carries the same name as the class.
- The constructor can take parameters (or not).

» The constructor never has a return type, not even void.

» Main() doesn't need to invoke any extra method to initialize the object when it's created; no Init() is necessary.

REMEMBER

If you provide your own constructor, C# no longer supplies a default constructor. Your constructor replaces the default and becomes the only way to create an instance of your class.

Constructing something

Try out a constructor thingie. Consider the classes from the following program, DemonstrateCustomConstructor:

```
// MyObject -- Create a class with a noisy custom constructor
//    and an internal data object.
public class MyObject
{
    // This data member is a property of the class (it's static).
    private static MyOtherObject _staticObj = new MyOtherObject();

    // This data member is a property of each instance.
    private MyOtherObject _dynamicObj;

    // Constructor (a real chatterbox)
    public MyObject()
    {
        Console.WriteLine("MyObject constructor starting");
        Console.WriteLine("(Static data member constructed before " +
                          "this constructor)");
        Console.WriteLine("Now create nonstatic data member dynamically:");
        _dynamicObj = new MyOtherObject();
        Console.WriteLine("MyObject constructor ending");
    }
}

// MyOtherObject -- This class also has a noisy constructor but
//    no internal members.
public class MyOtherObject
{
    public MyOtherObject()
    {
        Console.WriteLine("MyOtherObject constructing");
    }
}
```

The `Main()` function merely starts the construction process, as shown here:

```
static void Main(string[] args)
{
    Console.WriteLine("Main() starting");
    Console.WriteLine("Creating a local MyObject in Main():");
    MyObject localObject = new MyObject();
    Console.Read();
}
```

Executing this program generates the following output:

```
Main() starting
Creating a local MyObject in Main():
MyOtherObject constructing
MyObject constructor starting
(Static data member constructed before this constructor)
Now create nonstatic data member dynamically:
MyOtherObject constructing
MyObject constructor ending
Press Enter to terminate...
```


The following steps reconstruct what just happened:

1. The program starts, and `Main()` outputs the initial message and announces that it's about to create a local `MyObject`.
2. `Main()` creates a `localObject` of type `MyObject`.
3. `MyObject` contains a static member `_staticObj` of class `MyOtherObject`.

   REMEMBER

   All static data members are initialized before the first `MyObject()` constructor runs. In this case, C# populates `_staticObj` with a newly created `MyOtherObject` before passing control to the `MyObject` constructor. This step accounts for the third line of output.
4. The constructor for `MyObject` is given control. It outputs the initial message, `MyObject constructor starting`, and then notes that the static member was already constructed before the `MyObject()` constructor began:

   ```
   (Static data member constructed before this constructor)
   ```
5. After announcing its intention with `Now create nonstatic data member dynamically`, the `MyObject` constructor creates an object of class `MyOtherObject` using the new operator, generating the second `MyOtherObject constructing` message as the `MyOtherObject` constructor is called.
6. Control returns to the `MyObject` constructor, which returns to `Main()`.

Initializing an object directly with an initializer

Besides letting you initialize data members in a constructor, C# enables you to initialize data members directly by using initializers. Thus, you could write the BankAccount class as follows:

```
public class BankAccount
{
  // Bank accounts start at 1000 and increase sequentially.
  private static int _nextAccountNumber = 1000;

  // Maintain the account number and balance for each object.
  private int _accountNumber = ++_nextAccountNumber;
  private double _balance = 0.0;

  // ... other members ...
}
```

Here's the initializer business. Both _accountNumber and _balance are assigned a value as part of their declaration, which has the same effect as a constructor but without having to do the work in it.

Be clear about exactly what's happening. You may think that this statement sets _balance to 0.0 right now. However, _balance exists only as a part of an object. Thus, the assignment isn't executed until a BankAccount object is created. In fact, this assignment is executed every time an object is created.

Note that the static data member _nextAccountNumber is initialized the first time the BankAccount class is accessed; that's the first time you access any method or property of the object owning the static data member, including the constructor.

REMEMBER

After the static member is initialized, it isn't reinitialized every time you construct a BankAccount instance. That's different from the instance members. Initializers are executed in the order of their appearance in the class declaration. If C# encounters both initializers and a constructor, the initializers are executed before the body of the constructor.

Seeing that construction stuff with initializers

In the DemonstrateCustomConstructor program, move the call new MyOtherObject() from the MyObject constructor to the declaration itself, as follows (see the bold text), modify the second `WriteLine()` statement as shown, and then rerun the program:

```
public class MyObject
{
  // This member is a property of the class (it's static).
  private static MyOtherObject _staticObj = new MyOtherObject();

  // This member is a property of each instance.
  private MyOtherObject _dynamicObj = new MyOtherObject();  // <- Here.

  public MyObject()
  {
    Console.WriteLine("MyObject constructor starting");
    Console.WriteLine(
      "Both data members initialized before this constructor)");
    // _dynamicObj construction was here, now moved up.
    Console.WriteLine("MyObject constructor ending");
  }
}
```


Compare the following output from this modified program with the output from its predecessor, `DemonstrateCustomConstructor`:

```
Main() starting
Creating a local MyObject in Main():
MyOtherObject constructing
MyOtherObject constructing
MyObject constructor starting
(Both data members initialized before this constructor)
MyObject constructor ending
Press Enter to terminate...
```

Initializing an object without a constructor

Suppose that you have a little class to represent a `Student`:

```
public class Student
{
  public string Name { get; set; }
  public string Address { get; set; }
  public double GradePointAverage { get; set; }
}
```

A `Student` object has three public properties, `Name`, `Address`, and `GradePointAverage`, which specify the student's basic information. Normally, when you create a new

Student object, you have to initialize its Name, Address, and GradePointAverage properties like this:

```
Student randal = new Student();
randal.Name = "Randal Sphar";
randal.Address = "123 Elm Street, Truth or Consequences, NM 00000";
randal.GradePointAverage = 3.51;
```

If Student had a constructor, you could do something like this:

```
Student randal = new Student
  ("Randal Sphar", "123 Elm Street, Truth or Consequences, NM, 00000", 3.51);
```

Sadly, however, Student lacks a constructor, other than the default one that C# supplies automatically — which takes no parameters. You can simplify that initialization with something that looks suspiciously like a constructor — well, sort of:

```
Student randal = new Student
  { Name = "Randal Sphar",
    Address = "123 Elm Street, Truth or Consequences, NM 00000",
    GradePointAverage = 3.51
  };
```

The last two examples are different in this respect: The first one, using a constructor, shows parentheses containing two strings and one double value separated by commas, and the second one, using the new object-initializer syntax, has instead curly braces containing three assignments separated by commas. The syntax works something like this:

```
new LatitudeLongitude
  { assignment to Latitude, assignment to Longitude  };
```

The object-initializer syntax lets you assign to any accessible *set* properties of the LatitudeLongitude object in a code block (the curly braces). The block is designed to initialize the object. Note that you can set only accessible properties this way, not private ones, and you can't call any of the object's methods or do any other work in the initializer.

The object-initializer syntax is much more concise: one statement versus three. Also, it simplifies the creation of initialized objects that don't let you do so through a constructor. The new object-initializer syntax doesn't gain you much of anything besides convenience, but convenience when you're coding is high on any programmer's list. So is brevity. Besides, the feature becomes essential when you read about anonymous classes.

TIP

Use the new object-initializer syntax to your heart's content. The book uses it frequently, so you have plenty of examples. The help topic at `https://docs.microsoft.com/en-us/dotnet/csharp/programming-guide/classes-and-structs/how-to-initialize-objects-by-using-an-object-initializer` provides additional details.

Using Expression-Bodied Members

Expression-bodied members first appeared in C# 6.0 as a means to make methods and properties easier to define. In C# 7.0, expression-bodied members also work with constructors, destructors, property accessors, and event accessors.

Creating expression-bodied methods

The following example shows how you might have created a method before C# 6.0:

```
public int RectArea(Rectangle rect)
{
    return rect.Height * rect.Width;
}
```

REMEMBER

When working with an expression-bodied member, you can reduce the number of lines of code to just one line, like this:

```
public int RectArea(Rectangle rect) => rect.Height * rect.Width;
```

Even though both versions perform precisely the same task, the second version is much shorter and easier to write. The trade-off is that the second version is also terse and can be harder to understand.

Defining expression-bodied properties

Expression-bodied properties work similarly to methods: You declare the property using a single line of code, like this:

```
public int RectArea => _rect.Height * _rect.Width;
```

The example assumes that you have a private member named `_rect` defined and that you want to get the value that matches the rectangle's area.

Defining expression-bodied constructors and destructors

In C# 7.0, you can use this same technique when working with a constructor. In earlier versions of C#, you might create a constructor like this one:

```
public EmpData()
{
   _name = "Harvey";
}
```

In this case, the EmpData class constructor sets a private variable, _name, equal to "Harvey". The C# 7.0 version uses just one line but accomplishes the same task:

```
public EmpData() => _name = "Harvey";
```

Destructors work much the same as constructors. Instead of using multiple lines, you use just one line to define them.

Defining expression-bodied property accessors

Property accessors can also benefit from the use of expression-bodied members. Here is a typical C# 6.0 property accessor with both get and set methods:

```
private int _myVar;
public MyVar
{
   get
   {
      return _myVar;
   }
   set
   {
      SetProperty(ref _myVar, value);
   }
}
```

When working in C# 7.0, you can shorten the code using an expression-bodied member, like this:

```
private int _myVar;
public MyVar
{
   get => _myVar;
   set => SetProperty(ref _myVar, value);
}
```

Defining expression-bodied event accessors

As with property accessors, you can create an event accessor form using the expression-bodied member. Here's what you might have used for C# 6.0:

```
private EventHandler _myEvent;
public event EventHandler MyEvent
{
    add
    {
        _myEvent += value;
    }
    remove
    {
        _myEvent -= value;
    }
}
```

The expression-bodied member form of the same event accessor in C# 7.0 looks like this:

```
private EventHandler _myEvent;
public event EventHandler MyEvent
{
    add => _myEvent += value;
    remove => _myEvent -= value;
}
```

IN THIS CHAPTER

» Including constructors in a hierarchy

» Invoking the base-class constructor

» Differentiating between *is a* and *has a*

» Substituting one class object for another

Chapter 5
Inheritance: Is That All I Get?

Object-oriented programming is based on four principles: the capability to control access (encapsulation), inherit from other classes, respond appropriately (polymorphism), and refer from one object to another indirectly (interfaces).

Inheritance is a common concept. You are a human. You inherit certain properties from the class `Human`, such as your ability to converse and your dependence on air, food, and beverages. The class `Human` inherits its dependencies on air, water, and nourishment from the class `Mammal`, which inherits from the class `Animal`.

The capability to pass down properties is a powerful one. You can use it to describe items in an economical way. For example, if your son asks, "What's a duck?" you can say, "It's a bird that quacks." Despite what you may think, that answer conveys a considerable amount of information. Your son knows what a bird is, and now he knows all those same characteristics about a duck plus the duck's additional property of "quackness."

Object-oriented languages express this inheritance relationship by allowing one class to inherit properties from another. This feature enables object-oriented languages to generate a model that's closer to the real world than the model generated by languages that don't support inheritance. This chapter discusses C#

inheritance in detail so that you can understand the relationships between the various classes that you use.

REMEMBER

You don't have to type the source code for this chapter manually. In fact, using the downloadable source is a lot easier. You can find the source for this chapter in the `\CSAIO4D2E\BK02\CH05` folder of the downloadable source. See the Introduction for details on how to find these source files.

Why You Need Inheritance

Inheritance serves several important functions. You may think, for example, that inheritance reduces the amount of typing. In a way, it does — you don't need to repeat the properties of a `Person` when you're describing a `Student` class. A more important, related issue is the major buzzword *reuse.* Computer scientists have known for some time that starting from scratch with each new project and rebuilding the same software components makes little sense.

Compare the situation in software development to that of other industries. Think about the number of car manufacturers that start by building their own wrenches and screwdrivers before they construct a car. Of those who do that, estimate how many would start over completely and build all new tools for the next model. Practitioners in other industries have found that starting with existing screws, bolts, nuts, and even larger off-the-shelf components such as motors and compressors makes more sense than starting from scratch.

Inheritance enables you to tweak existing software components. You can adapt existing classes to new applications without making internal modifications. The existing class is inherited into — or, as programmers often say, *extended* by — a new subclass that contains the necessary additions and modifications. If someone else wrote the base class, you may not be able to modify it, so inheritance can save the day.

This capability carries with it a third benefit of inheritance. Suppose that you inherit from — extend — an existing class. Later, you find that the base class has a bug you must correct. If you modified the class to reuse it, you must manually check for, correct, and retest the bug in each application separately. If you inherited the class without changes, you can generally stick the updated class into the other application with little hassle.

INHERITANCE IS AMAZING

To make sense of their surroundings, humans build extensive taxonomies. For example, Fido is a special case of dog, which is a special case of canine, which is a special case of mammal — and so it goes. This ability to classify items shapes the human understanding of the world.

In an object-oriented language such as C#, you say that the class `Student` inherits from the class `Person`. You also say that `Person` is a base class of `Student` and that `Student` is a subclass of `Person`. Finally, you say that a `Student` IS_A `Person`. (Using all caps and an underscore is a common way of expressing this unique relationship.)

Notice that the IS_A property isn't reflexive: Although `Student` IS_A `Person`, the reverse isn't true. A `Person` IS_NOT_A `Student`. A statement such as this one always refers to the general case. A particular `Person` might be, in fact, a `Student` — but lots of people who are members of the class `Person` aren't members of the class `Student`. In addition, the class `Student` has properties that it doesn't share with the class `Person`. For example, `Student` has a grade-point average, but the ordinary `Person` quite happily does not.

The inheritance property is transitive. For example, if I define a new class `Graduate Student` as a subclass of `Student`, `GraduateStudent` is also a `Person`. It must be that way: If a `GraduateStudent` IS_A `Student` and a `Student` IS_A `Person`, a `GraduateStudent` IS_A `Person`.

But the biggest benefit of inheritance is that it describes the way life is. Items inherit properties from each other. There's no getting around it.

Inheriting from a BankAccount Class (a More Complex Example)

A bank maintains several types of accounts. One type, the savings account, has all the properties of a simple bank account plus the ability to accumulate interest. The following sections discuss the `BankAccount` class and its subclass, `SavingsAccount`, starting with a basic application and then looking at how the constructors and other features work.

Working with the basic update

It's important to start with the basics. The BankAccount class acts as the base class for the SimpleSavingsAccount program:

```
// BankAccount -- Simulate a bank account, each of which
//    carries an account ID (which is assigned
//    on creation) and a balance.
internal class BankAccount    // The base class
{
    // Bank accounts start at 1000 and increase sequentially.
    private static int _nextAccountNumber = 1000;

    // Maintain the account number for each object.
    private int _accountNumber;

    // Constructor -- Initialize a bank account with the next account
    //  ID and the specified initial balance (default to zero).
    internal BankAccount() : this(0) { }

    internal BankAccount(decimal initialBalance)
    {
        _accountNumber = ++_nextAccountNumber;
        Balance = initialBalance;
    }

    // Balance property.
    protected decimal Balance
        { get; set; }

    // Deposit -- any positive deposit is allowed.
    public void Deposit(decimal amount)
    {
        if (amount > 0)
        {
            Balance += amount;
        }
    }

    // Withdraw -- You can withdraw any amount up to the
    //    balance; return the amount withdrawn.
    public decimal Withdraw(decimal withdrawal)
    {
        if (Balance <= withdrawal) // Use Balance property.
        {
            withdrawal = Balance;
        }
```

```
            Balance -= withdrawal;
            return withdrawal;
        }

        // ToString - Stringify the account.
        public override string ToString()
        {
            return $"{_accountNumber} - {Balance:C}";
        }
    }
```

This example uses *chaining* to chain one constructor to another using `this`. When you see internal `BankAccount() : this(0) { }`, it means to call the next constructor in the chain using a value of `0` for the `initialBalance` parameter. Using this approach greatly reduces the amount of code you have to write, reduces the potential for error, and makes the code more maintainable. The second constructor obtains the next account number and sets the `Balance` property.

The `Balance` property has a `protected` access modifier because only the base class, `BankAccount`, and the derived class, `SavingsAccount`, will access it. Using this approach means that you can simplify the code and not have to maintain a separate internal variable of your own.

The three methods, `Deposit()`, `Withdraw()`, and `ToString()`, allow controlled public access of BankAccount features. `ToString()` overrides the base `ToString()` to display the account number and balance as a dollar amount.

The `SavingsAccount` class adds the ability to change the balance based on interest accumulation, as shown here:

```
internal class SavingsAccount : BankAccount   // The subclass
{
    private decimal _interestRate = 0;

    // InitSavingsAccount -- Input the rate expressed as a
    //    rate between 0 and 100.
    internal SavingsAccount(decimal interestRate) :
        this(0, interestRate) { }

    internal SavingsAccount(decimal initialBalance,
        decimal interestRate) : base(initialBalance)
    {
        _interestRate = interestRate / 100;
    }
```

```
    // AccumulateInterest -- Invoke once per period.
    public void AccumulateInterest()
    {
        Balance = Balance + (decimal)(Balance * _interestRate);
    }

    // ToString -- Stringify the account.
    public override string ToString()
    {
        return $"{base.ToString()} ({_interestRate:P})";
    }
}
```

As with BankAccount, SavingsAccount provides two constructors, one of which is chained to the other. SavingsAccount is a subclass of BankAccount, so it already has access to elements like a Balance. The only thing it needs to add is the ability to accumulate interest, which appears in AccumulateInterest(). Notice how the SavingsAccount class ToString() builds on the base class ToString(). Also note how the SavingsAccount() constructor calls initializeBalance() in the base class.

Main() does about as little as it can. It creates a BankAccount, makes a deposit, displays the account, creates a SavingsAccount, accumulates one period of interest, and displays the result, with the interest rate as shown here:

```
static void Main(string[] args)
{
    // Create a bank account and display it.
    BankAccount ba = new BankAccount(100M);
    ba.Deposit(100M);
    Console.WriteLine($"Account {ba.ToString()}");

    // Now a savings account
    SavingsAccount sa = new SavingsAccount(12.5M);
    sa.Deposit(100M);
    sa.AccumulateInterest();
    Console.WriteLine($"Account {sa.ToString()}");
    Console.Read();
}
```

You see the following output when you run this application:

```
Account 1001 - $200.00
Account 1002 - $112.50 (12.500%)
```

Tracking the BankAccount and SavingsAccount classes features

It can be hard to track precisely how the BankAccount and SavingsAccount classes work unless you single-step through them using the debugger. Another technique is to add some Console.WriteLine() method entries, as shown in the following listing (and in SimpleSavingsAccountTracked):

```
internal class BankAccount    // The base class
{
    // Bank accounts start at 1000 and increase sequentially.
    private static int _nextAccountNumber = 1000;

    // Maintain the account number for each object.
    private int _accountNumber;

    // Constructor -- Initialize a bank account with the next account
    //  ID and the specified initial balance (default to zero).
    internal BankAccount() : this(0)
    {
        Console.WriteLine("*** Called BankAccount Default Constructor ***");
    }

    internal BankAccount(decimal initialBalance)
    {
        _accountNumber = ++_nextAccountNumber;
        Balance = initialBalance;
        Console.WriteLine("*** Called BankAccount Constructor ***");
    }

    // Balance property.
    protected decimal Balance
        { get; set; }

    // Deposit -- any positive deposit is allowed.
    public void Deposit(decimal amount)
    {
        if (amount > 0)
        {
            Balance += amount;
            Console.WriteLine("*** Called BankAccount Deposit() ***");
        }
    }

    // Withdraw -- You can withdraw any amount up to the
    //    balance; return the amount withdrawn.
    public decimal Withdraw(decimal withdrawal)
```

```
    {
        if (Balance <= withdrawal) // Use Balance property.
        {
            withdrawal = Balance;
        }
        Balance -= withdrawal;
        Console.WriteLine("*** Called BankAccount Withdrawal() ***");
        return withdrawal;
    }

    // ToString - Stringify the account.
    public override string ToString()
    {
        Console.WriteLine("*** Called BankAccount ToString() ***");
        return $"{_accountNumber} - {Balance:C}";
    }
}

// SavingsAccount -- A bank account that draws interest
internal class SavingsAccount : BankAccount   // The subclass
{
    private decimal _interestRate = 0;

    // InitSavingsAccount -- Input the rate expressed as a
    //    rate between 0 and 100.
    internal SavingsAccount(decimal interestRate) :
        this(0, interestRate)
    {
        Console.WriteLine("*** Called SavingsAccount Constructor 1 ***");
    }

    internal SavingsAccount(decimal initialBalance,
        decimal interestRate) : base(initialBalance)
    {
        _interestRate = interestRate / 100;
        Console.WriteLine("*** Called SavingsAccount Constructor 2 ***");
    }

    // AccumulateInterest -- Invoke once per period.
    public void AccumulateInterest()
    {
        Balance = Balance + (decimal)(Balance * _interestRate);
        Console.WriteLine("*** Called SavingsAccount " +
            "AccumulateInterest() ***");
    }

    // ToString -- Stringify the account.
    public override string ToString()
```

```
        {
            Console.WriteLine("*** Called SavingsAccount ToString() ***");
            return $"{base.ToString()} ({_interestRate:P})";
        }
    }
```

The code in Main() is unchanged, although, you could certainly play around with it to see what happens. When you run this version of the code, you see the following output:

```
*** Called BankAccount Constructor ***
*** Called BankAccount Deposit() ***
*** Called BankAccount ToString() ***
Account 1001 - $200.00
*** Called BankAccount Constructor ***
*** Called SavingsAccount Constructor 2 ***
*** Called SavingsAccount Constructor 1 ***
*** Called BankAccount Deposit() ***
*** Called SavingsAccount AccumulateInterest() ***
*** Called SavingsAccount ToString() ***
*** Called BankAccount ToString() ***
Account 1002 - $112.50 (12.50%)
```

Creating and using the BankAccount object ba is straightforward. The code calls the constructor that accepts an initial amount, deposits $100.00, and then prints the result.

However, creating and using the SavingsAccount object, sa, requires a little more work. In this case, the code:

1. Calls the BankAccount constructor that accepts an initial amount first because that's the constructor called by the base(initialBalance) portion of the second SavingsAccount constructor.
2. Performs the tasks in the second SavingsAccount constructor because that's the constructor called by the this(0, interestRate) portion of the first SavingsAccount constructor.
3. Performs the tasks in the first SavingsAccount constructor (the one that accepts only an interest rate as input).
4. Makes a deposit using the BankAccount.Deposit() method (despite the fact that the call appears as sa.Deposit(100M)).
5. Accumulates interest using the SavingsAccount.AccumulateInterest() method because this method is unique to the SavingsAccount class.
6. Calls the SavingsAccount.ToString() override, which calls the BankAccount.ToString() override to print the savings account string.

REMEMBER

It's important to understand the order used to call the various constructors and methods because you could make bad assumptions otherwise. When working through a class construction, you can always add statements to see what is getting called and when it's getting called to better understand application flow. This approach really helps when trying to solve structural flaws in your application.

IS_A versus HAS_A — I'm So Confused_A

The relationship between SavingsAccount and BankAccount is the fundamental IS_A relationship in inheritance. In the following sections, you discover why. You also see what the alternative, the HAS_A relationship, would look like in comparison.

The IS_A relationship

The IS_A relationship between SavingsAccount and BankAccount is demonstrated by modifications to the class Program (shown in bold) in the SimpleSavingsAccount program from the preceding section (as found in SimpleSavingsAccount2):

```
class Program
{
    public static void DirectDeposit(BankAccount ba, decimal pay)
    {
        ba.Deposit(pay);
    }

    static void Main(string[] args)
    {
        // Create a bank account and display it.
        BankAccount ba = new BankAccount(100M);
        DirectDeposit(ba, 100M);
        Console.WriteLine($"Account {ba.ToString()}");

        // Now a savings account
        SavingsAccount sa = new SavingsAccount(12.5M);
        DirectDeposit(sa, 100);
        sa.AccumulateInterest();
        Console.WriteLine($"Account {sa.ToString()}");
        Console.Read();
    }
}
```

In effect, nothing has changed. The only real difference is that all deposits are now being made through the local method `DirectDeposit()`, which isn't part of class `BankAccount`. The arguments to this method are the bank account and the amount to deposit.

REMEMBER

Notice that `Main()` could pass either a bank account or a savings account to `DirectDeposit()` because a `SavingsAccount` IS_A `BankAccount` and is accorded all the same rights and privileges. Because `SavingsAccount` IS_A `BankAccount`, you can assign a `SavingsAccount` to a `BankAccount`-type variable or method argument.

Gaining access to BankAccount by using containment

The class `SavingsAccount` could have gained access to the members of `BankAccount` in a different way, as shown in the following code (and in `SimpleSavingsAccount3`):

```
internal class SavingsAccount
{
    private BankAccount _bankAccount;
    private decimal _interestRate = 0;

    // InitSavingsAccount -- Input the rate expressed as a
    //    rate between 0 and 100.
    internal SavingsAccount(decimal interestRate) :
        this(0, interestRate)
    { }

    internal SavingsAccount(decimal initialBalance,
        decimal interestRate)
    {
        _bankAccount = new BankAccount(initialBalance);
        _interestRate = interestRate / 100;
    }

    // AccumulateInterest -- Invoke once per period.
    public void AccumulateInterest()
    {
        _bankAccount.Balance = _bankAccount.Balance +
            (decimal)(_bankAccount.Balance * _interestRate);
    }
```

```
    public void Deposit(decimal amount)
    {
        _bankAccount.Deposit(amount);
    }

    public decimal Withdraw(decimal withdrawal)
    {
        return _bankAccount.Withdraw(withdrawal);
    }

    // ToString -- Stringify the account.
    public override string ToString()
    {
        return $"{_bankAccount.ToString()} ({_interestRate:P})";
    }
}
```

In this case, the class `SavingsAccount_` *contains* a data member `_bankAccount` (as opposed to inheriting from `BankAccount`). The `_bankAccount` object contains the balance and account number information needed by the savings account. The `SavingsAccount_` class retains the data unique to a savings account and *delegates* to the contained `BankAccount` object as needed. That is, when the `SavingsAccount` needs, say, the balance, it asks the contained `BankAccount` for it. Notice that this strategy requires the inclusion of instantiating `_bankAccount` within the second constructor and using _bankAccount anywhere that you might have seen `base` used in the past.

WARNING

This approach has several drawbacks. For one thing, you must change the access modifier for `Balance` in `BankAccount` to `public`, which means that it's no longer protected. Every time you make a class member more accessible, you add the potential for security issues. In addition, this version of `SavingsAccount` includes its own version of `Deposit()` and `Withdraw()`, which leads to code replication and potential errors, again increasing the potential for security issues. Here are some reasons you might use containment rather than inheritance:

- The new class doesn't need access to all the existing class members.
- The application requires loose coupling so that changes in the existing class don't ripple through to the new class.
- Runtime changes to the existing class won't affect the new class (an advanced programming technique not fully discussed in this minibook; see Book 3, Chapter 6), but you can read about it at `https://www.dotnetcurry.com/csharp/dynamic-class-creation-roslyn`).
- It's essential to limit access to private and protected members, and the new class won't require access to these members (actually improving security).

In this case, you say that the SavingsAccount_HAS_A BankAccount. Hard-core object-oriented jocks say that SavingsAccount *composes* a BankAccount. That is, SavingsAccount is partly composed of a BankAccount.

The HAS_A relationship

The HAS_A relationship is fundamentally different from the IS_A relationship. This difference doesn't seem so bad in the following application-code segment example:

```
// Create a new savings account.
BankAccount ba = new BankAccount()

// HAS_A version of SavingsAccount
SavingsAccount_ sa = new SavingsAccount_(ba, 5);

// And deposit 100 dollars into it.
sa.Deposit(100M);

// Now accumulate interest.
sa.AccumulateInterest();
```

The problem is that this modified SavingsAccount_ cannot be used as a BankAccount because it doesn't inherit from BankAccount. Instead, it *contains* a BankAccount — not the same concept. For example, this code example fails:

```
// DirectDeposit -- Deposit my paycheck automatically.
void DirectDeposit(BankAccount ba, int pay)
{
  ba.Deposit(pay);
}

void SomeMethod()
{
  // The following example fails.
  SavingsAccount_ sa = new SavingsAccount_(sa, 100);
  // ... continue ...
}
```

REMEMBER

DirectDeposit() can't accept a SavingsAccount_ in lieu of a BankAccount. No obvious relationship between the two exists, as far as C# is concerned, because inheritance isn't involved. Don't think, though, that this situation makes containment a bad idea. You just have to approach the concept a bit differently in order to use it.

When to IS_A and When to HAS_A

The distinction between the IS_A and HAS_A relationships is more than just a matter of software convenience. This relationship has a corollary in the real world.

For example, a Ford Explorer IS_A car. An Explorer HAS_A motor. If your friend says, "Come on over in your car" and you show up in an Explorer, he has no grounds for complaint. He may have a complaint if you show up carrying your Explorer's engine in your arms, however. (Or at least *you* will.) The class `Explorer` should extend the class `Car`, not only to give `Explorer` access to the methods of a `Car` but also to express the fundamental relationship between the two.

Unfortunately, the beginning programmer may have `Car` inherit from `Motor`, as an easy way to give the `Car` class access to the members of `Motor`, which the `Car` needs in order to operate. For example, `Car` can inherit the method `Motor.Go()`. However, this example highlights a problem with this approach: Even though humans become sloppy in their speech, making a car go isn't the same thing as making a motor go. The car's go operation certainly relies on that of the motor's, but they aren't the same thing — you also have to put the transmission in gear, release the brake, and complete other tasks. Perhaps even more than that, inheriting from `Motor` misstates the facts. A car simply isn't a type of motor.

REMEMBER

Elegance in software is a goal worth achieving in its own right. It enhances understandability, reliability, and maintainability.

Other Features That Support Inheritance

C# implements a set of features designed to support inheritance. The following sections discuss these features.

Substitutable classes

A program can use a subclass object where a base-class object is called for. In fact, you may have already seen this concept in one of the examples. `SomeMethod()` can pass a `SavingsAccount` object to the `DirectDeposit()` method, which expects a `BankAccount` object. You can make this conversion more explicit:

```
BankAccount ba;

// The original, not SavingsAccount_
SavingsAccount sa = new SavingsAccount();
```

```
// OK:
ba = sa;                    // Implicitly convert subclass to base class.
ba = (BankAccount)sa;       // But the explicit cast is preferred.
sa = (SavingsAccount)ba;    // An explicit cast is allowed.

// Not OK:
sa = ba;                    // No implicit conversion of base class to subclass
```

The first line stores a `SavingsAccount` object into a `BankAccount` variable. C# converts the object for you. The second line uses a cast to explicitly convert the object.

The final two lines attempt to convert the `BankAccount` object back into `SavingsAccount`. You can complete this operation explicitly, but C# doesn't do it for you. It's like trying to convert a larger numeric type, such as `double`, to a smaller one, such as `float`. C# doesn't do it implicitly because the process may involve a loss of data.

REMEMBER

The IS_A property isn't reflexive. That is, even though an Explorer is a car, a car isn't necessarily an Explorer. Similarly, a `BankAccount` isn't necessarily a `SavingsAccount`, so the implicit conversion isn't allowed. The explicit conversion is allowed because the programmer has indicated a willingness to "chance it."

Invalid casts at runtime

Generally, casting an object from `BankAccount` to `SavingsAccount` is a dangerous operation. Consider this example from `SimpleSavingsAccount4`:

```
class Program
{
    public static void ProcessAmount(BankAccount bankAccount)
    {
        // Deposit a large sum to the account.
        bankAccount.Deposit(10000.00M);

        // If the object is a SavingsAccount, collect interest now.
        SavingsAccount savingsAccount = (SavingsAccount)bankAccount;
        savingsAccount.AccumulateInterest();
    }

    static void Main(string[] args)
    {
        SavingsAccount sa = new SavingsAccount(100M, 12.5M);
        ProcessAmount(sa);
        Console.WriteLine(sa.ToString());
```

```
            BankAccount ba = new BankAccount(100M);
            ProcessAmount(ba);
            Console.WriteLine(ba.ToString());
            Console.Read();
        }
    }
```

ProcessAmount() performs a few operations, including invoking the AccumulateInterest() method. The cast of ba to a SavingsAccount is necessary because the bankAccount parameter is declared to be a BankAccount. The program compiles properly because all type conversions are made by explicit cast.

All goes well with the first call to ProcessAmount() from within Main(). The SavingsAccount object sa is passed to the ProcessAmount() method. The cast from BankAccount to SavingsAccount causes no problem because the ba object was originally a SavingsAccount anyway.

The second call to ProcessAmount() isn't as lucky, however. The cast to SavingsAccount cannot be allowed. The ba object doesn't have an AccumulateInterest() method. When you run this example, you see the following output when you use the Debug⇨Start Without Debugging command:

```
1001 - $11,362.50 (12.50%)

Unhandled Exception: System.InvalidCastException: Unable to cast object of
 type 'SimpleSavingsAccount.BankAccount' to type
 'SimpleSavingsAccount.SavingsAccount'. at
 SimpleSavingsAccount.Program.ProcessAmount(BankAccount bankAccount) in
 E:\CSAIO4D2E\BK02\CH05\SimpleSavingsAccount4\Program.cs:line 96 at
 SimpleSavingsAccount.Program.Main(String[] args) in
 E:\CSAIO4D2E\BK02\CH05\SimpleSavingsAccount4\Program.cs:line 107
Press any key to continue ...
```

WARNING

An incorrect conversion generates an error during the execution of the program (a *runtime error* in the form of an exception). Runtime errors are much more difficult to find and fix than compile-time errors. Worse, they can happen to a user other than you, which users tend not to appreciate.

Avoiding invalid conversions with the is operator

The ProcessAmount() method would work if it could ensure that the object passed to it is a SavingsAccount object before performing the conversion. C# provides two keywords for this purpose: is and as.

The is operator accepts an object on the left and a type on the right. The is operator returns true if the runtime type of the object on the left is compatible with the type on the right. Use it to verify that a cast is legal before you attempt the cast. You can modify ProcessAmount() in the previous section (as shown in SimpleSavingsAccount5) to avoid the runtime error by using the is operator:

```
public static void ProcessAmount(BankAccount bankAccount)
{
    // Deposit a large sum to the account.
    bankAccount.Deposit(10000.00M);

    // If the object is a SavingsAccount
    if (bankAccount is SavingsAccount)
    {
        // then collect interest now.
        SavingsAccount savingsAccount = (SavingsAccount)bankAccount;
        savingsAccount.AccumulateInterest();
    }
}
```

The added if statement checks the bankAccount object to ensure that it's of the class SavingsAccount. The is operator returns true when ProcessAmount() is called the first time. When passed a BankAccount object in the second call, however, the is operator returns false, avoiding the illegal cast. This version of the program doesn't generate a runtime error as shown here.

```
1001 - $11,362.50 (12.50%)
1002 - $10,100.00
```

TIP

A best practice is to protect all casts with the is operator to avoid the possibility of a runtime error. However, you should avoid casts altogether, if possible.

Avoiding invalid conversions with the as operator

The as operator works a bit differently from is. Rather than return a bool if the cast should work (but doesn't), it converts the type on the left to the type on the right. It safely returns null if the conversion fails — rather than cause a runtime error. You should always use the result of casting with the as operator only if it isn't null. So, using as looks like this:

```
SavingsAccount savingsAccount = bankAccount as SavingsAccount;
if (savingsAccount != null)
```

```
{
  // Go ahead and use savingsAccount.
}
// Otherwise, don't use it: generate an error message yourself.
```

REMEMBER

Generally, you should prefer `as` because it's more efficient. The conversion is already done with the `as` operator, whereas you must complete two steps when you use `is`: First test with `is` and then complete the cast with the cast operator. Unfortunately, `as` doesn't work with value-type variables, so you can't use it with types such as `int`, `long`, or `double` or with `char`. When you're trying to convert a value-type object, prefer the `is` operator.

GARBAGE COLLECTION AND THE C# DESTRUCTOR

C# provides a method that's inverse to the constructor: the *destructor*. It carries the name of the class with a tilde (~) in front. For example, the `~BaseClass()` method is the destructor for `BaseClass`.

C# invokes the destructor at some unknown time when it is no longer using the object. The default destructor is the only destructor that can be created because the destructor cannot be invoked directly. In addition, the destructor is always virtual.

When an inheritance ladder of classes is involved, destructors are invoked in reverse order of constructors. That is, the destructor for the subclass is invoked before the destructor for the base class.

The destructor method in C# is much less useful than it is in other object-oriented languages, such as C++, because C# has *nondeterministic destruction*. Understanding what that term means — and why it's important — requires some explanation.

The memory for an object is borrowed from the heap when the program executes the `new` command, as in `new SubClass()`. This block of memory remains reserved as long as any valid references to that memory are used by any running programs. You may have several variables that reference the same object.

The memory is said to be *unreachable* when the last reference goes out of scope. In other words, no one can access that block of memory after no more references to it exist. C# doesn't do anything in particular when a memory block first becomes unreachable. A low-priority system task executes in the background, looking for unreachable memory blocks. To avoid negatively affecting program performance, this garbage collector executes when little is happening in your program. As the garbage collector finds unreachable memory blocks, it returns them to the heap.

Normally, the garbage collector operates silently in the background. The garbage collector takes over control of the program for only a short period when heap memory begins to run out.

The C# destructor — for example, ~`BaseClass()` — is nondeterministic because it isn't invoked until the object is garbage-collected, and that task can occur long after the object is no longer being used. In fact, if the program terminates before the object is found and returned to the heap, the destructor is never invoked. *Nondeterministic* means you can't predict when the object will be garbage-collected. It could be quite a while before the object is garbage-collected and its destructor called.

C# programmers seldom use the destructor. C# has other ways to return borrowed system resources when they're no longer needed, using a `Dispose()` method, a topic that's beyond the scope of this book. (You can find the basics about `Dispose()` at `https://docs.microsoft.com/en-us/dotnet/standard/garbage-collection/implementing-dispose`.)

IN THIS CHAPTER

» Hiding or overriding a base class method

» Building abstract classes and methods

» Using `ToString()`

» Sealing a class from being subclassed

Chapter 6
Poly-what-ism?

In inheritance, one class adopts the members of another. Thus it's possible to create a class `SavingsAccount` that inherits data members, such as `account id`, and methods, such as `Deposit()`, from a base class `BankAccount`. That's useful, but this definition of inheritance isn't sufficient to mimic what's going on out there in the business world. (See Chapter 5 of this minibook if you don't know or remember much about class inheritance.)

A microwave oven is a type of oven, not because it looks like an oven, but rather because it performs the same functions as an oven. A microwave oven may perform additional functions, but it performs, at the least, the base oven functions, such as heating food. It's not important to know what the oven must do internally to make that happen, any more than it's important to know what type of oven it is, who made it, or whether it was on sale when purchased.

From a human vantage point, the relationship between a microwave oven and a conventional oven doesn't seem like such a big deal, but consider the problem from the oven's point of view. The steps that a conventional oven performs internally are completely different from those that a microwave oven may take.

The power of inheritance lies in the fact that a subclass doesn't *have* to inherit every single method from the base class just the way it's written. A subclass can inherit the essence of the base class method while implementing the details differently.

REMEMBER

You don't have to type the source code for this chapter manually. In fact, using the downloadable source is a lot easier. You can find the source for this chapter in the \CSAIO4D2E\BK02\CH06 folder of the downloadable source. See the Introduction for details on how to find these source files.

Overloading an Inherited Method

As described in the "Overloading a method doesn't mean giving it too much to do" section of Chapter 2 of this minibook, two or more methods can have the same name as long as the number or type of arguments differs (or as long as both differ). If you need a quick, but complete, summary of overloading, check out the article at https://www.geeksforgeeks.org/c-sharp-method-overloading/ as well. The following sections extend the concept of method overloading to inherited methods.

It's a simple case of method overloading

REMEMBER

Giving two methods the same name is *overloading*. The arguments of a method become a part of its extended name, as this example demonstrates:

```
public class MyClass
{
  public static void AMethod()
  {
    // Do something.
  }

  public static void AMethod(int)
  {
    // Do something else.
  }

  public static void AMethod(double d)
  {
    // Do something even different.
  }

  public static void Main(string[] args)
  {
    AMethod();
    AMethod(1);
    AMethod(2.0);
  }
}
```

C# can differentiate the methods by their arguments. Each of the calls within `Main()` accesses a different method.

REMEMBER

The return type isn't part of the extended name. You can't have two methods that differ only in their return types.

Different class, different method

Not surprisingly, the class to which a method belongs is also a part of its extended name. Consider this code segment:

```
public class MyClass
{
  public static void AMethod1();
  public void AMethod2();
}

public class UrClass
{
  public static void AMethod1();
  public void AMethod2();
}

public class Program
{
  public static void Main(string[] args)
  {
    UrClass.AMethod1();  // Call static method.

    // Invoke the MyClass.AMethod2() instance method:
    MyClass mcObject = new MyClass();
    mcObject.AMethod2();
  }
}
```

The name of the class is a part of the extended name of the method. The method `MyClass.AMethod1()` has nothing to do with `UrClass.AMethod1()`.

Peek-a-boo — hiding a base class method

So a method in one class can overload another method in its own class by having different arguments. As it turns out, a method can also overload a method in its own base class. Overloading a base class method is known as *hiding* the method.

Suppose that your bank adopts a policy that makes savings account withdrawals different from other types of withdrawals. Suppose, just for the sake of argument, that withdrawing from a savings account costs $1.50.

Taking the procedural approach, you could implement this policy by setting a flag (variable) in the class to indicate whether the object is a `SavingsAccount` or just a simple `BankAccount`. Then the withdrawal method would have to check the flag to decide whether it needs to charge $1.50, as shown here:

```
public class BankAccount
{
  private decimal _balance;
  private bool _isSavingsAccount;  // The flag

  // Indicate the initial balance and whether the account
  // you're creating is a savings account.
  public BankAccount(decimal initialBalance, bool isSavingsAccount)
  {
    _balance = initialBalance;
    _isSavingsAccount = isSavingsAccount;
  }

  public decimal Withdraw(decimal amountToWithdraw)
  {
    // If the account is a savings account ...
    if (_isSavingsAccount)
    {
      // ...then skim off $1.50.
      _balance -= 1.50M;
    }

    // Continue with the usual withdraw code:
    if (amountToWithdraw > _balance)
    {
      amountToWithdraw = _balance;
    }

    _balance -= amountToWithdraw;
    return amountToWithdraw;
  }
}

class MyClass
{
  public void SomeMethod()
  {
```

```
    // Create a savings account:
    BankAccount ba = new BankAccount(0, true);
  }
}
```

Your method must tell the BankAccount whether the object you're instantiating is a SavingsAccount in the constructor by passing a flag. The constructor saves that flag and uses it in the Withdraw() method to decide whether to charge the extra $1.50.

The more object-oriented approach hides the method Withdraw() in the base class BankAccount with a new method of the same name in the SavingsAccount class. The BankAccount and SavingsAccount classes of the HidingWithdrawal example show how this approach works:

```
// BankAccount -- A very basic bank account
internal class BankAccount
{
    internal BankAccount(decimal initialBalance)
    {
        Balance = initialBalance;
    }

    internal decimal Balance
        { get; private set; }

    internal decimal Withdraw(decimal amount)
    {
        // Good practice means avoiding modifying an input parameter.
        // Modify a copy.
        decimal amountToWithdraw = amount;

        if (amountToWithdraw > Balance)
        {
            amountToWithdraw = Balance;
        }

        Balance -= amountToWithdraw;
        return amountToWithdraw;
    }
}

// SavingsAccount -- A bank account that draws interest
internal class SavingsAccount : BankAccount
{
    private decimal InterestRate
        { get; set; }
```

```
    // SavingsAccount -- Input the rate expressed as a
    //    rate between 0 and 100.
    public SavingsAccount(decimal initialBalance, decimal interestRate)
    : base(initialBalance)
    {
        InterestRate = interestRate / 100;
    }

    // Withdraw -- You can withdraw any amount up to the
    //    balance; return the amount withdrawn.
    internal decimal Withdraw(decimal withdrawal)
    {
        // Take the $1.50 off the top.
        base.Withdraw(1.5M);

        // Now you can withdraw from what's left.
        return base.Withdraw(withdrawal);
    }
}
```

The two classes provide some basics for creating the accounts and withdrawing money. Notice that both classes have a `Withdraw()` method with precisely the same signature, so the `Withdraw()` method in `SavingsAccount` completely hides the `Withdraw()` method in `BankAccount`. Here's the `Main()` method used to exercise these two classes.

```
static void Main(string[] args)
{
    BankAccount ba;
    SavingsAccount sa;

    // Create a bank account and withdraw $100.
    ba = new BankAccount(200M);
    ba.Withdraw(100M);

    // Try the same trick with a savings account.
    sa = new SavingsAccount(200M, 12);
    sa.Withdraw(100M);

    // Display the resulting balance.
    Console.WriteLine("When invoked directly:");
    Console.WriteLine("BankAccount balance is {0:C}", ba.Balance);
    Console.WriteLine("SavingsAccount balance is {0:C}", sa.Balance);
    Console.Read();
}
```

Main() in this case creates a BankAccount object with an initial balance of $200 and then withdraws $100. Main() repeats the trick with a SavingsAccount object. When Main() withdraws money from the base class, BankAccount.Withdraw() performs the withdraw function with great aplomb. When Main() then withdraws $100 from the savings account, the method SavingsAccount.Withdraw() tacks on the extra $1.50.

TIP

Notice that the SavingsAccount.Withdraw() method uses BankAccount.Withdraw() rather than manipulate the balance directly. Because of this approach, the set member of Balance is private, rather than internal, reducing security risks. If possible, let the base class maintain its own data members.

Making the hiding approach better than adding a simple test

On the surface, adding a flag to the BankAccount.Withdraw() method may seem simpler than all this method-hiding stuff. After all, it's just four little lines of code, two of which are nothing more than braces.

The problems are manifold. One problem is that the BankAccount class has no business worrying about the details of SavingsAccount. More formally, it's known as breaking the encapsulation of SavingsAccount. Base classes don't normally know about their subclasses, which leads to the real problem: Suppose that your bank subsequently decides to add a CheckingAccount or a CDAccount or a TBillAccount. All those likely additions have different withdrawal policies, each requiring its own flag. After adding three or four different types of accounts, the old Withdraw() method starts looking complicated. Each of those types of classes should worry about its own withdrawal policies and leave BankAccount.Withdraw() alone. Classes are responsible for themselves.

Accidentally hiding a base class method

Oddly enough, you can hide a base class method accidentally. For example, you may have a Vehicle.TakeOff() method that starts the vehicle rolling. Later, someone else extends your Vehicle class with an Airplane class. Its TakeOff() method is entirely different. In airplane lingo, "take off" means more than just "start moving." Clearly, this is a case of mistaken identity — the two methods have no similarity other than their identical name. Fortunately, C# detects this problem.

C# generates an ominous-looking warning when it compiles the earlier `HidingWithdrawal` program example. The text of the warning message is long, but here's the important part:

```
'...SavingsAccount.Withdraw(decimal)' hides inherited member
  '...BankAccount.Withdraw(decimal)'.
  Use the new keyword if hiding was intended.
```

C# is trying to tell you that you've written a method in a subclass that has the same name as a method in the base class. Is that what you meant to do?

TIP

This message is just a warning — you don't even notice it unless you switch over to the Error List window to take a look. But you should sort out and fix all warnings. In almost every case, a warning is telling you about something that can bite you if you don't fix it.

The descriptor `new` (shown in bold below) tells C# that the hiding of methods is intentional and not the result of an oversight (and it makes the warning disappear):

```
internal new decimal Withdraw(decimal withdrawal)
{
    // Take the $1.50 off the top.
    base.Withdraw(1.5M);

    // Now you can withdraw from what's left.
    return base.Withdraw(withdrawal);
}
```

VIEWING WARNINGS AS ERRORS

It's important to fix warnings as you start creating the details of your application so that the errors the warnings point out don't become long-term issues. To make the warnings more visible, you can treat them as errors. To do so, choose Project ⇨ Properties. In the Build pane of your project's properties page, scroll down to Errors and Warnings. Set the Warning Level to 4, the highest level, which turns the compiler into more of a chatterbox. Also, in the Treat Warnings As Errors section, select All. (If a particular warning becomes annoying, you can list it in the Suppress Warnings box to keep it out of your face.)

When you treat warnings as errors, you're forced to fix the warnings — just as you would be forced to fix real compiler errors. This practice makes for better code. Even if you don't enable the Treat Warnings As Errors option, leave the Warning Level at 4 and select the Error List window after each build.

TIP

This use of the keyword new has nothing to do with the same word new that's used to create an object. (C# even overloads itself!)

Polymorphism

You can overload a method in a base class with a method in the subclass. As simple as this process sounds, it introduces considerable capability, and with capability comes danger.

Here's a thought experiment: Should you make the decision to call BankAccount.Withdraw() or SavingsAccount.Withdraw() at compile-time or at runtime? To illustrate the difference, the following example changes the previous HidingWithdrawal program in a seemingly innocuous way. (The HidingWithdrawalPolymorphically version streamlines the listing by leaving out the stuff that doesn't change.) The new version is shown here:

```
class Program
{
    public static void MakeAWithdrawal(BankAccount ba, decimal amount)
    {
        ba.Withdraw(amount);
    }

    static void Main(string[] args)
    {
        BankAccount ba;
        SavingsAccount sa;

        // Create a bank account, withdraw $100, and
        // display the results.
        ba = new BankAccount(200M);
        MakeAWithdrawal(ba, 100M);

        // Try the same trick with a savings account.
        sa = new SavingsAccount(200M, 12);
        MakeAWithdrawal(sa, 100M);

        // Display the resulting balance.
        Console.WriteLine("When invoked through intermediary:");
        Console.WriteLine("BankAccount balance is {0:C}", ba.Balance);
        Console.WriteLine("SavingsAccount balance is {0:C}", sa.Balance);
        Console.Read();
    }
}
```

The following output from this program may or may not be confusing, depending on what you expected:

```
When invoked through intermediary:
BankAccount balance is $100.00
SavingsAccount balance is $100.00
```

This time, rather than perform a withdrawal in `Main()`, the program passes the bank account object to the method `MakeAWithdrawal()`.

The first question is fairly straightforward: Why does the `MakeAWithdrawal()` method even accept a `SavingsAccount` object when it clearly states that it's looking for a `BankAccount`? The answer is obvious: "Because a `SavingsAccount` IS_A `BankAccount`." (See the "IS_A versus HAS_A — I'm So Confused_A" section of Chapter 5 of this minibook.)

The second question is subtle. When passed a `BankAccount` object, `MakeAWithdrawal()` invokes `BankAccount.Withdraw()` — that's clear enough. But when passed a `SavingsAccount` object, `MakeAWithdrawal()` calls the same method. Shouldn't it invoke the `Withdraw()` method in the subclass?

The prosecution intends to show that the call `ba.Withdraw()` should invoke the method `BankAccount.Withdraw()`. Clearly, the `ba` object is a `BankAccount`. To do anything else would merely confuse the state. The defense has witnesses back in `Main()` to prove that although the `ba` object is declared `BankAccount`, it is in fact a `SavingsAccount`. The jury is deadlocked. Both arguments are equally valid.

In this case, C# comes down on the side of the prosecution: The safer of the two possibilities is to go with the declared type because it avoids any miscommunication. The object is declared to be a `BankAccount` and that's that. However, that may not be what you want.

Using the declared type every time (Is that so wrong?)

In some cases, you don't want to choose the declared type. What you want is to make the call based on the *real type* — the runtime type — as opposed to the declared type. For example, you want to use the `SavingsAccount` stored in a `BankAccount` variable. This capability to decide at runtime is known as *polymorphism*, or *late binding*. Using the declared type every time is called *early binding* because it sounds like the opposite of *late binding*.

The term *polymorphism* comes from the Greek language: *Poly* means more than one, *morph* means transform, and *ism* relates to an ideology or philosophy. Consequently, polymorphism is the idea or concept of transforming a single object, `BankAccount`, into many different objects, `BankAccount` or `SavingsAccount` (in this case). Polymorphism and late binding aren't exactly the same concept — but the difference is subtle:

- *Polymorphism* refers to the general ability to decide which method to invoke at runtime.
- *Late binding* refers to the specific way a language implements polymorphism.

Polymorphism is the key to the power of Object-Oriented Programming (OOP). It's so important that languages that don't support it can't advertise themselves as OOP languages.

TECHNICAL STUFF

Languages that support classes but not polymorphism are *object-based languages.* Visual Basic 6.0 (not VB.NET) is an example of such a language.

Without polymorphism, inheritance has little meaning. As another example, suppose that you had written a great program that uses a class named `Student`. After months of design, coding, and testing, you release this application to rave reviews from colleagues and critics alike.

Time passes, and your boss asks you to add to this program the capability of handling graduate students, who are similar but not identical to undergraduate students. (The graduate students probably claim that they aren't similar in any way.) Suppose that the formula for calculating the tuition amount for a graduate student is completely different from the formula for an undergrad. Now, your boss doesn't know or care that, deep within the program, are numerous calls to the member method `CalcTuition()`. The following example shows one of those many calls to `CalcTuition()`:

```
void SomeMethod(Student s)  // Could be grad or undergrad
{
  // ... whatever it might do ...
  s.CalcTuition();
  // ... continues on ...
}
```

If C# didn't support late binding, you would need to edit `SomeMethod()` to check whether the `student` object passed to it is a `GraduateStudent` or a `Student`. The program would call `Student.CalcTuition()` when `s` is a `Student` and

GraduateStudent.CalcTuition() when it's a GraduateStudent. Editing SomeMethod() doesn't seem so bad, except for two problems:

- You're assuming use by only one method. Suppose that CalcTuition() is called from many places.
- CalcTuition() might not be the only difference between the two classes. The chances aren't good that you'll find all items that need to be changed.

Using polymorphism, you can let C# decide which method to call.

Using is to access a hidden method polymorphically

C# provides one approach to manually solving the problem of making your program polymorphic, using the keyword is. (The "Avoiding invalid conversions with the is operator" section of Chapter 5 of this minibook introduces is and its cousin as.) The expression ba is SavingsAccount returns true or false depending on the runtime class of the object. The declared type may be BankAccount, but which type is it really? The following code chunk uses is to access the SavingsAccount version of Withdraw() specifically (as found in HidingWithdrawalPolymorphically2):

```
public static void MakeAWithdrawal(BankAccount ba, decimal amount)
{
    if (ba is SavingsAccount)
    {
        SavingsAccount sa = (SavingsAccount)ba;
        sa.Withdraw(amount);
    }
    else
    {
        ba.Withdraw(amount);
    }
}
```

Now, when Main() passes the method a SavingsAccount object, MakeAWithdrawal() checks the runtime type of the ba object and invokes SavingsAccount.Withdraw().

TECHNICAL STUFF

As an alternative, the programmer could have performed the cast and the call for a SavingsAccount in the following single line:

```
((SavingsAccount)ba).Withdraw(amount);  // Notice locations of parentheses.
```

You often see this technique used in programs written by experienced developers who hate typing any more than necessary. Although you can use this approach, it's more difficult to read than when you use multiple lines, as shown in the example code. Anything written confusingly or cryptically tends to be more error-prone, too.

The `is` approach works, but it's a bad idea. It requires `MakeAWithdrawal()` to be aware of all the different types of bank accounts and which of them is represented by different classes. That puts too much responsibility on poor old `MakeAWithdrawal()`. Right now, your application handles only two types of bank accounts, but suppose that your boss asks you to implement a new account type, `CheckingAccount`, and it has different `Withdraw()` requirements. Your program doesn't work properly if you don't search out and find every method that checks the runtime type of its argument.

Declaring a method virtual and overriding it

As the author of `MakeAWithdrawal()`, you don't want to know about all the different types of accounts. You want to leave to the programmers who use `MakeAWithdrawal()` the responsibility to know about their account types and just leave you alone. You want C# to make decisions about which methods to invoke based on the runtime type of the object.

You tell C# to make the runtime decision of the version of `Withdraw()` by marking the base class method with the keyword `virtual` and marking each subclass version of the method with the keyword `override`.

The following example relies on polymorphism. It has output statements in the `Withdraw()` methods to prove that the proper methods are indeed being invoked. Here are the `BankAccount` and `SavingsAccount` classes of the `PolymorphicInheritance` program:

```
// BankAccount -- A very basic bank account
internal class BankAccount
{
    internal BankAccount(decimal initialBalance)
    {
        Balance = initialBalance;
    }

    internal decimal Balance
        { get; private set; }
```

Poly-what-ism?

```
    internal virtual decimal Withdraw(decimal amount)
    {
        decimal amountToWithdraw = amount;

        if (amountToWithdraw > Balance)
        {
            amountToWithdraw = Balance;
        }
        Console.WriteLine($"In BankAccount.Withdraw() for " +
            $"${amountToWithdraw}.");

        Balance -= amountToWithdraw;
        return amountToWithdraw;
    }
}

// SavingsAccount -- A bank account that draws interest
internal class SavingsAccount : BankAccount
{
    private decimal InterestRate
        { get; set; }

    // SavingsAccount -- Input the rate expressed as a
    //    rate between 0 and 100.
    public SavingsAccount(decimal initialBalance, decimal interestRate)
    : base(initialBalance)
    {
        InterestRate = interestRate / 100;
    }

    // Withdraw -- You can withdraw any amount up to the
    //    balance; return the amount withdrawn.
    internal override decimal Withdraw(decimal withdrawal)
    {
        // Take the $1.50 off the top.
        Console.WriteLine("Deductng the SavingsAccount fee.");
        base.Withdraw(1.5M);

        // Now you can withdraw from what's left.
        Console.WriteLine($"In SavingsAccount.Withdraw() for " +
            $"${withdrawal}.");
        return base.Withdraw(withdrawal);
    }
}
```

The `Withdraw()` method is marked as `virtual` in the base class `BankAccount`. Likewise, you see it marked override in the subclass `SavingsAccount`. This version of the example also adds some `Console.WriteLine()` calls so you can see what's happening. Here's the `Program` class code:

```
class Program
{
    public static void MakeAWithdrawal(BankAccount ba, decimal amount)
    {
        ba.Withdraw(amount);
    }

    static void Main(string[] args)
    {
        BankAccount ba;
        SavingsAccount sa;

        // Create a bank account, withdraw $100, and
        // display the results.
        Console.WriteLine("Withdrawal: MakeAWithdrawal(ba, ...)");
        ba = new BankAccount(200M);
        MakeAWithdrawal(ba, 100M);
        Console.WriteLine("BankAccount balance is {0:C}", ba.Balance);

        // Try the same trick with a savings account.
        Console.WriteLine("\r\nWithdrawal: MakeAWithdrawal(sa, ...)");
        sa = new SavingsAccount(200M, 12);
        MakeAWithdrawal(sa, 100M);
        Console.WriteLine("SavingsAccount balance is {0:C}", sa.Balance);
        Console.Read();
    }
}
```

Notice that all the decision-making code is removed from the `HidingWithdrawal-Polymorphically2` example. The output from executing this program is shown here:

```
Withdrawal: MakeAWithdrawal(ba, ...)
In BankAccount.Withdraw() for $100.
BankAccount balance is $100.00

Withdrawal: MakeAWithdrawal(sa, ...)
Deductng the SavingsAccount fee.
In BankAccount.Withdraw() for $1.5.
In SavingsAccount.Withdraw() for $100.
In BankAccount.Withdraw() for $100.
SavingsAccount balance is $98.50
```

TIP

Choose sparingly which methods to make virtual. Each one has a small cost in resource use and runtime speed, so use the `virtual` keyword only when necessary. It's a trade-off between a class that's highly flexible and can be overridden (lots of virtual methods) and a class that isn't flexible enough (hardly any virtuals).

Getting the most benefit from polymorphism

Much of the power of polymorphism springs from polymorphic objects sharing a common interface. For example, given a hierarchy of `Shape` objects — `Circles`, `Squares`, and `Triangles`, for example — you can count on all shapes having a `Draw()` method. Each object's `Draw()` method is implemented quite differently, of course. But the point is that, given a collection of these objects, you can freely use a `foreach` loop to call `Draw()` or any other method in the polymorphic interface on the objects.

C# During Its Abstract Period

A duck is a type of bird. So are the cardinal and the hummingbird. In fact, every bird out there is a subtype of bird. The flip side of that argument is that no bird exists that *isn't* a subtype of `Bird`. That statement doesn't *sound* profound, but in a way, it is. The software equivalent of that statement is that all `bird` objects are instances of the `Bird` subclasses — there's never an instance of class `Bird`. What's a bird? It's always a robin or a grackle or another specific species.

Different types of birds share many properties (otherwise, they wouldn't be birds), yet no two types share every property. If they did, they wouldn't be different types. For example, not all birds `Fly()` the same way (or possibly at all). Ducks have one style, cardinals another. The hummingbird's style is completely different. And ostriches are only interested in sticking their heads in the sand and not flying at all (or perhaps not — see `https://www.scienceworld.ca/stories/do-ostriches-really-bury-their-heads-sand/`). But if not all birds fly the same way and there's no such thing as an instance of a generic `Bird`, what the heck is `Bird.Fly()`? The `Bird.Fly()` method would need to be different for each subclass of `Bird`. The following sections discuss this issue in detail.

Class factoring

People generate taxonomies of objects by factoring out commonalities. To see how factoring works, consider the two classes `HighSchool` and `University`, shown in Figure 6-1. This figure uses the Unified Modeling Language (UML), a graphical language that describes a class along with the relationship of that class to others. UML has become universally popular with programmers and is worth learning (to a reasonable extent) in its own right.

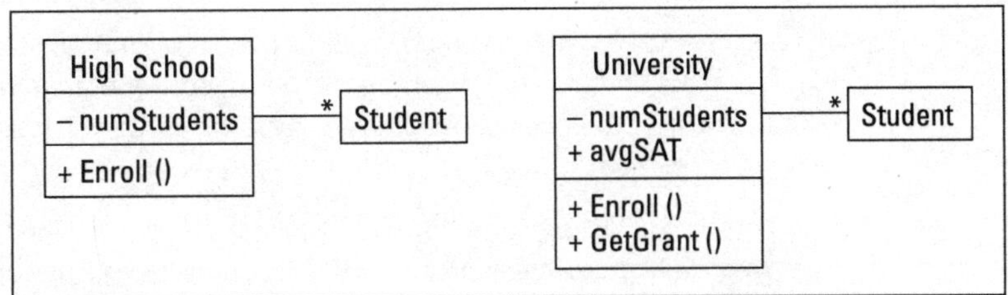

FIGURE 6-1: A UML description of the `HighSchool` and `University` classes.

High schools and universities have several similar properties (refer to Figure 6-1) — many more than you may think. Both schools offer a publicly available `Enroll()` method for adding `Student` objects to the school. In addition, both classes offer a private member, `numStudents`, which indicates the number of students attending the school. Another common feature is the relationship between students: One school can have any number of students — a student can attend only a single school at one time. Even high schools and most universities offer more than described, but only one of each type of member is needed for illustration.

In addition to the features of a high school, the university contains a method `GetGrant()` and a data member `avgSAT`. High schools have no SAT entrance requirements and students receive no federal grants.

Figure 6-1 is acceptable, as far as it goes, but some information is duplicated, and duplication in code (and UML diagrams) stinks. You can reduce the duplication by allowing the more complex class `University` to inherit from the simpler `HighSchool` class, as shown in Figure 6-2.

The `HighSchool` class is left unchanged, but the `University` class is easier to describe. You say that "a `University` is a `HighSchool` that also has an `avgSAT` and a `GetGrant()` method." But this solution has a fundamental problem: A university isn't a high school with special properties.

UML LITE

The Unified Modeling Language (UML) is an expressive language that's capable of clearly defining the relationships of objects within a program. One advantage of UML is that you can ignore the more specific language features without losing its meaning entirely. The essential features of UML are

- Classes are represented by a box divided vertically into three sections. The name of the class appears in the uppermost section.
- The data members of the class appear in the middle section, and the methods of the class in the bottom. You can omit either the middle or bottom section if the class has no data members or methods or if you want just a high-level classes-only view.
- Members with a plus sign (+) in front are public; those with a minus sign (–) are private. To provide protected and internal visibility, most people use the pound sign (#) and the tilde (~), respectively.

  A private member is accessible only from other members of the same class. A public member is accessible to all classes. See Chapter 4 in this minibook.
- The label `{abstract}` next to a name indicates an abstract class or method. An *abstract class or method* doesn't provide a full implementation, so you can only use it as a base class to create other classes.

  UML uses a different symbol for an abstract method, but doing so isn't essential. You can also just show abstract items in italics.
- An arrow between two classes represents a relationship between the two classes. A number above the line expresses cardinality — the number of items you can have at each end of the arrow. The asterisk symbol (*) means *any number*. If no number is present, the cardinality is assumed to be 1. Thus you can see that a single university has any number of students — a one-to-many relationship (refer to Figure 7-1).
- A line with a large, open arrowhead, or a triangular arrowhead, expresses the IS_A relationship (inheritance). The arrow points *up* the class hierarchy to the base class. Other types of relationships include the HAS_A relationship (a line with a filled diamond at the owning end).

To explore UML in depth, check out *UML 2 For Dummies*, by Michael Jesse Chonoles and James A. Schardt (Wiley).

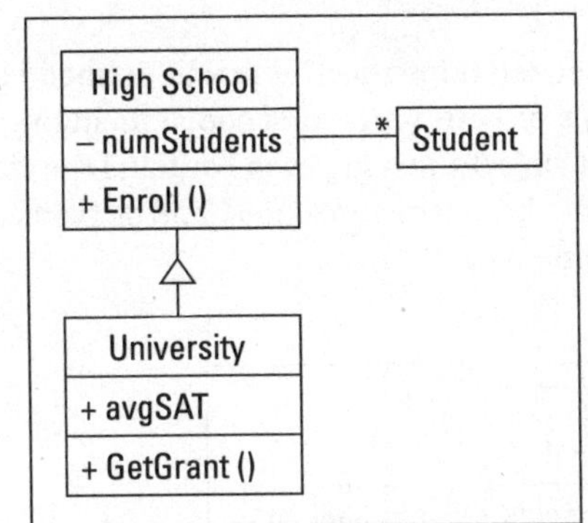

FIGURE 6-2: Inheriting HighSchool simplifies the University class but introduces problems.

You say, "So what? Inheriting works, and it saves effort." True, but the problems are more than stylistic trivialities. This type of misrepresentation is confusing to the programmer, both now and in the future. Someday, a programmer who is unfamiliar with your programming tricks will have to read and understand what your code does. Misleading representations are difficult to reconcile and understand.

In addition, this type of misrepresentation can lead to problems down the road. Suppose that the high school decides to name a "favorite" student at the prom. The clever programmer adds the `NameFavorite()` method to the `HighSchool` class, which the application invokes to name the favorite `Student` object.

But now you have a problem: Most universities don't name a favorite student. However, as long as `University` inherits from `HighSchool`, it inherits the `NameFavorite()` method. One extra method may not seem like a big deal. "Just ignore it," you say. However, one method is just one more brick in the wall of confusion. Extra methods and properties accumulate over time, until the `University` class is carrying lots of extra baggage. Pity the poor software developer who has to understand which methods are "real" and which aren't.

REMEMBER

Inheritances of convenience lead to another problem. The way it's written, Figure 6-2 implies that a `University` and a `HighSchool` have the same enrollment procedure. As unlikely as that statement sounds, assume that it's true. The program is developed, packaged up, and shipped off to the unwitting public. Months pass before the school district decides to modify its enrollment procedure. It isn't obvious to anyone that modifying the high school enrollment procedure also modifies the sign-up procedure at the local college.

To fix the source of the problem you must consider that a university isn't a particular type of high school. A relationship exists between the two, but neither IS_A or HAS_A are the right ones. Instead, both high schools and universities are special types of schools. That's what they have the most in common.

Figure 6-3 describes a better relationship. The newly defined class `School` contains the common properties of both types of schools, including the relationship they both have with `Student` objects. `School` even contains the common `Enroll()` method, although it's abstract because `HighSchool` and `University` usually don't implement `Enroll()` the same way.

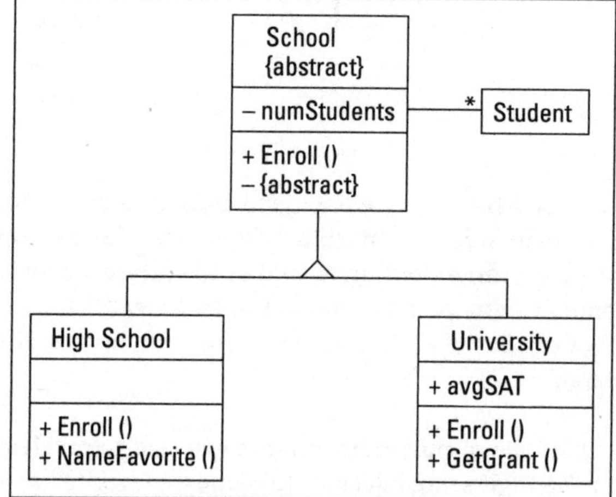

FIGURE 6-3: Base both `HighSchool` and `University` on a common `School` class.

The classes `HighSchool` and `University` now inherit from a common base class. Each contains its unique members: `NameFavorite()` in the case of `HighSchool`, and `GetGrant()` and `avgSAT` for the `University`. In addition, both classes override the `Enroll()` method with a version that describes how that type of school enrolls students. In effect, the example extracts a superclass, or base class, from two similar classes, which now become subclasses. The introduction of the `School` class has at least two big advantages:

- **It corresponds with reality.** A `University` is a `School`, but it isn't a `HighSchool`. Matching reality is nice but not conclusive.
- **It isolates one class from changes or additions to the other.** Adding the `CommencementSpeech()` method to the `University` class doesn't affect `HighSchool`.

This process of culling common properties from similar classes is known as *factoring*. This feature of object-oriented languages is important for the reasons described earlier in this minibook, plus one more: reducing redundancy.

WARNING

Factoring is legitimate only if the inheritance relationship corresponds to reality. Factoring together a class `Mouse` and `Joystick` because they're both hardware pointing devices is legitimate. Factoring together a class `Mouse` and `Display` because they both make low-level operating-system calls is not.

Factoring can and usually does result in multiple levels of abstraction. For example, a program written for a more developed school hierarchy may have a class structure more like the one shown in Figure 6-4.

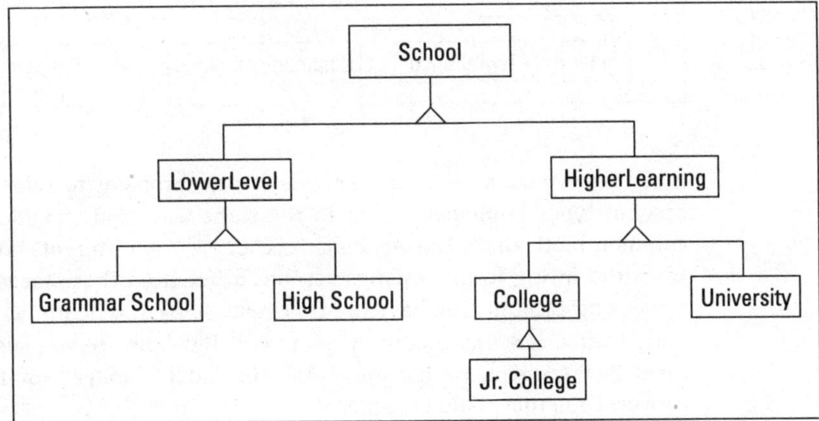

FIGURE 6-4: Class factoring usually results in added layers of inheritance hierarchy.

You can see that Figure 6-4 inserts a pair of new classes between `University` and `School`: `HigherLearning` and `LowerLevel`. It subdivides the new class `HigherLearning` into `College` and `University`. This type of multitiered class hierarchy is common and desirable when factoring out relationships. They correspond to reality, and they can teach you subtle features of your solution.

Note, however, that no Unified Factoring Theory exists for any given set of classes. The relationship shown in Figure 6-4 seems natural, but suppose that an application cared more about differentiating types of schools administered by local politicians from those that aren't. This relationship, shown in Figure 6-5, is a more natural fit for that type of problem. No correct factoring exists: The proper way to break down the classes is partially a function of the problem being solved.

The abstract class: Left with nothing but a concept

As intellectually satisfying as factoring is, it reveals a problem of its own. Revisit `BankAccount`, introduced at the beginning of this chapter. Think about how you may go about defining the different member methods defined in `BankAccount`.

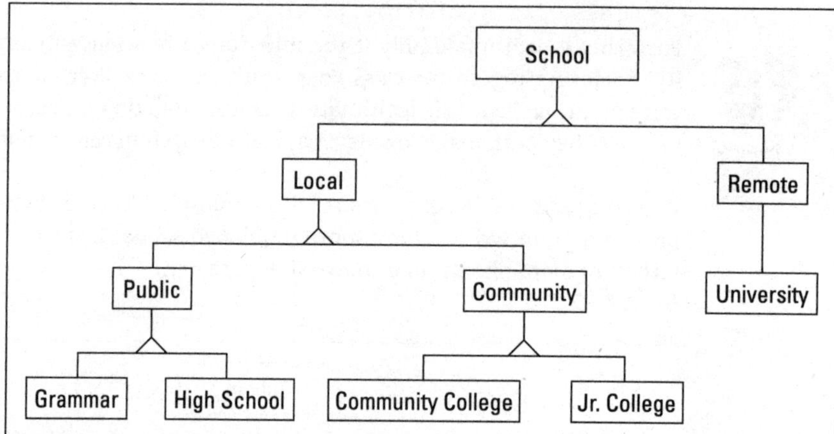

FIGURE 6-5: Breaking down classes is partially a function of the problem being solved.

Most `BankAccount` member methods are no problem to refactor because both account types implement them in the same way. You should implement those common methods in `BankAccount`. `Withdraw()` is different, however. The rules for withdrawing from a savings account differ from those for withdrawing from a checking account. You have to implement `SavingsAccount.Withdraw()` differently from `CheckingAccount.Withdraw()`. But how are you supposed to implement `BankAccount.Withdraw()`? Ask the bank manager for help. This is the conversation that could take place:

> "What are the rules for making a withdrawal from an account?" you ask, expectantly.
>
> "Which type of account? Savings or checking?" comes the reply.
>
> "From an account," you say. "Just an account."
>
> [Blank look.] (You might say a "blank bank look." Then again, maybe not.)

The problem is that the question doesn't make sense. No such thing as "just an account" exists. All accounts (in this example) are either checking accounts or savings accounts. The concept of an account is *abstract:* It factors out properties common to the two concrete classes. It's incomplete because it lacks the critical method `Withdraw()`. (After you delve into the details, you may find other properties that a simple account lacks.)

How do you use an abstract class?

Abstract classes are used to describe abstract concepts. An *abstract class* is a class with one or more abstract methods. An abstract method is a method marked `abstract` and has no implementation because it has no method body. You create the method body when you subclass from the abstract class. Consider the classes of the AbstractInheritance program:

```
// AbstractBaseClass -- Create an abstract base class with nothing
//    but an Output() method. You can also say "public abstract."
abstract public class AbstractBaseClass
{
    // Output -- Abstract method that outputs a string
    abstract public void Output(string outputString);
}

// SubClass1 -- One concrete implementation of AbstractBaseClass
public class SubClass1 : AbstractBaseClass
{
    override public void Output(string source) // Or "public override"
    {
        string s = source.ToUpper();
        Console.WriteLine($"Call to SubClass1.Output() from within {s}");
    }
}

// SubClass2 -- Another concrete implementation of AbstractBaseClass
public class SubClass2 : AbstractBaseClass
{
    public override void Output(string source)  // Or "override public"
    {
        string s = source.ToLower();
        Console.WriteLine($"Call to SubClass2.Output() from within {s}");
    }
}
```

The program first defines the class AbstractBaseClass with a single abstract Output() method. Because it's declared abstract, Output() has no implementation — that is, no method body. Two classes inherit from AbstractBaseClass: SubClass1 and SubClass2. Both are concrete classes because they override the Output() method with real methods and contain no abstract methods themselves.

TIP

A class can be declared abstract regardless of whether it has abstract members; however, a class can be concrete (not abstract) only when all abstract methods in any base class above it have been overridden with full methods.

The two subclass Output() methods differ in a trivial way: Both accept input strings, which they send back to users. However, one converts the string to all caps before output and the other converts it to all-lowercase characters. Here is the `Program` class for this example:

```
class Program
{
    public static void Test(AbstractBaseClass ba)
    {
        ba.Output("Test");
    }

    static void Main(string[] args)
    {
        // You can't create an AbstractBaseClass object because it's
        // abstract. C# generates a compile-time error if you
        // uncomment the following line.
        // AbstractBaseClass ba = new AbstractBaseClass();

        // Now repeat the experiment with SubClass1.
        Console.WriteLine("\ncreating a SubClass1 object");
        SubClass1 sc1 = new SubClass1();
        Test(sc1);

        // And, finally, a SubClass2 object
        Console.WriteLine("\ncreating a SubClass2 object");
        SubClass2 sc2 = new SubClass2();
        Test(sc2);
        Console.Read();
    }
}
```

This code looks much the same as the `PolymorphicInheritance` example earlier in the chapter. `Main()` instantiates an object of each of the subclasses and then calls the `Test()` method, which calls on the `Output()` method in each class. The following output from this program demonstrates the polymorphic nature of `AbstractInheritance`:

```
Creating a SubClass1 object
Call to SubClass1.Output() from within TEST

Creating a SubClass2 object
Call to SubClass2.Output() from within test
```

TIP

An abstract method is automatically virtual, so you don't add the `virtual` keyword to an abstract method.

Creating an abstract object — not!

Notice something about the AbstractInheritance program: It isn't legal to create an AbstractBaseClass object, but the argument to Test() is declared to be an object of the class AbstractBaseClass or one of its subclasses. It's the subclasses clause that's critical here. The SubClass1 and SubClass2 objects can be passed because each one is a concrete subclass of AbstractBaseClass. The IS_A relationship applies. This powerful technique lets you write highly general methods.

Sealing a Class

You may decide that you don't want future generations of programmers to be able to extend a particular class. You can lock the class by using the keyword sealed. A sealed class cannot be used as the base class for any other class. Consider this code snippet:

```
public class BankAccount
{
  // Withdrawal -- You can withdraw any amount up to the
  //    balance; return the amount withdrawn
  virtual public void Withdraw(decimal withdrawal)
  {
    Console.WriteLine("invokes BankAccount.Withdraw()");
  }
}

public sealed class SavingsAccount : BankAccount
{
  override public void Withdraw(decimal withdrawal)
  {
    Console.WriteLine("invokes SavingsAccount.Withdraw()");
  }
}

public class SpecialSaleAccount : SavingsAccount  // Oops!
{
  override public void Withdraw(decimal withdrawal)
  {
    Console.WriteLine("invokes SpecialSaleAccount.Withdraw()");
  }
}
```

This snippet generates the following compiler error:

```
'SpecialSaleAccount' : cannot inherit from sealed class 'SavingsAccount'
```

You use the `sealed` keyword to protect your class from the prying methods of a subclass. For example, allowing a programmer to extend a class that implements system security enables someone to create a security back door.

Sealing a class prevents another program, possibly somewhere on the Internet, from using a modified version of your class. The remote program can use the class as is, or not, but it can't inherit bits and pieces of your class while overriding the rest.

IN THIS CHAPTER

» Going beyond IS_A and HAS_A

» Creating and using interfaces

» Unifying class hierarchies with interfaces

» Managing flexibility via interfaces

Chapter 7

Interfacing with the Interface

A class can contain a reference to another class, which describes the simple HAS_A relationship. One class can extend another class by using inheritance — that's the IS_A relationship. The C# interface implements another, equally important association: the CAN_BE_USED_AS relationship. This chapter introduces C# interfaces and shows some of the numerous ways they increase the power and flexibility of object-oriented programming. Most importantly, you discover how to unify classes with interfaces to produce clearer application code with improved flexibility.

You don't have to type the source code for this chapter manually. In fact, using the downloadable source is a lot easier. You can find the source for this chapter in the `\CSAIO4D2E\BK02\CH07` folder of the downloadable source. See the Introduction for details on how to find these source files.

Introducing CAN_BE_USED_AS

If you want to jot a note, you can scribble it with a pen, type it into your Personal Digital Assistant (PDA) (a high performance handheld device used for business purposes that comes with a wide variety of add-ons such as bar code readers), or pound it out on your laptop's keyboard. You can fairly say that all three objects — pen, PDA, and computer — implement the `TakeANote` operation. Suppose that you use the magic of inheritance to implement this concept in C#:

```
abstract class ThingsThatRecord          // The base class
{
  abstract public void TakeANote(string note);
}

public class Pen : ThingsThatRecord      // A subclass
{
  override public void TakeANote(string note)
  {
    // ... scribble a note with a pen ...
  }
}

public class PDA : ThingsThatRecord      // Another subclass
{
  override public void TakeANote(string note)
  {
    // ... stroke a note on the PDA ...
  }
}

public class LapTop : ThingsThatRecord  // A third subclass
{
  override public void TakeANote(string note)
  {
    // ... tap, tap, tap ...
  }
}
```

TIP

If the term *abstract* has you stumped, see Chapter 6 of this minibook and, later in this chapter, read the discussion in the section "Abstract or concrete: When to use an abstract class and when to use an interface." If the whole concept of inheritance is a mystery, check out Chapter 5 of this minibook. The following simple method shows the inheritance approach working just fine:

```
void RecordTask(ThingsThatRecord recorder) // Parameter type is base class.
{
  // All classes that extend ThingsThatRecord have a TakeANote method.
  recorder.TakeANote("Shopping list");
  // ... and so on.
}
```

The parameter type is `ThingsThatRecord`, so you can pass any subclasses to this method, making the method quite general. That might seem like a good solution, but it has two big drawbacks:

- **A fundamental problem:** Do `Pen`, `PDA`, and `LapTop` truly have an IS_A relationship? Are those three items all the same type in real life? The issue is that `ThingsThatRecord` makes a poor base class here.
- **A purely technical problem:** You might reasonably derive both `LapTop` and `PDA` as subclasses of `Computer`. But nobody would say that a `Pen` IS_A `Computer`. You have to characterize a pen as a type of `MechanicalWritingDevice` or `DeviceThatStainsYourShirt`. But a C# class can't inherit from two different base classes at the same time — a C# class can be only one type of item.

So the `Pen`, `PDA`, and `LapTop` classes have in common only the characteristic that they CAN_BE_USED_AS recording devices. Inheritance doesn't apply.

Knowing What an Interface Is

An *interface* in C# resembles a class with no data members and nothing but abstract methods in older versions of C#, almost like an abstract class — almost:

```
interface IRecordable
{
  void TakeANote(string note);
}
```

Interfaces created in C# 8.0 and above can have default implementations for their members and also static members for common functionality, making the newer interfaces a little closer to a base class. The interface begins with the `interface` keyword. It contains nothing but abstract methods. It has no data members and no implemented methods.

TECHNICAL STUFF

Interfaces can contain a few other features, including properties (covered in Chapter 4 of this minibook), events (covered in Chapter 8 of this minibook), and indexers (covered in Chapter 7 of Book 1). Among the elements that a C# interface cannot exhibit when working with an older implementation are

- Access modifiers, such as `public` or `private` (see Chapter 4 of this minibook)
- Keywords such as `virtual`, `override`, or `abstract` (see Chapter 6 of this minibook)

- Data members (see Chapter 1 of this minibook)
- Implemented methods — nonabstract methods with bodies

When creating an interface using C# 8.0 or above, you can include these additional elements:

- Constants
- Operators
- Static constructors
- Nested types
- Static fields, methods, properties, indexers, and events
- Member declarations using the explicit interface implementation syntax
- Explicit access modifiers (the default access is public)

REMEMBER

There is a distinct separation between interface code created for versions of C# older than 8.0 and interface code created for versions of C# 8.0 and above. It's essential to know which version of C# you're using when working with interfaces, or you should assume that you need to follow the older rules. Unlike an abstract class, a C# interface isn't a class. It can't be subclassed.

How to implement an interface

To put a C# interface to use, you implement it with one or more classes or structures. The class and structure headings might look like this:

```
// Looks like inheritance, but isn't
class Pen : IRecordable
struct PenDescription : IRecordable
```

REMEMBER

A C# interface specifies that classes or structures which implement the interface must provide specific implementations. For example, any class that implements the `IRecordable` interface must provide an implementation for the `TakeANote` method. The method that implements `TakeANote` doesn't use the `override` keyword. Using an interface isn't like overriding a virtual method in classes. Class `Pen` might look like this:

```
class Pen : IRecordable
{
  public void TakeANote(string note)    // Interface method implementations
  {                                     // MUST be declared public.
```

```
        // ... scribble a note with a pen ...
    }
}
```

This example fulfills two requirements: Note that the class implements IRecordable and provides a method implementation for TakeANote().

The syntax indicating that a class inherits a base class, such as ThingsThatRecord, is essentially no different from the syntax indicating that the class implements a C# interface such as IRecordable:

```
public class PDA : ThingsThatRecord ...
public class PDA : IRecordable ...
```

TIP

Visual Studio can help you implement an interface. Hover the cursor over the interface name in the class heading. A little underline appears underneath the first character of the interface name — it's a Smart Tag. Move the cursor until a menu opens and then choose Implement Interface. Presto! A skeleton framework appears; you fill in the details.

Using the newer C# 8.0 additions

Microsoft added a lot of functionality to C# 8.0 interfaces, so it pays to spend a little more time reviewing them. The IRecordable8 program provides more than the interface code snippets you've seen so far so that you can gain an understanding of the C# 8.0 difference. This code requires use of the .NET Core template, rather than the .NET Framework template. In addition, you must choose .NET 6.0 when asked for the Target Framework in the Console Application Wizard. Here is the IRecordable interface used for this example:

```
public interface IRecordable
{
    // This is a default implementation.
    public string GetName()
    {
        return "Writing Device";
    }

    private static int _numDevices;
    public static int NumDevices
    {
        get { return _numDevices; }
        set { if (value >= 0) _numDevices = value; }
    }
```

```
    public static bool IsDeviceAvailable()
    {
        if (NumDevices > 0)
            return true;
        else
            return false;
    }

    string Description();

    void PerformWrite(string Stuff);
}
```

This example doesn't show everything you can do, but it provides you with some ideas about what is possible. Notice that the instance method, `GetName()`, has an implementation, as does the static property, `NumDevices`, and the static method, `IsDeviceAvailable()`. You don't have to implement any of these members in your class if the default implementations will work. It's essential that you create `NumDevices` as shown because interfaces don't support the auto-implemented properties that classes do. However, you don't see an implementation for either `Description()` or `PerformWrite()`, so you need to provide an implementation for them in your class. Consequently, this is what a class based on the `IRecordable` interface might look like:

```
internal class Pen : IRecordable
{
    internal Pen()
    {
        IRecordable.NumDevices += 1;
    }

    ~Pen()
    {
        IRecordable.NumDevices -= 1;
    }

    // Uncomment this method to obtain a specific
    // implementation.
    //public string GetName()
    //{
    //    return "Pen";
    //}

    public string Description()
    {
        return "A device used for writing by hand.";
    }
```

```
    private bool PenWriting
        { get; set; }

    public void PerformWrite(string Stuff)
    {
        if (PenWriting)
        {
            Console.WriteLine("Pen is writing.");
            Console.WriteLine($"The paper contains: {Stuff}.");
        }
        else
            Console.WriteLine("Pen isn't writing.");
    }

    public void StopWriting()
    {
        PenWriting = false;
        Console.WriteLine("Pen off paper.");
    }

    public void StartWriting()
    {
        PenWriting = true;
        Console.WriteLine("Pen on paper.");
    }
}
```

The Pen class provides implementations for both Description() and PerformWrite(). In addition, it provides custom properties and methods to make these actions happen. The need to start and stop writing, for example, applies to a pen because your hand must move onto the paper and off the paper as needed. The example has GetName() commented out so that you can see the default implementation in action. If you uncomment this code, you can use the specific implementation for this class instead.

REMEMBER

Notice that this example provides both a constructor and a finalizer that update the number of writing devices that are available. This value is part of the interface, so you call the interface to change it. Here is application code that is based on the Pen class.

```
static void Main(string[] args)
{
    Console.WriteLine($"Pen available? {IRecordable.IsDeviceAvailable()}");
    IRecordable myPen = new Pen();

    Console.WriteLine($"Pen available? {IRecordable.IsDeviceAvailable()}");
    ((Pen)myPen).StartWriting();
```

```
    myPen.PerformWrite("Hello There!");
    Console.WriteLine($"Using a {myPen.GetName()}.");
    ((Pen)myPen).StopWriting();
    myPen.PerformWrite("Goodbye");
    Console.ReadLine();
}
```

It's possible to call static interface methods from within your code as well as any classes you create. You don't have to instantiate an object to use them. So, the first check to `IRecordable.IsDeviceAvailable()` will provide a response of `False` because the code hasn't created a `Pen` object, `myPen`, yet.

If you want to use the interface features with `myPen`, you must create it as an `IRecordable` object. This means that you must tell the compiler that `myPen` is actually a `Pen` object every time you want to use one of the `Pen`-specific features, such as `StartWriting()`, or the compiler will complain. However, if you provide an override for an interface member in your class, the compiler will automatically use the override. Here's the default output from the example:

```
Pen available? False
Pen available? True
Pen on paper.
Pen is writing.
The paper contains: Hello There!.
Using a Writing Device.
Pen off paper.
Pen isn't writing.
```

How to name your interface

The .NET naming convention for interfaces precedes the name with the letter I. Interface names are typically adjectives, such as `IRecordable`.

Why C# includes interfaces

The bottom line with interfaces is that an interface describes a capability, such as Swim Safety Training or Class A Driver's License. A class implements the `IRecordable` interface when it contains a full version of the `TakeANote` method.

More than that, an interface is a *contract.* If you agree to implement every non-default member defined in the interface, you get to claim its capability. Not only that, but a client using your class in an application knows calling those methods is possible. Implementing an interface is a promise, enforced by the compiler. (Enforcing promises through the compiler reduces errors.)

Mixing inheritance and interface implementation

Unlike some languages, such as C++, C# doesn't allow *multiple inheritance* — a class inheriting from two or more base classes. Think of class HouseBoat inheriting from House and Boat. Just don't think of it in C#.

But although a class can inherit from only one base class, it can in addition implement as many interfaces as needed. After defining IRecordable as an interface, a couple of the recording devices looked like this:

```
public class Pen : IRecordable          // Base class is Object.
{
  public void TakeANote(string note)
  {
    // Record the note with a pen.
  }
}

public class PDA : ElectronicDevice, IRecordable
{
  public void TakeANote(string note)
  {
    // Record the note with your thumbs or a stylus.
  }
}
```

Class PDA inherits from a base class and implements an interface.

And he-e-e-re's the payoff

To begin to see the usefulness of an interface such as IRecordable, consider this example:

```
public class Program
{
  static public void RecordShoppingList(IRecordable recorder)
  {
    // Jot it down, using whatever device was passed in.
    recorder.TakeANote(...);
  }

  public static void Main(string[] args)
  {
    PDA pda = new PDA();
    RecordShoppingList(pda);  // Oops, battery's low ...
```

```
        Pen pen = new Pen();
        RecordShoppingList(pen);
    }
}
```

The IRecordable parameter is an instance of any class that implements the IRecordable interface. RecordShoppingList() makes no assumptions about the exact type of recording object. Whether the device is a PDA or a type of ElectronicDevice isn't important, as long as the device can record a note.

That concept is immensely powerful because it lets the RecordShoppingList() method be highly general — and thus possibly reusable in other programs. The method is even more general than using a base class such as ElectronicDevice for the argument type, because the interface lets you pass almost arbitrary objects that don't necessarily have anything in common other than implementing the interface. They don't even have to come from the same class hierarchy, which truly simplifies the designing of hierarchies, for example.

TECHNICAL STUFF

Some programmers and many older online articles use the term *interface* in more than one way. You can see the C# keyword interface and how it's used. People also talk about a class's *public interface*, or the public methods and properties that it exposes to the outside world. Most sources now use the term *Application Programming Interface* or *API* to specify the methods, events, and properties used to access a class. This book uses API to refer to this public part of a class.

Using an Interface

In addition to your being able to use a C# interface for a parameter type, an interface is useful as

- A method return type
- The base type of a highly general array or collection
- A more general kind of object reference for variable types

The previous section explains the advantage of using a C# interface as a method parameter. The following sections tell you about other interface uses.

As a method return type

You farm out the task of creating key objects you need to a factory method. Suppose that you have a variable like this one:

```
IRecordable recorder = null;  // Yes, you can have interface-type variables.
```

Somewhere, maybe in a constructor, you call a factory method to deliver a particular kind of IRecordable object:

```
recorder = MyClass.CreateRecorder("Pen");  // A factory method is often static.
```

where CreateRecorder() is a method, often on the same class, that returns not a reference to a Pen but, rather, an IRecordable reference:

```
static IRecordable CreateRecorder(string recorderType)
{
  if (recorderType == "Pen") return new Pen();
  ...
}
```

You can find more about the factory idea in the section "Hiding Behind an Interface," later in this chapter. But note that the return type for CreateRecorder() is an interface type.

As the base type of an array or collection

Suppose that you have two classes, Animal and Robot, and that both are abstract. You want to set up an array to hold both thisCat (an Animal) and thatRobot (a Robot). The only way is to fall back on type Object, the ultimate base class in C# and the only base class that's common to both Animal and Robot as well as to their subclasses:

```
object[] things = new object[] { thisCat, thatRobot };
```

That's poor design for lots of reasons. But suppose that you're focused on the objects' movements. You can have each class implement an IMovable interface:

```
interface IMovable
{
  void Move(int direction, int speed, int distance);
}
```

and then set up an array of IMovables to manipulate your otherwise incompatible objects:

```
IMovable[] movables = { thisCat, thatRobot };
```

The interface gives you a commonality that you can exploit in collections.

As a more general type of object reference

The following variable declaration refers to a specific, physical, concrete object (see the later section "Abstract or concrete: When to use an abstract class and when to use an interface"):

```
Cat thisCat = new Cat();
```

One alternative is to use a C# interface for the reference:

```
IMovable thisMovableCat = (IMovable)new Cat();  // Note the required cast.
```

Now you can put any object into the variable that implements IMovable. This practice has wide, powerful uses in object-oriented programming, as you can see in the next section.

Using the C# Predefined Interface Types

Because interfaces are extremely useful, you find a considerable number of interfaces in the .NET class library. Among the dozen or more interfaces in the System namespace alone are IComparable, IComparable<T>, IDisposable, and IFormattable. The System.Collections.Generics namespace (https://docs.microsoft.com/en-us/dotnet/api/system.collections.generic) includes IEnumerable<T>, IList<T>, ICollection<T>, and IDictionary<TKey, TValue>. And there are many more. Those with the <T> notation are generic interfaces. Book 1, Chapter 6 explains the <T> notation in the discussion of collection classes.

Two interfaces that are commonly used are IComparable and IEnumerable — largely superseded now by their generic versions IComparable<T> (read as "IComparable of T") and IEnumerable<T>.

The "Implementing the incomparable IComparable<T> interface" section, later in this chapter, shows you the IComparable<T> interface. This interface lets you compare all sorts of objects, such as Students, to each other, and enables the

Sort() method that all arrays and most collections supply. IEnumerable<T> makes the powerful foreach loop work. Most collections implement IEnumerable<T>, so you can iterate the collections with foreach. You can find an additional major use for IEnumerable<T>, as the basis for query expressions, described in Book 1.

Looking at a Program That CAN_BE_USED_AS an Example

Interfaces help you perform tasks in ways that classes can't because you can implement as many interfaces as you want, but you can inherit only a single class. The SortInterface program that appears in the following sections demonstrates the use of multiple interfaces and how you can use multiple interfaces effectively. To fully understand the impact of working with multiple interfaces, it's important to break the SortInterface program into sections to demonstrate various principles.

Creating your own interface at home in your spare time

The following IDisplayable interface is satisfied by any class that contains a Display() method (and declares that it implements IDisplayable, of course). Display() returns a string representation of the object that can be displayed using WriteLine().

```
// IDisplayable -- Any object that implements the Display() method
interface IDisplayable
{
  // Return a description of yourself.
  string Display();
}
```

The following Student class implements IDisplayable:

```
class Student : IDisplayable
{
    public Student(string name, double grade)
        { Name = name; Grade = grade; }
    public string Name { get; private set; }
    public double Grade { get; private set; }
```

```
    public string Display()
    {
        string padName = Name.PadRight(9);
        return $"{padName}: {Grade:N0}";
    }
}
```

Display() uses string interpolation (https://docs.microsoft.com/en-us/dotnet/csharp/language-reference/tokens/interpolated) to format the information. It relies on a numeric string formatter for the Grade information (https://docs.microsoft.com/en-us/dotnet/standard/base-types/standard-numeric-format-strings).

The following DisplayArray() method in the Program class (place it before Main()) takes an array of any objects that implement the IDisplayable interface. Each of those objects is guaranteed (by the interface) to have its own Display() method.

```
// DisplayArray -- Display an array of objects that implement
//   the IDisplayable interface.
public static void DisplayArray(IDisplayable[] displayables)
{
    foreach (IDisplayable disp in displayables)
        Console.WriteLine($"{disp.Display()}");
}
```

Implementing the incomparable IComparable<T> interface

C# defines the interface IComparable<T> this way (don't add this code to the SortInterface example):

```
interface IComparable<T>
{
  // Compare the current T object to the object 'item'; return a
  // 1 if larger, -1 if smaller, and 0 if the same.
  int CompareTo(T item);
}
```

A class implements the IComparable<T> interface by implementing a CompareTo() method. Notice that CompareTo() takes an argument of type T, a type you supply when you instantiate the interface for a particular data type, as in this example:

```
class SoAndSo : IComparable<SoAndSo>  // Make me comparable.
```

When you implement IComparable<T> for your class, its CompareTo() method should return 0 if the two items (of your class type) being compared are "equal" in a way that you define. If not, it should return 1 or −1, depending on which object is "greater."

It seems a little Darwinian, but you could say that one Student object is "greater than" another Student object if the subject student's grade-point average is higher. Implementing the CompareTo() method implies that the objects have a sorting order. If one student is greater than another, you must be able to sort the students from least to greatest. In fact, most collection classes (including arrays but not dictionaries) supply a Sort() method something like this:

```
void Sort(IComparable<T>[] objects);
```

This method sorts a collection of objects that implement the IComparable<T> interface. It doesn't even matter which class the objects belong to. For example, they could even be Student objects. Collection classes such as arrays or List<T> could even sort this updated version of the Student class (with changes shown in bold):

```
// Student -- Description of a student with name and grade
class Student : IComparable<Student>, IDisplayable   // Instantiation
{
  public Student(string name, double grade)
      { Name = name; Grade = grade; }
  public string Name { get; private set; }
  public double Grade { get; private set; }

  public string Display()
  {
      string padName = Name.PadRight(9);
      return $"{padName}: {Grade:N0}";
  }

  // Implement the IComparable<T> interface:
  // CompareTo -- Compare another object (in this case, Student objects)
  //   and decide which one comes after the other in the sorted array.
  public int CompareTo(Student rightStudent)
  {
    // Compare the current Student (call her 'left') against the other
    // student (call her 'right').
    Student leftStudent = this;

    // Generate a -1, 0 or 1 based on the Sort criteria (the student's
    // grade). You could use class Double's CompareTo() method instead.
    if (rightStudent.Grade < leftStudent.Grade)
```

```
    {
      Console.WriteLine($"{rightStudent.Name} < {leftStudent.Name}");
      return -1;
    }
    if (rightStudent.Grade > leftStudent.Grade)
    {
      Console.WriteLine($"{rightStudent.Name} > {leftStudent.Name}");
      return 1;
    }

    Console.WriteLine($"{rightStudent.Name} = {leftStudent.Name}");
    return 0;
  }
}
```

Sorting an array of `Students` is reduced to this single call:

```
// Where Student implements IComparable<T>
void MyMethod(Student[] students)
{
  Array.Sort(students); // Sort array of IComparable<Student>s
}
```

You provide the comparator (`CompareTo()`), and `Array` does all the work.

Creating a list of students

To test everything you've written so far, you need a list of students. The example provides a simple mechanism for doing so in a method called `CreateStudentList()` that relies on two fixed lists: `names` and `grades`. You place it at the end of the `Student` class. Here's the code you need:

```
// CreateStudentList - To save space here, just create
// a fixed list of students.
static string[] names = { "Homer", "Marge", "Bart", "Lisa", "Maggie" };
static double[] grades = { 0, 85, 50, 100, 30 };

public static Student[] CreateStudentList()
{
    Student[] students = new Student[names.Length];
    for (int i = 0; i < names.Length; i++)
    {
        students[i] = new Student(names[i], grades[i]);
    }
    return students;
}
```

As you can see, CreateStudentList() defines an array of students that has the same length as the names list and relies on the Student class constructor. For each name and grade pair, the code creates another entry in students and then returns the completed array to the caller.

Testing everything using Main()

At this point, you have everything needed to sort a list of students. All you need is some code in Main() to demonstrate the functionality. The following code tests your Student class:

```
static void Main(string[] args)
{
    // Sort students by grade...
    Console.WriteLine("Using Array.Sort() to sort.");

    // Get an unsorted array of students.
    Student[] students = Student.CreateStudentList();

    // Use the IComparable interface to sort the array.
    Array.Sort(students);

    // Now the IDisplayable interface to display the results.
    DisplayArray(students);

    // Use Language Integrated Query (LINQ) instead.
    Console.WriteLine("\r\nUsing LINQ to sort.");
    Student[] students2 = Student.CreateStudentList();
    students2 = students2.OrderBy(C => C).ToArray();
    DisplayArray(students2);

    Console.Read();
}
```

Main() begins by creating a student list. It then sorts the students using Array.Sort(), which actually calls the CompareTo() method in Student. The code then calls DisplayArray() so that you can see the sorted output.

For comparison purposes, this example also uses Language Integrated Query (LINQ) to sort the values. To use LINQ, you must add the using System.Linq; statement to the beginning of your code file. Again, this method relies on CompareTo(), but the process is different. You can read more about LINQ at https://docs.microsoft.com/en-us/dotnet/csharp/programming-guide/concepts/

linq/. For now, just know that it's a different type of sorting technique. Here's what you see when you run this application:

```
Using Array.Sort() to sort.
Homer < Marge
Homer < Bart
Marge > Bart
Homer < Lisa
Bart < Lisa
Marge < Lisa
Homer < Maggie
Bart > Maggie
Lisa     : 100
Marge    : 85
Bart     : 50
Maggie   : 30
Homer    : 0

Using LINQ to sort.
Homer < Bart
Maggie < Bart
Lisa > Bart
Marge > Bart
Bart = Bart
Bart = Bart
Lisa = Lisa
Marge < Lisa
Lisa = Lisa
Homer = Homer
Maggie > Homer
Lisa     : 100
Marge    : 85
Bart     : 50
Maggie   : 30
Homer    : 0
```

The output statements show the action of `Array.Sort()` when combined with `CompareTo()` for this particular class. You also see that LINQ requires more steps to get the job done, but produces the same result as `Array.Sort()`. The goal is to sort the list as quickly as possible.

Unifying Class Hierarchies

Figure 7-1 shows the `Robot` and `Animal` hierarchies. Some, but not all, of the classes in each hierarchy not only inherit from the base classes, `Robot` or `Animal`, but also implement the `IPet` interface (not all animals are pets).

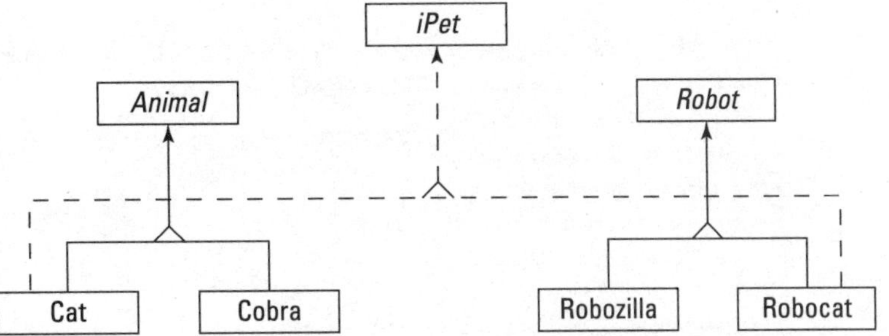

FIGURE 7-1: A tale of two class hierarchies and one interface.

The following code snippet shows how to implement the hierarchy. Note the properties in `IPet`. This code shows how you specify properties in interfaces using the approach that works for all versions of C# (the "Using the newer C# 8.0 additions" section of the chapter shows the newer C# 8.0 and above additions). If you need both getter and setter, just add `set;` after `get;`.

```
// Two abstract base classes and one interface
abstract class Animal
{
  abstract public void Eat(string food);
  abstract public void Sleep(int hours);
  abstract public int NumberOfLegs { get; }
  public void Breathe() { ... } // Nonabstract, implementation not shown.
}

abstract class Robot
{
  public virtual void Speak(string whatToSay) { ... } // Impl not shown
  abstract public void LiftObject(object o);
  abstract public int NumberOfLegs { get; }
}

interface IPet
{
  void AskForStrokes();
  void DoTricks();
  int NumberOfLegs { get; }  // Properties in interfaces look like this.
  string Name { get; set; }  // get/set must be public in implementations.
}

// Cat -- This concrete class inherits (and partially implements)
//    class Animal and also implements interface IPet.
class Cat : Animal, IPet
{
  public Cat(string name) { Name = name; }

  // 1. Overrides and implements Animal members (not shown).
  // 2. Provides additional implementation for IPet.
```

```
  // Inherits NumberOfLegs property from base class, thus meeting
  // IPet's requirement for a NumberOfLegs property.
  #region IPet Members
  public void AskForStrokes() ...
  public void DoTricks() ...
  public string Name { get; set; }
  #endregion IPet Members

  public override string ToString() { return Name; }
}

class Cobra : Animal
{
  // 1. Inherits or overrides all Animal methods only (not shown).
}

class Robozilla : Robot    // Not IPet
{
  // 1. Override Speak.
  public override void Speak(string whatToSay)
      { Console.WriteLine("DESTROY ALL HUMANS!"); }

  // 2. Implement LiftObject and NumberOfLegs, not all shown.
  public override void LiftObject(object o) ...
  public override int NumberOfLegs { get { return 2; } }
}

class RoboCat : Robot, IPet
{
  public RoboCat(string name) { Name = name; }

  // 1. Override some Robot members, not all shown:
  #region IPet Members
  public void AskForStrokes() ...
  public void DoTricks() ...
  public string Name { get; set; }
  #endregion IPet Members
}
```

The code shows two concrete classes that inherit from `Animal` and two that inherit from `Robot`. However, you can see that neither class `Cobra` nor class `Robozilla` implements `IPet` — probably for good reasons. Most people don't plan to watch TV with a pet cobra beside them on the couch, and a robozilla sounds nasty, too. Some of the classes in both hierarchies exhibit what you might call "petness" and some don't.

The point of this section is that any class can implement an interface, as long as it provides the right methods and properties. RoboCat can carry out the AskForStrokes() and DoTricks() actions and have the NumberOfLegs property, as can Cat in the Animal hierarchy — all while other classes in the same hierarchies don't implement IPet.

Hiding Behind an Interface

Often this book discusses code that (a) you write but (b) someone else (a client) uses in a program (you may be the client yourself, of course). Sometimes you have a complex or tricky class whose entire API you would truly rather not expose to clients. For various reasons, however, it includes some dangerous operations that nonetheless have to be public. (For example, you might not want to expose code for deleting records, but the client may really need that functionality unless you want to create a support group devoted to deleting records.) Ideally, you would expose a safe subset of your class's public methods and properties and hide the dangerous ones. C# interfaces can do that, too.

Here's a different Robozilla class, with several methods and properties that amateurs can use safely and enjoyably. But Robozilla also has some advanced features that can be, well, scary:

```
public class Robozilla  // Doesn't implement IPet!
{
  public void ClimbStairs();                    // Safe
  public void PetTheRobodog();                  // Safe? Might break it.
  public void Charge();                         // Maybe not safe
  public void SearchAndDestroy();               // Dangerous
  public void LaunchGlobalThermonuclearWar(); // Catastrophic
}
```

REMEMBER

You want to expose only the two safer methods while hiding the last three dangerous ones. Here's how you can do that by using a C# interface:

1. Design a C# interface that exposes only the safe methods:

```
public interface IRobozillaSafe
{
  void ClimbStairs();
  void PetTheRobodog();
}
```

2. Modify the Robozilla class to implement the interface. Because it already has implementations for the required methods, all you need is the IRobozillaSafe notation on the class heading:

```
public class Robozilla : IRobozillaSafe  ...
```

3. Give your clients a way to instantiate a new Robozilla, but return to them a reference to the interface. Now you can just keep Robozilla itself a secret from everybody and give most users the IRobozillaSafe interface. This example uses a static factory method added to class Robozilla:

```
// Create a Robozilla but return only an interface reference.
public static IRobozillaSafe CreateRobozilla(<parameter list>)
{
  return (IRobozillaSafe)new Robozilla(<parameter list>);
}
```

4. Clients then use Robozilla like this:

```
IRobozillaSafe myZilla = Robozilla.CreateRobozilla(...);
myZilla.ClimbStairs();
myZilla.PetTheRobodog();
```

It's that simple. Using the interface, they can call the Robozilla methods that it specifies — but not any other Robozilla methods. However, expert programmers can defeat this ploy with a simple cast:

```
Robozilla myKillaZilla = (Robozilla)myZilla;
```

Doing so is usually a bad idea, though. The interface has a purpose: to keep bugs at bay. In real life, programmers sometimes use this hand-out-an-interface technique with the complex DataSet class used in ADO.NET (https://docs.microsoft.com/en-us/dotnet/framework/data/adonet/ado-net-overview) to interact with databases. A DataSet can return a set of database tables loaded with records — such as a table of Customers and a table of Orders. (Modern relational databases, such as Oracle and SQL Server, contain tables linked by various relationships. Each table contains lots of records, where each record might be, for example, the name, rank, and serial number of a Customer.)

Unfortunately, if you hand a client a DataSet reference (even through a read-only property's get clause), the client can muddle the situation by reaching into the DataSet and modifying elements that you don't want modified. To prevent such mischief you can:

- Return a DataView object, which is read-only.
- Create a C# interface to expose a safe subset of the operations available on the DataSet. Then you can subclass DataSet and have the subclass (call it MyDataSet) implement the interface.
- Give clients a way to obtain an interface reference to a live MyDataSet object and let them have at it in relative safety — through the interface.

TIP

You usually shouldn't return a reference to a collection, either, because it lets anyone alter the collection outside the class that created it. Remember that the reference you hand out can still point to the original collection inside your class. That's why List<T>, for instance, provides an AsReadOnly() method. This method returns a collection that can't be altered:

```
private List<string> _readWriteNames = ...  // A modifiable data member
...
ReadonlyCollection<string> readonlyNames = _readWriteNames.AsReadOnly();
return readonlyNames; // Safer to return this than _readWriteNames.
```

Although it doesn't qualify as using an interface, the purpose is the same.

Inheriting an Interface

A C# interface can inherit the methods of another interface. However, interface inheritance may not always be true inheritance, no matter how it may appear. The following interface code lists a base interface, much like a base class, in its heading:

```
interface IRobozillaSafe : IPet   // Base interface
{
  // Methods not shown here ...
}
```

By having IRobozillaSafe "inherit" IPet, you can let this subset of Robozilla implement its own petness without trying to impose petness inappropriately on all of Robozilla:

```
class PetRobo : Robozilla, IRobozillaSafe // (also an IPet by inheritance)
{
  // Implement Robozilla operations.
  // Implement IRobozillaSafe operations, then ...
  // Implement IPet operations too (required by the inherited IPet interface).
}
...
```

```
// Hand out only a safe reference, not one to PetRobo itself.
IPet myPetRobo = (IPet)new PetRobo();
// ... now call IPet methods on the object.
```

The `IRobozillaSafe` interface inherits from `IPet`. Classes that implement `IRobozillaSafe` must therefore also implement `IPet` to make their implementation of `IRobozillaSafe` complete. This type of inheritance isn't the same concept as class inheritance. For instance, class `PetRobo` in the previous example can have a constructor, but no equivalent of a base-class constructor exists for `IRobozillaSafe` or `IPet`. Older interfaces don't have constructors (starting with C# 8.0, interfaces can have a static constructor as described at `https://docs.microsoft.com/en-us/dotnet/csharp/programming-guide/classes-and-structs/constructors#static-constructors`). More important, polymorphism doesn't work the same way with interfaces. Though you can call a method of a subclass through a reference to the base class (class polymorphism), the parallel operation involving interfaces (interface polymorphism) doesn't work: You can't call a method of the derived interface (`IRobozillaSafe`) through a base interface reference (`IPet`).

Although interface inheritance isn't polymorphic in the same way that class inheritance is, you can pass an object of a derived interface type (`IRobozilla-safe`) through a parameter of its base interface type (`IPet`). Therefore, you can also put `IRobozillasafe` objects into a collection of `IPet` objects.

Using Interfaces to Manage Change in Object-Oriented Programs

Interfaces are the key to object-oriented programs that bend flexibly with the winds of change. Your code will laugh in the face of new requirements.

REMEMBER

You've no doubt heard it said, "Change is a constant." When you hand a new program to a bunch of users, they soon start requesting changes. Add this feature, please. Fix that problem, please. (Although users aren't usually so polite; they'll likely snarl at you and say something like, "Who in the world implements a program without this feature?") The RoboWarrior has feature *X*, so why doesn't Robozilla? Many programs have a long shelf life. Thousands of programs, especially old Fortran and Cobol programs, have been in service for 20 or 30 years, or longer. They undergo lots of maintenance in that extended time span, which makes planning and designing for change one of your highest priorities.

Here's an example: In the Robot class hierarchy, suppose that all robots can move in one way or another. Robocats saunter. Robozillas charge — at least when operated by a power (hungry) user. And Robosnakes slither. One way to implement these different modes of travel involves inheritance: Give the base class, Robot, an abstract Move() method. Then each subclass overrides the Move() method to implement it differently:

```
abstract public class Robot
{
  abstract public void Move(int direction, int speed);
  // ...
}

public class Robosnake : Robot
{
  public override void Move(int direction, int speed)
  {
    // A real Move() implementation here: slithering.
    ... some real code that computes angles and changes
    snake's location relative to a coordinate system, say ...
  }
}
```

But suppose that you often receive requests to add new types of movement to existing Robot subclasses. "Please make Robosnake undulate rather than slither," maybe. Now you have to open up the Robosnake class and modify its Move() method directly.

REMEMBER

After the Move() method is working correctly for slithering, most programmers would prefer not to meddle with it. Implementing slithering is difficult, and changing the implementation can introduce brand-new bugs. If it ain't broke, don't fix it.

Making flexible dependencies through interfaces

There must be a way to implement Move() that doesn't require you to open a can of worms every time a client wants wriggling instead. You can use interfaces, of course! Look at the following code that uses HAS_A, a now-familiar relationship between two classes in which one class contains the other:

```
public class Robot
{
  // This object is used to implement motion.
  protected Motor _motor = new Motor(); // Refers to Motor by name
```

```
  // ...
}

internal class Motor { ... }
```

The point about this example is that the contained object is of type `Motor`, where `Motor` is a concrete object. (That is, it represents a real item, not an abstraction.) HAS_A sets up a dependency between classes `Robot` and `Motor`: `Robot` depends on the concrete class `Motor`. A class with concrete dependencies is tightly coupled to them: When you need to replace `Motor` with something else, code that depends directly on `Motor` like this has to change, too. Instead, insulate your code by relying only on the API of dependencies, which you can do with interfaces.

Abstract or concrete: When to use an abstract class and when to use an interface

In Chapter 6 of this minibook, the discourse about birds says, "Every bird out there is a subtype of `Bird`." In other words, a duck is an instance of a subclass `Duck`. You never see an instance of `Bird` itself — `Bird` is an abstraction. Instead, you always see concrete, physical ducks, sparrows, or hummingbirds. Abstractions are concepts. As living creatures, ducks are real, concrete objects. Also, concrete objects are instances of concrete classes. (A *concrete class* is a class that you can instantiate. It lacks the `abstract` keyword, and it implements all methods.)

REMEMBER

You can represent abstractions in two ways in C#: with abstract classes or with C# interfaces. The two have differences that can affect your choice of which one to use:

- **Use an abstract class** when you can profitably share an implementation with subclasses — the abstract base class can contribute real code that its subclasses can use by inheritance. For instance, maybe class `Robot` can handle part of the robot's tasks, just not movement.

  An abstract class doesn't have to be completely abstract. Though it has to have at least one abstract, unimplemented method or property, some can provide implementations (bodies). Using an abstract class to provide an implementation for its subclasses to inherit prevents duplication of code. That's always a good thing.

- **Use an interface** when you can't share any implementation for the most part or your implementing class already has a base class.

Most C# interfaces are purely, totally abstract. An older C# interface supplies no implementation of any of its methods (C# 8.0 and above allows a default implementation, which you can override or not, as needed). Yet it can also add flexibility that isn't otherwise possible. The abstract class option may not be available because you want to add a capability to a class that already has a base class (that you can't modify). For example, class Robot may already have a base class in a library that you didn't write and therefore can't alter. Interfaces are especially helpful for representing completely abstract capabilities, such as movability or displayability, that you want to add to multiple classes that may otherwise have nothing in common — for example, being in the same class hierarchy.

Doing HAS_A with interfaces

You discovered earlier in this chapter that you can use interfaces as a more general reference type. The containing class can refer to the contained class not with a reference to a concrete class but, rather, with a reference to an abstraction. Either an abstract class or a C# interface will work:

```
AbstractDependentClass dependency1 = ...;
ISomeInterface dependency2 = ...;
```

Suppose that you have an `IPropulsion` interface:

```
interface IPropulsion
{
  void Movement(int direction, int speed);
}
```

Class `Robot` can contain a data member of type `IPropulsion` instead of the concrete type `Motor`:

```
public class Robot
{
  private IPropulsion _propel;     // <--Notice the interface type here.

  // Somehow, you supply a concrete propulsion object at runtime ...
  // Other stuff and then:
  public void Move(int speed, int direction)
  {
    // Use whatever concrete propulsion device is installed in _propel.
    _propel.Movement(speed, direction); // Delegate to its methods.
  }
}
```

Robot's Move() method delegates the real work to the object referred to through the interface. Be sure to provide a way to install a concrete Motor or Engine or another implementer of IPropulsion in the data member. Programmers often install that concrete object — "inject the dependency" — by passing it to a constructor:

```
Robot r = new Robosnake(someConcreteMotor);  // Type IPropulsion
```

or by assigning it via a setter property:

```
r.PropulsionDevice = someConcreteMotor;       // Invokes the set clause
```

Another approach to dependency injection is to use a factory method (discussed in the "As a method return type" section, earlier in this chapter, and illustrated in the section "Hiding Behind an Interface"):

```
IPropulsion _propel = CreatePropulsion();     // A factory method
```

IN THIS CHAPTER

» Solving callback problems with delegates

» Using delegates to customize a method

» Using anonymous methods

» Creating events in C#

Chapter 8

Delegating Those Important Events

This chapter looks into a corner of C# that has been around since the birth of the language. The ability to create a *callback*, a method used to handle events, is essential for C# applications of all sorts. In fact, the callback appears in applications of every kind today. Even web-based applications must have some sort of callback mechanism to allow them to work properly.

The alternative is to hold up the application while you wait for something to happen, which means that the application won't respond to anything but the anticipated input. That's how the console applications used in examples to this point work. The `Console.Read()` call essentially stops the application until the user does something. A console application can work in this manner, but when a user could click any button on a form, you must have something better — a callback mechanism. In C#, you implement a callback by using a *delegate*, which is a description of what a callback method requires to handle an event. The delegate acts as a method reference type. In addition to callback methods, this chapter also helps you understand how to create and use delegates.

REMEMBER

You don't have to type the source code for this chapter manually. In fact, using the downloadable source is a lot easier. You can find the source for this chapter in the `\CSAIO4D2E\BK02\CH08` folder of the downloadable source. See the Introduction for details on how to find these source files.

E.T., Phone Home — The Callback Problem

If you've seen the Steven Spielberg movie *E.T., the Extraterrestrial* (1982), you watched the cute but ugly little alien stranded on Earth try to build an apparatus from old toy parts with which he could "phone home." He needed his ship to pick him up.

It's a big jump from *E.T.* to C#, but code sometimes needs to phone home, too. For example, you may have wondered how the Windows progress bar works. It's the horizontal "bar" that gradually fills up with coloring to show progress during a lengthy operation, such as copying files. The progress bar is based on a lengthy operation's periodic pause to "phone home." In programmerese, it's a *callback.* Usually, the lengthy operation estimates how long its task should take and then checks frequently to see how far it has progressed. Periodically, the progress bar sends a signal by calling a *callback method* back on the mother ship — the class that kicked off the long operation. The mother ship can then update its progress bar. The trick is that you have to supply this callback method for the long operation to use.

That callback method may be in the same class as the lengthy operation — such as phoning your sister on the other side of the house. Or, more often, it's in another class that knows about the progress bar — such as phoning Aunt Maxie in Minnesota. Somehow, at its start, the lengthy operation has been handed a mechanism for phoning home — sort of like giving your kid a cellphone so that they can call you at 10 p.m.

REMEMBER

This chapter talks about how your code can set up this callback mechanism and then invoke it to phone home when needed. Callbacks are used a lot in Windows programming, typically for a piece of code, down in your program's guts, to notify a higher-level module that the task has finished, to ask for needed data, or to let that module take a useful action, such as write a log entry or update a progress bar. However, the place where you use callbacks the most is with the user interface. When the user does something with the user interface, such as click a button, it generates an event. The callback method handles the event.

Defining a Delegate

C# provides *delegates* for making callbacks — and a number of other tasks. Delegates are the C# way (the .NET way, really, because any .NET language can use them) for you to pass around methods as though they were data. You're saying, "Here, execute this method when you need it" (and then handing over the method to execute). This chapter helps you get a handle on that concept, see its usefulness, and start using it yourself.

You may be an experienced coder who will recognize immediately that delegates are similar to C/C++ function pointers — only much, much better. Here are some things to consider when choosing delegates over function pointers:

- » Delegates are managed so that you don't have to worry about them hanging around to cause problems after you use them.
- » A delegate will always point to a valid function, whereas function pointers can point to any memory location.
- » When pointing to multiple callbacks, a function pointer's built-in iterator makes it easy to ensure that each callback is called every time.
- » It's possible to use delegates in either synchronous or asynchronous mode.
- » Delegates are type-safe and will always point to a method with the correct signature.

Think of a delegate as a vehicle for passing a callback method to a "workhorse" method that needs to call you back or needs help with that action, as in doing the same action to each element of a collection. Because the collection doesn't know about your custom action, you need a way to provide the action for the collection to carry out. Figure 8-1 shows how the parts of this scheme fit together.

A delegate is a data type, similar to a class. As with a class, you create an instance of the delegate type in order to use the delegate. Figure 8-1 shows the sequence of events in the delegate's life cycle as you complete these steps:

1. **Define the delegate type (in much the same way as you would define a class).**

   Sometimes, C# has already defined a delegate you can use. Much of the time, though, you'll want to define your own, custom delegates.

TECHNICAL STUFF

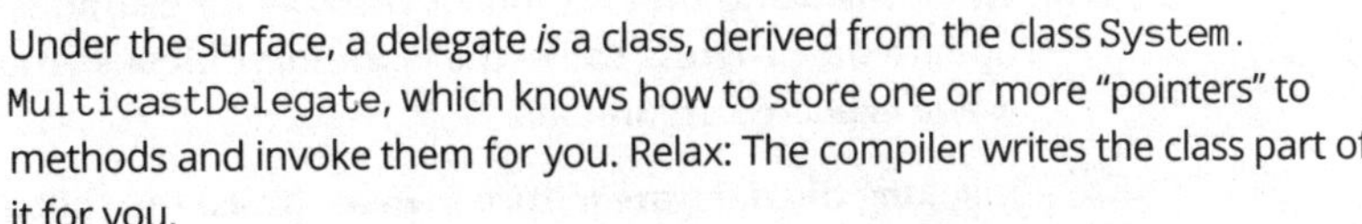

   Under the surface, a delegate *is* a class, derived from the class `System.MulticastDelegate`, which knows how to store one or more "pointers" to methods and invoke them for you. Relax: The compiler writes the class part of it for you.

2. **Create an instance of the delegate type — such as instantiating a class.**

REMEMBER

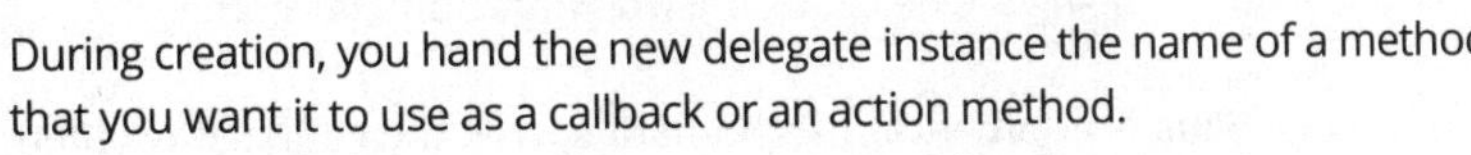

   During creation, you hand the new delegate instance the name of a method that you want it to use as a callback or an action method.

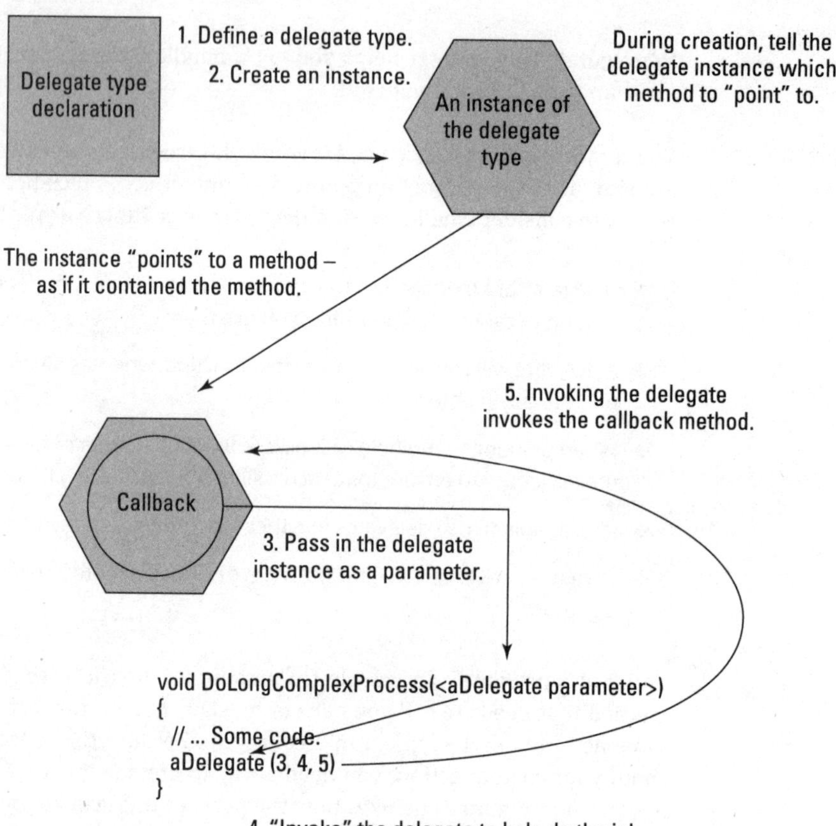

FIGURE 8-1: Sending your delegate to the bungee-jump on your behalf.

3. **Pass the delegate instance to a workhorse method, which has a parameter of the delegate type.**

   That's the doorway through which you insert the delegate instance into the workhorse method. It's like smuggling a candy bar into a movie theater — except that in this example, the movie theater expects, even invites, the contraband candy.

4. **When the workhorse method is ready — for example, when it's time to update the progress bar — the workhorse invokes the delegate, passing it any expected arguments.**

5. **Invoking the delegate in turn invokes (calls) the callback method that the delegate "points" to.**

   Using the delegate, the workhorse phones home.

This fundamental mechanism solves the callback problem — and has other uses, too. Delegate types can also be generic, allowing you to use the same delegate for different data types, much as you can instantiate a `List<T>` collection for `string` or `int`. Book 1 Chapter 8 covers the use of generic types in detail.

FUNCTION POINTERS IN C# 9.0

C# 9.0 adds the ability to use C++-like function pointers in place of delegates. A function pointer allows access to low-level Intermediate Language (IL) functionality that isn't accessible or is not accessed efficiently in C# today (see `https://docs.microsoft.com/en-us/dotnet/csharp/language-reference/proposals/csharp-9.0/function-pointers` for details). This book doesn't cover this low-level programming technique because of the specialness of its functionality. For example, if you were directly interacting with a C++ library or the Windows API, you might need this technique. Most developers will never need to use it in place of a delegate. However, you can find an example and some additional documentation at `https://riptutorial.com/csharp-9/learn/100009/function-pointers`.

Pass Me the Code, Please — Examples

In this section, you see a couple of examples — and solve the callback problem discussed at the beginning of this chapter.

Delegating the task

In this section, you walk through two examples of using a callback — a delegate instance phoning home, like *E.T.*, to the object that created it. But first take a look at some common variations on what you can use a callback delegate for:

REMEMBER

- **To notify the delegate's home base of an event:** A lengthy operation has finished or made some progress or perhaps run into an error. "Mother, this is E.T. Can you come get me at Elliot's house?"
- **To call back to home base to ask for the necessary data to complete a task:** "I'm at the store. Should I get white bread or wheat?"
- **More generally, to customize a method:** The method you're customizing provides a framework, and its caller supplies a delegate to do the work. "Take this grocery list to the store and follow it exactly." The delegate method carries out a task that the customized method needs done (but can't handle by itself). The customized method is responsible for invoking the delegate at the appropriate moment.

First, a simple example

The `SimpleDelegateExample` program demonstrates a simple delegate. The delegate-related parts of this example are highlighted in boldface.

```
class Program
{
    // Inside class or inside namespace
    delegate int MyDelType(string name);

    static void Main(string[] args)
    {
        // Create a delegate instance pointing to the CallBackMethod below.
        // Note that the callback method is static, so you prefix the name
        // with the class name, Program.
        MyDelType del = new MyDelType(Program.CallBackMethod);

        // Call a method that will invoke the delegate.
        UseTheDel(del, "hello");
        Console.Read();
    }

    // CallBackMethod -- A method that conforms to the MyDelType
    //    delegate signature (takes a string, returns an int).
    //    The delegate will call this method.
    public static int CallBackMethod(string stringPassed)
    {
        // Leave tracks to show you were here.
        // What's written here? stringPassed.
        Console.WriteLine($"CallBackMethod writes: {stringPassed}");

        // Return an int.
        return stringPassed.Length;  // Delegate requires an int return.
    }

    // UseTheDel -- A "workhorse" method that takes a MyDelType delegate
    //    argument and invokes the delegate. arg is a string to pass
    //    to the delegate invocation.
    private static void UseTheDel(MyDelType del, string arg)
    {
        if (del == null) return; // Don't invoke a null delegate!

        // Here's where you invoke the delegate.
        // What's written here? A number representing the length of arg.
        Console.WriteLine($"UseTheDel writes {del(arg)}");
    }
}
```

First you see the delegate definition. `MyDelType` defines a *signature*, which specifies the inputs and outputs that the method must provide. You can pass any method with the delegate that takes a `string` argument and return an `int`. Second, notice that the `CallBackMethod()` matches the delegate signature. Third, `Main()` creates an instance of the delegate, called `del`, and then passes the delegate instance to a "workhorse" method, `UseTheDel()`, along with some string data, `"hello"`, that the delegate requires. In that setup, here's the sequence of events:

1. `UseTheDel()` takes two arguments, a `MyDelType` delegate, and a `string` that it calls `arg`. So, when `Main()` calls `UseTheDel()`, it passes the delegate instance to be used inside the method. When you create the delegate instance, `del`, in `Main()`, you pass the name of the `CallBackMethod()` as the method to call. Because `CallBackMethod()` is static, you have to prefix the name with the class name, `Program`.
2. Inside `UseTheDel()`, the method ensures that the delegate isn't `null` and then starts a `WriteLine()` call. Within that call, before it finishes, the method invokes the delegate by calling `del(arg)`. `arg` is just something you can pass to the delegate, which causes the `CallBackMethod()` to be called.
3. Inside `CallBackMethod()`, the method writes its own message, including the string that was passed when `UseTheDel()` invoked the delegate. Then `CallBackMethod()` returns the length of the string it was passed, and that length is written out as the last part of the `WriteLine()` in `UseTheDel()`.

The output looks like this:

```
CallBackMethod writes: hello
UseTheDel writes 5
```

`UseTheDel()` phones home and `CallBackMethod()` answers the call.

Considering the Action, Func, and Predicate delegate types

All delegates represent a kind of function pointer, whether you use them to deal with events or not.You can divide delegates used specifically as function pointers into three types using three special keywords: `Action`, `Func`, and `Predicate`. All three are delegate types, but they have a special format, and you usually use them differently from standard delegates (as input to methods that require a function pointer, for example). Here's a quick overview of these delegate types:

- `Action`: Has one or more input parameters and no output parameters (so you use it with methods that return `void`). The Action delegates support up to 16 input arguments, as shown at `https://docs.microsoft.com/en-us/dotnet/api/system.action`.

- **Func**: Has zero or more input parameters and one output parameter. As with `Action`, `Func` has a limit of 16 input arguments, as shown at: `https://docs.microsoft.com/en-us/dotnet/api/system.func-1`.
- **Predicate**: Defines a specific set of criteria and determines whether the input object meets those criteria, returning `True` when the conditions are met and `False` otherwise. You can see more specifics about the `Predicate` type at `https://docs.microsoft.com/en-us/dotnet/api/system.predicate-1`.

You can see how these three kinds of delegates work in the `Program` class of the `ActionFuncPredicate` example:

```
class Program
{
    static void Main(string[] args)
    {
        // Define and execute the action.
        Action<int, int> showIntMath = new Action<int, int>(DisplayAdd);
        showIntMath(1, 2);

        // Define and execute the function.
        Func<int, int, int> doIntMath = new Func<int, int, int>(DoAdd);
        Console.WriteLine($"1 + 2 = {doIntMath(1, 2)}.");

        // Define and execute the predicate.
        Values theseValues = new Values() { value1 = 1, value2 = 2 };
        Predicate<Values> isValue = x => x.value1 + x.value2 == 3;
        Console.WriteLine($"The output is 3? {isValue(theseValues)}");
        Console.ReadLine();
    }

    static void DisplayAdd(int value1, int value2)
    {
        Console.WriteLine($"{value1} + {value2} = {value1 + value2}.");
    }

    static int DoAdd(int value1, int value2)
    {
        return value1 + value2;
    }
```

```
    internal struct Values
    {
        internal int value1;
        internal int value2;
    }
}
```

In all three examples, the code evaluates two int values: 1 and 2. All three examples use the delegate pattern in some manner, with Action and Func being the most direct presentations. Here are differences to consider in the implementation for this example:

- To create an Action, the code defines the DisplayAdd() method, which adds the two values and outputs their sum to the display.
- To create a Func, the code defines DoAdd(), which sums the two values and returns the result to the caller.
- The Predicate is a little more complex because the code must define a struct, Values, to hold the two values and then use a lambda expression, x => x.value1 + x.value2 == 3, to evaluate whether 1 + 2 really does add up to 3. The "Shh! Keep It Quiet — Anonymous Methods" section of the chapter talks more about lambda expressions, but essentially, x is an input object, and you work with it to determine what to provide as an output, which must always be a logical value when working with a Predicate.

When you execute this code, you see the following output:

```
1 + 2 = 3.
1 + 2 = 3.
The output is 3? True
```

A More Real-World Example

For a more realistic example than SimpleDelegateExample, the SimpleProgress example shows you how to write a little app that puts up a progress bar and updates it every time a lengthy method invokes a delegate. This example relies on a Windows Forms application, which means using a different template than you have in the past, so be sure to follow the procedure in the upcoming "Putting the app together," section to start your project.

The example displays a small dialog-box-style window with two buttons and a progress bar. When you load the solution example into Visual Studio and then build it, run it, and click the upper button, marked Click to Start, the progress bar runs for a few seconds. You see it gradually fill up, one-tenth of its length at a time. When it's completely full, you can click the Close button to end the program or click Click to Start again.

Putting the app together

To create the sample app on your own and experience a bit of Windows graphical programming, follow these steps, working first in *design mode,* in which you're just laying out the appearance of your app. First, create the project and position the necessary controls on your "window":

1. **Choose Create a New Project in the Start Window (choose File ⇨ Start Window if you don't see it).**

   You see the Create a New Project window.

2. **Choose C#, Windows, and Desktop in the drop-down lists that you see.**

   The wizard displays the list of project templates shown in Figure 8-2.

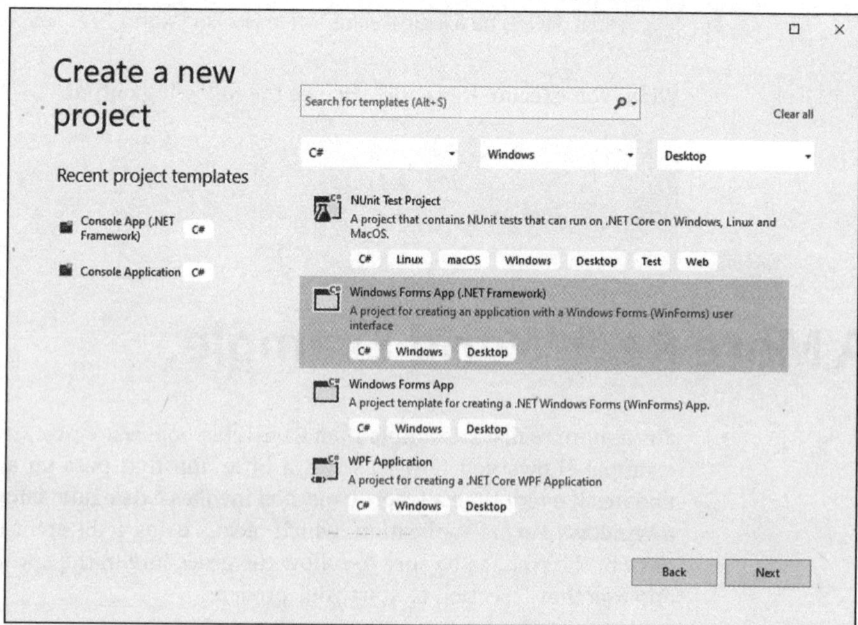

FIGURE 8-2: Choose the Windows Forms App (.NET Framework) template.

3. **Choose the Windows Forms App (.NET Framework) template and click Next.**

   You see a Configure Your New Project window that looks similar to the window you've been using to create Console applications.

4. **Type** SimpleProgress **in the Project Name field, ensure that the Place Solution and Project in the Same Directory check box is selected, and then click Create.**

   The first thing you see is the *form:* a window that you lay out yourself using several *controls.*

5. **Choose View ➪ Toolbox and open Common Controls group.**

   You see the list of controls shown in Figure 8-3.

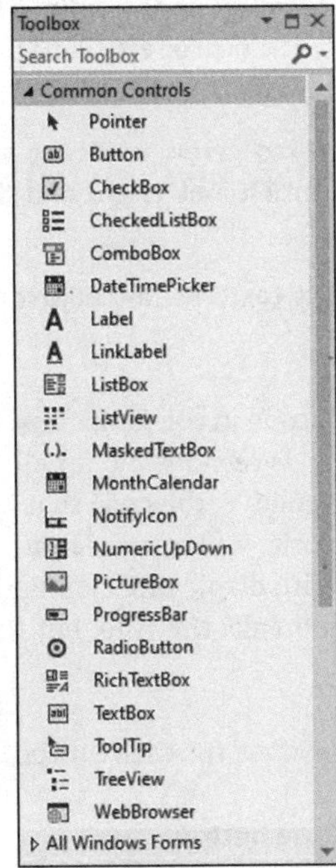

FIGURE 8-3: The Common Controls Group contains the controls you use most often.

6. **Drag a** `ProgressBar` **control to the form and drop it; then drag two** `Button`**s onto the form.**

7. **Position the buttons and the** `ProgressBar`**, and resize the window using the sizing handles so that the form looks somewhat like the one shown in Figure 8-4.**

   Note the handy guide lines that help with positioning.

FIGURE 8-4: Create the form you use to demonstrate the use of a progress bar.

Setting the properties and adding event handlers

Next, set properties for these controls: Choose View⇨Properties Window, select a control on the form, and set the control's properties:

1. **For the progress bar — named `progressBar1` in the code — make sure that the `Minimum` property is `0`, the `Maximum` property is `100`, the `Step` property is `10`, and the `Value` property is `0`.**
2. **For button1, change the `Text` property to `Click to Start` and drag the sizing handles on the button image until it looks right and shows all its text.**
3. **For button2, change the `Text` property to `Close` and adjust the button's size to your liking.**

TIP

In this simple example, you're putting all code in the *form* class. (The form is your window; its class — here, named `Form1` — is responsible for all things graphical.) Generally, you should put all "business" code — the code that does your calculations, data access, and other important work — in other classes. Reserve the form class for code that's intimately involved with displaying elements on the form and responding to its controls. This example breaks the rule, but the delegate works no matter where its callback method is.

Now, still in design mode, add a *handler method* for each button:

1. **On the form, double-click the new Close button.**

   This action generates a method in the "code behind the form" (or, simply, "the code-behind") — the code that makes the form work. It looks like this (you add the boldfaced code):

```
private void button2_Click(object sender, EventArgs e)
{
  Close();
}
```

TIP

To toggle between the form's code and its image, just change tabs in the main panel.

2. **Double-click the new Click to Start button to generate its handler method, which looks like the following in the code-behind:**

```
private void button1_Click(object sender, EventArgs e)
{
  UpdateProgressCallback callback =
    new UpdateProgressCallback(this.DoUpdate);

  // Do something that needs periodic progress reports. This
  // passes a delegate instance that knows how to update the bar.
  DoSomethingLengthy(callback);

  // Clear the bar so that it can be used again.
  progressBar1.Value = 0;
}
```

You see red underlines beneath `UpdateProgressCallback` and `DoSomethingLengthy()`, which indicate errors. Ignore these errors for now — later steps will fix them.

3. **Add the following callback method to the form class:**

```
private void DoUpdate()
{
  // Tells progress bar to update itself
  progressBar1.PerformStep();
}
```

The next section walks you through the remaining code, all of it on the form class. Later in the chapter, you see other variations on the delegate that's passed.

Looking at the workhorse code

The remaining bits of code tucked into the `Form1` class consist of the parts of the delegate life cycle, covered earlier in this chapter. You see the class and then the various delegate components. Here's the delegate declaration that you add immediately after the `Form1()` constructor:

```
// Declare the delegate. This one is void.
delegate void UpdateProgressCallback();
```

You also need a DoSomethingLengthy(), which is the workhorse for this application. It accepts an UpdateProgressCallback delegate as input.

```
// DoSomethingLengthy -- My workhorse method takes a delegate.
private void DoSomethingLengthy(UpdateProgressCallback updateProgress)
{
    // Set the total duration of the updates (4 seconds), number of updates
    // and the duration of each update interval.
    int duration = 4000;
    int intervals = 10;
    int updateInterval = duration / intervals;

    for (int i = 0; i <= intervals; i++)
    {
        // Do something time consuming.
        Thread.Sleep(updateInterval);

        // Update the progress bar.
        updateProgress();
    }
}
```

All this code does is sleep for the specified interval (simulating doing something time consuming) and then it updates the progress bar by calling updateProgress(). To make DoSomethingLengthy() work, you must also add another using statement to the top of your code:

```
using System.Threading;
```

It's helpful to look at the class declaration for this application because it's different from those used for console applications:

```
public partial class Form1 : Form
```

The partial keyword indicates that this file is only part of the full class. The rest can be found in the Form1.Designer.cs file listed in Solution Explorer. (Take a look at it.) Later, in the "Stuff Happens — C# Events" section, you revisit that file to discover a couple of things about *events*. Partial classes let you split a class between two or more files. The compiler generates the Form1.Designer.cs file, so don't modify its code directly. You can modify it indirectly, however, by changing elements on the form. Form1.cs is *your* part.

Shh! Keep It Quiet — Anonymous Methods

The word *anonymous* essentially means "something that lacks a name." America may have been in the desert on a horse with no name (`https://www.youtube.com/watch?v=na47wMFfQCo`), but programmers ride nameless methods instead. You can use anonymous methods in a variety of ways in C#, such as making delegate creation simpler. The following sections discuss anonymous methods, including some new uses presented with C# 9.0.

TIP

Microsoft is working on lambda additions for C# 10.0 that weren't available at the time of writing. You can read about them at `https://docs.microsoft.com/en-us/dotnet/csharp/language-reference/proposals/csharp-10.0/lambda-improvements`. Most of these improvements don't change the way lambdas work in any major way—they're mostly subtle changes that have the potential to make lambda use a little easier.

Delegating Those Important Events

Defining the basic anonymous method

After you have the gist of using delegates, take a quick look at Microsoft's *first* cut at simplifying delegates in C# 2.0 a couple of years ago. To cut out some of the delegate rigamarole, you can use an anonymous method, as shown in the `SimpleProgress2` example. Anonymous methods are just written in more traditional notation. Although the syntax and a few details are different, the effect is essentially the same whether you use a raw delegate, an anonymous method, or a lambda expression (a special kind of declaration for creating anonymous functions, as described at `https://docs.microsoft.com/en-us/dotnet/csharp/language-reference/operators/lambda-expressions`).

An anonymous method creates the delegate instance and the method it "points" to at the same time — right in place, on the fly, *tout de suite.* Here are the guts of the `DoSomethingLengthy()` method again, this time rewritten to use an anonymous method:

```
private void DoSomethingLengthy()
{
    // Set the total duration of the updates (4 seconds), number of updates
    // and the duration of each update interval.
    int duration = 4000;
    int intervals = 10;
    int updateInterval = duration / intervals;

    // Create delegate instance.
    UpdateProgressCallback anon = delegate ()
    {
```

```
        // Method 'pointed' to
        progressBar1.PerformStep();
    };

    for (int i = 0; i <= intervals; i++)
    {
        // Do something time consuming.
        Thread.Sleep(updateInterval);

        // Invoke the delegate.
        if (anon != null) anon();
    }
}
```

The code looks like standard delegate instantiations, except that after the = sign, you see the `delegate` keyword, any parameters to the anonymous method in parentheses (or empty parentheses if none), and the method body. The code that used to be in a separate `DoUpdate()` method — the method that the delegate "points" to — has moved inside the anonymous method — no more pointing. And this method is utterly nameless. You still need the `UpdateProgressCallback()` delegate type definition, and you're still invoking a delegate instance, named `anon` in this example. Consequently, even though there is no method name, the variable `anon` does have a name, and the method and variable are separate entities.

Using static anonymous methods

Code, including anonymous functions, are not without cost in terms of resources and speed. When you create an anonymous function, the hidden costs of doing so could include:

- Overhead for the delegate invocation
- Heap allocations for each of the arguments
- Heap allocations for the enclosing method created by a lambda expression

REMEMBER

Each of these overhead needs and allocations wouldn't really seem like much for an individual data item, but the code repeats them for each data item, which means that the cost can become high. You can read more about these issues at `https://devblogs.microsoft.com/premier-developer/dissecting-the-local-functions-in-c-7/`. C# 9.0 allows the use of the `static` keyword with anonymous functions, which disallows the capture of locals or instance state from containing scopes. By adding `static` to an anonymous method, you can reduce or eliminate any unintended allocations. The `WorkWithEats` class of the `StaticAnonymous` example shows how this technique works (note that you must set up your project to use C# 9.0 by adding the proper language entry to `StaticAnonymous.csproj`):

```
internal class WorkWithEats
{
    const string outString = "{0} is a {1}.";

    internal struct EatItem
    {
        internal string Name;
        internal string Category;
    }

    internal void CreateEats(Func<string, string, string> func)
    {
        List<EatItem> Eats = new List<EatItem>
        {
            new EatItem() {Name="Apple", Category="Fruit"},
            new EatItem() {Name="Bread", Category="Grain"},
            new EatItem() {Name="Asparagus", Category="Vegetable"},
            new EatItem() {Name="Hamburger", Category="Meat"}
        };

        foreach (var item in Eats)
            Console.WriteLine(func(item.Name, item.Category));
    }

    internal void ShowEats()
    {
        CreateEats(static (name, category) => string.Format(
            outString, name, category));
    }
}
```

This example begins saving memory by defining `outString` as a `const` (which means that you don't need to provide the usual object baggage). You can find a longer discussion of how the memory savings happen at `https://stackoverflow.com/questions/23529592/how-are-c-sharp-const-members-allocated-in-memory`. The `EatItem` `struct` makes it possible to use a `List<EatItem>` to hold all the required data in the `CreateEats()` method. The `CreateEats()` method accepts a `Func` as input (see the "Considering the `Action`, `Func`, and `Predicate` delegate types" section, earlier in this chapter, for details). It then creates a list of `EatItem` entries and uses `func` to display them.

The second thing to notice about this example is the `ShowEats()` method, which begins by calling `CreateEats()` with a lambda expression as input. However, notice that this is a `static` lambda expression, which isn't available before C# 9.0. The lambda expression accepts a `name` and a `category` as input, and then displays them using `outString` for formatting.

The WorkWithEats class does most of the work for this example. All that Main() does is create the appropriate object and start it, as shown here:

```
static void Main(string[] args)
{
    WorkWithEats myEats = new WorkWithEats();
    myEats.ShowEats();
    Console.ReadLine();
}
```

The output from this example mixes the formatting string and the various values, as shown here:

```
Apple is a Fruit.
Bread is a Grain.
Asparagus is a Vegetable.
Hamburger is a Meat.
```

Working with lambda discard parameters

Currently, when you create a parameter for a lambda expression, C# will complain if you don't actually use the parameter as part of the expression code. For example, the compiler will complain if you have a lambda expression like this:

```
var handler = (object Obj, EventArgs Args) => ShowDialog();
```

You can replace Obj and Args with underscores to show that they're *discard parameters* (parameters that you won't use) so that the compiler doesn't complain that you haven't used them during the compilation process. Using discard parameters makes your code clearer and easier to understand. In this case, you see that your call could use an object and EventArgs; it just doesn't. To use discard parameters, you modify your code like this:

```
var handler = (object _, EventArgs _) => ShowDialog();
```

Stuff Happens — C# Events

One more application of delegates deserves discussion in this section: the C# *event*, which is implemented with delegates. An event is a variation on a callback but provides a simpler mechanism for alerting the application whenever an important event occurs. An event is especially useful when more than one method is waiting for a callback. Events are widely used in C#, especially for connecting the objects in the user interface to the code that makes them work. The buttons in the `SimpleProgress` example, presented earlier in this chapter, illustrate this use.

The Observer design pattern

It's extremely common in programming for various objects in the running program to have an interest in events that occur on other objects. For example, when the user clicks a button, the form that contains the button wants to know about it. Events provide the standard mechanism in C# and .NET for notifying any interested parties of important actions.

TIP

The event pattern is so common that it has a name: the Observer design pattern. It's one of many common *design patterns* that people have published for anyone to use in their own code. To begin learning about other design patterns, you can consult *Design Patterns: Elements of Reusable Object-Oriented Software,* by Erich Gamma, Richard Helm, Ralph Johnson, and John Vlissides (Addison-Wesley Professional).

The Observer pattern consists of an Observable object — the object with interesting events (sometimes called the Subject) — and any number of Observer objects: those interested in a particular event. The observers register themselves with the Observable in some way and, when events of interest occur, the Observable notifies all registered observers. You can implement this pattern in numerous ways without events (such as callbacks and interfaces), but the C# way is to use events.

TIP

An alternative name for *observers* that you may encounter is *listeners.* Listeners listen for events. And that's not the last of the alternatives.

What's an event? Publish/Subscribe

One analogy for events is your local newspaper. You and many other people contact the paper to subscribe, and then the paper delivers current newspapers to you. The newspaper company is the Publisher, and its customers are Subscribers, so this variation of Observer is often called *Publish/Subscribe* pattern. That's the analogy used in the chapter, but remember that the Observer pattern *is* the Publish/Subscribe pattern, with different terminology. Observers are subscribers, and the Observable object that they observe is a publisher.

In C#, when you have a class on which interesting events arise, you advertise the availability of notifications to any classes that may have an interest in knowing about such events by providing an *event object* (usually public).

REMEMBER

The term *event* has two meanings in C#. You can think of the word *event* as meaning both "an interesting occurrence" and a specific kind of C# object. The former is the real-world concept, and the latter is the way it's set up in C#, using the `event` keyword.

How a publisher advertises its events

REMEMBER

To advertise for subscribers, a class declares a delegate and a corresponding event, something like this:

```
public class PublisherOfInterestingEvents
{
  // A delegate type on which to base the event. Should be
  // declared 'internal' if all subscribers are in the same assembly.
  public delegate void NewEditionEventHandler(object sender,
                                              NewEditionEventArgs e);
  // The event:
  public event NewEditionEventHandler NewEdition;
  // ... other code.
}
```

The delegate and event definitions announce to the world: "Subscribers welcome!" You can think of the `NewEdition` event as similar to a variable of the `NewEditionEventHandler` delegate type. (So far, no events have been sent. This is just the infrastructure for them.)

TIP

It's considered good practice to append `EventHandler` to the name of a delegate type that is the basis for events. A common example, which you can see in the `SimpleProgress` code example, discussed earlier in this chapter, is a `Button` advertising its various events, including a `Click` event. In C#, class `Button` exposes this event as

```
event _dispCommandBarControlEvents_ClickEventHandler Click;
```

where the second, long item is a delegate defined somewhere in .NET.

REMEMBER

Because events are used so commonly, .NET defines two event-related delegate types for you, named `EventHandler` and `EventHandler<TEventArgs>`. You can change `NewEditionEventHandler` in the previous code to `EventHandler` or to the generic `EventHandler<TEventArgs>`, and you don't need your own delegate type. The rest of this chapter uses the built-in `EventHandler<TEventArgs>` delegate type mentioned earlier, not `EventHandler` or a custom type, `NewEditionEventHandler`. You should prefer this form, too:

```
event EventHandler<NewEditonEventArgs> NewEdition;
```

How subscribers subscribe to an event

To receive a particular event, subscribers sign up something like this:

```
publisher.EventName +=
  new EventHandler<some EventArgs type here>(some method name here);
```

where publisher is an instance of the publisher class, EventName is the event name, and EventHandler<*TEventArgs*> is the delegate underneath the event. More specifically, the code in the previous example might be

```
myPublisher.NewEdition += new EventHandler<NewEditionEventArgs>(MyPubHandler);
```

Because an event object is a delegate under its little hood, the += syntax is adding a method to the list of methods that the delegate will call when you invoke it.

TIP

Any number of objects can subscribe this way (and the delegate will hold a list of all subscribed "handler" methods) — even the object on which the event was defined can subscribe, if you like. (And yes, this example shows that a delegate can "point" to more than one method.) In the SimpleProgress program, look in the Form1.Designer.cs file for how the form class registers itself as a subscriber to the buttons' Click events.

How to publish an event

When the publisher decides that something worthy of publishing to all subscribers has occurred, it *raises* (sends) the event. This situation is analogous to a real newspaper putting out the Sunday edition. To publish the event, the publisher would have code like this in one of its methods (but see the later section "A recommended way to raise your events"):

```
NewEditionEventArgs e =
  new NewEditionEventArgs(<args to constructor here>);

// Raise the event -- 'this' is the publisher object.
NewEdition(this, e);
```

Or for the Button example, though this is hidden in class Button:

```
EventArgs e = new EventArgs();  // See next section for more on this topic.
Click(this, e);                 // Raise the event.
```

In each of these examples, you set up the necessary arguments — which differ from event to event; some events need to pass along a lot of info. Then you raise the event by "calling" its name (like invoking a delegate!):

```
// Raising an event (distributing the newspaper)
eventName(<argumentlist>);
NewEdition(this, e);
```

REMEMBER

Events can be based on different delegates with different signatures, that have different parameters, as in the earlier NewEditionEventHandler example, but providing the sender and e parameters is conventional for events. The built-in EventHandler and EventHandler<TEventArgs> delegate types define them for you.

Passing along a reference to the event's sender (the object that raises the event) is useful if the event-handling method needs to get more information from it. Thus a particular Button object, button1, can pass a reference to the Form class the button is a part of. The button's Click event handler resides in a Form class, but the sender is the button: You would pass this.

REMEMBER

You can raise an event in any method on the publishing class. And you can raise it whenever appropriate. The "A recommended way to raise your events" section says more about raising events.

How to pass extra information to an event handler

The e parameter to an event handler method is a custom subclass of the System.EventArgs class. You can write your own NewEditionEventArgs class to carry whatever information you need to convey:

```
public class NewEditionEventArgs : EventArgs
{
  public NewEditionEventArgs(DateTime date, string majorHeadline)
    { PubDate = date; Head = majorHeadline; }
  public DateTime PubDate { get; private set; }
  public string Head { get; private set; }
}
```

You should implement this class's members as properties, as shown in the previous code example. The constructor uses the private setter clauses on the properties. Often, your event doesn't require any extra arguments, and you can just fall back on the `EventArgs` base class, as shown in the next section. If you don't need a special `EventArgs`-derived object for your event, just pass:

```
NewEdition(this, EventArgs.Empty);  // Raise the event.
```

A recommended way to raise your events

The earlier section "How to publish an event" shows the bare bones of raising an event. However, you should always define a special event raiser method, like this:

```
protected virtual void OnNewEdition(NewEditionEventArgs e)
{
  EventHandler<NewEditionEventArgs> temp = NewEdition;

  if (temp != null)
  {
    temp(this, e);
  }
}
```


Providing this method ensures that you always remember to complete two steps:

1. **Store the event in a temporary variable.**

   This step makes your event more usable in situations in which multiple "threads" try to use it at the same time. Threads divide your program into a foreground task and one or more background tasks, which run simultaneously (concurrently).

2. **Check the event for `null` before you try to raise it.**

   If it's `null`, trying to raise it causes an error. Besides, `null` also means that no other objects have shown an interest in your event (none is subscribed), so why bother raising it? *Always* check the event for `null`, regardless of whether or not you write this On*SomeEvent* method.

Making the method `protected` and `virtual` allows subclasses to override it. That's optional. After you have that method, which always takes the same form (making it easy to write quickly), you call the method when you need to raise the event:

```
void SomeMethod()
{
  // Do stuff here and then:
  NewEditionEventArgs e =
    new NewEditionEventArgs(DateTime.Today, "Peace Breaks Out!");
  OnNewEdition(e);
}
```

How observers "handle" an event

The subscribing object specifies the name of a *handler method* when it subscribes — it's the argument to the constructor (boldfaced):

```
button1.Click += new EventHandler<EventArgs>(button1_Click);
```

This line sort of says, "Send my paper to this address, please." Here's a handler for the NewEdition event:

```
myPublisher.NewEdition += new EventHandler<NewEditionEventArgs>(NewEdHandler);
...
void NewEdHandler(object sender, NewEditionEventArgs e)
{
  // Do something in response to the event.
}
```

REMEMBER

When you create a button click event handler in Visual Studio (by double-clicking the button on your form), Visual Studio generates the subscription code in the Form1.Designer.cs file. You shouldn't edit the subscription, but you can delete it and replace it with the same code written in your half of the partial form class. Thereafter, the form designer knows nothing about it.

In your subscriber's handler method, you do whatever is supposed to happen when your class learns of this kind of event. To help you write that code, you can cast the sender parameter to the type you know it to be:

```
Button theButton = (Button)sender;
```

WHEN TO DELEGATE, WHEN TO EVENT, WHEN TO GO ON THE LAMBDA

Events: Use events when you may have multiple subscribers or when communicating with client software that uses your classes.

Delegates: Use delegates or anonymous methods when you need a callback or need to customize an operation.

Lambdas: A *lambda expression* is, in essence, just a short way to specify the method you're passing to a delegate. You can use lambdas instead of anonymous methods.

and then call methods and properties of that object as needed. Because you have a reference to the sending object, you can ask the subscriber questions and carry out operations on it if you need to — like the person who delivers your newspaper knocking on your door to collect the monthly subscription fees. And, you can extract information from the e parameter by getting at its properties in this way:

```
Console.WriteLine(e.HatSize);
```

You don't always need to use the parameters, but they can be handy.

IN THIS CHAPTER

» Dealing with separately compiled assemblies

» Writing a class library

» Using more access-control keywords

» Working with namespaces

Chapter 9

Can I Use Your Namespace in the Library?

C# gives you a variety of ways to break code into meaningful, workable units. These methods include programmatic breaks, such as methods and classes, and structural breaks, such as libraries, assemblies, and namespaces.

You can use a method to divide a long string of code into separate, maintainable units. Use the class structure to group both data and methods in meaningful ways to further reduce the complexity of the program. This chapter also discusses use of partial classes and partial methods to break up things even further. Programs are complex already, and humans become confused easily, so we need all the help we can get.

C# provides another level of grouping: You can group similar classes into a separate library. Beyond writing your own libraries, you can use anybody's libraries in your programs. These programs contain multiple modules known as *assemblies.* This chapter describes libraries and assemblies.

Meanwhile, the access-control story in Chapter 4 of this minibook leaves a few untidy loose ends — the `protected`, `internal`, and `protected internal` keywords — and is slightly complicated further by the use of *namespaces*, another way to group similar classes and allow the use of duplicate names in two parts of a program. This chapter covers namespaces as well.

REMEMBER

You don't have to type the source code for this chapter manually. In fact, using the downloadable source is a lot easier. You can find the source for this chapter in the `\CSAIO4D2E\BK02\CH09` folder of the downloadable source. See the Introduction for details on how to find these source files.

Dividing a Single Program into Multiple Source Files

The programs in this book are for demonstration purposes only. Each program is no more than a few dozen lines long and contains no more than a few classes. An industrial-strength program, complete with all the necessary bells and whistles, can include hundreds of thousands of lines of code, spread over a hundred or more classes.

Consider an airline ticketing system: You have the interface to the reservations agent whom you call on the phone, another interface to the person behind the gate counter, the Internet (in addition to the part that controls aircraft seat inventory plus the part that calculates fares, including taxes); the list goes on and on. A program such as this one grows huge before it's all over. Putting all those classes into one big `Program.cs` source file quickly becomes impractical. It's awkward for these reasons:

- **You have to keep the classes straight.** A single source file can become extremely difficult to understand. Getting a grip on modules such as these, for example, is much easier:
  - `Aircraft.cs`
  - `Fare.cs`
  - `GateAgent.cs`
  - `GateAgentInterface.cs`
  - `ResAgent.cs`
  - `ResAgentInterface.cs`

  They also make the task of finding things easier.

» **The work of creating large programs is usually spread among numerous programmers.** Two programmers can't edit the same file at the same time; each programmer requires exclusive file access or else chaos ensues. You may have 20 or 30 programmers working on a large project at one time. One file containing a single class would limit 24 programmers to one hour of editing a day, around the clock. If you divide the program into multiple classes and then place each class into its own file, orchestrating the same 24 programmers becomes much easier.

» **Compiling a large file may take a considerable length of time.** You can draw out a coffee break for only so long before the boss starts getting suspicious. You certainly wouldn't want to rebuild all the instructions that make up a big system just because a programmer changed a single line. Visual Studio 2019 can rebuild a single project (an individual module of the whole program, which may contain numerous projects). That's quicker and easier than building an entire big program at one time.

For these reasons, the smart C# programmer divides a program into multiple `.cs` source files, which are compiled and built together into a single executable `.exe` file.

REMEMBER

A *project file* contains the instructions about which files should be used together and how they're combined. You can combine project files to generate combinations of programs that depend on the same user-defined classes. For example, you may want to link a write program with its corresponding read program. That way, if one changes, the other is rebuilt automatically. One project would describe the write program while another describes the read program. A set of project files is known as a *solution*. (The `FileRead` and `FileWrite` programs covered in Book 3 could rely on a single combined solution, but they don't.)

TIP

Visual C# programmers use the Visual Studio Solution Explorer to combine multiple C# source files into projects within the Visual Studio 2022 environment. Book 4 describes Solution Explorer.

Working with Global using Statements

At one time, you saw a few `using` directives in a file that applied to that file or to all the files associated with a class. Now, however, any complex application is going to contain a wealth of `using` statements that become hard to manage. C# 10.0 introduces the idea of a `global using` statement. The idea is that you place these `global using` statements into a separate file, where they're easy to find and manage, and that they affect the entire project. You need to create a .NET Core application to use them and ensure that you select .NET 6.0 as the framework. The

`GlobalUsing` example begins with the `GlobalUsing.cs` file, which contains all of the `global using` statements for the project. Use the following steps to add this file to the project you created (or simply review it using the downloadable source):

1. **Right-click GlobalUsing in Solution Explorer and choose Add⇨New Item.**

   You see the Add New Item dialog box shown in Figure 9-1. Notice that you can drill down into the Visual C# Items folder in the left pane to select the Code folder and make it easier to locate the item you need.

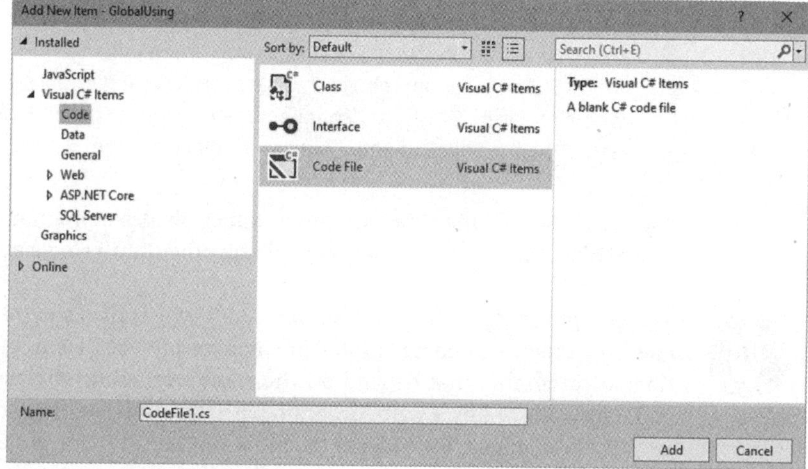

FIGURE 9-1: Use the Add New Item dialog box to add a new item to your project.

2. **Highlight the Code File item in the center pane.**

   You see a description of this item in the right pane.

3. **Type** GlobalUsing.cs **in the Name field and click Add.**

   Visual Studio adds the new file to your project.

Now you have a single place to go to see all the `using` statements for your application, except that these are `global using` statements because they affect the entire application. To see how this can work, type **global using System;** in the `GlobalUsing.cs` file. Now look at the `Program.cs` file and you see that the `using System;` statement is greyed out because Visual Studio recognizes that there is a global alternative. Remove this statement, compile the application, and you see it works just fine with the `global using` statement in place.

Dividing a Single Program into Multiple Assemblies

In Visual Studio, and in C#, Visual Basic .NET, and the other .NET languages, one project equals one compiled *module* — otherwise known as an *assembly* in .NET. The words module and assembly have somewhat different technical meanings, but only to advanced programmers. In this book, you can just equate the two terms.

Executable or library?

C# can produce two basic assembly types (there are others):

- **Executable (`.EXE`):** A program in its own right that contains a `Main()` method. You can double-click a `.EXE` file in File Explorer, for example, and cause it to run. This book is full of executables in the form of console applications. Executable assemblies often use supporting code from libraries in other assemblies.
- **Class library (`.DLL`):** A compiled library of functionality that can be used by other programs. All programs in this book also use libraries. For example, the `System` namespace (the home of classes such as `String`, `Console`, `Exception`, `Math`, and `Object`) exists in a set of library assemblies. Every program needs `System` classes. Libraries are housed in DLL assemblies.

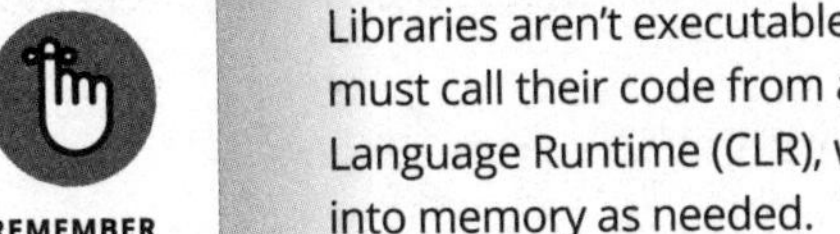

REMEMBER

Libraries aren't executable — you can't make them run directly. Instead, you must call their code from an executable or another library. The Common Language Runtime (CLR), which runs C# programs, loads library assemblies into memory as needed.

The important concept to know is that you can easily write your own class libraries. The "Putting Your Classes into Class Libraries" section of this chapter shows you how to perform this task.

Assemblies

Assemblies, which are the compiled versions of individual projects, contain the project's code in a special format, along with a bunch of *metadata*, or detailed information about the classes in the assembly.

This section introduces assemblies because they round out your understanding of the C# build process — and they come into play in the discussion of namespaces

and access keywords such as protected and internal. (You find these namespaces and these keywords covered later in this chapter.) Assemblies also play a big part in understanding class libraries. It's all covered in the later section "Putting Your Classes into Class Libraries."

The C# compiler converts the project's C# code to Common Intermediate Language (usually called IL) that's stored in the appropriate type of assembly file. IL resembles assembly language (one step beyond the 1s and 0s used in machine language) that hardcore programmers have used for decades to get down "close to the metal" because their higher-level languages couldn't do what they needed or the compilers couldn't produce the most efficient code possible.

One major consequence of compiling from .NET to IL, regardless of language, is that a program can use assemblies written in different languages. For example, a C# program can call methods in an assembly originally written in Visual Basic or C++ or the C# program can subclass a VB class.

Executables

You can run executable assemblies in a variety of ways:

- Run them in Visual Studio: Choose Debug➪Start Debugging (F5) or Debug➪Start without Debugging (Ctrl+F5).
- Double-click the assembly file (.EXE) in Windows Explorer.
- Right-click the file in Windows Explorer and choose Run or Open from the pop-up menu.
- Type the assembly's name (and path) into a console window.
- If the program takes arguments, such as filenames, from the command line, drag the files to the executable file in Windows Explorer.

A solution in Visual Studio can contain multiple projects — some .DLL and some .EXE. If a solution contains more than one .EXE project, you must tell Visual Studio which project is the *startup project*; the one runs from the Debug menu. To specify a startup project, right-click that project in Solution Explorer and choose Set As Startup Project. The startup project's name appears in boldface in Solution Explorer.

Think of a solution containing two .EXE assemblies as two separate programs that happen to use the same library assemblies. For example, you might have in a solution a console executable and a Windows Forms executable plus some libraries. If you make the console app the startup project and compile the code, you produce a console app. If you make the Windows Forms app the startup — well, you get the idea.

Class libraries

A *class library* contains one or more classes, usually ones that work together in some way. Often, the classes in a library are in their own namespaces. (The "Putting Classes into Namespaces" section, later in this chapter, explains namespaces.) You may build a library of math routines, a library of string-handling routines, and a library of input/output routines, for example.

Sometimes, you even build a whole solution that is nothing but a class library, rather than a program that can be executed on its own. (Typically, while developing this type of library, you also build an accompanying `.EXE` project to test your library during development. But when you release the library for programmers to use, you release just the `.DLL` (not the `.EXE`) — and documentation for it, which you can generate by writing XML comments in the code. XML comments are described in Book 4, which is all about Visual Studio.) The next section shows you how to write your own class libraries.

Putting Your Classes into Class Libraries

REMEMBER

The simplest definition of a *class library project* is one whose classes contain no `Main()` method. Can that definition be correct? It can and is. The existence of `Main()` distinguishes a class library from an executable. C# libraries are much easier to write and use than similar libraries were in C or C++.

The following sections explain the basic concepts involved in creating your own class libraries. Don't worry: C# does the heavy lifting. Your end of it is quite simple.

Creating the projects for a class library

You can create the files for a new class library project and its test application in either of two ways:

» **Create the class library project first and then add the test application project to its solution.** You might take this approach if you were writing a stand-alone class library assembly. The next section describes how to create the class library project.

» **Create a test application first and then add one or more library projects to its solution.** Thus you might first create the test application as a console application or a graphical Windows Forms (or Windows Presentation Foundation or as a Universal Application Platform) application. Then you would add class library projects to that solution.

This approach is the one to take if you want to add a supporting library to an ongoing application. In that case, the test application could be either the ongoing program or a special test application project added to the solution just to test the library. For testing, you set the test application project as the startup project as described in the earlier section "Executables."

Creating a stand-alone class library

If your whole purpose is to develop a stand-alone class library that can be used in various other programs, you can create a solution (`TestClass` in this case) that contains a class library project from scratch. Here's how simple it is:

1. **Choose Create a New Project.**

   You see the Create a New Project dialog box.

2. **Select C#, Windows, and Library from the drop-down lists.**

   The wizard displays the kinds of libraries you can create, including class libraries, as shown in Figure 9-2. Note that there are a number of Class Library templates for various uses. The example in this chapter uses a traditional Class Library template for Windows (shown highlighted in the figure).

3. **Select the Class Library (.NET Framework) entry and then click Next.**

   You see the Configure Your New Project window shown in Figure 9-3.

4. **Type** TestClass **in the Project Name field, clear Place Solution and Project in the Same Directory, and type** TestClassProject **in the Solution Name field.**

   The example uses `TestClass` as the project name.

   REMEMBER

   The reason you want separate solution and project directories is so that you can add a test application for your class library later. Using separate directories makes it easier to keep the various project elements separate.

5. **Click Create.**

   Visual Studio creates the new project for you. You see the `Class1.cs` file open so that you can begin adding code for your class library. After you have a class library project, you can add a test application project using the approach described in the next section.

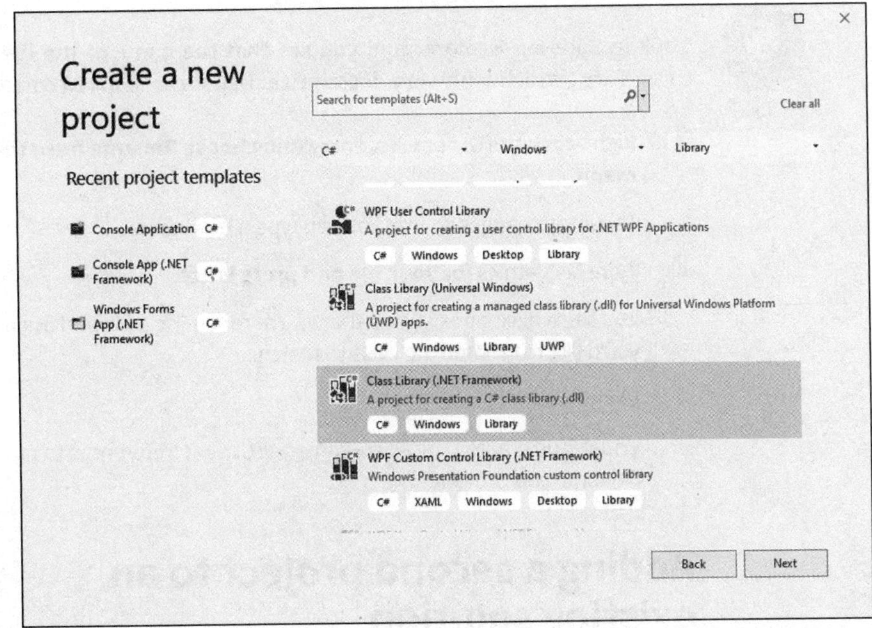

FIGURE 9-2: The Class Library (.NET Framework) is for use with Windows alone.

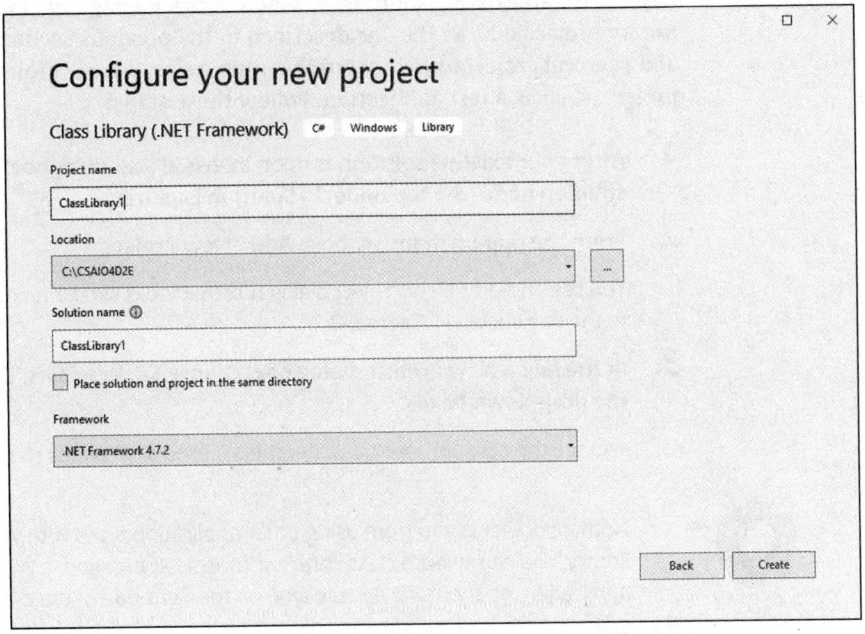

Configure your new project

Class Library (.NET Framework) C# Windows Library

Project name

ClassLibrary1

Location

C:\CSAIO4D2E

Solution name

ClassLibrary1

Place solution and project in the same directory

Framework

.NET Framework 4.7.2

Back Create

FIGURE 9-3: Configure the class as needed.

TIP

Look in Solution Explorer and you see that the name of the file for your class is `Class1.cs`, which isn't very descriptive. Use these steps to correct the situation:

1. **Right-click the `Class1.cs` entry and choose Rename from the context menu.**

   The entry changes so that you can type a new name.

2. **Type** DoMath.cs **for your file and press Enter.**

   You see a dialog box stating that you're renaming a file and asking whether you'd like to rename the class to match.

3. **Click Yes.**

   Visual Studio automatically renames all `Class1` references to match the new filename you provide.

Adding a second project to an existing solution

If you have an existing solution — whether it's an ongoing application or a class library project such as the one described in the previous section — you can easily add a second project to your solution: either a class library project or an executable project, such as a test application. Follow these steps:

1. **After your existing solution is open in Visual Studio, right-click the solution node (the top node) in Solution Explorer.**
2. **From the pop-up menu, choose Add⇨New Project.**

   You see an Add a New Project dialog box that looks similar (except for the title) to the one shown in Figure 9-2.

3. **In the Add a New Project dialog box, choose C#, Windows, Console from the drop-down boxes.**

   You see the console application templates used in previous chapters of the book.

   TIP

   Nothing prevents you from using other application types with your class library. You can select a class library, a console application, a Windows Forms application, or another available type on the right side of the dialog box.

4. **Choose the Console App (.NET Framework) template to create a standard C# Windows console application.**
5. **Click Next.**

You see the Configure Your New Project dialog box shown in Figure 9-4. Notice that this dialog box lacks many of the features of the one shown in Figure 9-3 because you're adding a project to an existing solution.

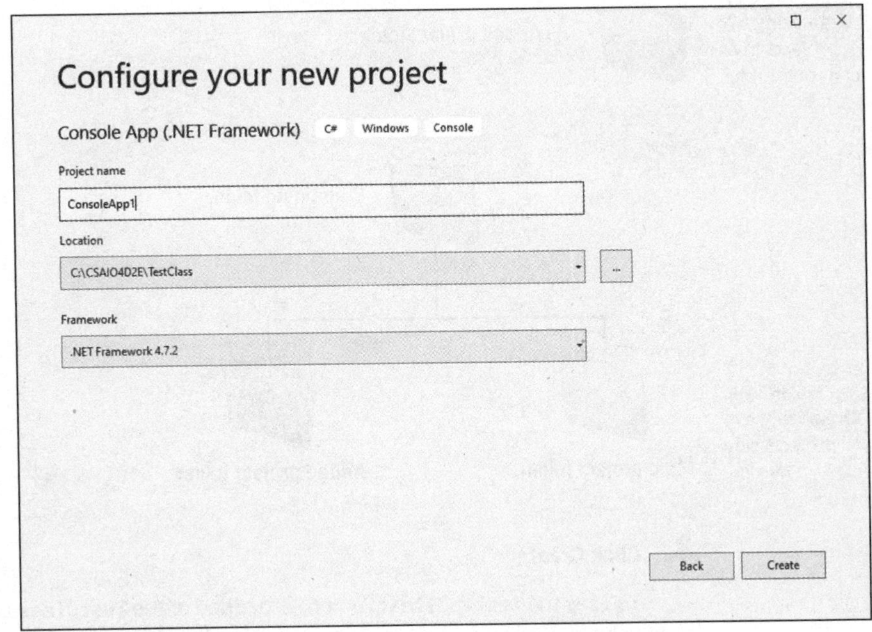

FIGURE 9-4: Configure the options for the application used to test the `DoMath` class.

6. **Type** TestApplication **in the Project Name field.**
7. **Keep** `\CSAIO4D2E\BK02\CH09\TestClassProject` **as the location for the example code.**

   You'll see two subfolders in the `TestClassProject` folder once you create this test application in the next step: `TestClass` and `TestApplication`. The location you choose depends on how you want to organize your solution. You can put the new project's folder in either of two places:

   - **All-in-one-folder:** Navigate into the main project folder, making the added project a subfolder. (See Figure 9-5.)
   - **Side-by-side:** Navigate to the folder that contains the main project folder so that the two projects are at the same level. (See Figure 9-6.)

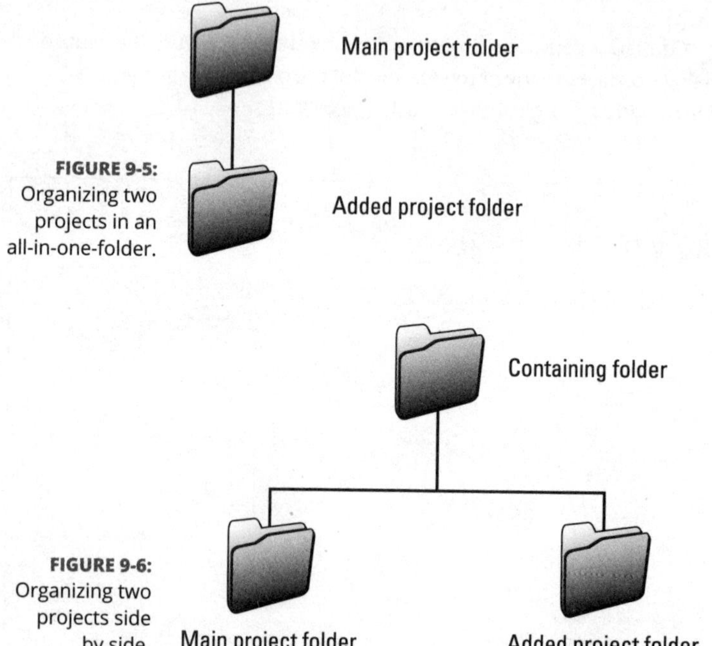

FIGURE 9-5: Organizing two projects in an all-in-one-folder.

FIGURE 9-6: Organizing two projects side by side.

8. **Click Create.**

   You see the `TestApplication` project added to the `TestClass` project in Solution Explorer, as shown in Figure 9-7. Both of these projects are part of the `TestClass` solution, which states that the highlight is currently on project 2 of 2 projects. Notice that each project lists the files used to implement it below the project entry. You can drill down into the file listing to see other dependencies. The projects are listed in alphabetical order by default to make them easier to find.

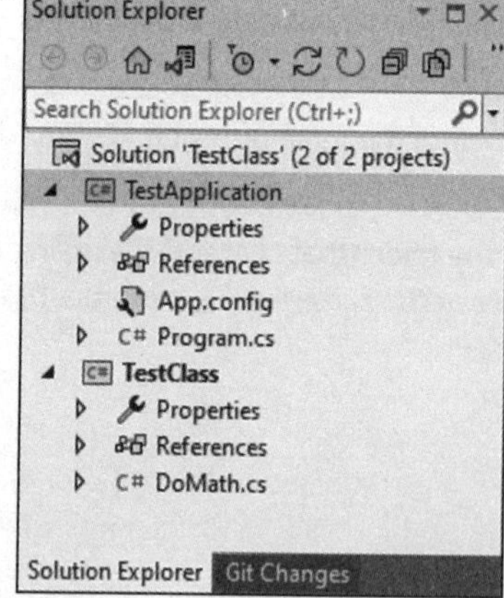

FIGURE 9-7: The projects used to create the TestClass solution are listed individually.

After you create TestApplication, right-click its entry in Solution Explorer and choose Set as StartUp Project from the context menu. Notice that TestApplication now appears in bold type to show that it's the application that the debugger will start when you run the application.

Creating the code for the library

After you have a class library project, create the classes that make up the library. The following TestClass example shows a simple class library:

```
namespace TestClass
{
    public class DoMath
    {
        public int DoAdd(int Num1, int Num2)
        {
            return Num1 + Num2;
        }

        public int DoSub(int Num1, int Num2)
        {
            return Num1 - Num2;
        }

        public int DoMul(int Num1, int Num2)
        {
            return Num1 * Num2;
        }

        public int DoDiv(int Num1, int Num2)
        {
            return Num1 / Num2;
        }
    }
}
```

Libraries can contain any C# type: class, structure, delegate, interface, and enumeration. You find structures discussed in Chapter 11 of this minibook, delegates appear in Chapter 8 of this minibook, interfaces are in Chapter 7 of this minibook, and Book 1, Chapter 10 discusses enumerations.

Notice that the access modifiers are all set to public in this case because the intent is to access the code from outside the assembly. However, when creating a class library, you follow the same access rules as you do for any other class and provide the individual elements with just the amount of access required to perform the required tasks.

REMEMBER

In class library code, you normally shouldn't catch exceptions. Let them bubble up from the library to the client code that's calling into the library. Clients need to know about these exceptions and handle them in their own ways. Book 1 covers exceptions.

The example code also shows that this file doesn't contain any `using` directives because it doesn't need any. Adding only the `using` directives you need makes your code:

- Simpler
- Less error prone
- Easier to maintain

Using a test application to test a library

By itself, the class library doesn't do anything, so you need a *test application*, a small executable program that tests the library code during development by calling its methods. In other words, write a program that uses classes and methods from the library. You see this behavior in the `TestApplication` program example.

REMEMBER

To use your class library from within the test application, you must add a reference to it. To perform this task, right-click References in the `TestApplication` section of Solution Explorer and choose Add Reference. You see a Reference Manager dialog box. Select the Projects\Solution tab so that you see `TestClass`, as shown in Figure 9-8. Select the box next to the `TestClass` entry and click OK. Visual Studio opens the References folder for `TestApplication`, and you see `TestClass` added to the list.

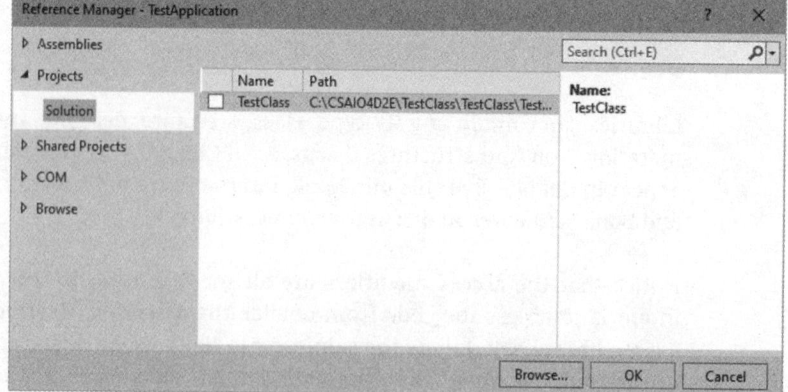

FIGURE 9-8: Add a reference for your class library.

It's time to create a test program. The following code appears in the `Program.cs` file for `TestApplication`, rather than in the `DoMath.cs` file:

```
using System;

// Add a reference to your class library.
using TestClass;

namespace TestApplication
{
    class Program
    {
        static void Main(string[] args)
        {
            // Create a DoMath object.
            DoMath math = new DoMath();

            // Test the DoMath library functions.
            Console.WriteLine($"6 + 2 = {math.DoAdd(6, 2)}");
            Console.WriteLine($"6 - 2 = {math.DoSub(6, 2)}");
            Console.WriteLine($"6 * 2 = {math.DoMul(6, 2)}");
            Console.WriteLine($"6 / 2 = {math.DoDiv(6, 2)}");
            Console.Read();
        }
    }
}
```

This application just creates an instance of `DoMath` and then exercises all the public methods within the class. To build this class and application, choose Build⇨Build Solution. Here's the output from the test application when you choose one of the options to run the application on the Debug menu:

```
6 + 2 = 8
6 - 2 = 4
6 * 2 = 12
6 / 2 = 3
```

TIP

Libraries often provide only `static` methods. In that case, you don't need to instantiate the library object. Just call the methods through the class.

Going Beyond Public and Private: More Access Keywords

Dividing a program into multiple assemblies, as discussed in the previous sections, has a bearing on which code in `AssemblyB` you can access from `AssemblyA`. The access-control examples in Chapter 4 of this minibook do a good job of illustrating what happens within a single assembly when you configure the access modifiers correctly. However, now you have two assemblies, so an `internal` access modifier says that `AssemblyB` can't access the internal members of `AssemblyA`; therefore, you need to make a change in how you configure the access modifiers. The following sections discuss how to use access modifiers when you have multiple assemblies.

Internal: For CIA eyes only

Suppose that a solution has these two projects:

- `InternalLimitsAccess`: An executable whose class `Congress` contains the `Main()` method that kicks off program execution. (No law requires the `Main()` class to be named `Program`.)
- `CIAAssembly`: The class library project.

In real life, the U.S. Congress has the annoying habit of expecting the Central Intelligence Agency (CIA) to reveal its secrets — just to members of Congress, of course. ("We won't leak your secrets — honest.") Meanwhile, those overly secretive spooks at the CIA have secrets they would prefer to hang on to. (Maybe they know the secret formula for Coca-Cola or Colonel Sanders's secret herbs and spices or a more sinister entity.) Exactly what Secret X is doesn't matter here, but the CIA wants to keep Secret X, well, secret. The following sections discuss how the CIA managed to hide its secrets.

Keeping Group B from knowing what Group A is doing

Everybody at the CIA needs to know Secret X. In the `CheckCIA` example, the CIA is divided into several classes — class `GroupA` and class `GroupB`. Think of them as sections of the CIA that (sometimes) communicate and share with each other. Suppose that `GroupA` is the holder of Secret X, so the group marked it `private`. The code looks something like this:

```
// In assembly InternalLimitsAccess:
class Congress
```

```
{
  static void Main(...)
  {
    // Code to oversee CIA
  }
}

// In assembly CIAAssembly:
public class GroupA
{
  private string _secretFormulaForCocaCola; // Secret X
  internal GroupA() { _secretFormulaForCocaCola = "lots of sugar";}
}

public class GroupB
{
  public void DoSomethingWithSecretX()
  {
    // Do something with Secret X, if only you could access it.
  }
}
```

Now GroupB can't see Secret X, but suppose that it has a legitimate need to know it. GroupA can, of course, bump Secret X to public status, but if it does, the secret isn't much of a secret anymore. If GroupB can see the secret, so can those snoops over in Congress. Even worse, CNN knows it too, not to mention Fox, ABC, and other networks. And you know how well those folks keep secrets. Oh, right — Russia can see Secret X, too.

REMEMBER

Luckily, C# also has the internal keyword. Using internal is just one step down from public and well above private. If you mark the GroupA class and its "public" methods — the ones that are visible outside the class — with the internal keyword instead, everybody at the CIA can see and access Secret X — as long as you either mark the secret itself (a data member) as internal or provide an internal property to get it with, as shown in this version (which appears in the CheckCIA example):

```
namespace CIAAssembly
{
    internal class GroupA
    {
        private string _secretFormulaForCocaCola; // Secret X
        internal GroupA() { _secretFormulaForCocaCola = "lots of sugar"; }
        internal string SecretX
        {
            get { return _secretFormulaForCocaCola; }
        }
    }
```

```
    public class GroupB
    {
        public void DoSomethingWithSecretX()
        {
            GroupA myAccess = new GroupA();

            // Do something with Secret X, now that we can see it:
            Console.WriteLine($"I know Secret X, which is" +
                $" {myAccess.SecretX.Length}" +
                $" characters long, but I'm not telling.");
        }
    }
}
```

Now class GroupB has the access it needs — and it isn't giving up the secret (even under threat of waterboarding). All it tells Congress, over in Main(), is that it knows Secret X, and Secret X has 11 characters. Here's that chunk of code:

```
class Congress
{
  static void Main(string[] args)
  {
    // Code to oversee CIA
    // The following line doesn't compile because GroupA isn't accessible
    // outside CIAAssembly. Congress can't get at GroupA over at CIA.

    // CIAAssembly.GroupA groupA = new CIAAssembly.GroupA();

    // Class Congress can access GroupB because it's declared public.
    // GroupB is willing to admit to knowing the secret, but it's
    // not telling -- except for a small hint.
    GroupB groupB = new GroupB();
    groupB.DoSomethingWithSecretX();
    Console.Read();
  }
}
```

From Main(), GroupA is now invisible, so an attempt to construct an instance of it doesn't compile. But because GroupB is public, Main() can access it and call its public method DoSomethingWithSecretX().

Adding secure access

Wait! CIA does have to talk to Congress about certain topics, but on a need-to-know basis, limited to selected members of Congress, of course. They can do so already, via GroupB, as long as they present the proper credentials, although you need to add them to the code:

```
public string DoSomethingWithSecretXUsingCredentials(string credentials)
{
    if (credentials == "congressman with approved access")
    {
        GroupA myAccess = new GroupA();

        return myAccess.SecretX;
    }
    return string.Empty;
}
```

The internal keyword makes classes and their members accessible only inside their own assembly. But within the assembly, the internal items are effectively "public" to all local classes.

You can mark a method inside an internal class as public, though it isn't truly public. A class member can't be more accessible than its class, so the so-called "public" member is just internal.

CIA can still keep its deepest, darkest secrets ultra-hush-hush by declaring them private inside their owning class. That strategy makes them accessible only in that class.

Protected: Sharing with subclasses

The main purpose of private is to hide information. In particular, private hides a class's internal implementation details. (Classes who know classes too intimately aren't the luckiest classes in the world. In fact, they're the unluckiest.) Classes with a lot of implementation details are said to be "too tightly coupled" with the classes they know too much about. If class A is aware of the internal workings of class B, A can come to rely too much on those details. If they ever change, you end up having to modify both classes.

The less the other classes — and assemblies — know about how class B performs its magic, the better. The "Access control to the rescue — an example" section of Chapter 4 of this minibook uses the example of a BankAccount class. The bank doesn't want forgetful folks or forgetful classes to be able to change a balance directly. That balance is properly part of the BankAccount class's implementation. It's private. BankAccount provides access to the balance — but only through a carefully controlled public interface. In the `BankAccount` class, the interface shared with the main application consists of three `internal` methods:

- `Balance`: Provides a read-only way to find out the current balance. You can't use `Balance` to modify the underlying balance.
- `Deposit()`: Lets someone outside the class add to the balance in a controlled way.
- `Withdraw()`: Lets someone (presumably the account owner) subtract from the balance, but within carefully controlled limits. `Withdraw()` enforces the business rule that you can't withdraw more than you have.

Access-control considerations other than `private`, `internal`, and `public` arise in programming. The previous section explains how the `internal` keyword opens a class — but only to other classes in its own assembly.

However, suppose that the `BankAccount` class has a subclass, `SavingsAccount` (described in the "Working with the basic update" section of Chapter 5 of this minibook). Methods in `SavingsAccount` need access to that balance defined in the base class. Of course, other classes, even in the same assembly, probably don't. Luckily, `SavingsAccount` can use the same public interface, the same access, as outsiders: using `Balance`, `Deposit()`, and `Withdraw()`.

Sometimes, though, the base class doesn't supply such access methods for its subclasses (and others) to use. What if the `_balance` data member in `BankAccount` is `private` and the class doesn't provide the `Balance` property? Enter the `protected` keyword: If the `_balance` instance variable in the base class is declared `protected` rather than `private`, outsiders can't see it — it's effectively private to them. But subclasses can see it just fine.

In the case of the Chapter 5 example, the `Balance` property is marked `protected`, which means that only `BankAccount` and `SavingsAccount` can see it. Access to balance information is provided through a public `override` of the `ToString()` method, which provides a controlled method of access. So, a caller outside of the assembly would only be able to deposit money, withdraw money, and get a balance — all in a controlled manner. The `SimpleSavingsAccountAssembly` example found in the downloadable source shows an assembly version of the program (further protecting the class functionality from prying eyes) and you can see how well it works with six small modifications of the original Chapter 5 code; the classes (two changes) and their constructors (four additional changes) must be made `public` to see them. When working with an assembly, you can no longer keep the classes and constructors `internal`, but the other assembly members are actually hidden better. In addition, you need to provide a reference and `using` directive for the BankAccount and SavingsAccount classes. The AccountLibrary project contains the classes, and the MyATM project contains Main().

Putting Classes into Namespaces

Namespaces exist to put related classes in one bag and to reduce collisions between names used in different places. For example, you may compile all math-related classes into a MathRoutines namespace. A single file can be (but isn't commonly) divided into multiple namespaces:

```
// In file A.cs:
namespace One
{
}

namespace Two
{
}
```

More commonly, you group multiple files. For example, the file Point.cs may contain the class Point, and the file ThreeDSpace.cs contains class ThreeDSpace to describe the properties of a Euclidean space (like a cube). You can combine Point.cs and ThreeDSpace.cs and other C# source files into the MathRoutines namespace (and, possibly, a MathRoutines library assembly). Each file would wrap its code in the same namespace. (It's the classes in those files, rather than the files themselves, that make up the namespace. Which files the classes are in is irrelevant for namespaces. Nor does it matter which assembly they're in: A namespace can span multiple assemblies.)

```
// In file Point.cs:
namespace MathRoutines
{
  class Point { }
}

// In file ThreeDSpace.cs:
namespace MathRoutines
{
  class ThreeDSpace { }
}
```

REMEMBER

If you don't wrap your classes in a namespace, C# puts them in the *global namespace*, the base (unnamed) namespace for all other namespaces. A better practice, though, is to use a specific namespace. The namespace serves these purposes:

- **A namespace puts oranges with oranges, not with apples.** As an application programmer, you can reasonably assume that the classes that comprise the `MathRoutines` namespace are all math related. By the same token, when looking for just the perfect math method, you first would look in the classes that make up the `MathRoutines` namespace.
- **Namespaces avoid the possibility of name conflicts.** For example, a file input/output library may contain a class `Convert` that converts the representation in one file type to that of another. At the same time, a translation library may contain a class of the same name. Assigning the namespaces `FileIO` and `TranslationLibrary` to the two sets of classes avoids the problem: The class `FileIO.Convert` clearly differs from the class `TranslationLibrary.Convert`.

Declaring a namespace

You declare a namespace using the keyword `namespace` followed by a name and an open and closed curly-braces block. The classes (and other types) within that block are part of the namespace:

```
namespace MyStuff
{
  class MyClass {}
  class UrClass {}
}
```

In this example, both `MyClass` and `UrClass` are part of the `MyStuff` namespace.

REMEMBER

Namespaces are implicitly `public`, and you can't use access specifiers on namespaces, not even `public`. Besides classes, namespaces can contain other types, including these:

- `delegate`
- `enum`
- `interface`
- `struct`

A namespace can also contain *nested namespaces,* which are namespaces within other namespaces, to any depth of nesting. You may have Namespace2 nested inside Namespace1, as in this example:

```
namespace Namespace1
{
  // Classes in Namespace1 here ...
  // Then the nested namespace:
  namespace Namespace2
  {
    // Classes in Namespace2
    public class Class2
    {
      public void AMethod() { }
    }
  }
}
```

To call a method in Class2, inside Namespace2, from somewhere outside Namespace1, you specify this line:

```
Namespace1.Namespace2.Class2.AMethod();
```

Imagine these namespaces strung together with dots as a sort of logical path to the desired item. "Dotted names," such as System.IO, look like nested namespaces, but they name only one namespace. So System.Data is a complete namespace name, not the name of a Data namespace nested inside System. This convention makes it easier to have several related namespaces, such as System.IO, System.Data, and System.Text, and make the family resemblance obvious. In practice, nested namespaces and namespaces with dotted names are indistinguishable.

TECHNICAL STUFF

Prefixing all namespaces in a program with your company name is conventional — making the company name the front part of multiple segments separated by dots: MyCompany.MathRoutines. (That statement is true if you have a company name; you can also use just your own name.) Adding a company name prevents name clashes if your code uses two libraries that happen to use the same basic namespace name, such as MathRoutines.

TIP

The Visual Studio New Project dialog box runs an Application Wizard that puts all code it generates in namespaces. The wizard names these namespaces after the project directory it creates. Look at any of the programs in this book, each of which was created by the Application Wizard. For example, the AlignOutput program is created in the AlignOutput folder. The name of the source file is Program.cs, which matches the name of the default class. The name of the namespace containing Program.cs is the same as that of the folder: AlignOutput.

Using file-scoped namespaces

The C# 10.0 development staff is attempting to clean up your files somewhat. The `global using` statement, described in the "Working with Global using Statements" section of this chapter, cleans up the vertical waste to some extent. A file-scoped namespace cleans up the horizontal waste by allowing you to specify a namespace without all the usual indentation, as shown in the `FileScopeNamespace` example and in the code here:

```
using System;

namespace FileScopeNamespace;
class Program
{
    static void Main(string[] args)
    {
        Console.WriteLine("Hello World!");
    }
}
```

The `FileScopeNamespace` entry now applies to the entire file. You must use a .NET Core application to make this work. In addition, you must add C# 10.0 support to your `FileScopeNamespace.csproj` file as shown below in bold:

```
<Project Sdk="Microsoft.NET.Sdk">

  <PropertyGroup>
    <OutputType>Exe</OutputType>
    <TargetFramework>net6.0</TargetFramework>
  </PropertyGroup>
  <PropertyGroup>
    <LangVersion>10.0</LangVersion>
  </PropertyGroup>

</Project>
```

Relating namespaces to the access keyword story

REMEMBER

In addition to helping package your code into a more usable form, namespaces extend the notion of access control presented in Chapter 4 of this minibook (which introduces the `public`, `private`, `protected`, `internal`, `protected internal` and `private protected` keywords). Namespaces extend access control by further limiting which members of a class you can access from where.

However, namespaces affect visibility more than accessibility. By default, classes and methods in NamespaceA are invisible to classes in NamespaceB, regardless of their access-control specifiers. But you can make one namespace's classes and methods visible to another namespace in a couple of ways. The bottom line is that you can access only what is visible to you and is public enough. This issue involves access control, extended earlier in this chapter and covered in the discussion of access specifiers in Chapter 4 of this minibook.

Determining whether the class and method you need are visible and accessible to you

To determine whether Class1 in NamespaceA can call NamespaceB.Class2.AMethod(), consider these two questions:

- **Is Class2 over in NamespaceB visible to the calling class, Class1?**

  This issue involves namespace visibility, discussed at the end of this list.

- **If the answer to the first question is True, are Class2 and its AMethod() also "public enough" for Class1 to access?**

  If Class2 is in a different assembly from Class1, it must be public for Class1 to access its members. Class2, in the same assembly needs to be declared at least internal. Classes can only be public, protected, internal, or private.

  Likewise, the Class2 method must have at least a certain level of access in each of those situations. Methods add the protected internal option to the list of access specifiers that classes have. Chapter 4 in this minibook and the earlier section "Going Beyond Public and Private: More Access Keywords" supply the gory details.

You need to answer Yes to both questions before Class1 can call the Class2 method.

Making classes and methods in another namespace visible

C# provides two ways to make items in NamespaceB visible in NamespaceA:

- **Fully qualify names from NamespaceB wherever you use them in NamespaceA.** This method results in code such as the following line, which starts with the namespace name and then adds the class and lists the method:

  ```
  System.Console.WriteLine("my string");
  ```

» **Eliminate the need for fully qualified names in** NamespaceA **by giving your files a** using **directive for** NamespaceB:

```
using System; // These are namespace names.
using NamespaceB;
```

Programs throughout this book make items in NamespaceB visible in NamespaceA with the using directive. The next two sections discuss full qualification and using directives.

Using fully qualified names

The namespace of a class is a part of the extended class name, which leads to the first way to make classes in one namespace visible in another. The FullyQualified example doesn't have any using directives to simplify referring to classes in other namespaces:

```
namespace MathRoutines  // Broken into two segments -- see below.
{
    class Sort
    {
        public void SomeMethod()
        {
            System.Console.WriteLine("In SomeMethod");
        }
    }
}

namespace Paint
{
    public class PaintColor
    {
        public PaintColor(int nRed, int nGreen, int nBlue) { }
        public void Paint()
        {
            System.Console.WriteLine("Painting");
        }
        public static void StaticPaint()
        {
            System.Console.WriteLine("Static Painting");
        }
    }
}

namespace MathRoutines  // Another piece of this namespace
```

```
{
    public class Test
    {
        static public void Main(string[] args)
        {
            // Create an object of type Sort from the same namespace
            // we're in and invoke a method.
            Sort obj = new Sort();
            obj.SomeMethod();

            // Create an object in another namespace -- notice that the
            // namespace name must be included explicitly in every
            // class reference.
            Paint.PaintColor black = new Paint.PaintColor(0, 0, 0);
            black.Paint();
            Paint.PaintColor.StaticPaint();
        }
    }
}
```

Normally, `Sort` and `Test` would be in different C# source files that you build together into one program. In this case, the two classes `Sort` and `Test` are contained within the same namespace, `MathRoutines`, even though they appear in different declarations within the file (or in different files). That namespace is broken into two parts.

The method `Test.Main()` can reference the `Sort` class without specifying the namespace because the two classes are in the same namespace. However, `Main()` must specify the `Paint` namespace when referring to `PaintColor`, as in the call to `Paint.PaintColor.StaticPaint()`. This process is known as *fully qualifying* the name.

Notice that you don't need to take any special steps when referring to `black.Paint()`, because the class of the `black` object is specified, namespace and all, in the `black` declaration. Here's the output from this example:

```
In SomeMethod
Painting
Static Painting
```

Working with partial classes

The term *partial class* brings up visions of people who can't make up their minds or who procrastinate, but it has nothing to do with either. A partial class allows flexibility in designing how the class is put together, the manner in which developers interact with it, and methods available for adding features later. The following sections describe partial classes in more detail.

Defining the purpose of partial classes

Normally you want to place all the code for a class within a single file so that you can see all of it at one time. In general, if a class is so large that you need to spread it out, perhaps a better class design will allow a smaller implementation. However, some classes are just large, and there isn't a lot you can do to make them smaller. With this idea in mind, you can create partial classes in the following circumstances and use them to good effect:

- The class is large enough to require the skills of multiple programmers, so you place the code in multiple files to allow each programmer access to part of the class.
- When working with automatically generated source (such as that from a designer), the code generator can create part of the class automatically, and a developer can provide handwritten code for the rest of the class. This is the approach used by Visual Studio to create Windows Forms, web service wrapper code, and a great many other application elements.
- A source generator can add functionality to an existing class (as described at `https://docs.microsoft.com/en-us/dotnet/csharp/roslyn-sdk/source-generators-overview`) using this technique.

Working with multiple files for a single class

Using partial classes is much like using a regular class except that you include the keyword `partial`. The `PartialParts` example shows how to create such classes. The `PartOne.cs` file of the example contains the first part of the `DoStuff` class:

```
namespace Parts
{
    public partial class DoStuff
    {
        internal int TheValue
            { get; private set; }

        public DoStuff()
        {
            TheValue = 0;
        }
```

```
        public override string ToString()
        {
            return $"The value is: {TheValue}.";
        }
    }
}
```

This part of the class contains an `internal` property, `TheValue`, a constructor, and an `override` for `ToString()`. The constructor simply sets `TheValue` to `0`. You use `ToString()` to obtain formatted output for `TheValue`.

The pieces of a partial class must be part of the same assembly and namespace. To make it easier to work with the `Parts` namespace and the `DoStuff` class, you need to add another file to the same project. Right-click the PartialParts project entry and choose Add⇨New Item from the context menu. When you see the Add New Item dialog box, highlight the Code File entry, type **PartTwo.cs** in the Name field, and click Add. When you see the new code file, you can add the following code:

```
using System;

namespace Parts
{
    public partial class DoStuff
    {
        public void DoAdd(int value)
        {
            if (value > 0)
                TheValue += value;
            else
                throw new ArgumentOutOfRangeException("value",
                    "Input must be greater than 0!");
        }

        public void DoSubtract(int value)
        {
            if (value > 0)
                if (value <= TheValue)
                    TheValue -= value;
                else
                    TheValue = 0;
            else
                throw new ArgumentOutOfRangeException("value",
                    "Input must be greater than 0!");
        }
    }
}
```

This part of the code adds two methods: DoAdd(), for adding values greater than 0 to TheValue; and DoSubtract(), for subtracting values greater than 0 from TheValue. The DoSubtract() method has the further restriction of not allowing TheValue to get below 0. In both cases, the methods throw an ArgumentOutOfRangeException when the user passes a value 0 or below. Now it's time to test this partial class using the following code:

```
static void Main(string[] args)
{
    DoStuff thisStuff = new DoStuff();

    try
    {
        thisStuff.DoAdd(-1);
    }
    catch (ArgumentOutOfRangeException e)
    {
        Console.WriteLine(e.Message);
    }

    try
    {
        thisStuff.DoAdd(5);
    }
    catch (ArgumentOutOfRangeException e)
    {
        Console.WriteLine(e.Message);
    }

    try
    {
        thisStuff.DoSubtract(1);
    }
    catch (ArgumentOutOfRangeException e)
    {
        Console.WriteLine(e.Message);
    }

    Console.WriteLine($"{thisStuff.ToString()}");
    Console.ReadLine();
}
```

`Main()` simply exercises class features, including the generation of the `ArgumentOutOfRangeException`. When you run this code, you see the following output:

```
Input must be greater than 0!
Parameter name: value
The value is: 4.
```

TIP

This technique also works fine with structures and interfaces. All the same rules apply as when you work with classes.

Working with Partial Methods

Starting with C# 9.0, you can create partial methods within your partial classes. A partial method is somewhat different from a partial class in that the implementation appears in just one place. There are other differences as well, which are discussed in the first section that follows. The second section shows a quick implementation of working with a partial method.

Defining what partial methods do

A partial method allows you to split a method into a signature part and potentially an implementation part. When a signature lacks an implementation, the compiler removes the signature during compile time, which means that the method doesn't even exist. However, you must provide an implementation for a partial method unless it meets these criteria:

- Lacks accessibility modifiers (including the default `private`)
- Returns `void`
- Doesn't contain any `out` parameters
- Avoids all the following modifiers:
  - `virtual`
  - `override`
  - `sealed`
  - `new`
  - `extern`
- A partial method must appear within a partial type, such as a partial class.

You can use partial methods in a number of circumstances to enhance the coding environment or to perform some tasks automatically. A partial method is useful in these circumstances:

- **Templates:** A development team is implementing a template. The template defines a full list of potential methods. However, the development team may not need all the methods and may therefore implement only some of them. The unimplemented methods simply don't appear in the output.
- **Source generators:** A source generator automatically creates an implementation during compilation based on declarations that the developer provides. The developer provides only a signature, which the source generator then fills out. Because there will be an implementation in the future, the developer can write code against the declared method. Working with source generators is well outside the scope of this book, but you can find a tutorial for creating one at `https://devblogs.microsoft.com/dotnet/introducing-c-source-generators/`.
- **Team development:** A single file might contain a full listing of all the methods for a class, which individual developers then implement in other files. Having a complete list of all possible methods in one place reduces confusion and helps coordinate team efforts. The single file is read-only except during design updates so that any number of developers can refer to it.

Creating a partial method

This section looks at the simplest implementation of a partial method. The signature part simply shows what the partial method will contain, such as this entry in the `PartOne.cs` file for the `DoStuff` class of the `PartialParts` example:

```
public partial void DoDivide(int value);
```

The implementation for this method appears in `PartTwo.cs` as:

```
public partial void DoDivide(int value)
{
    if (value > 0)
        TheValue = TheValue / value;
    else
        throw new ArgumentOutOfRangeException("value",
            "Input must be greater than 0!");
}
```

As with `DoAdd()` and `DoSubtract()`, the input value must be greater than `0`. Otherwise, `DoDivide()` will throw an `ArgumentOutOfRangeException`.

IN THIS CHAPTER

» Distinguishing between named and optional parameters

» Using optional parameters

» Declaring and using output parameters

» Implementing reference return types

Chapter 10

Improving Productivity with Named and Optional Parameters

Parameters, as you probably remember, are the inputs to methods. They're the values that appear as part of the method's signature. When the method returns a value (it doesn't always do so), the parameters provide the data required to generate the output value. Sometimes, the return values are parameters (`out` parameters), which confuses things.

In ancient versions of C# and most C-derived languages, parameters can't be optional (oddly enough, you find some examples of this ancient code lurking about online just waiting to make you feel hindered). Instead of making parameters optional, you are required to make a separate overload for every version of the method you expect your users to need. This pattern works well, but there are some problems that are explored in this chapter.

C# 4.0 and above have optional parameters. *Optional parameters* are parameters that have a default value right in the method signature. It's the same control-versus-productivity issue that Book 3, Chapter 6 shows you about the dynamic type. Optional parameters give you just enough rope to hang yourself. A programmer can easily make mistakes.

Exploring Optional Parameters

Optional parameters depend on having a default value set in order to be optional. For instance, if you're searching for a phone number by name and city, you can default the city name to your city, making the parameter optional.

```
public static string searchForPhoneNumber(string name, string city =
    "Columbus") {...}
```

The following sections discuss how to work with optional parameters in C#.

Working with optional value parameters

Here is the reason that optional parameters are so amazing. Consider the following code for the `addit()` method. It's silly, but it illustrates the realities of multiple overloads. So, previously you had this:

```
public static int addit(int z, int y)
{
    return z + y;
}

public static int addit(int z, int y, int x)
{
    return z + y + x;
}

public static int addit(int z, int y, int x, int w)
{
    return z + y + x + w;
}

public static int addit(int z, int y, int x, int w, int v)
{
    return z + y + x + w + v;
}
```

With optional parameters, you now have this:

```
public static int addit(int z, int y, int x = 0, int w = 0, int v = 0)
{
    return z + y + x + w + v;
}
```

If you need to add two numbers, you can do it easily.

```
int answer = addit(10, 4),
```

If you need to add four numbers, you have no problems, either.

```
int answer = addit(10, 4, 5, 12);
```

So why are optional parameters dangerous? Because sometimes default values can have unintended consequences. For instance, you don't want to make a `divideit()` method and set the default parameters to `0`. Someone could call it and get a hard to debug division by zero error. Just as you wouldn't set the `divideit()` method parameters to `0`, setting the optional values in `addit()` to `1` would be bad. This would mean that the each optional value would automatically add 1 to the sum as shown below.

```
public static int addit(int z, int y, int x = 1, int w = 1, int v = 1)
{
    // You CLEARLY don't want this
    return z + y + x + w + v;
}
```

And sometimes problems can be subtle, so use optional parameters carefully. For instance, say you have a base class and then derive a class that implements the base, like this:

```
public abstract class Base
{
    public virtual void SomeFunction(int x = 0)
    {...}
}

public sealed class Derived : Base
{
    public override void SomeFunction(int x = 1)
    {...}
}
```

What happens if you declare a new instance?

```
Base ex1 = new Base();
ex1.SomeFunction();                 // SomeFunction (0)

Base ex2 = new Derived();
ex2.SomeFunction();                 // SomeFunction (0)
Derived ex3 = new Derived();
ex3.SomeFunction();                 // SomeFunction (1)
```

What happened here? Depending on how you implement the classes, the default value for the optional parameter is set differently. The first example, `ex1`, is an instantiation of `Base`, and the default optional parameter is `0`. In the second example, `ex2` is cast to a type of `Derived` (which is legal because `Derived` is a subclass of `Base`), and the default value is also `0`. However, in the third example, `Derived` is instantiated directly, and the default value is `1`. This isn't expected behavior. No matter how you slice it, it's a gotcha and something to watch out for.

Avoiding optional reference types

A reference type, as Book 1 discusses, types a variable that stores a reference to actual data, instead of the data itself. Reference types are usually referred to as objects. New reference types are implemented with

- `class`
- `interface`
- `delegate`

These need to be built before you use them; class itself isn't a reference type, but the `Calendar` class is. There are three built-in reference types in the .NET Framework:

- String
- Object
- Dynamic

You can pass a reference type into a method just as you can pass a static type. It is still considered a parameter. You still use it inside the method as you do with any other variable.

But can reference types be passed, as value types can? Give it a try. For instance, if you had a `Schedule` method for your `Calendar` class, you could pass in the `CourseId`, or you could pass in the whole `Course`. It all depends on how you structure the application.

```
public class Course
{
    public int CourseId;
```

```
        public string Name;
        public void Course(int id, string name)
        {
            CourseId = id;
            Name = name;
        }
    }

    public class Calendar
    {
        public static void Schedule(int courseId)
        {
        }
        public static void Schedule(Course course)
        {
            // Something interesting happens here
        }
    }
```

In this example, you have an overloaded method for `Schedule` — one that accepts a `CourseId` and one that accepts a `Course` reference type. The second is a reference type, because `Course` is a class, rather than a static type, like the `int` of the `CourseId`.

What if you want the second `Schedule` method to support an optional `Course` parameter? Say, if you want it to create a `new Course()` by default, you omit the parameter. This would be similar to setting a static integer to `0` or whatever, wouldn't it?

```
        public static void Schedule(Course course = New Course())
        {
            // Implementation here
        }
```

This isn't allowed, however. Visual Studio allows optional parameters only on static types, and the compiler tells you so. (There are exceptions to this rule that aren't covered in the book, such as using nullable reference types in C# 8.0 or above as described at `https://docs.microsoft.com/dotnet/csharp/language-reference/builtin-types/nullable-reference-types`.) If you want to do this, you have to accept the `CourseId` in the `Schedule` method and construct a new `Course` in the body of the event.

Looking at Named Parameters

Hand in hand with the concept of optional parameters are named parameters. If you have more than one default parameter, you need a way to tell the compiler which parameter you're supplying! For example, look at the `addit()` method earlier in this chapter, after optional parameters are implemented:

```
public static int addit(int z, int y, int x = 0, int w = 0, int v = 0)
{
    return z + y + x + w + v;
}
```

Clearly, the order of the parameters doesn't matter in this implementation, but if this were in a class library, you might not know that the order of the parameters is a non-issue! How would you tell the compiler to skip `x` and `w` if you want to supply `v`? With named parameters, you can say

```
int answer = addit(z:3, y:7, v:4);
```

The non-optional parameters don't have to be named; the position is assumed because they're required anyway. Nonetheless, naming them is good practice. If you skip naming them, you have this instead:

```
int answer = addit(3, 7, v:4);
```

You have to admit that this is a little harder to read. One would have to go back to the method signature to figure out what is happening. C# 7.2 does provide an additional wrinkle. Normally, you can't have any positional arguments after using named arguments. However, starting with C# 7.2, you can do this:

```
int answer = addit(z:3, 7, v:4);
```

The `7` still relates to `y` because it appears in the correct position. However, now your code is exceptionally hard to read.

Using Alternative Methods to Return Values

Normally, you return values to the user by using the `return` keyword followed by the value. Some situations require an alternative method of returning the value. For example, if you're working with the Win32 API, you often need to use a parameter, rather than an actual return value, because of the way that Microsoft wrote the original C/C++ code. You may find other situations where you need to return multiple values and don't want to create a `struct`, `list`, or other object to return them. The following sections talk about these alternative methods to return values.

Output (out) parameters

Output parameters are parameters in the method signature that actually change the value of the variable that is passed into them by the user. The parameter references the location of the original variable, rather than create a working copy. Output parameters are declared in a method signature with the `out` keyword. You can have as many as you like (well, within reason), although if you use more than a few, you probably should use something else (a generic list, maybe?). An output parameter might look like this in a method declaration:

```
public static void Schedule(int courseId, out string name,
                            out DateTime scheduledTime)
{
    name = "something";
    scheduledTime = DateTime.Now;
}
```

Following the rules, you should be able to make one of these parameters optional by presetting a value. Unlike reference parameters (described in the "Returning values by reference" section of this chapter), it makes sense that output parameters don't support default values. The output parameter is exactly that — output, and setting the value should happen inside the method body. Because output parameters aren't expecting a value coming in anyway, it doesn't benefit the programmer to have default values.

Working with out variables

C# 7.0 changes the way return values work. You can now work with `out` variables in new ways. The "Output (out) parameters" section of the chapter discusses the common methods of working with the `out` variable using a traditional approach. However, consider the following example, which has just one `out` variable.

```
static void MyCalc(out int x)
{
    x = 2 + 2;
}
```

In this case, you can use a shorter way than shown in the previous section to obtain a result from MyCalc():

```
static void DisplayMyCalc()
{
    MyCalc(out int p);
    Console.WriteLine($"{nameof(p)} = {p}");
}
```

The output is a value of 4 because you set x to 4 within MyCalc() and x is returned as a changed value to the caller. However, you don't need to declare p before using it. The declaration occurs as part of the call to MyCalc().

TIP

Of course, if your method returns just one output parameter, it's normally best to use a return value instead. This example uses just one so that you get a better idea of how the new technique works.

REMEMBER

A more interesting addition to C# 7.0 is that you can now use the var keyword (where the compiler infers the variable's data type) with out parameters. For example, this call is perfectly acceptable in C# 7.0.

```
static void DisplayMyCalc()
{
    MyCalc(out var p);
    Console.WriteLine($"{nameof(p)} = {p}");
}
```

Returning values by reference

There may be a situation where you want to return a variable, rather than a value, to the caller. For example, returning a variable allows the caller to treat the value it contains as either a reference or a value. Using return by reference can become a little complicated though, so you need to understand all of the rules found at https://docs.microsoft.com/dotnet/csharp/programming-guide/classes-and-structs/ref-returns. You can return values by reference in older versions of C#. However, you have to create your code carefully to do it, as shown here:

```
int[] arrayData = { 1, 2 };
static ref int ReturnByReference()
{
    ref int x = ref arrayData[0];
    return ref x;
}
```

In C# 7.0 and above, you can reduce the code used to perform this task to this:

```
int[] arrayData = { 1, 2 };
static ref int ReturnByReference()
{
    return ref arrayData;
}
```

REMEMBER

However, notice that you're returning an entire array now, instead of a single `int` value. The array is a reference type; the `int` is a value type. You can't return value types by using this technique. To make returning a value type possible, you must pass it in as a parameter, like this:

```
myInt = 1;
static ref int ReturnByReference(ref int myInt)
{
    return ref myInt;
}
```

Dealing with null Parameters

Receiving a `null` value for a method parameter is problematic unless you provide some means of dealing with it. In the past, you needed to provide your own null argument checking for a method call, such as:

```
static void SayHello(String Name)
{
    if (null == Name)
        throw new ArgumentNullException("name");
    else
        Console.WriteLine($"Hello {Name}!");
}
```

There are two problems here. First, you might forget to add the required `null` checking code. Second, you're essentially writing the same code over and over again, which is quite annoying, and no one wants to be annoyed. C# 10.0 has an answer to the problem in the form of `null` parameter checking using the `!!` operator. So, this example code looks like this now:

```
static void SayHello(String Name!!)
{
    Console.WriteLine($"Hello {Name}!");
}
```

The result is that you get the same amount of work done, with half as much labor. When `SayHello()` receives a `null` input, it automatically throws an `ArgumentNullException`.

IN THIS CHAPTER

» Determining when to use structures

» Defining structures

» Working with structures

» Working with records

Chapter 11 Interacting with Structures

Structures are an important addition to C# because they provide a means for defining complex data entities, akin to records from a database. Because of the way you use structures to develop applications, a distinct overlap exists between structures and classes. This overlap causes problems for many developers because determining when to use a structure versus a class can be difficult. Consequently, the first order of business in this chapter is to discuss the differences between the two and offer some best practices.

Creating structures requires you to use the `struct` keyword. A structure can contain many of the same elements found in classes: constructors, constants, fields, methods, properties, indexers, operators, events, and even nested types. This chapter helps you understand the nuances of creating structures with these elements so that you can fully access all the flexibility that structures have to offer.

Even though structures do have a great deal to offer, the most common way to use them is to represent a kind of data record. The next section of this chapter discusses the structure as a record-holding object. You discover how to use structures in this manner for single records and for multiple records as part of a collection.

C# 9.0 introduced the new `record` type (with the `field` addition in C# 10.0), which is a kind of class with immutable features. Like classes, `records` are a reference type, rather than a value type like structures are. The final section of this chapter discusses the new `record` type and helps you understand how it differs from the structure and class.

REMEMBER

You don't have to type the source code for this chapter manually. In fact, using the downloadable source is a lot easier. You can find the source for this chapter in the `\CSAIO4D2E\BK02\CH11` folder of the downloadable source. See the Introduction for details on how to find these source files.

Comparing Structures to Classes

For many developers, the differences between structures and classes are confusing, to say the least. In fact, many developers use classes alone and forget about structures. However, not using structures is a mistake because they fulfill a definite purpose in your programming strategy. Using structures can make the difference between an application that performs well and one that does the job, but does so more slowly than it could.

REMEMBER

You find many schools of thought on the use of structures. This book doesn't even attempt to cover them all. It does give you a good overview of how structures can help you create better applications. After you have this information, you can begin using structures and discover for yourself precisely how you want to interact with them.

Considering struct limits

Structures are a value type, which means that C# allocates memory for them differently than classes. Most of the `struct` limits come from this difference. Here are some things to consider when you think about using a `struct` in place of a class. A structure

- Can have constructors, but not destructors. This means that you can perform all the usual tasks required to create a specific data type, but you don't have control over cleaning up through a destructor.
- Cannot inherit from other structures or classes (meaning they're stand-alone).
- Can implement one or more interfaces, but with the limits imposed by the elements they support (see "Including common struct elements," later in this chapter, for details).
- Cannot be defined as `abstract`, `virtual`, or `protected`.

Understanding the value type difference

When working with structures, you must remember that they're a value type, not a reference type like classes. This means that structures have certain inherent advantages over classes. For example, they're much less resource intensive. In addition, because structures aren't garbage-collected, they tend to require less time to allocate and deallocate.

TIP

The differences in resource use and in both allocation and deallocation time is compounded when working with arrays. An array of reference types incurs a huge penalty because the array contains just pointers to the individual objects. To access the object, the application must then look for it on the heap.

Value types are also deterministic. You know that C# deallocates them the moment they go out of scope. Waiting for C# to garbage-collect reference types means that you can't quite be sure how memory is used in your application.

Determining when to use struct versus class

Opinions abound as to when to use a `struct` versus a `class`. For the most part, it all ends up being a matter of what you're trying to achieve and what you're willing to pay in terms of both resource usage and application speed to achieve it. In most cases, you use `class` far more often than you use `struct` simply because `class` is more flexible and tends to incur fewer penalties in some situations.

As with all value types, structures must be boxed and unboxed when cast to a reference type or when required by an interface they implement. Too much boxing and unboxing will actually make your application run slower. This means that you should avoid using structures when you need to perform tasks with reference types. In this case, using a class is the best idea.

REMEMBER

Using a value type also changes the way in which C# interacts with the variable. A reference type is passed by reference during a call so that any changes made to the reference type appear in all instances that point to that reference. A value type is copied when you pass it because it's passed by value. This means that changes you make to the value type in another method don't appear in the original variable. This is possibly the most confusing aspect of using structures for developers because passing an object created by a class is inherently different from passing a variable created by a structure. This difference makes classes generally more efficient to pass than structures.

It's true that structures do have a definite advantage when working with arrays. However, you must exercise care when working with structures in collection types because the structure may require boxing and unboxing. If a collection works with objects, you need to consider using a class instead.

Avoid using structures when working with objects. Yes, you can place object types within a structure, but then the structure will contain a reference to the object, rather than the object itself. References reduce the impact of any resource and time savings that a structure can provide. Keep structures limited to other value types such as `int` and `double` when possible. Of course, many structures still use reference types such as `String`.

Creating Structures

Creating a structure is similar to creating a class in many respects. Of course, you use the `struct` keyword instead of the `class` keyword, and a structure has the limitations described in the "Considering struct limits" section, earlier in this chapter. However, even with these differences, if you know how to create a class, you can also create a structure. The following sections describe how to work with structures in greater detail.

Defining a basic struct

A basic `struct` doesn't contain much more than the fields you want to use to store data. For example, consider a `struct` used to store messages from people requesting the price of certain products given a particular quantity. It might look like this (also found in the `BasicStruct` example in the downloadable source):

```
public struct Message
{
    public int MsgID;
    public int ProductID;
    public int Qty;
    public double Price;
}
```

To use this basic structure, you might follow a process like this:

```
static void Main(string[] args)
{
    // Create the struct without new.
    Message myMsg;
```

```
    // Or, create it with new.
    //Message myMsg = new Message();

    // Create a message.
    myMsg.MsgID = 1;
    myMsg.ProductID = 22;
    myMsg.Qty = 5;

    // Compute the price.
    myMsg.Price = 5.99 * myMsg.Qty;

    // Display the struct on screen.
    Console.WriteLine(
        $"In response to Msg {myMsg.MsgID}, you can get {myMsg.Qty} " +
        $"of {myMsg.ProductID} for ${myMsg.Price}.");
    Console.ReadLine();
}
```

Note that the process used to create and use a structure is much the same as creating and using a class. In fact, you could possibly look at the two processes as being the same for the most part (keeping in mind that structures do have differences). For example, you can create a `struct` without using `new` as shown in the code, which is a benefit when `structs` are used in an array from a performance perspective. If you create a `struct` without using `new`, then you must initialize the fields before you use them. The output from this example looks like this:

```
In response to Msg 1, you can get 5 of 22 for $29.95.
```

REMEMBER

Obviously, this is a simplified example, and you'd never create code like this for a real application, but it does get the process you use across. When working with structures, think about the processes you use with classes, but with a few differences that can make structures far more efficient to use.

Including common struct elements

Structures can include many of the same elements as classes do. The "Defining a basic struct" section of the chapter introduces you to the use of fields. As previously noted, fields cannot be `abstract`, `virtual`, or `protected`. However, their default scope is `private`, and you can set them to `public`, as shown in the code. Obviously, classes contain far more than fields and so do structures. The following sections use the `StructWithElements` example to take you through the common `struct` elements so that you can use structures efficiently in your code.

Constructors

As with a `class`, you can create a `struct` with a constructor. Here's an example of the `Message struct` with a constructor included:

```
public struct Message
{
    public int MsgID;
    public int ProductID;
    public int Qty;
    public double Price;

    public Message(int msgId, int productId = 22, int qty = 5)
    {
        // Provided by the user.
        MsgID = msgId;
        ProductID = productId;
        Qty = qty;

        // Defined by the application.
        if (ProductID == 22)
            Price = 5.99 * qty;
        else
            Price = 6.99 * qty;
    }
}
```

Note that the constructor accepts default values, so you can use a single constructor in more than one way. When you use the new version of `Message`, IntelliSense shows both the default constructor (which, in contrast to a class, doesn't go away) and the new constructor that you created, as shown here:

```
Message myMsg2 = new Message(2);
Console.WriteLine(
    $"In response to Msg {myMsg2.MsgID}, you can get {myMsg2.Qty} " +
    $"of {myMsg2.ProductID} for ${myMsg2.Price}.");
```

The output from this part of the example is the same as for the `BasicStruct` example. Thanks to the use of default parameters, you can create a new message by simply providing the message number. The default parameters assign the other values. Of course, you can choose to override any of the values to create a unique object.

Constants

As with all other areas of C#, you can define constants in structures to serve as human readable forms of values that don't change. For example, you might choose to create a generic product constant like this:

```
public const int genericProduct = 22;
```

Creating a new message now might look like this:

```
Message myMsg3 = new Message(3, Message.genericProduct);
Console.WriteLine(
    $"In response to Msg {myMsg3.MsgID}, you can get {myMsg3.Qty} " +
    $"of {myMsg3.ProductID} for ${myMsg3.Price}.");
```

The new form is easier to read. However, it doesn't produce different results.

Methods

Structures can often benefit from the addition of methods that help you perform specific tasks with them. For example, you might want to provide a method for calculating the `Message Price` field, rather than perform the task manually every time. Using a method would ensure that a change in calculation method appears only once in your code, rather than each time the application requires the calculation. The `CalculatePrice()` method looks like this:

```
public static double CalculatePrice(double SinglePrice, int Qty)
{
    return SinglePrice * Qty;
}
```

Obviously, most calculations aren't this simple, but you get the idea. Moving the code to a method means that you can change the other parts of the code to make its meaning clearer. For example, the `Message()` constructor `if` statement now looks like this:

```
// Defined by the application.
if (ProductID == 22)
    Price = CalculatePrice(5.99, qty);
else
    Price = CalculatePrice(6.99, qty);
```

REMEMBER

Note that you must declare the `CalculatePrice()` method `static` or you receive an error message. A structure, like a class, can have both `static` and instance methods. The instance methods become available only after you create an instance of the structure.

Properties

You can also use properties with structures. In fact, using properties is the recommended approach in many cases because using properties lets you ensure that input values are correct. Fortunately, if you are using C# 7.0 or above and originally created public fields, you can turn them into properties quite easily using these steps:

1. **Place the cursor (insertion point) anywhere on the line of code you want to turn into a property.**

   In this case, place it anywhere on the line of code that reads: `public int MsgID;`. A screwdriver icon appears in the left margin of the editing area.

2. **Hover your mouse cursor over the top of the screwdriver to show the down arrow next to the icon, and click the down arrow.**

   You see options associated with the field. The highlighted option, Encapsulate Field: 'MsgID' (And Use Property), lets you turn MsgID into a property and use it appropriately in your code.

3. **Click the Encapsulate Field: 'MsgID' (And Use Property) option.**

   Visual Studio turns the field into a property by making the changes shown in bold in the following code:

```
private int msgID;
public int ProductID;
public int Qty;
public double Price;
public const int genericProduct = 22;

public int MsgID { get => msgID; set => msgID = value; }
```

TIP

At this point, you can work with the property as needed to safeguard your data. However, one other issue is still there. If you try to compile the code now, you see a CS0188 error code in the constructor telling you that you're trying to use the property before the fields are assigned. To correct this problem, change the assignment `MsgID = msgId;` in the constructor to `msgID = msgId;`. The difference is that you assign a value to the private field now, rather than use the public property.

Using supplemental struct elements

The "Including common struct elements" section, earlier in this chapter, discusses elements that you commonly use with both classes and structures to perform essential tasks. The `ColorList` example found in the following sections describes some supplemental elements that will enhance your use of structures.

Indexers

An indexer allows you to treat a structure like an array. In fact, you must use many of the same techniques with it, but you must also create a lot of the features from scratch because your structure indexer has flexibility that an array doesn't provide. Here's the code for a structure, `ColorList`, that has the basic features required for an indexer (note that you must add the `using System.Linq;` directive to the beginning of your code for this example):

```
public struct ColorList
{
    private string[] names;

    public string this[int i]
        { get => names[i]; set => names[i] = value; }

    public void Add(string ColorName)
    {
        if (names == null)
        {
            names = new string[1];
            names[0] = ColorName;
        }
        else
        {
            names = names.Concat<string>(
                new string[] { ColorName }).ToArray();
        }
    }

    public int Length
        { get => names.Length; }
}
```

REMEMBER

Starting from the top of the listing, an indexer implies that you have an array, list, or some other data structure somewhere in the `struct`, which is `names` in this case. To access names using an indexer, you must also create a `this` property of the type shown in the example. The `this` property enables you to access specific names array elements. Note that this example is using a really simple `this` property; a production version would add all sorts of checks, including verifying that `names` isn't `null` and that the requested value actually exists.

When working with an indexer associated with a class, you assign a starting value to the array. However, you can't do that in this case because this is a structure, so `names` remains uninitialized. However, you can override the default constructor, so you can initialize `names` there. The `Add()` method provides the solution. To add a new member to `names`, a caller must provide a `string` that adds the value to `names` as shown.

Note that when names is null, Add() first initializes the array and then adds the color to the first element (given that there are no other elements). However, when names already has values, the code concatenates a new single element string array to names. You must call ToArray() to convert the enumerable type used with Concat() to an array for storage in names.

To use ColorList in a real application, you must also provide a means of obtaining the array length. The read-only Length property accomplishes this task by exposing the names.Length property value. Here is an example of ColorList in action:

```
static void Main(string[] args)
{
    // Create a color list.
    ColorList myList = new ColorList();

    // Fill it with values.
    myList.Add("Yellow");
    myList.Add("Blue");

    // Display each of the elements in turn.
    for (int i = 0; i < myList.Length; i++)
        Console.WriteLine("Color = " + myList[i]);

    Console.ReadLine();
}
```

The code works much as you might expect for a custom array. You create a new ColorList, rely on Add() to add values to it, and then use Length within a for loop to display the values. Here's the output from this code:

```
Color = Yellow
Color = Blue
```

Operators

Structures can also contain operators. For example, you might choose to create a method for adding two ColorList structures together. You do that by creating a + operator. Note that you're creating, not overriding, the + operator, as shown here:

```
public static ColorList operator + (ColorList First, ColorList Second)
{
    ColorList Output = new ColorList();

    for (int i = 0; i < First.Length; i++)
        Output.Add(First[i]);
```

```
    for (int i = 0; i < Second.Length; i++)
        Output.Add(Second[i]);

    return Output;
}
```

You can't create an instance operator. It must appear as part of the `struct`, as shown. The process follows the same technique you use to create a `ColorList` in the first place. The difference is that you iterate through both `ColorList` variables to perform the task using a `for` loop. Here's some code that uses the + operator to add two `ColorList` variables.

```
// Create and fill a second color list.
ColorList myList2 = new ColorList();
myList2.Add("Red");
myList2.Add("Purple");

// Add the first list to the second.
ColorList myList3 = myList + myList2;

// Display each of the elements in turn.
Console.WriteLine("\r\nCombined Color Lists\r\n");
for (int i = 0; i < myList3.Length; i++)
    Console.WriteLine("myList3 Color = " + myList3[i]);
```

As you can see, `myList3` is the result of adding two other `ColorList` variables, not of creating a new one. The output is as you'd expect:

```
myList3 Color = Yellow
myList3 Color = Blue
myList3 Color = Red
myList3 Color = Purple
```

Working with Read-only Structures

Starting with C# 7.2, you can create read-only structures. The main reason to use a read-only structure is to improve application performance. The article at `https://devblogs.microsoft.com/premier-developer/the-in-modifier-and-the-readonly-structs-in-c/` demonstrates one way in which this performance improvement occurs. The point is that you can use such a structure to model complex data that the application can't change after it creates the structure.

TIP

A second, less obvious reason to use read-only structures is to provide thread safety. When working with huge amounts of data, the ability to move data between processors without concern for state changes is critical. You can also use read-only structures to provide a constant hash value for cryptographic needs. The `ReadOnlyStruct` example shows how to create a read-only structure like the one shown here (note that if you use the standard .NET Framework, you must add the `IsExternalInit` code shown in the "Working with init-only setters" section of Chapter 4 of this minibook, as well as set your language version in the `ReadOnlyStruct.csproj` file to a minimum of 7.2):

```
public readonly struct ReadOnlyData
{
    // Create properties to hold values.
    public readonly int Value { get; }

    // Define a constructor to assign values
    // to the properties.
    public ReadOnlyData(int n)
    {
        Value = n;
    }
}
```

To create a read-only structure, you add the `readonly` keyword before `struct`, as shown. The auto-constructed `Value` property is read-only by default. However, adding `readonly` to it reminds users that it isn't possible to assign a value to `Value` outside of the constructor. The following code shows how you might use a read-only structure:

```
static void Main(string[] args)
{
    // Define some data.
    int[] Data = Enumerable.Range(1, 5).ToArray();

    // Create the read-only structure.
    ReadOnlyData MyReadOnlyData = new ReadOnlyData(10);

    // Perform a task with the structure.
    int Result = 0;
    foreach (int n in Data)
    {
        Result += n + MyReadOnlyData.Value;
        Console.WriteLine(
            $"n = {n}\tValue = {MyReadOnlyData.Value}\t" +
            $"Result = {Result}");
    }
```

```
    Console.ReadLine();
}
```

To compile this code, you need to add `using System.Linq;` to the top of the file to make `Enumerable.Range()` accessible. When you run this code, you see the following output:

```
n = 1   Value = 10      Result = 11
n = 2   Value = 10      Result = 23
n = 3   Value = 10      Result = 36
n = 4   Value = 10      Result = 50
n = 5   Value = 10      Result = 65
```

TIP

As of C# 9.0, you can add an `init` accessor to your read-only structure, `public readonly int Value { get; init; }`, so that it allows an alternative method of assigning values to the properties, like this:

```
// Use a C# 9.0 construction.
ReadOnlyData MyReadOnlyData2 = new ReadOnlyData
{
    Value = 12
};
```

This approach is clearer than using the constructor to assign values to the structure properties. However, the end result is the same — you can't reassign values after the initial construction.

Working with Reference Structures

The previous section talks about a performance enhancement to using structures in the form of reduced access. The reference structure that first appears in C# 7.2 is another way to make structures more efficient and faster. In fact, you can combine this form of structure with a read-only structure to greatly improve structure performance, but at the cost of a huge loss of flexibility. The reference structure always remains on the stack, which means that you can't box it and put it on the heap, even accidentally. Consequently, a reference structure eliminates the potential for performance losses resulting from boxing and unboxing. However, this approach also comes with these limitations:

- No array element support
- Unable to declare it as a type of a field of a class or a non-ref `struct`
- No interface implementation

- No boxing to `System.ValueType` or `System.Object`
- Unable to use it as a type argument
- Ineligible for capture by a lambda expression or a local function
- Inaccessible in an async method
- No iterator support

All these limitations come as a result of not being able to move the structure from the stack to the heap. However, you can use a reference structure variable in a synchronous method such as those that return `Task` or `Task<TResult>`. The following code, found in the `RefStruct` example, shows how to create a reference structure:

```
public ref struct FullName
{
    public string First { get; set; }
    public string Middle { get; set; }
    public string Last { get; set; }

    public override string ToString()
    {
        return $"Name: {First} {Middle} {Last}";
    }
}
```

To use this structure, you work with it in essentially the same way as you do for any other structure, like this:

```
static void Main(string[] args)
{
    FullName ThisName = new FullName
    {
        First = "Sam",
        Middle = "L",
        Last = "Johnson"
    };

    Console.WriteLine(ThisName.ToString());
    Console.ReadLine();
}
```

Using Structures as Records

The main reason to work with structures in most code is to create records that contain custom data. You use these custom data records to hold complex information and pass it around as needed within your application. It's easier and faster to pass a single record than it is to pass a collection of data values, especially when your application performs the task regularly. The following sections show how to use structures as a kind of data record.

Managing a single record

Passing structures to methods is cleaner and easier than passing individual data items. Of course, the values in the structure must be related in order for this strategy to work well. However, consider the following method:

```
static void DisplayMessage(Message msg)
{
    Console.WriteLine(
        $"In response to Msg {myMsg.MsgID}, you can get {myMsg.Qty} " +
        $"of {myMsg.ProductID} for ${myMsg.Price}.");
}
```

TIP

In this case, the `DisplayMessage()` method receives a single input of type `Message` instead of the four variables that the method would normally require. Using the `Message` structure produces these positive results in the code:

- The receiving method can assume that all the required data values are present.
- The receiving method can assume that all the variables are initialized.
- The caller is less likely to create erroneous code.
- Other developers can read the code with greater ease.
- Code changes are easier to make.

Adding structures to arrays

Applications rarely use a single data record for every purpose. In most cases, applications also include database-like collections of records. For example, an application is unlikely to receive just one `Message`. Instead, the application will likely receive a group of `Message` records, each of which it must process.

TECHNICAL STUFF

You can add structures to any collection. However, most collections work with objects, so adding a structure to them would incur a performance penalty because C# must box and unbox each structure individually. As the size of the collection increases, the penalty becomes quite noticeable. Consequently, it's always a better idea to restrict collections of data records that rely on structures to arrays in your application when speed is the most important concern.

Working with an array of structures is much like working with an array of anything else. You could use code like this to create an array of Message structures:

```
// Display all the messages on screen.
Message[] Msgs = { myMsg, myMsg2 };
DisplayMessages(Msgs);
```

In this case, Msgs contains two records, myMsg and myMsg2. The code then processes the messages by passing the array to DisplayMessages(), which is shown here:

```
static void DisplayMessages(Message[] msgs)
{
    foreach (Message item in msgs)
    {
        Console.WriteLine(
            $"In response to Msg {myMsg.MsgID}, you can get {myMsg.Qty} " +
            $"of {myMsg.ProductID} for ${myMsg.Price}.");
    }
}
```

The DisplayMessages() method uses a foreach loop to separate the individual Message records. It then processes them using the same approach as DisplayMessage() in the previous section of the chapter.

Overriding methods

REMEMBER

Structures provide a great deal of flexibility that many developers assign exclusively to classes. For example, you can override methods, often in ways that make the structure output infinitely better. A good example is the ToString() method, which outputs a somewhat unhelpful (or something similar):

```
Structures.Program+Messages
```

The output isn't useful because it doesn't tell you anything. To garner anything useful, you must override the ToString() method by using code like this:

```
public override string ToString()
{
    // Create a useful output string.
    return "Message ID:\t" + MsgID +
        "\r\nProduct ID:\t" + ProductID +
        "\r\nQuantity:\t" + Qty +
        "\r\nTotal Price:\t" + Price;
}
```

Now when you call `ToString()`, you obtain useful information. In this case, you see the following output when calling `myMsg.ToString()`:

```
Message ID:     1
Product ID:     22
Quantity:       5
Total Price:    29.95
```

Using the New Record Type

Using structures as records proved so helpful that in C# 9.0 you find a new `record` type. Rather than force you to write a bunch of code to obtain the same effect, the record type combines the best features of structures and classes to provide you with the means of defining records along the same lines as those described in the "Using Structures as Records" section of the chapter. However, there are some significant differences as described in the sections that follow and shown in the `BasicRecord` example. Note that you must use the .NET Core template with .NET 5.0 for this example to obtain the proper support.

Comparing records to structures and classes

As previously mentioned, a record is a combination of a structure and a class with a little secret sauce added so that you experience the delicious taste of records without the coding. A record has these properties:

- The ability to define immutable properties so that a record is more secure than either a structure or class.
- A record uses value equality so that two records with the same structure and the same properties are the same. This differs from a class, which depends on reference equality (looking for pointers to the same memory location).

- You can use non-destructive mutation to create a new record (with different property values) based on an existing record. To perform this task, you use the `with` expression.
- Unlike many other C# objects, the record provides a `ToString()` method that displays:
  - The record type name
  - The names and values of public properties
- A record is a kind of class under the covers, so, unlike a structure, it supports inheritance hierarchies.

Working with a record

A record can look remarkably similar to a structure, except for the use of the `record` keyword, as shown here:

```
public record Person
{
    public string First { get; set; }
    public string? Middle { get; set; }
    public string Last { get; set; }
    public int? Age { get; set; }
}
```

TIP

The question marks after the type declaration for the `Middle` and `Age` properties means that these properties are nullable. You'll see how this works to your advantage a little later in this section. However, for now, try this code to work with the structure:

```
static void Main(string[] args)
{
    Person ThisPerson = new Person()
    {
        First = "Amanda",
        Middle = null,
        Last = "Langley",
        Age = null
    };

    Console.WriteLine(ThisPerson.ToString());
    Console.ReadLine();
}
```

Unlike classes and structures, a record provides the means to print itself out in a meaningful way through the ToString() method. Here's the default output you see:

```
Person { First = Amanda, Middle = , Last = Langley, Age =  }
```

However, you likely want to add a ToString() method, especially if you have nullable properties. The following ToString() method makes use of the nullable Age value to determine what to print:

```
public override string ToString()
{
    if (Age.HasValue)
        return $"{Last}, {First} {Middle}\r\nAge: {Age}";
    else
        return $"{Last}, {First} {Middle}\r\nAge Withheld";
}
```

Notice the use of the HasValue property to determine whether Age is null. The output now looks like this:

```
Langley, Amanda
Age Withheld
```

Using the positional syntax for property definition

Records provide a level of flexibility in declaration that you don't find with classes or structures. For example, you can create a positional declaration with relative ease, as shown here:

```
public record Person2(string First, string Middle, string Last, int? Age)
{
    public override string ToString()
    {
        if (Age.HasValue)
            return $"{Last}, {First} {Middle}\r\nAge: {Age}";
        else
            return $"{Last}, {First} {Middle}\r\nAge Withheld";
    }
}
```

This code is significantly shorter than the declaration in the previous section, yet it does the same thing with a little twist. You can now create the record using a shorter syntax as well:

```
Person2 NextPerson = new("Andy", "X", "Rustic", 42);
```

The record is instantiated on a single line without writing any code for a special constructor. The point is that you waste a lot less time writing code, yet get flexible records for data processing.

Understanding value equality

Like a structure, a record compares the kind of record and the values it contains when making an equality decision. This means that you can compare two different records quickly and easily. Here is an example of how this comparison works:

```
Person2 ThirdPerson = new("Andy", "X", "Rustic", 42);
Console.WriteLine($"NextPerson == ThirdPerson: " +
    $"{NextPerson == ThirdPerson}");
Console.WriteLine($"ReferenceEquals(NextPerson, ThirdPerson): " +
    $"{ReferenceEquals(NextPerson, ThirdPerson)}");
```

When you run this code, you see the following output:

```
NextPerson == ThirdPerson: True
ReferenceEquals(NextPerson, ThirdPerson): False
```

`NextPerson` and `ThirdPerson` are two completely different objects. However, you can compare them to verify that they contain the same record using the == operator. If this were a class, you'd need to compare the value of each property individually, which is time consuming and error prone.

Creating safe changes: Nondestructive mutation

There are times when two records might be almost the same, but just a little different. In such a case, you can mutate a current record into a new record using this technique:

```
Person2 FourthPerson = ThirdPerson with { Age = null };
Console.WriteLine(FourthPerson);
```

In this case, FourthPerson would be just like ThirdPerson, but with a different Age property value. When you run this code, you see the following output:

```
Rustic, Andy X
Age Withheld
```


Using the field keyword

The `get; set;` syntax used by auto-implemented properties is fine as long as you don't need to do anything other than get or set a value. Otherwise, you need to create a backing field and add a lot more code to your properties. C# 10.0 introduces the `field` keyword to reduce or eliminate the use of backing fields. For example, in the following record, it's possible to ensure that `Department` is stored in uppercase without resorting to the use of a backing field:

```
public record Person
{
    public string First { get; set; }
    public string? Middle { get; set; }
    public string Last { get; set; }
    public int? Age { get; set; }
    public string Department { get; set => field = value.ToUpper(); }
}
```

This feature only works if you configure your project to use C# 10.0 in the `.csproj` file like this:

```
<PropertyGroup>
  <LangVersion>10.0</LangVersion>
</PropertyGroup>
```

The field keyword makes it easy to keep things short and simple. You can use it with `get;`, `set;`, and `init;` as needed. Don't worry if you can't fit what you need on a single line. You can use an extended version like this as well:

```
public record Person
{
    public string First { get; set; }
    public string? Middle { get; set; }
    public string Last { get; set; }
    public int? Age { get; set; }
    public string Department { get;
        set
```

```
        {
            if (value.Trim() == "")
                throw new ArgumentException("No blank strings");
            field = value.ToUpper();
        }
    }
}
```

This second form still doesn't require the use of a backing field, and it tends to be shorter than the older version of the code. The point is that you shouldn't have to use backing fields very often anymore with C# 10.0 and the .NET 6.0 framework (it doesn't work with .NET 5.0).

3

Designing for C#

Contents at a Glance

IN THIS CHAPTER

» Designing for security

» Building secure Windows applications

» Digging into `System.Security`

Chapter 1
Writing Secure Code

Security is a big topic. Ignoring for a moment all the buzzwords surrounding security, you likely realize that you need to protect your application from being used by people who shouldn't use it. You also need to prevent your application from being used for things it shouldn't be used for.

At the beginning of the electronic age, security was usually performed by *obfuscation* (also called *security through obscurity*). If you had an application that you didn't want people peeking at, you just hid it, and no one would know where to find it. Thus, it would be secure. (Remember *War Games*, the movie in which the military assumed that no one would find the phone number needed to connect to its mainframes — but Matthew Broderick's character did?)

Using obfuscation obviously doesn't cut it anymore; now you need to consider security as an integral requirement of every system that you write. Your application might not contain sensitive data, but can it be used to get to other information on the machine? Can it be used to gain access to a network that it shouldn't? The answers to these questions matter.

The two main parts to security are authentication and authorization. *Authentication* is the process of making sure a user is authentic — that the user identity is genuine. The most common method of authentication is to require the use of a username and password, though other ways exist, such as thumbprint scans and *Multi-Factor Authentication*, or *MFA* (such as verifying an identity using a second device). (This book doesn't cover MFA, but you can read about it at `https://docs.microsoft.com/en-us/azure/active-directory/authentication/concept-mfa-howitworks`.) *Authorization* is the act of ensuring that a user has the authority to perform specific tasks. File permissions are a good example of this — users can't delete system-only files, for instance.

It's never possible to identify a specific user with complete assurance. Hackers steal usernames and passwords with ease. Biometric devices, such as thumbprint scanners, are also easy to beat. The article at `https://www.instructables.com/How-To-Fool-a-Fingerprint-Security-System-As-Easy-/` details just how easy it is to overcome thumbprint security. You can also find articles on how to circumvent technologies like facial recognition (`https://iopscience.iop.org/article/10.1088/1757-899X/1069/1/012047/meta`). In fact, no biometric authentication technique is foolproof today even though biometric authentication was once viewed as a panacea. The best you can ever hope to achieve is to authenticate a user identity, never the user. You don't actually ever know that you're dealing with a particular person; it could be a hacker in disguise. In this chapter, you discover the tools that are available in the .NET Framework to help you make sure that your applications are secure.

You don't have to type the source code for this chapter manually. In fact, using the downloadable source is a lot easier. You can find the source for this chapter in the `\CSAIO4D2E\BK03\CH01` folder of the downloadable source. See the Introduction for details on how to find these source files.

Designing Secure Software

Security takes a fair amount of work to correctly design. If you break the process into pieces, you find that it's a lot easier to accomplish. The Patterns and Practices team (a group of software architects at Microsoft who devise programming best practices) have created a systematic approach to designing secure programs, described in the following sections, that you should find straightforward.

Determining what to protect

Different applications have different *artifacts* (resources, data, identities, and so on) that need protection, but all applications have a common need to protect something. If you have a database in your application, that is the most important item to protect. If your application is a server-based application, the server should rate fairly high when you're determining what to protect.

SECURITY CHANGES FOR C# 9.0 AND ABOVE

Code Access Security (CAS) (`https://www.c-sharpcorner.com/UploadFile/84c85b/net-code-access-security-cas/`) is a method of securing an application by defining what the code can and cannot do. It's an older form of security that provides granular control over specific kinds of application access to resources. The idea is that a user can't circumvent security if the application itself lacks the required rights. CAS proved unpopular for a lot of reasons, but the main one is that it treats every user the same so that owners, managers, security professionals, and users all look the same.

Role-Based Security (`https://docs.microsoft.com/en-us/dotnet/standard/security/role-based-security`) focuses on individual users and the role being played by that user at any given time. It provides a level of flexibility that CAS can't provide. Because CAS is so unpopular, Microsoft has removed it starting with .NET 5.0 and above. This means that if you create a .NET Core application using C# 9.0 or above, CAS security isn't allowed any longer. The examples in this chapter use Role-Based Security techniques, but you can read about what to do with your older CAS applications at `https://docs.microsoft.com/en-us/dotnet/core/compatibility/core-libraries/5.0/code-access-security-apis-obsolete`. The point is that if you see a `SYSLIB0003` compile error, your application contains CAS and you need to do something about it.

REMEMBER

Even if your program is just a little single-user application, the software should do no wrong. An outsider shouldn't be able to use the application to break into the user's computer.

Documenting the components of the program

If you think this section's title sounds similar to part of the design process, you're right. A lot of threat modeling is just understanding how the application works and describing it well.

First, describe what the application does. This description becomes a functional overview. If you follow the commonly accepted Software Development Life Cycle (SDLC), the use cases, requirements, or user stories documents (depending on your personal methodology) should give you a good starting point.

Next, describe how the application accomplishes all those tasks at the highest level. A Software Architecture Overview (SAO) diagram is a useful way to do it. This diagram shows which machines and services do what in your software. Sometimes the SAO is a simple diagram. If you have a stand-alone Windows Forms (also known as WinForms) program, such as a game, that's all there is! A stand-alone program has no network connection and no communication between software parts. Therefore, the software architecture diagram contains only one instance.

Decomposing components into functions

After you create a document that describes what the software is doing and how, you need to break out the individual functional pieces of the software. If you've set up your software in a component fashion, the classes and methods show the functional decomposition. It's simpler than it sounds.

The end result of breaking the software into individual pieces is having a decent matrix of which components need to be protected, which parts of the software interact with each component, which parts of the network and hardware system interact with each component, and which functions of the software do what with each component.

Identifying potential threats in functions

After you create the list of components that you need to protect, you tackle the tough part: Put two and two together. Identifying threats is the process that gets the security consultants the big bucks, and it's almost entirely a factor of experience.

For instance, if your application connects to a database, you have to imagine that the connection could be intercepted by a third party. If you use a file to store sensitive information, the file could, theoretically, be compromised.

To create a threat model, you need to categorize the potential threats to your software. An easy way to remember the different categories of threats is as the acronym STRIDE:

- **_S_poofing identity:** Users pretend to be someone they are not.
- **_T_ampering with data or files:** Users edit something that shouldn't be edited.
- **_R_epudiation of action:** Users have the opportunity to say they didn't do something that they actually did do.
- **_I_nformation disclosure:** Users see something that shouldn't be seen.
- **_D_enial of service:** Users prevent legitimate users from accessing the system.
- **_E_levation of privilege:** Users get access to something that they shouldn't have access to.

All these threats must be documented in an outline under the functions that expose the threat. This strategy not only gives you a good, discrete list of threats but also focuses your security hardening on those parts of the application that pose the greatest security risk.

Building Secure Windows Applications

The .NET framework lives in a tightly controlled sandbox when running on a client computer. Because of the realities of this sandbox, the configuration of security policy for your application becomes important.

The first place you need to look for security in writing Windows applications is in the world of authentication and authorization. For example, gaining access to an application feature that the user shouldn't use is a security breach inside the application. Deleting a required file using operating system features is a security breach outside the application. You must also consider the user's role at any given time. In one situation, a user might work as a manager with access to sensitive data, but in another situation a user might perform tasks as a worker with no access to sensitive data.

When you're threat modeling, you can easily consider all the possible authentication and authorization threats using the STRIDE acronym. (See the earlier section "Identifying potential threats in functions" for more about STRIDE.)

Authentication using Windows logon

To be straightforward, the best way for an application to authorize a user is to make use of the Windows logon. Various arguments arise about this strategy and others, but the key is simplicity: Simple things are more secure.

For much of the software developed with Visual Studio, the application will be used in an office by users who have different roles in the company; for example, some users might be in the Sales or Accounting department. In many environments, the most privileged users are managers or administrators — yet another set of roles. In most offices, all employees have their own user accounts, and users are assigned to the Windows groups that are appropriate for the roles they play in the company.

REMEMBER

Using Windows security works only if the Windows environment is set up correctly. You can't effectively build a secure application in a workspace that has a bunch of Windows 10 machines with everyone logging on as the administrator, because you can't tell who is in what role.

Building a Windows application to take advantage of Windows security is straightforward. The goal is to check to see who is logged on (authentication) and then check that user's role (authorization). The following steps show you how to create the `SecureButton` application that protects the menu system for each user by showing and hiding buttons. Even though this sample application relies on the Windows Forms App template, the techniques also work with other application types, such as a Windows Presentation Foundation (WPF) app. To successfully run this code, you must have an environment that has Accounting, Sales, and Management user groups (even if they're fake and temporary).

1. **Choose Create a New Project.**

   You see the Create a New Project dialog box.

2. **Select C#, Windows, and Desktop in the drop-down list boxes that appear near the top of the form.**

   The wizard presents a list of appropriate templates.

3. **Highlight the Windows Forms App (.NET Framework) option and click Next.**

   This template creates the traditional WinForms application that runs on the Windows desktop. You see the Configure Your New Project dialog box.

4. **Type** SecureButton **in the Project Name field,** C:\CSAIO4D2E\BK03\CH01 **(or other appropriate location) in the Location field, and select Place Solution and Project in the Same Directory; then click Create.**

   Visual Studio presents a form you can use to design the WinForms app.

5. **Right-click** `Form1.cs` **in Solution Explorer and choose Rename from the context menu.**

   The name of the form changes into an edit box so that you can rename it.

6. **Type** SecureButtonTest **and press Enter.**

   The name of the form changes into something more descriptive.

7. **Highlight the form's Text property and type** Secure Button Test.

   You see the name at the top of the form change.

8. **Add four buttons to your form from the Toolbox — one for Sales Menu, one for Accounting Menu, one for Manager Menu, and one for Minimal Menu.**

   Figure 1-1 shows one method for configuring the form. You change the button caption using the `Text` property found in the Properties window for each of the buttons.

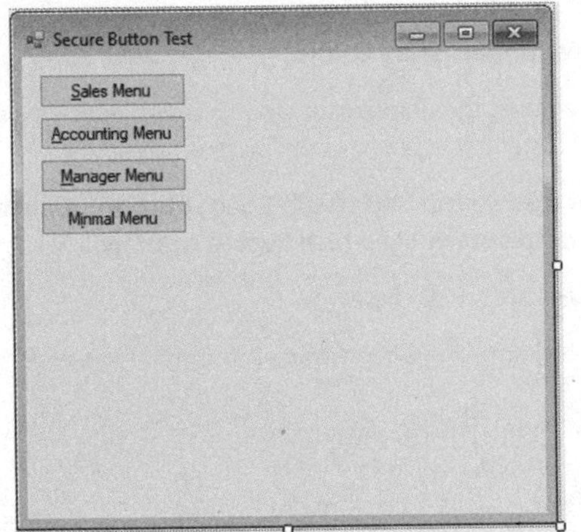

FIGURE 1-1: The Windows Security application sample.

9. **Set the** `(Name)` **property for each of the buttons to match their role name:** `SalesButton`, `AccountingButton`, `ManagerButton`, **and** `MinimalButton`.

   Giving the buttons a recognizable name makes them easier to work with.

10. **Set every button's visible properties to** `False` **so that they aren't shown on the form by default.**

    Even though Minimal Menu is the default, you don't make it visible unless the user is in that role.

11. **Double-click the form to reach the** `SecureButtonTest_Load` **event handler.**

12. **Above the** `Namespace` **statement, import the** `System.Security.Principal` **namespace this way:**

```
using System.Security.Principal;
```

13. **In the** `SecureButtonTest_Load` **event handler, instantiate a new** `Identity` **object that represents the current user with the** `GetCurrent` **method of the** `WindowsIdentity` **object by adding this bit of code:**

```
WindowsIdentity myIdentity = WindowsIdentity.GetCurrent();
```

14. **Get a reference to this identity with the** `WindowsPrincipal` **class:**

```
WindowsPrincipal myPrincipal = new WindowsPrincipal(myIdentity);
```

15. **Hover the mouse next to the** `using` **statements.**

    You see a light-bulb icon when using C# 7.0 or above. This icon tells you that there are ways to make your code more efficient.

16. Choose Remove Unnecessary Usings.

Visual Studio removes the unnecessary `using` statements. This action makes your code load faster and use resources more efficiently.

17. Finally, also in the `SecureButtonTest_Load` subroutine, code a little `If...Then` statement to determine which button to show.

The code changes are shown here:

```
private void SecureButtonTest_Load(object sender, EventArgs e)
{
    // Get the user's identity.
    WindowsIdentity myIdentity =
        WindowsIdentity.GetCurrent();

    // Obtain information about the user's rights.
    WindowsPrincipal myPrincipal =
        new WindowsPrincipal(myIdentity);

    // Determine which button to show based on
    // the user's rights.
    if (myPrincipal.IsInRole("Accounting"))
        AccountingButton.Visible = true;
    else if (myPrincipal.IsInRole("Sales"))
        SalesButton.Visible = true;
    else if (myPrincipal.IsInRole("Management"))
        ManagerButton.Visible = true;
    else
        MinimalButton.Visible = true;
}
```

In some cases, you don't need this kind of role diversification. Sometimes you just need to know whether the user is in a standard role, which `System.Security` provides for. Using the `WindowsBuiltInRole` enumerator, you describe actions that should take place when, for example, the administrator is logged on:

```
if (myPrincipal.IsInRole(WindowsBuiltInRole.Administrator))
{
    //Do something
}
```

Encrypting information

Encryption is, at its core, an insanely sophisticated process. A number of namespaces are devoted to different algorithms (see `https://docs.microsoft.com/en-us/dotnet/standard/security/cryptography-model` as an example). Because encryption is so complex, this book doesn't get into details. Nonetheless, it's important that you understand one cryptographic element for a key element of security: encrypting files. When you work with a file in a Windows Forms application, you risk having someone load it in a text editor and look at it, unless you have encrypted the file.

The common encryption scheme Advanced Encryption Standard (AES) is implemented in .NET in Visual Studio 2008 (C# 3.0) and above. Older versions of Visual Studio rely on the Data Encryption Standard (DES), which isn't the strongest encryption in these days of 64-bit desktop machines (the Microsoft documentation at `https://docs.microsoft.com/en-us/dotnet/api/system.security.cryptography.des` recommends against using DES). Use AES whenever possible to gain the highest level of encryption for your application. You can find the methods to encrypt for DES in the `DESCryptoServiceProvider` in the `System.Security.Cryptography` namespace.

Your program should never contain passwords and they shouldn't appear in configuration or other easily accessible files either. When encrypting a file, the user should always enter the password or attackers can easily break the encryption.

Deployment security

If you deploy your application using ClickOnce, you need to define the access level the application will request. *ClickOnce* is a method of publishing your application using the technique described in the article at `https://docs.microsoft.com/en-us/visualstudio/deployment/quickstart-deploy-using-clickonce-folder` (for .NET Core applications) and `https://docs.microsoft.com/en-us/visualstudio/deployment/how-to-publish-a-clickonce-application-using-the-publish-wizard` (for .NET Framework desktop applications). To define the requested security, choose Project⇨SecureButton Properties and select the Security tab shown in Figure 1-2.

Here, you can define the features that your application uses so that the user installing it receives a warning at installation rather than a security error when running the application.

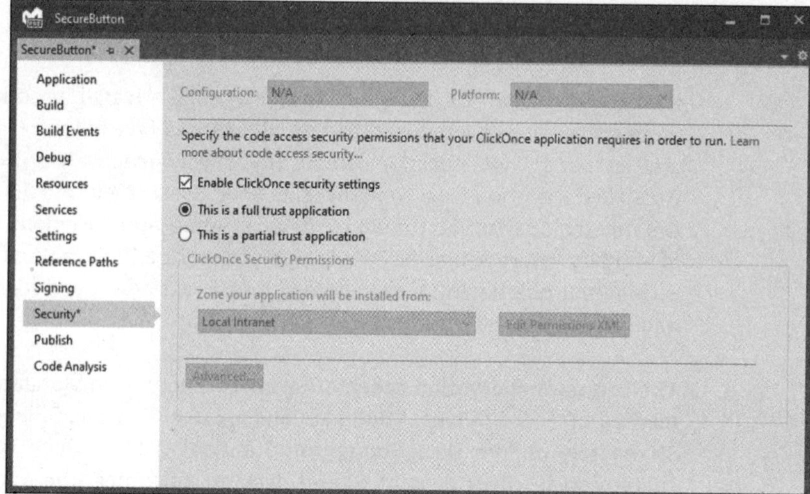

FIGURE 1-2: The Windows Security tab of the My Project configuration file.

Using System.Security

Although many of the security tools are built into the classes that use them, some classes defy description or classification. For that reason, `System.Security` is the holding pot for stuff that doesn't fit anywhere else.

The more common namespaces for `System.Security` are described in Table 1-1. I show how to use the `Security.Principal` namespace in the earlier section "Authentication using Windows logon."

TABLE 1-1 Common Namespaces in System.Security

Namespace	Description	Common Classes
Security	Base classes for security	CodeAccessPermission, SecureString
AccessControl	Sophisticated control for authorization	AccessRule, AuditRule
Authorization	Enumerations that describe the security of an application	CipherAlgorithmType
Cryptography	Contains several namespaces that help with encryption	CryptoConfig, DESCryptoServiceProvider
Permissions	Controls access to resources	PrincipalPermission, SecurityPermission
Policy	Defends repudiation with classes for evidence	Evidence, Site, Url
Principal	Defines the object that represents the current user context	WindowsIdentity, WindowsPrincipal

IN THIS CHAPTER

» Understanding the `System.Data` namespace

» Connecting to a data source

» Working with data from databases

Chapter 2
Accessing Data

Not to predispose you to the contents of this chapter, but you'll probably find that data access is the most important part of your use of the .NET Framework. You'll likely use the various features of the `System.Data` namespace more than any other namespace.

Unquestionably, one of the most common uses of Visual Studio is the creation of business applications. Business applications are about data. This is the black and white of development with Visual Studio. Understanding a little of everything is important, but complete understanding of the `System.Data` namespace is essential when you're building business applications.

Until the .NET Framework became popular in the 2003 time frame, most business applications built using Microsoft products used FoxPro or Visual Basic. C# has unquestionably replaced those languages as the business programmer's language of choice over the years. You can look at the data tools in C# in three ways:

- **Database connectivity:** Getting information out of and into a database is a primary part of the `System.Data` namespace.
- **Holding data in containers within your programs:** The `DataSet`, `DataView`, and `DataTable` containers are useful mechanisms for accomplishing the holding of data.

REMEMBER

Language Integrated Query (LINQ) enables you to get the data out of the data containers using a Structured Query Language (SQL)-like methodology rather than complicated object-oriented language (OOL). LINQ isn't actually based on SQL — it's a separate language, but if you know SQL, then you have a leg up on using LINQ.

- **Integration with data controls:** The `System.Web` and `System.Windows` namespaces function to integrate with the data controls. Data control integration uses database connectivity and data containers extensively. This makes data controls a great target for your reading in this chapter.

REMEMBER

You don't have to type the source code for this chapter manually. In fact, using the downloadable source is a lot easier. You can find the source for this chapter in the `\CSAIO4D2E\BK03\CH02` folder of the downloadable source. See the Introduction for details on how to find these source files.

Getting to Know System.Data

Data in .NET is different from data in any other Microsoft platform. Microsoft has and continues to change the way data is manipulated in the .NET Framework. ADO.NET, whose implementation is contained in the `System.Data` library, provides the common way to think about data from a development perspective:

- **Disconnected:** After you get data from a data source, your program is no longer connected to that data source. You have a copy of the data. This cures one problem and causes another:
  - You no longer have a row-locking problem. Because you have a copy of the data, you don't have to constrain the database from making changes.
  - You have the *last in wins* problem. If two instances of a program get the same data, and they both update it, the last one back to the database overwrites the changes made by the first program.
- **XML driven:** The data copy that's collected from the data source is XML under the hood. It might be moved around in a custom format when Microsoft deems it necessary for performance, but it is just XML either way, making movement between platforms, applications, or databases much easier.
- **Database-generic containers:** The containers don't depend on the type of database at all — they can be used to store data from anywhere.
- **Database-specific adapters:** Connections to the database are specific to the database platform, so if you want to connect to a specific database, you need the components that work with that database.

The process for getting data has changed a little, too. You used to have a connection and a command, which returned a `Recordset`. Now you have an adapter, which uses a connection and a command to fill a `DataSet` container. What has changed is the way the user interface helps you get the job done.

`System.Data` has the classes to help you connect to a lot of different databases and other types of data. These classes are broken up into the namespaces in Table 2-1.

TABLE 2-1 **The System.Data Namespaces**

Namespace	Documentation URL	Purpose	Most Used Classes
System.Data	`https://docs.microsoft.com/dotnet/api/system.data`	Classes common to all of ADO.NET	The containers DataSet, DataView, DataTable, DataRow
System.Data.Common	`https://docs.microsoft.com/dotnet/api/system.data.common`	Utility classes used by database-specific classes	DbCommand, DbConnection
System.Data.ODBC	`https://docs.microsoft.com/dotnet/api/system.data.odbc`	Classes for connections to ODBC databases such as dBASE	OdbcCommand, OdbcAdapter
System.Data.OleDb	`https://docs.microsoft.com/dotnet/api/system.data.oledb`	Classes for connections to OleDb databases such as Access	OleDbCommand, OleDbAdapter
System.Data.OracleClient	`https://docs.microsoft.com/dotnet/api/system.data.oracleclient`	Classes for connections to Oracle	OracleCommand, OracleAdapter
System.Data.SqlClient	`https://docs.microsoft.com/dotnet/api/system.data.sqlclient`	Classes for connections to Microsoft SQL Server	SqlCommand, SqlDataAdapter
System.Data.SqlTypes	`https://docs.microsoft.com/dotnet/api/system.data.sqltypes`	For referencing the native types common to SQL Server	SqlDateTime

Though there is a lot to the `System.Data` namespace and related tools, this chapter focuses on the way Visual Studio implements these tools. In previous versions of the development software of all makes and models, the visual tools just made things harder because of the black box problem.

The *black box problem* is that of having a development environment do some things for you over which you have no control. Sometimes it's nice to have things done for you, but when the development environment doesn't build them exactly how you need them, code is generated that isn't useful.

Fortunately, that isn't the case anymore. Visual Studio now generates completely open and sensible C# code when you use the visual data tools. You should be pleased with the results.

How the Data Classes Fit into the Framework

The data classes are all about information storage. Book 1 talks about collections, which are for storage of information while an application is running. Hashtables are another example of storing information. *Collections* hold lists of objects, and *hashtables* hold name and value pairs. The data containers hold data in larger amounts and help you manipulate that data. Here are the data containers:

- `DataSet`: Kind of the granddaddy of them all, the `DataSet` container is an in-memory representation of an entire database.
- `DataTable`: A single table of data stored in memory. `DataSet` containers are made up of `DataTable` containers.
- `DataRow`: Unsurprisingly, a row in a `DataTable` container.
- `DataView`: A copy of a `DataTable` that you can use to sort and filter data for viewing purposes.
- `DataReader`: A read-only, forward-only stream of data used for one-time processes, such as filling up list boxes. Usually called a *fire hose.*

Getting to Your Data

Everything in the `System.Data` namespace revolves around getting data from a database such as Microsoft SQL Server and filling these data containers. You can get to this data manually. Generally speaking, the process goes something like this:

1. You create an adapter.
2. You tell the adapter how to get information from the database (the connection).

3. The adapter connects to the database.
4. You tell the adapter which information to get from the database (the command).
5. The adapter fills the `DataSet` container with data.
6. The connection between the adapter and the database is closed.
7. You now have a disconnected copy of the data in your program.

Not to put too fine a point on it, but you shouldn't have to go through that process at all. Visual Studio does a lot of the data management for you if you let it. Best practice is to use as much automation as possible.

Using the System.Data Namespace

The `System.Data` namespace is another namespace that gets mixed up between the code world and the visual tools world. Though it is more of a relationship between the form controls and the `Data` namespace, it often seems that the data lives right inside the controls, especially when you're dealing with Windows Forms.

In the following sections, you deal primarily with the visual tools, which are as much a part of the C# experience as the code. First, you discover how to connect to data sources, and then you see how to write a quick application using one of those connections. Finally, you uncover a little of the code side.

To make all this work, you need to have some kind of schema set up in your database. It can be a local project of your own creation or a sample schema. The next section tells you how.

Setting up a sample database schema

To get started, direct your browser to `https://github.com/Microsoft/sql-server-samples/releases/tag/adventureworks2012`. If this URL doesn't work, search the web for *SQL Server 2012 samples* and find the nearest link. (If you want to use a newer version of the AdventureWorks database, you need to install a copy of SQL Server because these newer versions all rely on SQL Server backup (`.bak`) files. You can find these files at `https://github.com/Microsoft/sql-server-samples/releases/tag/adventureworks`.

Any of the sample schemas will work. If you want exactly the same one used in the examples here, choose the AdventureWorks2012 Online Transaction Processing (OLTP) Data File (`adventure-works-2012-oltp-data-file.mdf`). Other options may be a better fit for the work you're doing.

To install, download the MDF file and put it somewhere that makes sense to you. You'll eventually reference it in your project, so a local location like `C:\Databases` might be good if you have root directory access (or add the `Databases` folder to your user folder). If you're familiar with SQL Server, you can add a database to your local install and point to it there. In case you aren't a DBA, you can also point a data provider directly to a file. That's the approach used for the rest of this chapter.

Creating the data access project

Before you can do anything, you need to create your data access application. Of course, there will be a lot of configuring to do before you complete the task, but just start with the basics of the AccessData example using the following steps:

1. **Click Create a New Project.**

   You see the template selection page.

2. **Choose C#, and then Windows, and then Desktop from the three drop-down list boxes at the top.**

   The template list changes to show the specific templates that you selected.

3. **Highlight the Windows Forms App (.NET Framework) option; then click Next.**

   The Configure Your New Project page appears.

4. **Type** AccessData **in the Project Name field.**
5. **In the Location field, choose or type a place to put your projects (the example uses** `C:\CSAIO4D2E\BK03\CH02`**).**
6. **Select Place Solution and Project in the Same Directory and then click Create.**

   Visual Studio creates the AccessData solution for you.

Connecting to a data source

There is more to connecting to a database than establishing a simple connection to a SQL Server dataset these days. C# developers have to connect to mainframes, text files, unusual databases, web services, and other programs. All these disparate systems get integrated into windows and web screens, with create, read, update, and delete (CRUD) functionality to boot.

REMEMBER

Getting to these data sources is mostly dependent on the `Adapter` classes of the individualized database namespaces. Oracle has its own, as does SQL Server. Databases that are ODBC (Open Database Connectivity) compliant (such as Microsoft Access) have their own `Adapter` classes; the newer OLEDB (Object Linking and Embedding Database) protocol has one, too.

Fortunately, a wizard handles most of this. The Data Source Configuration Wizard is accessible from the Data Sources panel, where you spend much of your time when working with data. To get started with the Data Source Configuration Wizard, follow these steps:

1. **Choose View ➪ Other Windows ➪ Data Sources, or press Shift+Alt+D.**

   The Data Sources panel tells you that you have no data sources.

2. **Click the Add New Data Source link in the Data Sources panel.**

   You see the Data Source Configuration Wizard, shown in Figure 2-1. The wizard has a variety of data source types to choose from. The most interesting of these is the Object source, which gives you access to an object in an assembly to bind your controls to.

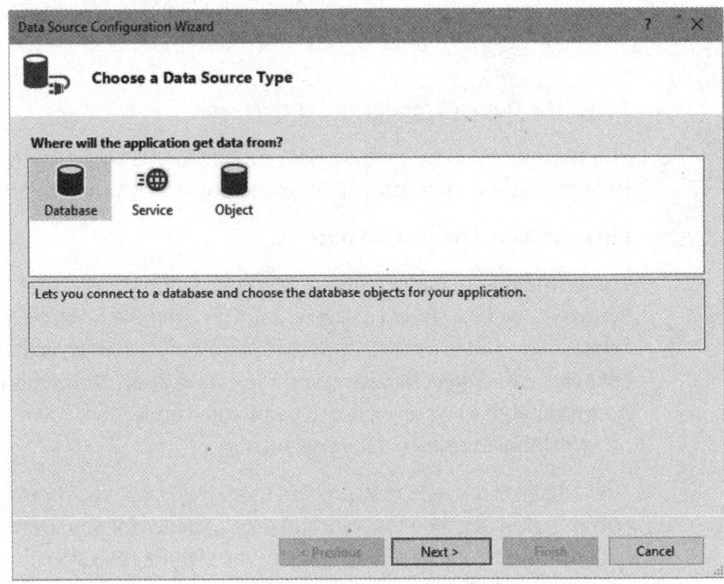

FIGURE 2-1: Choose a source type for the application data.

3. **Select the Database data source type and click Next.**

   You see the database model selections shown in Figure 2-2 (the figure shows a bare metal setup in which you don't have any database managers, including SQL Server, installed on your system, so you may see more options). As a minimum, you have access to the Dataset model.

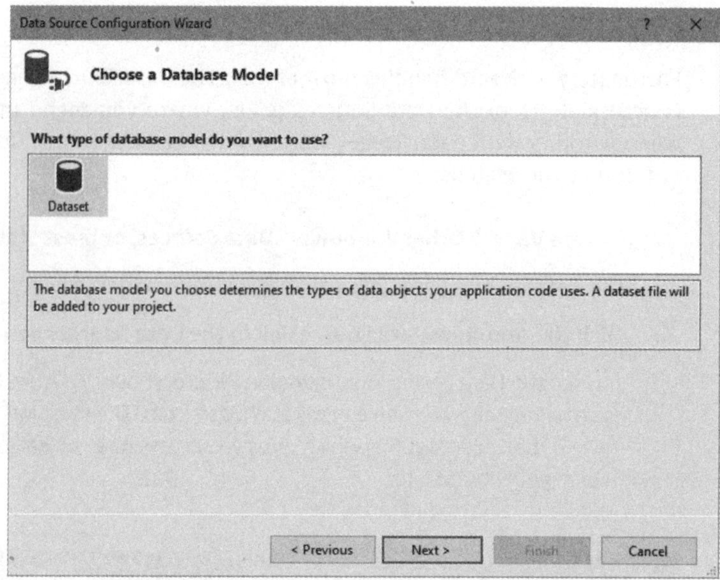

FIGURE 2-2: Choose a database model to use to model the data.

4. **Select the Dataset model and click Next.**

   You see the option to choose a data connection, as shown in Figure 2-3. Because this is a new application, you shouldn't see any connections.

5. **Click the New Connection button.**

   Visual Studio asks you to create a new connection by using the Choose Data Source dialog box, shown in Figure 2-4. This example relies on a direct connection to a Microsoft SQL Server Database File, which is the easiest kind of connection to create. Note that you can create direct connections to Microsoft Access database files as well, and can create connections to an assortment of other databases using a database adapter.

TIP

The Data Provider field may provide more than one data provider. The wizard normally chooses the most efficient data provider for you. However, other data providers may have functionality you require for a specific application type. Always verify that you select the best data provider for your particular application needs.

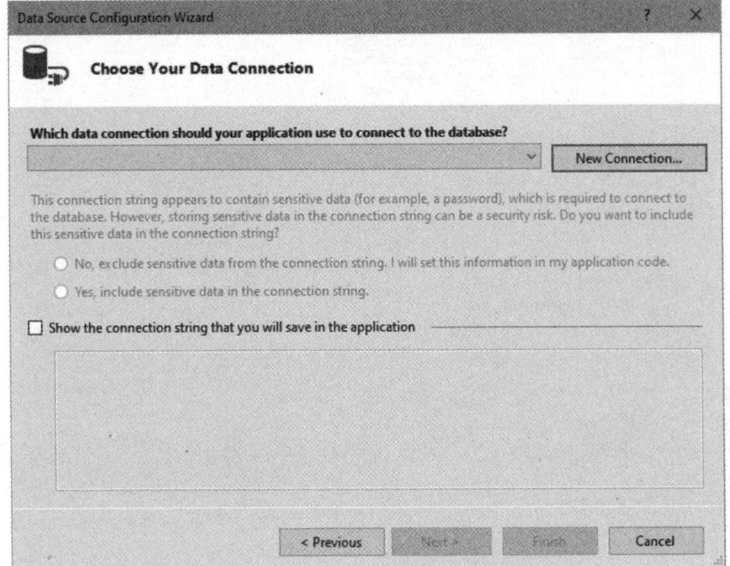

FIGURE 2-3: Choosing your data connection.

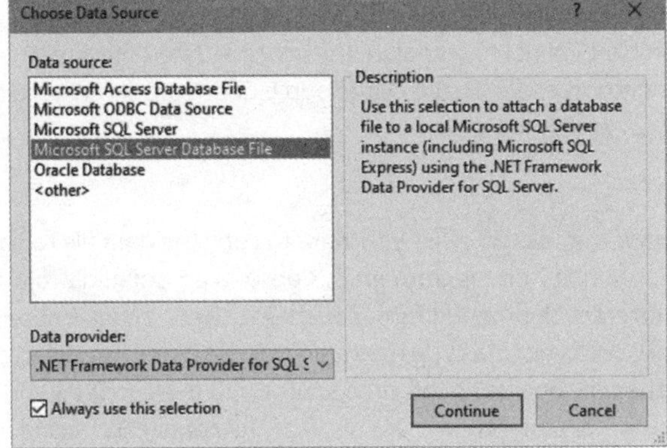

FIGURE 2-4: The Choose Data Source dialog box.

The steps that follow are specific to using a Microsoft SQL Server database file. Other types of data sources may require that you perform other steps to create a connection.

6. **Select Microsoft SQL Server Database File and click Continue.**

   You see the Add Connection dialog box, shown in Figure 2-5.

7. **Click Browse to display the Select SQL Server Database File dialog box, highlight the** `adventure-works-2012-oltp-data-file.mdf` **file that you downloaded earlier, and click Open.**

   It's important to note that this technique only works with `.mdf` files, not the `.bak` files you find in other locations. The wizard adds the location to the Database File Name field.

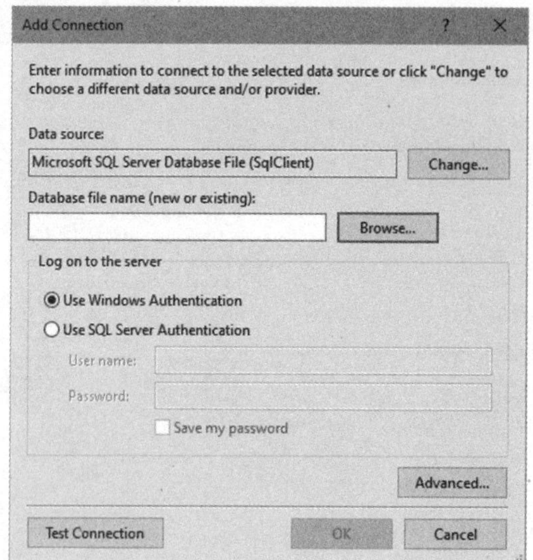

FIGURE 2-5: Specify the location of the database file used for this example.

8. **Click OK.**

   You may be asked by Visual Studio to upgrade the database file, which is totally fine. Simply click Yes to complete the process. After a few moments, you see the connection added to the Data Source Configuration Wizard dialog box, shown previously in Figure 2-5.

9. **Click Next.**

   The wizard may ask whether you want to copy the data file to your current project. If you're working through this book in an isolated project, that's fine. If you're on a development effort with others, check to make sure that it's appropriate to your life cycle methodology. For this example, click No because you're the only one using this data source and there isn't a good reason to create another copy. The wizard displays the connection string filename, such as adventure_works_2012_oltp_data_fileConnectionString, and asks whether you want to save it to the application.

10. **Click Next.**

    You see the Choose Your Database Objects and Settings dialog box. You can choose the tables, views, or stored procedures that you want to use.

11. **Under Tables, select Product and ProductCategory.**

    The Choose Your Database Objects and Settings dialog box should look similar to the one shown in Figure 2-6.

12. **Click Finish.**

    You're done! If you look at the Data Sources pane, you can see that a `DataSet` was added to your project with the two tables you requested.

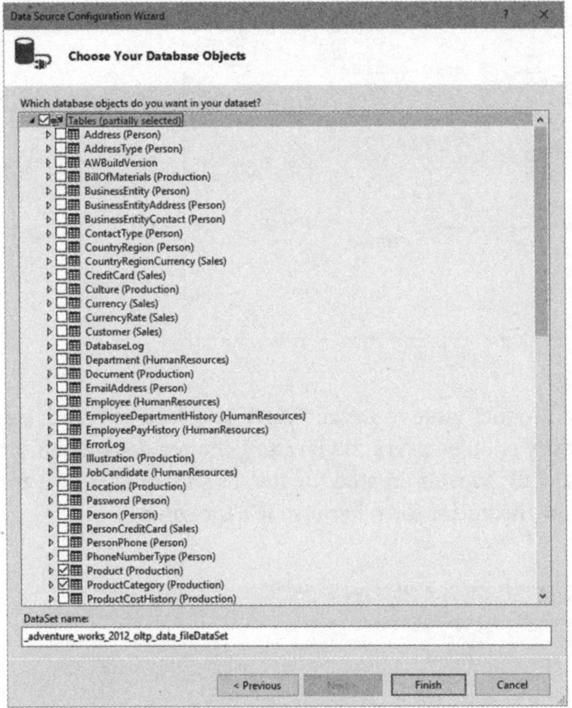

FIGURE 2-6: Selecting data objects.

By following the preceding steps, you create two significant entities in Visual Studio:

- » You create a connection to the database, shown in the Server Explorer. You find that it sticks around — it's specific to this installation of Visual Studio.
- » You also create a dataset, which is specific to this project and won't be there if you start another project.

Both of them are important, and they provide different functionality. In this chapter, you focus on the project-specific data source displayed in the dataset.

Working with the visual tools

The Rapid Application Development (RAD) data tools for C# in Visual Studio are usable and do what you need, and they write decent code for you. Select the Data Sources panel (View➪Other Windows➪Data Sources) and click a table in the panel; a drop-down arrow appears, as shown in Figure 2-7. Click it, and you see something interesting: A drop-down list appears, and you can then choose how that table is integrated into Windows Forms.

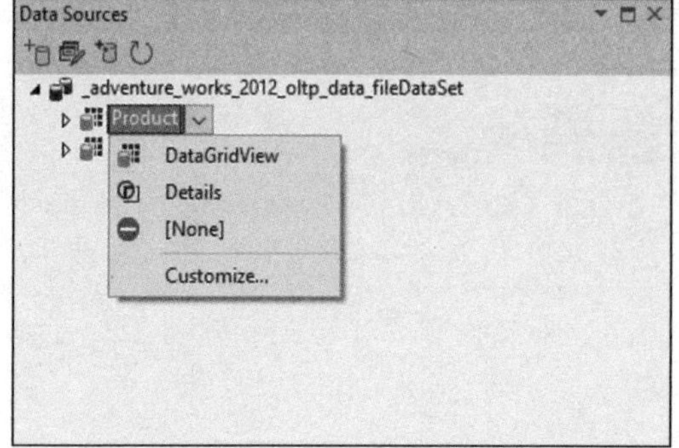

FIGURE 2-7: Table Options drop-down list.

Change the Product table to Details View. It's used to create a detail type form — one that easily enables users to view and change data. Then drag the table to the form, and Details View is created for you, as shown in Figure 2-8. (The screenshot doesn't show the entire form because it's too long.)

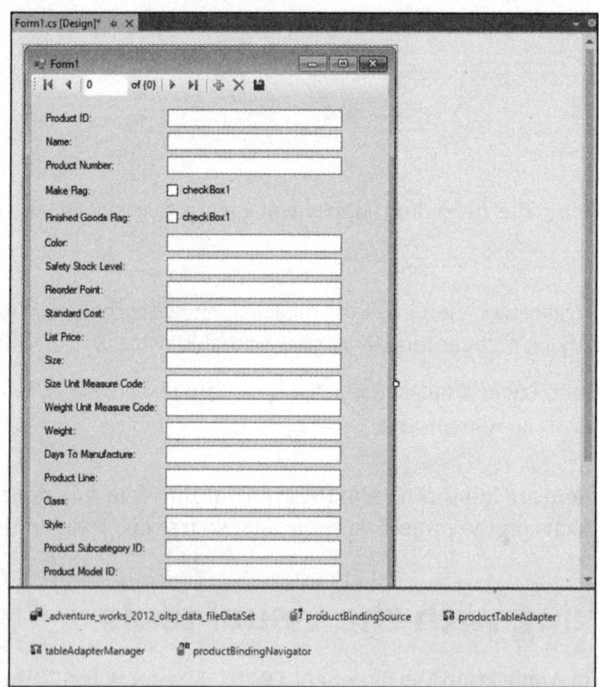

FIGURE 2-8: Creating a Parts Detail data form.

A whole lot of things happened when you dropped the table on your form:

- The fields and the field names were added.
- The fields are in the most appropriate format.

» The field name is a label.

» Visual Studio automatically adds a space where the case changes.

TIP

Note that each field gets a SmartTag that enables you to specify a query for the values in the text box. You can also preset the control that's used by changing the values in the Data Sources pane. Five completely code-based objects are added in the Component Tray at the bottom of the page:

» **DataSet**: `_adventure_works_2012_oltp_data_fileDataSet`

» **BindingSource**: `productBindingSource`

» **TableAdapter:** `productTableAdapter`

» **TableAdapterManager:** `tableAdapterManager`

» **BindingNavigator:** `productBindingNavigator`

The VCR Bar (technically called the `BindingNavigator`) is added to the top of the page. When you run the application, you can use the VCR Bar to cycle among the records in the table. Click the Start button to see the VCR Bar work. You can walk through the items in the database with no problems.

Writing data code

In most enterprise development environments, however, you won't be using the visual tools to build data access software. Generally, an infrastructure is already in place because enterprise software often has specific requirements, and the easiest way to manage those specifications is with unique and customized code. In short, some organizations don't want things done the way Microsoft does them.

Output of the visual tools

Visual tools often aren't used in enterprise environments because the code the tools put out is rather complicated. Double-click `Form1.Designer.cs` in Solution Explorer to see the code-behind for the form controls. Figure 2-9 shows what you see when you first get in there. The box marking the region near the top of the code window is marked as `Windows Form Designer generated code`, and you can't help but notice that the line number before that section is in the twenties and the number after that is in the seven hundreds. That's a lot of generated code.

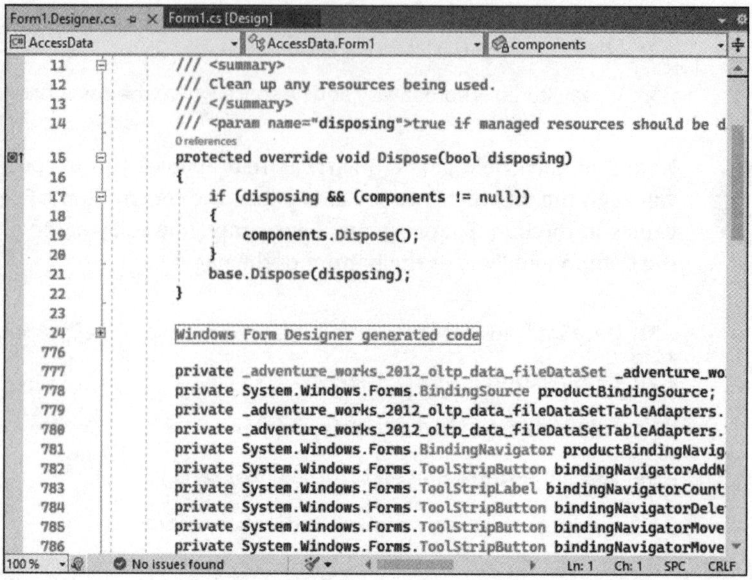

```
/// <summary>
/// Clean up any resources being used.
/// </summary>
/// <param name="disposing">true if managed resources should be d
protected override void Dispose(bool disposing)
{
    if (disposing && (components != null))
    {
        components.Dispose();
    }
    base.Dispose(disposing);
}

Windows Form Designer generated code

private _adventure_works_2012_oltp_data_fileDataSet _adventure_wo
private System.Windows.Forms.BindingSource productBindingSource;
private _adventure_works_2012_oltp_data_fileDataSetTableAdapters.
private _adventure_works_2012_oltp_data_fileDataSetTableAdapters.
private System.Windows.Forms.BindingNavigator productBindingNavig
private System.Windows.Forms.ToolStripButton bindingNavigatorAddN
private System.Windows.Forms.ToolStripLabel bindingNavigatorCount
private System.Windows.Forms.ToolStripButton bindingNavigatorDele
private System.Windows.Forms.ToolStripButton bindingNavigatorMove
private System.Windows.Forms.ToolStripButton bindingNavigatorMove
```

FIGURE 2-9: Generated code. Huh?

Nothing is wrong with this code, but it is purposely generic to support anything that anyone might want to do with it. Enterprise customers often want to make sure that everything is done the same way. For this reason, they often define a specific data code format and expect their software developers to use that, rather than the visual tools.

Basic data code

The code of the sample project is simple (you don't type this code, it was automatically generated for you):

```
using System;
using System.Windows.Forms;

namespace AccessData
{
    public partial class Form1 : Form
    {
        public Form1()
        {
            InitializeComponent();
        }

        private void productBindingNavigatorSaveItem_Click(object sender,
            EventArgs e)
        {
            this.Validate();
```

```
            this.productBindingSource.EndEdit();
            this.tableAdapterManager.UpdateAll(
                this._adventure_works_2012_oltp_data_fileDataSet);

        }

        private void Form1_Load(object sender, EventArgs e)
        {
            // TODO: This line of code loads data into the
            // '_adventure_works_2012_oltp_data_fileDataSet.Product'
            // table. You can move, or remove it, as needed.
            this.productTableAdapter.Fill(
                this._adventure_works_2012_oltp_data_fileDataSet.Product);

        }
    }
}
```

Although this code is fairly straightforward, it obviously isn't everything that you need. The rest of the code is in the file that generates the visual form itself, supporting the visual components.

The time may come when you want to connect to a database without using visual tools. The "How the Data Classes Fit into the Framework" section, earlier in this chapter, discusses the required steps and here is the code to go with it:

```
1. SqlConnection mainConnection = new SqlConnection();
2. mainConnection.ConnectionString =
   "server=(local);database=Assets_Maintenance;Trusted_Connection=True"
3. SqlDataAdapter partsAdapter = new SqlDataAdapter("SELECT * FROM Parts",
   mainConnection)
4. DataSet partsDataSet = new DataSet();
5. mainConnection.Open();
6. partsAdapter.Fill(partsDataSet);
7. mainConnection.Close();
```

TIP

This approach becomes useful especially when you want to build a web service or a class library — though you should note that you can still use the visual tools in those project types. The following paragraphs discuss this code a line at a time.

Line 1 sets up a new data connection, and line 2 populates it with the connection string. You can get this from your Database Administrator (DBA) or from the Properties panel for the data connection.

Line 3 has a SQL query in it. A Stored Procedure is a database artifact that allows you to use a parameterized query from ADO.NET, rather than dynamically generated SQL Strings. Don't use inline SQL for production systems.

Line 4 builds a new dataset. This is where the schema of the returned data is held and what you use to navigate the data.

Lines 5, 6, and 7 perform the magic: Open the connection, contact the database, fill the dataset using the adapter, and then close the database. It's all straightforward in this simple example. More complex examples make for more complex code.

After running this code, you would have the Products table in a `DataSet` container, just as you did in the visual tools in the earlier section, "How the Data Classes Fit into the Framework." To access the information, you set the value of a text box to the value of a cell in the `DataSet` container, like this:

```
TextBox1.Text = myDataSet.Tables[0].Rows[0]["name"]
```

To change to the next record, you need to write code that changes the `Rows[0]` to `Rows[1]`. As you can see, it would be a fair amount of code. That's why few people use the basic data code to get the databases. Either you use the visual tools or you use an Object Relationship Model of some sort, such as Entity Framework.

IN THIS CHAPTER

» Reading and writing data files

» Using the `Stream` classes

» Using the `using` statement

» Dealing with input/output errors

Chapter 3 Fishing the File Stream

Catching fish in a stream can prove to be quite a thrill to those who engage in fishing. Anglers often boast of the difficulty of getting that one special fish out of the stream and into a basket. Fishing the "file stream" with C# isn't quite so thrilling, but it's one of those indispensable programming skills.

File access refers to the storage and retrieval of data on the disk. This chapter covers basic text-file input/output. Reading and writing data from databases are covered in Chapter 2 of this minibook, and reading and writing information to the Internet are covered in Chapter 4.

REMEMBER

You don't have to type the source code for this chapter manually. In fact, using the downloadable source is a lot easier. You can find the source for this chapter in the `\CSAIO4D2E\BK03\CH03` folder of the downloadable source. See the Introduction for details on how to find these source files.

Going Where the Fish Are: The File Stream

The console application programs in this book mostly take their input from, and send their output to, the console. Programs outside this chapter have better — or at least different — things to bore you with than file manipulation. It's important not to confuse their message with the extra baggage of involved input/output (I/O). However, console applications that don't perform file I/O aren't very common.

The I/O classes are defined in the `System.IO` namespace. The basic file I/O class is `FileStream`. In days past, the programmer would open a file. The `open` command would prepare the file and return a *handle*. Usually, this handle was nothing more than a number, like the one they give you when you place an order at a Burger Shop. Every time you wanted to read from or write to the file, you presented this ID.

Streams

C# uses a more intuitive approach, associating each file with an object of class `FileStream`. The constructor for `FileStream` opens the file and manages the underlying handle. The methods of `FileStream` perform the file I/O.

TIP

`FileStream` isn't the only class that can perform file I/O. However, it represents your good ol' basic file that covers 90 percent of your file I/O needs. This primary class is the one described in this chapter.

The *stream* concept is fundamental to C# I/O. Think of a parade, which "streams" by you, first the clowns, and then the floats, and then a band or two, some horses, a troupe of `Customer` objects, a `BankAccount`, and so on. Viewing a file as a stream of bytes (or characters or strings) is much like a parade. You "stream" the data in and out of your program.

The .NET classes used in C# include an abstract `Stream` base class and several subclasses, for working with files on the disk, over a network, or already sitting as chunks of data in memory. Some stream classes specialize in encrypting and decrypting data; some are provided to help speed up I/O operations that might be slow using one of the other streams; and you're free to extend class `Stream` with your own subclass if you come up with a great idea for a new stream (although extending `Stream` is arduous). The "Exploring More Streams than Lewis and Clark" section, later in this chapter, gives you a tour of the stream classes.

TECHNICAL STUFF

In case you're looking for a good reason to upgrade to .NET 6.0 and C# 10.0, `FileStream` performance is one of them. According to articles like the one at `https://www.daveabrock.com/2021/05/23/dotnet-stacks-50/`, reading data from a file can be as much as 2.5 times faster, and writing data to a file can be as much as 5.5 times faster. The more detailed information at `https://devblogs.microsoft.com/dotnet/performance-improvements-in-net-6/#io` describes how this all works in detail. The article at `https://docs.microsoft.com/dotnet/core/compatibility/core-libraries/6.0/filestream-position-updates-after-readasync-writeasync-completion` tells you that part of the reason for the change is to make `ReadAsync` and `WriteAsync` thread safe so that you can perform file-oriented tasks using multiple threads. You don't have to worry about doing anything to get these really amazing changes; they come as the default in .NET 6.0 and C# 10.0.

Readers and writers

`FileStream`, the stream class you'll probably use the most, is a basic class. Open a file, close a file, read a block of bytes, and write a block — that's about all you have. But reading and writing files down at the byte level is a lot of work. Fortunately, the .NET class library introduces the notion of *readers* and *writers*. Objects of these types greatly simplify file (and other) I/O.

When you create a new *reader* (of one of several available types), you associate a stream object with it. It's immaterial to the reader whether the stream connects to a file, a block of memory, a network location, or the Mississippi. The reader requests input from the stream, which gets it from — well, wherever. Using *writers* is quite similar, except that you're sending output to the stream rather than asking for input. The stream sends it to a specified destination. Often that's a file, but not always. The `System.IO` namespace contains classes that wrap around `FileStream` (or other streams) to give you easier access:

- `TextReader`/`TextWriter`: A pair of abstract classes for reading characters (text). These classes are the base for two flavors of subclasses: `StringReader`/`StringWriter` and `StreamReader`/`StreamWriter`.

REMEMBER

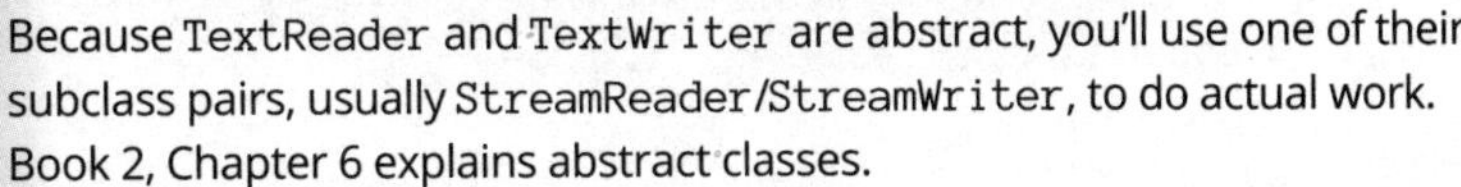

  Because `TextReader` and `TextWriter` are abstract, you'll use one of their subclass pairs, usually `StreamReader`/`StreamWriter`, to do actual work. Book 2, Chapter 6 explains abstract classes.

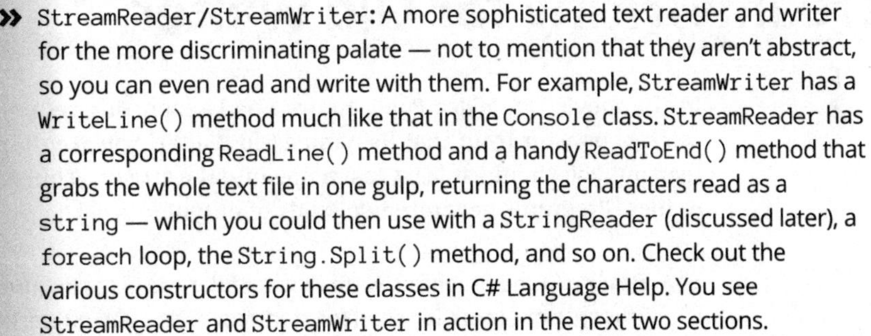

- `StreamReader`/`StreamWriter`: A more sophisticated text reader and writer for the more discriminating palate — not to mention that they aren't abstract, so you can even read and write with them. For example, `StreamWriter` has a `WriteLine()` method much like that in the `Console` class. `StreamReader` has a corresponding `ReadLine()` method and a handy `ReadToEnd()` method that grabs the whole text file in one gulp, returning the characters read as a `string` — which you could then use with a `StringReader` (discussed later), a `foreach` loop, the `String.Split()` method, and so on. Check out the various constructors for these classes in C# Language Help. You see `StreamReader` and `StreamWriter` in action in the next two sections.

One nice thing about reader/writer classes such as `StreamReader` and `StreamWriter` is that you can use them with any kind of stream. This makes reading from and writing to a `MemoryStream` no harder than reading from and writing to the kind of `FileStream` discussed in earlier sections of this chapter. (The "Exploring More Streams than Lewis and Clark" section later in this chapter covers `MemoryStream`.) See the later section "More Readers and Writers" for additional reader/writer pairs.

The following sections provide the `FileWrite` and `FileRead` programs, which demonstrate ways to use these classes for text I/O the C# way.

ASYNCHRONOUS I/O: IS IT WORTH WAITING FOR?

Normally, a program waits for a file I/O request to complete before continuing. Call a `read()` method, and you generally don't get control back until the file data is safely in the boat. This is known as *synchronous I/O.* Think of *synchronous* as meaning "while you wait."

The C# `System.IO` classes also support *asynchronous* I/O. Using asynchronous I/O, the `read()` call returns immediately to allow the program to continue doing something else while the I/O request is completed in the background. The program can check a "done" flag at its leisure to decide when the I/O has completed.

This is sort of like cooking hamburgers. Using synchronous I/O, you put the meat in the pan on the stovetop and stand there watching it until the meat has completely cooked before you go off and start cutting the onions that go on the burgers.

Using asynchronous I/O, you can start cutting up the onions while the hamburger patties are cooking. Every once in a while, you peek over to see whether the meat is done. When it is, you stop cutting, take the meat off the stove, and slap it on the buns.

StreamWriting for Old Walter

In the movie *On Golden Pond,* Henry Fonda spent his retirement years trying to catch a monster trout that he named Old Walter. You aren't out to drag in the big fish, but you should at least cast a line into the stream. This section covers writing to files. Programs generate two kinds of output:

- **Binary:** Some programs write blocks of data as bytes in pure binary format. This type of output is useful for storing objects in an efficient way — for example, a file of `Student` objects that you need to *persist* (keep on disk in a permanent file). See the later section "More Readers and Writers" for the `BinaryReader` and `BinaryWriter` classes.

TECHNICAL STUFF

A sophisticated example of binary I/O is the persistence of groups of objects that refer to each other (using the HAS_A relationship). Writing an object to disk involves writing identifying information (so its type can be reconstructed when you read the object back in), and then each of its data members, some of which may be references to connected objects, each with its own identifying information and data members. Persisting objects this way is called *serialization.*

» **Text:** Most programs read and write human-readable text: you know, letters, numbers, and punctuation, like Notepad. The human-friendly `StreamWriter` and `StreamReader` classes are the most flexible ways to work with the stream classes. For some details, see the earlier section "Readers and writers."

TECHNICAL STUFF

Human-readable data was formerly known as American Standard Code for Information Interchange (ASCII) text or, slightly later, American National Standards Institute (ANSI) text. These two monikers refer to the standards organization that defined them. However, ANSI encoding doesn't provide the alphabets east of Austria and west of Hawaii; it can handle only Roman letters, like those used in English. It has no characters for Russian, Hebrew, Arabic, Hindi, or any other language using a non-Roman alphabet, including Asian languages such as Chinese, Japanese, and Korean. The modern, more flexible Unicode character format is "backward-compatible" — including the familiar ANSI characters at the beginning of its character set, but still provides a large number of other alphabets, including everything you need for all the languages just listed. Unicode comes in several variations, called *encodings;* however, Unicode Transformation Format (8-Bit) (UTF8) is the default encoding for C#. You can read more about Unicode encodings at `https://unicodebook.readthedocs.io/unicode_encodings.html`. Other popular encodings are: UTF7, UTF16, and UTF32, where the number after UTF specifies the number of bits used in the encoding.

Using the stream: An example

The `FileWrite` example in this section reads lines of data from the console and writes them to a file of the user's choosing. The code begins by ensuring that the file doesn't already exist. If it does, the user is queried for another filename. The user can also create multiple files by providing a new filename at the completion of the current file. The program relies on blank entries to stop writing to a particular file and to stop creating new files. The following subsections break the code up into manageable pieces, but you can see everything in one chunk by reviewing the downloadable source.

Obtaining a StreamWriter

If you've been following along with the previous sections, you know that you need to create a `StreamWriter` as the first step to write data to a file. Here's the code the application uses:

```
private static StreamWriter GetWriterForFile(string fileName)
{
    StreamWriter sw;

    // Open file for writing in one of these modes:
    //   FileMode.CreateNew to create a file if it
```

```
    //      doesn't already exist or throw an
    //      exception if file exists.
    //   FileMode.Append to append to an existing file
    //      or create a new file if it doesn't exist.
    //   FileMode.Create to create a new file or
    //      truncate an existing file.

    //   FileAccess possibilities are:
    //      FileAccess.Read,
    //      FileAccess.Write,
    //      FileAccess.ReadWrite.
    FileStream fs = File.Open(fileName, FileMode.CreateNew, FileAccess.Write);

    // Generate a file stream with UTF8 characters.
    // Second parameter defaults to UTF8, so can be omitted.
    sw = new StreamWriter(fs, System.Text.Encoding.UTF8);
    return sw;
}
```

All this method really does is open a file for writing in a particular mode when the file doesn't exist. It then uses the `file handle` (the pointer to the file) to create a stream to write to it and returns this stream to the caller.

Writing data to the file using the StreamWriter

After you have a `StreamWriter` to use, you can output data to it. The `WriteFileFromConsole()` method shown here performs that task until it receives a blank input line from the user:

```
private static void WriteFileFromConsole(StreamWriter sw)
{
    Console.WriteLine("Enter text; enter blank line to stop");

    while (true)
    {
        // Read next line from Console; quit if line is blank.
        string input = Console.ReadLine();

        if (input.Length == 0)
        {
            break;
        }

        // Write the line just read to output file.
        sw.WriteLine(input);
    }
}
```

WRAP MY FISH IN NEWSPAPER

Sometimes, one class wraps itself around another class to make the wrapped class easier to use. This kind of wrapping one class around another is a useful software pattern — the `StreamWriter` *wraps* (contains a reference to) another class, `FileStream`, and extends the `FileStream's` interface with some nice amenities. The `StreamWriter` methods *delegate* to (call) the methods of the inner `FileStream` object. This is the HAS_A relationship discussed in Book 2 Chapter 5, so anytime you use HAS_A, you're wrapping. In effect:

1. You tell the `StreamWriter`, the wrapper, what to do.
2. The `StreamWriter` translates your simple instructions into the more complex ones needed by the wrapped `FileStream`.
3. `StreamWriter` hands these translated instructions to the `FileStream` for action.

Wrapping is a powerful, frequently used technique in programming. A `Wrapper` class looks like this:

```
class Wrapper
{
  private Wrapped _wrapped;
  public Wrapper(Wrapped w)
  {
    _w = w; // Now Wrapper has a reference to Wrapped.
  }
}
```

This example uses class `Wrapper`'s constructor to install the wrapped object, letting the caller provide the wrapped object. You might install it through a `SetWrapped()` method or by some other means, such as creating the wrapped object inside a constructor. You can also wrap one *method* around another, like so:

```
void WrapperMethod()
{
  _wrapped.DoSomething();
}
```

(continued)

(continued)

In this example, `WrapperMethod()`'s class HAS_A reference to whatever the `_wrapped` object is. In other words, the class wraps that object. `WrapperMethod()` delegates all or part of the evening chores to the `DoSomething()` method on the `_wrapped` object.

Think of wrapping as a way to translate one model into another. The wrapped item may be complicated enough that you want to provide a simpler version, or the wrapped item may have an inconvenient interface that you want to make over into a more convenient one. Generally speaking, wrapping illustrates the Adapter design pattern (see `https://www.tutorialspoint.com/design_pattern/adapter_pattern.htm` for details). You can see it in the relationship between `StreamWriter` and `FileStream`. In many cases, you can wrap one stream around another stream in order to convert one kind of stream into another.

Putting everything together

You now have a means of opening the file, creating a `StreamWriter` for it, and then outputting data to the `StreamWriter`. The `Main()` method puts everything together into a loop that allows working with multiple nonexisting files, as shown here:

```
static void Main(string[] args)
{
    StreamWriter sw = null;
    string fileName = "";

    // Get a non-existing filename from the user.
    while (true)
    {
        try
        {
            // Enter output filename (simply hit Enter to quit).
            Console.Write("Enter filename (Enter blank filename to quit): ");
            fileName = Console.ReadLine();

            if (fileName.Length == 0)
            {
                // No filename -- this jumps beyond the while loop. You're done.
                break;
            }

            // Call a method (below) to set up the StreamWriter.
            sw = GetWriterForFile(fileName);
```

```
            // Read one string at a time, outputting each to the FileStream.
            WriteFileFromConsole(sw);

            // Done writing, so close the file you just created.
            sw.Close(); // A very important step. Closes the file too.
            sw = null;  // Give it to the garbage collector.
        }
        catch (IOException ioErr)
        {
            // Error occurred during the processing of the file. Tell the user
            // the full name of the file and the default directory.

            // Directory class
            string dir = Directory.GetCurrentDirectory();

            // System.IO.Path class
            string path = Path.Combine(dir, fileName);
            Console.WriteLine($"Error on file {path}");

            // Now output the error message in the exception.
            Console.WriteLine(ioErr.Message);
        }
    }
    Console.Read();
}
```

TIP

Notice that the program nulls the sw reference after closing StreamWriter. A file object is useless after the file has been closed. It's good programming practice to null a reference after it becomes invalid so that you won't try to use it again. (If you do, your code will throw an exception, letting you know about it!) Closing the file and nulling the reference lets the garbage collector claim it (see Book 2 Chapter 5 to meet the friendly collector on your route) and leaves the file available for other programs to open.

REMEMBER

The exception handling used in this example provides complete information as to the cause of failure to open the file for writing. Because the user can't see what's going on with a file in most cases, it's important to provide good error trapping and handling.

TECHNICAL STUFF

WORKING WITH PATH CHARACTERS

Notice the string `path = Path.Combine(dir, fileName);` line in the catch block for the `Main()` method. The `Combine()` method is smart enough to realize that for a file like `c:\test.txt`, the path isn't in the current directory. `Path.Combine()` is also the safest way to ensure that the two path segments being combined will combine correctly, including a path separator character between them.

In Windows, the normal path separator character is \, but you can make the / character used on Linux systems work fine in most cases. You can obtain the correct separator for whatever operating system your code is running on, whether it's Windows or some brand of Linux, by using `Path.DirectorySeparatorChar`. The .NET Framework library is full of features like that, clearly aimed at writing C# programs that run on multiple operating systems.

Using some better fishing gear: The using statement

TECHNICAL STUFF

Now that you've seen `FileStream` and `StreamWriter` in action, it's important to point out the usual way to do stream writing in C# — inside a `using` statement:

```
using (<someresource>)
{
  // Use the resource.
}
```

The `using` statement is a construct that automates the process of cleaning up after using a stream. On encountering the closing curly brace of the `using` block, C# manages "flushing" the stream and closing it for you. (To *flush* a stream is to push any last bytes left over in the stream's buffer out to the associated file before it gets closed. Think of pushing a handle to drain the last water out of your . . . trout stream.) Employing `using` eliminates the common error of forgetting to flush and close a file after writing to it. Don't leave open files lying around. Without `using`, you'd need to write

```
Stream fileStream = null;
TextWriter writer = null;
try
{
  // Create and use the stream, then ...
}
finally
```

```
{
  stream.Flush();
  stream.Close();
  stream = null;
}
```

Note how the code declares the stream and writer above the `try` block (so they're visible throughout the method). It also declares the `fileStream` and `writer` variables using abstract base classes rather than the concrete types `FileStream` and `StreamWriter`. That's a good practice. The code sets them to `null` so that the compiler won't complain about uninitialized variables. The preferred way to write the key I/O code in the `FileWrite` example looks more like this:

```
// Prepare the file stream.
FileStream fs = File.Open(fileName,
                          FileMode.CreateNew,
                          FileAccess.Write);

// Pass the fs variable to the StreamWriter constructor in the using statement.
using (StreamWriter sw = new StreamWriter(fs))
{
  // sw exists only within the using block, which is a local scope.

  // Read one string at a time from the console, outputting each to the
  // FileStream open for writing.
  Console.WriteLine("Enter text; enter blank line to stop");

  while (true)
  {
    // Read next line from Console; quit if line is blank.
    string input = Console.ReadLine();

    if (input.Length == 0)
    {
      break;
    }

    // Write the line just read to output file via the stream.
    sw.WriteLine(input);

    // Loop back up to get another line and write it.
  }
} // sw goes away here, and fs is now closed. So ...

fs = null; // Make sure you can't try to access fs again.
```

The items in parentheses after the `using` keyword are its "resource acquisition" section, where you allocate one or more resources such as streams, readers/writers, fonts, and so on. (If you allocate more than one resource, they have to be of the same type.) Following that section is the enclosing block, bounded by the outer curly braces.

REMEMBER

The `using` statement's block is not a loop. The block only defines a local scope, like the `try` block or a method's block. (Variables defined within the block, including its head, don't exist outside the block. Thus the `StreamWriter sw` isn't visible outside the `using` block.) The "Focusing on scope rules" section of Book 1, Chapter 5 provides an introductory discussion of scope, but reading the entire chapter is helpful for a fuller understanding.

At the top of the preceding example, in the resource-acquisition section, you set up a resource — in this case, create a new `StreamWriter` wrapped around the already-existing `FileStream`. Inside the block is where you carry out all your I/O code for the file.

At the end of the `using` block, C# automatically flushes the `StreamWriter`, closes it, and closes the `FileStream`, also flushing any bytes it still contains to the file on disk. Ending the `using` block also *disposes* (signifies that the object is no longer needed to the garbage collector) the `StreamWriter` object — see the warning and the technical discussion coming up.

TIP

It's a good practice to wrap most work with streams in `using` statements. Wrapping the `StreamWriter` or `StreamReader` in a `using` statement, for example, has the same effect as putting the use of the writer or reader in a `try...finally` exception-handling block. (See Book 1, Chapter 9 for a discussion of exceptions.) In fact, the compiler translates the `using` block into the same code it uses for a `try...finally`, which guarantees that the resources get cleaned up:

```
try
{
  // Allocate the resource and use it here.
}
finally
{
  // Close and dispose of the resource here.
}
```

WARNING

After the `using` block, the `StreamWriter` no longer exists, and the `FileStream` object can no longer be accessed. The `fs` variable still exists, assuming that you created the stream outside the `using` statement, rather than on the fly like this:

```
using (StreamWriter sw = new StreamWriter(new FileStream(...)) ...
```

Flushing and closing the writer has flushed and closed the stream as well. If you try to carry out operations on the stream, you get an exception telling you that you can't access a closed object. Notice that in the `FileWriter` code earlier in this section the code sets the `FileStream` object, `fs`, to `null` after the `using` block to ensure the code won't try to use `fs` again. After that, the `FileStream` object is handed off to the garbage collector.

TECHNICAL STUFF

Specifically, `using` is aimed at managing the cleanup of objects that implement the `IDisposable` interface (see Book 2, Chapter 7 for information on interfaces). The `using` statement ensures that the object's `Dispose()` method gets called. Classes that implement `IDisposable` guarantee that they have a `Dispose()` method. `IDisposable` is mainly about disposing non-.NET resources, mainly stuff in the outside world of the Windows operating system, such as file handles and graphics resources. `FileStream`, for example, wraps a Windows file handle that must be released. (Many classes and `structs` implement `IDisposable`; your classes can, too, if necessary.)

This book doesn't delve into `IDisposable`, but you should plan to become more familiar with it as your C# powers grow. Implementing it correctly has to do with the kind of indeterminate garbage disposal mentioned briefly in Book 2, Chapter 5 and can be complex. So `using` is for use with classes and `structs` that implement `IDisposable`, which is something that you can check at `https://docs.microsoft.com/dotnet/standard/garbage-collection/using-objects`. It won't help you with just *any* old kind of object. *Note:* The intrinsic C# types — `int`, `double`, `char`, and such — do *not* implement `IDisposable`. Class `TextWriter`, the base class for `StreamWriter`, does implement the interface like this:

```
public abstract class TextWriter : MarshalByRefObject, IDisposable
```

When in doubt, check C# Language Help to see whether the classes or `structs` you plan to use implement `IDisposable`. You can always call `Dispose()` on any object that implements it to free up resources. It's also possible to call `myObject.Dispose()` to determine whether the object implements `IDisposable`. If you see an error, then the object doesn't implement `IDisposable`.

Pulling Them Out of the Stream: Using StreamReader

Writing to a file is cool, but it's sort of worthless if you can't read the file later. The following `FileRead` program puts the *input* back into the phrase *file I/O*. This program reads a text file like the ones created by `FileWrite` or by Notepad — it's sort of `FileWrite` in reverse:

```
static void Main(string[] args)
{
    // Get the name of a file to process. If the user doesn't
    // provide one, exit with an error code of -1.
    Console.Write("Enter the name of a text file to read: ");
    String filename = Console.ReadLine();
    if (filename.Length == 0)
    {
        Console.WriteLine("No filename provided, exiting.");
        Environment.Exit(-1);
    }

    // Verify that the file actually exists. If not, then exit
    // with a -2 error code.
    if (!File.Exists(filename))
    {
        Console.WriteLine("The File doesn't exit!");
        Console.ReadLine();
        Environment.Exit(-2);
    }

    // Open the file for processing by creaing a FileStream and
    // a StreamReader with a using statement.
    using (StreamReader sr = new StreamReader(filename))
    {
        Console.WriteLine("\nContents of File:");

        // Proces the file one line at a time.
        while (!sr.EndOfStream)
        {
            String input = sr.ReadLine();
            Console.WriteLine(input);
        }
    }

    Console.ReadLine();
}
```

The first thing you should notice about this example is just how much shorter it is than the `FileWrite` example. That's not because `FileWrite` bears all the burden and `FileRead` is on a luxury cruise. The `FileWrite` example is important because it demonstrates modularization techniques that you can employ for complex file situations. The `FileRead` example is important because it demonstrates the latest techniques in handling less complex file-handling situations. You could easily re-code `FileWrite` using this style and it would perform just as well.

This example also provides you with a different view of error trapping and handling. Rather than rely on exceptions (the error has aleady happened), it relies on built-in functions to determine whether an error is about to occur. Yes, that's right: This example has precognition! It also adds the use of external error codes. You can use these error codes in a batch file to perform tasks in batches without actually having to watch them complete one by one, slowly dropping off to sleep as you do and then banging your head on the keyboard. Rather, you use the error codes to create log entries that tell you when things don't work properly. Checking for things that could go wrong is generally faster than handling an exception and considered better programming practice.

Notice that this example also relies on a form of the `using` statement so that you can see it in action. Instead of creating a separate `FileStream`, this example relies on a special `StreamReader` constructor that accepts a filename as input. The `FileStream` is still created — you just don't have to mess with it.

During the file reading process, the `while` loop relies on a check of `!sr.EndOfStream` to determine when to stop reading data from the file. The `EndOfStream` property becomes true when the last bit of data is read from the file. In short, this example demonstrates a number of tricks you can use to make your code extremely short.

TIP

For an example of reading arbitrary *bytes* from a file — which could be either binary or text — see the `LoopThroughFiles` example in Book 1, Chapter 7. The program actually loops through all files in a target directory, reading each file and dumping its contents to the console, so it gets tedious if there are lots of files. Feel free to terminate it by pressing Ctrl+C or by clicking the console window's close box. See the discussion of `BinaryReader` in the next section.

More Readers and Writers

Earlier in this chapter, you see the `StreamReader` and `StreamWriter` classes that you'll probably use for the bulk of your I/O needs. However, .NET also makes several other reader/writer pairs available:

- `BinaryReader`/`BinaryWriter`: A pair of stream classes that contain methods for reading and writing each value type: `ReadChar()`, `WriteChar()`, `ReadByte()`, `WriteByte()`, and so on. (These classes are a little more primitive: They don't offer `ReadLine()`/`WriteLine()` methods.) The classes are useful for reading or writing an object in binary (not human-readable) format, as opposed to text. You can use an array of `bytes` to work with the binary data as raw bytes. For example, you may need to read or write the bytes that make up a bitmap graphics file.

Experiment: Open a file with a `.EXE` extension using Notepad. You may see some readable text in the window, but most of it looks like some sort of garbage. That's binary data.

The "Formatting the output lines" section of Chapter 7 in Book 1 includes an example, mentioned earlier, that reads binary data. The example uses a `BinaryReader` with a `FileStream` object to read chunks of bytes from a file and then writes out the data on the console in hexadecimal (base 16) notation, which is explained in that chapter. Although it wraps a `FileStream` in the more convenient `BinaryReader`, that example could just as easily have used the `FileStream` itself. The reads are identical. Although the `BinaryReader` brings nothing to the table in that example, it's used there to provide an example of this reader. The example does illustrate reading raw bytes into a *buffer* (an array big enough to hold the bytes read).

- `StringReader`/`StringWriter`: And now for something a little more exotic: simple reader and writer classes that are limited to reading and writing `string`s. They let you treat a `string` like a file, an alternative to accessing a `string`'s characters in the usual ways, such as with a `foreach` loop

```
foreach (char c in someString) { Console.Write(c); }
```

or with array-style bracket notation ([ ])

```
char c = someString[3];
```

or with `String` methods like `Split()`, Concatenate(), and `IndexOf()`. With `StringReader`/`StringWriter`, you read from and write to a `string` much as you would to a file. This technique is useful for long strings with hundreds or thousands of characters (such as an entire text file read into a `string`) that you want to process in bunches, and it provides a handy way to work with a `StringBuilder`.

When you create a `StringReader`, you initialize it with a `string` to read. When you create a `StringWriter`, you can pass a `StringBuilder` object to it or create it empty. Internally, the `StringWriter` stores a `StringBuilder` — either the one you passed to its constructor or a new, empty one. You can get at the internal `StringBuilder`'s contents by calling `StringWriter`'s `ToString()` method.

Each time you read from the string (or write to it), the "file pointer" advances to the next available character past the read or write. Thus, as with file I/O, you have the notion of a "current position." When you read, say, 10 characters from a 1,000-character string, the position is set to the eleventh character after the read.

The methods in these classes parallel those described earlier for the `Stream-Reader` and `StreamWriter` classes. If you can use those, you can use these.

Exploring More Streams than Lewis and Clark

File streams are not the only kinds of `Stream` classes available. The flood of `Stream` classes includes (but probably is not limited to) those in the following list. Note that unless otherwise specified, these stream classes all live in the `System.IO` namespace.

- `FileStream`: For reading and writing files on a disk.
- `MemoryStream`: Manages reading and writing data to a block of memory. You see this technique sometimes in unit tests, to avoid actually interacting with the (slow, possibly troublesome) file system. In this way, you can fake a file when testing code that reads and writes.

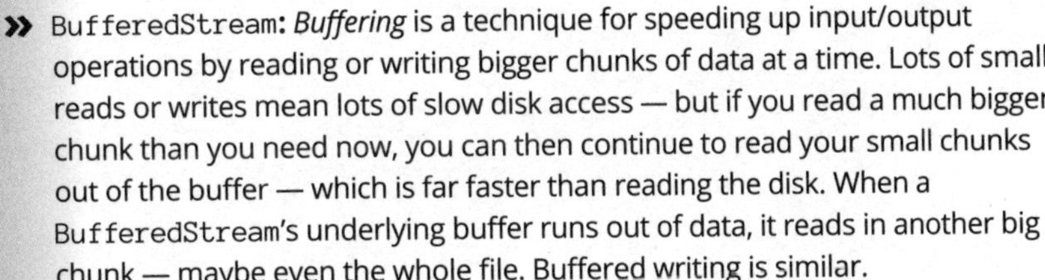

- `BufferedStream`: *Buffering* is a technique for speeding up input/output operations by reading or writing bigger chunks of data at a time. Lots of small reads or writes mean lots of slow disk access — but if you read a much bigger chunk than you need now, you can then continue to read your small chunks out of the buffer — which is far faster than reading the disk. When a `BufferedStream`'s underlying buffer runs out of data, it reads in another big chunk — maybe even the whole file. Buffered writing is similar.

  Class `FileStream` automatically buffers its operations, so `BufferedStream` is for special cases, such as working with a `NetworkStream` to read and write bytes over a network. In this case, you wrap the `BufferedStream` around the `NetworkStream`, effectively "chaining" streams. When you write to the `BufferedStream`, it writes to the underlying `NetworkStream`, and so on.

  When you're wrapping one stream around another, you're *composing streams*. (You can look it up in C# Language Help for more information.) The earlier sidebar, "Wrap my fish in newspaper," discusses wrapping.

- `NetworkStream`: Manages reading and writing data over a network. See `BufferedStream` for a simplified discussion of using it. `NetworkStream` is in the `System.Net.Sockets` namespace because it uses a technology called *sockets* to make connections across a network.
- `UnmanagedMemoryStream`: Lets you read and write data in unmanaged blocks of memory. *Unmanaged* means, basically, "not .NET" and not managed by the .NET runtime and its garbage collector. This is advanced stuff, dealing with interaction between .NET code and code written under the Windows operating system.
- `CryptoStream`: Located in the `System.Security.Cryptography` namespace, this stream class lets you pass data to and from an encryption or decryption transformation.

IN THIS CHAPTER

» Taking a tour of the `System.Net` namespace

» Using built-in tools to access the network

» Making the network tools work for you

Chapter 4
Accessing the Internet

The .NET Framework is designed from the ground up to take the Internet and networking in general into consideration. Not surprisingly, the emphasis on connectivity in every form is nowhere more clear than it is in the `System.Net` namespace (`https://docs.microsoft.com/dotnet/api/system.net`). The Internet takes first chair here, with web tools taking up 13 of the classes in the namespace.

`System.Net` is a big, meaty namespace, and finding your way around it can be difficult, so this chapter begins with an overview of the namespace. The chapter then discusses tasks that you perform often and shows the basics of performing them. Next, you find out about the tools to research complex features of the classes.

Networking is a big part of the .NET Framework, and all the functionality is in this namespace. An entire book can be (and has been) written on the subject. For the purposes of this introduction to networking with C#, this chapter shows you the following features:

- Getting a file from the network
- Sending email
- Logging transfers
- Checking the status of the network around your running application

Keep in mind that sockets, IPv6, and other advanced Internet protocols are important, but many developers don't currently use them every day. This chapter talks about the parts of the namespace that you will use every day. As always, there is more to discover about `System.Net`.

REMEMBER

You don't have to type the source code for this chapter manually. In fact, using the downloadable source is a lot easier. You can find the source for this chapter in the `\CSAIO4D2E\BK03\CH04` folder of the downloadable source. See the Introduction for details on how to find these source files.

Getting to Know System.Net

The `System.Net` namespace is full of classes that are confusing if viewed in the documentation, but make a lot of sense when used in an application. The namespace removes all the complexity of dealing with the various protocols used on the Internet.

There are more than 4,000 RFCs for Internet protocols (an *RFC* is a Request For Comments, a document that is sent to a standards body for review by peers before it becomes a standard). You can obtain copies of these RFCs in locations such as `https://www.rfc-editor.org/standards` and `http://www.faqs.org/rfcs/`. If you have to learn all the RFCs separately, you'll never complete your project. The `System.Net` namespace is about making network coding less painful.

`System.Net` isn't just for web projects. Like everything else in the base class library, you can use `System.Net` with all kinds of projects. You can

- » Get information from web pages on the Internet and use it on your programs.
- » Move files via the Internet using FTPs.
- » Send email easily.
- » Use more advanced network structures.
- » Secure communications over the Internet using the SSL protocol.

If you need to check on the connectivity of a computer from a Windows application, you can use `System.Net`. If you need to build a class that will download a file from a website, `System.Net` is the namespace you need. Just because most classes relate to the Internet doesn't mean that only web applications can use it. That's the magic of `System.Net`. Any application can be connected to another application through an Application Programming Interface (API) that you access using `System.Net` functionality. While some parts of the namespace function to make the development of web applications easier, the namespace in general is designed to make any application work with networks that adhere to web standards (including an intranet accessible within your organization).

How Net Classes Fit into the Framework

The `System.Net` namespace contains a large number of classes and smaller namespaces. The number of classes and namespaces increases with each version of the .NET Framework, so it pays to look after each update to see what new goodies are present. The number may seem overwhelming. However, if you look closely, you can see patterns. The following sections discuss the smaller namespaces and provide a listing of essential System.Net namespace classes.

Understanding the System.Net subordinate namespaces

When you view the System.Net documentation at `https://docs.microsoft.com/dotnet/api/system.net`, you see a few subordinate namespaces listed in the "See Also" section of the page. However, this isn't a complete list, and there really are a number of additional subordinate namespaces you need to know about, as shown in Table 4-1. The Latest Full Implementation column tells you the latest version of .NET that contains the full set of classes for the namespace. Later versions may remove some functionality from the namespace.

TABLE 4-1 **A Listing of Important System.Net-Associated Namespaces**

Namespace	Purpose	Latest Full Implementation	Link
`System.Net.Cache`	A *cache* provides the means to improve application performance by storing commonly used resources. This namespace works with the `WebRequest` and `HttpWebRequest` classes to improve web-based application speed by creating cache policies.	6.0	`https://docs.microsoft.com/dotnet/api/system.net.cache`
`System.Net.Configuration`	Manages the configuration settings for web-based applications. These settings affect all the other System.Net namespaces and classes.	4.8	`https://docs.microsoft.com/dotnet/api/system.net.configuration`

(continued)

TABLE 4-1 *(continued)*

Namespace	Purpose	Latest Full Implementation	Link
`System.Net.Http`	Provides the functionality needed to create HTTP applications. It's where you find the client, content, message, request, and response-oriented classes. The .NET Framework 5.0 provides some enhancements to this namespace.	6.0	`https://docs.microsoft.com/dotnet/api/system.net.http`
`System.Net.Http.Headers`	Contains the classes for managing the headers used with the `System.Net.Http` namespace. In many cases, these headers are defined as part of RFC 2616 (`http://www.faqs.org/rfcs/rfc2616.html`).	6.0	`https://docs.microsoft.com/dotnet/api/system.net.http.headers`
`System.Net.Mail`	Allows sending (not receiving) of email using the Simple Mail Transfer Protocol (SMTP). The classes follow RFC 2821 (`http://www.faqs.org/rfcs/rfc2821.html`) among other standards.	6.0	`https://docs.microsoft.com/dotnet/api/system.net.mail`
`System.Net.Mime`	Contains classes that provide Multipurpose Internet Mail Exchange (MIME) support for the `Content-Type`, `Content-Disposition`, and `Content-transfer-Encoding` headers used with the `SmtpClient` class. The classes follow RFC 2045 (`http://www.faqs.org/rfcs/rfc2045.html`) among other standards.	6.0	`https://docs.microsoft.com/dotnet/api/system.net.mime`
`System.Net.NetworkInformation`	Obtains network data that includes traffic data, network address information, and notification of address changes for the local computer. This is also where you find an implementation of the Ping utility (`https://docs.microsoft.com/dotnet/api/system.net.networkinformation.ping`) that allows verification of remote host status.	6.0	`https://docs.microsoft.com/dotnet/api/system.net.networkinformation`

Namespace	Purpose	Latest Full Implementation	Link
`System.Net.PeerToPeer`	Provides access to peer-to-peer networking functionality. It provides an implementation of the Peer Name Resolution Protocol (PNRP) discussed at `https://docs.microsoft.com/dotnet/framework/network-programming/peer-name-resolution-protocol`.	4.8	`https://docs.microsoft.com/dotnet/api/system.net.peertopeer`
`System.Net.PeerToPeer.Collaboration`	Enhances the `System.Net.PeerToPeer` namespace functionality. It provides the functionality needed for serverless managed collaboration sessions.	4.8	`https://docs.microsoft.com/dotnet/api/System.Net.PeerToPeer.Collaboration`
`System.Net.Security`	Allows secure communication using network streams. This namespace received significant updates in .NET 5.0 and .NET 6.0.	6.0	`https://docs.microsoft.com/dotnet/api/System.Net.Security`
`System.Net.Sockets`	Implements Windows Sockets (Winsock) functionality (see `https://docs.microsoft.com/windows/win32/winsock/getting-started-with-winsock` for details), which allows firm control over network communications.	4.8	`https://docs.microsoft.com/dotnet/api/System.Net.Sockets`
System.Net.WebSockets	Implements Web Sockets (WebSocket) functionality (see `https://docs.microsoft.com/aspnet/core/fundamentals/websockets` for details), which allows two-way persistent communication channels over TCP connections. The .NET Framework 6.0 provides some enhancements to this namespace.	6.0	`https://docs.microsoft.com/dotnet/api/System.Net.WebSockets`

Working with the System.Net classes

The `System.Net` classes are well named, and you will note that a few protocols get a number of classes each. After you translate the entry names, you can narrow down what you need based on the way the protocol is named:

- `Authentication` and `Authorization`: These classes provide security.
- `Cookie`: This class manages cookies from web browsers and usually is used in ASP.NET pages.
- `DNS` (Domain Name Services): These classes help to resolve domain names into IP addresses.
- `Download`: This class is used to get files from servers.
- `EndPoint`: This class helps to define a network node.
- `FileWeb`: This brilliant set of classes describes network file servers as local classes.
- `FtpWeb`: This class is a simple File Transfer Protocol implementation.
- `Http` (HyperText Transfer Protocol): This class is the web protocol.
- `IP` (Internet Protocol): This class helps to define network endpoints that are specifically Internet related.
- `NetworkCredential`: This class is another security implementation.
- `Service`: This class helps manage network connections.
- `Socket`: This class deals with the most primitive of network connections.
- `Upload`: This set of classes helps you upload information to the Internet.
- `Web`: These classes help with the World Wide Web — largely implementations of the `http` classes that are more task oriented.

This list is extensive because the classes build on each other. The `EndPoint` classes are used by the `socket` classes to define certain network specifics, and the `IP` classes make them specific to the Internet. The `Web` classes are specific to the World Wide Web. You will rarely use the highest-level classes, but it's often tough to see what is needed when. Most of the functions that you use every day, though, are encapsulated within the namespaces found in Table 4-1.

Using the System.Net Namespace

The `System.Net` namespace is *code oriented*, which means that few implementations are specifically for user interfaces. Almost everything that you do with these classes is behind the scenes. You have few drag-and-drop user controls — the `System.Net` namespace is used in the Code View. To demonstrate this fact, the examples in the remainder of the chapter build a Windows Forms application that has the following requirements:

- » Check the network status.
- » Get a specific file from the Internet.
- » Email it to a specific email address (or addresses).
- » Log the whole transaction.

Checking the network status

First, you need to inform the user about network connectivity using the `Network-Tools` example. To begin, create a Windows Forms application using the same steps as found in the "Creating the data access project" section of Chapter 2 of this minibook (making the requisite changes for example name and location), and then follow these steps when you see the form displayed:

1. **Add a `StatusStrip` control to the lower left of the form by dragging it from the Menus & Toolbars group of the Toolbox.**

   The `StatusStrip` automatically takes up the entire bottom area of the form.

2. **Select the SmartTag that appears on the left side of the `StatusStrip` and add three `StatusLabels`.**

   Figure 4-1 shows how the dropdown entries appear when you click the down arrow in the box.

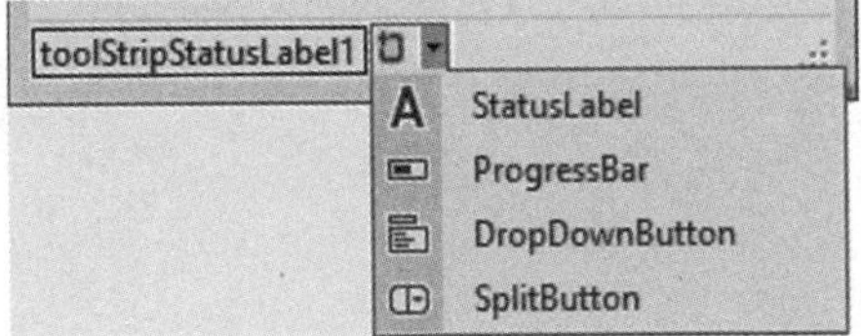

FIGURE 4-1: Many controls come with SmartTags that let you configure them easily.

3. **Select each** `StatusLabel` **in turn and configure it for displaying network and application status.**

   Configure your `StatusLabel` controls like this:

   - `toolStripStatusLabel1`: Set `(Name)` to `NetStatus` and `Text` to `Not Connected`.
   - `toolStripStatusLabel2`: Set `(Name)` to `PictureStatus` and `Text` to `Not Downloaded`.
   - `toolStripStatusLabel3`: Set `(Name)` to `EmailStatus` and `Text` to `No Email Sent.0`

   Figure 4-2 shows how your `StatusStrip` should appear at this point.

FIGURE 4-2: Configure the `StatusStrip` to provide the user with useful information.

4. **Double-click the form.**

   Visual Studio creates the `Form1_Load()` method and displays the Code Editor for you.

5. **Reference the** `System.Net` **namespace by adding the line** `using System.Net.NetworkInformation;` **to the top of the code.**

6. **Add the following code to** `Form1_Load()` **to test whether the network is available and display it on the status bar:**

```
private void Form1_Load(object sender, EventArgs e)
{
    if (NetworkInterface.GetIsNetworkAvailable())
    {
        NetStatus.Text = "Connected";
    }
    else
    {
        NetStatus.Text = "Disconnected";
    }
}
```

That's all there is to it. The `NetworkInformation` class contains a bunch of information about the status of the network, current IP addresses, the gateway being used by the current machine, and more.

TIP

Keep in mind that the `NetworkInformation` class will work only on a local machine. If you use this class in an ASP.NET Web Forms application, you will get information about the server.

Downloading a file from the Internet

You can get a file from the Internet in one of several ways, and one of the most common is by using hypertext transfer protocol (HTTP). You can find something to download from HTTP sites across the web today, so it's an important protocol to know. To build an application that uses HTTP, start with the example from the previous section and follow these steps:

1. **Drag a** `Button` **control onto the form from the Toolbox.**
2. **Type** &Download **in the button's** `Text` **property and** btnDownload **in the button's** `(Name)` **property.**
3. **Double-click the button.**

   Visual Studio creates the `btnDownload_Click()` method and displays the Code Editor for you.
4. **Add the following imports to the top of the coding area:**

   ```
   using System.Net;
   using System.IO;
   ```
5. **Create a new method called** `DownloadFile` **that accepts a** `remoteFile` **and a** `localFile` **as type** `string`**.**
6. **Type the following code into the** `DownloadFile()` **method:**

   ```
   private void DownLoadFile(string remoteFile, string localFile)
   {
       // Create the stream and request objects.
       FileStream localFileStream = File.Create(localFile);
       HttpWebRequest httpRequest =
           (HttpWebRequest)WebRequest.Create(remoteFile);

       // Configure the request.
       httpRequest.Method = WebRequestMethods.Http.Get;

       // Configure the response to the request.
       WebResponse httpResponse = httpRequest.GetResponse();
   ```

```
        Stream httpResponseStream = httpResponse.GetResponseStream();
        byte[] buffer = new byte[1024];

        // Process the response by downloading data.
        int bytesRead = httpResponseStream.Read(buffer, 0, 1024);
        while (bytesRead > 0)
        {
            localFileStream.Write(buffer, 0, bytesRead);
            bytesRead = httpResponseStream.Read(buffer, 0, 1024);
        }

        // Close the streams.
        localFileStream.Close();
        httpResponseStream.Close();

        // Update the status strip.
        PictureStatus.Text = "Picture Downloaded";
    }
```

The code follows a process of establishing a connection, configuring the connection, configuring a response to that connection, and then performing a task. In this case, the task is to download a file from the HTTP site. You must always close the streams when you finish performing a task.

7. **Call the** `DownloadFile()` **method from the** `btnDownload_Click()` **event handler by using the following code:**

```
private void btnDownload_Click(object sender, EventArgs e)
{
    // Obtain the file.
    DownLoadFile(@"http://blog.johnmuellerbooks.com/" +
        "wp-content/uploads/2014/06/cropped-country01-1.jpg",
        @"c:\temp\Country_Scene.jpg");
}
```

To use this example, you must replace the first string with the location of a file on your HTTP site and the second string with the location on your hard drive where you want the file to go. In this HTTP example, the `WebRequest` and `WebResponse` classes in the `System.Net` namespace are fully utilized to create the more complete `HttpWebRequest` and properties such as the method of download.

In fact, the toughest part of this process is dealing with a `FileStream` object, which is still the best way to move files and is not specific to the `System.Net` namespace. Streams are discussed in Chapter 3 of this minibook, which covers the `System.IO` namespace, but they have significance to the network classes too.

Streams represent a flow of data of some kind, and a flow of information from the Internet qualifies.

That's what you are doing when you get a web page or a file from the Internet — gathering a flow of data. If you think about it, it makes sense that this is a flow, because the status bar in an application shows a percentage of completion. Just like pouring water into a glass, the flow of data is a stream, so the concept is named `Stream`.

Emailing a status report

Email is a common requirement of networked systems. This example works fine with your personal email, but you need to know the SMTP server address (required when you set up your email application), your username, and your password to make it work. If you are working in an enterprise environment, you are going to write a larger-scale application to handle all email requirements, rather than make each individual application email-aware. However, if you are writing a stand-alone product, it might require email support.

1. **Add four `TextBox` controls named `EmailAddress`, `SMTPServer`, `Username`, and `Password`, and four `Label` controls to the default form in Design View.**

   Your form should look similar to the one shown in Figure 4-3.

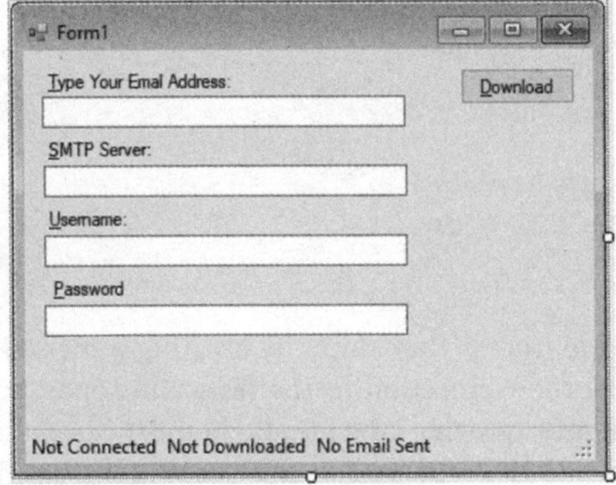

FIGURE 4-3: Configuring the form to accept email information.

2. **Change to Code View.**
3. **Add the following imports to the top of the coding area:**

```
using System.Net.Mail;
```

4. **Create a new method called** `SendEmail()` **that accepts** `fromAddress`, `toAddress`, `subject`, **and** `body`, **all of type** `string`.

   It should accept the from email address, the to email address, the subject of the email, and the body of the email.

5. **Type the following code into the** `SendEmail()` **method:**

```
private void SendEmail(string fromAddress, string toAddress,
    string subject, string body)
{
    // Define the message.
    MailMessage message =
        new MailMessage(fromAddress, toAddress, subject, body);

    // Configure the credentials.
    NetworkCredential Creds =
        new NetworkCredential(Username.Text, Password.Text);

    // Create the connection and send the message.
    SmtpClient mailClient = new SmtpClient(SMTPServer.Text)
    {
        Credentials = Creds
    };
    mailClient.Send(message);

    // Release the message and client.
    message = null;
    mailClient = null;

    // Update the status strip.
    EmailStatus.Text = "Email Sent";
}
```

The example follows a process that starts by creating a message. It then creates a client that provides the connection to the host and sends the message to the host. Notice that you must provide credentials (in most cases) to access the STMP server, and that you add these as part of the `SmtpClient` configuration as `Credentials`. The last step is to release the message and client so that the garbage collector can reclaim them.

After you have written your method, you need to call it after the file is downloaded in the `btnDownload_Click()` event handler. Change the code of that subroutine to the following to call that method:

```
private void btnDownload_Click(object sender, EventArgs e)
{
    // Obtain the file.
    DownLoadFile(@"http://blog.johnmuellerbooks.com/" +
        "wp-content/uploads/2014/06/cropped-country01-1.jpg",
        @"c:\temp\Country_Scene.jpg");

    // Send a success message.
    SendEmail(EmailAddress.Text, EmailAddress.Text,
        "HTTP Successful", "Picture Successfully Downloaded");
}
```

The example uses the value of the `EmailAddress` text box twice: once for the to address, and once for the from address. This isn't always necessary, because you may have a situation in which you want the email to come only from a webmaster address or to go only to your address.

To run the application, provide your email address, SMTP server address, username, and password in the fields of the form. When you click Download, the application should download the file to the local drive and then email you to inform you that the download is complete. You will also see status information at the bottom of the application. A host of things can go wrong with network applications, though, and you should be aware of them. Here are a few:

- For most network activity, the machine running the software must be connected to a network. This isn't a problem for you as the developer, but you need to be conscious of the end users, who may need connectivity to have access to the features they want to use. Use of the network status code can help inform users about the availability of those features.
- Firewalls and other network appliances sometimes block network traffic from legitimate applications. Some examples of this include:
  - Network analysis features of .NET are often blocked on corporate servers. If the server is available to the public, these openings can cause holes for hackers to crawl through.
  - Speaking of hackers, make sure that if you use incoming network features in your application, you have adequately secured your application. More on this can be found in the excellent book *Writing Secure Code*, Second Edition, by Michael Howard and David C. LeBlanc (published by Microsoft Press).
  - Email is especially fragile. Often, Internet service providers will block email from an address that is not registered on a mail server. This means that if you are using your localhost server, your ISP might block the email.

» Network traffic is notoriously hard to debug. For instance, if the sample application works, but you never receive an email from the SmtpServer you coded, what went wrong? You may never know.

Logging network activity

This brings you to the next topic, which is network logging. Because network activity problems are so hard to debug and reproduce, Microsoft has built in several tools for the management of tracing network activity.

What's more, as with the ASP.NET tracing available, the `System.Net` namespace tracing is completely managed using the configuration files. To be able to use the functions, therefore, you don't need to change and recompile your code. In fact, with a little management, you can even show debug information to the user by managing the `config` files your application uses.

Each kind of application has a different kind of configuration file. For Windows Forms applications, which you are using here, the file is called `app.config` and is stored in the development project directory. When you compile, the name of the file is changed to the name of the application, and it's copied into the `bin` directory for running.

If you open your `app.config` file now by double-clicking its entry in Solution Explorer, you see that it has practically nothing in it (as shown in Listing 4-1). This is fairly new for .NET, which used to have very involved configuration. You will add some content to the configuration to get tracing turned on. Note that your `.NETFramework,Version` version number may vary from the one shown.

LISTING 4-1: The Default app.config File

```
<?xml version="1.0" encoding="utf-8" ?>
<configuration>
    <startup>
        <supportedRuntime version="v4.0"
                          sku=".NETFramework,Version=v4.7.2"/>
    </startup>
</configuration>
```

First, you need to add a new source for the `System.Net` namespace. Next, you add a switch to the `switches` section for the source you added. Finally, you add a `sharedlistener` to that section and set the file to flush the tracing information automatically. The finished `app.config` file, with the additions in bold, is shown in Listing 4-2.

LISTING 4-2: The Finished app.config File

```
<?xml version="1.0" encoding="utf-8" ?>
<configuration>
    <startup>
        <supportedRuntime version="v4.0"
                           sku=".NETFramework,Version=v4.5.2"/>
    </startup>
    <system.diagnostics>
      <sources>
        <source name="System.Net">
          <listeners>
            <add name="System.Net"/>
          </listeners>
        </source>
      </sources>
      <switches>
        <add name="System.Net" value="Verbose" />
      </switches>
      <sharedListeners>
        <add name="System.Net"
             type="System.Diagnostics.TextWriterTraceListener"
             initializeData="my.log"/>
      </sharedListeners>
      <trace autoflush="true" />
    </system.diagnostics>
</configuration>
```

Run the application again and watch the Output window. Advanced logging information is shown there because of your changes to the configuration file. Additionally, a log file was written. In the development environment, this is in the bin/debug directory of your project. You might have to click the Show All Files button at the top of the Solution Explorer to see it.

In that folder, you should see the file named `my.log`, where the `SharedListener` you added to the `app.config` file directed the logging information. Listing 4-3 shows how the content of this file could appear. The specific URLs, reference numbers, and other object values will differ in your output, but you should see something similar to the output shown here (which has been edited for brevity):

```
System.Net Verbose: 0 : [15048] Entering WebRequest::Create(http://blog.
   johnmuellerbooks.com/wp-content/uploads/2014/06/cropped-country01-1.jpg)
System.Net Verbose: 0 : [15048] Entering HttpWebRequest#33675143::HttpWebRequest
   (http://blog.johnmuellerbooks.com/wp-content/uploads/2014/06/
   cropped-country01-1.jpg#-113598309)
System.Net Information: 0 : [15048] Current OS installation type is 'Client'.
```

```
System.Net Information: 0 : [15048] RAS supported: True
System.Net Verbose: 0 : [15048] Exiting HttpWebRequest#33675143::
   HttpWebRequest()
System.Net Verbose: 0 : [15048] Exiting WebRequest::Create()    ->
   HttpWebRequest#33675143
System.Net Verbose: 0 : [15048] Entering HttpWebRequest#33675143::GetResponse()
...
System.Net Information: 0 : [15048] HeaderCollection#39451090::Get(MIME-Version)
System.Net Information: 0 : [15048] HeaderCollection#39451090::Get(From)
System.Net Information: 0 : [15048] HeaderCollection#39451090::Get(To)
System.Net Information: 0 : [15048] HeaderCollection#39451090::Get(Date)
System.Net Information: 0 : [15048] HeaderCollection#39451090::Get(Subject)
System.Net Information: 0 : [15048] HeaderCollection#26753075::Get(Content-Type)
System.Net Information: 0 : [15048] HeaderCollection#26753075::Get(Cont
   ent-Transfer-Encoding)
System.Net Information: 0 : [15048] HeaderCollection#26753075::Get(Cont
   ent-Transfer-Encoding)
System.Net Information: 0 : [15048] HeaderCollection#26753075::Get(Cont
   ent-Transfer-Encoding)
System.Net Verbose: 0 : [15048] Exiting SmtpClient#13869071::Send()
```

Reading this file, you can see that the reference numbers that match the requests on the server all appear, dramatically improving the ease of debugging. Also, because everything is in order of action, finding out exactly where the error occurred in the process is much easier.

One of the more interesting entries is the series of three commands used to retrieve each block of data for the picture. The `ConnectStream` exits the previous read, enters a new read, and then downloads the data like this (along with the actual binary data):

```
System.Net Verbose: 0 : [15048] Exiting ConnectStream#47891719::Read()   ->
   Int32#1024
System.Net Verbose: 0 : [15048] Entering ConnectStream#47891719::Read()
System.Net Verbose: 0 : [15048] Data from ConnectStream#47891719::Read
```

IN THIS CHAPTER

» Understanding the System.Drawing namespace

» Determining where the drawing classes fit

» Creating a simple game application using System.Drawing

Chapter 5
Creating Images

No one is going to write the next edition of *Bioshock* using C# directly (although, you might do so using third-party products like Unity Gaming Services, https://unity.com/). It just isn't the kind of language you use to write graphics-intensive applications like shoot-'em-up games.

Still, C# packs a fair amount of power into the System.Drawing classes. (This chapter focuses on the Windows Forms method of creating graphics — the WPF method is different.) Though these classes are somewhat primitive in some areas, and using them might cause you to have to write a few more lines of code than you should, there isn't much that these classes can't do with sufficient work.

The drawing capability provided by the .NET Framework is divided into four logical areas by the namespace design provided by Microsoft. All the general drawing capability is in the System.Drawing namespace. Then there are some specialized namespaces:

» System.Drawing.2D has advanced vector drawing functionality.

» System.Drawing.Imaging is mostly about using bitmap graphic formats, like .bmp and .jpg files.

» System.Drawing.Text deals with advanced typography.

This chapter focuses on the base namespace and covers only the basics of drawing in C#. (Discussing every aspect of drawing could easily fill an entire book.)

REMEMBER

You don't have to type the source code for this chapter manually. In fact, using the downloadable source is a lot easier. You can find the source for this chapter in the \CSAIO4D2E\BK03\CH05 folder of the downloadable source. See the Introduction for details on how to find these source files.

Getting to Know System.Drawing

Even at the highest level, graphics programming consists of drawing polygons, filling them with color, and labeling them with text — all on a canvas of some sort. Unsurprisingly, this leaves you with four objects that form the core of the graphics code you write: graphics, pens, brushes, and text.

SYSTEM.DRAWING AND .NET CORE APPLICATIONS

You can't use System.Drawing with .NET Core applications. Instead, you must use the System.Drawing.Common namespace, which has somewhat less functionality, as you can see in articles like the one at https://www.hanselman.com/blog/how-do-you-use-systemdrawing-in-net-core. However, you do gain access to common features such as the following:

- System.Drawing.Bitmap
- System.Drawing.BitmapData
- System.Drawing.Brush
- System.Drawing.Font
- System.Drawing.Graphics
- System.Drawing.Icon

This book doesn't cover System.Drawing.Common in any depth because its use is similar to System.Drawing (only less capable). However, one thing you need to do to use it is add NuGet support for System.Drawing.Common to your application. To perform this task, you choose Tools➪NuGet Package Manager➪Manage NuGet Packages, enter **System.Drawing.Common** in the search field, and then add it to your application. Here's what you'll see:

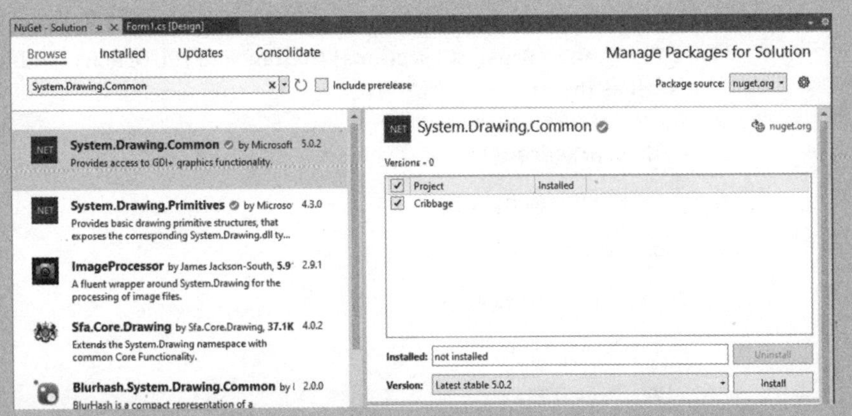

When working with non-Windows systems, you must also install the `libgdiplus` library (`https://www.mono-project.com/docs/gui/libgdiplus/`) on the host system to obtain `System.Drawing.Common` support because it isn't installed by default. If you move to .NET 6, the `System.Drawing.Common` namespace is supported only on Windows systems.

If you decide that you simply can't live with the limitations of `System.Drawing.Common`, some articles, such as the one at `https://photosauce.net/blog/post/5-reasons-you-should-stop-using-systemdrawing-from-aspnet`, discuss alternatives. You add these alternatives to your project using NuGet, just as you do for `System.Drawing.Common`, but the programming techniques will differ from `System.Drawing` use, so you'd be starting from scratch, which isn't possible for upgrade projects in many cases. The point is that you do have options available when working with .NET Core applications.

Graphics

Generally speaking, the `Graphics` class creates an object that is your canvas. All the methods and properties of the `Graphics` object are designed to make the area you draw upon more appropriate for your needs.

Also, most of the graphics- and image-related methods of other classes in the framework provide the `Graphics` object as output. For instance, you can call the `System.Web.Forms.Control.CreateGraphics` method from a Windows Forms application and get a `Graphics` object back that enables you to draw in a form control in your project. You can also handle the `Paint` event of a form, and check out the `Graphics` property of the event.

`Graphics` objects use pens and brushes (discussed later in this chapter, in the "Pens" and "Brushes" sections) to draw and fill. `Graphics` objects have methods such as these:

- `DrawRectangle`
- `FillRectangle`
- `DrawCircle`
- `FillCircle`
- `DrawBezier`
- `DrawPolygon`
- `DrawLine`

These methods accept pens and brushes as parameters. You might think, "How can a circle help me?" but you must remember that even complex graphic objects such as those found in *Halo Infinite* (`https://www.halowaypoint.com/`) are made up of circles and triangles — thousands of them. The trick to useful art is using math to put together lots of circles and triangles until you have a complete image. The sample application described later in this chapter is a simple example of just that.

Pens

You use pens to draw lines and curves. Complex graphics are made up of polygons, and those polygons are made of lines, and those lines are generated by pens. Pens have properties such as

- `Color`
- `DashStyle`
- `EndCap`
- `Width`

You get the idea: You use pens to draw things. These properties are used by the pens to determine how things are drawn.

Brushes

Brushes paint the insides of polygons. Though you use the pens to draw the shapes, you use brushes to fill in the shapes with gradients, patterns, or colors. Brushes are usually passed in as parameters to a `Fill`*`Whatever`* method of the pen objects. In most cases, the fill for the object comes first so that it doesn't overlap the object edges; then the pen draws the outline. The filling and the outlining use two different methods. (The brush object always stays inside the lines, though.)

Don't look for the `Brush` class (which is a base class), however. It's a holding area for the real brushes, which have kind of strange names. Brushes are made to be customized, but you can do a lot with the brushes that come with the framework as is. Some of the brushes include

- `SolidBrush`
- `TextureBrush`
- `HatchBrush`
- `PathGradientBrush`

Although the pens are used to pass into the `Draw` methods of the `Graphics` object, brushes are used to pass into the `Fill` methods that form polygons and other shapes.

Text

Text is painted with a combination of fonts and brushes. Just like polygons, the `Font` class uses brushes to fill in the lines of a text operation.

`System.Drawing.Text` has collections of all the fonts installed in the system running your program, or installed as part of your application. `System.Drawing.Font` has all the properties of the typography, such as

- Bold
- Size
- Style
- Underline

The `Graphics` object, again, provides the writing of the text on the canvas.

How the Drawing Classes Fit into the Framework

The `System.Drawing` namespace breaks drawing into two steps:

1. **Create a `System.Drawing.Graphics` object.**
2. **Use the tools in the `System.Drawing` namespace to draw on it.**

It seems straightforward, and it is. The first step is to get a `Graphics` object. `Graphics` objects come from two main places — existing images and Windows Forms.

To get a `Graphics` object from an existing image, look at the `Bitmap` object. The `Bitmap` object is a great tool that enables you to create an object using an existing image file. This gives you a new palette that is based on a bitmap image (a JPEG file, for example) that is already on your hard drive. It's a convenient tool, especially for web images.

```
Bitmap currentBitmap = new Bitmap(@"c:\images\myImage.jpg");
Graphics palette = Graphics.FromImage(currentBitmap);
```

Now the object `palette` is a `Graphics` object whose height and width are based on the image in `currentBitmap`. What's more, the base of the `palette` image looks exactly like the image referenced in the `currentBitmap` object.

You can use the pens, brushes, and fonts in the `Graphics` class to draw directly on that image, as though it were a blank canvas. It's possible to use a font to put text on images before showing them on web pages and to use other `Graphics` elements to modify the format of images on the fly, too.

Another way to get a `Graphics` object is to get it from Windows Forms. The preferred method is to catch the `Paint` event and use its `Graphics` object. However, you can also use the `System.Windows.Forms.Control.CreateGraphics()` method, but this approach means that the drawing could disappear when the control needs to refresh. This method gives you a new palette that is based on the drawing surface of the control being referenced. If it's a form, it inherits the height and width of the form and has the form background color. You can use pens and brushes to draw right on the form.

When you have a `Graphics` object, the options are endless. Sophisticated drawing isn't out of the question, though you would have to do a ton of work to create graphics like you see in *Halo* using Visual Studio. (There isn't a Master Chief class that you can just generate automatically.)

Nonetheless, even the most complex 3D graphics are just colored polygons, and you can make those with the `System.Drawing` namespace. The following sections build a cribbage board with a `Graphics` object, pens, brushes, and fonts.

Using the System.Drawing Namespace

Good applications come from strange places. Many people enjoy games, and one favorite in the United States (and many other places) is the card game cribbage (see some instruction on the basics at `https://www.dummies.com/games/card-games/cribbage/the-basics-of-cribbage/`). Say that you're on vacation and have the urge to play. You have the cards, but not a cribbage board.

You do have your laptop, Visual Studio, and the `System.Drawing` namespace. After just a few hours of work, you could build an application that serves as a working cribbage board! The `Cribbage` example in the following sections isn't quite complete (which would require a whole lot of code), but it does include enough code to get you started, and it's operational enough to let you play a game.

Getting started

Cribbage is a card game where hands are counted up into points, and the first player to score 121 points wins. It's up to the players to count the points, and the score is kept on a board.

Cribbage boards are made up of two lines of holes for pegs, usually totaling 120, but sometimes 60 holes are used and you play through twice. Figure 5-1 shows a typical cribbage board. Cribbage boards come in a bunch of styles — check out `www.cribbage.org` if you're curious; it has a great gallery of almost 100 boards, from basic to whimsical.

In this example, you create the board image for an application that keeps score of a cribbage game — but it wouldn't be beyond C# to write the cards into the game, too! So the board for this application has 40 holes on each of three pairs of lines, which is the standard board setup for two players playing to 120, as shown in Figure 5-2. The first task is to draw the board and then to draw the pegs as the players' scores — entered in text boxes — change.

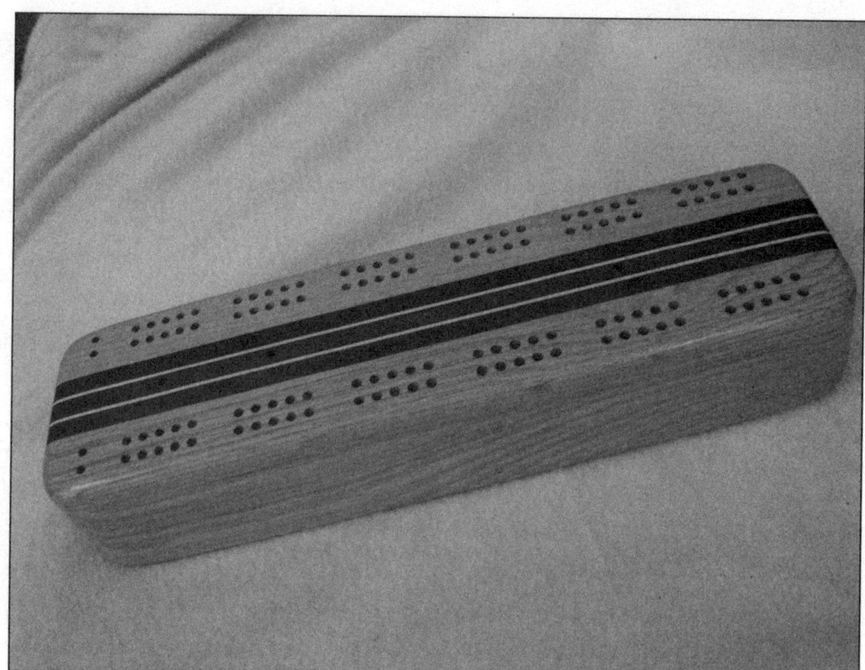

FIGURE 5-1: A traditional cribbage board.

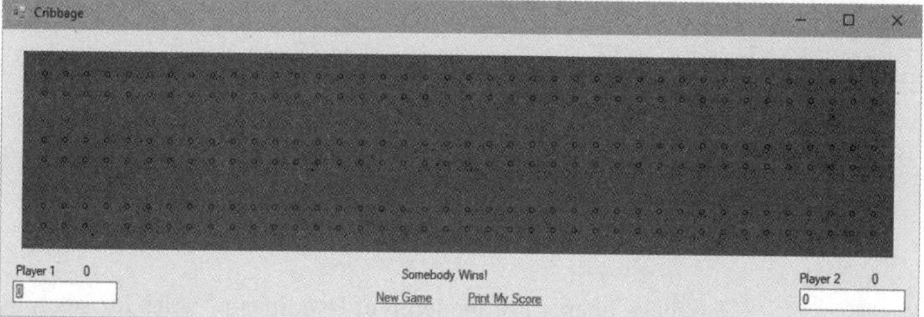

FIGURE 5-2: The digital cribbage board.

The premise is this: The players play a hand and enter the resulting scores in the text box below their respective names (refer to Figure 5-2). When the score for each hand is entered, the score next to the player's name is updated, and the back peg is moved on the board (making the current front peg, the back peg). The next time that same player scores a hand, the back peg is moved forward past the front peg the number of points scored, and the front peg becomes the back peg. The inventor of cribbage was paranoid of cheating, and the back peg makes this less likely. If you're unfamiliar with cribbage, you may want to check out the rules at `http://www.cribbage.org/`.

Setting up the project

To begin, create a playing surface. You set up the board shown in Figure 5-2 without drawing the board itself — you see later how to paint it with `System.Drawing` objects. Your board should look like Figure 5-3 when you're ready to start creating business rules. The various controls, from left to right (top to bottom), are named Player1Points (`Label`), Player1 (`TextBox`), WinMessage (`Label`), StartGame (`LinkLabel`), PrintMe (`LinkLabel`), Player2Points (`Label`), and Player2 (`TextBox`). (It also helps to set the `FormBorderStyle` property to `FixedSingle`.)

FIGURE 5-3: The basic board.

Handling the score

The following method, which handles score changes, is called from the text boxes' `Leave` event handlers. The reason you don't use the `TextChanged` event handler is that you want to be sure that the user has fully entered the score before you process it. Otherwise, each digit entered would count as another score addition. The method is purposely generic to make it easier to use the same code for both players.

```
// Fields used to keep track of score.
private int Player1LastTotal = 0;
private int Player2LastTotal = 0;

private void HandleScore(TextBox scoreBox, Label points,
    Label otherPlayer, ref Int32 lastScore)
{
    try
    {
        if (0 > Int32.Parse(scoreBox.Text) |
            Int32.Parse(scoreBox.Text) > 27)
        {
            // Display an error message and ensure the errant
            // score textbox has focus.
```

```
            scoreBox.Focus();
            WinMessage.Text = "Score must be between 0 and 27";
        }
        else
        {
            // Clear any error message.
            WinMessage.Text = "";

            // Update the last score.
            lastScore = Int32.Parse(points.Text);

            // Add the score written to the points
            points.Text = (Int32.Parse(points.Text) +
                Int32.Parse(scoreBox.Text)).ToString();

            // Reset the score text.
            scoreBox.Text = "0";

            // Change the focus to the next player.
            if (scoreBox.Name == "Player1")
                Player2.Focus();
            else
                Player1.Focus();
        }
    }
    catch (System.FormatException ext)
    {
        // Something other than a number
        if (scoreBox.Text.Length > 0)
        {
            scoreBox.Focus();
            WinMessage.Text = "Score must be a number";
        }
    }
    catch (Exception ex)
    {
        // Eek!
        scoreBox.Focus();
        MessageBox.Show("Something went wrong!  " + ex.Message);
    }

    // Check the score
    if (Int32.Parse(points.Text) > 120)
    {
        // Make it possible to print the score.
        PrintMe.Visible = true;

        if (Int32.Parse(points.Text) /
            Int32.Parse(otherPlayer.Text) > 1.5)
```

```
        {
            WinMessage.Text = scoreBox.Name + " Skunked 'em!!!";
        }
        else
        {
            WinMessage.Text = scoreBox.Name + " Won!!";
        }
        WinMessage.Visible = true;
    }
}
```

The code begins by creating two variables to hold the player score totals. `HandleScore()` accepts the current score, as found in the current player's `TextBox`, and the totals for both players. It then checks the current score to ensure that it's in the right format and within the correct value range. Instead of using `Int32.Parse()` and an exception handler, you could also use `Int32.TryParse()`, which doesn't produce an exception, but also requires additional handling because now you have to check whether the conversion is successful. After the new score is verified, its value is added to the correct player's score and then the new score is reset to `0`. The next player's `TextBox` then receives the focus.

Now that the scores are updated, it's time to check the totals. When the total for a particular player exceeds 120 points, the game is over. The game displays one of two messages depending on how much the one player tromped the other.

Creating an event connection

Of course, if you have something that's associated with an event, you must have event handlers. Select each of the player `TextBox` controls in turn, click the Events button, and then double-click the Leave event to produce an event handler, as shown in Figure 5-4.

Now that you have the required event handlers, you can add the following code to them:

```
private void Player1_Leave(object sender, EventArgs e)
{
    // Handle the score.
    HandleScore(Player1, Player1Points, Player2Points,
        ref Player1LastTotal);

    // Update the board.
    Form1.ActiveForm.Invalidate();
}
```

```
private void Player2_Leave(object sender, EventArgs e)
{
    // Handle the score.
    HandleScore(Player2, Player2Points, Player1Points,
        ref Player2LastTotal);

    // Update the board.
    Form1.ActiveForm.Invalidate();
}
```

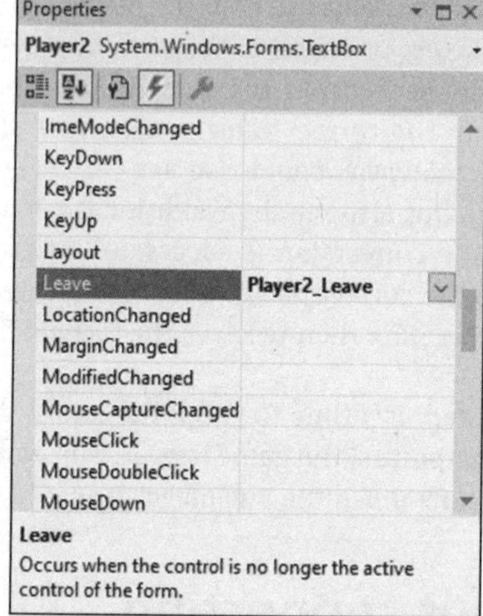

FIGURE 5-4: Add a Leave event handler for each of the TextBox controls.

Note that you must pass the private field used to hold the player's previous score by reference. Otherwise, the fields won't update.

In addition, you must call `Form1.ActiveForm.Invalidate()`. Otherwise, the board won't redraw, which means that you won't see the pins move.

Drawing the board

The application needs to paint right on a form to create the image of the board for the cribbage application. This means gaining access to the `Graphics` object through the `PaintEventArgs` object passed to the application during each redraw event. From there, you need to complete these tasks:

- Paint the board brown using a brush.
- Draw six rows of little circles using a pen.

» Fill in the hole if that is the right score.

» Clean up your supplies.

The following method redraws the board every time it gets called. To make the method purpose more understandable, the code calls it `CribbageBoard_Paint()`.

```
private void CribbageBoard_Paint(object sender, PaintEventArgs e)
{
    // Obtain the graphics object.
    Graphics g = e.Graphics;

    // Create the board
    SolidBrush brownBrush = new SolidBrush(Color.Brown);
    g.FillRectangle(brownBrush, new Rectangle(20, 20, 820, 180));

    // Paint the little holes.
    // There are 244 little holes in the board.
    // Three rows of 40 times two, with the little starts and stops on
    // either end.
    // Let's start with the 240.
    int rows = 0;
    int columns = 0;
    int scoreBeingDrawn = 0;
    Pen blackPen = new Pen(Color.Black, 1);
    SolidBrush blackBrush = new SolidBrush(Color.Black);
    SolidBrush redBrush = new SolidBrush(Color.Red);

    // There are 6 rows, then, at 24 and 40, 80 and 100, then 140 and 160.
    for (rows = 40; rows <= 160; rows += 60)
    {
        // There are 40 columns. They are every 20
        for (columns = 40; columns <= 820; columns += 20)
        {
            // Calculate score being drawn
            scoreBeingDrawn = ((columns - 20) / 20) +
                ((((rows + 20) / 60) - 1) * 40);

            // Draw Player1
            // If score being drawn = Player1 fill, otherwise draw
            if (scoreBeingDrawn == Int32.Parse(Player1Points.Text))
            {
                g.FillEllipse(blackBrush, columns - 2, rows - 2, 6, 6);
            }
            else if (scoreBeingDrawn == Player1LastTotal)
            {
                g.FillEllipse(redBrush, columns - 2, rows - 2, 6, 6);
            }
```

Creating Images

```
            else
            {
                g.DrawEllipse(blackPen, columns - 2, rows - 2, 4, 4);
            }

            // Draw Player2
            // If score being drawn = Player2 fill, otherwise draw
            if (scoreBeingDrawn == Int32.Parse(Player2Points.Text))
            {
                g.FillEllipse(blackBrush, columns - 2, rows + 16, 6, 6);
            }
            else if (scoreBeingDrawn == Player2LastTotal)
            {
                g.FillEllipse(redBrush, columns - 2, rows + 16, 6, 6);
            }
            else
            {
                g.DrawEllipse(blackPen, columns - 2, rows + 16, 4, 4);
            }
        }
    }

    // Perform the required cleanup.
    g.Dispose();
    brownBrush.Dispose();
    blackPen.Dispose();
}
```

Aside from the math, note the decision making. If the score being drawn is the score in the label, fill in the hole with a black peg. If it's the last score drawn, fill in the hole with a red peg. Otherwise, well, just draw a circle.

REMEMBER

To make the `CribbageBoard_Paint()` event handler work properly, you must associate it with the form. In Design View, select `Form1`. Click the Events button at the top of the Properties window to display the list of events associated with `Form1` (see Figure 5-4 as an example). Click the drop-down list box for the `Paint` event and choose the `CribbageBoard_Paint` entry.

Printing the score

You may decide that you really need evidence as to how the game really went. Fortunately, you can print the game board when you're done. The `PrintMe` link, combined with a `PrintDocument` component, will allow you to do just that with a minimum of fuss. Just drag and drop the PrintDocument component to your form and you see it appear at the bottom in its own area as printDocument1. This component doesn't have a visual interface. You need event handlers for both PrintMe and printDocument1, which you can create by double-clicking them. Then you add the following code to the event handlers:

```
// Define a variable to hold the bitmap to print.
private Bitmap memoryImage;

private void PrintMe_LinkClicked(object sender,
    LinkLabelLinkClickedEventArgs e)
{
    // Create a graphics object.
    Graphics thisPage = this.CreateGraphics();
    Size thisSize = this.Size;
    memoryImage = new Bitmap(thisSize.Width, thisSize.Height, thisPage);

    // Copy the form image to memory.
    Graphics memoryGraphics = Graphics.FromImage(memoryImage);
    memoryGraphics.CopyFromScreen(this.Location.X, this.Location.Y,
        0, 0, thisSize);

    // Print the document.
    printDocument1.Print();
}

private void printDocument1_PrintPage(object sender,
    System.Drawing.Printing.PrintPageEventArgs e)
{
    // Ensure the image will fit on the paper by
    // resizing it.
    e.Graphics.DrawImage(memoryImage, 0, 0,
        memoryImage.Width/2, memoryImage.Height/2);
}
```

Two processes are happening in PrintMe_LinkClicked(). First, you create a bitmap to hold the image that you want to print in memory. Second, you fill that image with the form graphic onscreen. When you have the form image in memory, you can print it.

The printDocument1_PrintPage() method simply takes the memory image and draws it on the printer canvas. You see the result as a copy of the printed form.

Starting a new game

The last thing you need to do is create some method for starting a new game, which is where the `LinkLabel`, `StartGame`, comes into play. The following code sets everything up for a new game:

```
private void StartGame_LinkClicked(object sender,
    LinkLabelLinkClickedEventArgs e)
{
    // Set the scores to zero.
    Player1.Text = "0";
    Player2.Text = "0";
    Player1Points.Text = "0";
    Player2Points.Text = "0";
    Player1LastTotal = 0;
    Player2LastTotal = 0;

    // Reset the text and hide the print link.
    WinMessage.Text = "";
    PrintMe.Visible = false;
}
```

It's tough to fathom, but this is exactly how large-scale games are written. Admittedly, big graphics engines make many more If-Then decisions, but the premise is the same.

Also, large games use bitmap images sometimes, rather than draw all the time. For the cribbage-scoring application, for example, you could use a bitmap image of a peg rather than fill an ellipse with a black or red brush!

IN THIS CHAPTER

» Understanding dynamic typing

» Defining variables

» Staying flexible by being dynamic

» Making static operations dynamic

Chapter 6 Programming Dynamically!

Dynamic programming is another one of those buzzwords that really doesn't have a clear definition. At its loosest, it means developing something in such a way that the program makes more decisions about the way it runs while running, rather than when you compile it.

Scripting languages are a great example of this type of programming. When you write something in JavaScript (`https://developer.mozilla.org/docs/Web/JavaScript/Reference`), you don't compile it at all — all the decisions are made at runtime. Ruby (`https://www.ruby-lang.org/`) is another good example: Most of the time, an entire program can just be typed into a command prompt and run right from there.

REMEMBER

When you declare a variable in a dynamically typed language, you don't have to say what type you are making that variable. The compiler will just figure it out for you. In a static language, such as earlier versions of C#, you do have to say what type you are making that variable. However, starting with C# 3.0, the `var` keyword lets you leave the decision of which type to use to the compiler.

Microsoft originally promised that dynamic types would never be in C#, but later decided that the feature had to be added. Why? Mostly it's because of the development requirements for Microsoft Office. Office uses COM, the pre-.NET structure for Microsoft applications. Additionally, the WinRT API is not based in managed code and supports JavaScript, one of the original dynamic languages. They probably added dynamic support looking forward to WinRT as well.

COM and WinRT expects that the languages that use it (like VB Classic and C++) will have dynamic types. This made developing for Microsoft Office difficult for C# programmers, which was exactly opposite of what Microsoft wanted to happen. The end result? The dynamic type.

Shifting C# Toward Dynamic Typing

So-called "dynamic languages" are a trend that keeps coming back, like ruffled tux shirts. *Dynamic languages* are languages that allow for loose typing, rather than static. The concept got started in the 1960s with the List Processing (LISP) language. Dynamic languages came back in the late 1980s for two reasons: network management scripting and the artificial intelligence craze. Thanks to the web, the buzzword is back yet again.

The World Wide Web, for those of you who aren't old enough to remember, was built on View Source and dynamic languages. Microsoft's original web development language, Active Server Pages, was built on VBScript (`https://www.guru99.com/introduction-to-vbscript.html`) — a dynamic language.

The web is better with a dynamic programming environment, so the trend is probably here to stay this time (until the next big thing, anyway). C# isn't the only language that is adding dynamic language features, and dynamic type isn't the only language feature that has been added to make it more appealing for web programmers. Several dynamic languages have been around for a while, like these:

- LISP
- Perl
- Scheme
- Smalltalk
- Visual Basic

Although some of these aren't as popular as they once were, they are still out there and have pushed the trend in the newer languages. You can see this trend in all the new or refurbished languages that have dynamic type systems that have popped up over the last ten years. Many of them have roots in the web, while others are being newly used for the web:

- Cold Fusion
- Groovy
- JavaScript
- Lua
- Newspeak
- PHP
- Python
- Ruby

Some of these languages support multiple coding styles. For example, even though Python supports a dynamic typing system, it can use the object-oriented, imperative, functional programming, and procedural coding styles. It's important to realize that the typing system doesn't necessarily affect the coding style used by a language.

Developers who work in dynamic languages often use them for practically everything except highly structured team-build kinds of environments. Uses include:

- Data analysis using data science techniques
- Artificial intelligence, machine learning, and deep learning
- Scripting infrastructure for system maintenance
- Building tests
- One-use utilities
- Scripting other applications
- Building websites
- Biology
- Games

Dynamic languages are popular for these kinds of tasks for two reasons. First, they provide instant feedback, because you can try a piece of code outside the constraints of the rest of the program you are writing. Second, you can start building your higher-level pieces of code without building the plumbing that makes it work.

For instance, Ruby has a command-line interface that you can simply paste a function into, even out of context, and see how it works. There is even a web version at https://www.tutorialspoint.com/execute_ruby_online.php. You can type code right in there, even if there are classes referenced that aren't defined, because Ruby will just take a guess at it. If you want a more organized environment that relies on Python, you can find it with Google Colaboratory (Colab for short) at https://colab.research.google.com/notebooks/intro.ipynb.

This ease of online use moves nicely into the next point, which is that a dynamic language enables you to build a class that refers to a type that you haven't defined elsewhere. For example, you can make a class to schedule an event, without actually having to build the underlying Event type first.

All of this lends itself to a language that is a lot more responsive to change. You can make a logic change in one place and not have to dig through reams of code to fix all the type declarations everywhere. Add this to optional and named parameters (see Book 2 Chapter 10) and you have a lot less typing to do when you have to change your program.

Other benefits to dynamic languages in general show up as you use them more. For instance, macro languages are usually dynamically typed. If you've tried to build macros in previous versions of Visual Studio, you know what a pain it is to use a static language. Making C# (and Visual Basic, for that matter) more dynamic not only makes it a better language for extending Visual Studio but also gives programmers the capability to include the language in the programs they write so that other developers can further extend those applications.

Employing Dynamic Programming Techniques

By now, you must be asking why all this talk about dynamic code is important to C# developers. When you define a new variable, you can use the dynamic keyword, and C# will let you make assumptions about the members of the variable. For example, if you want to declare a new Course object, you do it like this:

```
Course newCourse = new Course();
newCourse.Schedule();
```

This is, of course, assuming that you have a `Course` class defined somewhere else in your program, like this:

```
class Course
{
    public void Schedule()
    {
        // Something fancy here
    }
}
```

But what if you don't know what class the new object will be? How do you handle that? You could declare it as an `Object`, because everything derives from `Object`, right? Here's the code:

```
Object newCourse = new Object();
```

Not so fast, my friend, if you make your next line this:

```
newCourse.Schedule();
```

Note that the squiggly line appears almost immediately, and you get the famous "object does not contain a definition for `Schedule...`" error in the design time Error List. However, you can do this:

```
dynamic newCourse = SomeFunction();
newCourse.Schedule();
```

All this code needs to have is the stub of a function that returns some value, and you are good to go. What if `SomeFunction()` returns a string? Well, you get a runtime error. But it will still compile!

About now you may be thinking: "This is a *good* thing? How!?!" For the time being, you can blame COM. You see, COM was mostly constructed using C++, which has a variant type. In C++, you could declare a variable to be dynamic, like this:

```
VARIANT newCourse;
```

It worked just like the dynamic type, except C# wasn't invented yet. Because a lot of the objects in COM used `VARIANT` out parameters, it was really tough to handle Interop using .NET. (*Interop* is short for interoperability, where you're trying to get two pieces of code to talk with each other.) Because Microsoft Office is mostly made of COM objects, and because it isn't going to change any time soon, and because Microsoft wants us all to be Office developers one day, bam, you have the dynamic type.

Say, for instance, that your `newCourse` is a variant `out` parameter from a method in a COM class. To get the value, you have to declare it an Object, like this:

```
CourseMarshaller cm = new CourseMarshaller(); // a COM object
int courseId = 4;
Object newCourse;
cm.MakeCourse(courseId, out newCourse);
// and now we are back to square one
newCourse.Schedule(); // This causes a 'member not found exception'
```

The last line will not compile, even if the Schedule method exists, because you can't assume that `newCourse` will always come back as a `Course` object, because it is declared a variant. You're stuck. With a dynamic type, though, you're golden once again, with this code:

```
CourseMarshaller cm = new CourseMarshaller(); // a COM object
int courseId = 4;
dynamic newCourse;
cm.MakeCourse(courseId, newCourse);
newCourse.Schedule(); // This now compiles
```

However, if `newCourse` comes back as something that doesn't have a `Schedule()` method, you get a runtime error. But there are `try...catch` blocks for runtime errors. Nothing will help the code compile without the `dynamic` keyword.

Putting Dynamic to Use

When C# encounters a dynamically typed variable, like the variables you created earlier, it changes everything that variable touches into a *dynamic operation*. This dynamic conversion means that when you use a dynamically typed object in an expression, the entire operation is dynamic.

Classic examples

Here are six examples of how a dynamic operation works. Say you have the dynamic variable `dynamicVariable`. Because the dynamic variable will pass through all six examples, they will all be dispatched dynamically by the C# compiler.

1. `dynamicVariable.someMethod("a", "b", "c");`: The compiler binds the method `someMethod` at runtime, since `dynamicVariable` is dynamic. No surprise.

2. `dynamicVariable.someProperty = 42;`: The compiler binds the property `someProperty` just like it did in the first method.

3. `var newVar = dynamicVariable + 42;`: The compiler looks for any overloaded operators of + with a type of `dynamic`. Lacking that, it outputs a dynamic type.

4. `int newNumber = dynamicVariable;`: This is an implicit conversion to `int`. The runtime determines whether a conversion to `int` is possible. If not, it throws a type mismatch error.

5. `int newNumber = (int) dynamicVariable;`: This is an explicit cast to `int`. The compiler encodes this as a cast — you actually change the type here.

6. `Console.WriteLine(dynamicVariable);`: Because there is no overload of `WriteLine()` that accepts a dynamic type explicitly, the entire method call is dispatched dynamically.

Making static operations dynamic

If the compiler chooses to make a static operation dynamic — as it did in item 6 in the preceding section — the compiler rebuilds the code on the fly to have it handle the dynamic variable. What does that mean for you? Glad you asked.

Take item 6, `Console.WriteLine(dynamicVariable);`. This piece of code forces the compiler to build intermediary code, which checks for the type of variable at runtime in order to come up with something that is writable to the console. The compiled code first checks whether the input is a static type that it knows. Next, it checks for a type present in the program. Then it will just try a few things that might work. It will fail with an error if it finds nothing.

If you must use this approach to creating code as a developer, at least you can get the job done. But remember that it's slower than molasses in January (or even slower). This is why `Variant` got such a bad rap in Visual Basic Classic. Dynamic is something you don't use until you need it. It puts a tremendous strain on the machine running the program, especially if all variables are dynamic.

Understanding what's happening under the covers

Using dynamic programming techniques doesn't have to be hard. In fact, you can do so with just three functional lines of code by using this simple method:

```
class C
{
    public dynamic MyMethod(dynamic d)
```

```
    {
        return d.Foo();
    }
}
```

This is pretty straightforward stuff — a method that accepts a dynamic class and returns the results of the type's `Foo` method. Not a big deal. Here is the compiled C# code:

```
class C
{
    [return: Dynamic]
    public object MyMethod([Dynamic] object d)
    {
        if (MyMethodo__SiteContainer0.p__Site1 == null)
        {
            MyMethodo__SiteContainer0.p__Site1 =
              CallSite<Func<CallSite, object, object>>
              .Create(new CSharpCallPayload(
                CSharpCallFlags.None, "Foo", typeof(object), null,
                new CSharpArgumentInfo[] {
              new CSharpArgumentInfo(CSharpArgumentInfoFlags.None,
            null) }));
        }
        return MyMethodo__SiteContainer0.p__Site1
          .Target(MyMethodo__SiteContainer0.p__Site1, d);
    }

    [CompilerGenerated]
    private static class MyMethodo__SiteContainer0
    {
      public static CallSite<Func<CallSite, object, object>> p__Site1;
    }
}
```

Most developers wouldn't want to try to break this code down. Fortunately, they don't have to. That's what compilers are for, right?

Running with the Dynamic Language Runtime

There is more to dynamic languages than just the dynamic typing. You can do some powerful things. As with all power, you have to be careful not to misuse it.

The Dynamic Language Runtime — shown in Figure 6-1 — is a library added to the .NET Framework specifically to provide for adding dynamic languages (like Ruby) to the Visual Studio fold (like IronRuby), or to add dynamic language features to existing static languages (like C# 4.0).

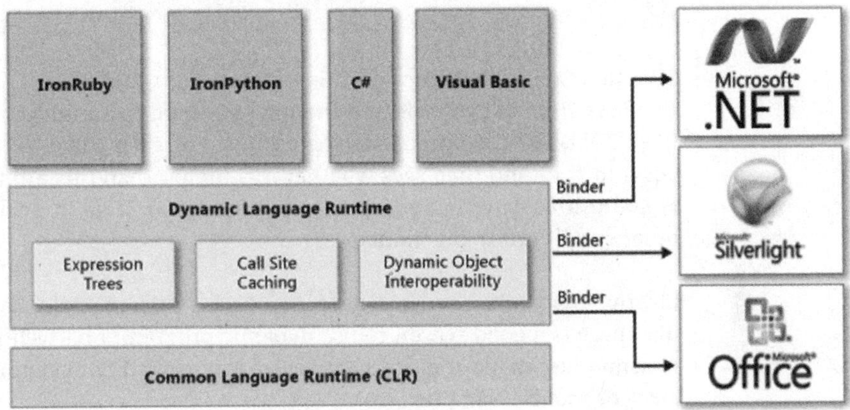

FIGURE 6-1: The Dynamic Language Runtime.

The runtime helps the compiler to construct code in the compiled assembly that will make a lot of choices dynamically. The code block at the end of the preceding section is an example of the simplest kind. Of course, C# has similar features, so you can use dynamic programming techniques. Here's the code:

```
static dynamic f(dynamic x)
{
    return Math.Sqrt(x) + 5.0 * Math.Pow(x, 3.0);
}

static void Main(string[] args)
{
    dynamic[] array = new Array[11];

    for (int i = 0; i < 11; i++)
    {
        array[i] = Console.ReadLine();
    }

    for (int i = 10; i>=0; i--)
    {
        dynamic y = f(array[i]);
        if (y > 400.0)
        {
            Console.WriteLine(string.Format("{0} TOO LARGE", i));
        }
        else
```

```
            {
                Console.WriteLine("{0} : {1}", i, array[i]);
            }
        }

        Console.ReadKey();
    }
```

Two functions are defined in this example: `f()` and `Main()`. `Main()` accepts 11 numbers from the console and then moves them to an integer array using a `for` loop. Next, the code processes the entries. For each value in the array, it sets `y` equal to `f(x)` and then sees whether it is higher than this arbitrary value (which is 400 in this case, but you could use any value). If so, it prints "TOO LARGE"; otherwise, it prints the number.

Clearly, you could have just used `double` for this example, so it may not seem like there is a good reason to use dynamic programming techniques. But, use of dynamic just made the program easier to create. Try changing the array to an array of `double`, like this:

```
Double[] array = new Double[11];
```

Now the call to `ReadLine()` doesn't work. You'll just cast it to a `double`. Nope, can't do that; you have to use `TryParse`. You get the picture. Static types are hard to code with. Dynamic types are easier to code with.

What's the other side of this? Well, obviously, if the user enters a non-numeric string, the program outputs a runtime error, and that's bad. If you statically type everything, you can trap that error much more easily and handle it right on user input.

Add to that the reality that C# is making runtime decisions about every single variable throughout the entire run of the program. That's a whole lot of extra processing that you could have avoided if you had just done that static typing.

The take-home here is that using dynamic types makes your programming job much easier and your troubleshooting job much harder. If you are writing a utility script for your own use and don't care if it occasionally crashes with a type mismatch, use dynamic. If you are writing a backup script for a hospital and the lives of thousands are at stake, static types are likely better.

FINDING IRONPYTHON AND IRONRUBY

Microsoft originally created both IronPython and IronRuby to compete with offerings provided by others for other software frameworks. You found them included in your copy of Visual Studio. However, because the languages didn't prove quite as popular as Microsoft had hoped, you won't find them in Visual Studio by default any longer. Fortunately, you can still find both languages online. The IronPython site appears at `http://ironpython.net/`, and the IronRuby site is at `http://ironruby.net/`. Both languages enjoy a small community of support and some level of third-party support, but don't expect to get much help from Microsoft.

Fortunately, installing IronPython and IronRuby support into your copy of Visual Studio isn't hard. You can use NuGet to do it. The instructions appear at `https://www.nuget.org/packages/IronPython` for IronPython and at `https://www.nuget.org/packages/IronRuby` for IronRuby.

Using Static Anonymous Functions

A problem with dynamic programming techniques is that lambdas and anonymous functions can capture local field values and instance information, which may create error situations for your application because the compiler makes some assumptions that aren't correct. For example, the function may create an offset in an output value based on the previous state of the function. C# 9.0 and above allows you to get past this problem by adding the `static` keyword to lambdas and anonymous functions. Here are some of the trade-offs to consider when using the `static` keyword:

- You can now access static members, including constants, of an enclosing scope.
- You can't access these members of an enclosing scope:
  - `nameof()`
  - Local variables
  - Parameters
  - `this`
  - base

- Accessibility rules change to match those of static members of an enclosing scope.
- There's no guarantee that the static anonymous function will actually appear as a static method in the metadata after compilation because this detail is left to the compiler.
- A non-static anonymous function can capture state from the enclosing static anonymous function, but it can't capture state from outside the enclosing static anonymous function scope.

4

A Tour of Visual Studio

Contents at a Glance

» Surveying the available versions

» Setting up Visual Studio

» Understanding projects and solutions

» Exploring the different types of projects

Chapter 1
Getting Started with Visual Studio

Writing applications using a text editor and then compiling them at the command line is a thing of the past. Today, you use an *Integrated Development Environment (IDE)*, which is a program that provides a platform for development, to create C# applications. An IDE helps to make development easier.

Programmers who are used to starting with a blank screen and a command line often dismiss an IDE as a slow, bogged-down waste of time. However, Visual Studio really does make working with C# faster and more pleasant. It's quick, easy to use, agile, and smart. If you're truly determined to use a command-line interface, consider using a Read, Evaluate, Print, and Loop (REPL) environment such as CShell (`http://cshell.net`), discussed in the "Using IDE alternatives" sidebar, later in this chapter.

True, you don't have to use an IDE to program, but if you're going to use one, it should be Visual Studio. It was purposely built to write C# code, and it's made to construct programs for all the platforms that .NET now supports, including Windows.

TIP

Other options exist, however. MonoDevelop (https://www.monodevelop.com/) is a tool built for Linux users to write .NET code, but it works in Windows. When working on the Mac, you might use Visual Studio for the Mac (https://visualstudio.microsoft.com/vs/mac/). You might even choose a browser-based IDE, such as OnlineGBD (https://www.onlinegdb.com/online_csharp_compiler), which actually allows you to develop your C# code using your Android tablet. If you really want to twist your brain into a knot, check out Rextester (https://rextester.com/), where you can select from any of a large number of languages to develop with using a browser interface. (Just select the language you want from the Language drop-down list.) These tools are all free.

Of course, you can also get the Visual Studio Community edition free. All the examples in this book will work with this particular IDE, so you should get the Community edition unless you need the advanced features of a paid version of Visual Studio or require one of the other products for some other reason. This chapter introduces you to the various versions of Visual Studio and discusses the C# projects available to you.

Versioning the Versions

Visual Studio has lots of different versions. The reason is its famous licensing problem. If Microsoft just sold the whole package for what it was worth, only the Fortune 50 could afford it, and it would cut out about 99 percent of its audience. If Microsoft makes a lot of different versions and tries to incorporate the features that different groups of people use, it can capture nearly 100 percent of the audience. This chapter discusses the features and benefits of all the major editions.

An overview of Visual Studio 2022 updates

Some of the changes in Visual Studio 2022 affect all editions. For example, you can now create applications for these platforms using various C# templates:

- Windows
- Android
- iOS
- Linux

USING IDE ALTERNATIVES

One of the complaints about using an IDE is that it's not very interactive. An IDE provides a static environment where you type code, build it, and then run it to test it. Yes, IDE features can point out things like syntax errors, but you really don't get any feedback until you've written a lot of code. Other languages, such as Scala, provide a read–eval–print loop (REPL) environment in which feedback is more or less instantaneous. Fortunately, CShell provides you with a REPL for C#. Of course, this approach works only for relatively simple code. If you want to use the REPL for something a bit more complicated, you must provide the code in a script file, but then, you're starting to work in something more akin to the IDE environment again. Consequently, CShell is a great solution for those times when you need to test simple ideas for your C# application quickly, and then move them to your actual application within Visual Studio.

Another approach to the whole issue of static coding environments is the literate programming approach provided by products such as Jupyter Notebook (`https://jupyter.org/`). This product includes a C# plug-in (`https://github.com/jupyter/jupyter/wiki/Jupyter-kernels`) that you can use to write code. *Literate programming* is a report-like technique originally advanced by Donald Knuth to create an environment suitable for scientific research (`https://www-cs-faculty.stanford.edu/~knuth/lp.html`). More important, it provides you with the means for creating coding examples that are suitable for group discussions of a much larger project. Unlike CShell, you can write relatively complex coding examples using Jupyter Notebook, but you also lose some of the advantages of using a REPL.

The bottom line is that this book uses an IDE because that's the traditional approach to writing C# code and the approach that you use most of the time when writing applications for any environment. However, you should keep these alternatives in mind when the IDE just won't do the job for you.

- macOS
- Other technologies and platforms (see the list at `https://docs.microsoft.com/en-us/visualstudio/releases/2022/compatibility#developOther` for details). Many of these other technologies and platforms won't affect your C# development.

REMEMBER

The biggest news, however, is that Visual Studio 2022 is a fully 64-bit environment now, which means that you can make fuller use of all the functionality that your system provides. In addition, Visual Studio 2022 is noticeably faster in some areas than it was in the past. Fortunately, your 32-bit applications continue to run fine in the new environment.

As you read through this book, you also find mentions of .NET 6.0 updates that affect how you code. Some of the updates are significant, and you notice them immediately. Other updates are subtle, but you can find them if you look. You can see a list of .NET 6.0 updates at `https://devblogs.microsoft.com/dotnet/announcing-net-6-preview-7/`. What may surprise you is how many of these updates you have already noticed without really being aware of them because they're under the covers.

TIP

Whether you call it IntelliSense, IntelliCode, or something else altogether, this feature of Visual Studio saves you time by helping you make corrections to your code as you type and also by making suggestions. In this version of Visual Studio, you definitely want to remember the Tab key because pressing Tab allows you to complete major code segments quickly, easily, and without error. At the end of the day, you may amaze yourself at your productivity after you get used to the new IntelliSense (the name used in this book) features. It's the most noticeable and welcome feature for many developers.

The new debugging support will bedazzle you with all sorts of gizmos, charts, graphs, blinking lights, and pizzazz of every sort. However, you may find that you really don't use much of it unless you work on a large project. The debugger does tell you more about what is wrong with your application, and this feature does save time. For the most part, however, you find that you use the same debugging techniques as in the past with just a bit more help from the IDE.

Community edition

The Community edition is the free version of Visual Studio. It's made for hobbyists, classrooms, and academic research, but many professional programmers use it as their edition of choice for small personal projects, or for working on open source projects. Microsoft also targets this edition to small organizations that have five or fewer developers. So if you work for a small company, you might not need anything more than this edition, which means that C# development will remain free.

Although the Community edition is a little less functional than the Professional edition, you can compile every code example in this book by using the Community edition. It has the power of the .NET Framework, which is also free, and gives you a significant means of learning C#. From a development platform perspective, the Community edition supports everything that all the other editions support, including

- Windows Desktop
- Universal Windows Platform, or UWP (formerly known as Universal Windows Apps)

- Universal Application Platform (UAP)
- Web (ASP.NET)
- Azure development
- Cloud development
- Office 365
- Business Applications
- Apache Cordova
- C++ Cross-Platform Library Development
- Python
- Node.js
- .NET Core
- Git support
- Docker Tools

TIP

New to Visual Studio versions 2019 and above are cross-platform tools that help you create applications for all the non-Windows platforms that C# now supports. Here are the features you can expect:

- Remote iOS Simulator for Windows
- The ability to share code between Android and iOS using Xamarin (`https://dotnet.microsoft.com/apps/xamarin`), a platform for building iOS and Android apps using C# and .NET
- Native iOS and Android UI Designers
- Xamarin.Forms

In the past, the various Express and academic editions gave people a taste of what they could do with C#, but tended to move them toward the paid Professional edition. With Visual Studio 2022, Microsoft takes a different route and gives you everything needed to fully experience C#. You even have access to many advanced debugging and diagnostic tools, testing tools, and cross-platform templates. The chart at `https://www.visualstudio.com/vs/compare/` provides a full comparison.

REMEMBER

What the Community edition lacks is enterprise-level support. It's important to note that Microsoft defines an enterprise as an entity having more than 250 PCs or more than $1 million U.S. dollars in annual revenue. If you find that you need enterprise-type support but don't have an enterprise-sized organization, you need the Professional edition. However, for most developers, the Community edition provides everything needed to discover and use the wonders of C#.

Professional edition

Besides designing the Professional edition to work in a larger, enterprise environment, Microsoft endowed the Professional edition with one necessary addition: CodeLens (`https://docs.microsoft.com/visualstudio/ide/find-code-changes-and-other-history-with-codelens`). This feature is designed to help you look at your code in a detailed manner. Think about it as a sort of magnifying glass for code. You can use CodeLens to perform these sorts of tasks:

- Find references to your code wherever they might exist.
- Review the code history and determine how changes might affect your code.
- Manage the branches in your code.
- Determine who made code changes.
- Contact other team members about changes using Lync or Skype.
- Track linked code reviews and linked bugs.
- Locate and manage unit tests for your code.

Enterprise edition

There is a huge difference in functionality between the Professional edition and the Enterprise edition. Yes, the Community edition, Professional edition, and Enterprise edition can all create the same kinds of projects, but the tools required to design, build, test, and manage really large projects reside in the Enterprise edition. For example, all the architectural features, such as Architectural Layer Diagrams and Architecture Validation, are part of the Enterprise edition. If you want to validate your design, you need Live Dependency Validation, which is a truly amazing feature described at `https://docs.microsoft.com/visualstudio/modeling/validate-code-with-layer-diagrams`.

The management features are also designed around the huge project environment. For example, Code Clone (`https://docs.microsoft.com/previous-versions/hh205279(v=vs.140)`) provides the means to detect duplicate code in your project. After all, when a project is huge, multiple developers are apt to come up with the same way to perform specific tasks. Ensuring that you don't have to maintain multiple copies of the same code reduces costs and makes the code easier to manage (not to mention that it eliminates some of the nastier bugs).

You also receive some truly advanced functionality for performing diagnostics and debugging your code. In addition, the Enterprise edition contains additional cross-platform support. However, where the Enterprise edition truly shines is with testing tools. When working with the Community edition or Professional edition, all you get is unit testing. However, the Enterprise edition provides all these other forms of testing:

- Live Unit Testing
- IntelliTest
- Microsoft Fakes (Unit Test Isolation)
- Code Coverage
- Snapshot Debugger
- Time Travel Debugging (see the walkthrough at `https://docs.microsoft.com/windows-hardware/drivers/debugger/time-travel-debugging-walkthrough`)

TIP

There are also new cross-platform development features (starting in Visual Studio 2019) that help you create applications that work across multiple platforms. This includes Xamarin support, as shown here:

- Embedded Assemblies
- Xamarin Inspector
- Xamarin Profiler

MSDN

The Microsoft Developer Network (MSDN) subscription is by far the best way to get Microsoft products. It may seem as though setting up a development environment to develop anything of significance would be impossibly expensive. This is not necessarily the case.

The MSDN subscription is exactly what it sounds like — a subscription to a majority of the Microsoft products that matter. For around $1,199.00 for the first year and $799.00 a year after that for a Professional edition subscription, you get access to everything you need. This isn't actually an edition of Visual Studio. (You can learn more about the various subscription costs for the Visual Studio component at `https://visualstudio.microsoft.com/subscriptions/` and the MSDN Platforms component at `https://visualstudio.microsoft.com/msdn-platforms/`.)

That MSDN Platforms fee sounds like a lot, but think about it this way: Even if you do only one project a year on your own time, your investment will pay off. Considering the fact that Visual Studio alone is half of that, and it gets a revision every two years or so, it's a bargain. Along with Visual Studio Professional, you also get subscriptions to a wealth of software that would take pages to list here, but you can see a complete list at `https://visualstudio.microsoft.com/vs/pricing-details/`.

Installing Visual Studio

Visual Studio Community edition installs much like any other Windows program. First, assure yourself that your machine can run Visual Studio. Then you run the setup program that you download from the Microsoft site at `https://www.visualstudio.com/vs/community/` and make a few decisions. Then you wait. Visual Studio is big. It takes a while. The official minimum requirements for Visual Studio 2022 are shown in this list:

- **Operating system:**
  - Windows 10 version 1909 or higher: Home, Professional, Education, and Enterprise (Team, LTSB, and S are not supported)
  - Windows Server 2016: Standard and Datacenter
  - Windows Server 2019: Standard and Datacenter
- **Hardware:**
  - 1.8 GhZ or faster 64-bit quad-core (or better) processor
  - 4GB of RAM (16GB of RAM recommended)
  - 20GB of available hard drive space (50GB recommended)
  - 5400 RPM drive
  - Video card that supports a minimum display resolution of 720p (1280 by 720; higher resolution recommended)

WARNING

Remember that Visual Studio 2022 is a 64-bit-only IDE, so if you plan to continue working with a 32-bit platform or an older version of Windows, you might want to consider continuing to use Visual Studio 2019, which still comes with C# 9.0 support. You can find the Visual Studio 2019 requirements, which are significantly less than Visual Studio 2022, at `https://docs.microsoft.com/en-us/visualstudio/releases/2019/system-requirements`. Note that there is a very long list of platforms that Visual Studio 2022 doesn't support, such as ARM processors, Windows Server Core, Windows Minimal Server, Windows containers, virtual machine environments, multiple simultaneous user environments, and so on. If you have any doubt about your setup, make sure to consult the requirements at `https://docs.microsoft.com/visualstudio/releases/2022/system-requirements`.

You can run on the configuration shown below, but you may find that some features run slowly and a few don't run at all. Here's a more realistic base configuration for Visual Studio Community edition:

- 3.4 GHz 64-bit 8-core processor
- 64-bit Windows 10 with 8GB of RAM
- 250GB of available space on a solid-state drive (SSD)
- Wide Extended Graphics Array (WXGA) (1366 × 768) or higher display adapter
- Dual monitors (or a laptop with an external monitor) with one being a touchscreen

Breaking Down the Projects

After you have run the setup program and set your default settings, you just need to start a project and get your fingers dirty. All the project types (except maybe one or two) in the first three minibooks were Console applications, meaning they are meant to be run at the command prompt. Many more projects are available. Notice the main kinds of projects in the Visual Studio New Project dialog box, shown in Figure 1-1. You control which projects you see by selecting options in the three drop-down list boxes at the top.

The following list shows the project types installed as part of Visual Studio Community edition for C# developers.

- **Cloud:** Scalable services that run on Microsoft Azure (`https://azure.microsoft.com/`). You can create a number of service, web application, job, and mobile application types. This is also where you find Blazor (`https://dotnet.microsoft.com/apps/aspnet/web-apps/blazor`), Angular (`https://angular.io/`), React.js (`https://reactjs.org/`), and Redux (`https://redux.js.org/`) templates.

Getting Started with Visual Studio

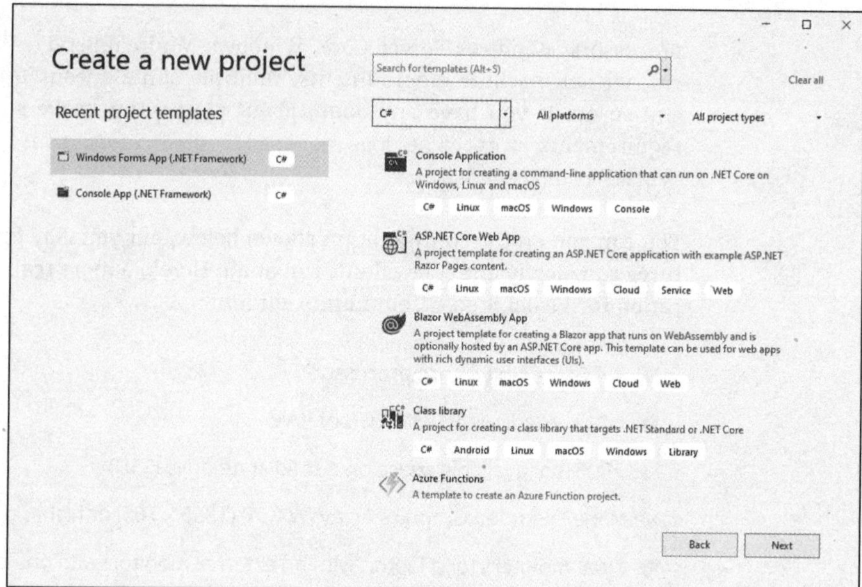

FIGURE 1-1: The Visual Studio Community edition provides lots of project types.

- **Console:** There are two kinds of console applications: .NET Core (which supports Linux, macOS, and Windows) and .NET Framework (which supports desktop development).
- **Desktop:** Rich client applications that compile into `.EXE`s and run right on your computer. Microsoft Word is a Windows application. Most of the templates create applications that run on Windows, but some templates let you create applications for the Universal Windows Platform (UWP) and Xbox.
- **Extensions:** You can use the templates in this category to create extensions for Visual Basic, so it does anything special that you need it to do. This category may be blank when you first look at it. You need to install additional tools and features by clicking the supplied link to provide entries here.
- **Games:** Creating games using Visual Studio and C# is possible, but it's not necessarily an easy task. The article at `https://narrasoft.com/is-c-a-good-tool-for-game-development/` provides you with some insights into how to perform this task. This category may be blank when you first look at it. You need to install additional tools and features by clicking the supplied link to provide entries here.
- **IoT (Internet of Things):** Allows you to create applications that interact with devices that support specific interfaces. You can read more about C# and IoT at `https://dotnet.microsoft.com/apps/iot`. This category is likely to be blank when you first look at it. The article at `https://docs.microsoft.com/dotnet/iot/intro` provides information on how to install the required support.

» **Library:** Libraries make it possible to store code for use in multiple projects. Of course, you have to have the right library for the kind of project you want to create. The templates in this list support all the project types you can create using C#.

» **Machine Learning:** The ability to use computers to interact with humans in an intelligent way is a major part of what machine learning offers. Machine learning relies heavily on huge amounts of data and complex data, which means you must have a robust machine to even begin working with machine learning apps locally (there are online options). This category is likely to be blank when you first look at it. The sites at `https://dotnet.microsoft.com/apps/machinelearning-ai/ml-dotnet` and `https://dotnet.microsoft.com/apps/machinelearning-ai` provide information on how to get started with machine learning.

» **Mobile:** Creating applications that run on multiple devices is a necessity today. The templates in this category let you create apps for Windows, iOS, and Android. This category may be blank when you first look at it. You need to install additional tools and features by clicking the supplied link to provide entries here.

» **Office:** You use the templates in this category to create Office and SharePoint applications. If you want to develop for Office 365, you need the special developer license discussed at `https://docs.microsoft.com/visualstudio/subscriptions/vs-m365`. Desktop development requires that you install the support that comes with your Office product. This category will be blank unless you install the required support.

» **Other:** Templates that don't fit anywhere else appear in this category. This category is normally blank unless you install some type of specialized support.

» **Service:** Some types of applications have no user interface. Instead, they sit in the background and wait for requests from a client. These applications are services and Windows is packed with them (just open the Services app to see them). These templates let you create services specifically designed for your application in addition to Windows services.

» **Test:** Unit tests that help you check the functionality of your application using automation.

» **UWP:** Single-page applications that rely on the UWP. This app type has no predefined controls or layout.

» **Web:** Websites that require a web server to run. (A web server is included with Visual Studio for development purposes.) Microsoft.com is an example of a web application.

TIP

The default projects that you obtain with any copy of Visual Studio 2022 are the tip of the iceberg. These are the projects that Microsoft assumes that you will likely use most. However, Visual Studio 2022 can support a huge number of other project types that this book doesn't cover. You install them using NuGet (see `https://docs.microsoft.com/nuget/consume-packages/install-use-packages-visual-studio` for details).

Exploring the Create a New Project dialog box

You start all new projects by using the New Project dialog box, shown in Figure 1-1. It's possible to access this dialog box in a number of ways. The most common technique is to choose Create a New Project when Visual Studio starts. However, you can also choose File ⇨ New ⇨ Project. When adding a new project to an existing solution, you can also right-click the solution entry in Solution Explorer and choose Add ⇨ New Project.

To make it easier to choose a template, you see the templates you've used recently listed on the left side. You can simply select one of these entries and click Next to continue the wizard. You can also search for templates by criteria using the search field at the top. Otherwise, you can select entries in the three drop-down list boxes to choose a template that way.

What you see after you choose a template depends on the wizard for that template. However, Microsoft has attempted to standardize the wizards to some extent. You usually see three (or sometimes more) important text boxes when you click Next after choosing a template:

- **Name:** The name of this project.
- **Location:** The path to the project file.
- **(Optional) Solution:** Determines whether the new project is part of the existing solution or is part of a new solution.
- **Solution Name:** The name of the solution. Solutions are collections of projects.
- **Framework:** The version of the .NET Framework you want to use.

There is sometimes a third or fourth page of the wizard, asking you for additional information. Just follow the prompts and you'll soon see the IDE, where you can begin editing your code.

Understanding solutions and projects

Visual Studio project files, and the solutions that love them, are a constant topic of interest to Microsoft developers. You work on one solution at a time, with a number of projects within. How you organize your solutions and their projects will make or break you when it comes time to find something.

You can think of solutions as folders that hold projects. They're just folders with special properties. The second page of the wizard has a special check box entitled Place Solution and Project in the Same Directory. You deselect this option when you want to add multiple projects to a single solution and want each project to have its own directory within the solution. Keeping projects separate makes it easier to reuse a project in another application.

Projects are where you put the code files for your programs. They store all kinds of things, like references to the .NET Framework, resources like graphics or files, and what file should be used to start the project.

Solutions do the same thing for projects that projects do for files. They keep the projects in a folder and store certain properties. For instance, they store which project should be started when debugging starts.

Neither the project nor the solutions have much to do with a finished program. They are just simple organizational structures for Visual Studio. The installation of the finished program is determined by the setup project.

In reality, the solution is more than a folder. It's a file in a folder that is used by Visual Studio to manage the developer experience. So, inside the folder for the solution is a file describing the projects within and then a bunch of folders containing the projects themselves.

There are files for the projects, too — files that describe the resources and references for the project. They are all XML files that contain text references to the values that you set using Visual Studio. Normally, you don't need to look at the solution or project files. The results of any organization you perform appears in Solution Explorer. Figure 1-2 shows a typical example of a simple application setup consisting of a solution (`CheckCIA`) and two projects (`CIAAssembly` and `InternalLimitsAccess`). Each of the projects contains the files associated with that project, such as `CIAAssembly.cs` in the `CIAAssembly` project.

Getting Started with Visual Studio

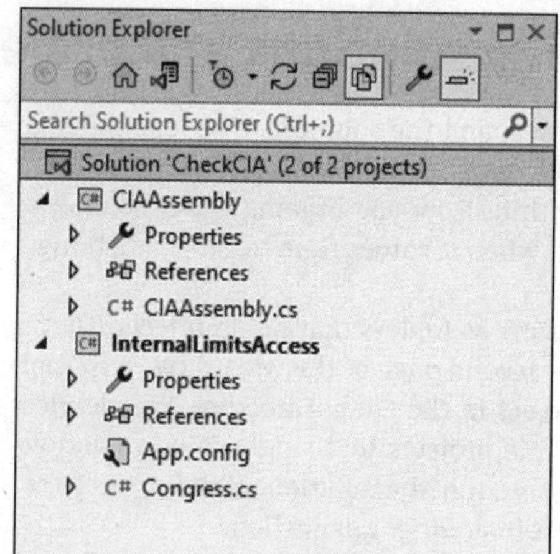

FIGURE 1-2: Solutions and projects appear in Solution Explorer.

IN THIS CHAPTER

» Using the designer

» Exploring Solution Explorer

» Coding with Code View

» Using the Tools menu

» Working with the debugger

Chapter 2
Using the Interface

Integrated Development Environments, or IDEs, are the Swiss army knife of the programmer's toolkit. IDEs provide a mechanism for storing program code, organizing and building it, and looking at finished products with design editors. IDEs make things happen and, in the bargain, cut hours from a task.

Visual Studio is impressive; it is massive. It would be tough to cover all Visual Studio features in a single book, much less a single chapter. In fact, you're unlikely to ever use all the Visual Studio features.

Rather than try to cover everything, this chapter gives you the chance to experience only the features of Visual Studio that you'll realistically use every day. Of course, continuing to explore the IDE and discovering new stuff is important — don't just stop with the content of this chapter. It provides only a brief overview of some of the astonishing features in the tool. You can discover more about the IDE at `https://docs.microsoft.com/visualstudio/get-started/visual-studio-ide`.

REMEMBER

You don't have to type the source code for this chapter manually. In fact, using the downloadable source is a lot easier. You can find the source for this chapter in the `\CSAIO4D2E\BK04\CH02` folder of the downloadable source. See the Introduction for details on how to find these source files.

Designing in the Designer

One thing that is integrated into an IDE is a way to edit files graphically, sometimes called a Graphic Development Environment or *designer*. Visual Studio allows you to graphically edit many different types of code bases and provides adjunct tools for the further management of said code bases. In short, the designer is the drag-and-drop element of the Visual Studio world. It isn't always the best way to develop a program, but it sure can help sometimes.

For each major type of project that Visual Studio maintains (except console applications and application elements without a visual interface, such as services), there is a designer. The designer handles the What You See Is What You Get portion of the experience and usually the behind-the-scenes markup code. In addition to the designers that Microsoft provides, you can also create your own custom editors and designers using the material found at `https://docs.microsoft.com/visualstudio/extensibility/creating-custom-editors-and-designers` as a starting point. Custom editors and designers enable you to work with application code in new ways and to support languages other than those that Visual Studio supports natively.

The problem is that because of the necessities of the software development world, different designers all work a little differently. A significant difference exists between HTML and XAML, for example, so the web designer and the WPF Designer don't look or act the same. Visual Studio gives you several visual designers to help develop applications, including these commonly used designers:

- Class designer
- Data View
- Web Forms
- Universal Windows Platform (UWP) application
- Windows Forms
- Windows Presentation Foundation (WPF)

Universal Windows Platform (UWP) application

Microsoft is getting into the run-anywhere game late — very late, but it's doing it with style. This type of application relies on the Windows Runtime (WinRT) to provide services across a multitude of devices that include your desktop, smartphone, Xbox, and other platforms. Book 5, Chapter 5 offers a good overview of this new method of creating Windows applications, but you should view this method more as an adjunct to what you have done in the past, rather than a complete replacement, because it's simply not practical to throw out your entire existing code base for software that is less capable. Because UWP applications run everywhere, they can't access the full potential of a desktop machine. It's more like writing a 32-bit application with serious limits, rather than a robust 64-bit application that can take on heavy tasks such as machine learning and serious database management. Each application type has a place in your developer Toolbox.

Much of the setup for a UWP application is the same as for any other project you've created so far in the book. However, there are a few differences, such as the need to select a target version of Windows for your app and also select the minimum acceptable version of Windows. You also have to configure your system for Developer Mode, which is covered in Book 5, Chapter 5. The initial display that you see also differs from other application-creation processes in that it gives you a series of steps to follow, as shown in Figure 2-1.

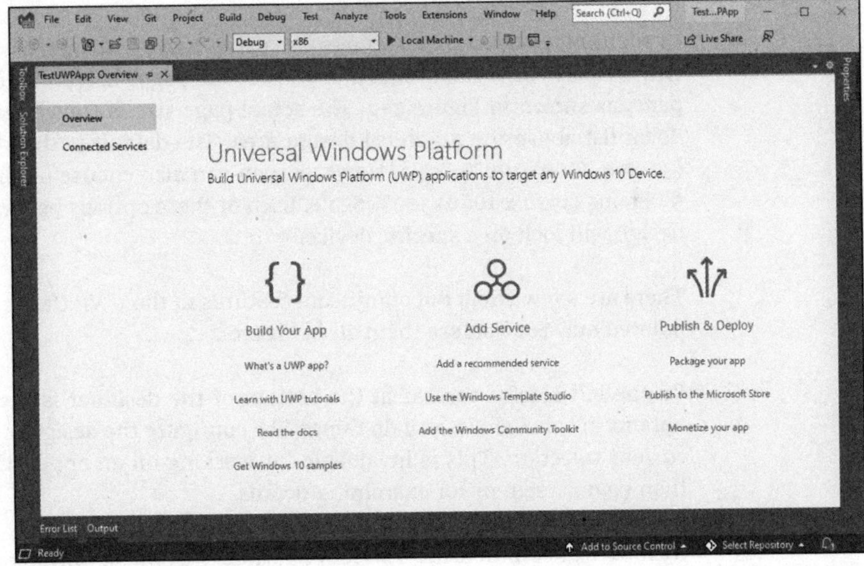

FIGURE 2-1: Creating a UWP application is a process that Visual Studio helps with.

The core of the user interface design experience is a language called Extensible Application Markup Language (XAML, pronounced *zammel*), which (unsurprisingly) is an XML-derived domain-specific markup language for the creation of user interfaces. In the designer, shown in Figure 2-2, the design is in the top frame and the underlying code is in the bottom frame.

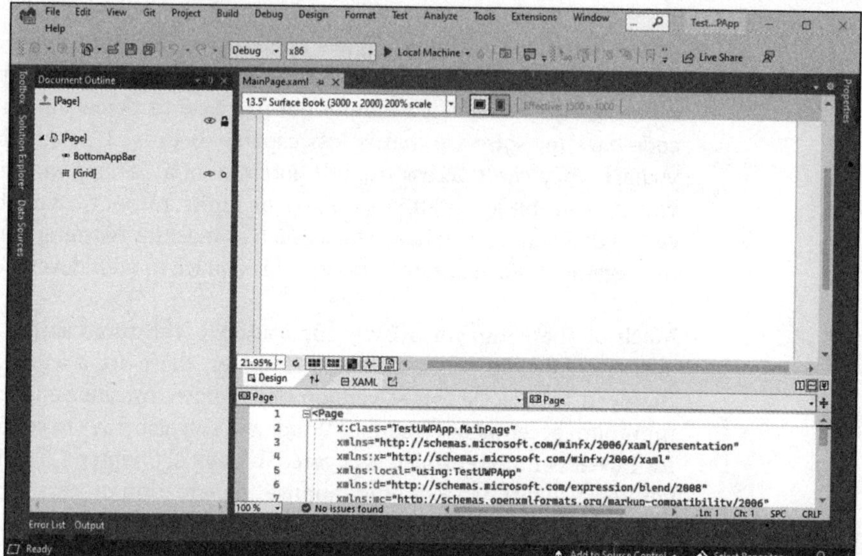

FIGURE 2-2: UWP applications rely on the use of pages to display information.

In addition, you design the application using pages. Each page is designed to work with displays of various sizes and you see the pages listed in a Document Outline pane, as shown in Figure 2-2. The actual page size is controlled using the drop-down list above the graphical design area. The default is the 13.5" Surface Book (3000 x 2000) 200% Scale. However, you can also choose other devices, such as 5" Phone (1920 x 1080) 300% Scale. Each of these options helps you see how your design will look on a specific device.

There are a few small but significant features in the UWP Designer that should be pointed out. You can see them all in Figure 2-2.

On the left side of the bar at the bottom of the designer is the Zoom field. The options in this field let you do things like configure the designer to zoom to fit the current selection. This is invaluable for working on an application that is bigger than your screen, or for examining details.

Next to the Zoom field are a series of buttons that make working with the designer easier. Here are the buttons in order of appearance:

- **Refresh:** Ensures that the design area shows any changes to the XAML and vice versa.
- **Show Snap Grid:** Toggles the snap grid. Using the snap grid helps you place controls more accurately and with less effort.

- **Snapping to Gridlines:** Determines how controls are placed on the form. Using gridline snapping means that controls automatically appear on specific boundaries, which makes placing the controls even easier. However, you also have a little less flexibility in placing controls precisely as you'd like them.
- **Toggle Artboard Background:** Controls the background shown behind the form you're creating. The default is a gray background like the one shown in Figure 2-1. You can also choose a black background that makes form features pop out better but can also be harder on the eyes.
- **Snapping to Snaplines:** Controls use of the lines *(snaplines)* that appear when you place controls on the form that show how one control aligns with another. Using snaplines makes it easier for you to align the controls and gives your form a more pleasing appearance. However, snapping to the snaplines can also make it harder to place controls precisely where you want them.
- **Control Display Options:** You can choose to display all the controls in the Toolbox (the default) or just the controls that apply to a particular platform. Using the Only Display Platform Controls option can improve the stability of the development environment and keep your eyes from going just a bit nuts trying to figure out what is what in the design area.

At the left side of the dividing line between the Design and XAML frames is a little double-arrow icon. Clicking this icon changes whatever is in the bottom frame to be in the top frame, and vice versa.

On the right side of the same dividing line are three buttons that determine the kind of split you have — a vertical split, a horizontal split (which is the default), or no split (so that the designer or Code Editor take the full space). Some people like the code. Some people like the designer. Some people prefer a mixture of the two. You determine how you want to use the tools.

Windows Presentation Foundation (WPF)

Windows Presentation Foundation is covered in some depth in Book 5, but for now you should know that it is the current focus of Microsoft's Windows desktop development experience. Yes, you still see a lot of Windows Forms development, but newer applications rely on either WPF or UWP. Book 5 talks all about WPF, so you can read more about it there. Figure 2-3 shows the WPF Designer, which has a striking similarity to the UWP Designer shown in Figure 2-2.

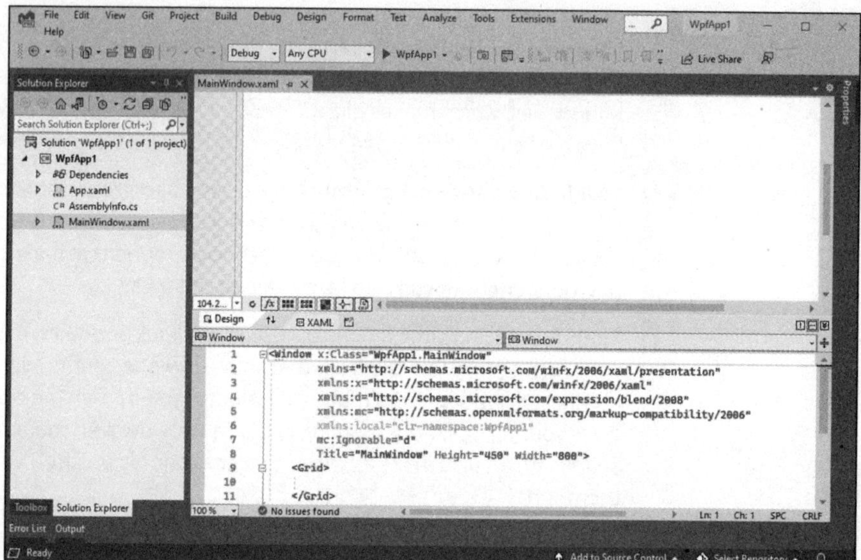

FIGURE 2-3: The WPF Designer.

REMEMBER

When creating a WPF application, you decide which version of the .NET Framework to use: .NET Core 3.1, .NET 5.0, or .NET 6.0. The framework version determines the features available to your application and somewhat controls its appearance. Figure 2-3 shows what you see when working with .NET 6.0. Notice that you see a window, not pages, as when working with the UWP Designer. You also don't select a device size.

You can click the design in the designer and move things around, if you want, or use the designer to select things and edit the properties in the Properties panel (covered in the upcoming section "Paneling the Studio"). Additionally, if you change something in the code area, you'll see the change in the design. It's a good system. The following list contains some button differences between the WPF Designer and the UWP Designer:

- **Effects (*fx*):** Toggles user interface effects. Turning the effects off does make the user interface a little less interesting but also conserves processing power for more productive uses.
- **Disable Project Code:** Enables or disables use of XAML code to display form content. Sometimes the XAML that appears in the bottom window in Figure 2-3 has errors in it. You can disable the project code to allow for fixing these errors without crashing the designer.

Windows Forms

The main difference between the Windows Forms Designer and the WPF Designer is the lack of a code panel in Windows Forms. Although there is code backing up Windows Forms, you don't get to edit it directly. The Windows Forms Designer performs this task for you and places the code in a special designer file, such as `Form1.Designer.cs` for a default project.

The topic of Windows Forms isn't covered in any detail in this book (there are a few projects, such as the network status example in Book 3, Chapter 4 and the image example in Book 3, Chapter 5). Even though it's still an active development platform, most developers are moving to WPF instead, so it pays to spend more time working with an environment that developers use for new projects. WPF performs the same programming duties as Windows Forms but is the newer technology. The Windows Forms Designer is shown in Figure 2-4.

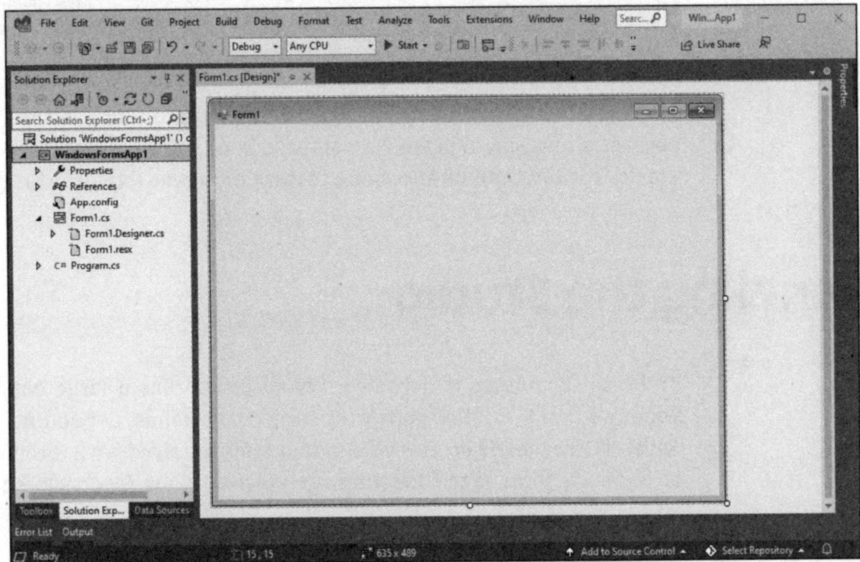

FIGURE 2-4: The Windows Forms Designer.

Data View

Data View is usually used with the Server Explorer and is part of an in-studio representation of SQL Management Studio. You can view and edit data tables in SQL Server (and other) database management systems right inside Visual Studio. An example is shown in Figure 2-5; in this case, you see the Show Table Data view of the Address (Person) table of the AdventureWorks2012 database.

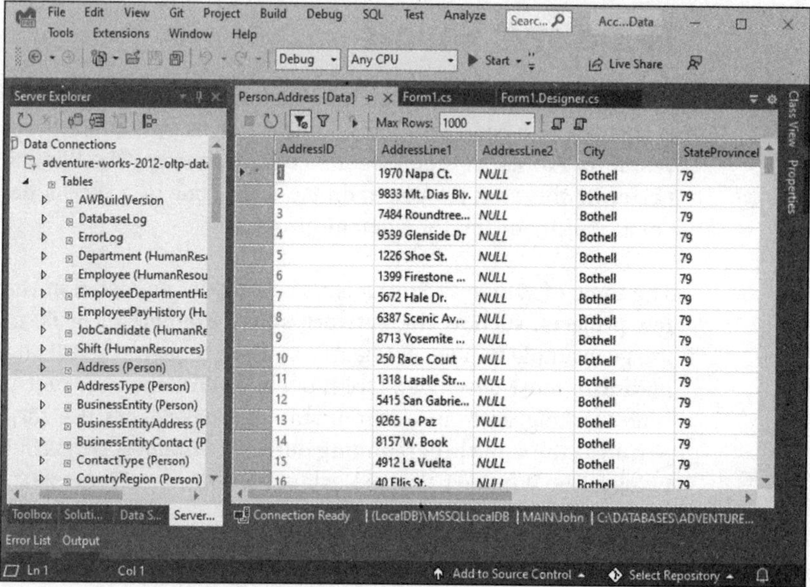

FIGURE 2-5: When you use Data View, who needs SQL Management Studio?

There is a remarkable amount of power here, and there just isn't enough space to cover it all. Again, this isn't a database book, so you may want to read the MSDN entries for the Data Connections feature of Server Explorer for more details.

Paneling the Studio

To be as flexible as it needs to, Visual Studio has a large collection of modular windows that are called *panels* (or sometimes panes, depending on whom you talk with). These panels do everything that isn't involved with directly editing a design or code. They manage files, manage objects, show feedback, show properties, do all sorts of stuff.

Visual Studio has more than 30 panels. You normally access them using either the View menu, such as View⇨Solution Explorer to see the Solution Explorer pane, or the Debug/Windows menu, such as Debug⇨Windows⇨Breakpoints to see the Breakpoints pane. There isn't room to discuss them all here, so the chapter covers only the five you use most often.

Solution Explorer

Solution Explorer (see Figure 2-6) manages solutions, projects, and files. Even though solutions consist mostly of files and folders, managing a solution is a somewhat more complex operation than it seems at first blush.

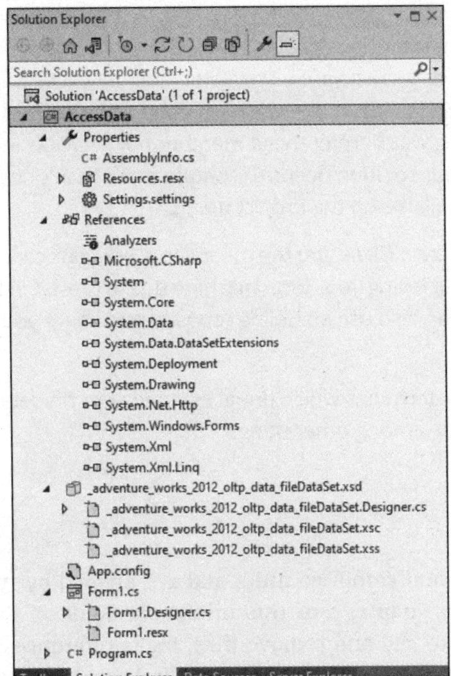

FIGURE 2-6: The explorer of solutions.

Solutions

For solutions themselves, Solution Explorer provides a number of important tools (accessible by right clicking the solution entry), including the following:

- **Solution Management:** Allows you to build, rebuild, or clean a solution. In addition, you can perform analysis that shows how your application runs.
- **Configuration Manager:** Provides a useful interface for what is basically a settings file in the solution itself. You can specify whether Release or Debug compilation is desired for your build here, if you want all debugging information stored with your file. You can tell the compiler whether you want the software built for 32-bit systems or 64-bit systems too. You can also reach Configuration Manager from the Build menu.
- **Manage and Restore NuGet Packages:** Lets you add new packages to your solution to extend the functionality that Visual Studio supplies. You can also restore existing packages to the solution as needed.
- **Add Projects:** Displays dialog boxes that you can use to add new projects to the existing solution.

- **Project Dependencies:** Choosing Set Startup Projects displays a dialog box that shows how your projects are interrelated and describes the way in which your projects depend on each other. It has a tab for the build order, too. When you're getting weird "referenced member not available in object" errors, check here first. Your solution needs to contain more than one project for this command to be available on the Project menu.
- **Create Git Repository:** Gives you the means to store your code online. This feature ensures that losing your local machine doesn't result in losing your code as well. You can also use an online repository to share your code with others.
- **Property Pages:** Determines which project should start on debug and where source files are kept, among other things.

Projects

Projects are the individual compiled units and are divided by type. You can find more about projects in Chapter 1 of this minibook. Solution Explorer brings to projects the capability to add and remove files, make references and services, set up a class diagram, open the representative Windows Explorer folder, and set properties. All this information is saved in the Project file. The Project file is just an XML file. There are a few key characteristics of the file:

- It includes a PropertyGroup for each build type. This is because you can set different properties for each type of executable.
- It contains an ItemGroup that has all the references in it, including required Framework versions, and another set of ItemGroups that have the project load details.
- The file includes the import of the project general details and the Target collections. You can actually edit the file manually to make a custom build environment.

You likely won't modify your Project file, but it's important that you know it can be done, and that Microsoft has inline comments. They expect the file to get changed.

Files

Files are a lot less exciting. They are pretty much exactly what you expect. They host the source code of the program being developed. Solution Explorer manages the files in the project basically the way Windows Explorer does. Solution Explorer lists the files and folders and allows them to be opened in the designer or the Code Editor.

TIP

Solution Explorer also knows what files to show. If the file isn't in the project, but happens to be sitting in the folder for the project, it won't show in the Explorer. If you can't find a file, try clicking the Show All Files button in the gray button bar at the top of the Explorer. The hidden files will show up grayed out but still won't compile into the project. You can add them to the project if you want.

Properties

The Properties panel (see Figure 2-7) is a simple, flexible tool that allows you to update those endless lists of details about everything in development projects. The panel is basically a window with a two-column-wide data grid. It reads properties in key/value pairs and allows for easy view and edit.

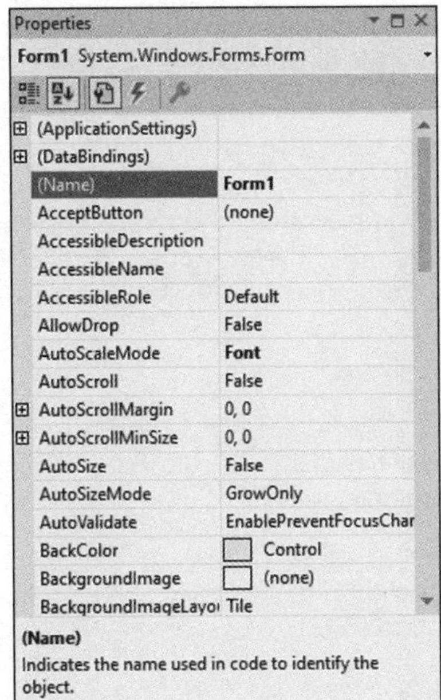

FIGURE 2-7: Modifying object properties.

You can find details about everything in your application here. If you click nearly anything in Visual Studio and press F4 to bring up the Properties panel (refer to Figure 2-7), you will get properties. Try it with these fun selections:

- Files in Solution Explorer
- Database connections
- A text box in a WPF project

- An XML tree node
- An item in Class View

If there is any metadata about something, the properties are in the Properties panel. It's a great tool.

The Toolbox

One of the great misunderstood tools is the Toolbox (see Figure 2-8). On the surface, the Toolbox seems so simple. The design-time controls for a given file type are available to drag and drop. Still, there is one important thing you need to remember about the Toolbox: It displays only controls that are appropriate to the file in focus. So if you're running a Windows Form in the designer, you won't see a database table available to drop. Keep in mind that the Toolbox is context sensitive. It works only when it has a file to work on.

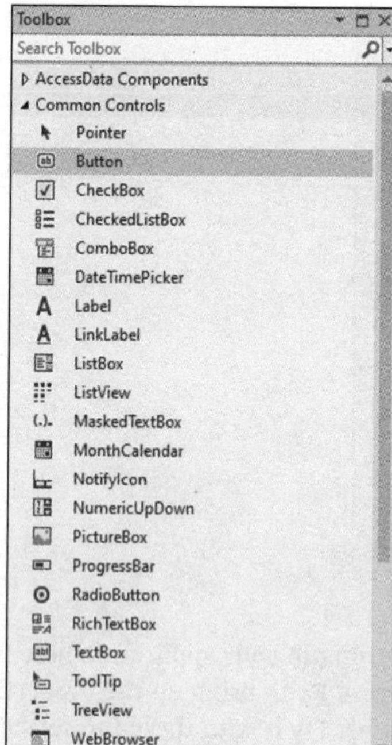

FIGURE 2-8: The Toolbox, with tools.

There is one other interesting property of the Toolbox: It can be used to store text clippings, which can be useful for demonstrations and presentations. It is also handy for storing often-used pieces of code. To do so, follow these steps:

1. **Open a code file.**

   Anything will do, `.cs` file, `.xaml` file, whatever.

2. **Highlight a piece of code.**
3. **Make sure the Toolbox is open and then drag the selected code to the General section of the TextBox.**

   The copied code becomes a tool.

4. **Open up another blank code file.**
5. **Drag the new tool into the code.**

   The copied code now appears in the code file.

Server Explorer

REMEMBER

Server Explorer (see Figure 2-9) enables developers to access important services on the local or a remote machine. These could be anything from the Microsoft Passport to Microsoft Message Queue (MSMQ) but generally include two types of services:

- Managed services
- Database connections

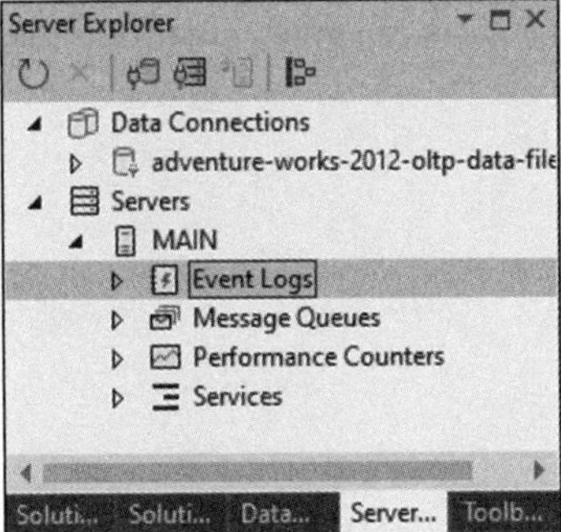

FIGURE 2-9: Server Explorer.

Managed services

Managed services include services such as the Event Logs and MSMQ, which you need to look at to test parts of your application. Internet Information Services, for example, is a managed service that shows up in the list. To get a server into Server Explorer, follow these steps:

1. **Right-click Servers.**
2. **Click the Add Server button.**
3. **Type the machine name or IP number of the server you want to add.**
4. **If you want to use different credentials than you used to log on (for a different account, for instance), click Connect Using a Different User Name and enter the new credentials.**
5. **Click OK.**

Play around with the services you see. There are a lot of features in this panel that this book doesn't cover.

Data connections

Above the Services in Figure 2-9 are the data connections. These are data connections that have been made on previous projects, which Visual Studio keeps around in case you need them for any other projects. Although keeping these connections around seems like a bit of a security risk, it sure as heck is convenient.

The goal is to reduce the dependency on SQL Management Console (the old method for managing the database for developers), and it does a darn good job. The key issue is access to the data model (table names and columns) and stored procedures; developing a program without access to the database is tough. In a new connection, these database objects are given default folders:

- Database diagrams
- Tables
- Views
- Stored Procedures
- Functions
- Types
- Synonyms
- Assemblies

The key thing you should try is to open a Stored Procedure (you can do this by double-clicking it in the Data Sources panel — which is available in a solution that has data connections). When you do so, you can easily edit SQL code, with indenting and colorization, right in Visual Studio. Use this. It's really neat.

Class View

The last of the five main panels is Class View. As discussed in Books 1 and 2, everything in the .NET Framework is an object. The classes that make up the framework — all derivatives of `Object` — are viewable in a tree view. The Class View is the home for that tree view (see Figure 2-10).

From the Class View, you can look at all the members of a class and access the inline documentation, which gives you an overview of the framework and custom classes that make up your project.

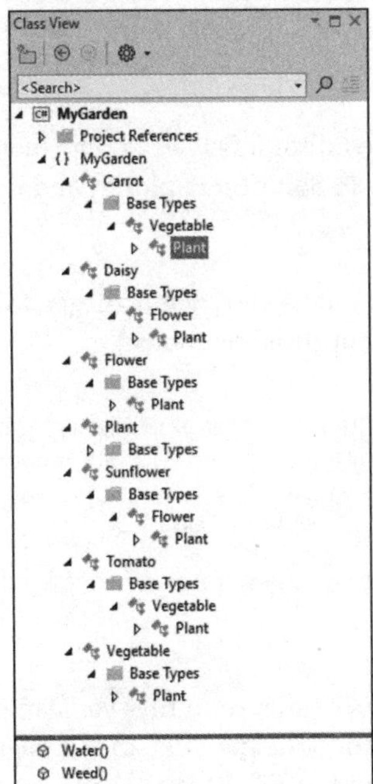

FIGURE 2-10: A view with Class.

Coding in the Code Editor

There is a lot to the Code Editor in Visual Studio. This is where you spend most of your time. Code Editor has two primary tools:

- **The Editor itself:** The first is the screen on which you edit the code — the Code Editor.
- **Auxiliary windows:** The second are the little auxiliary windows that do a lot of useful things that don't directly relate to the code.

Exercising the Code Editor

The Code Editor is where you edit code. It doesn't matter what type of code; all of it is edited here. You use the Code Editor to create class libraries, and it provides a smart interface for ensuring your class libraries have a good chance of working. If you are in XML, it works like an XML editor (such as the lower half of the view in Figure 2-2, shown previously).

You can get to a code file in the Code Editor a few ways. The most common way is to double-click on a source code file in Solution Explorer, and it will open in Code Editor.

If you are viewing something in the designer, you can get to the code-behind related to the file in question by any of three methods:

- Click the View Code button in Solution Explorer after highlighting a file in the list.
- Right-click the design surface and select View Code.
- Double-click a control in the designer to generate an event for that control and be moved to Code View.

You'll find yourself using all three over time. Note that you can get directly to the code-behind files by clicking the little triangle next to a designer file and then double-clicking the code files nested within. (This feature works with auto-generated files, but won't open the code-behind associated with the auto-generated file.)

Autocompleting with IntelliSense

IntelliSense (sometimes also called AutoComplete, IntelliCode, or other names just to confuse you) is Microsoft's autocompletion feature, and it's a prominent part of the Code Editor. You find IntelliSense whether you want to or not. In Code

View, click inside a class and press Ctrl+spacebar. Everything you are allowed to type there shows up in a big list.

The nice thing is, IntelliSense is context-sensitive. Type **Console** and press the dot (`.`). All available members of the `Console` class appear. IntelliSense keeps you honest and prevents having to remember the two-million-odd members of the .NET Framework on a day-by-day basis.

IntelliSense helps with method signatures, too. Continue the line you started earlier by adding `WriteLine` — in other words, type **(Console.WriteLine)** — and then check out the IntelliSense. It will tell you all the overloads for the member in question. Use the up and down arrows to move between these members. It's slick.

Outlining

Visual Studio will auto-outline your code for you. Notice the little box with a minus sign (–) next to every namespace, class, and method in the Code Editor. Those are close-up sections of the code for readability. It might not seem like much now, but when you have 2,200 lines of code in there, you will be glad.

You can create your own outlining, too. Preceding a section that you want to outline, type **#region** on a new line. At the end of the section, type **#endregion**. This newly defined section — regardless of whether it's at an existing outline point — will get a new outline mark. If a comment is added after a `region` statement, it will show in the collapsed outline.

TIP

You can expand or collapse a region by clicking the + sign or the - sign next to the `#region` entry. Collapse a region to focus your time on the code that requires change. Expand a region to make the hidden code appear again so you can work on it.

Exploring the auxiliary windows

A number of windows affect text input and output in order to solve certain problems. As a group, they don't really have a name, so some developers call them auxiliary windows. Here are a few of them:

- **The Output window:** You use the Output window regularly for two things:
  - **Build logging:** Every time you build, the Output window tracks all the linking and compiling that go on under the sheets and shows any errors that might come up.

You can use errors listed in the Output window to navigate the code. The buttons in the Output box assist with getting around the code based on the messages in the window.

- **Debug statements:** The second use of the Output window is as a means of seeing debug statements. If you use a `Debug.Write()` statement in your code, the Output window is where it will go. Additionally, if you use `Console.Write()`, but are running a Windows Forms application, for instance, the text will go to the Output window.

» **The Immediate window:** This window does exactly what one would expect it to do: take action immediately. In debug mode, you can use the Immediate window to send commands to the program as it is running, to change the state, or evaluate operations. Try the following to see how the Immediate window works:

1. **Open any executable project.**
2. **Put a breakpoint somewhere in the code by clicking in the gray bar running down the side of Code View.**

   A red dot appears.
3. **Choose Debug ⇨ Start Debugging or press F5.**

   The program should stop at the spot you selected.
4. **Select the Immediate window.**

   If you don't see the Immediate window displayed by default, choose Debug ⇨ Windows ⇨ Immediate or press Ctrl+D,I.
5. **Type** ? this.

   See the IntelliSense menu?
6. **Type a . (dot).**

   You see a listing of all the things you can do with the `this` object (which may be nothing if you're not in a class) at the particular point you're at in the code. The ? command means to print whatever the object contains.

That's what the Immediate window is for. You can do more than print values, too. You can change variable values and modify the execution of your program. It is a powerful part of your debugging Toolbox.

» **The Breakpoints window:** If you're still running the last example, you can display the Breakpoints window by pressing Ctrl+D,B. The Breakpoints window appears, and any breakpoints you add will be in it (see Figure 2-11).

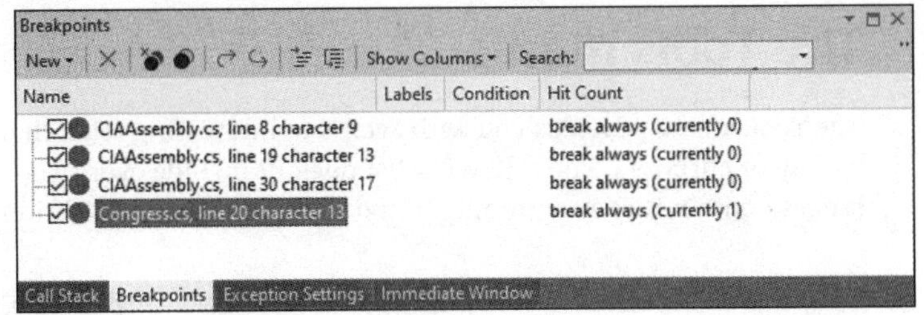

FIGURE 2-11: The Breakpoints window.

What's cool here is that you can right-click any breakpoint and completely alter the properties of that breakpoint by choosing Settings from the context menu. Try it — the important options are described in this list:

- **Location:** Specifies the location of the line of code that should host the breakpoint. This is convenient if you have filters set and you find you need to shift a line back.
- **Condition:** You can teach the breakpoint to stop at this line only if a certain variable is a specific value.
- **Hit Count:** Stop here only after the *x*th time it is hit.
- **Filter:** It's similar to Condition, except that you can use system values such as `MachineName`, `ProcessName`, `ProcessId`, `ThreadName`, and `ThreadId`. It's useful for multiprocessor development, among other things.
- **Actions (not shown):** You can do more than just stop on a breakpoint — instead, you can do something like print a value to the Output window, or even run a test script.

» **The Task List window:** While coding, have you ever wanted to tell the developer working after you that something still needs to be done? To make this happen, create a comment and start it with `//TODO:`. Adding a TODO comment makes it appear as a task in the Task List window (found on the View menu). Double-clicking the task in the Task List takes you to the line where the task was set, so you don't have to search for it.

Using the Tools of the Trade

Any overview chapter always has topics that just don't fit in any category. This chapter presents a double handful of tools that you want to know about.

The Tools menu

The Tools menu provides you with access to interesting tools that you can use for a variety of purposes. The following list doesn't include every Tools menu entry, but it does contain those commonly found in the Community edition of Visual Studio.

- **Get Tools and Features:** Displays the Visual Studio Installer, where you find new features to add to Visual Studio, plus any Microsoft-supplied updates for the base product.
- **Connect to Database:** See the "Server Explorer" section, earlier in this chapter.
- **Connect to Server:** Discussed in the "Server Explorer" section.
- **SQL Server (only when SQL Server is installed):** Provides a menu containing tasks that you perform specifically with SQL Server, rather than any other data source.
- **Code Snippets Manager:** Code snippets make it possible to reuse bits of code in your application. See `https://docs.microsoft.com/en-us/visualstudio/ide/code-snippets` for additional details.
- **Choose Toolbox Items:** This tool helps you manage the items in the Toolbox. You can add or remove a variety of components, including .NET, WPF, COM, and Silverlight.
- **NuGet Package Manager:** Manages Visual Studio Add-ins. Add, remove, enable, and disable.
- **Create GUID:** Creates a Globally Unique ID (GUID), one of those 25-character codes that are supposed to be unique over the next 2,500 years or something.
- **External Tools:** Enables you to add separate EXE files to the Tools menu, such as Notepad, NUnit, or other tools, that add functionality to Visual Studio.
- **Command Line:** Displays a Windows command-prompt window or a PowerShell window in which you can interact with your application, Visual Studio, C#, or other tools. Both windows open in the current project's folder, so you don't have to look for it on the drive.
- **Import and Export Settings:** Helps you move projects between development tools. You can store your current settings in a file in the `Users\<User Name>\AppData\Local\Microsoft\VisualStudio\<Version Number>\Settings` directory or change current settings to another batch of settings. You can share settings with other developers.
- **Customize:** Enables you to alter the look and feel of Visual Studio's menus and toolbars, including which toolbars are visible and the commands that they contain.
- **Options:** Alters the way Visual Studio works. Options are covered in some depth in Chapter 3 of this minibook. Set Visual Studio up to look and work the way you like.

Building

Previous chapters of this book discuss the basics of building a project. A few other options in the Build menu deserve at least a small explanation, including the following:

- **Rebuild:** This checks all the references throughout the project. It then removes any existing compiled files and compiles the project from scratch. It's useful if your development computer has changed configuration since your last build.
- **Clean:** This actually deletes not only the EXEs and DLLs created as part of your project (but not your code files), but also all DLLs that were copied into your project by references that were set to that mode.
- **Batch Build:** This enables you to build release and debug versions (for instance), or 32 and 64 bit (as another example) at the same time.
- **Configuration Manager:** Use this to set the order and mode in which you build your projects. The most common configurations are DEBUG (for code in progress) and RELEASE (for finished code).

Using the Debugger as an Aid to Learning

You might be surprised to discover how many professional developers learn new techniques, which is by looking at other people's code. It might seem like cheating, but it's actually the smart way to do things because someone else has already done all the hard work. Of course, trying to figure out how a particularly subtle programming technique works could consume days if you just look at the code. It's much easier to determine how the code works when seeing it in action, which is precisely why the debugger is an aid to learning. By running the code and stepping through it a bit at a time, you not only discover new programming techniques but also develop a better sense of precisely how C# works.

The example in this section relies on the cribbage application you first discover in Book 3, Chapter 5. However, the techniques work with any code, and you shouldn't feel the need to work through any particular example. The following sections fill in the details for you.

Stepping through code

The first step in working with the debugger as an aid to learning is to set one or more breakpoints in the code. For example, you might want to see how the

`CribbageBoard_Paint()` method works for the Cribbage application. To perform this task, you simply click the gray stripe that runs along the left side of the Code Editor. The breakpoint appears with a red dot in the left margin and the piece of code highlighted (normally in red as well).

The next step is to start the debugger by pressing F5 or choosing Debug ⇨ Start Debugging. You stop at the first breakpoint that the application encounters, which may not be the first breakpoint you set or the first breakpoint in the code. In fact, it's often revealing to see where you do end up because the location of a breakpoint tells you how the application starts, including what tasks it must perform and in what order it performs them.

Stepping through the code comes next. You see where the instruction pointer moves as the application executes code. You have three options for stepping through code:

- **Step Into:** Executes the next line of code. When the code is a method call, the instruction pointer goes to that method so that you see the internal workings of that method. Of course, you must have the method's source code in order to see how it works.
- **Step Over:** Executes the next line of code without entering any method calls. The content of a method call still executes, but you see the result of the method call, rather than how the method call actually works. The method call becomes a black box.
- **Step Out:** Moves to the next level up (after completing execution of the current method) and then executes the next line of the caller's code. If you have seen what you want to see inside a method call, clicking this button will move out of the method so that you can see the next line of code in the next level of the application (unless you're already at the top level of the application).

Going to a particular code location

When the application is running, you may not want to single step through every line of code. Yes, you want to stop at a certain breakpoint, but then you decide that you don't really want to stay there and execute the code line by line. In this case, you can hover the mouse next to the line of code that you do want to stop at next. You see a green right-pointing arrow like the one shown in Figure 2-12.

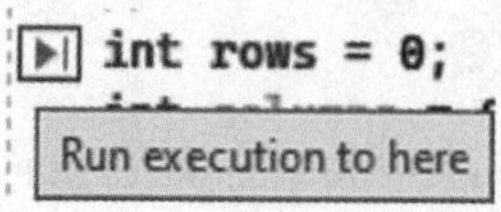

```
int rows = 0;
```

Run execution to here

FIGURE 2-12: Executing to a line of code.

When you click the right-pointing arrow, the code from the existing instruction pointer location to the location you point to will execute. You see the results of the execution, but not the individual steps. In some cases, this technique will help you get past problematic pieces of code where timing prevents you from truly seeing how the code executes.

Watching application data

Understanding how data changes over time is an essential part of learning with the debugger. You have access to a number of windows to help you do this. For example, you can include `Debug` and `Trace` statements in your code and then view their output in the Output window. To include `Debug` and `Trace` statements, you must add `using System.Diagnostics;` to the top of your application code. Use `Debug` statements when you want to output values only for debug releases of your application. Use `Trace` statements when you want to output values for both debug and release versions of your application.

Whenever you execute an application, the Locals window shown in Figure 2-13 contains a list of the local (rather than the global) variables. The local variables are those that are set in the current method and are likely the variables you use most often in well-designed code.

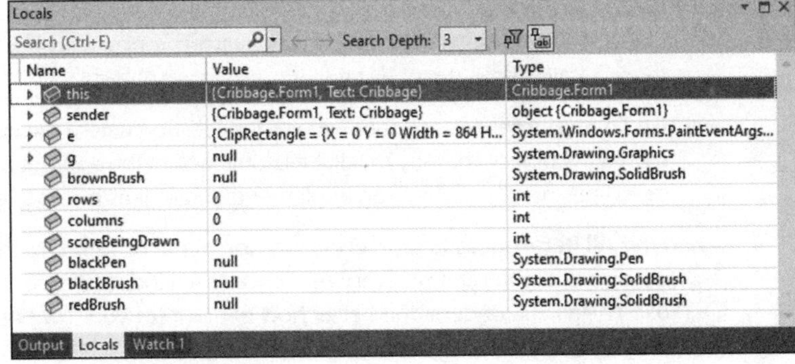

FIGURE 2-13: Use the Locals window to see local variable values.

The right-pointing arrow next to a variable entry tells you that you can drill down to find more information. In fact, in some situations, you can drill down quite a few levels before you finally reach the end. Some objects are really complex. Viewing the content of objects helps you understand them better and often provides insights into how to better use them to create robust applications.

If a particular variable doesn't appear in the Locals window or you want to view a particular object element in more detail as the code executes, you can use the Watch window, shown in Figure 2-14, instead. You type the variable you want to watch in the window. As the code executes, you see the value change. The Watch window also allows entry of expressions such as `radius * 2` or `employee == null`.

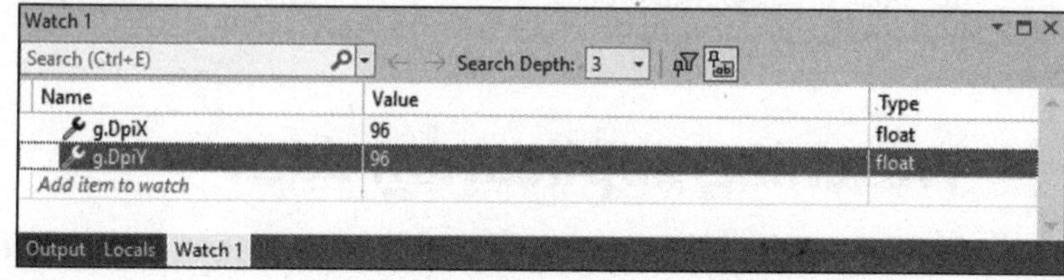

FIGURE 2-14: Use the Watch window to create custom variable views.

Viewing application internals

Learning to right-click in Visual Studio is a valuable aid in learning. Whenever you see anything that looks interesting, right-click it. The context menu tells you the sorts of things you can do with the object. For example, you might right-click a class and choose one of the detail view entries for it in the context menu. The internal view options you use most are

- **Peek Definition:** Shows the definition for the requested object in a small window within the current code window. The definition tells you more about the object.
- **Go To Definition:** Opens the file containing the definition for the requested object. This approach may take you away from your application, but you get more details about the object and its associated objects.
- **Go To Implementation:** Takes you to the location where the code implements the object, thereby making it usable within the application. A definition describes the object, while an implementation makes it a usable, real object.
- **Find All References:** Shows every location in the code where the object is used so that you can find every reference to it. Finding where an object is used helps you understand better how to use it for your own needs.

IN THIS CHAPTER

» Setting environment options

» Changing menus and commands

» Developing project template

Chapter 3

Customizing Visual Studio

In Chapters 1 and 2 of this minibook, you see how to install Visual Studio and make a new project. You also see the bits that the user interface gives you. The fun's over. Now you get to make it work for you.

Visual Studio offers a dizzying array of options for customization. Used poorly, these options have the real potential to make the lives of you and your coworkers miserable. Used correctly, they have the potential to double your productivity.

At its most basic, customization involves setting options to better match your environment, style, and work patterns. These options include everything from your code visibility to source control. The idea is to configure Visual Studio's options to your exact specifications.

The next step is to improve the usability of the application to match your day-to-day operations. One of the best overall ways to accomplish this is to change the button toolbar and the menus to make what you use every day more available.

Finally, you take a short deep dive into the Project and File templates of Visual Studio. Did you know that when you create a new XAML file (for example) or C# Class file that the contents of that file are controlled by a template and are editable? No? Well, you do now!

All these things put together amount to a rather flexible Integrated Development Environment (IDE). Although the flexibility is nice, the goal is to set a configuration that matches your style. Only you know what that configuration is. This chapter tells you what the software can do and gives you the tools to make the changes.

REMEMBER

You don't have to type the source code for this chapter manually. In fact, using the downloadable source is a lot easier. You can find the source for this chapter in the `\CSAIO4D2E\BK04\CH03` folder of the downloadable source. See the Introduction for details on how to find these source files.

Setting Options

Choose the Tools ⇨ Options menu item to open the Options dialog box, which looks like Figure 3-1 (the number of pages you see depends on the Visual Studio features you have installed). (The Environment section may be opened to show its content when you open the dialog box; click the arrow next to the section header to see other entries.) It is generally designed to set Boolean type options like Show This or Provide That or to change paths to resources where Visual Studio will store certain files.

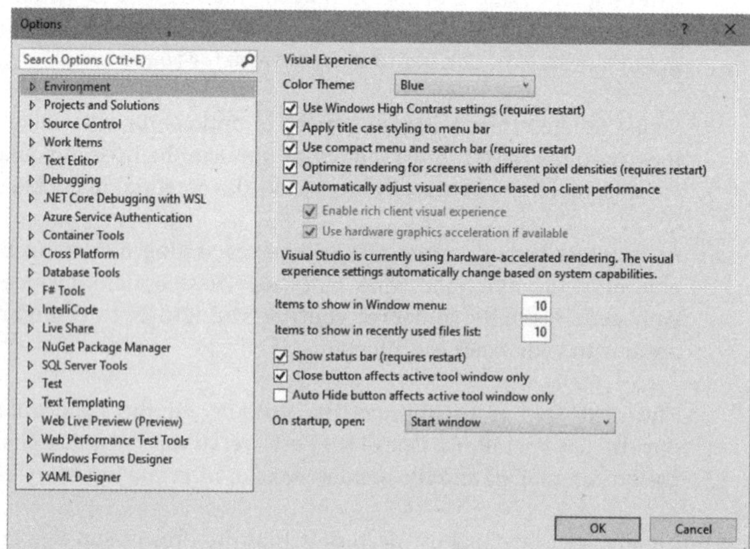

FIGURE 3-1: The default Options screen.

Those details are all well and good, but the goal of this chapter is to introduce the other things that the options provide. The following sections start with adjustments to your environment, describe the remarkable language options, and then explore some neat stuff.

Environment

The Environment section is where you begin in the Options dialog box. Sections here include the font details of code-editing screens, key mappings, and the Really Simple Syndication (RSS) feed settings for the Start window.

The Environment\Fonts and Colors settings will probably be of interest only when you need them for a presentation or you have a special visual need (such as color blindness or an inability to see small type). Sixteen points is the size of choice for most developers. There are a number of "code friendly" fonts out there, and this is where you select them.

Defining the Start window

The *Start window* is the first graphical element you see when you start Visual Studio. You find this setting in the Environment\General page. The On Startup, Open drop-down list box contains these options:

- **Start Window:** The default option is to open the Start window so that you can open a recent solution, create a new solution, obtain code from an online repository, or open either a remote or local project or solution that you haven't opened recently (or perhaps at all).
- **Most Recent Solution:** This option ignores the Start window completely and gets you right to work. If you want, you can still view the Start window by closing the solution (use File⇨Close Solution). Use this option if you tend not to view the Start window content.
- **Empty Environment:** This option opens Visual Studio without doing anything at all. Use this option when you don't know how you'd like to start your session but find it annoying when Visual Studio tries to make the decision for you.

Keyboard commands

The most useful settings in the Options dialog box are the Environment\Keyboard settings. This is where you make Visual Studio feel like Visual C# 2005 through the use of keyboard mappings.

TIP

Keyboard mappings are key combinations you set to run commands from the keyboard rather than by clicking your mouse. For example, one commonly used mapping is Ctrl+C, which copies material in the same way that clicking the Edit menu and then clicking Copy does. Many developers feel that using keyboard mapped commands makes the development experience faster and easier.

The keyboard settings essentially enable you to set keyboard commands for any menu selection in Visual Studio. The Apply the Following Additional Keyboard Mapping Scheme drop-down list enables the key mappings to be different, if you happen to like the mappings of other development environments.

Language

The term *language* doesn't mean the Environment\International Settings page settings that enable you to change the display language of Visual Studio if you have additional language packs installed (although that is neat). It refers to the *programming* languages you work in with Visual Studio. The Text Editor section is where you can provide settings for each of these programming languages.

The Text Editor options change the way the Code Editor behaves. All the languages that Visual Studio supports out of the box appear in the tree view under the main heading and allow you to alter general options, tabbing, formatting, sometimes advanced options, and miscellaneous features of the text editor.

For instance, look at Text Editor\C#. To open the C# section, click the right-pointing arrow next to Text Editor and then the right-pointing arrow next to C#. The first view in the Options panel is the General view. Here you can change the default options for statement completion, various behavior settings, and what the Code Editor should display aside from the code. The other panels you can use are

- **Scroll Bars:** This section contains options for how and when Visual Studio displays scroll bars. You have individual settings for horizontal and vertical scroll bars. All the annotation options also appear on this page.
- **Tabs:** This section is for people who are obsessive about the tabbing of their source code. The Tabs panel determines how many spaces make up a tab, and whether Visual Studio should insert them automatically.
- **Advanced:** This section should probably be called *Miscellaneous*. Everything that doesn't fit into other categories is here. In this section, handling comments, interface implementation, and refactoring details all have a check box that basically says, "If you don't like it when Visual Studio does this, click here."

» **Code Style:** This section has a number of subsections that all define how Visual Studio presents and formats code.

- **General:** Contains all the options for defining how Visual Studio presents `this` object entries.
- **Formatting:** Formatting in C# is very in-depth. Generally, C# coders are a little persnickety about the look of their code. Visual Studio does a lot of work to help make your code look the way you want it, but you have to tell it what to do. Options for formatting include: General (automatic formatting features); Indentation; Newlines; Spacing; and Wrapping.
- **Naming:** This page contains options for determining when and how Visual Studio alerts you to potential naming issues in your code. For example, there is an option for ensuring that you start all interface names with the letter I. If you create an interface that doesn't have a name that begins with I, the compiler reports it as a Required Style error at the Severity Level you prefer.

» **IntelliSense:** This section determines how IntelliSense works within the editor. For example, you can determine whether to include completion lists as part of the IntelliSense selections.

Neat stuff

Here's a short list of rarely used features. Right now, they probably won't make a lot of sense, but you will remember them when you need them later.

» To implement a new source control provider, first install the package (for instance, Turtle for CodePlex's SVN implementation, or Team System) and then go to Source Control in Options to pick the one you want to use.

» Many people recommend that you store your projects in a short file path, like `C:\Projects`. You can change where you store projects in the Projects and Solutions\Locations section in the Options dialog box.

» The NuGet Package Manager is an essential part of Visual Studio because it lets you add specialized functionality. Visual Studio ships with just one source (albeit an extensive one). However, you can add more sources as needed in the NuGet Package Manager\Package Sources section. For an example of another source you might want to use, check out the article at `https://www.grapecity.com/componentone/docs/uwp/online-getting-started/config-nugetpackage.html`.

» You can teach Visual Studio to open a file with a given extension in a certain file editor using the Text Editor / File Extension section of the Options panel.

Creating Your Own Templates

Older versions of Visual Studio required that you rely on various hacks to create custom templates. Visual Studio 2019 and above provide a much better, much easier approach to working with custom templates using the Visual Studio IDE so that you don't have to worry about hacking into anything. The following sections provide quick methods for creating both project and item templates of your own.

Developing a project template

Just setting up a project can take a while. If you commonly use a particular project configuration, performing all the required work just once makes more sense than doing it every time you create a new project. The following steps help you create a custom project template that contains both a console application and a class file. However, you can use this approach for creating any sort of custom project template that you require.

1. **Click Create a New Project.**

   You see a selection of project templates.

2. **Highlight the Console App (.NET Framework) entry and click Next.**

   You see the Configure Your New Project page of the wizard.

3. **Type** ConsoleAndClass **in the Project Name field, select a location for this project, check Place Solution and Project in the Same Directory, and choose a .NET Framework version. Click Create.**

   Visual Studio creates a new project for you. At this point, you can provide any generic project-specific changes you need to include. However, remember that you're not creating a full-fledged application — you're creating a template, a sort of a blank.

4. **Right-click the ConsoleAndClass project in Solution Explorer and choose Add ⇨ New ⇨ Item from the context menu.**

   Visual Studio displays the Add New Item dialog box.

5. **Select the Class Entry and click Add.**

   There is no need to give the class a specific name because you'll rename it when you use the template.

6. **Perform any required class configuration.**

   If you configure your classes in a certain way every time, this is the time to make the required changes. The goal is to save time.

7. **Choose File ⇨ Save All.**

The reason you don't bother to compile your template is that it really shouldn't contain anything to compile — just the configuration for an application you want to create later.

8. **Choose Project ⇨ Export Template.**

You see the Choose Template Type page, shown in Figure 3-2. This is where you choose between a project and an item template, and which elements you want to appear in the template.

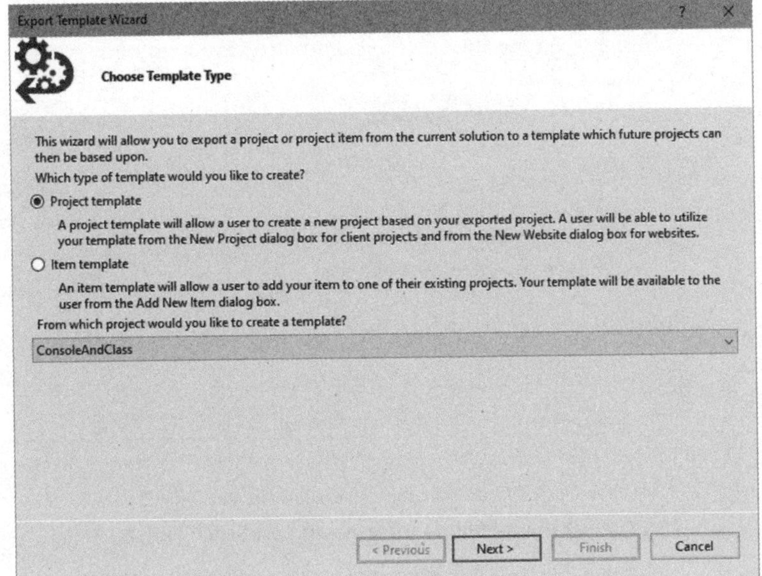

FIGURE 3-2: Determine whether you want to create a project or item template.

9. **Select Project Template and click Next.**

The wizard presents the Select Template Options page, shown in Figure 3-3. This is where you provide definitions for the template name, how to use it, and any graphics you want associated with the template. Note that the Output Location field is automatically defined for you, and you can't change it. Your template will appear in a `.zip` file, but you'll be able to access it like any other template. Here are some suggestions for the various field entries:

- Choose a name that defines precisely what the template will do, such as Console and Class Combined.
- Provide a template description that adds to the class name, such as "This template creates a .NET Framework console application with a class added."

- Make sure that the icon image is distinctive so that your template sticks out in the list. The example uses a red clock icon to signify that the template will save time.
- Create a screenshot for the preview image field if your template is graphical in nature. Otherwise, you really don't need an entry in this field.

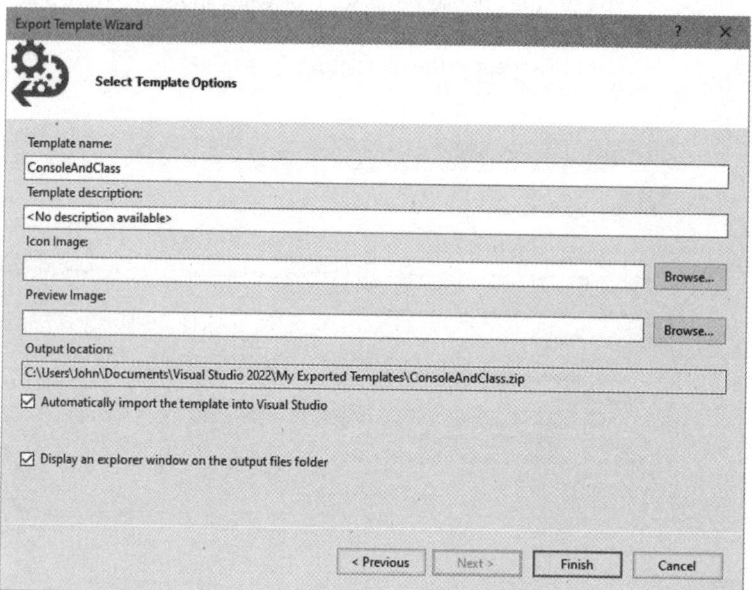

FIGURE 3-3: Provide enough information for others to use your template.

10. Fill out the template information and click Finish.

TIP

The wizard opens a copy of Explorer for you to the folder containing your template, such as `C:\Users\`*`<User Name>`*`\Documents\Visual Studio 2022\My Exported Templates`. You can copy the template to the Clipboard and store it in another location if you plan to share it with others. It's also possible to make template modifications by hacking into the files, something you should probably avoid unless you really do need to make changes.

REMEMBER

Make sure to close any projects and restart Visual Studio after creating a new project template. At this point, you can use your template to create new projects. However, template filtering doesn't work with user-defined templates, so you must set the filters to All Languages, All Platforms, and All Project Types to see your template, which will normally appear at the top of the list, as shown in Figure 3-4. If you don't see your template, you can search for it using the Search for Templates field at the top of the Create a New Project dialog box.

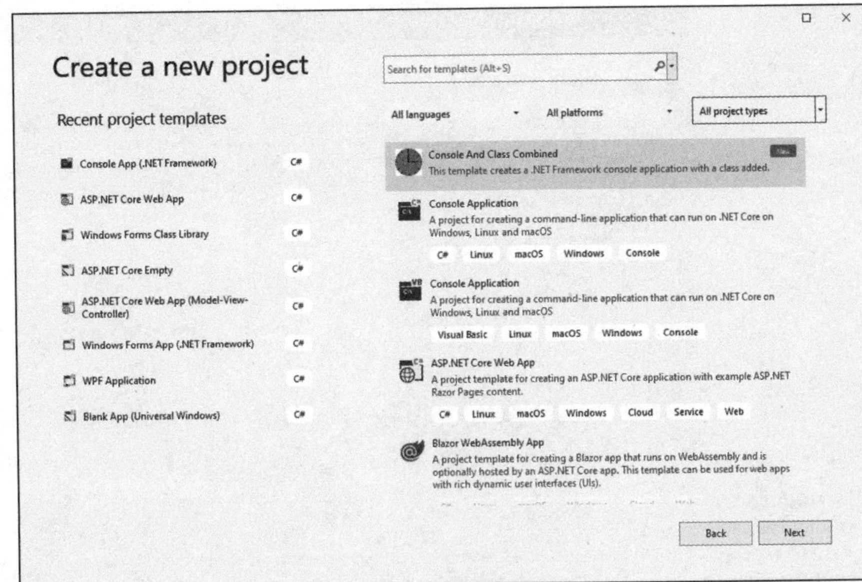

FIGURE 3-4: Your template will normally appear first in the list after you remove all filtering.

Developing an item template

Creating an item template is similar to creating a project template. You begin by creating a project, just as you do in the previous section. Follow these steps to create an item template (which differs from a project template):

1. **Choose Project⇨Export Template.**

   You see the Choose Template Type page of the Export Template Wizard, shown previously in Figure 3-2.

2. **Select Item Template and choose a project, if necessary; then click Next.**

   The wizard displays the Select Item to Export page, shown in Figure 3-5.

3. **Select one of the items to export, such as AssemblyInfo.cs if you have a common set of configuration items you add to a project; then click Next.**

   You see the Select Item References page, shown in Figure 3-6. This is where you ensure that the item template will have the specific references needed to perform correctly.

WARNING

In some cases, you can avoid potential future conflicts by not selecting any of the references at all, but doing so would mean that the item would have to work with literally any version of the .NET Framework. Many items you export will require a reference to `System` as a minimum. If you have any doubts, check the actual code files for the item you want to export to determine when a specific reference version is needed.

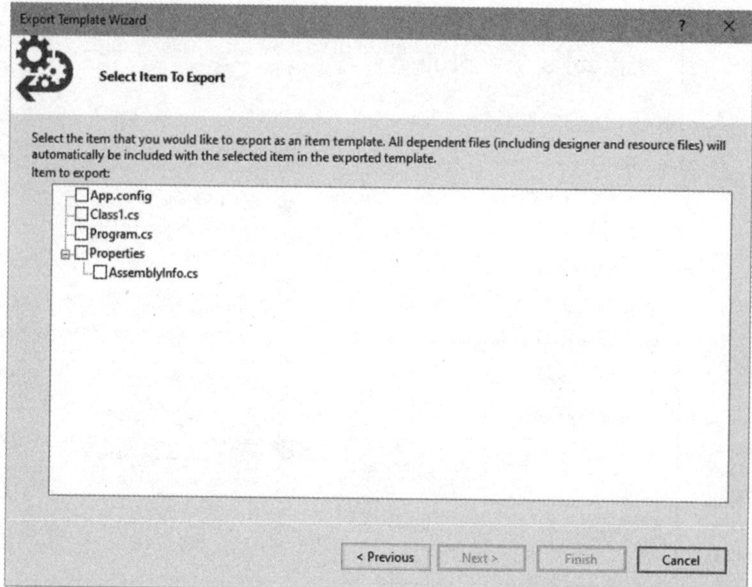

FIGURE 3-5: Determine which item to export from the project.

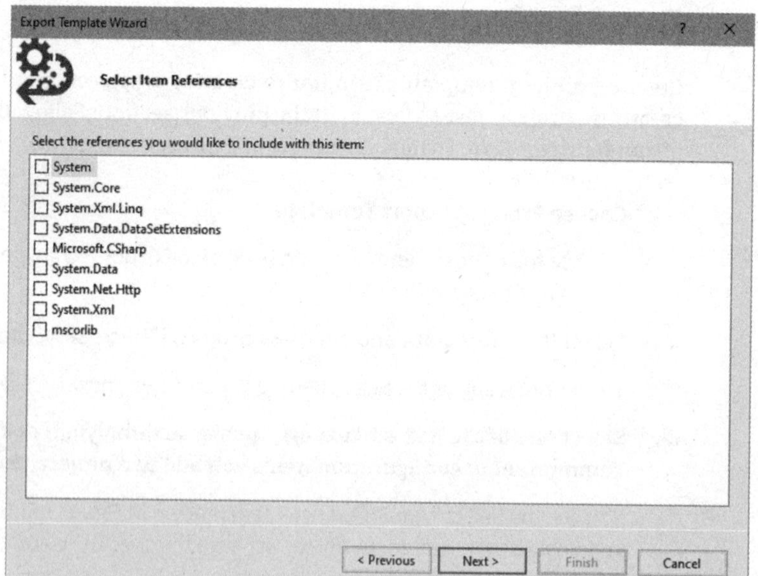

FIGURE 3-6: Select the references needed to use your item successfully.

4. **Select any required references and then click Next.**

   You see the Select Template Options page, shown in Figure 3-3.

5. **Fill out the required information for each field and then click Finish.**

   The wizard opens a copy of Explorer to the folder containing your template, such as `C:\Users\`*`<User Name>`*`\Documents\Visual Studio 2022\My Exported Templates`. The template will appear in a `.zip` file.

REMEMBER

Make sure that you close any projects and restart Visual Studio after creating a new item template. At this point, you can right-click the project entry in Solution Explorer and choose Add⇨New Item from the context menu. You'll see the new item templates you created in the Add New Item dialog box.

5

Windows Development with WPF

Contents at a Glance

IN THIS CHAPTER

» Taking a first look at WPF and what it can do for you

» Working with XAML

» Building your first WPF application

» Comparing XAML to C#

Chapter 1
Introducing WPF

WPF, or Windows Presentation Foundation, is a graphical system for rendering user interfaces. It provides great flexibility in how you can lay out and interact with your applications. With Common Language Runtime (CLR) at its core, you can use C# or any other CLR language to communicate with user-interface elements and develop application logic. The advantages of WPF for your application are its rich data binding and visualization support and its design flexibility and styling.

WPF enables you to create an application that is more usable to your audience. It gives you the power to design an application that would previously take extremely long development cycles and a calculus genius to implement. Now you can implement difficult things like graphics and animations in as few as three lines of code! This chapter introduces you to key WPF concepts as well as common application patterns used in the software industry today.

REMEMBER

You don't have to type the source code for this chapter manually. In fact, using the downloadable source is a lot easier. You can find the source for this chapter in the `\CSAIO4D2E\BK05\CH01` folder of the downloadable source. See the Introduction for details on how to find these source files.

Understanding What WPF Can Do

WPF's graphics capabilities make it the perfect choice for data visualization. Take, for instance, the standard drop-down list (or combo box). Its current use is to enable the user to choose a single item from a list of items. For this example, suppose you want the user to select a car model for purchase.

The standard way of displaying this choice is to display a drop-down list of car model names from which users can choose. There is a fundamental usability problem with this common solution: Users are given only a single piece of information from which to base their decision — the text that is used to represent the item in the list.

For the power user (or car fanatic), this may not be an issue, but other users need more than just a model name to make an educated decision on the car they want to purchase. This is where WPF and its data visualization capabilities come into play.

You can provide a template to define how each item in the drop-down list is rendered. The template can contain any visual element, such as images, labels, text boxes, tooltips, drop shadows, and more!

Figure 1-1 shows a typical display of a combo box. This control has limitations: It can relay to the user only a single piece of information, the text used to represent the car model (yes, you could add graphics to the combo box using low-level programming techniques beyond the ken of mere mortals, but most people wouldn't want to). It's possible for you to display images of the car models in a separate control based on the selection in the list, but this still mandates users to make their selection before seeing exactly what it is they are choosing. In contrast, WPF has the flexibility to display many pieces of information in each combo box item, like a one-stop shop for all the information the user will need to make their decision. (See Figure 1-2 for a WPF combo box.)

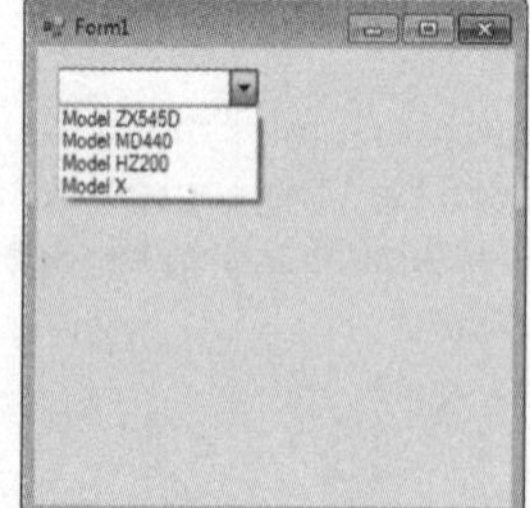

FIGURE 1-1: A typical combo box.

Figure 1-2 shows a sample combo box in WPF. The way the combo box item is rendered is defined using a data template. (Chapter 3 of this minibook covers data templates.) Each item in this combo box is rendered to provide the user with a visual cue along with multiple data fields. Displaying all this information enables users to make an educated decision about the choice they are making.

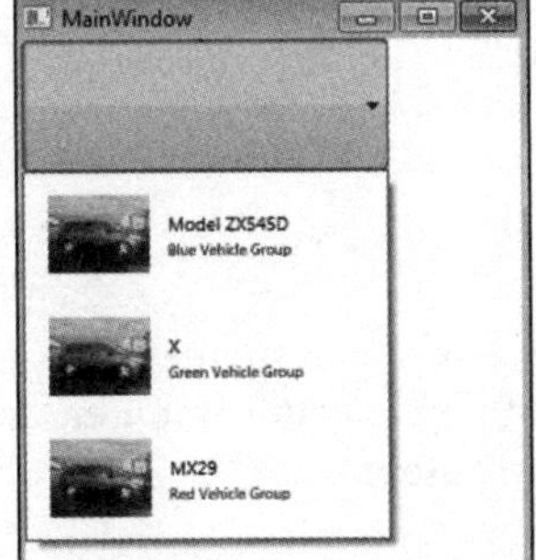

FIGURE 1-2: Visualizing data — a WPF combo box.

Introducing XAML

WPF enables you to build user interfaces declaratively. Extensible Application Markup Language (XAML; pronounced zammel) forms the foundation of WPF. XAML is similar to HTML in the sense that interface elements are defined using a tag-based syntax.

TECHNICAL STUFF

XAML is XML-based, and as such, it must be well formed, meaning all opening tags require closing tags, and all elements and attributes contained in the document must validate strictly against the specified schemas.

By default, when creating a WPF application in Visual Studio 2010 and above, the following schemas are represented in generated XAML files:

- `http://schemas.microsoft.com/winfx/2006/xaml/presentation`: This schema represents the default Windows Presentation Framework namespace.
- `http://schemas.microsoft.com/winfx/2006/xaml`: This schema represents a set of classes that map to CLR objects.

Most CLR objects can be expressed as XAML elements (with the exception of abstract base classes and some other nonabstract base classes used strictly for inheritance purposes in the CLR). XAML elements are mapped to classes; attributes are mapped to properties or events.

At runtime when a XAML element is processed, the default constructor for its underlying class is called, and the object is instantiated; its properties and events are set based on the attribute values specified in XAML. The next section reviews more XAML basics and gets you started on the path of WPF application development.

Diving In! Creating Your First WPF Application

Now it's time to get comfortable, so stop for a moment, go grab a caffeinated beverage, sit in a comfortable chair, pull up to your computer, and get ready to go! To create your first project, follow these steps:

1. **Open Visual Studio.**
2. **Click Create a New Project.**

   You see the list of available projects.
3. **Select C#, Windows, and Desktop in the filter list.**

   Visual Studio presents a list of Windows Desktop project types.
4. **Highlight WPF App (.NET Framework) and click Next.**

   You see the Configure Your New Project page of the wizard, shown in Figure 1-3.
5. **Type** MyFirstWPFApplication **in the Project Name field, select Place Solution and Project in the Same Directory, and then click Create.**

   Visual Studio creates a new WPF project for you and displays both the designer and the Code Editor with a default application defined. The WPF Application template creates two XAML files along with their respective code-behind files: `App.xaml` (`App.xaml.cs`) and `MainWindow.xaml` (`MainWindow.xaml.cs`), as shown in Figure 1-4. At this point, you can start adding code to the example application.

`App.xaml` represents the entry point of the application. This is where application-wide (globally scoped) resources and the startup window are defined (see Listing 1-1).

FIGURE 1-3: Configuring the WPF project.

FIGURE 1-4: WPF Application solution structure.

TECHNICAL STUFF

The resources are contained in a keyed collection of reusable objects. Resources can be created and retrieved using both XAML and C#. Resources can be anything — data templates, arrays of strings, or brushes used to color the background of text boxes. Resources are also *scoped*, meaning that they can be available to the entire Application (global), to the Window, to the User Control, or even to only a specific control.

LISTING 1-1: App.xaml

```
<Application x:Class="MyFirstWPFApplication.App"
             xmlns="http://schemas.microsoft.com/winfx/2006/xaml/presentation"
             xmlns:x="http://schemas.microsoft.com/winfx/2006/xaml"
             xmlns:local="clr-namespace:MyFirstWPFApplication"
             StartupUri="MainWindow.xaml">
    <Application.Resources>

    </Application.Resources>
</Application>
```

Listing 1-1 displays the XAML that was generated by the WPF App (.NET Framework) template in Visual Studio. Note that the WPF namespaces are defined. The namespace that represents the CLR objects will be distinguished in the XAML file with the x prefix.

The `StartupUri` value defines the window that will be displayed before the application is executed. In this case, the `MainWindow.xaml` window will be displayed.

The `x:Class` attribute defines the C# code-behind file of this XAML file. If you open `App.xaml.cs`, you see that its class name is `App` and it inherits from the `Application` class (which is the root element of the XAML file).

TECHNICAL STUFF

C# uses namespaces to organize and locate classes. To create objects from a specific namespace, you use the "using" syntax at the top of your class definitions. Similar to C#, XAML also requires you to declare which namespaces are used in the document. Namespaces are typically defined as an attribute within the root element of the document; the root element is the first XML tag in the XAML document. XAML uses XML syntax to define a namespace — "xmlns" means "XML namespace," and it's typically followed by a colon (:) and then an alias. This alias is the shorthand reference to the namespace throughout the XAML document; it's what you use to instantiate an object from a class in that namespace.

For instance, if you want to add the namespace MyTemplates.DataTemplates from the assembly `MyTemplates.dll`, you could define the namespace as

```
xmlns:myDTs="clr-namespace:MyTemplates.DataTemplates;assembly=MyTemplates.dll"
```

You are then able to instantiate an object from the MyTemplates.DataTemplates namespace as follows:

```
<myDTs:myClass></myDTs:myClass>
```

Declaring an application-scoped resource

To help you understand the creation and use of a global application-scoped resource, this section shows you how to create a resource that holds a string used in the application. An application-scoped resource is available to all Windows and user controls defined in the project. Follow these steps:

1. **Add the `System` namespace located in the `mscorlib.dll` assembly by adding the following namespace to the `App.xaml` root element (see Listing 1-2):**

   ```
   xmlns:sys="clr-namespace:System;assembly=mscorlib"
   ```

   The `mscorlib.dll` assembly is where the `String` class is located. The `String` class is now available for use throughout the `App.xaml` document.

2. **Create the resource between the `Application.Resource` tags; add the following `String` class element:**

   ```
   <sys:String x:Key="Purpose">Hello WPF World!</sys:String>
   ```

   This element instantiates an object of type `String`, initialized to the value `Hello WPF World!`, and keyed off of the key Purpose. This resource is now available throughout the `MyFirstWPFApplication` application by requesting the resource "Purpose" (see Listing 1-2).

LISTING 1-2: Updated App.xaml with Resource and System Namespace Defined

```
<Application x:Class="MyFirstWPFApplication.App"
             xmlns="http://schemas.microsoft.com/winfx/2006/xaml/presentation"
             xmlns:x="http://schemas.microsoft.com/winfx/2006/xaml"
             xmlns:local="clr-namespace:MyFirstWPFApplication"
             xmlns:sys="clr-namespace:System;assembly=mscorlib"
             StartupUri="MainWindow.xaml">
    <Application.Resources>
        <sys:String x:Key="Purpose">Hello WPF World!</sys:String>
    </Application.Resources>
</Application>
```

TECHNICAL STUFF

You may observe that the `Application.Resource` tag looks kind of odd. `Application.Resources` doesn't define a class as most XAML elements do. It's actually assigning a value to the `Resources` property of its containing `Application` object.

This type of tag is called a *property element*, an XML element that represents a property (or attribute) of an object. Property elements are used when complex objects are assigned to a property of an object that can't be expressed as a simple string value. Property elements must be contained within the tags of the parent element — in this case, within the `Application` tags.

Making the application do something

If you run the application as is, not much happens beyond the display of an empty window. The empty window is the one defined in `MainWindow.xaml`.

REMEMBER

`App.xaml` is the entry point of the WPF application. Within `App.xaml`, the `StartupUri` value defines the window displayed on application startup. In this case, the `StartupUri` value is `MainWindow.xaml`.

Add a label to `MainWindow.xaml` that displays the purpose of the String you defined in Resources. Just follow these steps:

1. **Open** `MainWindow.xaml`.
2. **Between the `Grid` tags, define a grid with a single row and single column by adding the following XAML markup:**

```
<Grid.ColumnDefinitions>
    <ColumnDefinition></ColumnDefinition>
</Grid.ColumnDefinitions>
<Grid.RowDefinitions>
    <RowDefinition></RowDefinition>
</Grid.RowDefinitions>
```

   Each column and row is defined by the `ColumnDefinition` and `RowDefinition` element contained within the `Grid.ColumnDefinitions` and `Grid.RowDefinitions` properties, respectively. If you want to add more columns, you simply add another `ColumnDefinition` element to the `Grid.ColumnDefinitions` Property Entity. The same goes for adding rows: You add an additional `RowDefinition` element to the `Grid.RowDefinitions` Property Entity.

3. **Directly below the** `Grid.RowDefinitions` **Property entity, create a label using the following XAML:**

```
<Label x:Name="lblPurpose" Content="{StaticResource Purpose}"
    FontSize="25" Grid.Row="0" Grid.Column="0"/>
```

This markup instantiates a WPF `Label` object accessible to the code-behind file (`MainWindow.xaml.cs`) using the variable `lblPurpose`. The `Content` attribute contains the text that is to be displayed in the label; in this case, you use the Application Resource that you defined in the preceding section by retrieving it using its key value, which is `Purpose`. The label text is rendered with a font size of 25 units and is to be located in the grid in the first row and first column.

WOW! That line of XAML really packs quite the punch! Here's some of what is going on in there:

- `x:Name`: This attribute assigns a variable name to the object being created by the XAML tag. This enables you to access the object from the code-behind file. In this case, the variable name of the label object being instantiated is `lblPurpose`.
- `Content`: The value assigned to this attribute can be of any type. By default, you can assign it a `string` value, and it will render as you would think a standard label would render. In the WPF reality, `Content` can be composed of anything: a string, an image, an instance of a user control, a text box, and so on. For more info, see Chapter 2 of this minibook.
- `FontSize`: The size of the font of the label. It is important to note that the size isn't denoted in points; it's expressed in Device Independent Units. WPF gets away from the concepts of pixels and points and moves to a universal sizing strategy. Think of Device Independent Units as more of a relative size than a pixel. For instance, if the containing element of the label were 100 units by 100 units, the label would render as ¼ of that size.
- `Grid.Row`: Identifies the grid row in which to render the label. Grid row collections are zero based, meaning that the first row is row 0, the second row is row 1, and so on. You should also note that the `Label` class doesn't contain a property named `Grid`. What you see here is the concept of attached properties. An *attached property* is a way to assign the context of a current control relative to the properties of a containing control. In this case, you assign the label to appear in the first row (row index 0) of its containing grid. Also observe that the label is located within the `Grid` tags; this is how the containing `Grid` element is located.
- `Grid.Column`: Similar to `Grid.Row`, this attached property identifies the grid column in which to render the label. Together with `Grid.Row`, both properties identify the cell where the label is located. In this case, you assign the label to render in the first column of its containing grid. Grid column collections are also zero based.

Go ahead and run your application. You now see Hello WFP World! displayed in the label on your Window. Congratulations! You have just created your first WPF application!

Whatever XAML Can Do, C# Can Do Better!

Anything that you can implement using XAML can be implemented in C#. This is not true in reverse; not everything you can do in C# can be done in XAML. C# is the obvious choice for performing business logic tasks with procedural code that can't be expressed in XAML. In the following steps, you create an identical WPF application to the one you created in the preceding section, this time using C# to implement its functionality:

1. **Choose File⇨Close Solution to close the current solution if necessary.**
2. **Click Create a New Project.**

   You see the list of available projects.
3. **Select C#, Windows, and Desktop in the filter list.**

   Visual Studio presents a list of Windows Desktop project types.
4. **Highlight WPF App (.NET Framework) and click Next.**

   You see the Configure Your New Project page of the wizard, shown in Figure 1-3.
5. **Type** MyFirstCodeOnlyWPFApplication **in the Project Name field, select Place Solution and Project in the Same Directory and then click Create.**

   Visual Studio creates the Solution and Project structure.
6. **Open** `App.xaml.cs`.
7. **Override the** `OnStartup` **method to include the creation of the Purpose application resource by adding the following code to the** `App` **class:**

```
protected override void OnStartup(StartupEventArgs e)
{
    // Create and add the Purpose application resource
    string purpose = "Hello WPF World, in C#";
    this.Resources.Add("Purpose", purpose);
    base.OnStartup(e);
}
```

8. **Open** `MainWindow.xaml` **and give the** `Grid` **element a name by adding the following attribute shown in bold:**

```
<Grid x:Name="gridLayout">

</Grid>
```

9. **Open `MainWindow.xaml.cs`, and in the default constructor, after the `InitializeComponents` method call, add the following code shown in bold:**

```
public MainWindow()
{
    InitializeComponent();

    // Define grid column and row
    this.gridLayout.ColumnDefinitions.Add(new ColumnDefinition());
    this.gridLayout.RowDefinitions.Add(new RowDefinition());

    // Obtain label content from the application resource, Purpose
    string purpose = this.TryFindResource("Purpose") as string;
    Label lblPurpose = new Label();
    lblPurpose.Content = purpose;
    lblPurpose.FontSize = 25;

    // Add label to the grid
    this.gridLayout.Children.Add(lblPurpose);

    // Assign attached property values
    Grid.SetColumn(lblPurpose, 0);
    Grid.SetRow(lblPurpose, 0);
}
```

Run the application and observe that the resulting product is similar to that obtained in the section "Diving In! Creating Your First WPF Application," earlier in this chapter.

IN THIS CHAPTER

» Laying out applications

» Using layout panels

» Working with the `Grid`

» Implementing display-only, input, and list-based controls

Chapter 2

Understanding the Basics of WPF

As Chapter 1 of this minibook explains, Windows Presentation Foundation (WPF) not only brings a dramatic shift to the look and feel of Windows applications but also changes the manner of development. The days of dragging and dropping controls from the Toolbox onto a form are long gone. Even though you can still drag and drop in WPF, you will find yourself better off and much happier if you work in XAML directly.

What was once difficult is now relatively simple. For example, in traditional Windows applications, when the user changes the size of the form, the controls typically stay huddled in their corner, and a large area of empty canvas is displayed. The only cure for this was a lot of custom code or expensive third-party controls. WPF brings the concept of *flow layout* from the web into the Windows world.

In the GDI/GDI+ world of WinForms, modifying a control's style or building complex looks was a Herculean feat. WPF has completely redefined the control paradigm, giving you, the developer, the freedom to make a control do unimaginable tasks — including playing a video on a button face. However, keep in mind that just because you *can* do something doesn't mean you *should!*

In this chapter, you work with WPF's layout process to control the layout of your application. This chapter also introduces you to the various WPF controls.

REMEMBER

You don't have to type the source code for this chapter manually. In fact, using the downloadable source is a lot easier. You can find the source for this chapter in the `\CSAIO4D2E\BK05\CH02` folder of the downloadable source. See the Introduction for details on how to find these source files.

Using WPF to Lay Out Your Application

Traditional Windows Forms development deals in absolutes. Position and size for controls are decided at design time and are based on the resolution of the developer's machine. When applications are deployed to users, the form that looked great on the developer's machine could now look very different (and possibly be downright unusable) because of hardware resolution differences.

Instead of depending on screen resolution, WPF measures UIElements in Device Independent Units (DIUs) that are based on the system Dots Per Inch (DPI). This enables a consistent look between many different hardware configurations.

WPF layout is based on relative values and is adjusted at runtime. When you place controls in a layout container (see the next section), the rendering engine considers the height and width only as "suggested" values. Location is defined in relation to other controls or the container. Actual rendering is a two-step process that starts with measuring all controls (and querying them for their preferred dimensions) and then arranging them accordingly.

NEW TECH, NEW TERMS

It seems that every time Microsoft introduces a new technology, developers have to learn a whole new set of terms. WPF is no different! At the root of the change are forms and controls in Windows Forms (WinForms). Here are some of the new terms:

- A *form* in WinForms is referred to as a *window* in WPF.
- Anything placed on a WinForms form is called a *control* (when it has a visual interface) or a *component* (when it doesn't), whereas items placed on a WPF window are referred to as *UIElements*.
- *Panels* are WPF UIElements used for layout.
- A *control* in WPF is a UIElement that can receive focus and respond to user events.
- A *content* control in WPF can contain only a single item, which can in turn be another UIElement.
- The WPF Window class is a specialized `Content` control.

Arranging Elements with Layout Panels

Designing a window begins with a layout control, or panel. Panels are different than `Content` controls in that they can hold multiple items, and depending on the panel, a significant amount of plumbing is taken care of for you.

Panels control how UIElements relate to each other and to their containing UIElement and do not dictate absolute positioning. Most application windows require some combination of panels to achieve the required user interface, so it's important to understand them all. Older forms of WPF ship with six core panels, which are described in the sections that follow:

UIElement	UI Panel?	Description
`Canvas`	Yes	Creates an area in which to position child elements using coordinates relative to the Canvas area.
`DockPanel`	Yes	Defines an area in which to position child elements relative to each other either horizontally or vertically.
`Grid`	Yes	Allows precise positioning of child elements using rows and columns as in an HTML table. The `Margin` property allows fine positioning.
`StackPanel`	Yes	Arranges the child elements into a single line that is positioned either horizontally or vertically.
`UniformGrid`	No	Arranges the children in a grid using equal cell sizes.
`WrapPanel`	Yes	Positions child elements in a sequential position from left to right. You can also arrange elements top to bottom when the `Orientation` is vertical. As more child elements are added, the `WrapPanel` breaks the line and begins placing the children on the next line. Consequently, smaller displays use more lines to show the child elements.

Newer forms of WPF add these panels as well:

UIElement	UI Panel?	Description
`TabPanel`	No	Defines the layout of tab buttons in a `TabControl`.
`ToolBarOverflowPanel`	No	Arranges the content within a `ToolBar` control.

UIElement	UI Panel?	Description
`VirtualizingPanel`	No	Used as a base class for creating panels that can virtualize their children (where the interface the user sees is selected from a larger number of data items based on the items the user can actually see, which ultimately makes the application work faster and use less memory).
`VirtualizingStackPanel`	Yes	Arranges and virtualizes content on a single line that is oriented either horizontally or vertically.

The Stack panel

Stack panels place UIElements in *stacks.* Items are placed in either a vertical pile (the default), like a stack of DVDs, or a horizontal arrangement, like books on a shelf. It is important to understand that the order items appear in the XAML is the order they appear in the panel — the first UIElement in the XAML appears at the top (vertical) or on the far left (horizontal). The following code contains the XAML for the Vertical Stack panel, shown in Figure 2-1. You can also find it in the `StackPanel` example found in the downloadable source code. Notice that you have a `StackPanel` containing another `StackPanel`, which is a good way to create complex layouts. The `pnlContainer <StackPanel>` element replaces the `<Grid>` element that Visual Studio provides by default.

```
<StackPanel x:Name="pnlContainer">
    <StackPanel Name="pnlStack" Grid.Row="0" Orientation="Vertical">
        <Button Content="A Button"/>
        <Button Content="Another Button"/>
        <TextBlock Text="This is a text block"/>
        <Button Content="Short"/>
        <Button Content="Really Long Button Label"/>
    </StackPanel>
</StackPanel>
```

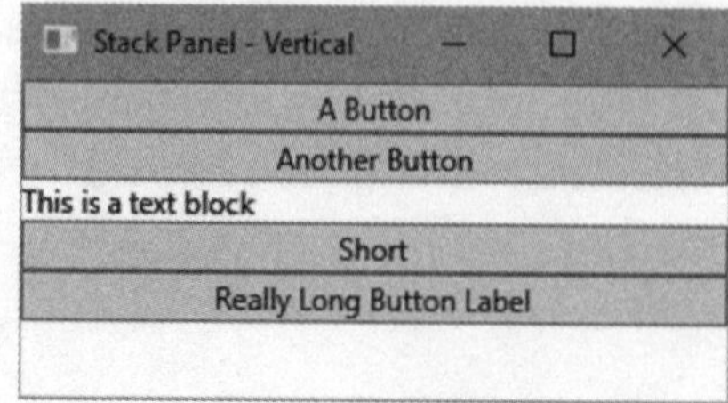

FIGURE 2-1: Vertical Stack panel.

EFFECTS OF WINDOWS CHROME ON WPF APPLICATIONS

When working with Windows Forms applications, you could depend on a relatively consistent appearance of the window elements of your application between Windows versions and even devices. Properties, like those shown in the following figure, make it easy to control whether certain features appear, such as the `ControlBox`, `MimimizeBox`, and `MaximizeBox`, appear as part of the application. In addition, it's easy to find articles, such as `https://help.syncfusion.com/windowsforms/form/titlebar`, that describe precisely how to change the appearance of the window used to house your application using simple and straightforward programming techniques.

The same can't be said of WPF applications, which rely on Windows *chrome*, the themes used to make applications appear a certain way depending on a combination of user settings, operating system version, and device (and perhaps other factors as well). Consequently, you can no longer depend on your application to have a certain appearance, and you must also consider the WPF screenshots in this book as suggestions rather than as actual visual tools that you can depend on.

The problem with WPF and its successors, and its effect on your application, is longstanding. At first, developers looked for ways to make their WPF applications look Metro-styled on Windows 7 (see `https://newbedev.com/making-wpf-applications-look-metro-styled-even-in-windows-7-window-chrome-theming-theme`). They then wanted to introduce some consistency in title bar appearance between Windows 8 (where the title is centered) and Windows 10 (where the title is left-justified) by making simple

(continued)

(continued)

modifications to their code like the one suggested at `https://www.codeproject.com/Questions/897719/How-Can-I-Set-The-Alignment-Of-Title-In-The-Window`. Unfortunately, there is nothing simple about modifying the appearance of the window provided by a WPF application, as described at `https://social.msdn.microsoft.com/Forums/sqlserver/en-US/bd88d47b-be11-431a-9967-1bc052174b2f/how-to-set-alignment-for-window-title?forum=wpf`. You need to write a great deal more code, as shown at `https://docs.microsoft.com/en-us/dotnet/api/system.windows.shell.windowchrome`.

Of course, you must also consider whether it's even a good idea to interact with and change the chrome for your WPF application. The idea is that the application should appear like every other application on a particular version of Windows for a certain device. In other words, the ability to act as a chameleon is considered a good idea in some circles, despite introducing a plethora of user questions and support issues. So, when you view the screenshots for WPF and Universal Windows Platform (UWP) applications in this book, consider them more as suggestions than as what you'll actually see on your system.

You may find that you want to have the ability to change the orientation of the controls based on the user's device or device orientation. To do this, you can add a button to the existing code, as shown here in bold:

```
<StackPanel Name="pnlContainer">
    <StackPanel Name="pnlStack" Grid.Row="0" Orientation="Vertical">
        <Button Content="A Button"/>
        <Button Content="Another Button"/>
        <TextBlock Text="This is a text block"/>
        <Button Content="Short"/>
        <Button Content="Really Long Button Label"/>
    </StackPanel>
    <StackPanel Name="pnlStack1" Grid.Row="1" Orientation="Vertical">
        <Button x:Name="cmdOrientation" Content="Set Horizontal"
            Click="cmdOrientation_Click"/>
    </StackPanel>
</StackPanel>
```

The new `cmdOrientation` button appears at the bottom of the display, as shown in Figure 2-2, which also shows the application in horizontal mode. The horizontal layout shown in Figure 2-2 illustrates the clipping that can take place when the sum of the preferred sizes of controls in a container is larger than the container can hold.

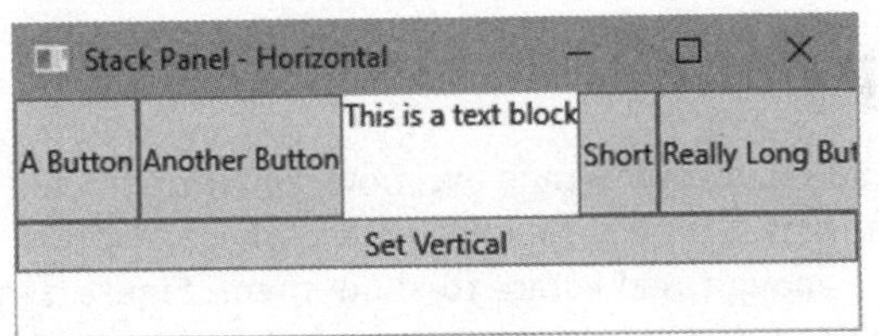

FIGURE 2-2: Horizontal layout showing clipped content.

Orientation (as well as all other properties) can be changed at runtime, as illustrated by the following code. The button at the bottom of the window changes the orientation, the button label, and the window title in the click event. Chapter 4 shows a better way of coding button click events using various code-behind techniques.

```
private void cmdOrientation_Click(object sender, RoutedEventArgs e)
{
    Button button = sender as Button;
    if (button.Content.ToString() == "Set Vertical")
    {
        pnlStack.Orientation = Orientation.Vertical;
        pnlStack.MinHeight = 0;
        button.Content = "Set Horizontal";
        Title = "Stack Panel - Vertical";
    }
    else
    {
        pnlStack.Orientation = Orientation.Horizontal;
        pnlStack.MinHeight = 50;
        button.Content = "Set Vertical";
        Title = "Stack Panel - Horizontal";
    }
}
```

The use of a second `StackPanel` allows the `cmdOrientation Button` to retain its vertical orientation, even when the other controls assume a horizontal orientation. When you plan to change orientation, you need to work with the various controls carefully to obtain the results you want.

TIP

Notice also that the code changes the `pnlStack.MinHeight` value as needed to provide a good appearance onscreen. It's important to provide a pleasing appearance without creating user interface problems on smaller devices. Experimentation will help you choose the values for any tweaks in the user interface appearance, but often it's better to use the default values that WPF provides.

The Wrap panel

The WrapPanel automatically wraps overflow content onto the next line(s). This is different from how a typical toolbar works, where overflow items are hidden when there isn't enough real estate to show them. Figure 2-3 shows the same content controls from the StackPanel example (a mixture of buttons and a text block) in a WrapPanel. (You can also find this code in the WrapPanel example in the downloadable source.) The initial XAML for the WrapPanel sample is in the following code:

```
<StackPanel Name="pnlContainer" Width="80">
    <WrapPanel Name="pnlWrap" Grid.Row="0">
        <Button Content="A Button"/>
        <Button Content="Another Button"/>
        <TextBlock Text="This is a text block"/>
        <Button Content="Short"/>
        <Button Content="Really Long Button Label"/>
    </WrapPanel>
    <WrapPanel Name="pnlWrap1" Grid.Row="1">
        <Button x:Name="cmdWidth" Content="Set Wide"
                Click="cmdWidth_Click"/>
    </WrapPanel>
</StackPanel>
```

Note that even with the WrapPanel, if the container can't hold the widest item (the last button in the example), some clipping will take place. This example uses pnlContainer to show the effect of a WrapPanel given the amount of display space by making the container narrower and wider with the following code, which you can test by clicking the Set Wide button at the bottom of the window:

```
private void cmdWidth_Click(object sender, RoutedEventArgs e)
{
    Button button = sender as Button;
    if (button.Content.ToString() == "Set Wide")
    {
        pnlContainer.Width = 350;
        button.Content = "Set Narrow";
        Title = "Wrap Panel - Wide";
    }
    else
    {
        pnlContainer.Width = 80;
        button.Content = "Set Wide";
        Title = "Wrap Panel - Narrow";
    }
}
```

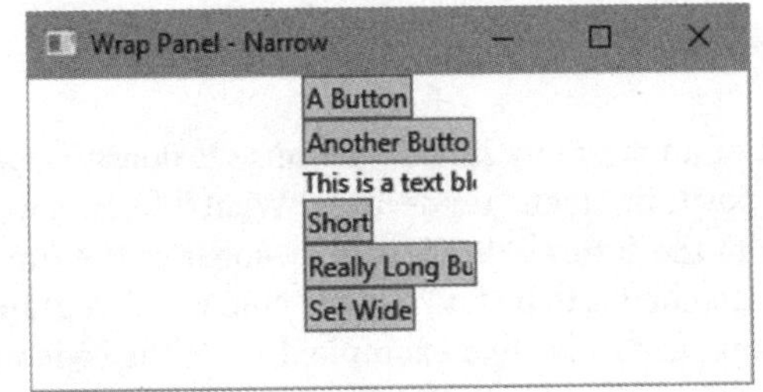

FIGURE 2-3: Two Wrap panels housed in a StackPanel.

The Dock panel

The DockPanel, as demonstrated in the DockPanel example in the downloadable source, uses attached properties (see Chapter 1 of this minibook) to "dock" child UIElements. An important thing to remember is that child elements are docked in XAML order, which means that if you have two items assigned to the left side (through DockPanel.Dock="left"), the first UIElement *as it appears* in the XAML gets the far left wall of the panel, followed by the next item. Here is the code used to create a DockPanel.

```
<DockPanel LastChildFill="True">
    <Button DockPanel.Dock="Left" Content="Far Left"/>
    <Button DockPanel.Dock="Left" Content="Near Left"/>
    <Button DockPanel.Dock="Top" Content="Top"/>
    <Button DockPanel.Dock="Bottom" Content="Bottom"/>
    <Button Content="Fill"/>
    <Button Content="Fill More"/>
</DockPanel>
```

Figure 2-4 shows the output from this example. The Dock panel also has a setting called LastChildFill. If this is true, the last element in XAML will fill the remaining real estate. Elements (prior to the last XAML element) that do not have a Dock setting specified will default to DockPanel.Dock="Left".

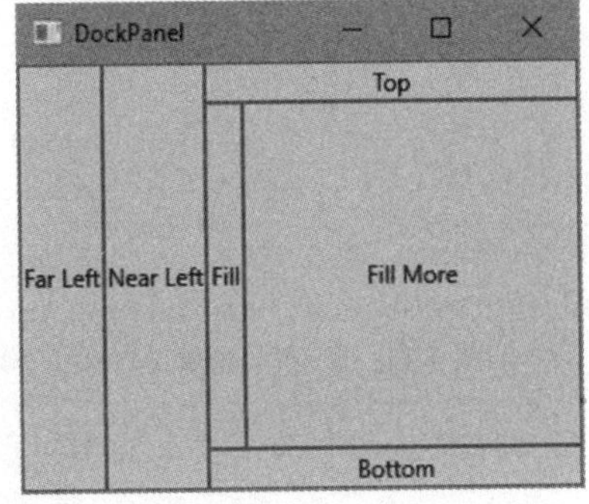

FIGURE 2-4: A Dock panel fills in controls in the area specified in XAML order.

Canvas

The Canvas is a bit of an anomaly in WPF because it doesn't use flow layout but goes back to fixed position layout rendering. "What?!" you say. "I thought flow layout was the way of the future!" Well, it is . . . most of the time. In some cases, part of your application needs to be laid out the "old way." A graphical application used to design floor plans is a perfect example. Here's the code to create a `Canvas` (also found in the `Canvas` example in the downloadable source).

```
<Canvas>
    <Rectangle Canvas.Left="40" Canvas.Top="40" Height="53"
               Name="rectangle1" Stroke="Black" Width="96"
               Fill="#FFE22323"/>
    <Ellipse Canvas.Left="28" Canvas.Top="142" Height="80"
             Name="ellipse1" Stroke="Black" Width="161"
             Fill="#FF0000FA"/>
    <Ellipse Canvas.Left="96" Canvas.Top="14" Height="108"
             Name="ellipse2" Stroke="Black" Width="78" Fill="#FFE5D620"/>
</Canvas>
```

Figure 2-5 shows the output of this example. Items are placed (or drawn) on the canvas relative to any side, and layering is handled through z-order. The *z-order* defines which items are drawn first, which second, and so on.

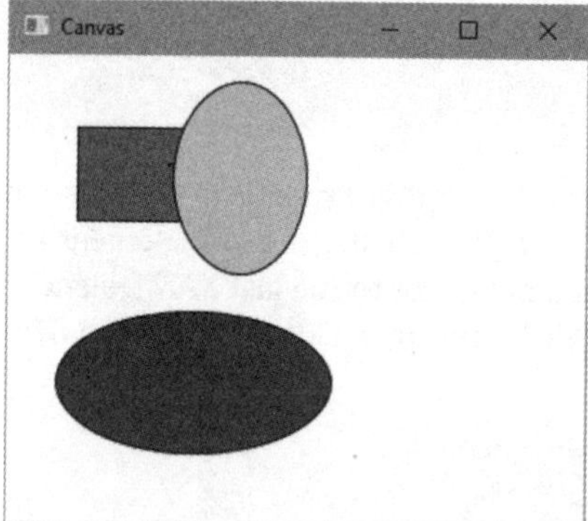

FIGURE 2-5: Canvas sample.

The Grid

Chapter 1 of this minibook introduces the `Grid`, which is the most common starting point to screen design. The `Grid` is, in fact, the default panel in a Window when you add a new WPF Window to your project.

The `Grid` divides the layout area with rows (`RowDefinitions`) and columns (`ColumnDefinitions`). The difference between the `Grid` and the `UniformGrid` is that the `Grid` allows for sizing of the cells by defining `RowDefinition Height` and `ColumnDefinition Width`. The following code shows how to create definitions for rows and columns by using the `Grid.RowDefinitions` and `Grid.ColumnDefinitions` tags.

```
<Grid>
    <Grid.RowDefinitions>
        <RowDefinition Height="2*"/>
        <RowDefinition Height="3*"/>
    </Grid.RowDefinitions>
    <Grid.ColumnDefinitions>
        <ColumnDefinition Width="*"/>
    </Grid.ColumnDefinitions>
</Grid>
```

Sizing rows and columns

There are three `GridUnitTypes` used for defining heights and widths:

- `Pixel`: Fixed size in Device Independent Units (DIUs).

  You define a fixed height or width based on DIUs by specifying a number in the definition. This goes against the `FlowLayout` grain, but there are certainly valid reasons to do this, such as when a graphic image on a window doesn't scale well (up or down) and needs to be a fixed size. Fixed sizing should be used with caution because it can limit the effectiveness of the user interface. If the content is dynamic or needs to be localized, the controls could clip the content or wind up leaving a lot of wasted space.

- `Auto`: Size is based on the preferred size of the contents.

  The `Auto` definition allows the row or column to determine how large (or small) it can be based on its content. This is decided during the measure stage of the layout process.

» **∗ (star):** Size uses all remaining space.

The ∗ (star) tells the rendering engine, “Give me all you’ve got! I’ll take it all!” Each star defined gets an equal portion of what’s left after all other sizing options have been computed. To achieve proportional sizing, multipliers can be added, as shown in the following code (you can also find this code in the `Grid` example):

```
<Grid>
    <Grid.RowDefinitions>
        <RowDefinition Height="2*"/>
        <RowDefinition Height="3*"/>
    </Grid.RowDefinitions>
    <Grid.ColumnDefinitions>
        <ColumnDefinition Width="*"/>
        <ColumnDefinition Width="*"/>
    </Grid.ColumnDefinitions>
    <Border Grid.Row="0" Grid.Column="0" BorderBrush="Black"
            BorderThickness="1" HorizontalAlignment="Stretch"
            VerticalAlignment="Stretch">
        <TextBlock Text="0,0"/>
    </Border>
    <Border Grid.Row="0" Grid.Column="1" BorderBrush="Black"
            BorderThickness="1" HorizontalAlignment="Stretch"
            VerticalAlignment="Stretch">
        <TextBlock Text="0,1"/>
    </Border>
    <Border Grid.Row="1" Grid.Column="0" BorderBrush="Black"
            BorderThickness="1" HorizontalAlignment="Stretch"
            VerticalAlignment="Stretch">
        <TextBlock Text="1,0"/>
    </Border>
    <Border Grid.Row="1" Grid.Column="1" BorderBrush="Black"
            BorderThickness="1" HorizontalAlignment="Stretch"
            VerticalAlignment="Stretch">
        <TextBlock Text="1,1"/>
    </Border>
</Grid>
```

For example, in Figure 2-6, the first row uses 40 percent (2⁄5) of the available space and the second row uses the remaining 60 percent (3⁄5).

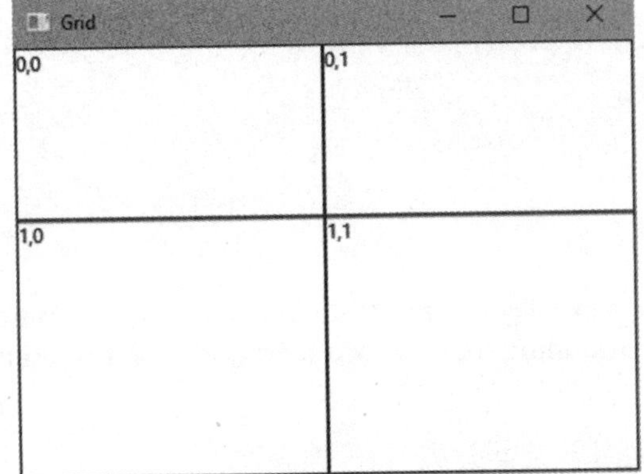

FIGURE 2-6: Basic `Grid` with proportional (*) row heights.

RowSpan and ColumnSpan

Similar to HTML tables, content in a `Grid` can span rows or columns by using the `Grid.RowSpan` and `Grid.ColumnSpan` attached properties, as shown in the following code (also found in the `Grid2` example):

```
<Grid>
    <Grid.RowDefinitions>
        <RowDefinition Height="2*"/>
        <RowDefinition Height="3*"/>
        <RowDefinition Height="5*"/>
    </Grid.RowDefinitions>
    <Grid.ColumnDefinitions>
        <ColumnDefinition Width="*"/>
        <ColumnDefinition Width="*"/>
    </Grid.ColumnDefinitions>
    <Border Grid.Row="0" Grid.Column="0" Grid.ColumnSpan="2"
            BorderBrush="Black" BorderThickness="1"
            HorizontalAlignment="Stretch" VerticalAlignment="Stretch">
        <TextBlock Text="0,0 - 0,1"/>
    </Border>
    <Border Grid.Row="1" Grid.Column="0" Grid.RowSpan="2"
            BorderBrush="Black" BorderThickness="1"
            HorizontalAlignment="Stretch" VerticalAlignment="Stretch">
        <TextBlock Text="1,0 - 2,1"/>
    </Border>
    <Border Grid.Row="1" Grid.Column="1" BorderBrush="Black"
            BorderThickness="1" HorizontalAlignment="Stretch"
            VerticalAlignment="Stretch">
        <TextBlock Text="1,1"/>
    </Border>
```

Understanding the Basics of WPF

```
    <Border Grid.Row="2" Grid.Column="1" BorderBrush="Black"
            BorderThickness="1" HorizontalAlignment="Stretch"
            VerticalAlignment="Stretch">
        <TextBlock Text="2,1"/>
    </Border>
</Grid>
```

Figure 2-7 shows a grid layout with the border controls spanning both columns in the first row and spanning the next two rows in the first column.

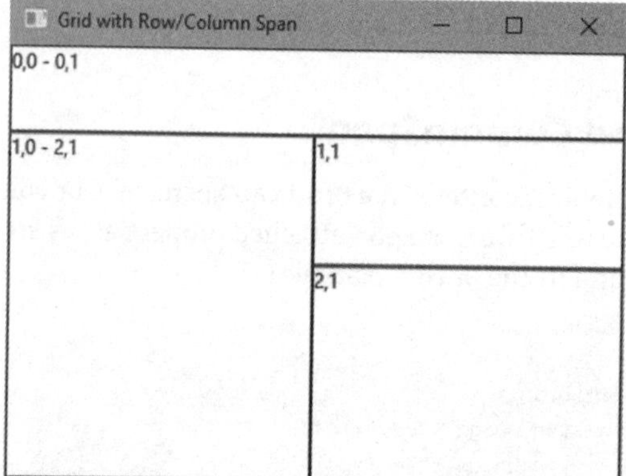

FIGURE 2-7: Grid with row and column spans.

Horizontal and vertical alignment within parent container's layout slot

You align an element within a container's layout slot by setting the `VerticalAlignment` and `HorizontalAlignment` properties. Horizontal settings are `Center`, `Left`, `Right`, and `Stretch`. Vertical options are `Center`, `Top`, `Bottom`, and `Stretch`. `Stretch` specifies the element to fill all available space. Explicit sizing of elements overrides the `Stretch` setting.

Content alignment within Content controls

The same options can be used for setting the alignment of the content within a `Content` control by using the `HorizontalContentAlignment` and `VerticalContentAlignment` properties in the control.

Margin versus padding

Margins create space around a UIElement and its parent container. Margin values start with the left and rotate clockwise (which is different from CSS, just to keep you on your toes). You can also use some abbreviations. Setting the value as one number makes a uniform margin; setting the value to two numbers (comma separated) sets the left and right margins to the first number and the top and bottom margins to the second.

```
<Button Margin="2,4,2,4" Content="Push Me"/> <!--L,T,R,B-->
<Button Margin="2,4" Content="Push Me"/> <!--LR,TB-->
<Button Margin="2" Content="Push Me"/> <!--LTRB-->
```

Padding increases spacing around UIElements inside a `Block`, `Border`, `Control`, or `TextBlock`. Imagine a picture surrounded by a strip of blue border material, which in turn is inside a frame. Suppose that the picture area (think of it as a container) has a small margin on all sides so that the actual picture is never in contact with the blue border. That's the concept of `Margin`. The blue border itself is extra padding outside the picture area. That's the concept of `Padding`. Think of `Margin` as an inside space and `Padding` as an outside space. This XAML shows something similar: a `TextBlock` and four buttons sitting inside a `StackPanel` with a `Border` around it, using both `Margin` and `Padding` (you can also find this code in the `MarginAndPadding` example):

```
<Border Background="LightBlue" BorderBrush="Black" BorderThickness="5"
        Padding="15">
    <StackPanel Background="White" HorizontalAlignment="Center"
                VerticalAlignment="Top">
        <TextBlock Margin="10,10" FontSize="18"
                   HorizontalAlignment="Center">
            HorizontalAlignment Sample
        </TextBlock>
        <Button HorizontalAlignment="Left">Button 1 (Left)</Button>
        <Button HorizontalAlignment="Right">Button 2 (Right)</Button>
        <Button HorizontalAlignment="Center">Button 3 (Center)</Button>
        <Button HorizontalAlignment="Stretch">Button 4 (Stretch)</Button>
    </StackPanel>
</Border>
```

The `Border` surrounds a light blue area of padding at `15` units. The `TextBlock` inside the white rectangle surrounded by blue shows a narrow `Margin` of `10` on each side as shown in white around the text "Horizontal Alignment Sample." (The Buttons have no margin.) Figure 2-8 shows what you see as output.

Shared size groups

Most complex windows require multiple panels to achieve the desired user experience. This can introduce erratic windows if the size of the content in one grid is different from that of the other.

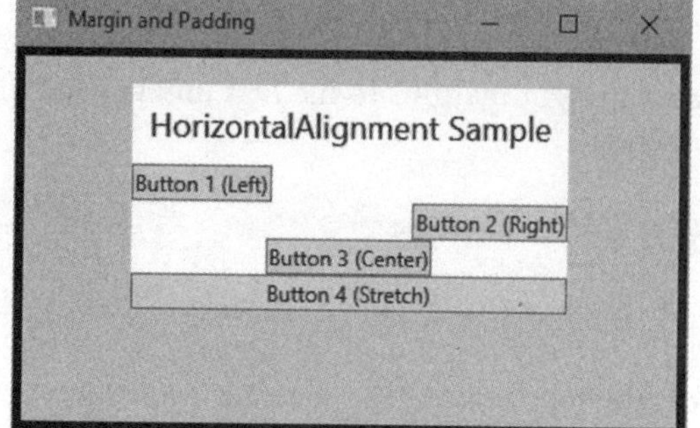

FIGURE 2-8: An example using `Margin` and `Padding`.

Fortunately, there is a simple solution. By setting the `Grid.IsSharedSizeScope` attached property on the *parent* grid, all the child grids can define `Rows` and `Columns` that subscribe to a `SharedSizeGroup`, and the rendering engine will ensure that they are sized correctly. The following code provides an example that uses shared sizing (you can also find the code in the `SharedSize` example):

```
<Grid Grid.IsSharedSizeScope="True">
    <Grid.RowDefinitions>
        <RowDefinition Height="Auto"/>
        <RowDefinition Height="Auto"/>
        <RowDefinition Height="Auto"/>
        <RowDefinition Height="Auto"/>
        <RowDefinition Height="Auto"/>
        <RowDefinition Height="Auto"/>
    </Grid.RowDefinitions>
    <Grid Grid.Row="0" Grid.RowSpan="3" Grid.Column="0">
        <Grid.RowDefinitions>
            <RowDefinition Height="Auto"/>
            <RowDefinition Height="Auto"/>
            <RowDefinition Height="Auto"/>
        </Grid.RowDefinitions>
        <Grid.ColumnDefinitions>
            <ColumnDefinition Width="Auto" SharedSizeGroup="Header"/>
            <ColumnDefinition Width="*"/>
        </Grid.ColumnDefinitions>
        <Label Grid.Row="0" Grid.Column="1" Grid.ColumnSpan="2"
               Content="Zoo Animals"
               HorizontalContentAlignment="Center"/>
        <Label Grid.Row="1" Grid.Column="0" Content="Hippopotamus"
               HorizontalContentAlignment="Stretch"/>
        <TextBox Grid.Row="1" Grid.Column="1"
                 HorizontalAlignment="Stretch" BorderThickness="2"/>
        <Label Grid.Row="2" Grid.Column="0" Content="Giraffe"
               HorizontalContentAlignment="Stretch"/>
        <TextBox Grid.Row="2" Grid.Column="1"
                 HorizontalAlignment="Stretch" BorderThickness="2"/>
```

```
    </Grid>
    <Grid Grid.Row="3" Grid.RowSpan="3" Grid.Column="0">
        <Grid.RowDefinitions>
            <RowDefinition Height="Auto"/>
            <RowDefinition Height="Auto"/>
            <RowDefinition Height="Auto"/>
        </Grid.RowDefinitions>
        <Grid.ColumnDefinitions>
            <ColumnDefinition Width="Auto" SharedSizeGroup="Header"/>
            <ColumnDefinition Width="*"/>
        </Grid.ColumnDefinitions>
        <Label Grid.Row="0" Grid.Column="1" Grid.ColumnSpan="2"
               Content="Pets" HorizontalContentAlignment="Center"/>
        <Label Grid.Row="1" Grid.Column="0" Content="Cats"
               HorizontalContentAlignment="Left"/>
        <TextBox Grid.Row="1" Grid.Column="1"
                 HorizontalAlignment="Stretch" BorderThickness="2"/>
        <Label Grid.Row="2" Grid.Column="0" Content="Dogs"
               HorizontalContentAlignment="Left"/>
        <TextBox Grid.Row="2" Grid.Column="1"
                 HorizontalAlignment="Stretch" BorderThickness="2"/>
    </Grid>
</Grid>
```

Figure 2-9 shows the output of this example, which shows that all the content is now aligned.

FIGURE 2-9: Multiple `Grid`s with shared sizing.

Putting it all together with a simple data entry form

For complex data entry forms, the `DataGrid` is the most appropriate form to use. (For more information, see the section "Exploring Common XAML Controls," later in this chapter.) The data entry form in the DataEntryForm example uses multiple grids to achieve the desired look. The text boxes are contained in columns with star sizing so that they will grow and shrink with the form. Also notice how the buttons stay in the same relative position as the form size changes. Here is the XAML used to build the window shown in Figure 2-10.

```
<Grid Background="FloralWhite">
    <Grid.RowDefinitions>
        <RowDefinition Height="Auto"/>
        <RowDefinition Height="Auto"/>
        <RowDefinition Height="Auto"/>
        <RowDefinition Height="Auto"/>
        <RowDefinition Height="Auto"/>
        <RowDefinition Height="10"/>
        <RowDefinition Height="Auto"/>
    </Grid.RowDefinitions>
    <Grid.ColumnDefinitions>
        <ColumnDefinition Width="Auto"/>
        <ColumnDefinition Width="Auto"/>
        <ColumnDefinition Width="*"/>
        <ColumnDefinition Width="Auto"/>
    </Grid.ColumnDefinitions>
    <Label Grid.Row="0" Grid.Column="0" Grid.RowSpan="2" Content="Name"
           HorizontalAlignment="Stretch" HorizontalContentAlignment="Center">
        <Label.LayoutTransform>
            <RotateTransform Angle="-90"/>
        </Label.LayoutTransform>
    </Label>
    <Label Grid.Row="0" Grid.Column="1" Content="First:"
           HorizontalAlignment="Stretch" HorizontalContentAlignment="Right"/>
    <TextBox Grid.Row="0" Grid.Column="2" HorizontalAlignment="Stretch"/>
    <Label Grid.Row="1" Grid.Column="1" Content="Last:"
           HorizontalAlignment="Stretch" HorizontalContentAlignment="Right"/>
    <TextBox Grid.Row="1" Grid.Column="2" HorizontalAlignment="Stretch"/>
    <Label Grid.Row="2" Grid.Column="1" Content="Address:"
           HorizontalAlignment="Stretch" HorizontalContentAlignment="Right"/>
    <TextBox Grid.Row="2" Grid.Column="2" HorizontalAlignment="Stretch"/>
    <Label Grid.Row="3" Grid.Column="1" Content="City:"
           HorizontalAlignment="Stretch" HorizontalContentAlignment="Right"/>
    <TextBox Grid.Row="3" Grid.Column="2" HorizontalAlignment="Stretch"/>
    <Button Grid.Row="3" Grid.Column="3" Content="Lookup" Margin="3,0,3,0"/>
    <Label Grid.Row="4" Grid.Column="1" Content="State:"
           HorizontalAlignment="Stretch" HorizontalContentAlignment="Right"/>
    <Grid Grid.Row="4" Grid.Column="2">
        <Grid.RowDefinitions>
            <RowDefinition Height="*"/>
        </Grid.RowDefinitions>
        <Grid.ColumnDefinitions>
```

```
            <ColumnDefinition Width="*"/>
            <ColumnDefinition Width="Auto"/>
            <ColumnDefinition Width="2*"/>
        </Grid.ColumnDefinitions>
        <TextBox Grid.Row="0" Grid.Column="0" HorizontalAlignment="Stretch"/>
        <Label Grid.Row="0" Grid.Column="1" Content="Zip:"
               HorizontalAlignment="Right"/>
        <TextBox Grid.Row="0" Grid.Column="2" HorizontalAlignment="Stretch"/>
    </Grid>
    <Grid Grid.Row="6" Grid.Column="0" Grid.ColumnSpan="3">
        <Grid.RowDefinitions>
            <RowDefinition Height="Auto"/>
        </Grid.RowDefinitions>
        <Grid.ColumnDefinitions>
            <ColumnDefinition Width="*"/>
            <ColumnDefinition Width="Auto"/>
            <ColumnDefinition Width="Auto"/>
        </Grid.ColumnDefinitions>
        <Button Grid.Row="0" Grid.Column="1" Content="Save" Margin="3,0"/>
        <Button Grid.Row="0" Grid.Column="2" Content="Close" Margin="3,0"/>
    </Grid>
</Grid>
```

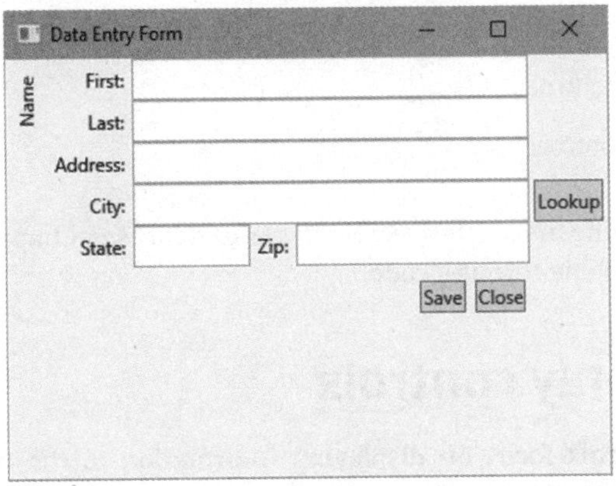

FIGURE 2-10: Simple data entry form.

And yes, that's a *lot* of XAML! One of the many great things about WPF is the flexibility to create just about any look and feel you can dream up. But sometimes (well, most of the time), it will take a lot of angle brackets.

In addition to using XAML for layout, you can do all the examples shown exclusively in code. Fixed sizing is specified by assigning a number to the `Width` property of the `ColumnDefinition` or `RowDefinition`. Assigning `Auto` or `*` is more complicated because the `Width` property is of type `GridLength`, as shown in the following code.

```
// Set to Auto sizing
column1 = new ColumnDefinition();
column1.Width = new GridLength(1, GridUnitType.Auto);
// Set to Star sizing
column2 = new ColumnDefinition();
column2.Width = new GridLength(1, GridUnitType.Star);
```

Exploring Common XAML Controls

A significant number of controls ship out of the box with Visual Studio 2022 (and more and more vendor-supplied controls are available for free download and purchase). This section covers the more commonly used controls. Many developers prefer to divide the available controls into three categories:

- Display-only controls
- Basic input controls
- List-based controls

All the controls in this section are bindable to data (see Chapter 3 in this minibook) and modifiable through code.

Display-only controls

Four main controls focus on displaying information to the user, as shown in Figure 2-11 (and the `DisplayControls` example):

- `Image`: The `Image` control displays images (of type `.bmp`, `.gif`, `.ico`, `.jpg`, `.png`, `.wdp`, and `.tiff`). To preserve the image's aspect ratio, set the `Width` *or* `Height`, but not both. This will cause the rendering engine to scale the image appropriately, potentially saving a significant amount of memory.

Note, by the way, that you can put images almost anywhere in WPF — for example, on a button, in a label, or inline in a paragraph of text. And it's quite easy. It's not so fancy in Figure 2-11, but you should know about this possibility.

The following code shows the XAML to load an image that shows a fancy-looking bit of color. Only the `Width` is set.

```
<Image Grid.Row="0" Grid.Column="0" Width="100" >
    <Image.Source>
        <BitmapImage UriSource="/Images/Colorblk.gif"/>
    </Image.Source>
</Image>
```

» `TextBlock` and `Label`: Both the `TextBlock` and the `Label` controls are designed to provide text or other content to the user with a few distinctions. The `TextBlock` control is designed to be the lightweight "little brother" to the label, deriving directly from UIElement.

The `Label` control provides access-modifier capability and also derives from `ContentControl`, which opens up additional possibilities. Placing an underscore (_) before a letter enables the access modifiers. To provide an underscore in the `Label`, use a double underscore. In XAML, because it is essentially XML, the underscore is used because an ampersand (which is what you use in WinForms) would break the XAML. The `Target` attribute specifies the control to receive focus when the access modifier is keyed. You have to use a binding expression to actually trigger an action, which is covered in Chapter 3 of this minibook.

Both the `TextBlock` and `Label` controls are illustrated in the following code:

```
<TextBlock Grid.Row="1" Grid.Column="0" Margin="5,0"
           HorizontalAlignment="Right" Text="Text_Block:"/>
<TextBox Grid.Row="1" Grid.Column="1" Margin="5,0"
         HorizontalAlignment="Stretch" Text="TextBox 1"/>
<Label Grid.Row="2" Grid.Column="0" Margin="5,0"
       HorizontalAlignment="Stretch"
       HorizontalContentAlignment="Right"
       Content="_Label__Content:"
       Target="{Binding ElementName=SampleTextBox}"/>
<TextBox Name="SampleTextBox" Grid.Row="2" Grid.Column="1"
         Margin="5,0"
         HorizontalAlignment="Stretch" Text="TextBox 2"/>
```

In the sample, the *L* in the `Label` content is the access modifier, and the double underscore adds an underscore character to the rendered output.

» ProgressBar: The final display-only control described here is the progress bar. Although technically a descendant of the RangeBase class, it does not enable user input as the slider does (see the next section). The following code shows a progress bar sample. To have the bar in perpetual motion, set the IsIndeterminate property to True:

```
<ProgressBar Grid.Row="3" Grid.Column="0" Maximum="100"
          Minimum="1" Value="50" IsIndeterminate="False"
          Height="20" Width="300" Grid.ColumnSpan="2"
          Foreground="Blue" Background="White"/>
```

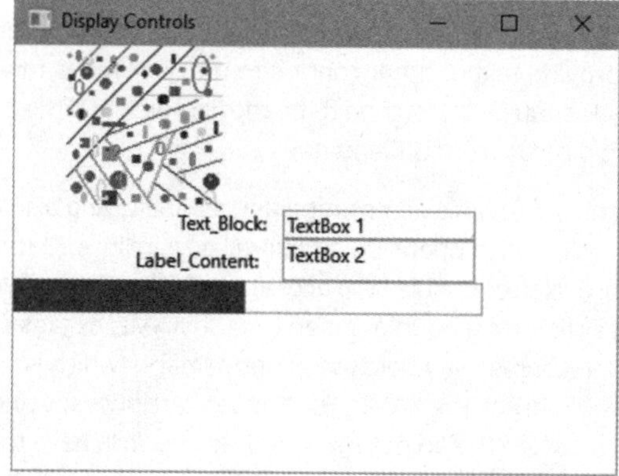

FIGURE 2-11: Display-only controls.

Basic input controls

The workhorses of line-of-business applications are the basic input controls. You find some of these on practically every window you create, and they are very straightforward. Figure 2-12 shows all these controls on a single window. Here are the basic input controls (also shown in the InputControls example):

» TextBox and PasswordBox: The TextBox and PasswordBox both allow for the input of standard text into the window. The PasswordBox obfuscates the characters typed (using either the default system password character or a developer-specified character) and is used for collecting sensitive information. The TextBox exposes its contents through the Text property, the PasswordBox through the Password property.

```
<StackPanel Grid.Row="0">
    <TextBox Text="Some Text"/>
    <PasswordBox PasswordChar="X" Password="Some Text"/>
</StackPanel>
```

- `CheckBox`: Check boxes represent Boolean values through the `IsChecked` property. The `IsChecked` property is nullable, which provides for three-state display (True, False, Unknown). Use a horizontally oriented `StackPanel` to lay `CheckBoxes` out horizontally, with some margin to separate the boxes:

```
<StackPanel Grid.Row="1" Orientation="Horizontal">
  <CheckBox IsChecked="True"
            Content="true" Margin="15,15"/>
  <CheckBox IsChecked="false"
            Content="False" Margin="15,15"/>
  <CheckBox IsChecked="{x:Null}" Content="Null" Margin="15,15"/>
</StackPanel>
```

- `RadioButton`: Radio buttons allow for a single selection within a range of choices. The choices are determined by the `GroupName` property. After one of the radio buttons is selected, the group can be entirely deselected only programmatically.

```
<StackPanel Grid.Row="2" Orientation="Horizontal">
  <RadioButton GroupName="RBSample" IsChecked="true"
               Content="Red" Margin="15,15"/>
  <RadioButton GroupName="RBSample"
               Content="White" Margin="15,15"/>
  <RadioButton GroupName="RBSample"
               Content="Blue" Margin="15,15"/>
</StackPanel>
```

- `Slider`: The slider control is a ranged input control. Similar to the `ProgressBar`, the control takes `Minimum`, `Maximum`, and `Interval` values. (An *interval* is the distance between changes from the minimum value to the maximum value.) Additionally, you can specify to show ticks, the location, and the tick frequency. *Ticks?* Those are the value lines that show on sliders.

```
<StackPanel Grid.Row="3">
    <Slider Interval="1" Minimum="1" Maximum="10"
            IsSnapToTickEnabled="True"
            TickPlacement="BottomRight" TickFrequency="1"/>
</StackPanel>
```

- `DatePicker`: The `DatePicker` control provides a concise method for getting (or displaying) date information by combining a `TextBox` with a `Calendar` control. Included in the many options is the capability to select multiple dates for a range of dates.

```
<StackPanel Grid.Row="4">
    <DatePicker/>
</StackPanel>
```

» Calendar: The difference between the Calendar control and the DatePicker is that the Calendar control is always in full display mode whereas the DatePicker's default look is similar to a text box.

```
<StackPanel Grid.Row="5">
    <Calendar/>
</StackPanel>
```

» Button: The Button control doesn't really fit in with the other controls in this section because it's more of an action control. Buttons respond to a user's click. To use this control, you begin with the XAML shown here:

```
<StackPanel Grid.Row="6">
    <Button Content="Click Me" Click="Button_Click" Width="60"/>
</StackPanel>
```

However, to make this control work, you must also provide code-behind code in the .cs file. The connection between this code and the XAML comes from the Click attribute. Here is the code-behind, which displays only a simple message box in this case.

```
private void Button_Click(object sender, RoutedEventArgs e)
{
    MessageBox.Show("Hello World");
}
```

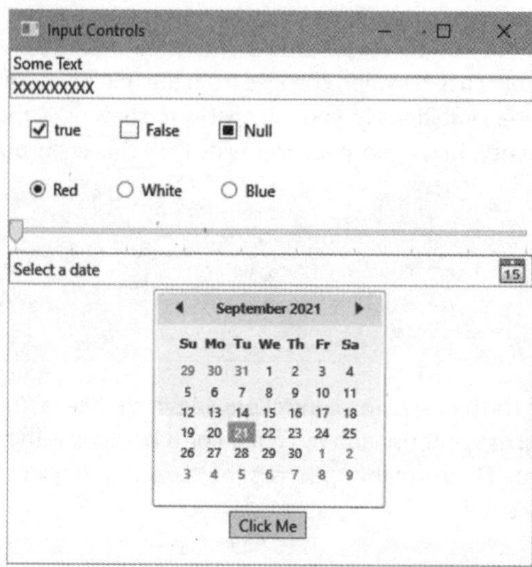

FIGURE 2-12: All the basic input controls.

List-based controls

The list-based controls (also referred to as `Item` controls) add an incredible amount of flexibility. As discussed in Chapter 1 of this minibook, the list-based controls no longer have to rely on data tricks or other magic to make the content meaningful to the user but can be templated to show greater details about the items contained.

Data binding is covered in great detail in Chapter 3 of this minibook, but the controls don't do anything unless you have something to show. In this case, the `ListBasedControls` example takes an extremely simple approach, the control content is hard coded. However, you do have other options, and it's important to know that you do. Here are the list-based controls:

- ComboBox and `ListBox`: The `ListBox` and the ComboBox in the sample below present a group of list items. However, you have other choices, including buttons and menu items. The main difference between the two controls is that the ComboBox displays a single item with a drop-down selector (see Figure 2-13), and the `ListBox` shows the entire list of items up to the allowed space and then scrolls the rest. The ComboBox can be set up to enable selecting items that are *not* in the list, as well as editing the items in the list.

```
<ComboBox Grid.Column="0" Height="20" Width="100"
        HorizontalAlignment="Stretch" VerticalAlignment="Top">
    <ListBoxItem Content="One"/>
    <ListBoxItem Content="Two"/>
    <ListBoxItem Content="Three"/>
    <ListBoxItem Content="Four"/>
    <ListBoxItem Content="Five"/>
</ComboBox>
<ListBox Grid.Column="1" Height="150" Width="100"
        HorizontalAlignment="Stretch" VerticalAlignment="Top">
    <ListBoxItem Content="One"/>
    <ListBoxItem Content="Two"/>
    <ListBoxItem Content="Three"/>
    <ListBoxItem Content="Four"/>
    <ListBoxItem Content="Five"/>
</ListBox>
```

» `TreeView`: The `TreeView` is a hierarchical `ItemsControl` much like Windows Explorer. The nodes (or branches) can be expanded or contracted, giving a nice user interface into any multilevel data. (See Figure 2-13.) The sample uses hard-coded data, but with a simple hierarchical template, tree views can be bound just as any other control can.

```
<TreeView Name="myTreeViewEvent" >
    <TreeViewItem Header="Employee1" IsSelected="True">
        <TreeViewItem Header="Jesper Aaberg"/>
        <TreeViewItem Header="Employee Number">
            <TreeViewItem Header="12345"/>
        </TreeViewItem>
        <TreeViewItem Header="Work Days">
            <TreeViewItem Header="Monday"/>
            <TreeViewItem Header="Tuesday"/>
            <TreeViewItem Header="Thursday"/>
        </TreeViewItem>
    </TreeViewItem>
    <TreeViewItem Header="Employee2">
        <TreeViewItem Header="Dominik Paiha"/>
        <TreeViewItem Header="Employee Number">
            <TreeViewItem Header="98765"/>
        </TreeViewItem>
        <TreeViewItem Header="Work Days">
            <TreeViewItem Header="Tuesday"/>
            <TreeViewItem Header="Wednesday"/>
            <TreeViewItem Header="Friday"/>
        </TreeViewItem>
    </TreeViewItem>
</TreeView>
```

» `DataGrid`: The `DataGrid` has five base column types:

- `DataGridTextColumn`: For `Text`
- `DataGridCheckBoxColumn`: For `Boolean`
- `DataGridComboBoxColumn`: For `ListItems`
- `DataGridHyperlinkColumn`: For displaying `Links`
- `DataGridTemplateColumn`: For designing custom columns

The `DataGrid` can be set to `AutoGenerate` the columns based on the data it is bound to. It then uses reflection to determine the best column type based on the data. Because this control relies on data binding, you see it demonstrated further in Chapter 3.

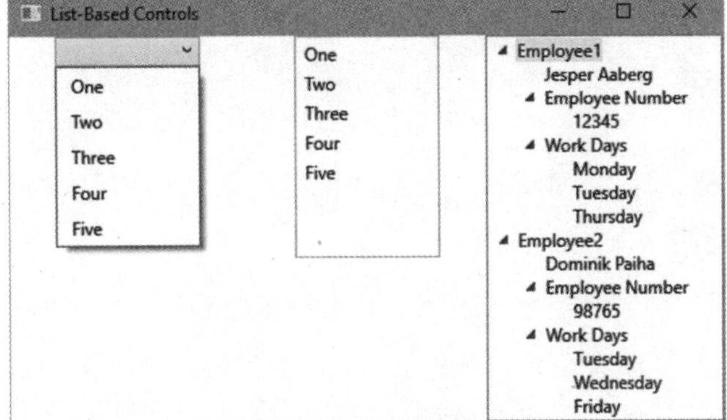

FIGURE 2-13: The ComboBox (left), `ListBox` (center), and `TreeView` (right) controls.

IN THIS CHAPTER

» Understanding dependency properties

» Working with binding modes

» Defining an example binding object

» Making sense out of data

Chapter 3
Data Binding in WPF

Data binding allows data from your application objects (the binding source) to be displayed in your user-interface elements (the binding target). What this means is that you can bind the Text property of a TextBox (for example) to the Name property of an instance of your Car class. Depending on the binding mode used when setting up the relationship, changes in the Text property value of the TextBox can automatically update the underlying Name property of your Car object (and vice versa) without requiring any additional code.

It's no mystery these days that most applications deal with data. As a WPF developer, you have full creative reign on how data is presented and how information entered by your user can be validated and used to update your underlying objects. One of WPF's strengths is its rich data binding support. This chapter walks you through the details.

REMEMBER

You don't have to type the source code for this chapter manually. In fact, using the downloadable source is a lot easier. You can find the source for this chapter in the \CSAIO4D2E\BK05\CH03 folder of the downloadable source. See the Introduction for details on how to find these source files.

Getting to Know Dependency Properties

Data binding happens when you set up a relationship between a binding source property and binding target property. The binding target object must be a `DependencyObject`, and the target property must be a `DependencyProperty`.

Understanding dependency properties is crucial to obtaining a firm grasp on WPF technology. Dependency properties are found in objects that inherit from `DependencyObject`. At its root, a dependency property extends the functionality of a regular property that already exists on a CLR object by adding a set of services that is also known as the WPF Property System. (Together, `DependencyObject` and `DependencyProperty` make up this property system.) Dependency properties can have their values determined by multiple input sources, meaning that their values can be obtained through a `Style` or a data binding expression. Dependency properties act like regular properties, but they allow you to set values based on the following:

- **A default value:** These are predefined on the property.
- **A calculated expression (similar to CSS, Cascading Style Sheets, expressions in the web world):** This can be a data binding expression or a reference to resources defined in the application.
- **Data binding:** This actually is built upon the preceding bullet using binding expressions on the binding source object.
- **Property value inheritance:** Not to be confused with object inheritance, property value inheritance allows values set on parent properties to be propagated down to its children. For instance, if you set `FontSize` values on the `Window` element (the root element), child elements such as `TextBlock` and `Label` automatically inherit those font property values. You can see another example of this by reviewing the concept of attached properties introduced in Chapter 1 of this minibook.
- **Styling:** Each style typically contains setters to set one or more property values.

The WPF property system also provides built-in property value change notification and property value validation functionality, which is reviewed in the section "Editing, Validating, Converting, and Visualizing Your Data," later in this chapter.

At the end of the day, dependency properties give the developer the capability to set property values directly in XAML as well as in code. The advantage to this is that you can keep your code clean and leave initializing object property values to XAML.

Exploring the Binding Modes

You have full control over how the binding relationship you create behaves. Multiple types of binding modes are available to you in WPF. These include the following:

- **The** `OneTime` **binding mode** is used when you want the source property to only initially set the target property value. Subsequent changes to the source property are not reflected in the target property. Similarly, changes to the target property are not reflected in the source property.
- **The** `OneWay` **binding mode** is typically used for read-only properties. In this binding mode, data from the source property sets the initial value of the target property. Subsequent changes to the source property will automatically update the binding target property value. Conversely, any subsequent changes made to the target property value are not reflected in the source property.
- **The** `OneWayToSource` **binding mode** is essentially the opposite of the `OneWay` binding mode. In this binding mode, data from the source property initializes the target property value. Subsequent changes to the source property value will not update the target property. However, updates to the target property value will automatically update the source property value.
- **The** `TwoWay` **binding mode** merges the functionality of the `OneWay` and `OneWayToSource` binding modes. In this binding mode, the source property value initializes the target property value. Subsequent changes to the source property value update the target property value. Similarly, updates to the target property value will update the source property value.

Investigating the Binding Object

Bindings can be defined using code or XAML. Here you begin with the XAML version. To see how to bind data to your UI elements, you first define a test set of data to work with.

Defining a binding with XAML

Just follow these steps to create a binding with XAML (also found in the `BindingSample1` example in the downloadable source):

1. **Create a new WPF App (.NET Framework) project and name it** `BindingSample1`.
2. **Define a simple** `Car` **class by adding a new** class template file **to your solution named** `Car.cs` **and code it as follows (note that you don't need any** `using` **directives in this case):**

```
namespace BindingSample1
{
    public class Car
    {
        private string _make;

        public string Make
        {
            get { return _make; }
            set { _make = value; }
        }

        private string _model;

        public string Model
        {
            get { return _model; }
            set { _model = value; }
        }

        public Car() { }
    }
}
```

3. **In** `MainWindow.xaml`**, replace the grid with one that defines a double column and single row grid; then add a label in each grid cell, like this:**

```
<Grid>
    <Grid.ColumnDefinitions>
        <ColumnDefinition></ColumnDefinition>
        <ColumnDefinition></ColumnDefinition>
    </Grid.ColumnDefinitions>
```

```
    <Grid.RowDefinitions>
        <RowDefinition></RowDefinition>
    </Grid.RowDefinitions>
    <Label x:Name="lblCarMake" Grid.Row="0" Grid.Column="0"
           Content="{Binding Path=Make, Mode=OneTime}"/>
    <Label x:Name="lblCarModel" Grid.Row="0" Grid.Column="1"
           Content="{Binding Path=Model, Mode=OneTime}"/>
</Grid>
```

Look at the `Content` dependency property value. The information contained within the curly braces defines the binding for the content to be displayed in the labels. The next section describes what this `Binding` expression means, but first you need some data to bind to.

4. **Open the `MainWindow.xaml.cs` code-behind file and create a method called `GenerateData()` in the `MainWindow` class that instantiates a `Car` object and assigns it to the `DataContext` of the window, like this:**

TECHNICAL STUFF

```
private void GenerateData()
{
    Car car1 = new Car() { Make = "Athlon", Model = "XYZ" };
    this.DataContext = car1;
}
```

`DataContext` defines the root object relative to which all child elements obtain their values (as long as the `DataContext` value on the child elements isn't directly set via XAML or code — this property is an example of property value inheritance; its value is obtained from its parent element unless otherwise specified).

5. **Call the `GenerateData()` method in the `MainWindow()` constructor method (`public MainWindow()`), immediately following `InitializeComponents()` call.**

Now, looking back to the XAML file (`MainWindow.xaml`), the first label `lblCar-Make` will bind to the `DataContext`'s `Make` property. The value is retrieved from the property specified in the binding's `Path` component. Similarly, the second label, `lblCarModel`, will bind to the `DataContext`'s `Model` property as specified in the binding expression's `Path` property. Each of these bindings is using a `OneTime` mode, which means that the label content will be bound only once, regardless of the underlying object property being bound to changes.

TECHNICAL STUFF

The Path component of the XAML Binding expression simply tells the XAML processor to take its value from a specific property of its DataContext. The Path value can also express properties that are nested, such as in the case of nested complex objects. In these cases, you use dot notation to reach the desired property, such as Property.SomeObject.SomeOtherProperty.

6. **Run the application.**

   You can see that the labels now display the Make and Model of the Car object that was assigned to the DataContext of the window. (See Figure 3-1.)

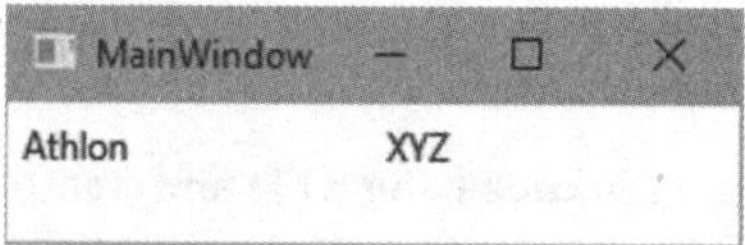

FIGURE 3-1: Data binding to properties of a DataContext.

Defining a binding with C#

You can also use C# to define bindings. The DataBinding1CSharp example shows how to perform this task. To demonstrate C# data binding, remove the Content attribute entirely from both labels in the XAML file. The label markup should now resemble the following:

```
<Label x:Name="lblCarMake" Grid.Row="0" Grid.Column="0"/>
<Label x:Name="lblCarModel" Grid.Row="0" Grid.Column="1"/>
```

Modify the GenerateData() method in MainWindow.xaml.cs to implement the Binding definitions in code. To do this, you must instantiate Binding objects directly. The constructor of the Binding object takes in the string Path value. Use the BindingOperations class to apply the Binding to the Content dependency property of your labels.

TECHNICAL STUFF

BindingOperations is a helper class provided to you by WPF. It has static methods that give you the power to add and clear data binding definitions on application elements.

The following code shows you how to define the Binding objects and assign the binding to the Content of the labels:

```
private void GenerateData()
{
    Car car1 = new Car() { Make = "Athlon", Model = "XYZ" };

    Binding makeBinding = new Binding("Make");
    makeBinding.Mode = BindingMode.OneTime;
```

```
        BindingOperations.SetBinding(lblCarMake,
           Label.ContentProperty, makeBinding);

        Binding modelBinding = new Binding("Model");
        modelBinding.Mode = BindingMode.OneTime;
        BindingOperations.SetBinding(lblCarModel,
           Label.ContentProperty, modelBinding);

        this.DataContext = car1;
    }
```

Note that this change also requires the use of the following `using` directives:

```
using System.Windows;
using System.Windows.Controls;
using System.Windows.Data;
```

Run the application and observe that it runs the same way as when the bindings were defined using XAML.

REMEMBER

Dependency properties are typically defined with the suffix *Property*, but you see them this way only when navigating MSDN documentation and accessing them through code. In XAML, you specify dependency property attributes by dropping the *Property* suffix from the name.

Editing, Validating, Converting, and Visualizing Your Data

In the preceding section, you got a taste of binding syntax and saw data appear on the screen. This section builds on this knowledge and shows you the SimpleBinding2 example that includes updating data from user-interface elements, as well as updating the user interface with changes happening to objects behind the scenes. To create an environment in which updates can occur, follow these steps:

1. **Create a new WPF Application project and name it** `BindingSample2`.
2. **Right-click the project entry in Solution Explorer and choose Add ⇨ Existing Item from the context menu.**

   You see the Add Existing Item dialog box.

3. **Highlight the `Car.cs` file located in the `BindingSample1` folder and click Add.**

   Visual Studio adds the `Car` class file to your project.

4. **Double-click `Car.cs` in Solution Explorer.**

   You see the file open in the editor.

5. **Change the `BindingSample1` namespace to `BindingSample2`.**

   The `Car` class is now ready for use in this example.

   In this example, you display the make and model of a `Car` object (the `DataContext`) in `TextBox` controls. This control enables you to edit the values of the `Car` properties. You will also use a `TwoWay` data binding mode so that changes made from the user interface will be reflected in the underlying `Car` object, and any changes made to the `Car` object from code-behind will be reflected in the user interface.

6. **Define two buttons, one that shows a message box containing the current value of the `DataContext` and another that forces changes to the `DataContext` through code-behind using the following code:**

```
<Grid>
    <Grid.ColumnDefinitions>
        <ColumnDefinition></ColumnDefinition>
        <ColumnDefinition></ColumnDefinition>
    </Grid.ColumnDefinitions>
    <Grid.RowDefinitions>
        <RowDefinition></RowDefinition>
        <RowDefinition></RowDefinition>
    </Grid.RowDefinitions>

    <StackPanel Orientation="Horizontal" Grid.Row="0"
                Grid.Column="0">
        <Label Content="Make"/>
        <TextBox x:Name="lblCarMake"  VerticalAlignment="Top"
           Text="{Binding Path=Make, Mode=TwoWay}"
           Width="200" Height="25"/>
    </StackPanel>

    <StackPanel Orientation="Horizontal" Grid.Row="0"
                Grid.Column="1" >
        <Label Content="Model"/>
        <TextBox x:Name="lblCarModel"  VerticalAlignment="Top"
```

```
            Text="{Binding Path=Model, Mode=TwoWay}"
            Width="200" Height="25"/>
    </StackPanel>

    <Button x:Name="btnShowDataContextValue"
            Click="btnShowDataContextValue_Click"
            Content="Show Current Data Context Value"
            Grid.Row="1" Grid.Column="0"/>

    <Button x:Name="btnChangeDataContextValue"
            Click="btnChangeDataContextValue_Click"
            Content="Change Data Context Value with Code-Behind"
            Grid.Row="1" Grid.Column="1"/>
</Grid>
```

7. **In the code-behind file,** `MainWindow.xaml.cs`**, add the following methods:**

```
private void GenerateData()
{
    Car car1 = new Car() { Make = "Athlon", Model = "XYZ" };
    this.DataContext = car1;
}

private void btnShowDataContextValue_Click(object sender,
                                           RoutedEventArgs e)
{
    Car dc = this.DataContext as Car;
    MessageBox.Show("Car Make: " + dc.Make + "\nCar Model: "
                    + dc.Model);
}

private void btnChangeDataContextValue_Click(object sender,
                                             RoutedEventArgs e)
{
    Car dc = this.DataContext as Car;
    dc.Make = "Changed Make";
    dc.Model = "Changed Model";
}
```

8. **In the constructor for** `MainWindow()`**, add a call to the** `GenerateData()` **method immediately following the** `InitializeComponents()` **call.**

9. **Run this application.**

You see that the values from the `DataContext` display properly in the `TextBox` controls. Feel free to change the values in the `TextBox` controls. For instance, change the `Make` value to `Athlon X`, and the model to `ABC`. When you finish with your edits, click the Show Current Data Context Value button. The changes you made to the values in the `TextBox` are now reflected in the underlying `DataContext` object. (See Figure 3-2.)

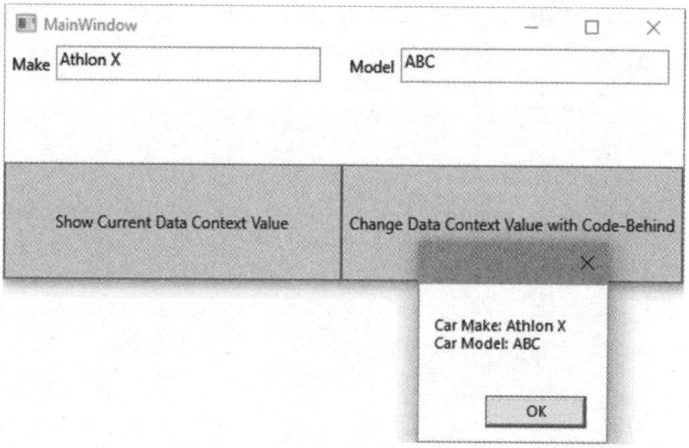

FIGURE 3-2: Editing data using a TwoWay binding mode.

10. **Click OK to get rid of the message box.**

If you look in the `Click` event handler of the Change Data Context Value With Code-Behind button (`btnChangeDataContextValue_Click()`), you will note that the `DataContext` `Car` object properties will be changed to `Changed Make` and `Changed Model`, respectively.

11. **Click the Change Data Context Value With Code-Behind button.**

Hmmm. Nothing is happening. What's up with that? If you click the Show Current Data Context Value button, you see that the properties have in fact been changed. Because you're using a TwoWay binding, your settings should automatically update your UI, right? Wrong! This is where another feature of WPF, the concept of `INotifyPropertyChanged`, comes into play.

`INotifyPropertyChanged` is a simple interface that allows your objects to raise an event that notifies its subscribers (namely your application) that a property value on the object has changed. Client applications subscribe to these events and update the user interface with the new values only when changes occur.

A similar interface exists for collections as well — the `INotifyCollectionChanged` interface. WPF also provides a generic class called `ObservableCollection<T>` that already implements `INotifyCollectionChanged` for you. When creating an `ObservableCollection` or your own collection that implements `INotifyCollectionChanged`, you need to ensure that the objects that will be contained within the collection also implement `INotifyPropertyChanged` interface.

The `INotifyPropertyChanged` interface contains a single event that must be implemented. This event is called `PropertyChanged`, and its parameters are the object that owns the property that has changed (the sender), and the string name of the property that has changed.

12. **Stop the application, open your `Car` class, and add the `using System.ComponentModel;` statement to allow access to `INotifyPropertyChanged`.**

13. **Type** : INotifyPropertyChanged **after `internal class Car` to add the required interface to your class.**

    Note that `INotifyPropertyChanged` has a red underline beneath it. You see this underline because your class doesn't implement the required members. This event happens every time you add a new interface, so knowing the fastest way to handle it is a good idea.

14. **Right-click `INotifyPropertyChanged`, choose Quick Actions and Refactorings from the context menu, and click Implement Interface.**

    Visual Studio adds the following code for you:

    ```
    public event PropertyChangedEventHandler PropertyChanged;
    ```

    For the application to be notified of the changes that occur in `Car` objects, the `PropertyChanged` event must be fired each time a property value has changed.

15. **To implement this in the `Car` class, create a helper method called `NotifyPropertyChanged` that takes in a string property name and fires the `PropertyChanged` event for the object instance and the name of the property that has changed, like this:**

    ```
    private void NotifyPropertyChanged(string propertyName)
    {
        if (PropertyChanged != null)
        {
            this.PropertyChanged(this,
                  new PropertyChangedEventArgs(propertyName));
        }
    }
    ```

Checking to see whether PropertyChanged is not null essentially means you're checking to see whether anyone is listening (subscribed) to the PropertyChanged event.

16. **Modify the Set methods in each of the public properties on the Car object to call the NotifyPropertyChanged helper method each time the property value has changed; edit the public properties, like this:**

```
private string _make;

public string Make
{
    get { return _make; }
    set
    {
        if (_make != value)
        {
            _make = value;
            NotifyPropertyChanged("Make");
        }
    }
}

private string _model;

public string Model
{
    get { return _model; }
    set
    {
        if (_model != value)
        {
            _model = value;
            NotifyPropertyChanged("Model");
        }
    }
}
```

17. **Run the application again.**

Now when you click the Change Data Context Value with Code-Behind button, the changed values get reflected automatically in the TextBox elements. This is due to the combination of the TwoWay binding mode as well as the implementation of INotifyPropertyChanged. (See Figure 3-3.)

ELEMENT BINDING

In this chapter, you bind `Label` and `TextBox` controls to properties of underlying objects. You're not limited to this scenario; you can bind to just about anything from primitive variables to property values gleaned from other UIElements. Element binding in particular has its own component in the `Binding` expression. For instance, suppose that you have a `TextBox` and `Label` control in your window. You'd like to have the `Content` of the `Label` automatically update with the changing value of the `Text` property of the `TextBox`. The XAML code to accomplish element binding between the `TextBox` and the `Label` looks similar to

```
<Label x:Name="lblCarMake"
     Content="{Binding ElementName=txtCarMake, Path=Text}"/>
<TextBox x:Name="txtCarMake" Width="200" Height="25"/>
```

The C# code to define this binding looks similar to

```
Binding b = new Binding("Text");
b.ElementName = "txtCarMake";
BindingOperations.SetBinding(lblCarMake, Label.ContentProperty, b);
```

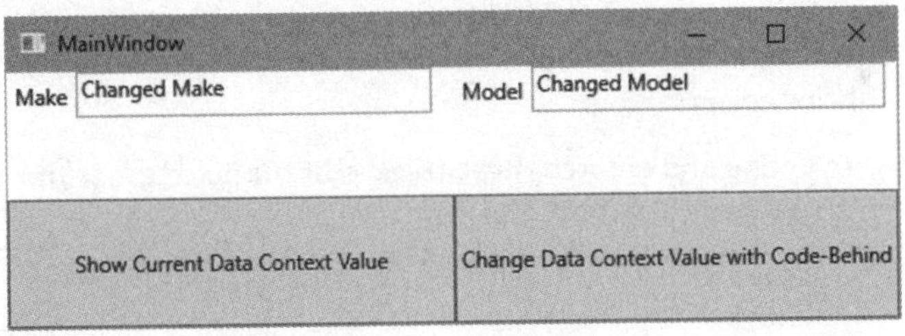

FIGURE 3-3: TwoWay data binding with `INotifyPropertyChanged`.

Validating data

It's good practice to validate any input provided to you from the user. People aren't perfect, and some people can be downright malicious. WPF provides a built-in framework for data validation and error notification. It's available to you through the implementation of the `IDataErrorInfo` interface on your classes shown in the `BindingSample2Validate` example. You can add validation to the `Car` class you already created in `BindingSample2` from the preceding section. Just follow these steps to add validation to your `Car` class:

1. **Open the `Car.cs` file and edit the class to also implement the `IDataErrorInfo` interface, like this:**

   ```
   public class Car : INotifyPropertyChanged, IDataErrorInfo
   ```

   Implementing this interface adds the following methods to the `Car` class:

   ```
   public string Error => throw new NotImplementedException();

   public string this[string columnName] =>
       throw new NotImplementedException();
   ```

2. **Edit the `Get` method of the `Error` property to return null by modifying the code to look like this:**

   ```
   public string Error => null;
   ```

   Now it's time to add some validation rules to the properties of the `Car` object. The `Car Make` and `Model` properties should enforce the rule that they must always be at least three characters in length. The `public string this[string columnName]` method is used by the `DataBinding` engine to validate the properties of the object as they are changed, based on the name of the property (which is what they mean by `columnName` in the method signature). This method returns any error messages related to the property being edited.

3. **To define and enforce these rules, edit the `public string this[string columnName]` method, like this:**

   ```
   public string this[string columnName]
   {
       get
       {
           string retvalue = null;
           if (columnName == "Make")
           {
               if (String.IsNullOrEmpty(this._make)
                       || this._make.Length < 3)
               {
                   retvalue = "Car Make must be at least 3 " +
                               "characters in length";
               }
           }

           if (columnName == "Model")
           {
   ```

```
            if (String.IsNullOrEmpty(this._model)
                        || this._model.Length < 3)
            {
                retvalue = "Car Model must be at least 3 " +
                                    "characters in length";
            }
        }

        return retvalue;
    }
}
```

In `MainWindow.xaml`, the `Make` and `Model` properties are bound to `TextBox` controls in the user interface. Note that you must also add another using directive to the class:

```
using System;
```

4. **To enable the text being entered into the TextBoxes to be validated against the constraints defined on the underlying property, edit the binding expressions in each** `TextBox`**, as shown in bold:**

```
<StackPanel Orientation="Horizontal" Grid.Row="0"
            Grid.Column="0">
    <Label Content="Make"/>
    <TextBox x:Name="txtCarMake" VerticalAlignment="Top"
       Text="{Binding Path=Make, Mode=TwoWay,
               UpdateSourceTrigger=PropertyChanged,
               ValidatesOnDataErrors=True,
               ValidatesOnExceptions=True}"
       Width="200" Height="25"/>
</StackPanel>

<StackPanel Orientation="Horizontal" Grid.Row="0"
            Grid.Column="1" >
    <Label Content="Model"/>
    <TextBox x:Name="txtCarModel" VerticalAlignment="Top"
       Text="{Binding Path=Model, Mode=TwoWay,
               UpdateSourceTrigger=PropertyChanged,
               ValidatesOnDataErrors=True,
               ValidatesOnExceptions=True}"
       Width="200" Height="25"/>
</StackPanel>
```

TECHNICAL STUFF

UpdateSourceTrigger identifies when the validation calls take place. In this example, validations occur as the text is changing, and UpdateSourceTrigger is fired when the underlying object property fires the PropertyChanged event.

ValidatesOnDataErrors is what enables the IDataErrorInfo validation method to be called on the property.

ValidatesOnExceptions will invalidate the TextBox if the underlying data source throws an exception, such as when, for instance, you have an integer property and the user enters a string. WPF automatically throws the exception that the input string was not in the correct format.

5. **Run the Sample and remove all text from the Make and Model TextBox controls.**

   You see that the TextBox controls are now rendered in red; as you enter text into the TextBox, as soon as you reach three characters, the red stroke disappears.

   The red stroke is sufficient to indicate that an error has occurred, but it's of little use to the users because they're not informed of the details of the error. A simple way to display the error is to add a tooltip on the TextBox. Do this by adding a Style resource to your window that defines a style that will trigger the tooltip when the data is in an invalid state.

6. **Add the following XAML directly below the Window tag at the top of MainWindow.xaml, like this to provide an error tooltip:**

```
<Window.Resources>
    <Style x:Key="errorAwareTextBox" TargetType="{x:Type TextBox}">
        <Style.Triggers>
            <Trigger Property="Validation.HasError" Value="true">
                <Setter Property="ToolTip"
            Value="{Binding RelativeSource={x:Static RelativeSource.Self},
            Path=(Validation.Errors)[0].ErrorContent}"/>
            </Trigger>
        </Style.Triggers>
    </Style>
</Window.Resources>
```

7. **Add a Style attribute to your TextBox, like this:**

```
    Style="{StaticResource ResourceKey=errorAwareTextBox}"
```

   Now when you run the application and remove the text from the TextBox controls, the TextBox displays a tooltip with the actual error message when you hover the mouse over the element. (See Figure 3-4.)

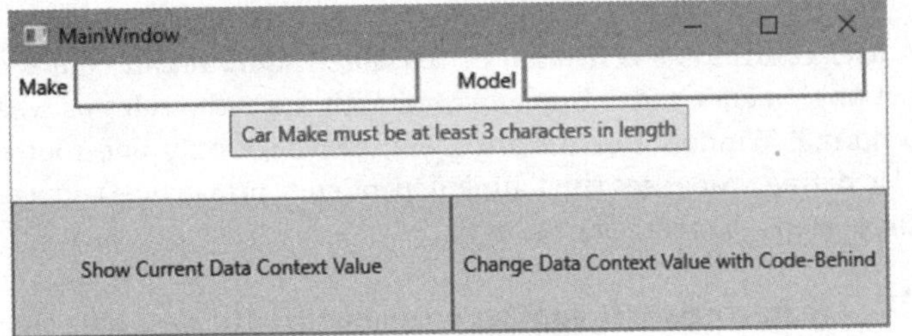

FIGURE 3-4: Displaying error messages using Styles.

Converting your data

WPF provides you with the capability to create an intuitive user interface. Sometimes this means allowing users to enter data in different formats that make sense to them, giving you the responsibility of translating the user's data entry into a format allowable by your data source. The same is true vice versa; you want to translate data from your data source into a more intuitive form for the user. A popular use-case for this type of conversion is the string representation of a date value, or if you want to display a red or green circle instead of the values True or False. WPF makes converting data easy by providing a simple interface called `IValueConverter` to implement. This interface contains two methods:

- `Convert`: This method obtains values from the data source and molds them to the form to be displayed to the user onscreen.
- `ConvertBack`: This method does the opposite — it takes the value from the user interface and molds it into a form that the data source expects.

Be sure to note that with these methods, you're not held to the same data type as the value being bound. For instance, your data source property being bound can be a Date data type, and the `Convert` method can still return a string value to the user interface.

To demonstrate this feature, create a new WPF application project called `BindingSample3`. This project is a dashboard application that can show the status of servers on the network. In this project, you implement two user controls, `RedX` and `GreenCheck`. You also create a value converter named `BooleanToIconConverter` that converts a `Boolean False` value to display the `RedX` control and converts a `True` value to display the `GreenCheck` control. These values indicate whether the server is available.

REMEMBER

A user control is a collection of reusable XAML. It can be made up of any number of elements and is implemented with the same rules as when you implement a normal Window (for instance, you can have only one root element). You can also define properties (including dependency properties!) on user controls. Follow these steps to create your sample:

1. **Create a new WPF application named** `BindingSample3`**.**
2. **Add a new User Control (WPF) to the project by choosing Project ⇨ Add User Control and name it** `GreenCheck.xaml`**.**
3. **Replace the** `Grid` **found in** `GreenCheck.xaml` **with this XAML:**

```
<Canvas x:Name="CheckCanvas" Width="50.4845" Height="49.6377"
           Canvas.Left="0" Canvas.Top="0">

    <Path x:Name="CheckPath" Width="43.4167" Height="45.6667"
          Canvas.Left="0" Canvas.Top="1.3113e-006"
          Stretch="Fill" Fill="#FF006432"
          Data="F1 M 19.0833,45.6667L 43.4167,2.16667L 38,
            1.3113e-006L 19.0833,42.5833L 2.41667,25.3333L 0,
            27.9167L 17.4167,44.25"/>
</Canvas>
```

You're not expected to come up with things like the `CheckPath` off the top of your head. (The `<Path>` is what describes how the check mark is drawn.) Various designer tools help you to draw items graphically and export your final graphics in a XAML format. Expression Design was the tool used to create the user controls in this example.

TIP

Unfortunately, Microsoft decided not to maintain Expression Design, so now you have to get it from a third party such as `http://expressiondesign4.com/` or `https://github.com/leeenglestone/ExpressionDesign4`. If you don't like Expression Design, you can find a list of alternative tools at `https://alternativeto.net/software/microsoft-expression-design/`.

4. **Add another User Control (WPF) to the project; name it** `RedX.xaml`**.**
5. **Replace the** `Grid` **in the** `RedX.xaml` **file with this XAML:**

```
<Canvas Width="44.625" Height="45.9394">

    <Path x:Name="Line1Path" Width="44.625" Height="44.375"
          Canvas.Left="0" Canvas.Top="0" Stretch="Fill"
          Fill="#FFDE0909"
          Data="F1 M 0,3.5L 3.5,0L 44.625,41L 42.125,44.375"/>
```

```
    <Path x:Name="Line2Path" Width="43.5772" Height="45.3813"
          Canvas.Left="0.201177" Canvas.Top="0.55809"
          Stretch="Fill"
          Fill="#FFDE0909" Data="F1 M 3.7719,45.9394L 0.201177,
            42.5115L 40.353,0.55809L 43.7784,2.98867"/>

</Canvas>
```

6. **Add a new class called** `BooleanToIconConverter.cs`.

7. **Add the following using directive to your class:**

```
using System.Windows.Data;
```

8. **Have the** `BooleanToIconConverter` **implement the** `IValueConverter` **interface.**

   The code should now contain the `Convert()` and `ConvertBack()` methods.

9. **Modify the** `Convert()` **method so that it looks like this:**

```
public object Convert(object value, Type targetType,
    object parameter, CultureInfo culture)
{
    if (value == null)
    {
        return value;
    }

    if ((bool)value == true)
    {
        return new GreenCheck();
    }
    else
    {
        return new RedX();
    }
}
```

10. **Add a new class called** `ServerStatus.cs`.

11. **Add three properties: the Server name, a Boolean indicator if the server is up, and a number of currently connected users, as shown here:**

```
public class ServerStatus
{
    public string ServerName { get; set; }
    public bool IsServerUp { get; set; }
```

```
    public int NumberOfConnectedUsers { get; set; }

    public ServerStatus() { }
}
```

12. In `MainWindow.xaml.cs`, **create the** `GenerateData()` **method shown here:**

```
private void GenerateData()
{
    ServerStatus ss = new ServerStatus()
    {
        ServerName = "HeadquartersApplicationServer1",
        NumberOfConnectedUsers = 983,
        IsServerUp = true
    };

    ServerStatus ss2 = new ServerStatus()
    {
        ServerName = "HeadquartersFileServer1",
        NumberOfConnectedUsers = 0,
        IsServerUp = false
    };

    ServerStatus ss3 = new ServerStatus()
    {
        ServerName = "HeadquartersWebServer1",
        NumberOfConnectedUsers = 0,
        IsServerUp = false
    };

    ServerStatus ss4 = new ServerStatus()
    {
        ServerName = "HQDomainControllerServer1",
        NumberOfConnectedUsers = 10235,
        IsServerUp = true
    };

    List<ServerStatus> serverList = new List<ServerStatus>();
    serverList.Add(ss);
    serverList.Add(ss2);
    serverList.Add(ss3);
    serverList.Add(ss4);

    this.DataContext = serverList;
}
```

This code initializes a list of a few `ServerStatus` objects and makes that list the `DataContext` of the `Window`.

13. **Add a call to** `GenerateData()` **immediately after the call to the** `InitializeComponent()` **method in the** `Window` **constructor).**

14. **Save and build your application.**

    You do this step so that the user control classes that you've defined are available to your XAML files.

15. **Add the following** `Window.Resources` **to** `MainWindow.xaml` **before the** `Grid`**:**

```
<Window.Resources>
    <local:BooleanToIconConverter
        x:Key="BooleanToIconConverter"/>

    <DataTemplate x:Key="ServerTemplate">
        <Border BorderBrush="Blue" Margin="3" Padding="3"
                BorderThickness="2" CornerRadius="5"
                Background="Beige">

            <StackPanel Orientation="Horizontal">

                <Label Content="{Binding
                    Path=IsServerUp,
                    Converter={StaticResource
                        BooleanToIconConverter}}"/>

                <StackPanel Orientation="Vertical"
                        VerticalAlignment="Center">

                    <TextBlock FontSize="25"
                        Foreground="Goldenrod"
                        Text="{Binding Path=ServerName}"/>

                    <TextBlock FontSize="18"
                        Foreground="BlueViolet"
                        Text="{Binding
                            Path=NumberOfConnectedUsers}"/>
                </StackPanel>

            </StackPanel>
        </Border>
    </DataTemplate>

</Window.Resources>
```

16. **Add the following code to the** `Grid` in `MainWindow.xaml`:

```
<Grid>
    <Grid.ColumnDefinitions>
        <ColumnDefinition/>
    </Grid.ColumnDefinitions>
    <Grid.RowDefinitions>
        <RowDefinition/>
    </Grid.RowDefinitions>

    <ListBox x:Name="lstServers" Width="490" Height="350"
             ItemsSource="{Binding}" Grid.Row="0" Grid.Column="0"
             ItemTemplate="{StaticResource
                ResourceKey=ServerTemplate}"/>
</Grid>
```

The first thing to note in `MainWindow.xaml` is that the namespace for the local assembly (`BindingSample3`) was added to the `Window` (identified by the namespace definition in the `Window` tag with the prefix `local`). This enables you to instantiate classes that are defined in the current assembly in XAML, such as `BooleanToIconConverter`.

```
<Window x:Class="BindingSample3.MainWindow"
    xmlns="http://schemas.microsoft.com/winfx/2006/xaml/presentation"
    xmlns:x="http://schemas.microsoft.com/winfx/2006/xaml"
    xmlns:d="http://schemas.microsoft.com/expression/blend/2008"
    xmlns:mc="http://schemas.openxmlformats.org/markup-compatibility/2006"
    xmlns:local="clr-namespace:BindingSample3"
    mc:Ignorable="d"
    Title="MainWindow" Height="400" Width="500">
```

In the `Window` resources, you initialize an instance of your `BooleanToIconConverter`, which is available to you through the local namespace.

```
<local:BooleanToIconConverter x:Key="BooleanToIconConverter"/>
```

The next `Window` resource that is defined is a data template. This data template provides a way to look at the data associated with a server's current status. The data template is defined as follows:

```
<DataTemplate x:Key="ServerTemplate">
    <Border BorderBrush="Blue" Margin="3" Padding="3"
            BorderThickness="2" CornerRadius="5"
            Background="Beige">
```

```
        <StackPanel Orientation="Horizontal">

            <Label Content="{Binding
                Path=IsServerUp,
                Converter={StaticResource
                    BooleanToIconConverter}}"/>

            <StackPanel Orientation="Vertical"
                    VerticalAlignment="Center">

                <TextBlock FontSize="25"
                    Foreground="Goldenrod"
                    Text="{Binding Path=ServerName}"/>

                <TextBlock FontSize="18"
                    Foreground="BlueViolet"
                    Text="{Binding
                        Path=NumberOfConnectedUsers}"/>
            </StackPanel>

        </StackPanel>
    </Border>
</DataTemplate>
```

Chapter 1 of this minibook states that one of the main reasons to adopt WPF as a user-interface technology is its data visualization flexibility. Data templates enable you to represent data contained in an object by using any number of XAML elements. The world is your oyster, and you can get as creative as you want to relay application information to your user in the most usable, intuitive fashion by using data templates.

Analyze the `ServerTemplate` data template. This data template represents the display of an instance of a `ServerStatus` object. Look at the `Label` element in the data template.

The `Content` property of the label is bound to the Boolean `IsServerUp` property of the `ServerStatus` object. You'll also notice that there is another component to the binding expression, called `Converter`. This is where the Boolean value (`IsServerUp`) gets passed into the `BooleanToIconConverter` and is rendered as the `RedX` or the `GreenCheck` user control, depending on its value.

The rest of the data template simply outputs the server name of the `ServerStatus` object in yellow and the number of connected users in blue-violet.

Within the `Grid` on the window, a `ListBox` control is defined that displays a list of servers on the network. Look at the definition of the `ListBox`:

```
<ListBox x:Name="lstServers" Width="490" Height="350"
         ItemsSource="{Binding}" Grid.Row="0" Grid.Column="0"
         ItemTemplate="{StaticResource
            ResourceKey=ServerTemplate}"/>
```

TECHNICAL STUFF

WPF provides a number of controls called `ItemsControls` that allow you to bind collections of objects to them. Examples of `ItemsControls` are `ListBox` and `ComboBox` (among others). Collections are bound to an `ItemsControl` through the `ItemsSource` attribute. A data template can also be applied to each object being bound through the `ItemsControl` `ItemTemplate` attribute.

Through Property Value inheritance, the `ItemsSource` of the `ListBox` is defaulted to the `DataContext` of `Window`. The empty `{Binding}` element simply states that it will use the current binding of its parent, which uses recursion up the element tree until it reaches a place where a binding is set. Remember that in the `GenerateData()` method, you're setting the `DataContext` binding to the list of servers to the `Window` itself, so the `ListBox` will inherit that list as its `ItemSource`.

The data template you defined in resources to describe a `ServerStatus` object renders each object being bound. You see this through the `ItemTemplate` attribute that uses the `StaticResource` to point to the `ServerTemplate` defined in resources. Now when you run the application, you see the ServerStatus data presented in a visually pleasing way! (See Figure 3-5.)

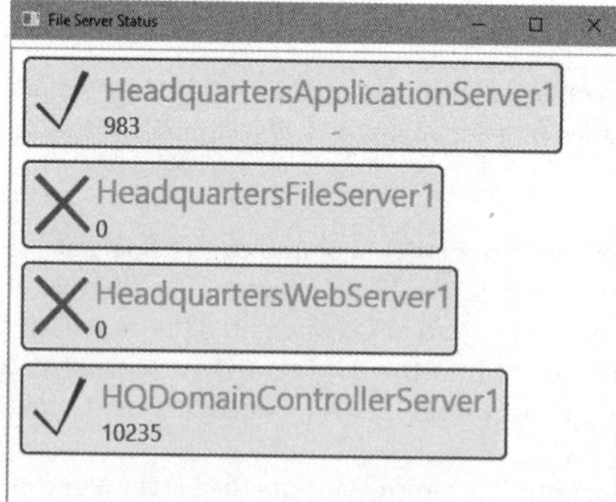

FIGURE 3-5: Rendering a collection of data using a value converter and data templates.

Finding Out More about WPF Data Binding

This chapter is not meant to be inclusive of all functionality possible through WPF's amazing data binding support. Other aspects of WPF data templates worth looking into include these concepts:

- Using `DataTemplateSelector`, which is a base class that allows you to render a data template based on some logical condition.
- Using data templates as a means to provide data adding/editing capabilities to the user.
- Switching a data template at runtime at the preference of the user. This allows users to switch a data template at will. For instance, in a `ListBox`, you may display only summary information; however, you can provide a button in your data template that will enable users to switch between the summary template and a more detailed template on demand.

IN THIS CHAPTER

» Understanding the command types

» Using built-in commands

» Using custom commands

» Using routed commands

Chapter 4
Practical WPF

Even though WPF still supports the direct event-handler wire-up (for example, through the `OnClick` event), WPF introduces a much better mechanism for responding to user events. It significantly reduces the amount of code you have to write and adds testability to your application. Traditional event handling is all contained in the code-behind for your form, which is extremely difficult to test in an automated fashion.

Software patterns have been around for a long time, first brought to the forefront by the classic tome *Design Patterns: Elements of Reusable Object-Oriented Software* (Addison-Wesley) by Erich Gamma, Richard Helm, Ralph Johnson, and John Vlissides — commonly referred to as the "Gang of Four." Software has evolved, and many new patterns have been developed over the years. One of the most effective user interface patterns developed for WPF is the Model-View-View Model (MVVM) pattern (commonly referred to as ViewModel, see `https://docs.microsoft.com/archive/msdn-magazine/2009/february/patterns-wpf-apps-with-the-model-view-viewmodel-design-pattern`). Using the ViewModel pattern in your WPF applications will improve software reuse, testability, readability, maintainability, and most of the other "-ilities" as well. (You run across other design patterns throughout this whole book.)

This chapter concentrates on yet another pattern, the Command Pattern, which can provide an effective middle ground between directly wiring things up and using an intermediary to make the connection between data and the view. Using the command pattern brings order to directly wiring things up, but is less difficult to implement than MVVM. The chapter begins by comparing the Command

Pattern to traditional event handling. It then discusses three command types: built-in, custom, and routed.

REMEMBER

You don't have to type the source code for this chapter manually. In fact, using the downloadable source is a lot easier. You can find the source for this chapter in the `\CSAIO4D2E\BK05\CH04` folder of the downloadable source. See the Introduction for details on how to find these source files.

Commanding Attention

The Command Pattern has been around since, well, forever, and you most likely use it every day. Copy and Paste commands are example implementations of the pattern built into Windows and most Windows applications. WPF provides a significant number of built-in commands and also allows for completely customized commands! The following sections provide you with additional information about how commands can work in WPF.

Traditional event handling

Traditional handling of user events (and still supported in WPF) is through an event handler. When the button on the Window is clicked, the code in the event handler (which has to be in the code-behind file) will execute. Here is an example of the WPF for using event handling (also found in the TraditionalEventHandling example in the downloadable source):

```
<Grid>
    <Grid.RowDefinitions>
        <RowDefinition Height="30"/>
        <RowDefinition Height="30"/>
    </Grid.RowDefinitions>

    <TextBox Name="Message" Grid.Row="0" HorizontalAlignment="Left"
             Width="200" Height="20"/>
    <Button Name="ClickMe" Grid.Row="1" HorizontalAlignment="Center"
            Content="Click Me" Click="ClickMe_Click"/>
</Grid>
```

REMEMBER

Note how the `Button` is connected to the code-behind by using the `Click` event. The mechanism used here is quite simple, but you must perform it for each control individually, making an error likely in some cases. Any change to the code-behind necessitates a change to every location at which the event handler is referenced in the XAML as well. The actual event-handler code is equally easy to figure out because it follows the technique used for Windows Forms applications:

```
private void ClickMe_Click(object sender, RoutedEventArgs e)
{
    MessageBox.Show(Message.Text);
}
```

By placing this code in the code-behind event handler, the business logic is now mixed with the user interface code, mixing concerns. To be fair, nothing in the framework *makes* one put the code in the code-behind; it just seems to always end up there. (You can, of course, separate your business logic into classes outside of your code-behind.)

This problem gets compounded when additional UIElements are added to the window that need to execute the same code. The common fix for this situation is to refactor the code in the original event handler into a separate method and have the event handlers for the related UIElements call the new method. The new method can even be moved into the Business Layer, separating concerns and allowing for testability.

The other issue is one of user experience. Often, menus and buttons need to be actively enabled or disabled based on the condition of the data (or some other condition/user action) in the window.

In this example, the `ClickMe` button remains enabled all the time because the application doesn't provide any code to enable or disable it based on the content of the `Message` text box. Realistically, the user interface should disable `ClickMe` automatically whenever `Message` is blank. Users tend to click active items repeatedly when given the option, wondering why nothing is happening. The command pattern as implemented in WPF cleanly and easily resolves both issues.

ICommand

The `ICommand` interface provides the contract for a command that a particular class will execute. It specifies the conditions required so that the command can execute. When those conditions are met, a class implementing `ICommand` executes the command. `ICommand` (which is the base interface for all commands discussed here) defines two event handlers and one event, as shown here.

```
bool CanExecute(object parameter);
void Execute(object parameter);
event EventHandler CanExecuteChanged;
```

ROUTEDCOMMAND VERSUS ROUTEDUICOMMAND

The only difference between RoutedCommand and RoutedUICommand is that RoutedUICommand adds a Text property used to decorate the bound controls' content uniformly. MenuItems pick up this property automatically and assign it to the Header property. Buttons (and other UIElements) need a bit of binding kung fu, such as the following XAML snippet, to get the Text into the Content property by binding the Content property to Command.Text.

```
Content="{Binding RelativeSource={RelativeSource Mode=Self}, Path=Command.
    Text}"
```

Perhaps the most powerful feature of WPF commands is the capability to determine at runtime whether the bound controls can execute. (See the next section for a detailed discussion.) The following list describes the ICommand elements in more detail.

- CanExecute is run by the CommandManager whenever focus changes, the PropertyChanged or CollectionChanged events are raised, or on demand through code. If the event handler returns false, all UIElements bound to that command are disabled.
- Execute contains the code that executes when the user action is processed or the command is executed through code.
- CanExecuteChanged accesses a mechanism supplied by INotifyCollectionChanged and INotifyPropertyChanged that determines when CanExecute is required.

Routed commands

The ICommand interface doesn't provide the entire goodness of commands in WPF. The RoutedCommand class (and its first descendant, RoutedUICommand) takes advantage of event routing to provide additional power.

The CanExecute event handler raises the PreviewCanExecute event, and the Execute event handler raises the PreviewExecuted event. These events are raised just prior to the CanExecute and Execute handlers and bubble up the element tree until an element with the correct command binding is located. This approach is useful to allow the control of commands at a higher level, while the fine-grained elements still control the CanExecute and the Execute event handlers.

Routed commands also expose a collection of InputGestures — keystrokes or other gestures that fire the Execute event handler. You use InputGestures to assign hot-key combinations to commands, such as Ctrl+S for saving.

Using Built-In Commands

WPF provides a number of built-in commands that you can use with little or no code (see the list at https://docs.microsoft.com/dotnet/api/system.windows.input). The most common set used by line-of-business-developers is wrapped up in the ApplicationCommands library. The advantage of using the built-in commands is that all the plumbing is taken care of for you. For example, the CanExecute and Execute event handlers are already implemented. All you have to do is bind them to UIElements through XAML, as shown in the BuiltIn-Commands example.

TIP

You may end up running the example code several times or have items on the Clipboard from other uses. To ensure that you begin with a clear Clipboard for this example, add the following call after InitializeComponent(); in the MainWindow() constructor:

```
Clipboard.Clear();
```

The sample shown in the following code and Figure 4-1 uses the ApplicationCommands.Copy and ApplicationCommands.Paste commands to facilitate Clipboard manipulation in your application. As a side note, WPF allows you to abbreviate the built-in commands by dropping the container name (ApplicationCommands), so Copy and Paste are legitimate abbreviations for the command bindings ApplicationCommands.Copy and ApplicationCommands.Paste.

```
<Grid>
    <Grid.RowDefinitions>
        <RowDefinition Height="40"/>
        <RowDefinition Height="30"/>
        <RowDefinition Height="30"/>
    </Grid.RowDefinitions>

    <Menu Grid.Row="0" HorizontalAlignment="Left" Name="menu1">
        <MenuItem Command="Copy">
            <MenuItem.Style>
                <Style TargetType="{x:Type MenuItem}">
                    <Setter Property="Foreground" Value="Black"/>
                    <Style.Triggers>
                        <Trigger Property="IsEnabled" Value="True">
```


Practical WPF

```
                    <Setter Property="Foreground" Value="Red"/>
                    <Setter Property="FontSize" Value="16"/>
                </Trigger>
            </Style.Triggers>
        </Style>
    </MenuItem.Style>
</MenuItem>

<MenuItem Command="Paste">
    <MenuItem.Style>
        <Style TargetType="{x:Type MenuItem}">
            <Setter Property="Foreground" Value="Black"/>
            <Style.Triggers>
                <Trigger Property="IsEnabled" Value="True">
                    <Setter Property="Foreground" Value="Red"/>
                    <Setter Property="FontSize" Value="16"/>
                </Trigger>
            </Style.Triggers>
        </Style>
    </MenuItem.Style>
</MenuItem>
</Menu>

<TextBox Grid.Row="1" HorizontalAlignment="Left" Width="200"/>
<TextBox Grid.Row="2" HorizontalAlignment="Left" Width="200"/>
</Grid>
```

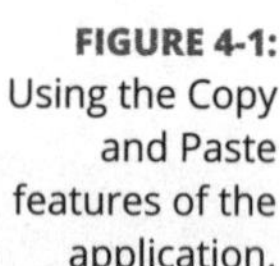

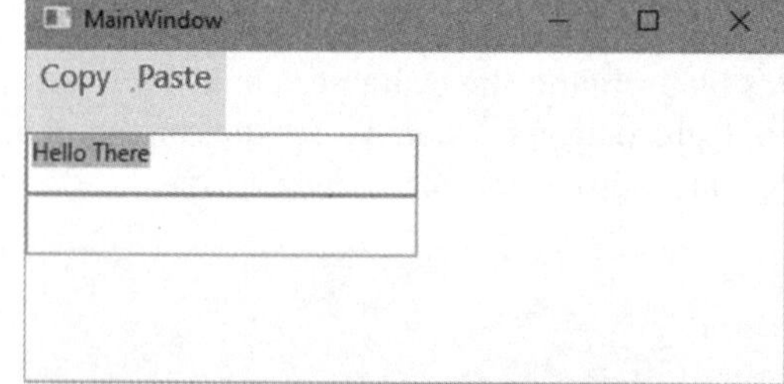

FIGURE 4-1: Using the Copy and Paste features of the application.

TIP

The example contains a bit of trick code that makes it easier to see changes in the UI. Notice how it uses `MenuItem.Style` to change how the menu items appear normally or when they have the focus. Normally, the `Setter` configures `Property="Foreground"` to `Value="Black"`, so you see black lettering. However, `Trigger` watches for `Property="IsEnabled"` to become `True`. When this occurs, the color of the text changes to `Red`. The code also changes the size of the menu by using `Property="FontSize"` and `Value="16"`. Of course, you can use this technique for all sorts of purposes, not only to make UI testing easier.

When the UIElement with focus supports the Clipboard `Copy` action *and* there are items selected that can be copied to the Clipboard, any elements bound to the `Copy` command are enabled.

When the UIElement with focus supports the Clipboard `Paste` action *and* there is data in the Clipboard that is supportable by the element with focus, any elements bound to the `Paste` command are enabled.

Using Custom Commands

You can use custom commands in all sorts of ways. For example, you might decide to implement the `ApplicationCommands.Copy` command by using a `Button` instead of a `MenuItem`. When you try using just the `Command` property, as you do with a `MenuItem`, it doesn't work. You need to create the connectivity that a `MenuItem` possesses, but a `Button` doesn't, by using a custom command. The following sections show the simplest method for creating a custom command. You can also see this code in the CustomCommands example in the downloadable source.

Defining the interface

This example uses two custom buttons, one labeled Copy and another labeled Paste. It also has two text boxes, one to hold the source text and another to hold the destination text. Destination is set for read-only use because the example copies from the source to the destination to keep things simple. You use the buttons as you did the menu items in the previous example. However, the connectivity isn't nearly as automated this time. The following code shows the interface for this example:

```
<Grid>
    <Grid.RowDefinitions>
        <RowDefinition Height="40"/>
        <RowDefinition Height="30"/>
        <RowDefinition Height="30"/>
    </Grid.RowDefinitions>

    <StackPanel Grid.Row="0" Orientation="Horizontal"
                HorizontalAlignment="Left">
        <Button Content="Copy" Command="ApplicationCommands.Copy"/>
        <Button Content="Paste" Command="ApplicationCommands.Paste"/>
    </StackPanel>

    <TextBox Name="Source" Grid.Row="1" HorizontalAlignment="Left"
             Width="200"/>
```

```
    <TextBox Name="Destination" Grid.Row="2" HorizontalAlignment="Left"
             Width="200" IsReadOnly="True"/>

</Grid>
```

Creating the window binding

To make the example code work, you must create a binding between the controls and the underlying code-behind. You have a number of ways in which to create a binding, and this example shows the most common. In the following code, you define the `Window.CommandBindings` as a series of `CommandBinding` elements. Note that the `Command` attributes here match the `Command` attributes used for the two buttons in the previous section:

```
<Window.CommandBindings>
    <CommandBinding Command="ApplicationCommands.Copy"
                    Executed="CommandBinding_Executed"
                    CanExecute="CommandBinding_CanExecute"/>
    <CommandBinding Command="ApplicationCommands.Paste"
                    Executed="CommandBinding_Executed"
                    CanExecute="CommandBinding_CanExecute"/>
</Window.CommandBindings>
```

When you type certain attribute names, such as `Executed`, the IDE automatically asks whether you want to create the associated event handler. If you allow the automatic creation, the event handler will appear in the code-behind for you. The temptation is to create a unique event handler for each of the command entries, but this would be a mistake because doing so makes maintenance harder. Instead, you want to use a single event handler for everything, as shown in the next section.

Ensuring that the command can execute

Now that you have controls and binding from the controls to an event handler, you need to create the event-handler code. In this case, you first need to determine whether executing the command is even possible. The buttons will automatically enable or disable as needed based on the value of `e.CanExecute` in the following code:

```
private void CommandBinding_CanExecute(object sender,
    CanExecuteRoutedEventArgs e)
{
    string Name = ((RoutedCommand)e.Command).Name;

    if (Name == "Copy")
```

```
    {
        if (Source == null)
        {
            e.CanExecute = false;
            return;
        }

        if (Source.SelectedText.Length > 0)
            e.CanExecute = true;
        else
            e.CanExecute = false;
    }
    else if (Name == "Paste")
    {
        if (Clipboard.ContainsText() == true)
        {
            e.CanExecute = true;
        }
        else
        {
            e.CanExecute = false;
        }
    }
}
```

REMEMBER

Note that you must convert the incoming `e.Command` value to a name string as shown in the code so that you can test for a particular command. The command `Name` is a simple string that contains either `Copy` or `Paste` in this case. The values you see depend on how you configure the `Command` attributes for your application controls.

The determiner for execution differs in each case. The `Copy` button won't work if the user hasn't selected some text. Likewise, it's not possible to paste text to the destination when the `Clipboard` lacks data of the correct type. Note that you must use `Clipboard.ContainsText()` to ensure that the user hasn't copied an image or some other type of data.

Performing the task

Now that you have all the connections defined between the window and the code-behind, you can begin coding the actual task. First you must add the `Clipboard.Clear();` call after `InitializeComponent();` in the `MainWindow()` method, as you did for the previous example.

The next step is to handle the Executed event. A single event handler works with both buttons, as shown here:

```
private void CommandBinding_Executed(object sender,
    ExecutedRoutedEventArgs e)
{
    String Name = ((RoutedCommand)e.Command).Name;

    if (Name == "Copy")
    {
        Clipboard.SetText(Source.SelectedText);
    }
    else if (Name == "Paste")
    {
        Destination.Text = Destination.Text + Clipboard.GetText();
    }
}
```

As with the CommandBinding_CanExecute() method in the previous section, this code begins by obtaining the name of the button that the user clicked. It uses this information to select a course of action. The goal is to copy text from Source and place it on Clipboard, or to copy text from Clipboard and place it in Destination.

REMEMBER

You normally wouldn't make the code this simple. The example does so to keep from hiding the workings of the code-behind as it relates to the Window controls. When you first start the application, neither button is activated.

Typing some text and then selecting some of it enables the Copy button, as shown in Figure 4-2. Note that the button doesn't become enabled when you type the text; it's the act of selecting the text that enables it. This is the same action that occurs when you use menu controls in the previous example.

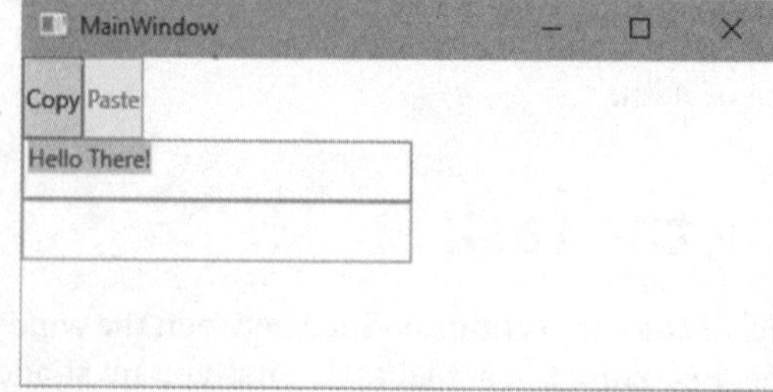

FIGURE 4-2: Selecting the text enables the Copy button.

When you click Copy, both the Copy and the Paste buttons are enabled. This action occurs because the text remains highlighted in the source text box. When you click Paste, the Copy button remains enabled. Normally, an application would place the focus on the pasted location, disabling the Copy button. As previously mentioned, this example does things simply so that you can see how the connections work. Clicking in the source text box (so that the text is no longer highlighted) does disable the Copy button.

Using Routed Commands

Routed commands require a little more effort, but they also allow you to perform custom actions that `ICommand` doesn't support. This example does something simple: displays a message box. However, the technique shown works for complex applications as well. The following sections demonstrate how you can use routed commands for both buttons and menus. You can also see this code in the RoutedCommands example in the downloadable source.

Defining the Command class

The center of the exercise is the `RoutedUICommand` object, `cmdSayHello`. It provides the resource needed to make the command available. However, to make this object work properly, it must appear within its own class within the `RoutedCommands` namespace (rather than as part of the `MainWindow` class).

REMEMBER

To interact with your `Command` class, you first must create it and then choose Build⇨Rebuild Solution to ensure that the class is visible to XAML. Otherwise, you might find that the XAML you write has blue underlines beneath the various command callouts for no apparent reason. Here is the code used to create the `Command` class:

```
public static class Command
{
    public static readonly RoutedUICommand cmdSayHello =
        new RoutedUICommand("Say Hello Menu", "DoSayHello",
            typeof(MainWindow));
}
```

WARNING

Note that the `Command` class and the `cmdSayHello` field are both static and that `cmdSayHello` is also `readonly`. If you don't create your `Command` class in this manner, WPF will refuse to recognize it. Unfortunately, your application will fail in odd ways, and finding this particular bug can be quite difficult. If you find that your application simply crashes in odd ways, you need to verify that you have created your `Command` class correctly.

Making the namespace accessible

Modern versions of Visual Studio automatically add the code required to make your namespace accessible as `local`. The actual entry appears as `xmlns:local="clr-namespace:RoutedCommands"` in this case. Here is the full code so that you see where to look for the namespace declaration:

```
<Window x:Class="RoutedCommands.MainWindow"
    xmlns="http://schemas.microsoft.com/winfx/2006/xaml/presentation"
    xmlns:x="http://schemas.microsoft.com/winfx/2006/xaml"
    xmlns:d="http://schemas.microsoft.com/expression/blend/2008"
    xmlns:mc="http://schemas.openxmlformats.org/markup-compatibility/2006"
    xmlns:local="clr-namespace:RoutedCommands"
    mc:Ignorable="d"
    Title="MainWindow" Height="200" Width="400">
```

If you don't have such an entry already in your XAML code, you must create one. Otherwise, your application won't be able to find your custom commands.

Adding the command bindings

As with the `ApplicationCommands` entries used with buttons, you must provide command bindings in order to access your custom commands. The following code shows the command bindings used for this example:

```
<Window.CommandBindings>
    <CommandBinding Command="local:Command.cmdSayHello"
                    CanExecute="CommandBinding_CanExecute"
                    Executed="CommandBinding_Executed"/>
</Window.CommandBindings>
```

REMEMBER

Note how the example code declares the `CommandBinding`. The `CanExecute` and `Executed` entries are much the same as in the previous section. However, the `Command` entry accesses the `local` namespace as `local:Command.cmdSayHello`, where `Command` is the name of the class used to hold the `RoutedUICommand` object and `cmdSayHello` is the name of the object.

Developing a user interface

You can use custom commands with any control that normally supports a click-type event. This example uses both a menu and a button to access the custom command, but you have many other options. The following code creates the application interface, which looks much like the other examples in this chapter:

```
<Grid>
    <Grid.RowDefinitions>
        <RowDefinition Height="40"/>
        <RowDefinition Height="30"/>
        <RowDefinition Height="30"/>
    </Grid.RowDefinitions>

    <Menu Grid.Row="0" HorizontalAlignment="Left" Name="menu1">
        <MenuItem Command="local:Command.cmdSayHello"/>
    </Menu>

    <TextBox Name="NameStr"  Grid.Row="1" HorizontalAlignment="Left"
             Width="200"/>
    <Button Grid.Row="2" Content="Say Hello"
            HorizontalAlignment="Right"
            Command="local:Command.cmdSayHello"/>
</Grid>
```

TIP

Note that the `MenuItem` element of the `Menu` control doesn't provide a textual entry for the user to see. On the other hand, the `Button` does provide this information in the form of the `Content` property. Even though the `MenuItem` lacks this information, it still displays `Say Hello Menu`. This information comes from the `RoutedUICommand` object declaration. When creating your `RoutedUICommand` object, it pays to provide a default text definition that works well with menus and then use custom text for other controls as needed.

Developing the custom command code-behind

Creating code for your custom command is almost an anticlimax because it works the same as when working with `ICommand`. You still need to define code for the `CanExecute` and `Executed` event handlers, such as the code shown here:

```
private void CommandBinding_CanExecute(object sender,
    CanExecuteRoutedEventArgs e)
{
    if ((NameStr != null) && (NameStr.Text.Length > 0))
        e.CanExecute = true;
    else
        e.CanExecute = false;
}

private void CommandBinding_Executed(object sender,
    ExecutedRoutedEventArgs e)
{
    MessageBox.Show("Hello " + NameStr.Text);
}
```

Obviously, this is a really simple example, but the technique works fine for complex setups as well. Note that you don't need to create different code for menus or buttons (or other controls, for that matter). Everyone uses the same code. Also note that you don't need to perform any special wire-ups to make the application work.

When you first start the application, the menu and button are both disabled. However, when you type text into the text box, both controls become enabled, as shown in Figure 4-3. Clicking either control produces a message box similar to the one shown in Figure 4-4.

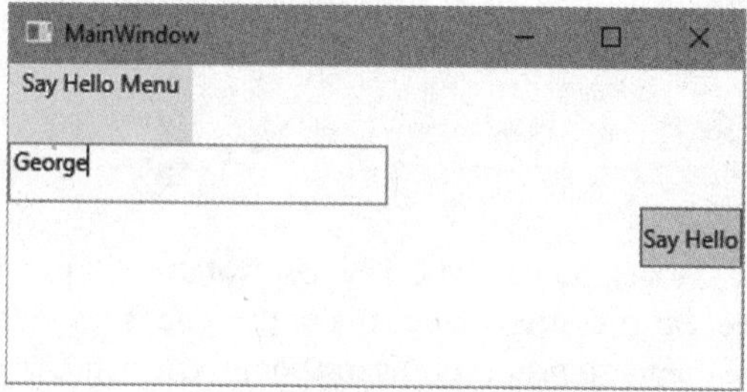

FIGURE 4-3: Typing a name (or other text) enables both the button and the menu.

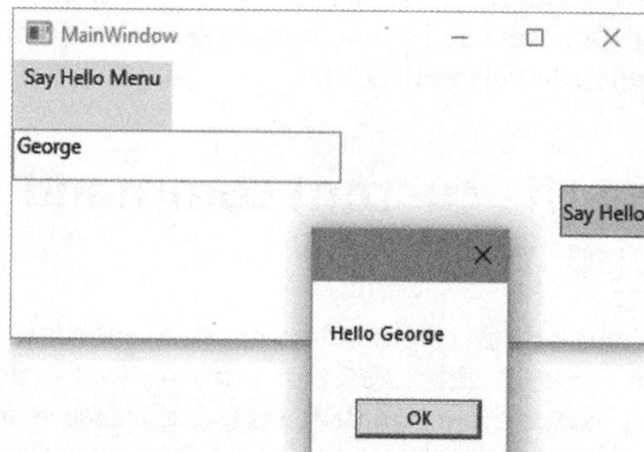

FIGURE 4-4. Clicking either control produces simple output.

REMEMBER

The moment you clear the text, the button and menu item become disabled again, so you know that the `CanExecute` event handlers work as expected. The main idea to take from this chapter is that WPF provides multiple methods for defining commands that you can use to create robust applications.

IN THIS CHAPTER

- » Understanding the Universal Windows Platform (UWP)
- » Using UWP to your advantage
- » Developing a simple UWP app
- » Working with .NET Core applications in general

Chapter 5
Programming for Windows 10 and Above

The Universal Windows Platform (UWP) epitomizes the new direction of development for Windows 10 and above machines. What started in Windows 10 should see additional use in Windows 11. Windows 10 is a robust version of Windows that corrects many of the problems found in versions like Vista and Windows 8. You find Windows used in over 1.3 billion machines according to sources like *PC Magazine* (`https://www.pcmag.com/reviews/microsoft-windows-10`) and 78 percent of Windows installations are Windows 10. In fact, Windows still claims 75 percent of the desktops out there (with macOS accounting for around 17 percent and Linux, in its various forms, taking up the rest). So, the question on your mind might be why a new kind of application is needed if it's going to affect so few people. The answer is that most people don't just sit at a desktop system anymore — they want the same app to work on their desktop, tablet, laptop, and smartphone anywhere they might be. So, UWP represents Microsoft's way of heading in this direction because it supports multiple platforms that include Windows 10/11, Windows 10/11 Mobile, Xbox One, and Hololens. So, the first part of this chapter helps fill in the details for you so that you can look oh so smart the next time you talk with your peers over cocktails at the company party.

Of course, there are billions (perhaps more) lines of more traditional Windows code out there — the kind used for most of the applications in this book. So you might be a little reticent about throwing them all out and starting from scratch. After all, your boss may not have been in a particularly good mood lately. The second part of this chapter is all about when using UWP for new development makes sense.

No chapter about the UWP would be complete without an example, so the chapter's third section provides you with UWP basics that are better than a simple Hello World application. For example, you discover how to set your Windows 10 and above machine up for Developer Mode. Of course, you won't find Developer Mode in older versions of Windows, so if you have one of those older versions, stop here, because you really can't write a UWP application — Visual Studio 2022 won't let you!

The final section of the chapter tells you more about the mysteries of .NET Core development. It focuses on .NET 6 because this is the latest and most feature-rich version of the .NET Framework. Again, if you're using your rusty, trusty old version of Visual Studio, nothing will work in this section —you really do need Visual Studio 2022.

REMEMBER

You don't have to type the source code for this chapter manually. In fact, using the downloadable source is a lot easier. You can find the source for this chapter in the `\CSAIO4D2E\BK05\CH05` folder of the downloadable source. See the Introduction for details on how to find these source files.

What is the Universal Windows Platform (UWP)?

You can look at UWP in a number of ways. From a simplistic perspective, it provides another method of creating a Windows client application. So, theoretically, it's just another in a long series of efforts on the part of Microsoft to make using Windows easier or better in some way, but still, it's just a client application development technology.

Like all newer Windows apps created by C# developers, UWP apps have access to the Win32 API. However, the access is granted through a special `WindowsApp.lib` library file, as described at `https://docs.microsoft.com/en-us/previous-versions/mt186421(v=vs.85)`, specialized DLLs (`https://docs.microsoft.com/en-us/previous-versions/mt186422(v=vs.85)`), and the .NET Framework (`https://docs.microsoft.com/en-us/dotnet/api/?view=dotnet-uwp-10.0`).

In other words, you have new methods for doing the same old things you've always done. Paul Thurrott (a well-known, longtime technical reviewer) (`https://www.thurrott.com/dev/206351/microsoft-confirms-uwp-is-not-the-future-of-windows-apps`) says outright that UWP isn't the absolute future of Windows app development; many UWP features will be made available through other avenues.

REMEMBER

The reasons to use UWP don't stem from a magical new application type or specialized libraries that will allow you to look like Super Programmer, the killer of all client problems. You use UWP to create WinCore apps that run the same across multiple devices and provide access to the app through the Microsoft store. In short, this is one tool in a toolbox, not the entire toolbox, as you might believe from some Microsoft hype. Even so, UWP provides you with this set of interesting and useful features:

- **Modern UI:** Whether users actually like tiles that blare out their messages in a multimedia frenzy or not remains to be seen (look at discussions like the ones found at `https://www.reddit.com/r/windows/comments/on98u0/why_do_people_hate_live_tiles/` and `https://mspoweruser.com/windows-10s-live-tiles-vestigial-time-go/` if you have any doubts). UWP apps can rely on live tiles, push notifications, and user activities that interact with Windows Timeline and Cortana's Pick Up Where I Left Off functionality. The problem is whether users actually find the modern UI practical.
- **Adaptable:** Many devices offer multiple modes of operation, such as orientation, and these devices have differing functionality, such as screen sizes, and UWP applications can accommodate all of it. This adaptability comes from the Model-View-ViewModel (MVVM) design pattern described at `https://docs.microsoft.com/windows/uwp/data-binding/data-binding-and-mvvm`.
- **Install and uninstall preciseness:** A huge problem with Windows apps as a whole is that they cause *machine rot,* the condition in which the OS must be installed from scratch because the various applications have modified it in some way. UWP supposedly disallows programming techniques that cause machine rot.
- **Lifecycle-based development:** Unlike many forms of Windows development, the developer has stronger control over the lifecycle of a UWP app. It's now possible to control the deployment, update, installation, and even uninstallation of the application.
- **Reduced development time:** This feature comes with a caveat: The learning curve for true UWP development is huge, and there is no way to reduce it. However, after you get into the UWP mindset, you can save development time in these ways:
  - Control over the development cycle means that less time is spent in application management.

UWP AND THE REGISTRY

UWP apps supposedly avoid machine rot by disallowing certain practices, such as registry access. However, a UWP app can still use the registry through an extension app (see `https://docs.microsoft.com/answers/questions/285798/how-can-i-edit-the-registry-with-c-uwp.html` for details), so some machine rot is inevitable. Windows developers will need to develop entirely new methods of working with devices that used to require registry access. For example, instead of garnering USB access through a registry setting (see the message thread at `https://social.msdn.microsoft.com/Forums/en-US/eac2ddff-1984-4d83-8029-07843855dd26/how-to-write-registry-key-at-uwp-app-install-time`), the developer will have to rely on recognized APIs, such as the one described at `https://github.com/Microsoft/Windows-universal-samples/tree/main/Samples/CustomUsbDeviceAccess`. The problem is that registry use is so ingrained in the Windows developer psyche that changes of this sort will take a long time, assuming that they happen at all.

- The adaptable nature of UWP means that you write the application once, not once for each device you want to support.
- Administrators spend less time trying to configure and adapt the application, so developers spend less time producing fixes.
- Users have a consistent look and feel on every device, so developers spend less time correcting UI functionality.
- Development issues surrounding UWP are theoretically eased by the UWP Bridges toolkits (`https://mspoweruser.com/microsoft-details-the-new-universal-windows-platform-at-build-2015/`). However, only the Desktop Bridge receives much attention, such as in the message thread at `https://stackoverflow.com/questions/65737039/how-to-package-a-wpf-net-core-app-with-xamlislands-and-desktop-bridge`.

» **Security:** A UWP app declares the resources it needs, and the user must allow that access. This is akin to the same functionality in Android apps.

» **Common API:** If your application doesn't use any special low-level features, it can run on any device that runs Windows 10 and above.

» **Strong language support:** UWP applications can rely on C#, C++, Visual Basic, and JavaScript for development at the same time (rather than use a single language for the entire application). However, you can't get by with just one language as in the days of yore because you need a second language for the UI: WinUI, XAML, HTML, or DirectX.

Devices Supported by the UWP

For development purposes, you must have a Windows 10 or above system. Most developers will use a desktop system because the Visual Studio 2022 interface requires a lot of screen real estate to use effectively. My personal experiences trying a laptop for development didn't work out well, but I'm sure that some people will find that a laptop works fine for their needs. What really surprised me was the reader who decided to write code using their smartphone. I'm not sure how they got that to work, but I suspect they spend a lot of time squinting after a programming session. The point is, you need Windows to develop UWP apps.

Using UWP apps is another story. The official Microsoft line is that UWP apps run on any device that supports Windows 10 or above, including Windows 10/11, Windows 10/11 Mobile, Xbox One, and Hololens. You can also connect your app to external devices (see `https://docs.microsoft.com/en-us/windows/uwp/devices-sensors/` for details). However, this is only part of the story. By using Xamarin (`https://dotnet.microsoft.com/apps/xamarin`) add-ins for Visual Studio 2022, it's possible to expand UWP development to these platforms:

- iOS (`https://www.apple.com/ios/ios-15/`)
- Android (`https://www.android.com/`)
- tvOS (`https://developer.apple.com/tvos/`)
- watchOS (`https://www.apple.com/watchos/watchos-8/`)
- macOS (`https://www.apple.com/macos/`)

With Xamarin support, you suddenly have access to a host of extremely popular devices that would be inconceivable for most Windows developers to even think about writing apps to support. Even though most of the products in this list are from Apple, don't discount the Android support. As described in *Android Application Development All-in-One For Dummies*, 3rd Edition, by Barry Burd and John Paul Mueller (Wiley), Android appears on a huge number of device types, including IoT devices like smart thermostats, watches, and even cars.

Whether you can actually make a UWP app work on your car is another story. (Anyone who has come up with a unique UWP app for something like a car should contact me at `John@JohnMuellerBooks.com`.) Android Developer Studio (`https://developer.android.com/studio`) comes with templates that Xamarin (`https://docs.microsoft.com/en-us/xamarin/android/`) doesn't currently appear to replicate. However, Xamarin most definitely supports Android wearables (`https://docs.microsoft.com/en-us/xamarin/android/wear/get-started/intro-to-wear`).

So, trying to pin down a precise list of devices that UWP supports is a little difficult. The answer to the question of support comes down to a mix of tools you're willing to use and the requirements of the device that you want to support. In addition, your coding skill will have a great deal to do with the success you see because UWP development in these other areas definitely requires thinking outside the box.

Creating Your Own UWP App

It's time to try your hand at UWP development. The following sections take you through the basic development process that you follow when working with UWP. Part of this process is setting up Developer Mode, which you have to do only once for each development machine you use.

Configuring Developer Mode

You can't create any sort of UWP project without setting Developer Mode on. The moment you finish a UWP project setup, you see the dialog box shown in Figure 5-1 if you haven't set up Developer Mode already. Consequently, this is one of the few sections in the minibook you absolutely can't skip unless you choose not to develop UWP apps. The following sections tell you more about Developer Mode.

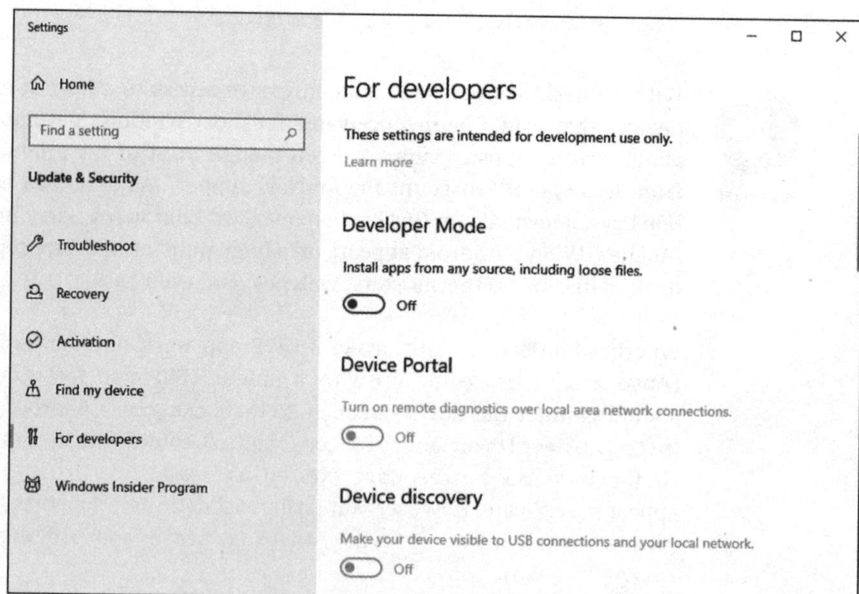

FIGURE 5-1: You can't create a UWP app without setting Developer Mode on.

Defining Developer Mode

Developer Mode provides the means for developers to gain additional access to their system's functionality when creating apps that could eventually end up in the Microsoft Store or on another device, such as a tablet. Microsoft actively discourages anyone from enabling Developer Mode (`https://docs.microsoft.com/windows/apps/get-started/enable-your-device-for-development`) unless actually needed for development purposes. For example, you wouldn't enable Developer Mode to fix your system.

When creating certain kinds of applications for Windows 8, a developer had to apply for a developer license from Microsoft, `https://docs.microsoft.com/en-us/previous-versions/windows/apps/hh974578(v=win.10)`, which could turn into a messy and annoying process at times (`https://superuser.com/questions/496104/windows-8-developer-license`). So, part of the reason for Developer Mode in Windows 10 and above is to avoid the whole licensing issue.

The reason for a development license and now Developer Mode is that developers need to work with apps that aren't necessarily signed or from an official source. Apps from an official source are vetted to ensure that they behave properly and don't represent a security risk, so allowing unsigned apps on a system presents the potential for damaging the system and its data. As part of granting this right, the system also enables Secure Shell (SSH) support (`https://www.ssh.com/academy/ssh`) for your system, so now there is the potential for outside access. When you turn Developer Mode on, you see the dialog box shown in Figure 5-2, warning you of the possible implications. You need to click Yes to complete the process.

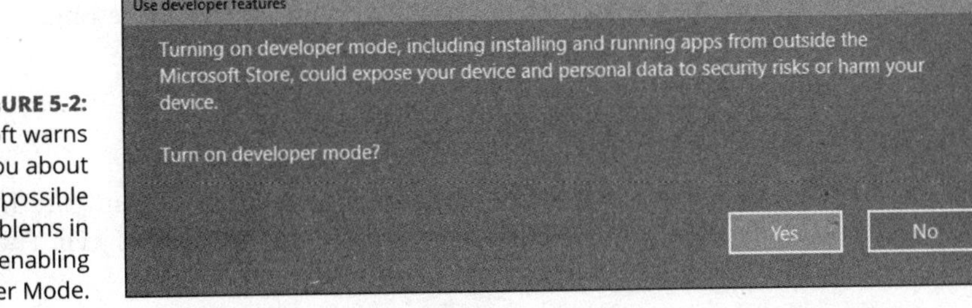

FIGURE 5-2: Microsoft warns you about the possible problems in enabling Developer Mode.

WARNING

This process of working with unsigned apps from unofficial sources is called *sideloading* (`https://docs.microsoft.com/windows/application-management/sideload-apps-in-windows-10`). An individual user might allow sideloading by default, but larger organizations could disallow sideloading through various policies. If you experience problems during the development process with sideloading apps, type **Group Policy** in the search area and press Enter. You see the Local Group Policy Editor, shown in Figure 5-3, which lets you drill down into the

Computer Configuration\Administrative Templates\Windows Components\App Package Deployment folder. Setting these policies to Enabled should fix the problem for you. However, remember that you pay a price in security by making these changes because now your system will likely accept any application from any source with your permission.

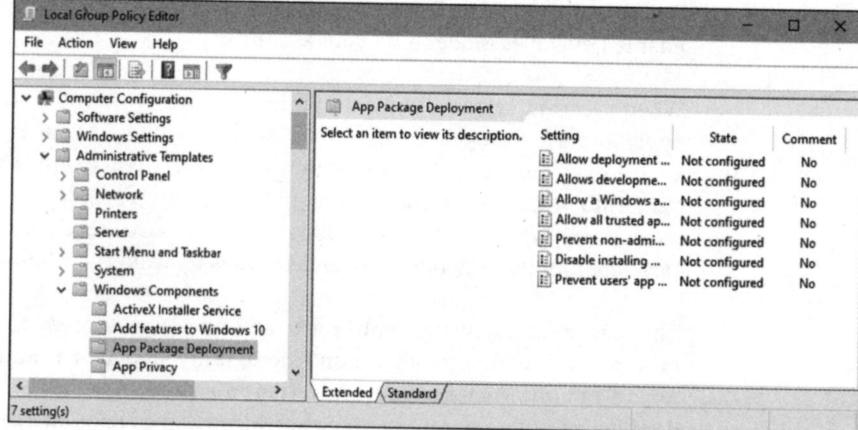

FIGURE 5-3: Make sure that local group policies don't get in the way of sideloading apps.

Locating Developer Mode in the Settings app

You may need to change the developer settings from time to time. However, as long as you have Developer Mode set to On, Visual Studio 2022 will never display the Settings app again. So, you need to look for it manually. To perform this task, type **Developer Settings** in the search field on the Windows taskbar, and you see the results shown in Figure 5-4. Select the Developer Settings entry that appears at the top to display the screen shown in Figure 5-1.

Working with the device settings

Besides making it possible to sideload apps, you can also configure Developer Mode to allow other activities that have security implications as well. The following list describes these features:

- **Windows Device Portal:** The Windows Device Portal (WDP) (`https://docs.microsoft.com/windows/uwp/debug-test-perf/device-portal`) is a web server that
  - Lets you configure and manage the settings for the device over a network or USB connection
  - Provides a localhost option for device configuration purposes

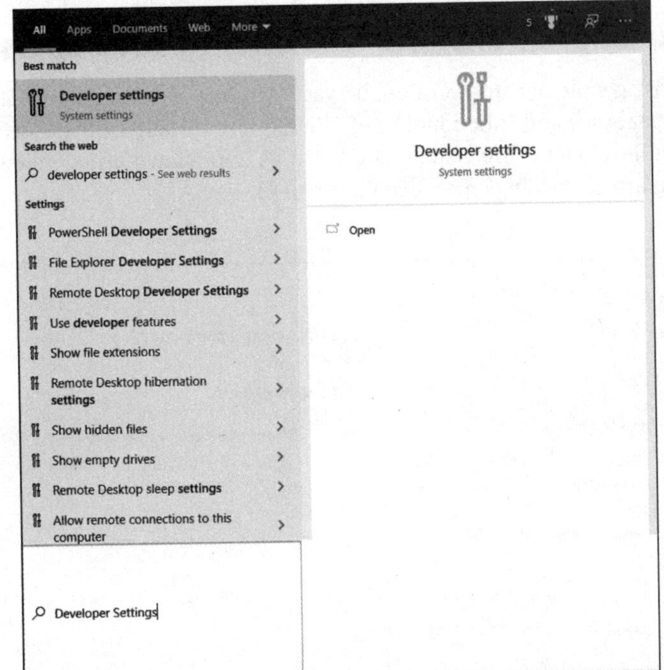

FIGURE 5-4: Using the search field on the taskbar makes it easy to find the Developer Settings.

   - Enables troubleshooting of your apps using supplied diagnostic tools
   - Allows viewing of the real-time performance of your Windows device

- **Device Discovery:** This feature allows device discovery and enables SSH support. Before you can interact with another device, you have to discover it programmatically (`https://docs.microsoft.com/windows/uwp/launch-resume/discover-remote-devices`). Fortunately, you have a number of means of discovering devices through various discovery techniques and filtering methodologies.

WARNING

The For Developers page of the Settings app contains a considerable number of other settings that you can review at `https://docs.microsoft.com/windows/apps/get-started/developer-mode-features-and-debugging`. The main focus of all these settings is that you gain a certain level of access in exchange for reduced security. As a consequence of these changes, your system may also become less reliable because the software that gets installed isn't vetted by anyone, for the most part. As part of configuring your system to use Developer Mode, you have to consider the ramifications of each settings change on system performance as well.

Making File Explorer friendlier to developers

Most people are unaware of the vast number of settings available to control the appearance and functionality of File Explorer. Many of these settings could make the developer's life easier. The Settings app shows an overview of settings that can affect the developer (see Figure 5-5).

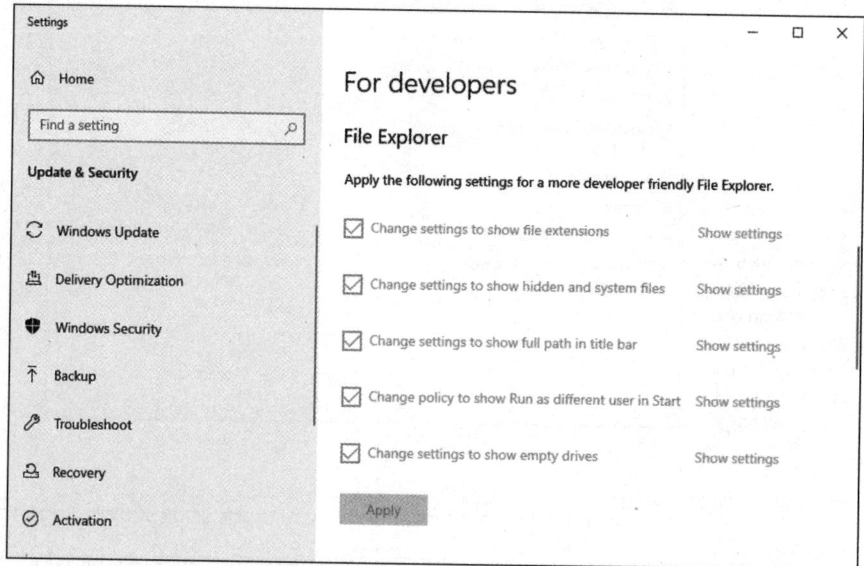

FIGURE 5-5: The Settings app provides an overview of developer-related settings for File Explorer.

These settings can appear in a variety of places in Windows, which is why it's so convenient to have them in one place. However, you may find that these settings don't quite provide everything you need, so you can click Show Settings to the right of the item you want to change, such as Change Policy to Show "Run as Different User" in Start (Figure 5-5), and see the details. In this case, you see a Microsoft Management Console (MMC) like the one shown in Figure 5-6 that allows you significantly more control over how File Explorer appears and works.

Notice that the Show "Run as Different User" Command on Start option is Enabled. Most of the settings appear as Not Configured, which means they use the Windows default setting. A setting is in an absolute condition only if you configure it.

Employing Remote Desktop

WARNING

The Remote Desktop settings allow for running an application on one system and debugging it (among other things) on another. However, there is another group of settings that present a higher security risk. It's the kind of settings group you'd use for two systems that aren't connected to the Internet. As shown in Figure 5-7, the default setup does allow for connections with Remote Desktop with Network Level Authentication (because the check mark is grayed out). However, it doesn't allow direct connections from other computers (because the check mark is filled in). If you click Apply, the recommended setting is applied. You can also deselect the check mark by clicking it, and the Apply button will become disabled.

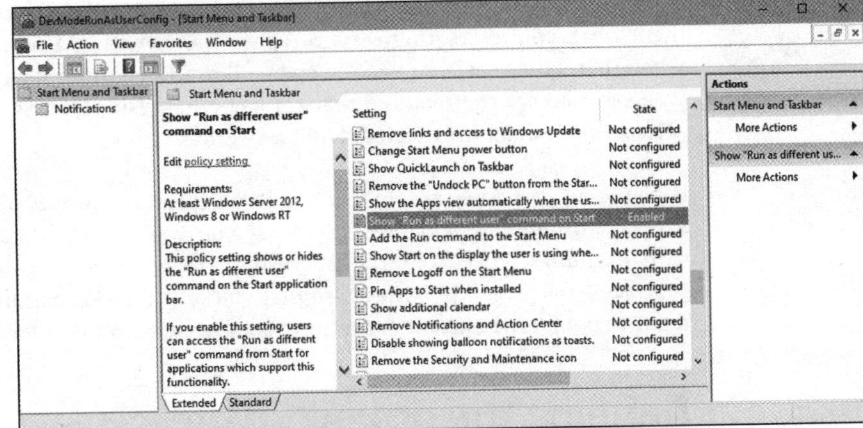

FIGURE 5-6: The actual settings for Developer Mode appear in a number of places, such as MMC.

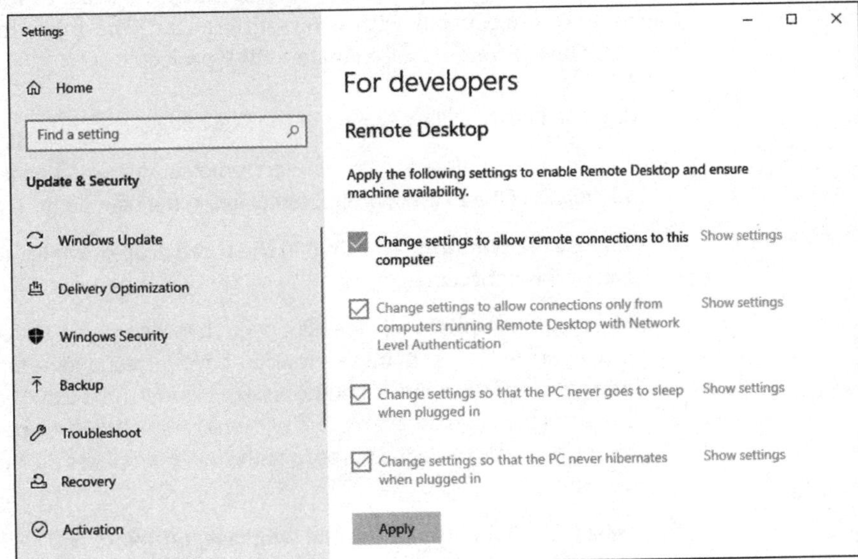

FIGURE 5-7: Use the Remote Desktop settings with care.

Using PowerShell

The PowerShell setting changes the execution policy to allow unsigned scripts to run locally. Remote scripts would still require that you sign them. So, if you click Apply in this For Developers area, you can run your local PowerShell scripts during development without problem.

TIP

You might find it necessary to run both local and remote scripts without signing them when you're creating certain types of apps within a remote environment. When that's the case, you need to open a PowerShell prompt as an administrator (you can't access the required registry key otherwise), type **Set-ExecutionPolicy -ExecutionPolicy Unrestricted**, and press Enter.

If you want to know more about the Set-ExecutionPolicy command, type **help Set-ExecutionPolicy** and press Enter. If you want to get detailed information with examples, check out the Microsoft site at `https://go.microsoft.com/fwlink/?LinkID=113394`. Note also that you type **Get-ExecutionPolicy** and press Enter to obtain the current execution policy as an administrator.

Defining the project

The process for creating a UWP project is much the same as for any other Visual Studio 2022 project, but with a few differences. The following steps help you through these differences. To create a UWP project:

1. **Choose Create a New Project in the Start Page.**

   You see the usual list of recent project templates in the left pane and a (optionally) filtered list of project templates in the right pane.

2. **Choose C#, Windows, and UWP in the three drop-down list boxes at the top of the right pane.**

   The project template list in the right pane changes to show the UWP templates (see Figure 5-8). Most of these templates have corresponding templates for other kinds of development purposes. For example, you can create a Class Library in the Windows Forms and WPF environments. These newer UWP templates serve the same purpose as the older templates do, but with a UWP twist.

3. **Select the Blank App (Universal Windows) template and click Next.**

   You see the Configure Your New Project page. It contains the Project Name and Location fields that you've used in the past to create other projects.

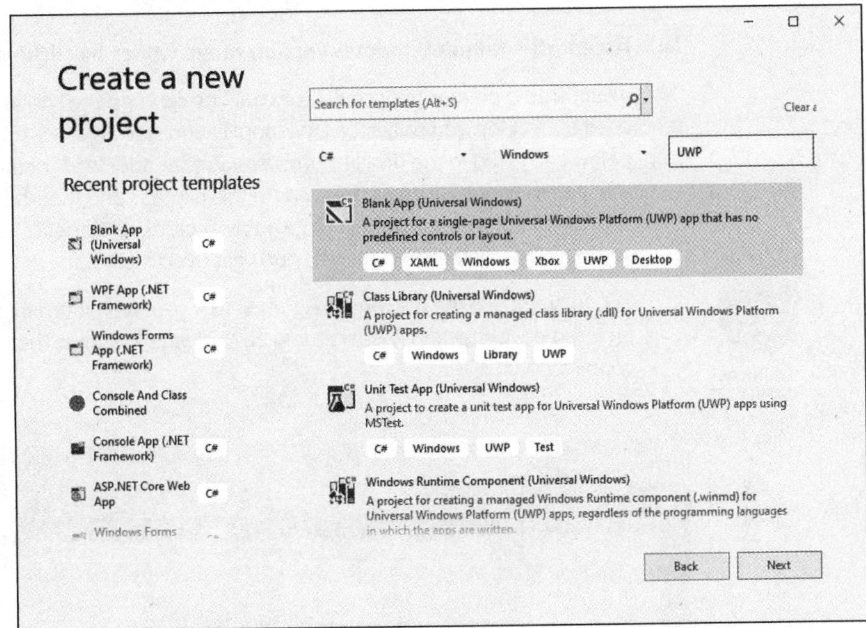

FIGURE 5-8: A listing of UWP templates.

4. **Type** MyUWPCalc **in the Project Name field, provide a location for your project, select the Place Solution and Project in the Same Directory box, and then click Create.**

   So far, there is nothing different in this step from any other project you have created. However, things change when you click Create. Now you see the New Universal Windows Platform Project dialog box, shown in Figure 5-9.

   You use this dialog box to determine the *target version* for your app, the one that you prefer that users have, and the *minimum version* for your app, the one that is less acceptable but still usable. If someone who doesn't have a version of Windows within this range tries to download and install your app, the Windows Store will refuse to allow it. This step is where the process of controlling the life cycle of your app starts. You get to choose which versions of Windows are acceptable. Figure 5-9 shows the default range, but you should look at the other versions for both drop-down list boxes (Target Version and Minimum Version).

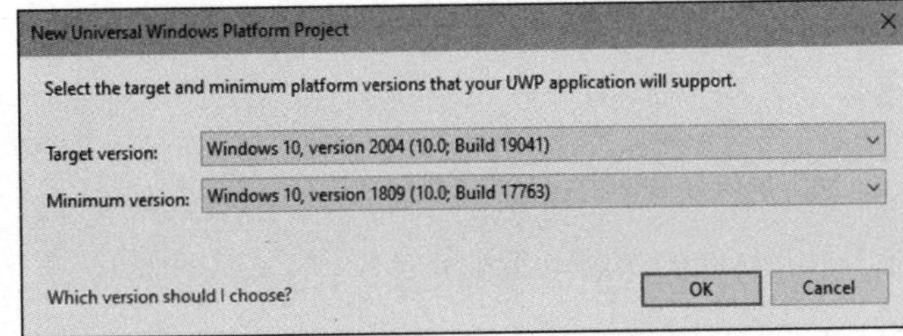

FIGURE 5-9: A UWP project requires some additional configuration.

5. **Accept the default Windows version range values by clicking OK.**

   Visual Studio creates the project for you. The center pane shows the process used to develop and publish a UWP application (see Figure 5-10). The links below each step in the process provide you with additional details. Remember that you may not follow all the steps in this process and that the Microsoft-supplied links tend to support large application development. This chapter shows you something simpler, so don't get overwhelmed!

TECHNICAL STUFF

   You may not see the content of Figure 5-10 if your development system lacks an Internet connection. Visual Studio 2022 always assumes that you have a live connection.

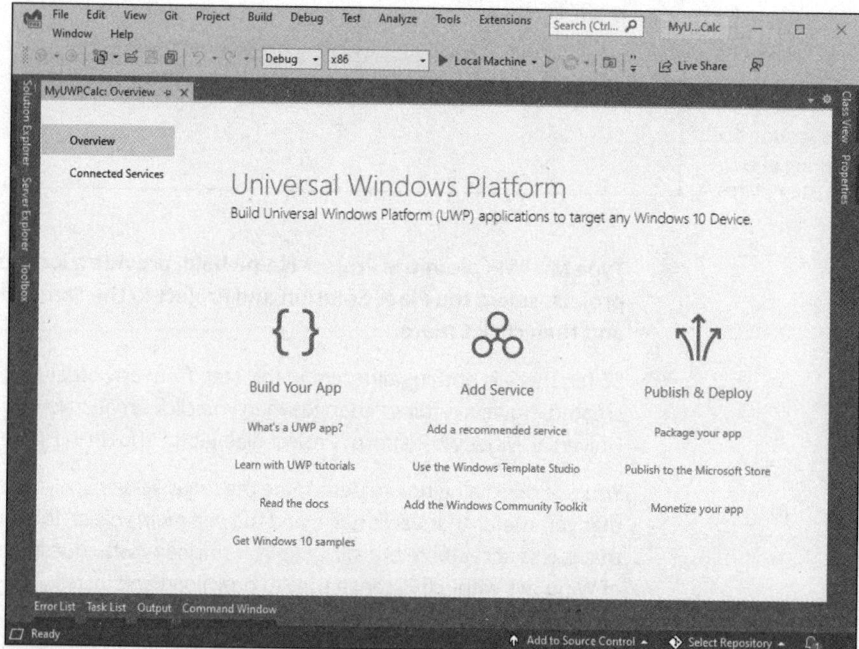

FIGURE 5-10: After completing the project wizard, you see a list of development steps.

Creating an interface

Use the same techniques you use for WPF when crafting your UWP application. You start with the `MainPage.xaml` file XAML, as shown here:

```
<Grid>
    <Grid.Resources>
        <Style TargetType="TextBlock">
            <Setter Property="FontSize" Value="14"/>
            <Setter Property="FontFamily" Value="Arial"/>
        </Style>
```

```
    </Grid.Resources>
    <Grid.RowDefinitions>
        <RowDefinition Height="50"/>
        <RowDefinition Height="50"/>
        <RowDefinition Height="*"/>
    </Grid.RowDefinitions>
    <StackPanel Orientation="Horizontal" Grid.Row="0">
        <TextBlock Text="Input: " Height="40" Width="150"/>
        <TextBox x:Name="Input" Text="0" Height="40" Width="200"/>
    </StackPanel>
    <StackPanel Orientation="Horizontal" Grid.Row="1">
        <TextBlock Text="Result: " Height="40" Width="150"/>
        <TextBox x:Name="Result" Text="0" Height="40" Width="200"
                 IsReadOnly="True"/>
    </StackPanel>
    <StackPanel Orientation="Horizontal" Grid.Row="2"
                VerticalAlignment="Top" HorizontalAlignment="Center">
        <Border BorderBrush="Black" BorderThickness="2" Padding="2">
            <Button x:Name="Add" Content="+" Click="DoMath"/>
        </Border>
        <Border BorderBrush="Black" BorderThickness="2" Padding="2">
            <Button x:Name="Sub" Content="-" Click="DoMath"/>
        </Border>
        <Border BorderBrush="Black" BorderThickness="2" Padding="2">
            <Button x:Name="Mul" Content="*" Click="DoMath"/>
        </Border>
        <Border BorderBrush="Black" BorderThickness="2" Padding="2">
            <Button x:Name="Div" Content="/" Click="DoMath"/>
        </Border>
        <Border BorderBrush="Red" BorderThickness="2" Padding="2">
            <Button x:Name="Clr" Content="X" Click="DoMath"/>
        </Border>
    </StackPanel>
</Grid>
```

This example sets a few more of the resources for the app than previous examples in the book do. For example, it shows how to configure the `FontSize` and `FontFamily` so that your app has a specific appearance, and so that you can ensure that the text is readable for your target audience.

As with a WPF application, you configure the `UIElements` by combining various containers. This app uses a `<Grid>` combined with a number of `<StackPanel>` containers. The input and output require two rows, while the controls consume a third. The result is a very flexible interface that can adapt to a number of format factors without giving up an organized appearance.

TIP

This example uses a `<Border>` around each `<Button>` to provide a nicer appearance. The effect isn't the same as adding the `BorderBrush`, `BorderThickness`, and `Padding` attributes directly to a `<Button>`. When using a `<Border>`, the `<Button>` remains the same size, and the surrounding border is placed around it. Otherwise, what you end up with is a really tiny button that your users will have to squint to see, greatly increasing the cost for glasses in your organization. Figure 5-11 shows how the UI looks.

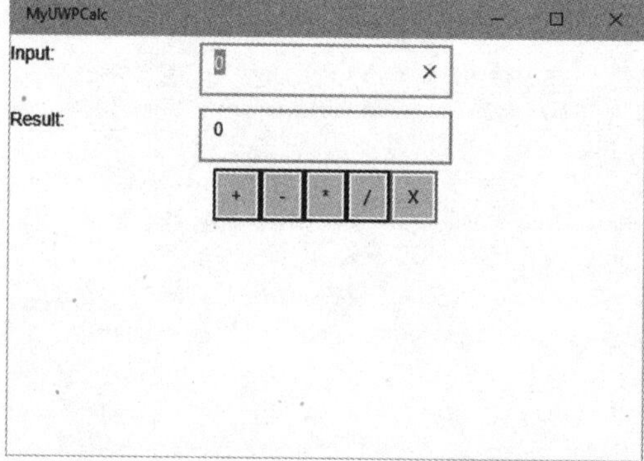

FIGURE 5-11: The app interface is very flexible and should work well for most devices.

The appearance in Figure 5-11 can be deceiving because you're getting a desktop view. The way to overcome this issue is to select a device type in the designer from the drop-down list box at the top. The default is a 13.5" Surface Book (3000 x 2000). The designer shows you how this version of the app looks for that device, as shown in Figure 5-12.

However, you might also need to support the app on a 6" Phone (1920 x 1080) format, so you can select that option from the drop-down list box. (It's also possible to switch between landscape and portrait modes.) Figure 5-13 shows the result of selecting that option using precisely the same code.

TIP

Note that the designer supports a zoom feature that defaults to showing the entire display on the select device. To actually see what you're doing in many cases, you need to change the zoom setting in the lower-left corner of the designer (set to 17.56% in Figure 5-13).

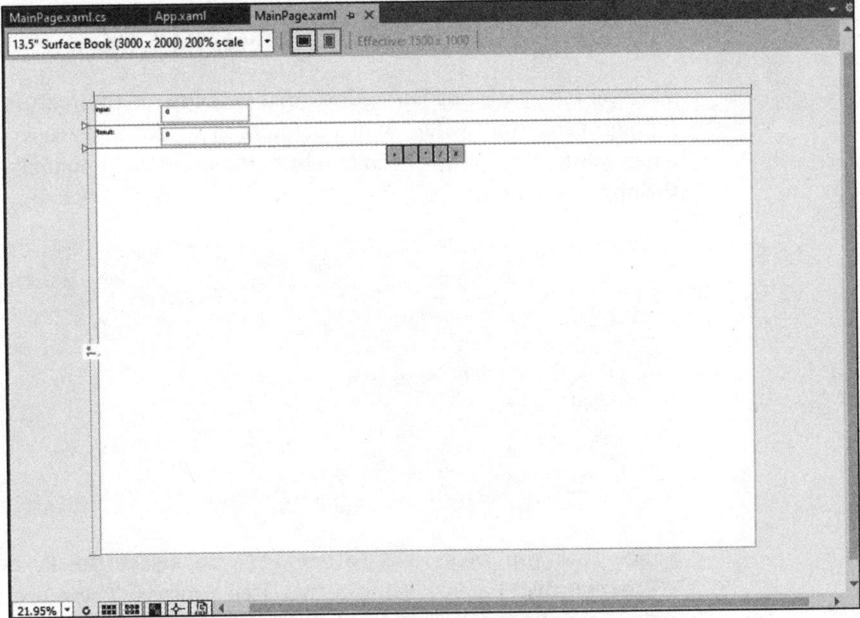

FIGURE 5-12: The example app shown in a 13.5" Surface Book (3000 x 2000) form.

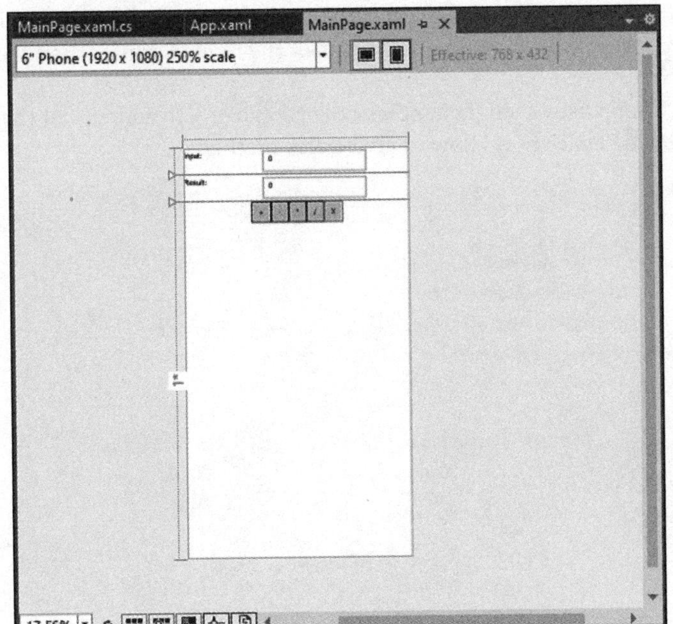

FIGURE 5-13: The example app shown in a 6" Phone (1920 x 1080) form.

Adding some background code

The app has a UI, but isn't functional yet. One of the features of this app is to highlight the input value, which defaults to 0, so that the user merely has to type a new value. The following code selects the input value to make this happen when the app first starts:

```
public MainPage()
{
    this.InitializeComponent();

    // Set the input up to allow easy entry.
    Input.SelectAll();
    Input.Focus(FocusState.Keyboard);
}
```

Notice that you must use `SelectAll()` to select the `0`, and then give the `UIElement` the `Focus()` using a two-step process. There are a lot of examples online that show calling `Focus()` by itself (which displays an error), but you must provide `Focus()` with a specific kind of state to use, which is `FocusState.Keyboard` in this case. The other common kind of focus for an app is `FocusState.Pointer`, which changes the focus of the mouse, rather than the keyboard.

The app uses a single handler called `DoMath()` to address all the buttons. The following code shows how to create this method:

```
private void DoMath(object sender, RoutedEventArgs e)
{
    // Obtain the current values.
    Double NewValue = 0;
    Double.TryParse(Input.Text, out NewValue);
    Double ExistingValue = 0;
    Double.TryParse(Result.Text, out ExistingValue);

    // Perform a task based on which button is pressed.
    switch (((Button)sender).Name)
    {
        case "Add":
            ExistingValue += NewValue;
            break;
        case "Sub":
            ExistingValue -= NewValue;
            break;
        case "Mul":
            ExistingValue *= NewValue;
            break;
```

```
        case "Div":
            ExistingValue /= NewValue;
            break;
        case "Clr":
            ExistingValue = 0;
            break;
    }

    // Output the result.
    Result.Text = ExistingValue.ToString();

    // Set the input up for the next entry.
    Input.Text = "0";
    Input.SelectAll();
    Input.Focus(FocusState.Keyboard);
}
```

The code begins by obtaining the current values of the `Input` and `Result` `UIElements` as `Double` values. The use of `Double.TryParse()` means that the user can enter any non-numeric value and not cause an app crash. Both `NewValue` and `ExistingValue` will contain a useful number or `0`, depending on the input.

The next step is to determine which `Button` the user clicked and then act upon it. To make this happen, you must cast `sender` as a `Button`, and then obtain the `Name` property from it, as shown in the code. The code shows how to perform the appropriate task afterward.

Finally, the code outputs the result to screen. It then sets up `Input` to receive the next value from the user.

Choosing a test device

When working with a UWP app, you have multiple options for testing. The Run button sports the drop-down list shown in Figure 5-14, in which you can choose the device you want to use for testing purposes. Here are the options you have:

- **Local Machine:** This is the default option that produces a window similar to that shown in Figure 5-11. You use this option to create your application, test it for functionality, and work out any bugs before deploying it elsewhere.
- **Remote Machine:** You can deploy the app to another machine that has a network connection to your local machine. To make this work, you'll need to install Remote Tools for Visual Studio 2022 (`https://visualstudio.microsoft.com/vs/preview/`) and ensure that the remote device allows Developer Mode setups. For example, when working with an Android device,

you must specifically configure the device for Developer Mode before any sort of remote activity can happen.

» **Device:** This option specifically applies to devices that you connect to your system through a USB port. As with the Remote Machine option, you need to have Remote Tools for Visual Studio 2022 installed on your local machine, and the device has to have Developer Mode enabled.

» **Download New Emulators:** This option takes you to a website where you can download an emulator to use in place of a physically connected device.

WARNING

All the emulators that are available as of this writing are for Windows 8, and they don't work on Windows 10 and above for many people. The message thread at `https://stackoverflow.com/questions/37209666/windows-phone-8-8-1-emulator-not-working-after-windows-10-upgrade` tells you more about this issue. The bottom line is that you need to ensure that your emulator will work with Windows 10/11 and that you have it configured correctly.

FIGURE 5-14: The Run button includes options for alternative deployments.

Working with .NET Core Applications

Most of the applications in this book rely on the .NET Framework 4.7.2, which supports Windows and only Windows. A .NET Core application is one that supports Linux, macOS, and Windows through various means. The concept of creating the application is the same, but the setup is slightly different and the resulting executables are different as well. The easiest way to see the .NET Core templates included with Visual Studio 2022 is to select C#, All Platforms, and All Project Types, then type **.NET Core** in the search box. You see a very long list of available .NET Core templates, as shown in Figure 5-15.

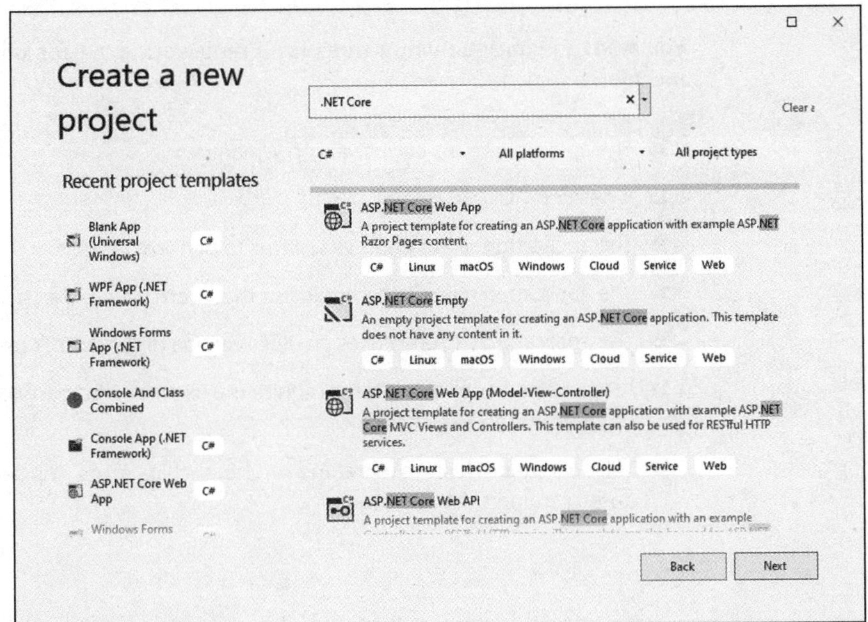

FIGURE 5-15: Locating the .NET Core templates is made easier using a search.

As you look through the list, you find some familiar entries, such as Console Application and Class Library. The output is the same in this case: a `.dll` file. Many of the templates have something to do with web development, a topic discussed in Book 6. Missing from this list is anything with a GUI similar to that found for a Windows Forms, WPF, or even a UWP application. Here, in a nutshell, is when you should use .NET Core:

- There is a cross-platform compatibility need that doesn't rely on a GUI.
- The application relies on microservices, Docker containers, or both.
- An application needs to provide high performance and scalability.
- There is a requirement to run multiple .NET versions on the same server.
- The application relies heavily on a command-line interface to meet administrative needs.
- A particular new C# language feature isn't found in the .NET Framework 4.7.2 (as demonstrated several times in this book).

You want to continue using the .NET Framework 4.7.2 for other needs, which include:

- The application runs exclusively on Windows.
- A desktop GUI is involved.
- The application uses Windows services to perform tasks.
- The application relies on technologies that aren't part of the .NET Core.
- The application currently uses an older version of the .NET Framework 4.7.2.
- At least some application tasks require the use of a third-party library that requires the .NET Framework.
- The application deploys to a cloud service, such as Azure App Service, that doesn't support the .NET Core.

6 Web Development with ASP.NET

Contents at a Glance

IN THIS CHAPTER

» **Working with the ASP.NET core templates**

» **Building your first web application using ASP.NET core**

Chapter 1
Creating a Basic ASP.NET Core App

In the beginning, things were simple. Developers used HTML tags to build web pages in a very basic manner. These pages weren't flexible, they broke easily, and there wasn't a good way to update them, but they were simple and extremely easy to understand. Today, things are flexible and updateable, but they're much harder to understand and they still break easily at times. This said, ASP.NET core applications are designed to work with vast quantities of data in a variety of ways that provide automation that those early developers couldn't contemplate, and this chapter is your introduction to them. It begins by introducing you to some of the templates (of which there are more than a few confusing options, so listen up). All the chapters in this part of the book are specific to Visual Studio 2022 and above.

Creating an ASP.NET core application requires a lot of files, so the second section of this chapter helps you wade through them. Nothing is worse than the feeling that you shouldn't touch something because you don't know what it's connected to. After all, you could possibly cause a complete meltdown of the Internet (but then again, probably not). During this whole process, you create your first ASP.NET Core Web Application and actually see it do something more than say Hello World (not a lot more, but something more). In the end, you gain an appreciation for what all those files do and why you really do want to touch them.

REMEMBER

You don't have to type the source code for this chapter manually. In fact, using the downloadable source is a lot easier. You can find the source for this chapter in the \CSAIO4D2E\BK06\CH01 folder of the downloadable source. See the Introduction for details on how to find these source files.

Understanding the ASP.NET Core Templates

As with other forms of development in Visual Studio 2022, ASP.NET Core sports a number of specialized templates to meet various developmental needs. As with other templates, the goal is to help you get started with a project with the minimum of effort. Essentially, these templates help you avoid the blank-page syndrome (where looking at a blank screen causes brain freeze) that many developers face. The following sections describe each of the templates in more detail so you have some idea of which template to use for a particular purpose.

Starting with nothing using ASP.NET Core Empty

This is the most basic template in the list. It doesn't provide any sort of content when you create it. However, this doesn't mean that the template doesn't include any files. Depending on how you configure the template using the wizard (as described in the "Creating the project" section, later in this chapter), you actually get quite a few files, but they mostly affect the actual running of the resulting website rather than provide any kind of content, as shown in Figure 1-1. In the figure, you see the files for an ASP.NET Core Empty template that relies on the .NET Core 3.1 and has no HTTP or Docker support. (Docker provides the means to package and share both applications and code with others.)

Figure 1-2 shows the same ASP.NET Core Empty template, but this time it uses NET 6.0 and supports both HTTPS and Docker. The way you configure even an empty project is important because the support files that the template provides are different depending on the selections you make. For example, this second version of the template supplies a `Secrets.json` file that contains sensitive application information (see `https://docs.microsoft.com/aspnet/core/security/app-secrets` for details).

As you go through the list of files, you notice that the `Startup.cs` file is missing from Figure 1-2. This is because you installed Docker support, and Docker will take care of application startup needs. However, this is the only file missing between the two setups. Otherwise, adding features adds files.

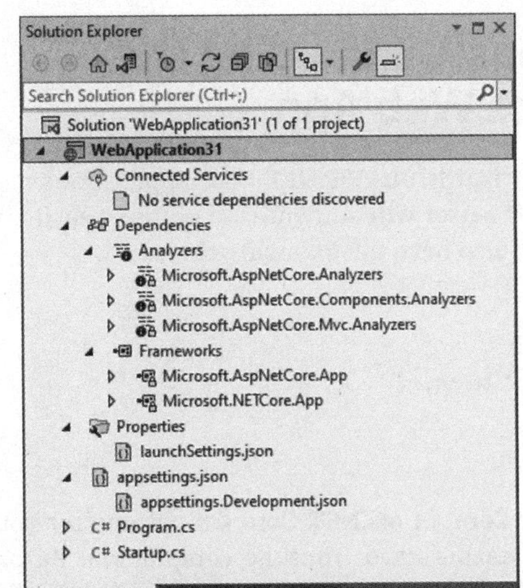

FIGURE 1-1: Even an empty template provides you with a considerable number of files.

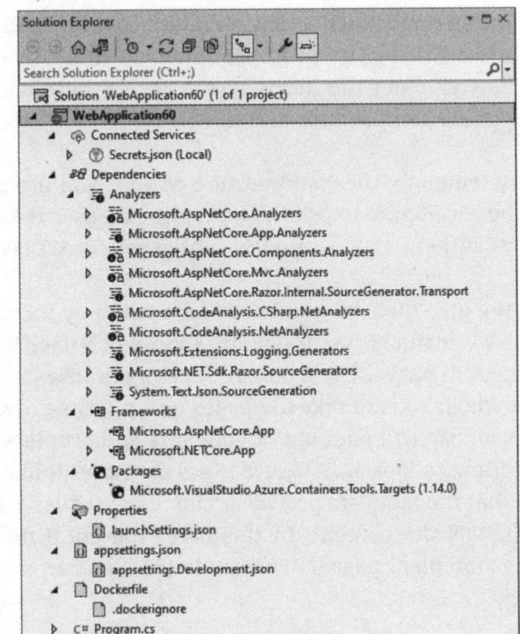

FIGURE 1-2: The version of .NET and app features both contribute to the file structure of the project.

REMEMBER

Of course, you still don't have any sort of content. All these entries in Solution Explorer support the application in some way. This is why the chapter begins by noting that things were a lot simpler when working with HTTP pages in the old days. As the chapter progresses and you read more in this part of the book, you discover that all those files are making it easier for you to provide the kind of content that people expect today — content that HTTP pages couldn't provide.

Creating a basic app using the ASP.NET Core Web App

The project template wizards for ASP.NET Core applications vary a little. These wizards ask you how the user will authenticate on the website, with a default of no authentication. You also have the following choices:

- Individual accounts
- Microsoft identity platform
- Windows

If you select the .NET Core 3.1 or .NET Core 5.0 options for your template, you also see an option to enable Razor runtime compilation. Razor helps you create server-side dynamic pages using a syntax that looks a lot like C#. It's really a simple syntax, view engine, that displays your web pages as you create them. Enabling runtime compilation means that you can see UI changes in real time without restarting your application. Oddly enough, selecting .NET Core 6.0 as your target framework hides this option because it's enabled by default. Chapter 2 of this minibook tells you about the Razor syntax for C# developers, so you don't need to worry about the complexities of it now.

As with the empty template, the configuration options you use greatly affect the number of files you see. Figure 1-3 shows a project that uses the .NET 6.0 Framework and Windows authentication, and it's configured for HTTPS.

TIP

If you're getting the idea that the number of files will only increase as you begin using more ASP.NET features, you're right. Soon you'll feel buried neck deep, perhaps even deeper, in pages. The pages all serve a purpose, and the best way to avoid getting overwhelmed is to take the pages one at a time. If you try to look at the whole picture, smoke will pour out of your ears and people will wonder about you. The main addition to look at in Figure 1-3 is the Pages folder, which contains the basic content that the template provides. The `.cshtml` files contain Razor code that makes up the website content. In this case, you get a main page (`index.cshtml`), a privacy statement page (`Privacy.cshtml`), and an error message page (`Error.cshtml`).

You may be wondering where the authentication page is because it doesn't appear in the Pages folder. How authentication takes place depends on the sort of authentication you choose, but it's scripted in the `Pages\Shared` folder. For example, if you choose individual accounts, you find a `_LoginPartial.cshtml` with the logic required to log a user into the system. The main page will have an additional Log In option that displays a separate page for logging into the website. This is the kind of page that you see on most websites today.

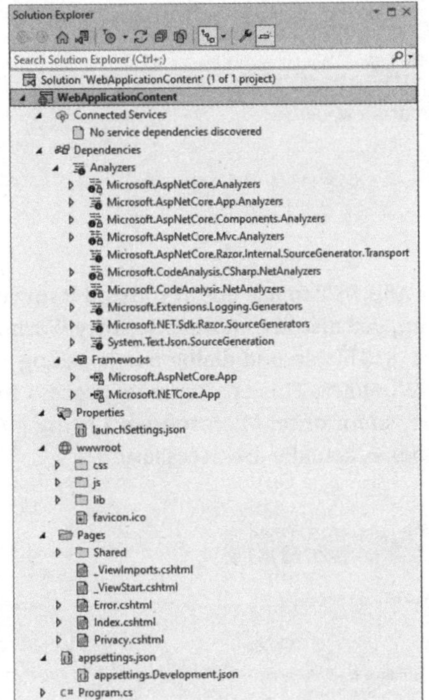

FIGURE 1-3: The Web App template provides you with basic content as a starting point.

Fumbling around with HTTPS-enabled sites

For most people, security can seem complex and like one of those things that you can't quite get right on the first try. This is especially true when security has multiple parts to it, as with a website. Consequently, it can feel more like you're fumbling with the security settings instead of adjusting them with some level of authority.

WARNING

When you choose the HTTPS option, which is the likely one for everything except the empty template, you see a Trust ASP.NET Core SSL Certificate dialog box like the one shown in Figure 1-4 when you run the application the first time. This message box is giving you the opportunity to use a generated SSL certificate so that you don't have to buy one just for development purposes. If you already have a certificate, you want to use it for your development to ensure that everyone is using the correct certificate. To use your certificate, install it using the instructions at `https://docs.microsoft.com/aspnet/core/security/authentication/certauth`.

Trust ASP.NET Core SSL Certificate

This project is configured to use SSL. To avoid SSL warnings in the browser you can choose to trust the self-signed certificate that ASP.NET Core has generated.

Would you like to trust the ASP.NET Core SSL certificate?

Don't ask me again

Yes No

FIGURE 1-4: Use the generated SSL certificate or install your own.

Installing a certificate for ASP.NET to use doesn't install it on your system. When you start the application up, you also see another Security Warning dialog box like the one shown in Figure 1-5. This second dialog box is asking whether you want to trust the certificate in Windows. This is a separate process from installing the certificate in Visual Studio, so for once, Microsoft isn't being purposely obtuse or annoying. Both message boxes actually are necessary.

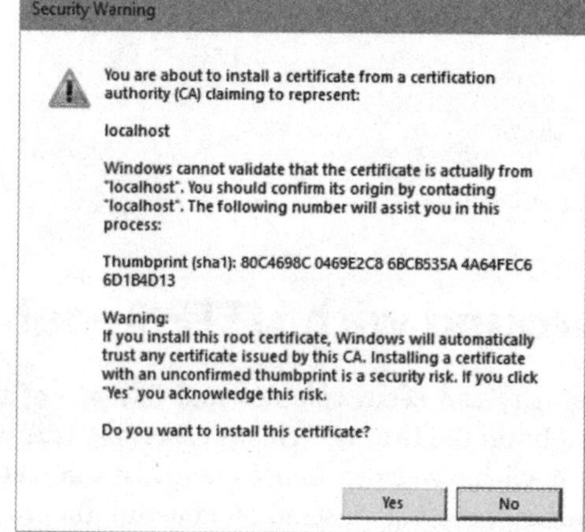

FIGURE 1-5: You must install any certificate you use in Windows as well as Visual Studio.

TIP

At some point, you may want to remove the Windows SSL certificate that you installed, but how to do that seems to be a deep, dark secret. The article at `https://docs.microsoft.com/dotnet/framework/wcf/feature-details/how-to-view-certificates-with-the-mmc-snap-in` tells you how to open the Microsoft Management Console (MMC) and install the Certificates snap-in. You want the snap-in for the local computer (there are several options). The certificate you want appears in the `Certificates\Personal\Certificates` folder as localhost. To remove the certificate, choose Action⇨Delete. You can also perform all sorts of other tasks, such as exporting the certificate should you need it later.

Building in business logic using ASP.NET Core App (Model-View-Controller)

If you have a really large project that presents the same data in multiple ways, you really want to use the Model-View-Controller (MVC) paradigm as part of your design (`https://docs.microsoft.com/aspnet/core/mvc/overview`). This paradigm breaks up your application into three parts:

- **Model:** Provides access to all the data-related elements of your application. The data can come from anywhere. In fact, you may generate part of the data as part of the model logic. The model doesn't consider how the data is used or even organized —it simply makes the data available. Consequently, a `Customer` object may retrieve some bits of a database, and a `Billing` object may retrieve other bits from the same database.
- **View:** Determines how the user sees the data. The same data might appear in multiple views, organized in different ways. For example, the same data may appear in a detail or table view. Users often control how the data is presented, so the same data may appear in a nearly infinite number of ways.
- **Controller:** Defines the business logic used to make the model and view work together in a manner that reflects company policies, legal requirements, and application needs. As you might expect, the controller provides the control required to keep chaos at bay and ensure that the user has a good computing experience that doesn't open any security holes.

Breaking the application into three pieces in this manner makes it possible for a large team to work efficiently because the various members aren't as likely to get in each other's way. Graphic artists who work on views don't need to interact with the model; all they need to know is that the data is available for use in a particular format. Likewise, database administrators can work with the model without worrying about user-interface concerns. Developers and security professionals can deal with controller issues separately from everyone else.

The downside of all this flexibility is that even more files are interconnected in even more complicated ways, as shown in Figure 1-6. Now you have separate folders for Controllers, Models, and Views — each of which has its own set of files. The figure doesn't show the usual `Connected Services`, `Dependencies`, or `Properties` folders content. It's about the same as that for other templates described so far in the chapter.

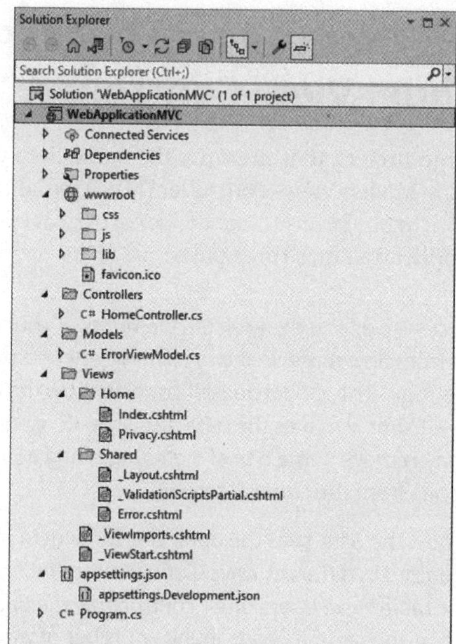

FIGURE 1-6: Separating functionality in MVC means yet more files.

Oddly, this template's default content doesn't vary from the content provided with other templates. In other words, you get more files for the same content. The difference is solely in the level of flexibility that this template provides.

Developing a programming interface using ASP.NET Core Web API

A lot of development depends on the use of Representational State Transfer (REST) today. Relying on an API means that the client portion of an application can reside anywhere. In addition, an API opens the possibility of third parties making use of the same data to create other applications or to perform similar tasks. The ASP.NET Core Web API is somewhat different from other templates in this chapter in that the focus is on the API and a few of the configuration requirements are different. For example, when setting up an authentication type, you have access only to the Microsoft identity platform or Windows.

TIP

There is a good reason to use either the .NET 5.0 or .NET 6.0 Framework with this template: You gain access to OpenAPI (`https://www.openapis.org/`) support. If you have ever tried using APIs from various third parties in the same application, you know that each API will come with its own quirks, which proves confusing, at best, when you write code. Using OpenAPI standardizes how developers describe APIs so that they become significantly easier to use. If you plan to create an API for use by third parties, enabling OpenAPI support is to your benefit. Figure 1-7 shows the files that you typically see when using the ASP.NET Core Web API with .NET 6.0 Framework, HTTPS enabled, no authentication, and OpenAPI support enabled.

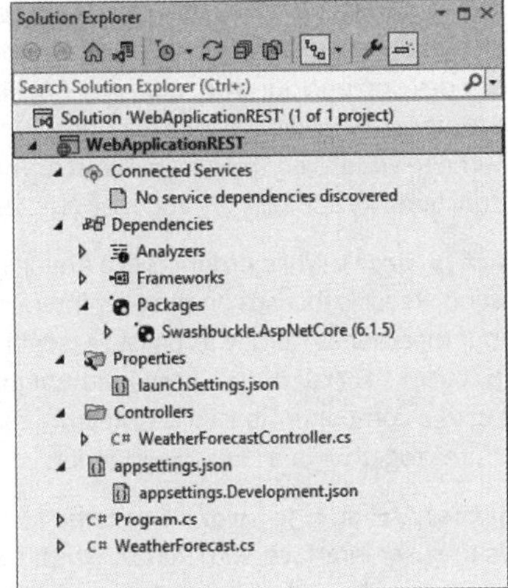

FIGURE 1-7: The ASP.NET Core Web API focuses on the API, not the client.

When you run this application, you see a web page that lets you play with the API. It's a fun API to try out, and who doesn't want to know the weather? Of course, now you're looking at the URL in your browser and wondering what Swagger is all about. No, it has nothing to do with pirates (`https://www.pinterest.com/ligeiahabanero/pirateswagger/`). OpenAPI is based on the Swagger Specification (`https://swagger.io/specification/`) originally created by SmartBear (`https://smartbear.com/`), where you can read a number of articles written by this book's author (`https://smartbear.com/blog/authors/john-mueller/`).

An overview of those other weird templates

When looking through the list of potential templates, you see some templates, such as ASP.NET Core gRPC Service. These templates let you work with third-party, open source software to create solutions that work with other third-party software. This book doesn't cover these open source solutions. However, here is an overview of the solutions that are installed with Visual Studio 2022:

- **gRPC (`https://grpc.io/`):** A *Remote Procedure Call (RPC)* occurs when a client makes a call to a server for various kinds of services or resources, such as performing tasks or accessing data. The advantage of RPC is that a client can make a call without knowing anything about the host network. All that is needed are the call particulars. Using gRPC enables RPC calls in any environment. You can use this service to perform load balancing, trace activity, check system health, and authenticate users, among other tasks.

- **Angular (`https://angular.io/`):** You use Angular to create complex enterprise-level apps that incorporate features, such as dashboards, that would take a long time to develop on your own. Consider Angular as a kind of super template service for those who like the look and feel of Angular apps and don't have a lot of time to code everything from scratch. You can get a better idea of Angular functionality at `https://angular.io/features`.
- **React.js (`https://reactjs.org/`):** While products like Angular focus on building an overall solution, React.js focuses on the user interface. The idea is to get a user interface put together as quickly as possible (see the tutorial at `https://reactjs.org/tutorial/tutorial.html`) without loss of flexibility or speed. This product uses a component-based architecture that lets you snap user-interface features together in a Lego-like manner.
- **React.js and Redux (`https://redux.js.org/`):** This template combines React.js, which provides the user interface, with Redux, which provides the means to store application state. Now it's possible for an application to have a memory of sorts so that a user can move from device to device and pick up at the same point where it left off in the last session without any loss of data or time.

Developing a Basic Web App

It's time to try your hand at creating an ASP.NET Core application. This application will involve a little more than saying Hello World, but not much more. The intent is to get you started with something simple that helps emphasize what a simple web application might look like. It's guaranteed to be easier than overcoming the learning curve of a lot of online examples, but also to help you over the learning curve as well. You can find this application in the `BasicWebApplication` example in the downloadable source.

Creating the project

This example starts with an empty project. Because of all the various permutations available, the example creates a specific website instead of providing more general information (as is found in previous sections of this chapter). Using an empty project and the specific steps help you see how to add various features to an application and then play around with it. Plus, you can avoid some of the complexities of figuring out predefined code for the moment. Follow these steps to create a new empty project:

1. **On the Start page, click Create a New Project.**

   You see the usual list of templates on the Create a New Project page that appears.

2. **Select C#, All Platforms, and Web from the three drop-down list boxes at the top of the right pane.**

   The list of templates now shows all the ASP.NET Core applications you can create, plus a number of other web-specific projects not covered in the book.

3. **Highlight the ASP.NET Core Empty template and then click Next.**

   You see the Configure Your New Project dialog box, shown in Figure 1-8.

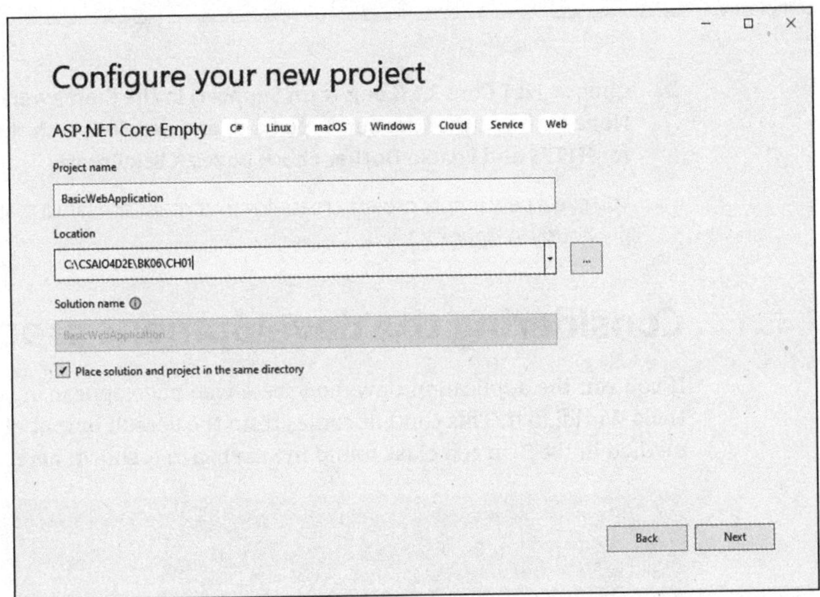

FIGURE 1-8: Configure your new project with identifying information.

4. **Type** BasicWebApplication **in the Project Name field and a location in the Location field, and select the Place Solution and Project in the Same Directory box. Click Next.**

   You see the Additional Information page, shown in Figure 1-9. This example keeps things as simple as possible by restricting the number of features the template provides. After you complete this example, you should try other options to see how they affect the starting project you receive.

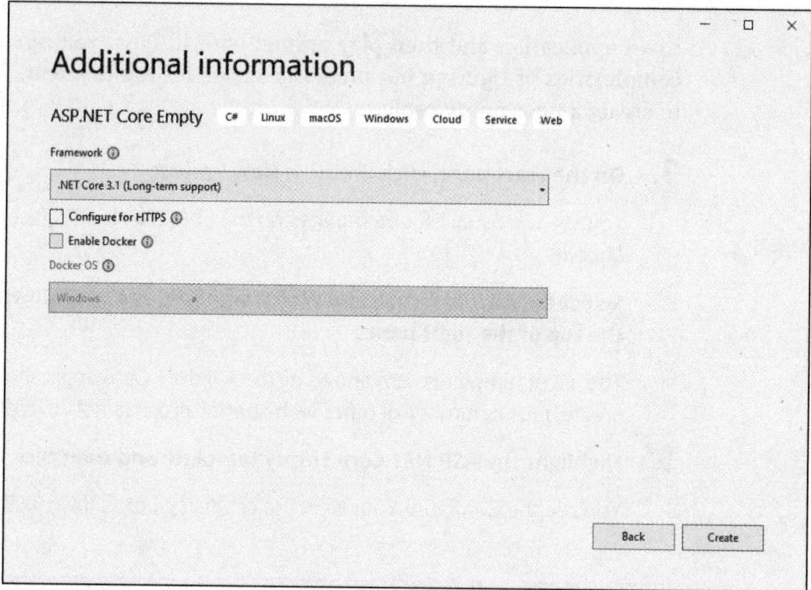

FIGURE 1-9: The example uses fewer template features to reduce project complexity.

5. **Choose .NET Core 3.1 (Long-term Support) in the Framework field, choose None in the Authentication Type field, and deselect both the Configure for HTTPS and Enable Docker check boxes. Click Create.**

   You see a new empty project created with content similar to that shown previously in Figure 1-1.

Considering the development process

If you run the application now, you see a web page appear in your browser with Hello World! in it. This content comes from the default output of the `Configure()` method in the `Startup` class found in `Startup.cs`, shown here:

```
// This method gets called by the runtime. Use this method to configure the
// HTTP request pipeline.
public void Configure(IApplicationBuilder app, IWebHostEnvironment env)
{
    if (env.IsDevelopment())
    {
        app.UseDeveloperExceptionPage();
    }

    app.UseRouting();

    app.UseEndpoints(endpoints =>
    {
```

```
        endpoints.MapGet("/", async context =>
        {
            await context.Response.WriteAsync("Hello World!");
        });
    });
}
```

Essentially, all this code does is create the home page, which is mapped to /, and writes Hello World! to it. If you want to add a page, you need to add another endpoint using `endpoints.MapGet()`. To see how this works for yourself, try adding the following code directly below the first endpoints.MapGet() call:

```
endpoints.MapGet("/page2/", async context =>
{
    await context.Response.WriteAsync("This is the second page.");
});
```

When you start the application now and change the URL in your browser to read: `http://localhost:11623/page2` (the port number, 11623, will vary by system), you see the next message, "This is the second page." While this addition is interesting, it's not particularly helpful in creating a website. It is helpful in understanding endpoints.

Adding web content

This example won't do any fancy interaction with databases or require a degree in web design. Instead, the example will serve some static content so that you can see a next step in the process of working with ASP.NET Core. Follow these steps to add some static web content.

1. **Right-click the BasicWebApplication entry in Solution Explorer and choose Add⇨New Folder.**

   You see a new folder added to the hierarchy.

2. **Type** wwwroot **and press Enter.**

   The folder icon changes to a world icon.

3. **Right-click the wwwroot folder and choose Add⇨New Item from the context menu.**

   You see the Add New Item dialog box, shown in Figure 1-10.

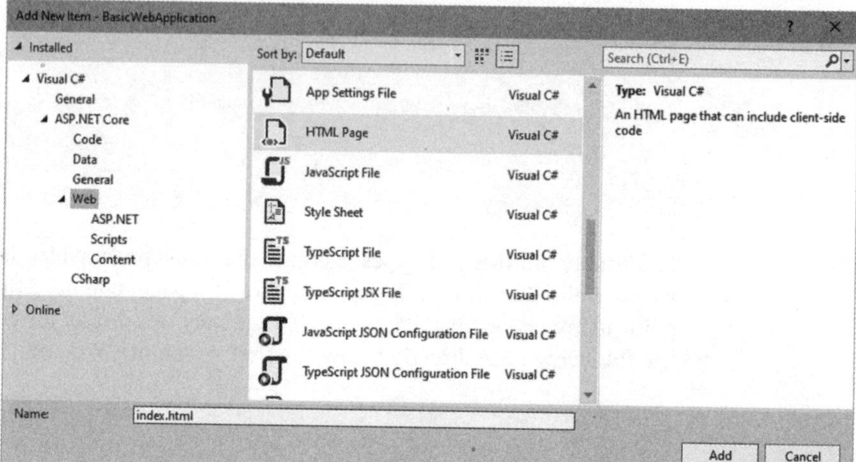

FIGURE 1-10: Add a new item to the wwwroot folder.

4. **Drill down to locate the** `Visual C#\ASP.NET Core\Web` **folder, and then highlight the HTML Page entry. Type** index.html **in the Name field and click Add.**

WARNING

The name and capitalization of this first file is essential. For example, if you type `Index.html`, the example may not work. The application is designed to look for these four files:

- default.htm
- default.html
- index.htm
- index.html

5. **Change the content of the default HTML page (such as** `index.html`**) as shown in bold below so that you can verify that it works:**

```
<!DOCTYPE html>
<html>
<head>
    <meta charset="utf-8"/>
    <title>Test Page</title>
</head>
<body>
    <p>This is some test content.</p>
</body>
</html>
```

At this point, you have a web page to use, but it isn't connected to the application. You need to make these connections in `Startup.cs`.

6. **Select** `Startup.cs`**. Comment out the entire** `app.UseEndpoints()` **section. Add the following code below right after the** `app.UseRouting()` **call:**

```
app.UseDefaultFiles();
app.UseStaticFiles();
```

The `UseDefaultFiles()` call tells your application to look for index.html. There are a lot of ways to change this configuration, but one way is to create a list of options and then pass those options to the `UseDefaultFiles()` call. The article at `https://docs.microsoft.com/aspnet/core/fundamentals/static-files` provides some additional insights on how to create a list of options.

The `UseStaticFiles()` call enables the use of static files, such as CSS, JavaScript, and HTML, with your application. As with `UseDefaultFiles()`, you can modify the behavior of static file usage by supplying a list of options with the `UseStaticFiles()` call.

At this point, you can start adding functionality to the `wwwroot` folder to create a completely static website similar to any other static website out there.

Making some basic changes to the first page

You can add JavaScript and CSS to your static pages, just as you would with any other website. However, for now, you just add a little additional content so that you can see the next step. Chapter 2 begins taking you through use of Razor files, but here you stick with static content. Begin by adding `page2.html` to your project using Steps 3 and 4 of the previous section. Modify the code for this page so that it looks like this:

```
<!DOCTYPE html>
<html>
<head>
    <meta charset="utf-8"/>
    <title>Second Page</title>
</head>
<body>
    <p>This is the second page.</p>
    <p>
        Click
        <a href="index.html">here</a>
        to return to the home page.
    </p>
</body>
</html>
```

Creating a Basic ASP.NET Core App

Now make a connection between page2.html and index.html by adding the code in bold to the index.html page:

```
<!DOCTYPE html>
<html>
<head>
    <meta charset="utf-8"/>
    <title>Test Page</title>
</head>
<body>
    <p>This is some test content.</p>
    <p>Click
        <a href="page2.html">here</a>
        to see the second page.
    </p>
</body>
</html>
```

Now when you run the application, you can switch between the home page and the second page without effort simply by clicking the link. Yes, this is a very simple application, but it demonstrates a number of ASP.NET Core features that you'll find helpful later.

IN THIS CHAPTER

» Understanding how Razor fits into the picture

» Working with variables in Razor

» Making decisions using Razor

» Storing and cycling through data

Chapter 2
Employing the Razor Markup Language

As mentioned in Chapter 1 of this minibook, Razor is Microsoft's language for implementing dynamic web content. While Chapter 1 shows how to create static content, most websites today use dynamic content so that updating them is easier. Using Razor is sort of like mixing C#, HTML, and some older technologies reminiscent of Active Server Pages (ASP) (`https://docs.microsoft.com/en-us/troubleshoot/iis/asp-support-windows`). The first part of this chapter discusses how this mix occurs and shows you some basics.

As with C#, any discussion of Razor needs to begin with using variables to store data. This means understanding the Razor data types, how to work with operators, and how to convert one data type to another. The information you obtained in Book 1, "The Basics of C# Sharp Programming," and especially in Chapters 2 through 4, will help you in this minibook.

The next three parts of the chapter discuss how to work with and manipulate data using a combination of logical statements, arrays, and loops. If you've read through Chapters 5 through 7 of Book 1, you'll find the information in these three parts of the chapter quite familiar because Razor is based on C# and follows the C# rules. However, there are differences between Razor and C# that these parts of the chapter help point out.

REMEMBER

You don't have to type the source code for this chapter manually. In fact, using the downloadable source is a lot easier. You can find the source for this chapter in the \CSAI04D2E\BK06\CH02 folder of the downloadable source. See the Introduction for details on how to find these source files.

Avoiding Nicks from Razor

Trying to comprehend a new technology can be difficult, and the learning curve often feels artificially steep. In fact, it feels like those early days of shaving when being unfamiliar with the razor makes one nick their skin constantly. The following sections help you avoid the nicks by bringing the learning curve down a little. To make this process easier, create an ASP.NET Core Web App using the template wizard and insights contained in the "Creating a basic app using the ASP.NET Core Web App" section of Chapter 1 of this minibook. You don't need to add anything to the resulting project; it's just helpful to have the files available for viewing. Use the .NET 3.1 (Long-term Support) framework and select None for Authentication type; deselect the Configure for HTTPS option, and select the Enable Razor runtime-compilation option. As an alternative, you can use the `RazorPageOverview` example found in the downloadable source.

Comparing Razor to its predecessors

There is a long list of technologies that precede Razor, representing a sort of a flavor-of-the-year march toward where the technology sits today. It starts with classic Active Server Pages (ASP), moves through various incarnations of that technology, through Model-View-Controller (MVC), to Razor today. If you've been a developer for long, the subtle but continuing changes in technology could drive you a bit nuts. In fact, when you go online to various tutorial sites such as W3Schools (`https://www.w3schools.com/asp/default.ASP`), even they have a hard time condensing the technology and making it easier to understand. When you start looking at ASP.NET tutorials (`https://www.tutorialspoint.com/asp.net/asp.net_first_example.htm`), you begin to see bits and pieces of what eventually became Razor. For example, both use the `@page` directive (look at the top of `Index.cshtml` in your project to see this directive), but Razor uses it in a slightly different manner, which is the source of much of the confusion out there about Razor.

The comparison you see most often is between MVC and Razor. Microsoft currently recommends using Razor to reduce complexity (`https://docs.microsoft.com/dotnet/architecture/porting-existing-aspnet-apps/comparing-razor-pages-aspnet-mvc`). Note that there is an MVC-like approach in Razor, except that Microsoft uses different terms for the various components because using different terms makes technology look new and shiny. So, the MVC action is now a handler, the MVC ViewModel is now a `PageModel`, and the view is now a Razor Page. When working in MVC, these elements appear in three different locations and you need to modify them individually, which makes MVC error prone because people forget to do things unless they have a string tied around their finger. When working with Razor, the handler and `PageModel` appear in a single file, while the view appears in a separate file, all under the Pages folder in the project. Here are some other differences between MVC and Razor:

- **Simpler pages:** A Razor page does have some connectivity to other files, but it's very close to a Web Forms setup in that you have the nonshared content in a single `.cshtml` file with a code-behind file.
- **Focus:** Many developers view Razor as the optimal solution for HTML views. They see MVC as an optimal solution for a Representational State Transfer (REST) API or a Service-Oriented Architecture (SOA). The technology you choose depends on the sort of website you want to create. Razor is typically the simple solution for simple problems.
- **Less code:** In comparing similar coding examples between Razor and MVC, you often find that the Razor code is a little shorter (not much) and a little simpler. However, little differences tend to pile up when you're working on a website of any size and complexity.

WARNING

One of the issues that will cause most developers woe is the fact that Visual Studio doesn't come with a designer for Razor pages. In Book 5, Chapter 2 you see a process for working with XAML to create WPF applications. To create an application, you drag and drop components onto the canvas. Book 5, Chapter 5 shows the same process for UWP applications. Unfortunately, when working with ASP.NET Core, you're left to write code manually. The only website development that Visual Studio 2022 offers with a designer is the older Web Forms templates, which require a special setup, as described in the "Gaining access to the Web Forms templates" sidebar.

Considering the actual file layout

A Razor website uses a number of files that may seem a little daunting at first, but they make sense after you take them apart rather than attempt to view them as a whole. Here is the list of files for the website in the order in which they're typically used to create the presentation:

- `Program.cs`: Contains the `Main()` method and application startup code. This code includes the creation of a `IHostBuilder` object, `webBuilder`, which actually starts the website using the `Startup` class found in `Startup.cs`.

» `Startup.cs`: Defines the website's underlying configuration. This is where the application adds Razor pages to the site and determines how those pages will interact. The "Developing a Basic Web App" section of Chapter 1 of this minibook shows you some of what goes on in the `Startup` class, such as adding `UseEndpoints()` calls and substituting calls to `app.UseDefaultFiles();` and `app.UseStaticFiles();` to support the use of static HTML files on a site. The calls made within this class determine the characteristics of the website interactions.

GAINING ACCESS TO THE WEB FORMS TEMPLATES

You can still use Web Forms with Visual Studio 2022, complete with a new designer. The problem is that this support is hidden from view and you need to know the secret handshake (shhh!). Begin by closing Visual Studio and opening the Visual Studio Installer. At the right side of the installation screen, you see a long list of optional components. Within the ASP.NET and Web Development group is the Additional Project Templates (Previous Versions) option shown in the first figure.

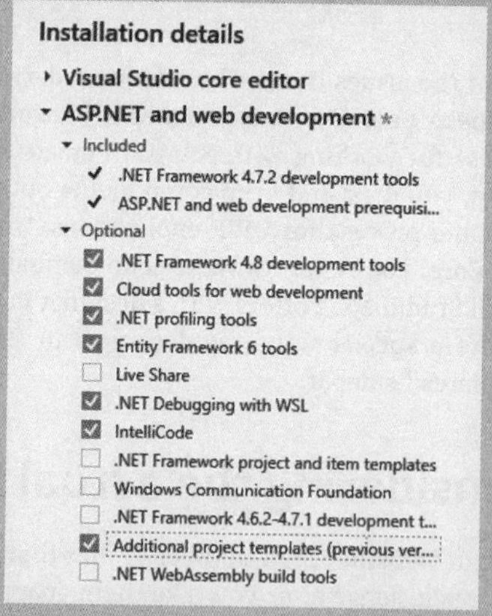

Installation details

- ▸ **Visual Studio core editor**
- ▾ **ASP.NET and web development** *
  - ▾ Included
    - ✔ .NET Framework 4.7.2 development tools
    - ✔ ASP.NET and web development prerequisi...
  - ▾ Optional
    - [x] .NET Framework 4.8 development tools
    - [x] Cloud tools for web development
    - [x] .NET profiling tools
    - [x] Entity Framework 6 tools
    - [ ] Live Share
    - [x] .NET Debugging with WSL
    - [x] IntelliCode
    - [ ] .NET Framework project and item templates
    - [ ] Windows Communication Foundation
    - [ ] .NET Framework 4.6.2-4.7.1 development t...
    - [x] Additional project templates (previous ver...
    - [ ] .NET WebAssembly build tools

Select this option and then click Modify. The installer will work away for a while, and then you'll be able to open Visual Studio again. The Create a New Project page of the new project wizard will now contain ASP.NET projects, including the ASP.NET Web Forms Site template, as shown in the second figure.

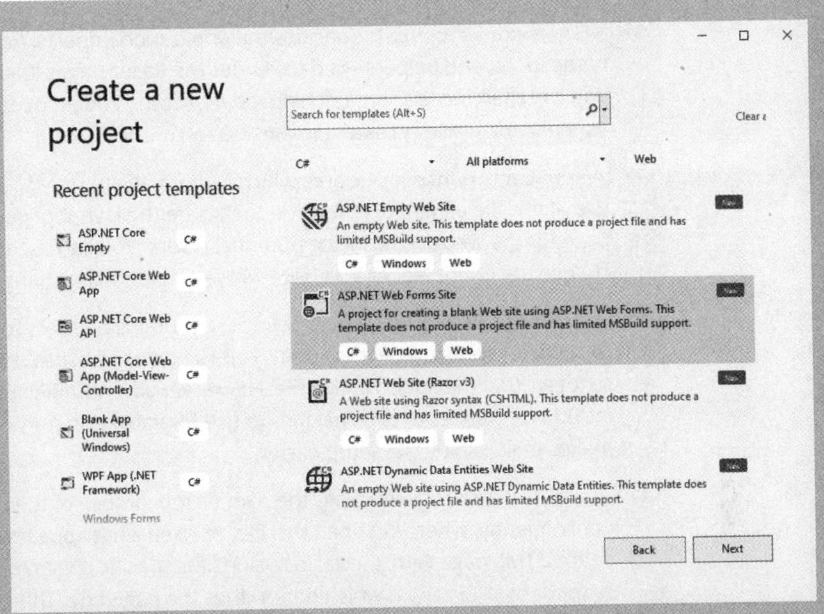

Visual Studio 2022 comes with two designers for the older Web Forms configuration: Legacy Web Forms designer (which is what you used in the past) and Web Live Preview (explained at `https://devblogs.microsoft.com/visualstudio/design-your-web-forms-apps-with-web-live-preview-in-visual-studio-2022/`). You transition between the two by choosing Tools➪Options to open the Options dialog box, and then you drill down into the Web Forms Designer settings, as shown in the third figure.

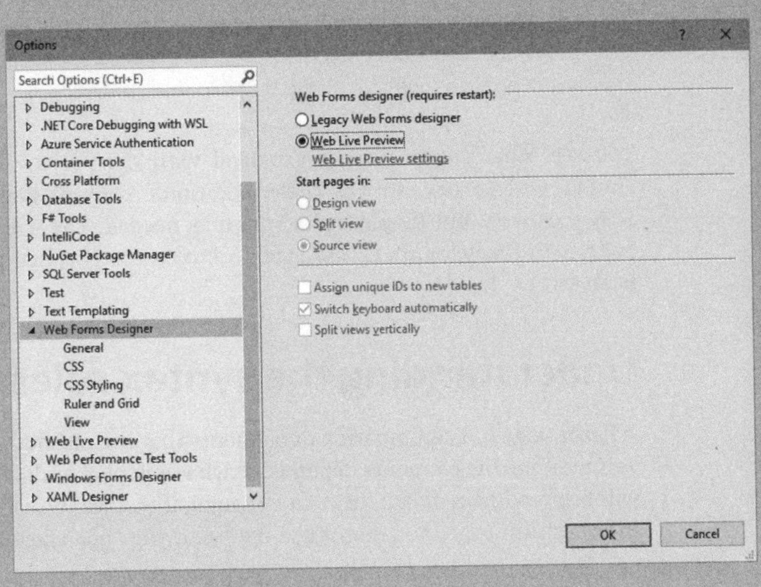

- _ViewImports.cshtml: Specifies the application imports, Razor page namespace, and helpers used to render the Razor pages (@addTagHelper). You can read more about tag helpers at https://docs.microsoft.com/aspnet/core/mvc/views/tag-helpers/intro.
- _ViewStart.cshtml: Declares which layout page to use for a website. The use of this file eliminates the need to declare the layout page in every content page for the website, reducing potential errors. You can use this feature to change the entire feel of a website with a single coding change.
- _ValidationScriptsPartial.cshtml: Contains pointers to the scripts used to validate the Razor page content. You see older websites that have the scripts actually included in this file. Newer versions of ASP.NET core pages include references to external files to use for validation purposes, which makes maintaining the setup easier.
- _Layout.cshtml: Determines the overall appearance of the Razor pages. Consequently, when you open this file, you see what appears to be an entire HTML page with special inclusions for specific page content, such as @ViewData["Title"], which determines the page title. This is also where you find common page elements, such as the navbar used to move between pages. However, this file doesn't contain any actual content — it's simply the layout used to contain the specific page layout.
- index.cshtml: Defines the first content page for a website. In all cases, the content appears within a layout specified by the layout document, which is usually _Layout.cshtml.
- index.cshtml.cs: Contains the code-behind for the associated content page. The code-behind performs tasks such as handling user-interface events and performing some types of dynamic page setups. Razor pages are based on the PageModel class (https://docs.microsoft.com/dotnet/api/microsoft.aspnetcore.mvc.razorpages.pagemodel).

You see other content pages provided with the project that include Privacy.cshtml and Error.cshtml. These additional content pages work the same as index.cshtml, but they're called upon as needed. There is a link from the home page to Privacy.cshtml. The Error.cshtml file is called upon only when there is an error.

Understanding the syntax rules for C#

A Razor page is a combination of elements that include both HTML and code. How you combine the elements depends on what you plan to do. However, all your code will begin with an at sign (@). For example, if you want to add a date to the default Index.cshtml page, you might use the following code shown in bold:

```
<div class="text-center">
    <h1 class="display-4">Welcome</h1>
    <p>It's @DateTime.Now.ToLongDateString()</p>
    <p>Learn about <a href="https://docs.microsoft.com/aspnet/core">
        building Web apps with ASP.NET Core
    </a>.</p>
</div>
```

Notice that this paragraph uses a combination of an HTML tag, `<p>`, plain text, and a call to `@DateTime.Now.ToLongDateString()`. The date will change every time someone loads the page. After that, however, it remains static. A lot of content falls into this category, and you should use this technique whenever possible to make things simple. The output of this call comes in the following form:

```
It's Friday, October 15, 2021
```

REMEMBER

Of course, you can create changing content and perform all sorts of other tasks. All the entries for performing code-related tasks on a page begin with `@`. If you actually need to show the `@` sign on a page, you use `@@` instead. In that case, Razor views the `@@` as an `@` and doesn't process the text that comes afterward as code.

There are some special rules for working with code on a Razor page, but the code appears as a form of C# and uses C# syntax rules. You could just as easily get the long date in your C# console application using `DateTime.Now.ToLongDateString()` as you can when working with Razor. So, it's important not to overthink how to do things.

Working with some Razor basics

Many sources online (such as `https://docs.microsoft.com/aspnet/core/razor-pages/`) show lots of ways to write code in Razor, but few of them look at simple tasks, which can mean that they can be quite hard to comprehend. To avoid frustration, you need something easier. The following sections look at two basic tasks that you might perform on any web page.

Making output mundane

The previous section showed a simple way to display the current date on your page. You actually have multiple ways to work with simple kinds of output depending on what you want to do. For example, you can add a field to your code to perform more complex kinds of output like this:

```
@{
    var showString = "This is a string.";
}
```

You can then use showString in your page like this:

```
<p id="StringOutput">@showString</p>
```

The creation of showString can include any level of complexity needed to provide the data required. However, at its root, showString is simply an output that provides online data.

You can also create custom classes to interact with your Razor page. For example, you might create a class like this one in Index.cshtml.cs:

```
public class CodeBehind
{
    public string aString = "This is a code-behind string.";
}
```

REMEMBER

To use this class in your code, you must first create an instance of it like this:

```
@{
    var codeBehind = new CodeBehind();
}
```

You then use the instance variable, codeBehind, on your page like this:

```
<p id="StringOutput2">@codeBehind.aString</p>
```

TIP

Notice that you access the CodeBehind class instance variable, aString, through the Razor page instance variable codeBehind. You can access instance methods in the same manner. If your custom class uses static fields or methods, you don't have to create an instance variable. As with any C# code, you can access static fields or methods without creating an instance variable first.

Changing web page data

Sometimes you just need to make a simple change to a web page and don't really want to create a complex design that will make your friends envious. Web pages are static, unlike applications on desktops that can be as dynamic as they want. Consequently, you need some means of requesting an update from the server or provide client-side code to make the change locally, but the fact is that you need some means of changing the web page content through a request. The easiest way to perform this task using Razor is to create code-behind. In this case, the code appears in Index.cshtml.cs as part of the IndexModel class like this:

```
public string changingString { get; set; }

public void OnGet()
{
    changingString = "This is the changing string.";
}

public void OnPost()
{
    changingString = "The string has changed.";
}
```

The focus of this code is the `changingString` property, which is set by `OnGet()` during the initial page request. Whenever your browser requests a new page, the code-behind looks at `OnGet()` to see whether there's something special to do. Later, when you request a change, you can use the post method in your page code to call on `OnPost()`, which assigns a new value to `changingString`. The code in `Index.cshtml` looks like this:

```
<p>@Model.changingString</p>
<form method="post">
    <button>Click to Change Text</button>
</form>
```

Mind you, that `<form>` really is around the individual `<button>`, not around the page as a whole. Notice that you use `@Model.changingString` to access `changingString`. A good many online examples show `@changingString`, which doesn't work at all (although it might have in the past). The `<button>` is just a simple HTML button without any sort on `onclick` handler added to it, so it doesn't look like it should work, but it actually does.

Of course, you might need to provide multiple buttons — imagine that! The simple post method doesn't work in this case, but you have another option with a very small change. You give the `OnPost()` method a more specific name, one that has a handler name to go with it. So, the following code has `OnPostView1()` and `OnPostView2()`:

```
public void OnPostView1()
{
    changingString = "The string has changed.";
}

public void OnPostView2()
{
    changingString = "Another Change!";
}
```

Now you need another method for accessing the methods. You get this method by simply adding the asp-page-handler attribute to the <form> tag, as shown here:

```
<form asp-page-handler="view1" method="post">
    <button>Click to Change Text</button>
</form>
<form asp-page-handler="view2" method="post">
    <button>Try Another Change</button>
</form>
```

REMEMBER

The value added to the asp-page-handler attribute is somewhat counterintuitive. Notice that it's just view1 or view2, not OnPostView1 or OnPostView2. The OnPost part of the reference is addressed by the method="post" attribute. If you were to use method="get" instead, the method names in your code-behind would need to be OnGetView1() and OnGetView2() instead. The use of this approach also changes the URL for the page. When a user clicks the first button, the URL changes to http://localhost:18975/?handler=view1. Likewise, when the user clicks the second button, the URL changes to http://localhost:18975/?handler=view2. (Note that the port number, 18975, will vary by system.) The bottom line is that you can have as many buttons as needed on a Razor page and use this simple approach to manage them.

Creating Variables

Variables in Razor follow the same course as variables in C#. You have access to the same data types, the same operators, and so on. However, you may find yourself using them differently. In many cases, variables provide assistance with creating content. For example, you might want to know whether someone is using view1 from the examples earlier in the chapter. In this case, you can simply test the content of changingString and place it in a bool in the Index.cshtml file, like this:

```
@{
    bool isView1 = Model.changingString == "The string has changed.";
}
```

This sort of test helps you decide how to process information. You can use this sort of testing to change the content of the page after each reload. It helps you do things like decide whether the user is logged into the website or if there is a connection to the database you need. The web page content can change to meet specific demands without having to rely on code-behind to do it.

Keeping Things Logical

The pattern for working with logical statements in Razor is very much the same as working with logical statements in C#, but with a slight twist. As with all code in a `.cshtml` page, you must precede the logical structure with an @ sign. The following sections discuss the basic logical statements and how to use them as part of a Razor page.

Starting simply by using if

The "Creating Variables" section, earlier in this chapter, discusses how to create variables in Razor. You can use these variables in all sorts of ways, but one of the most common methods is to modify the page appearance to meet specific conditions. The following `@if` statement uses the `isView1` variable created earlier to change the appearance of the page:

```
@if(isView1)
{
    <p>Using View1</p>
}
else
{
    <p>Not Using View1</p>
}
```

Notice that this looks about the same as any other `if` statement in C#. However, the output is different. In this case, you see that the selection of a particular logical path results in HTML output rather than the execution of code. Also note that the `else` clause of the `if` statement lacks the @ sign.

Sleeping at the switch

Razor supports switches, which can save you considerable time typing. Say you create an `int` named `ViewNumber` like this:

```
@{
    int ViewNumber;
    if (Model.changingString == "This is the changing string.")
        ViewNumber = 0;
    else if (Model.changingString == "The string has changed.")
        ViewNumber = 1;
    else
        ViewNumber = 2;
}
```

The `if` statement appears normal in this case because it appears within an `@` block. The code places a value in `ViewNumber` that corresponds to the current text in `changingString`. You can use a `switch` to process `ViewNumber`, like this:

```
@switch(ViewNumber)
{
    case 0:
        <p>Using Original View</p>
        break;
    case 1:
        <p>Using View 1</p>
        break;
    case 2:
        <p>Using View 2</p>
        break;
    default:
        <p>Unrecognized View</p>
        break;
}
```

Except for the `@` sign and the use of HTML tags, the `switch` statement in this example could appear in any C# file. All the same rules apply as when working with C#, so you don't have to do anything weird except remember that `@` sign and the fact that you can do something interesting with the HTML.

Implementing Loops

As you might expect, Razor implements loop processing using the same techniques that you use in C#. The difference is in how you process the data and the outcome of any tasks you perform. The following sections show how to create an array, so you have source data to process, and then how to process the data using a number of different techniques.

Creating an array

An array in Razor can take any form that you use in C#. Of course, you need to create it within an `@` block or use an existing array of values. Here's an example of creating an array for use within the example:

```
@{
    string[] Colors =
        { "Red", "Orange", "Yellow", "Green", "Blue", "Violet" };
}
```

As you can see, there is nothing weird here. The same techniques you use to create a C# array normally apply here as well.

Performing tasks a specific number of times using for

The `Colors` array created in the previous section provides a perfect way to test `for` loop processing in Razor. The following code uses the `Colors` array as a source and displays each of the colors in turn:

```
<h3>Colors</h3>
<ul class="text-left">
@for (var i = 0; i < Colors.Length; i++)
{
    <li>Color @i is @Colors[i]</li>
}
</ul>
```

As with the previous examples, you need to use the @ sign before you create the `for` loop. In addition, this example shows how you might process a source array so that it appears correctly onscreen. Remember that you can use all the same techniques as you normally use with a `for` loop to process data in C#.

Processing an unknown number of times using foreach and while

The essential difference between a `for` loop and both `foreach` and `while` is that the former processes data a known number of times, while the latter process data an unknown number of times until they're finished. In many cases, the choice of looping mechanism comes down to style and preference. Some developers like one form and other developers like another form. Here is the same output provided in the previous example using a `foreach` statement.

```
<h3>Colors Using Foreach</h3>
@{
    int counter = 0;
}
```

```
<ul class="text-left">
@foreach (string item in Colors)
{
    <li>Color @counter is @item</li>
    counter++;
}
</ul>
```

The example begins by declaring an `int` variable, `counter`, to keep track of the color number. It then uses the `@foreach` loop to process the `Colors` array. The differences you should notice in this version of the example are the technique used to produce the output and the fact that the example freely mixes HTML and C# code.

IN THIS CHAPTER

» Defining serialized data basics

» Developing a data generator and API

» Consuming the generated data and showing it onscreen

» Seeing the applications in action

Chapter 3 Generating and Consuming Data

Cereal is what you eat for breakfast; *serialization* is what you do with local data in XML or flat-file format. If you eat the former, the latter might make more sense. This chapter delves into data serialization and deserialization, which are incredibly useful tools for all sorts of purposes because the combination of these two techniques lets you work with structured data in a manner that doesn't require in-depth knowledge of database management. Throughout this chapter, you use the `WeatherForecast` project to generate weather data that is then serialized to create a usable data store (albeit not a very fancy one). The `RetrieveWeatherForecast` project queries the API created by the `WeatherForecast` project, deserializes it, and displays it onscreen. The first two parts of this chapter help you understand the current trends in data stores and the concept of serialization better.

REMEMBER

You don't have to type the source code for this chapter manually. In fact, using the downloadable source is a lot easier. You can find the source for this chapter in the `\CSAIO4D2E\BK06\CH03` folder of the downloadable source. See the Introduction for details on how to find these source files.

Understanding Why These Projects Are Important

At one point in history, companies relied on local data stores, with some users spending their entire day entering information into a database and other users spending their entire day trying to find ways to use the data. A developer had to be concerned about providing interfaces that implemented Create, Read, Update, and Delete (CRUD) principles. C# developers can still find tutorials demonstrating such applications online, such as the one at `https://docs.microsoft.com/aspnet/core/tutorials/razor-pages/razor-pages-start`.

TIP

When you look at how data is used today, it doesn't normally rely on local data stores with manually input data. According to Forbes (`https://www.forbes.com/sites/bernardmarr/2018/05/21/how-much-data-do-we-create-every-day-the-mind-blowing-stats-everyone-should-read/`) and SeedScientific (`https://seedscientific.com/how-much-data-is-created-every-day/`), the probabilities are that no one sat at a terminal and manually input the data you're using today. So, it becomes more important to know how to display information from these vast data stores than how to input the data manually, even though both are important.

Most data isn't even handled by humans anymore. Consider the seemingly human-intensive act of predicting the weather. It turns out that most weather data today is generated based on information collected by sensors (see `https://www.wunderground.com/about/data`, `https://agrimetsoft.com/knn-wg` and `https://www.ipcc-data.org/guidelines/pages/weather_generators.html`). In other words, no human has touched the data.

Consuming data has also changed. The chances are that you'll grab someone else's data using an API. For example, you can grab data from many different weather sites, including the MeteoMatics site at `https://www.meteomatics.com/en/weather-api/`. There is no chance whatsoever that these sites will allow you to change their data, but they do want you to consume their data, which means that you need to concentrate on simple applications that let users view the data in a prescribed manner.

It isn't possible to demonstrate complex weather forecast-generation techniques in a single chapter because most weather generators today rely on advanced machine learning and deep learning techniques. However, the `WeatherForecast` project gives you some idea of how such a program could work from a very basic perspective. The `RetrieveWeatherForecast` project demonstrates how to query an API and then present the information it provides onscreen in a basic manner. The point of these two projects is that you don't have to create extraordinarily complex coding scenarios to create truly useful applications that work with today's data.

Serialized Data Isn't for Breakfast

In some respects, serializing data is much like eating breakfast. You begin with a whole bowl of data and put it on disk one bite at a time, just as you eat cereal one bite at a time. The idea is to make the data manageable and more organized so that manipulating it is easier. When you work with a collection of objects in memory, a single object, the collection, contains other objects that you access. Each of these objects has a set of properties that contain data. Serialization breaks up each of the pieces so that you now have some means of storing the data on disk. The common storage methods are

- **Comma-Separated Value (CSV):** Breaks up the data into rows, with one row for each object in the collection, and columns, with one column for each property in the objects. You end up with a table consisting of rows and columns that look very much like what you might write down on paper to organize data yourself. This kind of storage normally requires that each object in the collection be of the same type and have the same properties defined. An advantage of this form of data storage is that it can be extremely space efficient for large quantities of data, which is why you see many datasets used for data science stored in this manner.
- **Extensible Markup Language (XML):** Starts at the root with the collection object, creating main nodes for each of the objects and subnodes for each of the properties. You end up with a tree-like structure that can adapt to any form that the data might take and can become quite descriptive of the relationship between data elements and the data itself. You normally use this form of storage when the data isn't well structured and a collection could contain different objects with different properties in each object. It also works well for data that is naturally hierarchical. An advantage of this form of storage is that it allows storage of data attributes in a fully retrievable manner.
- **JavaScript Object Notation (JSON):** Creates dictionary-like entries for each object. In many respects, JSON and XML are similar because they're both self-describing, use a hierarchical format, and can be fetched using a `XMLHttpRequest` call. However, JSON differs from XML in that JSON
  - Doesn't use an end tag
  - Is shorter most of the time
  - Is quicker to read and write
  - Can use arrays

REMEMBER

Each of these storage methods has other advantages and disadvantages. For example, CSV files are easily damaged in ways that might be hard to detect, while XML is bulky and consumes a lot of space. Both types of storage are easily moved between platforms and you see both of them used extensively online. The point of using data-storage techniques like this is to ensure that your data remains accessible even if the application is discarded at some point. Both data formats are kinds of text, which is the universal format across systems and was the first format used to store information before people got fancy.

To serialize data, you must describe to the application how to interpret it — how to take bites. There are many ways to accomplish this task, and the approach you choose depends on your data format. In many cases, you begin by simply defining the object you create as serializable and then use special coding techniques to write these objects to disk. The compiler provides a great deal of help in this case, and the code is easy to understand (as long as you don't delve too deeply into that behind-the-scenes code).

Developing a Data Generator and API

Data generators take information from some source or randomly define data elements and put it into a form that's convenient for any of a number of purposes, such as analysis. A data generator can spawn textual data, but it can also produce graphical, aural, and other sorts of data. The form of data depends on the needs of the user consuming it. The following sections discuss how to use an existing Visual Studio 2022 project to create a data generator that also acts as an API that a browser or other application can query.

Creating the WeatherForecast project

The first thing you need is a project to use. This project will rely on an existing Visual Studio 2022 template with some modifications that you normally make when creating a data generator. To create the project, follow these steps:

1. **Click Create a New Project in the Visual Studio 2022 start window.**

   You see a list of templates to use.

2. **Choose C#, All Platforms, and Web in the drop-down list boxes. Locate the ASP.NET Core Web API template, shown in Figure 3-1.**

TECHNICAL STUFF

Notice that the list of environments that the template supports includes desktop operating systems and cloud-based setups. An API can normally run anywhere it has the required support and can service consumers from any browser, which makes APIs extremely versatile. However, you normally start an API locally before moving it to the cloud.

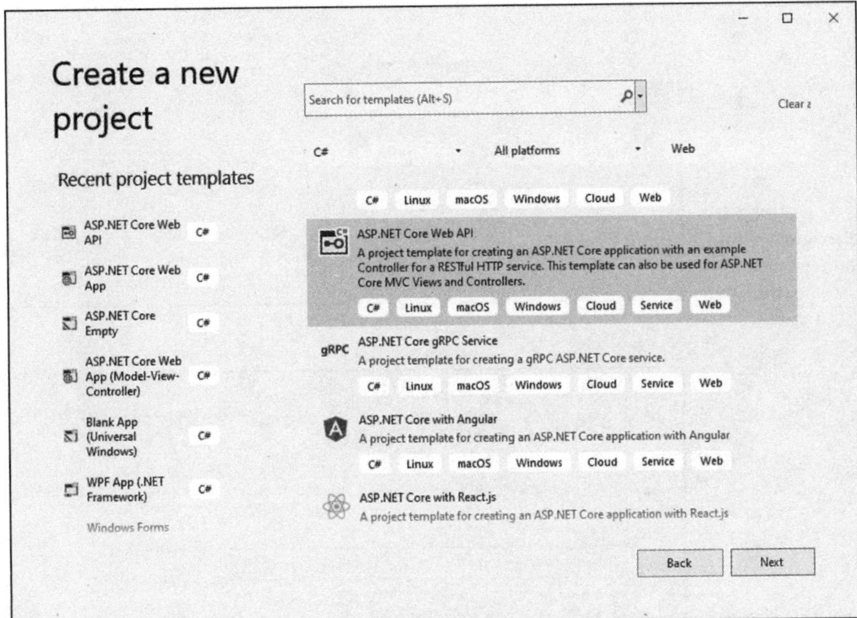

FIGURE 3-1: Locate the ASP.NET Core Web API template.

3. **Highlight the ASP.NET Core Web API template and click Next.**

   You see the Configure Your New Project dialog box, shown in Figure 3-2.

4. **Type** WeatherForecast **in the Project Name field and select a location for the project on your hard drive. Make sure that you select the Place Solution and Project in the Same Directory entry, and then click Next.**

   You see the Additional Information dialog box, shown in Figure 3-3.

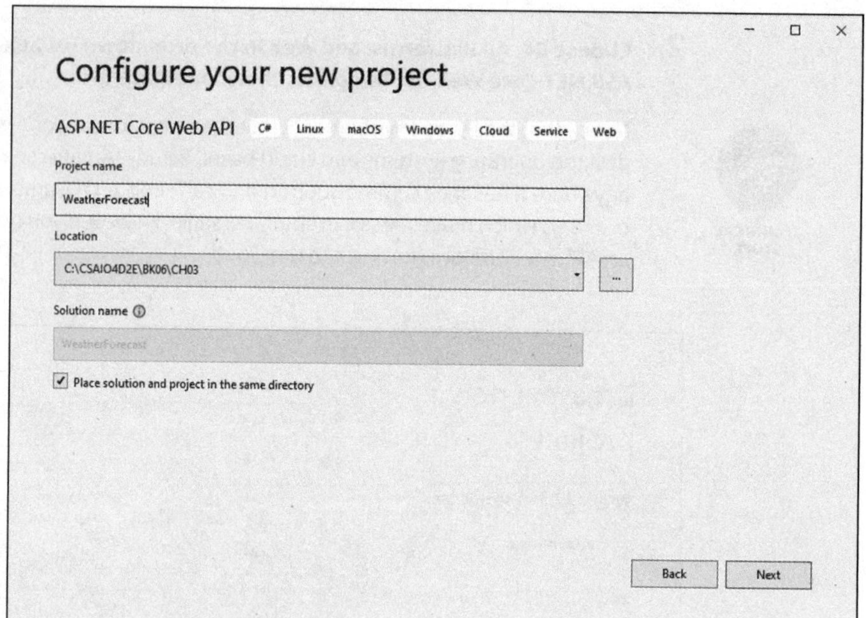

FIGURE 3-2: Provide a name and location for the API.

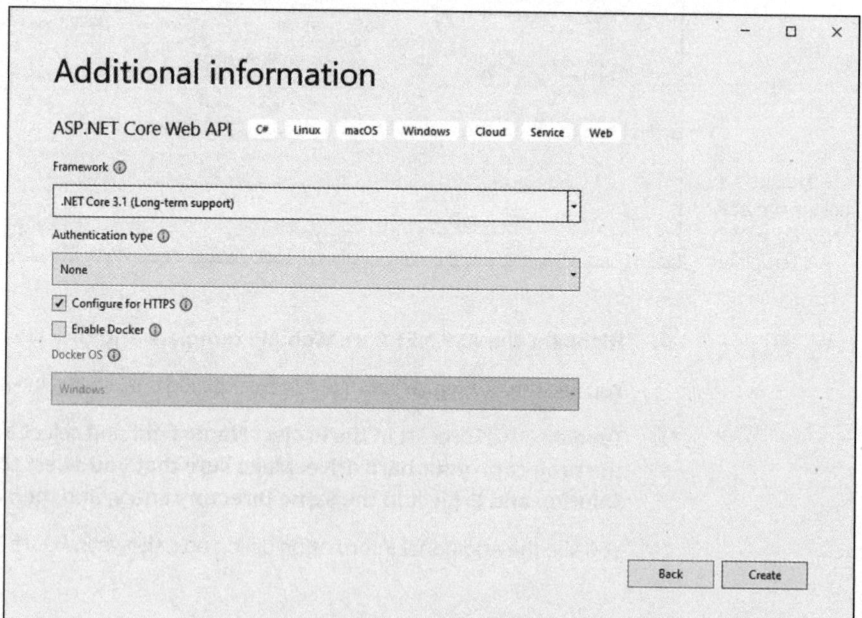

FIGURE 3-3: Select the additional requirements for the API.

5. **Select .NET Core 3.1 (Long-term Support) in the Framework field and None in the Authentication Type field, and select Configure for HTTPS.**

TIP

Public APIs, which number now in the hundreds of thousands (or perhaps even millions), usually don't require any authentication. Private and paid APIs usually do requirement authentication, but this authentication may not take the form of a logon dialog box. Instead, the client passes a special token to the API for verification. Consequently, you may not actually use the standard authentication features for your API very often. Think about how you want clients to authenticate before you create the project.

WARNING

It is standard practice to use Secure Sockets Layer (SSL) security for APIs of any sort because it's incredibly hard to trust the data the client receives otherwise (see `https://www.bluehost.com/resources/does-my-website-need-ssl-learn-the-benefits-of-ssl-for-website-security/` and `https://www.kaspersky.com/resource-center/definitions/what-is-a-ssl-certificate` for details). Deselecting the Configure for HTTPS check box is such a bad idea that it's hard to understand why Microsoft would even include it in this case. The bottom line is, if you want your client to feel comfortable, always use SSL.

6. **Click Create.**

Visual Studio 2022 creates a new web API project for you.

Making the data believable

The default API provided by the Visual Studio 2022 generates weather information randomly. In other words, this is fake data that you could use for testing purposes, but it isn't based on any real data, nor does it rely on machine learning techniques to compute a forecast. Rather, it's just values. However, the default setup is lacking in two ways:

- The dates don't reflect any sort of progression normally associated with weather forecasts. Normally, you see one-, seven-, and ten-day forecasts. Some setups even offer hourly forecasts, but there is always some sort of progression, which the example lacks.
- It's hard to believe weather data that claims that it's scorching at 20 degrees below zero, yet the default setup will try its best to convince you that it is indeed scorching. Ignore that icicle hanging off your nose; you're really overheated!

The code you need to change to make the output more realistic appears in the `Controllers` folder as `WeatherForecastController.cs`. Open this file and make the changes shown here:

```
[HttpGet]
public IEnumerable<WeatherForecast> Get()
{
    return Enumerable.Range(1, 10).Select(index => GetWeatherForecast())
      .ToArray();
}

private int DaysToAdd = 0;

public WeatherForecast GetWeatherForecast()
{
    var rng = new Random();

    WeatherForecast thisForecast = new WeatherForecast();
    thisForecast.Date = DateTime.Now.AddDays(DaysToAdd);
    DaysToAdd += 1;
    thisForecast.TemperatureC = rng.Next(-20, 40);
    switch (thisForecast.TemperatureC)
    {
        case int n when (n < -14):
            thisForecast.Summary = Summaries[0];
            break;
        case int n when (n >= -14 && n < -7):
            thisForecast.Summary = Summaries[1];
            break;
        case int n when (n >= -7 && n < 0):
            thisForecast.Summary = Summaries[2];
            break;
        case int n when (n >= 0 && n < 6):
            thisForecast.Summary = Summaries[3];
            break;
        case int n when (n >= 6 && n < 12):
            thisForecast.Summary = Summaries[4];
            break;
        case int n when (n >= 12 && n < 18):
            thisForecast.Summary = Summaries[5];
            break;
        case int n when (n >= 18 && n < 24):
            thisForecast.Summary = Summaries[6];
            break;
        case int n when (n >= 24 && n < 30):
            thisForecast.Summary = Summaries[7];
            break;
        case int n when (n >= 30 && n < 36):
```

```
            thisForecast.Summary = Summaries[8];
            break;
        case int n when (n >= 36):
            thisForecast.Summary = Summaries[9];
            break;
    }

    return thisForecast;
}
```

The `public IEnumerable<WeatherForecast> Get()` method is shorter than the original source. It doesn't actually define any data now, but it does create an array of weather predictions. The `Enumerable.Range(1, 10)` method creates a ten-day forecast, which is more believable than the five-day forecast created by default (although if you look hard enough, you can likely find some website that does provide a five-day forecast).

The `WeatherForecast GetWeatherForecast()` method defines the weather forecasts one day at a time. To create progressive days, the code calls `DateTime.Now.AddDays(DaysToAdd)` with a variable, `DaysToAdd`, that is incremented by `1` during each pass. The temperature in degrees Celsius is a randomly generated number. The temperature in degrees Fahrenheit is calculated in the `WeatherForecast.cs` file using `public int TemperatureF => 32 + (int)(TemperatureC / 0.5556);`. Calculated data often appears as part of the output of a data generator. Finally, the code uses a switch to define a `Summary` value based on the actual temperature (rather than randomly generating it as before). So, when the temperature nears 86 degrees Fahrenheit, the forecast will tell you that it's sweltering and not freezing.

Looking at the API configuration

It's important to know how to contact your API. To discover this information, open the `launchSettings.json` file found in the `Properties` folder. There are two important settings in this file that you can't ignore even if you want to use the defaults in every other way. The first is `"sslPort": 44327`. The number that follows `sslPort` specifies the port number used to access your web service. You can ignore the `applicationUrl` setting because you won't use it to access the API; only the `sslPort` setting matters. This means that you'll use `https://localhost:4432/7/` as the base URL to access this web service. (The port number, 4432, varies by system.)

REMEMBER

The second setting you need to know is `"launchUrl": "weatherforecast"`. This setting defines where your client can find the actual API. Consequently, the full URL for accessing the API is `https://localhost:44327/weatherforecast`. This is an essential bit of information because you need it later when creating the client.

Checking the API for functionality

You can check your API before you develop the client. The output won't be very exciting, but you can see that the API works as expected. The following sections explain how to check your API for functionality.

Viewing the data in a browser

The first place you want to look for API functionality is your browser. Choose Debug⇨Start Without Debugging. The first thing you'll normally see is a dialog box asking whether you want to install an SSL certificate for your project, as shown in Figure 3-4.

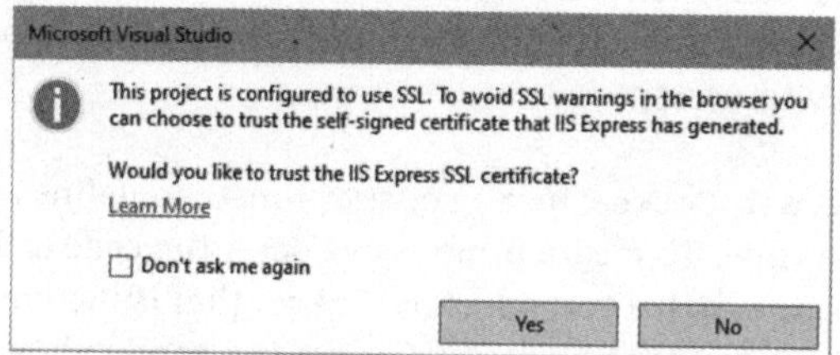

FIGURE 3-4: Determine whether you want to install the SSL certificate.

Unless you really enjoy having your browser ask you about the website you're testing over and over until you finally go crazy, you'll click Yes. Because the certificate is working only with your project, you don't need to worry much about opening huge security holes in your system.

Immediately after you click Yes, Windows will usually display another dialog box asking whether you're sure you want to install the certificate, as shown in Figure 3-5. Obviously, Visual Studio 2022 and Windows don't talk, so you have to answer essentially the same question twice.

Just about the time you start to think that you may never see your API in action, a browser window comes up and you see the serialized JSON data shown in Figure 3-6. The background code for your API automatically takes care of the serialization for you based on the array created by the `public IEnumerable<WeatherForecast> Get()` call. There are a lot of fancy reasons for this happening, such as the addition of the `[HttpGet]` attribute to the method call, which you can read about at `https://docs.microsoft.com/aspnet/core/mvc/controllers/routing` and `https://docs.microsoft.com/dotnet/api/microsoft.aspnetcore.mvc.httpgetattribute`, but the main thing to know is that it simply works as it should without any additional coding on your part.

FIGURE 3-5: Make Windows feel better by answering the question a second time.

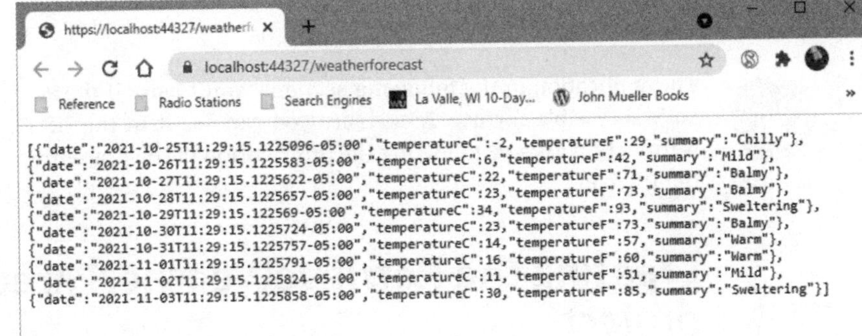

FIGURE 3-6: The browser output shows serialized weather forecast data.

Locating the IIS icon

If you've followed the process outlined in previous sections of this chapter, you now have a service. For a service to be useful, it must continue running until you don't need it any longer. In the Windows Notification Area, you see an IIS Express icon like the one shown in Figure 3-7. Right-clicking this icon displays a list of the running websites. In addition, you see controls for interacting with the websites.

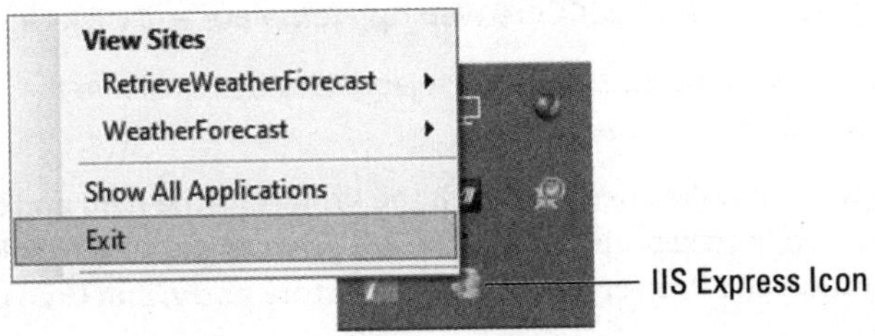

FIGURE 3-7: Look for the IIS Express icon in the Notification Area to see which applications are running.

TIP

Knowing about the IIS Express icon is very important because developers often spend a great deal of time looking for errors in their website code, only to find that the service isn't running. You can save yourself time and embarrassment by looking for this icon.

Creating a Consumer Website

After you have an API to use, you need an application to consume it. Because of how APIs work, the application need not be a web application — you could also use a console application, a desktop application, or any other application that interacts with data. It's amazing to think that your service could be used by anyone, anywhere. Given that this is a chapter on web development, however, the following sections focus on using the `WeatherForecast` API from a web application named `RetrieveWeatherForecast`.

REMEMBER

The application in the following sections won't work if the `WeatherForecast` API isn't accessible for use. Make sure you can see it in the IIS Express icon in the Notification Area by following the information in the preceding section, "Locating the IIS icon."

Creating the RetrieveWeatherForecast project

To begin using the `WeatherForecast` API, you need a web application. Follow these steps to create the example web application:

1. **Click Create a New Project in the Visual Studio 2022 start window.**

   You see a list of templates to use that are similar to the ones shown previously in Figure 3-1.

2. **Choose C#, All Platforms, and Web in the drop-down list boxes. Locate the ASP.NET Core Web App template.**

3. **Highlight the ASP.NET Core Web App template and click Next.**

   You see a Configure Your New Project dialog box similar to the one shown previously in Figure 3-2.

4. **Type** RetrieveWeatherForecast **in the Project Name field and select a location for the project on your hard drive. Make sure to select the Place Solution and Project in the Same Directory entry, and then click Next.**

   You see an Additional Information dialog box similar to the one shown previously in Figure 3-3.

5. **Select .NET Core 3.1 (Long-term Support) in the Framework field and None in the Authentication Type field, and then select Configure for HTTPS.**

   Because this is likely a critical business application, using SSL makes sense in this situation. Whether you use SSL for informational sites depends on the perceived risk from the client interacting with the data. When in doubt, use SSL.

6. **Click Create.**

   Visual Studio 2022 creates a new web app project for you.

Developing a user interface

Because you have no designer to use for ASP.NET Core Web App applications, it's somewhat important to use a little trial and error in putting the interface together. Most people have a hard time visualizing what the website will eventually look like based solely on the code, so making a few changes and then viewing the website is the best option you have. The following sections tell you more about creating a user interface for this example.

TIP

If you make changes to the interface, they may not always show up, which is really frustrating. Unfortunately, if the web application site is kept running, you may see the old code, not the new code. To prevent major hair loss, stop the application website (not the `WeatherForecast` service website) after each change to your code. You can stop it by clicking Stop Site, as shown in Figure 3-8 in the IIS Express icon in the Notification Area (described in the "Locating the IIS icon" section of the chapter).

Browse Applications
https://localhost:44361/
http://localhost:41208/
Stop Site

View Sites
RetrieveWeatherForecast
WeatherForecast
Show All Applications
Exit

FIGURE 3-8: Stop the site so that you can see changes to your user-interface code.

Adding the basic user-interface elements

This section's example uses a simple HTML table to display the data onscreen. However, the table comes in two sections: the container, which appears in the `Index.cshtml` file; and the data, which appears in the `Index.cshtml.cs` file. This section focuses on the container, as shown here:

```
@page
@model IndexModel
```

```
@{
    ViewData["Title"] = "The Weather Page";
}

<div class="text-center">
    <h1 class="display-4">Welcome to the Weather Page</h1>
    <table class="text-left" border="1" style="width:100%;" cellpadding="4">
        <tr>
            <th>Date</th>
            <th>Temperature (C)</th>
            <th>Temperature (F)</th>
            <th>Summary</th>
        </tr>
        @Html.Raw(Model.myData)
    </table>>
</div>
```

The changes include giving the page a new title and top-level heading. To make the data easier to see, you set some `<table>` tag attributes: `border`, `style`, and `cellpadding`. You may find that you want to make other changes to the appearance of the table as well.

Because the column headings don't change, you can also add them as part of the `Index.cshtml` file. In fact, you should always place non-changeable elements in the web page code rather than the code-behind.

The data for this example is provided by the `@Html.Raw(Model.myData)` entry. The code-behind replaces this code with the actual data obtained from the `WeatherForecast` API.

Understanding the need for raw HTML

The code-behind for your web page always assumes that a string is a string and not HTML. So, if you output something like `<p>This is a string</p>` from the code-behind, what you see on the web page is the string and both the opening and closing tags. Obviously, this isn't what you were expecting to happen on a web page, especially given that the web page is already full of tags. Consequently, the `Model.myData` output in the previous section would be flawed if you didn't do something with it as part of the display process.

This is where the `@Html.Raw()` call comes into play (see `https://docs.microsoft.com/dotnet/api/system.web.mvc.htmlhelper.raw` for more details). It tells ASP.NET to display the data in `Model.myData` as HTML rather than as pure text. The call is part of an entire interface named `IHtmlHelper`, which you can read more about at `https://docs.microsoft.com/dotnet/api/system.web.mvc.htmlhelper`.

Getting and deserializing the data

It's finally time to show how the various elements of this example are put together to display information onscreen. The following sections help you get through the process of working through deserialization and then display as HTML output.

Adding the WeatherForecast class

To deserialize the data from the `WeatherForecast` API, you need a class that describes the data. Fortunately, you already have such a class. It appears in the `WeatherForecast` project. Use these steps to add the class to your `RetrieveWeatherForecast` project:

1. **Right-click the RetrieveWeatherForecast entry in Solution Explorer and choose Add⇨Existing Item from the context menu.**

   You see an Add Existing Item dialog box.

2. **Navigate to the WeatherForecast project folder, as shown in Figure 3-9, and highlight `WeatherForecast.cs`. Click Add.**

   You see the `WeatherForecast.cs` file added to your project.

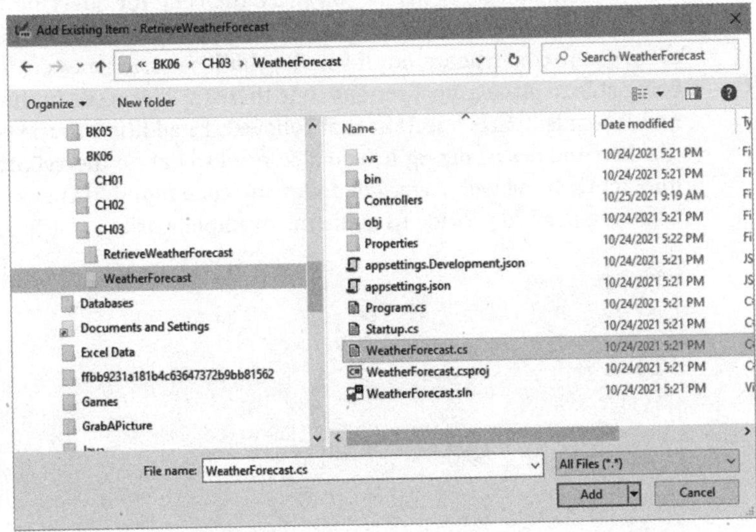

FIGURE 3-9: Add the `WeatherForecast` class to your project.

REMEMBER

There is only one problem with the file you've just imported. The variable names are all initial capitalized, such as `Date`. However, if you look at Figure 3-6, shown previously, you see that the variables are lowercase, such as `date`. Because C# is a case-sensitive language, you need to make the variables in the copy of

WeatherForecast.cs that you just imported into your RetrieveWeatherForecast project lowercase as well, so it now appears like this:

```
using System;

namespace RetrieveWeatherForecast
{
    public class WeatherForecast
    {
        public DateTime date { get; set; }

        public int temperatureC { get; set; }

        public int temperatureF => 32 + (int)(temperatureC / 0.5556);

        public string summary { get; set; }
    }
}
```

Building the essential code

When the web page loads, it calls OnGet() in the code-behind to obtain any needed information, so this is where you place the code for querying the WeatherForecast API. You might initially be tempted to place this code in the RetrieveWeatherForecast constructor, but if you do, you'll see error messages talking about not being able to place asynchronous code there (as discussed in the "Getting past the multithreaded parts" section that follows). In addition to the code for retrieving the data and deserializing it, you also need to define the myData variable used to interact with the web page. The following code found in index.cshtml.cs shows what you need to provide to make the example work:

```
[BindProperty]
public String myData { get; set; }

public async Task OnGet()
{
    // Create a client object to retrieve the data.
    HttpClient client = new HttpClient();

    // Tell the client object where to obtain the data
    // and what format the data will appear in.
    client.BaseAddress =
        new Uri("https://localhost:44327/weatherforecast");
    client.DefaultRequestHeaders.Accept.Add(
        new MediaTypeWithQualityHeaderValue("application/json"));
```

```
    // Provide a default response and then obtain the data.
    myData = "No Weather Report Today";
    HttpResponseMessage getData =
        await client.GetAsync("https://localhost:44327/weatherforecast");

    // If the data access was a success, then read it from the response
    // and display it onscreen.
    if (getData.IsSuccessStatusCode)
    {
        String data = getData.Content.ReadAsStringAsync().Result;

        // Deserialize the JSON data as a WeatherForecast array.
        WeatherForecast[] JSONData =
            JsonSerializer.Deserialize<WeatherForecast[]>(data);

        // Output each weather forecast as a row in a table.
        myData = "";
        foreach (WeatherForecast Item in JSONData)
        {
            myData += "<tr>";
            myData += "<td>" + Item.date.ToLongDateString() + "</td>";
            myData += "<td>" + Item.temperatureC + "</td>";
            myData += "<td>" + Item.temperatureF + "</td>";
            myData += "<td>" + Item.summary + "</td>";
            myData += "</tr>";
        }
    }

    await Task.Delay(1000);
}
```

In addition to the added code, you must also supply these `using` declarations at the beginning of the file.

```
// Added Using Statements
using System.Net.Http;
using System.Net.Http.Headers;
using Microsoft.AspNetCore.Mvc;
using System.Threading.Tasks;
using System.Text.Json;
```

Notice that `myData` is defined as a standard property. You need to make it `public` so that the web page can access it. In addition, you need to add the `[BindProperty]` attribute to bind the property to the web page. as described at `https://docs.microsoft.com/aspnet/core/mvc/models/model-binding`.

The process of querying the API begins with creating an `HttpClient` object, `client`, and configuring it for use. As shown in the code, for client to work at all with JSON data, you must configure the `BaseAddress` and `DefaultRequestHeaders.Accept` properties. The `BaseAddress` points to the URL for the API. However, you must also tell the client to accept `"application/json"` data by adding a `MediaTypeWithQualityHeaderValue` object to `DefaultRequestHeaders.Accept`.

The actual request response appears in a `HttpResponseMessage` object, `getData`, after the client calls `GetAsync()` with the required URL. A successful query will set `getData.IsSuccessStatusCode` to `true`, not OK or 200 as you might expect if you work with HTML requests very often.

There still isn't any data to work with. You retrieve the data by calling `getData.Content.ReadAsStringAsync().Result`. However, you still need to deserialize the resulting string by calling `JsonSerializer.Deserialize<WeatherForecast[]>()`. This is where the need for lowercase variables comes into play because the deserialization won't succeed otherwise. At this point, `JSONData` contains an array of weather forecasts that you can then process into HTML tags and data using a `foreach` loop.

Getting past the multithreaded parts

You can't use the default `OnGet()` supplied with the template. The reason for this is that the calls to the web API are multithreaded and asynchronous. If you were to use the default `OnGet()`, you'd never see the data because `OnGet()` would return too soon. So, the problem is one of getting everyone to cooperate.

The first part of this process is to use the `await` operator (`https://docs.microsoft.com/dotnet/csharp/language-reference/operators/await`) each time you make an asynchronous call. Consequently, you see `await client.GetAsync("https://localhost:44327/weatherforecast")` in the code, not just the call to `GetAsync()`. Unfortunately, this modification makes the code compile, but it doesn't fix the problem of `OnGet()` returning too soon.

The second part of the process is to change the return type of `OnGet()` from `void` to `Task`. Except, you never see anything returned in the code, so how does this even work? The final piece is the call to `await Task.Delay(1000)`, which provides an output that tells `OnGet()` that it's time to return. The example uses 1000 milliseconds, but you may have to increase this value for more complex API interactions.

Seeing the application in action

After completing the previous sections in the chapter, at this point you can finally run the application and see a result. Make sure that you have both the `WeatherForecast` and the `RetrieveWeatherForecast` projects open, and that the `WeatherForecast` service is running (as described in the "Locating the IIS icon" section of the chapter). Otherwise, the example won't work. Choose Debug⇨Start Without Debugging. You see the weather forecast (simulated) for the next ten days, as shown in Figure 3-10 (your data likely won't match).

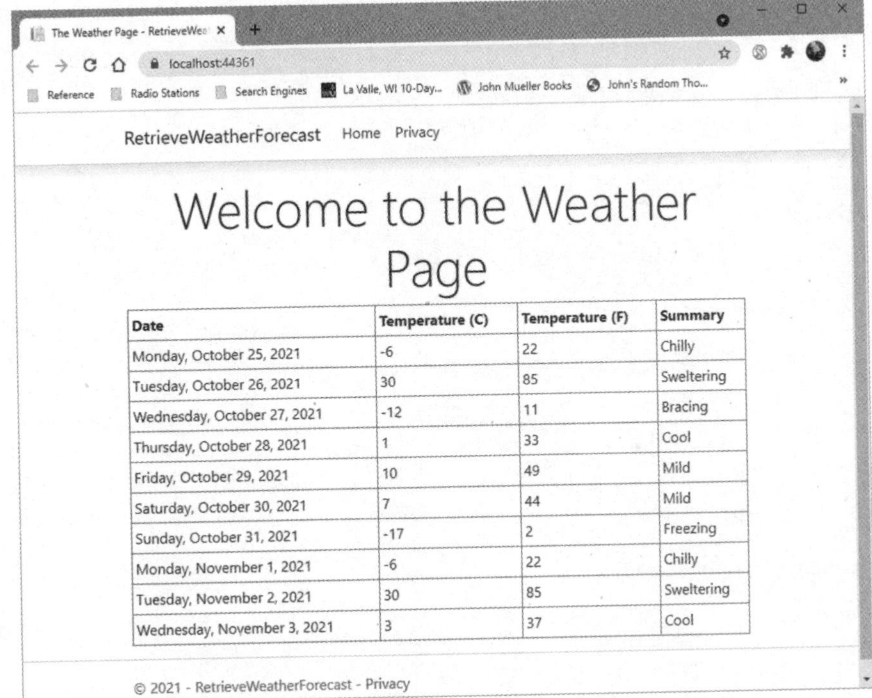

FIGURE 3-10: See the generated weather forecast from the `Weather Forecast` API.

Even though this is a simplistic view of web design, it's what happens in a great many instances today. Organizations are only too happy to use data generated by someone else when it suits their needs, and the techniques shown in this chapter help you obtain the required access to the data.

Index

Symbols & Numerics

A

B

C

D

E

F

G

H

I

J

K

L

M

N

O

S

T

U

V

W

X

Y

Z

About the Author

John Mueller is a freelance author and technical editor. He has writing in his blood, having produced 120 books and more than 600 articles to date. The topics range from networking to artificial intelligence and from database management to heads-down programming. Some of his current books include discussions of data science, machine learning, and algorithms. His technical editing skills have helped more than 70 authors refine the content of their manuscripts. John has always been interested in development and has written about a wide variety of languages, including a highly successful C++ book. Be sure to read John's blog at `http://blog.johnmuellerbooks.com/`. You can reach John on the Internet at `John@JohnMuellerBooks.com`. John also has a website at `http://www.johnmuellerbooks.com/` and you can download the source code for this book from `http://www.johnmuellerbooks.com/source-code/`. Be sure to follow John on Amazon at `https://www.amazon.com/John-Paul-Mueller/e/B004MOD0YS/`.

Dedication

To Rebecca, never forgotten, never far away — I'll love you forever.

Acknowledgments

Thanks to my wife, Rebecca. Even though she is gone now, her spirit is in every book I write, in every word that appears on the page. She believed in me when no one else would.

Rod Stephens has been a friend and colleague for many years now. His technical edit of this book was quite thorough, and I greatly appreciate his efforts. Rod took the time to talk with me about book topics through e-mail as I wrote about them. He offered insights on how to write better examples and more easily understood text, and he supplied access to resources that might not otherwise appear here.

Matt Wagner, my agent, deserves credit for helping me get the contract in the first place and taking care of all the details that most authors don't really consider. I always appreciate his assistance. It's good to know that someone wants to help.

A number of people read all or part of this book to help me refine the approach, test application code, verify the extensive text, and generally provide input that all readers wish they could have. These unpaid volunteers helped in ways too numerous to mention here. I especially appreciate the efforts of Eva Beattie, who provided general input, read the entire book, and selflessly devoted herself to this project.

Finally, I would like to thank Kelsie Baird, Susan Christophersen, and the rest of the editorial and production staff at John Wiley & Sons, Inc. for their unparalleled support of this writing effort.

Publisher's Acknowledgments

Acquisitions Editor: Kelsey Baird

Project Manager and Copy Editor: Susan Christophersen

Technical Editor: Rod Stephens

Production Editor: Mohammed Zafar Ali

Cover Image: © Casimiro PT/Shutterstock